FROM MĀSHĀ'ALLĀH TO KEPLER

Theory and Practice in Medieval and Renaissance Astrology

FROM MĀSHĀ ʾALLĀH TO KEPLER

Theory and Practice in Medieval and Renaissance Astrology

Edited by Charles Burnett and Dorian Gieseler Greenbaum

SOPHIA CENTRE PRESS

Cover image: the horoscope of the creation of the world, dedicated to the future Henry VIII, including a world map, the four winds, the signs of the zodiac (in gold), the planets in their degrees of exaltation (except Mercury) and the twelve astrological places: I (beginning of) life; II moveable property and helpers; III siblings, short journeys and religions; IV parents, immoveable property and ships; V children and entertainment; VI illnesses and servants; VII marriage and controversies; VIII death and inheritance; IX religion and long journeys; X rulership and profession; XI friends and hope; XII enemies and large animals.

First published in 2015.

Sophia Centre Press
University of Wales, Trinity Saint David,
Ceredigion, Wales SA48 7ED, United Kingdom.
www.sophiacentrepress.com

ISBN 978-1-907767-06-7

British Library Cataloguing in Publication Data.
A catalogue card for this book is available from the British Library.

Printed in the UK by Lightning Source.

Dedication

In memoriam
Giuseppe Bezza
21 September 1946 – 18 June 2014
amico nostro, caro et docto

CONTENTS

Abstracts

Giuseppe Bezza

Saturn–Jupiter Conjunctions and General Astrology: Ptolemy, Abū Ma'shar and Their Commentators

This essay explores the tradition of Saturn–Jupiter conjunctions in astrological techniques, from its beginnings in the use of the 'revolution of the year' in natal astrology, to its transference into general astrology by early Arabic astrologers. Commentaries on both Ptolemy and Abū Ma'shar deal with this doctrine. The first part of the essay looks at the conjunctionist theories of Abū Ma'shar and locates them in natural movements as described by Aristotle, but with Abū Ma'shar's own interpretation and hierarchy. He relates his scheme to the influence of heavenly bodies on earth. Scholastic philosophers took similar positions in discussing the influence and value of the planets, particularly the superior planets as a cause of stability. The closer to the prime mover the greater the planet's perfection. Superior planets could also be guides to inferior ones applying to them by aspect, as Albertus Magnus claims. Later writers such as Nifo and Ciruelo privileged not the superior planets but the luminaries, following the Ptolemaic tradition. Others, such as Ibn Riḍwān, Naibod, Cardano and Kepler discussed conjunctionist theory with respect to doctrines in the (pseudo-) Ptolemaic *Centiloquium*.

Jean-Patrice Boudet

From Baghdad to Civitas Solis*: Horoscopes of Foundations of Cities*

In the original Italian version of *La Città del Sole* (1602) and the Latin version of *Civitas Solis* (1637), Tommaso Campanella refers to two slightly different horoscopes of the City of the Sun. The second one is a real masterpiece of utopian astrology and a noteworthy achievement of Medieval and Renaissance research on the ideal city. This paper tries to find the earlier versions of this dream and reconstitute some of its experimentations. In contrast with most of the Ancient and Byzantine Greek horoscopes of cities, the foundation chart of Baghdad seems to show the difference between an ideal horoscope and an election of the better moment to initiate a major political event. We have some astrological indications about foundations of other cities in the Medieval Middle East but for the Latin Middle Ages, the material is poor and no original horoscope of a city is preserved from this period. However, Giovanni and Filippo Villani seem to refer to a real horoscope of Florence which could have been cast by Cecco of Ascoli († 1327), and the Cinquecento may be considered as the golden age of the horoscopes of cities, with a remarkable competition between the main Italian urban states and their champions in this matter—Luca Gaurico, Girolamo Cardano and Francesco Giuntini—who copied and modified a largely common astrological practice with an important manipulation. Almost all of these horoscopes are not properly catarchic, but try to explain *a posteriori* the major historical events of the cities. Between the two opposite exceptions of Baghdad and the City of the Sun, the great majority of foundation horoscopes seem to be attempts for retrospective and historical analysis.

Bernadette Brady
Galileo's Astrological Philosophy
Within the history of science questions have been asked as to the source of Galileo's approach to his natural philosophy. This paper addresses these questions through a consideration of Galileo's astrological papers known as the *Astrologica nonnulla*. This paper argues that the Arabic style of astrology used by Galileo was in itself a challenge to Aristotle's physics. This style of astrology emerged in the ninth century in parallel with Islamic occasionalism and was focused on recording the changeability of the planets in the heavens and reducing them to a number value. This reductionism was undertaken to achieve a level of predictability in the believed incalculable Aristotelian sublunar realm. This paper suggests that this style of astrology provided Galileo with the thinking space which allowed him to work outside the Aristotelian-dominant world view.

Geoffrey Cornelius
Interpreting Interpretations: The Aphorism in the Practice of the Renaissance Astrologers
How may we interpret the interpretations of the astrologers? This hermeneutic question is approached through the ubiquitous astrological device of the aphorism. Underlying the apparently arbitrary assemblage of these pithy maxims we discern a thematic methodology of exemplary connotation and metaphor. Theory and practice need to be distinguished, which permits going beyond the

often merely nominal Aristotelian-Ptolemaic gloss by which Renaissance astrologers might justify their craft. This reveals a poetic and divinatory form, wherein the meaning of the aphorism is determined by its context, the temporality and linguistic mood of its interpretation, viz. whether speculative and conjectural, the subjunctive of prediction, or assigned and revealed, the indicative of the casebook demonstration. This 'divinatory stochastic' analysis necessitates a reading-against the historical and theoretical view of astrology as proto-science. The problem of competing interpretations is illustrated with reference to a horoscope study by Girolamo Cardano, where it is suggested that contemporary scholarship, to the extent that it lacks an appreciation of astrological practice, has not adequately addressed the task of interpreting the astrologers' interpretations.

Meira Epstein
Curriculum by Design: Ibn Ezra's Astrological Texts
Ibn Ezra's astrological works have been called encyclopaedic, standing out as an integrated corpus that covers all disciplines of the astrological doctrine, from the fundamental to the advanced. Over the centuries, typical astrological texts have functioned as compendia of contemporary knowledge and served in the transmission of this discipline from one generation to the next. At first glance, Ibn Ezra's work appears to have the same characteristics, yet a closer look reveals another agenda of teaching and instruction in the form of a comprehensive curriculum. Internal evidence for this is found in the language of the text, the structured topics, the cross-references from one book to another, and the sequence of the books. Yet intriguing external evidence comes from the timing and the locale of their composition. All these lead to a deduction that this corpus was composed 'on demand', as a complete curriculum for a specific audience seeking this kind of knowledge. The art and skill of teaching include not only imparting information but understanding student needs, where difficulties may lie, anticipating confusion and providing effective methods of learning. Ibn Ezra demonstrates all that throughout his writings. The cumulative effect of such instances, combined with textual evidence, proves the teaching agenda that underlies this corpus.

Miquel Forcada
Astrology in al-Andalus during the 11th and 12th Centuries: Between Religion and Philosophy
This article studies the history of astrology in al-Andalus during the period when scientific activity reaches its peak. During the eleventh century, astrological production grows in quantity and quality but so does anti-astrological literature. The advent into power of the North African dynasties in the late eleventh century prompts the decline of astrological practice due to religious reasons. During the second half of the twelfth century, the Aristotelian philosophers likewise adopt an anti-astrological stance based on scientific considerations. The article analyzes, on the one hand, the arguments in favor of astrology found in eleventh century sources from al-Andalus, namely a chapter of the memoirs written by the Zirid king of Granada, ʻAbd Allah b. Buluggīn (r. 1075–1090). On the other hand, it surveys the anti-astrological arguments of the religious scholars of the eleventh century that hastened astrology's decline, focusing on three major authors, Ibn ʻAbd al-Barr (978–1071), Abū l-Walīd al-Bājī (1012–1081) and Ibn Ḥazm (991–1064), and their relationship with the anti-astrological discourse of philosophers like Ibn Bājja (d. 1139) and Ibn Rushd (d. 1198). The article also studies the place of astrology in the scientific practice of this time.

Dorian Gieseler Greenbaum
Kepler's Personal Astrology: Two Letters to Michael Maestlin
This essay explores a small portion of a personal astrological correspondence between Johannes Kepler and Michael Maestlin. It deals with a series of letters between the two on the births of their two sons, born ten days apart. Kepler and Maestlin discuss the boys' nativities, their hopes and expectations for their newborn sons, and the astrological interpretations to be drawn from the birthcharts. While Kepler's astronomical works have been frequently discussed by scholars, his astrological texts have received much less attention. With the Kepler Commission's recent publication (2009) of Kepler's astrological charts with additional theoretical and practical treatises on astrology and its practice, it is possible to examine Kepler's work in astrology in greater depth. These letters between Kepler and Maestlin illustrate Kepler's personal connection to astrology and his use of it for his own family.

Robert Hand

Evidence in Bonatti for the Practical Application of Certain Astrological Techniques

This paper will present some preliminary findings, as well as a demonstration of a methodology from my PhD dissertation entitled 'The Use of Military Astrology in Late Medieval Italy: The Textual Evidence' (Catholic University of America, 2013). The object of the dissertation is to show how the evolution of material presented in astrological writings, its quantity, its specificity, and its level of technical complexity, evolved in the hands of medieval Italian astrologers with respect to what they received from their predecessors in late Greek and Arabic astrology. Among the most important of these predecessors are Sahl ibn Bishr (d. ca. 822); al-Kindī (d. 870); possibly 'Alī ibn Abi l-Rijāl (fl. 1036 or 1062), known to the Latin world as Haly Abenragel; as well as 'Alī ibn Aḥmad al-'Imrānī (d. ca. 955), known to the Latin world as Haly Emrani. The medieval Italians in question are Guido Bonatti (ca. 1210–ca. 1290) principally, and Laurentius Bonincontrius (1410–1502). I hope to demonstrate that a close examination of the evolution of astrological method from these earlier authors to Bonatti, Bonincontrius and others after him, can be used by historians as a source of evidence from within the astrological tradition regarding the purposes for which astrology was employed. For reasons to be explained in the article I have chosen the use of astrology in conflict and warfare.

Stephan Heilen

Paul of Middelburg's Prognosticum *for the years 1484 to 1504*

This contribution is a case-study of one of the most influential conjunctionist texts of the Renaissance. Despite its importance, this text has hitherto received very little scholarly attention. Paul of Middelburg (1445–1533) first published his *Prognosticum* for the years 1484 to 1504 in August 1484. Its objects were two upcoming, rare astronomical events, the conjunction of Saturn and Jupiter in Scorpio in November 1484 and a total solar eclipse in Aries in March 1485. Unlike the countless annual predictions that were published by Renaissance astronomers (including Paul himself), this prediction covers twenty years, the approximate value of the periodicity of Saturn-Jupiter-conjunctions which had been standardized in the Perso-Arabic theory of the so-called 'Great Conjunctions' as the period of influence of each Saturn–Jupiter conjunction on the sublunar world. The present contribution aims at providing a detailled summary of the text and discussing its major characteristics.

Jan P. Hogendijk

Al-Bīrūnī on the Computation of Primary Progression (tasyīr)

This article concerns the astrological 'Book 11' of the Masudic Canon, one of the most important works of medieval Islamic astronomy, written by al-Bīrūnī between 1030 and 1040. In sections 1–4 of Chapter 5 of his 'Book 11', al-Bīrūnī deals with the astrological doctrine of primary progression (*tasyīr*) and presents a geometric introduction, followed by a number of approximate and exact computations with proofs. The sections have been published in Arabic: we present English translation and commentary with some worked examples. The doctrines of al-Bīrūnī involve the concept of 'astrological (ecliptic) longitude', which was reintroduced in the 20th century in the Dutch astrological school headed by Theo J. J. Ram (1884–1961).

Piergabriele Mancuso

Cosmological Traditions in Judeo-Byzantine South Italy: A Preliminary Analysis

Between the eighth and the tenth centuries, the Jews of southern Italy, at that time under the political and cultural influence of Byzantium, experienced a time of cultural renaissance, best represented by the composition in Hebrew—a language that the diaspora had neglected as a tool of scientific transmission in favour of local vernaculars, especially Arabic—of work on various disciplines, from historiography through mathematics to astrology and astronomy. In an attempt to reconcile the tenets of Ptolemy with the cosmological traditions preserved in the Bible and especially in the rabbinical writings (particularly the Talmud), Shabbatai Donnolo, a tenth century polymath from Apulia, the 'heel' of Italy's boot, examined and interpreted the *Baraita of Samuel,* an anonymous text produced probably in Palestine in the eighth century and mainly elaborating on Ptolemaic astrological teaching, and *Sefer Yetzirah,* another anonymous work dating to between the third and sixth centuries whose cosmology, however, did not abide by any known tradition, especially the writing of Ptolemy. The result of Donnolo's analysis is the 'deconstruction' of the two texts, especially *Sefer Yetzirah,* and the definition of a new, plausibly coherent, view of the universe and the cosmos dominated by a hierarchies of entities and celestial creatures.

Josefina Rodríguez-Arribas
Quantitative Concepts in Hellenistic and Medieval Astrology
My research in this article regarding the concept of 'power/strength' and three other minor quantitative/countable terms in Hellenistic and medieval astrology confirms the conclusions of my previous article on the concept of 'testimony' ('The Testimonies in Medieval Astrology: Finding Degrees of Certitude in Astrological Judgments', in *Doxa, Études sur les formes et la construction de la croyance,* ed. Pascale Hummel [Paris: Philologicum, 2010], pp. 115–33). In the ensemble of medieval manuscripts on the science of the stars, writers frequently considered the relationship between astronomy and astrology and the different status that each one held in the medieval classification of sciences. All medieval scientists considered astronomy a science, which means that it was considered evident and relying on clear proofs, whereas astrology, even for its practitioners, seemed to rely more upon experience and tradition, and its conclusions were approximate and, frequently, fallible. For this reason, astrologers devised different systems in order to establish degrees of certainty in the judgements that they could formulate about the positions or configurations of the elements in a horoscope. These systems left an imprint in the astrological terminology of Hellenistic and especially medieval texts, which I have analysed in my two articles.

H. Darrel Rutkin
Giuliano Ristori and Filippo Fantoni on Pseudo-Prophets, Great Conjunctions and Other Astrological Effects
In his lectures of the 1540s on Ptolemy's *Tetrabiblos* at the University of Pisa, Giuliano Ristori (1492–1556) identified Girolamo Savonarola as the pseudo-prophet predicted by the Great Conjunction in Scorpio of 1484, as others had identified Martin Luther. Although his successor at Pisa, Filippo Fantoni (ca. 1530–1591), used Ristori's lectures as the basis of his own Ptolemy course there—delivered in 1585 during Galileo's student years—Fantoni made no such identification. Rather, manuscript evidence reveals that Fantoni scratched out Savonarola's name quite emphatically in the text of Ristori's

lectures. In this essay, I will begin by describing the teaching of astrology at the University of Pisa in the 16th century. Then I will transcribe and analyze the text of Ristori's identification from MS Riccardiana 157 and of Fantoni's modification from MS Conventi Soppressi B.VII.479 of the Biblioteca Nazionale Centrale in Florence.

Julio Samsó
Astrology in Morocco towards the End of the Fourteenth Century and the Beginning of the Fifteenth Century
This paper analyses two astrological sources written in Morocco towards the end of the fourteenth and beginning of the fifteenth centuries: the commentary on an astrological poem by Ibn Abī l-Rijāl (11th c.) written by Ibn Qunfudh al-Qusanṭīnī (1339–1407) and the 'Book on rains and prices' authored by Abū ʿAbd Allāh al-Baqqār (fl. 1418). The former can be considered as an example of standard medieval Islamic astrology, while the latter is far more primitive, as it contains one of the few Arabic texts related to the 'system of the crosses' for astrological prediction, which seems to derive, ultimately, from a late Latin source used in the Iberian Peninsula and the Maghrib before the arrival of Muslim conquerors in 711. This system continued to be used in al-Andalus not only at the beginning of the 9th century but also in the 11th century and, obviously, in Morocco in the 15th century.

Petra G. Schmidl
Elections in Medieval Islamic Folk Astronomy
Elections usually describe an astrological method for choosing the most appropriate time for an important event—e.g., when to start a journey, or when to get married—by using the constellations. A specific sort of elections is found in medieval Islamic folk astronomical texts. There are lists included that usually relate the heliacal or cosmic rising of a lunar mansion to specific human enterprises that are either recommended or rejected during this period of approximately 13 days of the year.

Taking Ibn Raḥīq's text written in 11th century Hejaz as an example, this article will introduce in detail the specific character of these non-standard or non-mathematical lunar elections. It will provide some background information for integrating this text into the astronomical traditions of Medieval Islam, and add some other examples to illustrate that Ibn Raḥīq's text is not an isolated phenomenon.

Shlomo Sela
Abraham Ibn Ezra's Interpretation of Astrology according to the Two Versions of the Book of Reasons
In the framework of his astrological corpus, Abraham Ibn Ezra (ca. 1089–ca. 1161) composed two treatises which bear the same title: *Sefer ha-Ṭeʿamim,* the *Book of Reasons*. They were written to accomplish a similar although not identical purpose: to offer 'reasons', 'explanations', or 'meanings', of the raw astrological concepts formulated in two different introductions to astrology also composed by him: the two versions of *Reshit Ḥokhmah, Beginning of Wisdom*. Ibn Ezra's astrological treatises as a rule are infused with a didactic character and do not make any pretension of innovation. But the two versions of the *Book of Reasons* represent a special case: providing the 'reasons' behind the astrological doctrines presented in another text presupposes a more creative approach, a more innovative explanatory strategy, and a more resourceful reorganization of the available data. The main purpose of this article is to bring to light the main characteristics of Ibn Ezra's interpretive strategy: his approach to the creation of a new comprehensive Hebrew astrological vocabulary; his attitude towards his sources; his explanations of astrological doctrines; his attempt to interpret astrology in the light of the branches of science of his times and to bring astrology into harmony with them.

Graeme Tobyn
Dr Reason and Dr Experience: Culpeper's Assignation of Planetary Rulers in The English Physitian
Culpeper's herbal *The English Physitian* (1652) and its enlarged edition of the following year is unusual in its consistent attribution of a planetary correspondence for each plant, for which 'astrological botany' it became the subject of negative scrutiny by historians of the herbal. While astrology was traditionally linked to the medical art, its influence did not normally extend to the identification of specific remedies needed in a given case by their astrological 'rulers'. Culpeper was using a macrocosm-microcosm analogy that was an aspect of the cosmology of Paracelsian medicine. This was applied both to the gathering of the herbs under a propitious sky

and their clinical use according to astrological concepts of sympathy and antipathy. The astrological authors among the cited sources for the herbal, notably Antoine Mizauld, appear to have contributed little to Culpeper's correspondences. Analysis of these according to his explicit or implicit justifications in the text show that a herb might correspond to a planet because it strengthens the organ ruled by the planet, or by the doctrine of signatures or because its manifest qualities are shared by the planet. Over half of the herbs have no such correspondence and are often linked according to their medicinal actions on target organs, a link frequently supported by their visual appearance according to a doctrine of signatures.

Steven Vanden Broecke
Self-governance and the Body Politic in Renaissance Annual Prognostications
This paper tries to sidestep two dominant interpretations of the early modern prognostication. On the one hand, historians have suggested that these texts are best interpreted as printed commodities in an early modern information economy, providing individuals with a tool for fine-tuning the rationality of their acquisitive actions by taking in credible knowledge of the future. On the other hand, historians have also portrayed the early Renaissance prognostication as a site where 'popular' fears and anxieties, stimulated by the objective uncertainty and disorder of an entire age, manifested themselves in the form of 'pessimistic' predictions which could easily cross over into the language and imagery of apocalyptic prophecy. As an alternative, I lay out evidence that early prognostication culture is best interpreted as part of a late medieval culture of political governance which had begun to carve itself out within the older theological discourse of divine care and guidance of his people. Contrary to what is often suggested, prognosticators did not seek to protect individual readers from celestially induced misfortune. Instead, they tried to inject a measure of stability and rationality inside the constant play of celestially induced passions and effects (both unfortunate and fortunate). At the same time, early prognostication culture also testifies to a novel interest in the body politic, rather than the more homogeneous and universal social body of Christ, as the ultimate focus of its attention. The ideal reader of the prognostication was expected to identify himself as a member of the natural realm of

elements, plants and animals, of the social body of Christendom, and of a body politic consisting of different social estates under the guidance of specific secular rulers.

FROM MĀSHĀ'ALLĀH TO KEPLER: THEORY AND PRACTICE IN MEDIEVAL AND RENAISSANCE ASTROLOGY

INTRODUCTION

Charles Burnett and Dorian Gieseler Greenbaum

The history of modern scholarship in astrology has gone through several changes of viewpoint since its inception at the end of the nineteenth century. Esteemed scholars such as Franz Cumont and Auguste Bouché-Leclercq, whose books remain staples of scholarship in astrology, wrote from the perspective of astrology as a scorned and discarded part of the past, worthy perhaps of some historical notice, but ultimately a 'wretched subject'.[1] By the middle of the twentieth century, however, the field, still mostly denigrated but now beginning to be considered worthy of study on its own merits, attracted a new, still high-calibre generation of scholars, including Otto Neugebauer, David Pingree and John North. By the end of the twentieth century scholars such as Anthony Grafton, Francesca Rochberg and Wolfgang Hübner continued in the tradition of excellent scholarship, but now fully acknowledged the cultural importance and value of astrology. The twenty-first century has seen a continuation of this trend and, importantly, emphasises the viewpoint of astrology not as a failed science and intellectually bankrupt scam on the public, but as a crucial part of social, scientific and cultural history.

However, although astrology's reputation continues to be rehabilitated within specialised areas of scholarship, its outer reputation in general has not kept pace (see, for example, the work of Richard Dawkins). In addition, there is still a tendency within astrological scholarship to concentrate on the social context of astrology, the attacks on astrologers and their craft, and on astrological iconography and symbolism within other fields like religion, i.e., largely to look on astrology from the outside. This book aims to remedy that

[1] Taken from the rebuttal by Otto Neugebauer, 'The Study of Wretched Subjects', (*Isis* 42, 1951: p. 111), to George Sarton's comments on E. S. Drower's *The Book of the Zodiac (Sfar Malwasia)* (*Isis* 41, 1950: p. 374), in which Sarton used the term 'wretched' to describe 'omens, debased astrology and miscellaneous nonsense'.

tendency. Its intention is to look at the subject from the inside: the ideas and techniques of astrologers themselves. What did *astrologers* write about astrology and how did they teach their subject and practise their craft? What changes occurred in astrological theory and practice over time and from one culture to another? What cosmological and philosophical frameworks did astrologers use to orient their practice? What place did astrology have in universities and academies?

The genesis of this book was a conference at the Warburg Institute, London, in 2008. 'From Masha'allah to Kepler: The Theory and Practice of Astrology in the Middle Ages and Renaissance' took place at the Institute on 13–15 November of that year. The conference itself was a convivial and stimulating exchange of ideas on the theory and practice of astrology from the eighth to the seventeenth centuries, covering large areas of time, space and intellectual endeavour.

As conveners of the conference, we saw a need for scholars to present information and analysis of topics in the history of astrology which have often been overlooked by the usual study of this field. These topics included, especially, the theory, practice and application of astrology, placed in context and elucidated by the actual practitioners of astrology in the medieval period and Renaissance. To this end, we are remarkably pleased at the variety both in topics and in the geographical areas covered by the essays. Papers range geographically from Morocco to England, from al-Andalus to Baghdad. Some of them concentrate on the presentation of specific texts in astrology which have not heretofore been published, for example the contribution of Stephan Heilen. Folk and popular astrology is covered by Petra Schmidl and Graeme Tobyn. Jan Hogendijk presents an astronomical text which was used in astrological practice. An astrologer's interpretation of astrology is covered by Shlomo Sela. Astrology in specific geographical areas is explored by Miquel Forcada, Julio Samso and Piergabriele Mancuso. Other essays deal with the examination and analysis of particular techniques used in the astrology of this period: these include the papers of Giuseppe Bezza, Jean-Patrice Boudet, Robert Hand, Josefina Rodríguez-Arribas and Dorian Greenbaum. Some cover the teaching of astrology: Darrel Rutkin and Meira Epstein. Still others contemplate problems in the theory or philosophy of astrology which have not been explored by scholars before now, such as the essays of Bernadette Brady, Geoffrey Cornelius and Steven Vanden Broecke. In fact, though, these narrow classifications sometimes do not do the authors' works justice, because their essays range over several different classifications—philosophy, teaching and practice—or development of an astrological doctrine as well as its practical application. For this reason we decided to present the articles in alphabetical order, rather than by genre.

Despite these varying approaches, all of the contributions have at least one thing in common: a rigorous approach to the subject material, ignited by the obvious passion the speakers have for their chosen topics. In sum, the volume addresses a number of gaps in the history of scholarship in this field and, we hope, will be a useful addition to the libraries of scholars and interested readers in the history of astrology.

We thank Nicholas Campion for offering and generously supporting the publication of these papers by the Sophia Centre Press, and to Jean-Patrice Boudet for providing some of the funds to produce this volume. We also thank Meira Epstein for her rapid and effective assistance in formatting some articles containing Hebrew script. In addition, we thank our copy-editor, Marcia Butchart, and production editor, Jennifer Zahrt. Finally, we are grateful to Helena Avelar and Luís Ribeiro for their inspiration and help in finding the cover image for us.

Almost at the end of this long editing process, we were saddened to learn of the death of our dear colleague and friend, Giuseppe Bezza. His vast knowledge of the history and practice of astrology, coupled with his unfailing kindness and generosity, will be sorely missed, and his expertise hard to replace. We dedicate this volume to his memory.

Finally, due to both avoidable and unavoidable delays, the essays in this volume have languished for far too long on various hard drives until now. As the editors, we are very pleased indeed to present them to the public at last.

Charles Burnett, Warburg Institute
Dorian Gieseler Greenbaum, University of Wales Trinity Saint David

SATURN–JUPITER CONJUNCTIONS AND GENERAL ASTROLOGY: PTOLEMY, ABŪ MA'SHAR AND THEIR COMMENTATORS

Giuseppe Bezza

At the beginning of the first book of the *Summa Anglicana*, John of Ashenden explains the reasons that made him write a treatise on the prognostication of general events:

> Many ancient and modern astrologers wrote good treatises on weather forecasting and general events, but they all omitted something in their judgements. Ptolemy, who is the most worthy of them, explains the general rules of prognostication, which are based on the observation of eclipses, the quarters of the year, and the conjunctions and oppositions of the Sun and the Moon; but he does not mention the great conjunctions and the revolutions of the world-year. Albumasar, in his *Great Introduction*, presents many noteworthy rules about changes in the weather, but his explanation does not proceed in an ordered way. And, though his treatment of the great conjunctions is exhaustive, he is not convincing about eclipses and is silent on their judgements. Alkindi proceeds in a well-ordered way, but he says nothing about great conjunctions and eclipses. Dorotheus, Aomar and Gerdis [*sic*] mention nothing about the great conjunctions and the eclipses, although the rules they present are useful. As for Robert of Lincoln and the moderns, they make judgements according to the essential and accidental dignities of the planets only for weather conditions. Thus nobody has discussed general events in a way adequate for the purpose of the doctrine. Since I think it is possible to obtain from these books a true natural method about the change of weather and general events, it is my intention, in this treatise, to weigh up all the rules of the ancients according to the natural order of the doctrine.[1]

[1] 'Maxima vero causa quare hoc opus agressus sum est ista quia modo sunt multi astrologi antiqui et moderni multa et bona de tempestate aeris et de his quæ contingunt in mundo documenta scribunt et modum pronosticandi docent; sed inter omnes nullum invenio quin in suis libris omittant aliqua quæ in huiusmodi iudiciis forent necessaria et iudicantibus multipliciter possent valere. Ptolemæus quem inter omnes reputamus valentiorem in libro quadripartiti valde rationabilis procedit: in hac enim materia docet

This concise survey may not be complete, but it accurately represents the point of view of medieval astrologers. For this reason, some years later Pierre d'Ailly, at the beginning of his *Elucidarium*, repeats *verbatim* John of Ashenden's general considerations.[2] We can see, within the branches of astrology, how that of general astrology is based, above all, on Arabic sources. Peter of Abano and Nicole Oresme are two clear examples. Ptolemy's authority, however, as John of Ashenden remarks, is limited to the treatment of eclipses and syzygies, which represents only a small part of the predictive arsenal. On the other hand, Arabic astrologers are the principal authorities with regard to the great conjunctions and the revolutions of the world-years. These techniques may belong to Arabic astrology, but their roots lie within certain doctrines of Greek astrology, specifically natal techniques which were transferred to Arabic doctrines of general astrology.

---

regulas generales pronosticandi per eclipsim, deinde per quartas anni et postmodum per coniunctiones et oppositiones luminarium, deinde per eorum quadraturas, sed de coniunctionibus magnis videlicet sextum sententiarum [*legendum: centum viginti coniunctiones*] planetarum et de revolutionibus annorum mundi nihil penitus determinat. Albumasar tamen in maiori introductorio multas de temperie dat regulas notabiles, eas non tamen ponit in aliquo ordine, et licet de coniunctionibus magnis pertractet, de eclipsi luminarium parum loquitur nec earum iudicia manifestat. Alchindus vero quamvis notabiliter procedat, nihil tamen loquitur de coniunctionibus magnis nec de eclipsibus. Messahalla etiam quasi totaliter de magnis effectibus pertractat. Sed Dorotheus et Aomar et Gerdis (sic) paucas regulas sed notabiles, de eclipsibus vero et magnis coniunctionibus nihil loquuntur. Linconiensis autem et moderni secundum dignitates planetarum et essentiales et accidentales tantummodo de aeris mutatione iudicant, et sic discurrendo per singulos nullus eorum de temperie sufficienter loquitur. Et quia de eorum libris via naturalis et recta pro temperie ut mihi videre posset elici, eorum omnium sententias ac regulas secundum naturalem ordinem in hoc libro meo pro operis facilitate iudicandi pro posse meo iudicabo' (*Summa astrologiæ iudicialis de accidentibus mundi quæ anglicana vulgo nuncupatur, Ioannis Eschuidi viri anglici eiusdem scientiæ astrologiæ peritissimi* [Venice, 1489], I, dist. 1, sig. A 2r, col. b).

[2] Pietro d'Abano, *Concordantia astronomie cum theologia. Concordantia astronomie cum hystorica narratione. Et elucidarium duorum precedentium, domini Petri de Aliaco cardinalis Cameracensis* (Venice, 1490), sig. e1v.

- praecognatio per astronomiam
  - astronomicum circa stellarum motus
  - effectrix circa stellarum actiones
    - futurorum praedictio
      - universalis
        - causae universales
        - causae particulares
      - particularis
        - causae particulares
    - institutio
      - in stellarum signorumque habitudines per ipsas et ad invicem

Fig. 1: Ptolemaei doctrina.

PIETRO D'ABANO
Conciliator, diff. X; *Lucidator*, diff. I

- scientia quantitatum figurarum ordinationis et motuum corporum vel scientia totius
- scientia iudiciorum
  - exercitativa
    - de revolutionibus
      - de 120 coniunctionibus temporum
        Albumasar, Messahalae, Haly eben Ragel, Abraham duplex, Johannes Hispalensis
      - de revolutione anni secundum introitum solis in caput arietis vel ex coniunctione seu oppositione solis praecedente
        Ptholomeus, Albumasar, Haly eben Regel, Abraham duplex, Johannes Hyspalensis
      - de mutatione
        Alkindi
    - de nativitatibus et eorum revolutionibus
    - de interrogationibus
    - de electionibus
  - introductiva ad iudicia

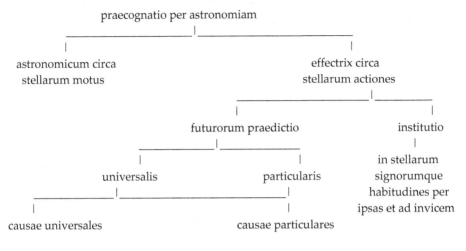

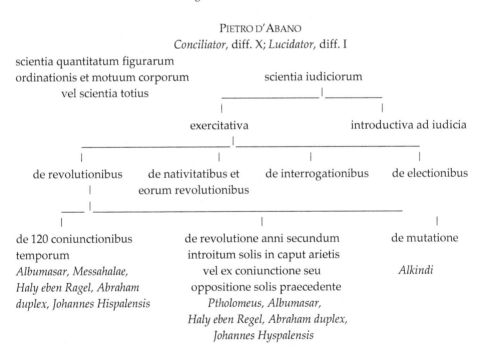

NICOLE ORESME
Livre de divinacions, ch. 2

astrologie

- mouvements, signes, mesures des corps du ciel
- qualitez, influences, puissances naturelles
- revolucions des astres, conjonctions des planetes
    - grans conjonctions
    - mutations du temps
    - humeurs du corps humain
- nativitez
- interrogacions
- elections

Fig. 2: Petrus Aponensis, Oresme.

From Greek doctrines to Arabic astrology

In the first two centuries of its history, Arabic astrology was deeply under Persian influence. Most of the astronomers and astrologers of the Abbasid period were Persian and transferred the characteristic elements of their tradition to the newborn Arabic astrology. In addition, a few technical terms from Persian astrology came into the Arabic lexicon. For the most part these are terms related to the doctrine of the length of life, like *kadkhudhāh* and *haylāj*, from which astrologers measured the substance of life and its ups and downs. Other terms, like *fardār*, *jar bakhtār*, *sālkhudhāh* are related to the periods following the birth, to the good or poor quality of future events. These terms and techniques do not come from Persian astrology, nor are they the result of the elaboration of Sassanid astrologers but, instead, are a fundamental part of Greek genethlialogy. We can find all of them in the principal Greek sources available to the Persian astrologers, primarily Dorotheus, Ptolemy and Vettius Valens. What is original to Persian and Arabic astrology is the transfer of these and other terms and techniques of genethlialogical astrology to general astrology through a mimetic process.

These terms belong to the branch of genethlialogy which Pingree called 'continuous astrology': παράδοσις (Latin *perfectio/profectio*, Arabic *intihā'*, translated by Zebelenos as τελείωσις), which revolves the years of the nativity according to the regular cycle of the twelve zodiacal signs and overlaps with the περίπατος, *directio, tasyīr*. In this way certain divisions, μερισμοί, are produced (Arabic *qismāt*, and the lord of *qisma* is the *qāsim* (transliterated by Zebelenos as χασίμ), distributor (ἐπιμερίζων in the Greek version of Abū Ma'shar's *De revolutionibus nativitatum*, διοικητὴς in Zebelenos).[3] These are the premisses on which the judgement of the revolution of the years proceeds. Arabic astrology transferred all these methods from genethlialogy to general astrology. So, the revolution of the years—not of the nativity, but of the world—became one of the foundation stones of historical and political astrology.

It is hard to imagine that this shift from genethlialogical to general techniques occurred under the influence of Greek astrology. Greek astrological literature is rich in the field of genethlialogy and interrogations, but poor in judgements about general events. The second book of Ptolemy's *Quadripartitum* is the greatest authority: here, eclipses and syzygies are the basic elements of the doctrine, and it is not possible to develop any regular cycle. On the contrary, the doctrine of the revolutions of the world-years, borrowed from Greek genethlialogy, is based on a regular sequence of motions of the superior planets, Saturn and Jupiter. The purpose of this doctrine was to give a cosmic model of historical development and political and religious changes. General astrology as it developed in the first period of Arabic science was strongly affected by Indian and Persian elements. It took the Greek structure of the doctrine of nativities as a template, transferring it from the microcosm, i.e., the human being, to the environment surrounding him. So, genethlialogical enquiries concerning future events described by Dorotheus, Ptolemy, Vettius Valens, Paul of Alexandria and others, were modified for the wider social environment. The doctrine of the revolution of the years, created by Greek astrologers with respect to the human being, was now transferred, with all its elements, to general astrology. In this way, the conjunctionist doctrine becomes a theory provided with a marvellous regularity, capable of establishing planetary periodisation and able to explain the course of history.

This doctrine is based on a hierarchy of causes that Abū Ma'shar arranges in six steps: the first four are the great, middle and small conjunctions of Saturn and Jupiter and the conjunction of Saturn and Mars in the sign of Cancer; the

[3] Cf. Giuseppe. Bezza, 'Il trattato sulle natività di Eleuterio Zebeleno di Elis', *MHNH, Revista Internacional de Investigación sobre Magia y Astrología Antiguas*, 2 (2002), pp. 257–300.

fifth and the sixth are the syzygies of the luminaries: the conjunction or the opposition of the Sun and Moon before the beginning of each season and in each month.[4] Abū Ma'shar justifies this hierarchical order by referring to the three natural movements described in Aristotle's *De cælo* (I, 2; 268 b20): 'All simple motion must be motion either from or towards or around the centre.'[5] Abū Ma'shar changes the order of these movements, by putting movement around the centre first, movement away from the centre, second, and movement towards the centre third.[6] The middle movement, away from the centre, is appropriate to the Sun, since it is in the middle of the planets, according to the Chaldean order. The spheres of the superior planets move around the centre, and the spheres of the inferior planets towards the centre. Therefore, the Sun divides the planets into two classes, and each of them can be understood as having a clearly distinct nature.

In some ways Abū Ma'shar's interpretation of the Aristotelian definition of natural motions appears defective, but his aim is to present a theory of his own about the specific influence of the stars. This theory describes the celestial bodies as analogous to terrestrial ones because their changing phases and conditions are the same; some philosophers described this vicissitude as a *tasrīf*—an alternation produced from a change of direction, analogous to the declension of the noun.[7]

Ibn al-Nadīm tells us of analogies that Sahl ibn Ḥārūn (d. 859–860), one of the directors of the House of Wisdom (Bayt al-Ḥikma), a little earlier than Abū Ma'shar, conceived between the natural world and the world of letters: just as the Arabic noun has three declensions, so must three be the number of natural motions: one moves away from the centre, like fire; another towards the centre, like earth; the third around the centre, like the celestial bodies.[8] These three motions are analogous to the motions of terrestrial things but they are, in their

---

[4] Abū Ma'shar, *On Historical Astrology. The Book of Religions and Dynasties (On the Great Conjunctions)*, ed. and trans. Keiji Yamamoto and Charles Burnett (Boston, Köln, Leiden: Brill, 2000), I, 1 [12–15], [19–20], vol. I, pp. 10–11, 18–19.

[5] Aristotle, *On the Heavens*, trans. J.L. Stocks (Oxford: The Clarendon Press, 1922).

[6] Abū Ma'shar, *On Historical Astrology*, I, 1 [7–10], vol. I, pp. 6–9, 607.

[7] Paul Kraus, *Jâbir ibn Hayyân. Contribution à l'histoire des idées scientifiques dans l'Islam. Jâbir et la science grecque* (Paris: Les Belles Lettres, 1986), p. 241 and n. 6.

[8] Ibn al-Nadīm, *Fihrist*, Arabic, ed. Gustav Flügel, repr. (Beirut: Khayats, 1964), p. 10; English trans., Bayard Dodge (New York and London: Columbia University Press), p. 19.

origin, celestial motions.

Triadic structure and the influence of heavenly bodies

These three motions, *ad centrum, a centro, circa centrum,* says Abū Ma'shar, are natural: *al-ḥarakāt al-ṭabī'īya; ḥaraka, motus,* signifies, in philosophical language, the gradual transition from a potential to an actual state. It is natural, *ṭabī'īya,* because it does not originate from an external cause, but belongs to the intelligence that moves the planet in its sphere.[9] In his foundation of a rational astrology, Abū Ma'shar emphasizes the differentiation of natures, of the planets as well as of the signs and elements, made in accordance with a triadic structure within time. In this way he explains why there are twelve zodiacal signs: because the signs indicate the four elements, their number must represent the elements themselves at the beginning, the middle and the end of their effects on terrestrial beings.[10] In the first chapter of the first book of *De magnis coniunctionibus,* the triadic structure takes on a qualitative sense, and each of the three terms is inherent in each one of the three superior planets: the beginning, *ibtidā',* to Saturn; the culmination, *intihā',* to Jupiter; the dissolution, *inḥiṭāṭ,* to Mars.[11]

Abū Ma'shar says: 'The first division (*qism,* division in the sense of natural disposition) …[12] and its influence (*ta'thīr*) is related to the first natural movement.' The Latin version translates *ta'thīr* as *effectus,* and this translation is consistent with the meaning of the Arabic word. In fact, the *ta'thīrāt* are the physical impressions that inferior bodies receive from the superior ones. When al-Qabīṣī refers to the physical effects of the planets—for example, that Jupiter produces heat and moisture, Mars heat and dryness, and so on—the verb used is *athara,* 'to make a mark on', 'to have an effect on'. So, the word *ta'thīr* has the same meaning as ποιητικὸν <τῆς οὐσίας> in Ptolemy's *Quadripartitum.* It follows that the nature, as well as the proper and specific power of the planets, is based on their positions in their orbits, but this assumption is inconsistent with

---

[9] Abū Ma'shar, *On Historical Astrology,* vol. I, p. 6, lines 42–43.

[10] Abū Ma'shar al-Balkhī, *Liber introductorii maioris ad scientiam judiciorum astrorum,* ed. Richard Lemay (Naples: Istituto universitario orientale, 1995), vol. II, p. 119 (Arabic); vol. V, p. 72 (Latin translation of John of Seville).

[11] Abū Ma'shar, *On Historical Astrology,* vol I, p. 6, lines 47–54.

[12] Ibid., I, 1 [7], vol. I, p. 6, l. 44, p. 7.

the general concepts of Ptolemaic astrology.[13]

In the second chapter of the first book of the *Quadripartitum*, Ptolemy describes the specific actions of the Sun, Moon, fixed stars and planets. These last produce, by their transits, a great number of changes in the weather—πλείστας ἐπισημασίας—that is to say, sudden alterations in the regular and natural course of the seasons and of the generation and growth of living beings, which is provided for by the actions of the luminaries. The Greek anonymous commentator explains that the action of the Sun on the environment is always constant, since its nature cannot be altered at all. Nevertheless, the planets can change, somewhat, the quality of the Sun's action; if they cooperate, the quality will be more intense. If they do not cooperate or they thwart the Sun's action, the quality will be weaker.[14] Then Ptolemy says that the virtue of the Sun prevails over that of the Moon, and the virtue of the Moon over that of the other stars. After this, he makes a specific statement concerning the planets' action: the way the planets perform their operations, he says, is indistinct—ἀσημότερον—and περιοδικώτερον. Robbins translates this adverbial form as 'at greater intervals',[15] but the right meaning is 'intermittent' or 'recurrent'. So, the action of the stars, since it makes πλείστας ἐπισημασίας, can produce some irregularities and deviations from the common course of nature, just as an ἐπισημασία means a symptom of illness in the human body. Finally, Ptolemy explains in more detail the means by which the planets operate: their appearances, occultations and motions in latitude.[16] There are general rules about the *modus influendi* of the

---

[13] Cf. Francesco Cigalini, *Coelum sydereum ... secundum globorum cœlestium numerum, cursum et influxum emensuratum* ... (Como, 1655), Book III, p. 176: 'sunt autem opera stellarum secundum naturam, non secundum mathematicen'. This work was written about one century before its publication. See the preface of Marco Cigalini.

[14] For the text of the Greek commentator, and the different versions of the edition of Hieronymus Wolf, see the Appendix.

[15] Robbins' version of Ptolemy's *Tetrabiblos*, (Cambridge, MA: Harvard University Press, 1980 [1940]), I.2 (p. 9): 'For though the sun's power prevails in the general ordering of quality, the other heavenly bodies aid or oppose it in particular details, the moon more obviously and continuously, as for example when it is new, at quarter, or full, and the stars at greater intervals and more obscurely'. The best translation is by Antonio Gogava: 'De reliquis autem est incertior et intervallis rarior' (*Cl. Ptolemæi Pelusiensis Mathematici Operis Quadripartiti, in latinum sermonem traductio, adiectis libris posterioribus, Antonio Gogava Graviens interprete*, (Louvain, 1548), sig. B1r).

[16] This is the meaning of πρόσνευσις, cf. the Greek anonymous commentator:

planets, where appearances and occultations should be understood both in relation to the Sun and to the horizon. Moreover, with the term περιοδιώτερον, Ptolemy means that the operation of the planets, since it is dependent on their relations with the luminaries, is neither regular nor constant, but subordinate.

In the first chapters of the second book, Ptolemy goes on to define in a similar way the action exerted by the planets in the context of the first cause of general events, namely eclipses.[17]

Hierarchies of the planets: why Saturn–Jupiter conjunctions are powerful

On the other hand, the position of the scholastic philosophers was very similar to the assertion of Abū Maʿshar.[18] According to the concise phrasing of Michele Zanardo, who wrote a scholastic treatise on the universe in the first years of the seventeenth century, since the order of the spheres declares the divine wisdom, the same order shows their celestial perfection.[19] Saint Thomas, for example, affirms that the superior planets are the cause of stability and continuance in time, more than the inferior ones, and therefore Saturn indicates what is steady and stable (*De cælo* II, 18, 468). The effects of the planets in the sublunar world are related to the order of their spheres and Thomas repeats this judgment in the twelfth book of his *Metaphysica*. The closer the planet is to the first heaven, the greater its influence on the earth. The ascending order of the planets signifies

---

'προσνεύσεις appellat motus in latitudinem' (*In Claudii Ptolemaei quadripartitum enarrator ignoti nominis*, ed. and trans. Hieronymus Wolf [Basel, 1559], p. 5 [see Appendix]).

[17] Valentin Naibod is the author of the best commentary of this Ptolemaic chapter, cf. *Enarratio elementorum astrologiæ, in qua præter Alcabicij expositionem atque cum Ptolemæi principiiis collationem, rejectis sortilegiis et absurdis vulgoque receptis opinionibus, de vera artis præceptorum origine et usu disseritur* (Cologne, 1560), pp. 354–59; *Valentini Naibodæ Mathematici præclarissimi in Claudii Ptolemæi Quadripartitæ Constructionis Apotelesmata Commentarius novus et Eiusdem Conversio nova*, ms. London, British Library, Sloane A 216 XVI G, fols 31r–34v.

[18] For a full description of the different views in Scholastic philosophy cf. *Commentarii Collegii Conimbricensis S.I. in quatuor libros de cœlo, meteorologicos et parva naturalia Aristotelis Stagiritæ* (Cologne, 1596), 2, 5, 2, 1.2.3., pp. 269–73 and Antonio Rubio, *Commentarij in libros Aristotelis Stagiritæ de cœlo et mundo: una cum dubijs et quæstionibus in schola agitari solitis* (Cologne, 1626), 2, 5, 4, pp. 187–92.

[19] Michele Zanardo, *Universum Cæleste de omnibus et singulis quæ ad naturam cælestium spherarum, ab empyreo usque ad spheram elementorum faciunt, disputans, ac concludens* (Venice, 1619), pp. 17–18.

not only the ascending degree of their celestial perfection, but also the degree of their effective virtue.

We can conclude that the spheres of the planets nearest to the prime mover have a greater perfection; the containing sphere is more perfect than the contained one.[20] The sphere of Saturn is more perfect than that of Jupiter, the sphere of Jupiter more perfect than that of Mars, and so on. Nevertheless, the sphere of the Sun is nobler than the spheres of the planets but, according to the concept of perfection based on the container theory, the superior planets perform their actions in a more universal and permanent way. Thus, their influence on terrestrial beings is more powerful.

Therefore there are two concepts to be considered: that of the nobility of the substance and that of formal perfection. The first is based on the intrinsic nature of the celestial bodies, like light and magnitude; for this reason the Sun is the noblest among the celestial bodies. The second is a consequence of the statement that *rerum ordo divinam sapientiam prædicat*. Both these concepts are present in Medieval Scholasticism. Buridan, though he admits that the Sun is the noblest substance, repeats the distinction of Thomas on the hierarchy of the celestial bodies: the three superior planets rule living beings and the generation of all things, the three inferior planets rule their movements and alterations. Thus, the greater perfection belongs to the superior planets.[21] This distinction is essential, since it allows the conception of a universal law on the distinct causality of the individual celestial bodies.

In the twelfth book of his *Metaphysica* Thomas describes the effects of the planets on the sublunar world according to the order of their spheres: the star of Saturn indicates permanence and steadiness; the star of Jupiter the condition of all beings and their completion; strength and protection from what is harmful proceed from the star of Mars. The three superior planets have a clearly determined effect on the development of beings while the Sun, which is the universal principle of development and movement, shows its operations through the motion of the spheres of the inferior planets. We know that the star of Venus has an effect on generation so that the being acquires its perfection,

---

[20] On the idea of celestial perfection based on the container theory, cf. Edward Grant, *Planets, Stars, and Orbs: The Medieval Cosmos, 1200–1687* (Cambridge: Cambridge University Press, 1996), pp. 220ff.

[21] Buridan, *Metaphysica*, XII, qu. 12.

and the star of Mercury has an effect on multiplication, i.e., the distinction of beings according to their species; finally, the Moon acts on matter and produces its changes.[22]

This hierarchy appears as a true order of nature. Restoro of Arezzo (fl. thirteenth century), in eight long chapters of his *Composizione del mondo*, describes it in a metaphorical way: this order is analogous to the order which has been established gradually in a kingdom and makes it free from danger. Saturn was the first man, who built up houses and roads and cultivated the soil. After Saturn, Jupiter appeared, as a prophet who teaches the way of God, because Jupiter signifies the one who warns while Saturn is the one who is warned. But the kingdom is not safe if criminals are not punished—if 'li malfatori non sono puniti'—so Mars appeared, with his armed knights. At that moment appropriate conditions arise for the entrance of the Sun, like the king, into the kingdom; then Venus, like the queen, and 'capetana delle donne'; then Mercury, 'colli suoi filosofi e colle scienze de tutte l'arti'. Finally the Moon, 'capetano... povarissimo... con una sua gente povarissima e vile, come so' viandanti e messi e corrieri'.[23]

We find this metaphor again in Paolo Veneto's physical and moral description of the seven planets,[24] and also in one of the commentators on

---

[22] 'Et inde est quod effectus planetarum apparent in istis inferioribus secundum ordinem eorundem. Nam primi tres superiores videntur ordinari ad ea quæ pertinent ad existentiam rei secundum seipsam: nam ipsa stabilitas esse rei attribuitur Saturno, perfectio autem rei et bona habitudo correspondet Jovi. Virtus autem rei, secundum quod se contra nociva tuetur, et ea propellit, correspondet Marti. Tres vero planete alti videntur proprium effectum habere ad motum ipsius rei existentis, ita quod Sol sit ut universale principium motus, et propter hoc eius operatio in motionibus inferioribus apparet. Venus autem videtur quasi proprium effectum habere magis determinatum, idest generationem, per quam aliquid consequitur speciem et ad quam scilicet omnes motus alii ordinantur in istis inferioribus. Mercurius autem videtur proprium effectum habere in multiplicatione, idest distinctione individuorum in una specie et propter hoc varios habet motus. Et ipse etiam cum naturis omnium planetarum miscetur, ut astrologi dicunt. Lunæ autem proprie competit immutatio materiæ, et dispositio ipsius ad recipiendum omnes impressiones cælestes, et propter hoc videtur quasi esse deferens impressiones cælestes, et applicans inferiori materiæ' (Thomas Aquinas, *Metaphysica*, XII, 9, 2561).

[23] Restoro d'Arezzo, *La composizione del mondo colle sue cascioni*, ed. Alberto Morino (Florence: Accademia della Crusca, 1976), II, 2,1–8; pp. 63–97.

[24] Paolo Veneto, *Liber de compositione mundi* (Lyon, 1525), capp. 10–16. 'emperciò che le

Ptolemy's *Quadripartitum*, Giuliano Ristori. In his explanation of the planetary hierarchy of Abū Ma'shar, he describes the descending order of the spheres like a progressive formation of an ideal kingdom. The first movement, the movement round the middle, is the cause of preservation, perpetuity and eternity of generation; thus, the three superior planets are the principle of every alteration in the cosmos, as well as its conservation and permanence. The second movement, *a medio*, is the movement of the Sun and it is necessary that its action be consequent to the operations of the three superior planets. Since their operations affect dogmas and kingdoms it is necessary for someone to govern, rule and establish kingdoms and their laws and religious dogma. For this reason the Sun signifies the king, princes, and emperors. The third movement, *ad medium*, is related to the three inferior planets since it is necessary, after the empire, dogmas, etc., are established, that they be maintained through unions and associations, science and the arts, messengers and travel; so unions are related to Venus, science and the arts to Mercury, the rest to the Moon.[25]

---

stelle, secondo che pónono e dicono li savi, hano a significare le genti e li animali'. This description is, in fact, a translation of Restoro d'Arezzo.

[25] Giuliano Ristori, *Lectura super Ptolomei quadripartitum reverendi ac eximij magistri Iuliani Ristori Pratensis per me Amerigum Troncianum, dum eum publice legeret in almo Pisauri gimnasio currente calamo collecta*, ms. Florence, Bibl. Riccardiana, lat. 157, Lectio LXI, fol. 176r. For more on this text see Darrel Rutkin's essay in this volume. Noteworthy is Bonincontri's long quotation of Abū Ma'shar's three natural motions (Abū Ma'shar, *On Historical Astrology*, vol. II, pp. 5–6, lines 44–56, 35–42) made in his explanation of Aphorism 62 of the *Centiloquium*: 'Albumasar, prima differentia *de magnis coniunctionibus*, dicit quod "unaquaque divisio individuorum altiorum ad unamquamque divisionem motuum relata est naturalium propter fortitudinem affinitatis seu convenientie earum ad illas et propter successionem effectus impressionum earum in mundo generationis et corruptionis. Et cum primus motus naturalium moveretur supra medium, motus autem secundus movetur a medio et motus tertius moveatur ad medium, relata est prima divisio planetarum altiorum et effectus eorum ad motum primum naturalium qui est super medium propter eius altitudinem et propter proximitatem eius ab eis et longitudinem eius a motu naturali tertio qui est ad medium et ideo facta est ei ex hac parte significatio super res temporis prolixi propter affinitatem vel convenientiam eius cum motu primo et prolixitate eius motus, unde relata est ad longiorem planetis superioribus in mundogenerationis et corruptionis, qui est Saturnus, significatio super res inceptibiles ut sunt vices et quicquid fit in temporibus prolixis eo quod est ei inceptio pre ceteris individuis circularibus in sublimi. Et relata est ad planetam secundum [cum]

Giuliano Ristori tries to reconcile Ptolemy and those who follow the conjunctionist doctrine. The order of nature, he says, is twofold: *quoad nos* and *quoad naturam*. We say that first, with respect to us, the luminaries have more light and therefore more action; secondly, with respect to nature, the superior planets are nobler than the luminaries, because they are closer to the first being [Prime Mover], and therefore their effects are more powerful.[26] Furthermore, the same proportion is found between the luminaries and the superior planets as between a large crystal and a small diamond: in the crystal there is a larger quantity and greater virtue, but in the diamond there is more effectiveness.[27]

---

in ordine nexus, qui est Iuppiter, significatio super augumento [*sic*] et conservatione generationis mortisque et cuiuslibet rei que sunt in terra (?) horumque similia que sunt perfectiones finium inceptionum precedentium vel que sunt longi temporis. Relata est quoque ad planetam tertium in ordine nexus, qui est Mars, significatio super bella et victorias et horum similia que sunt quasi descensiones et veluti diminutiones exitus rerum et finis earum et fines rerum significant solutiones principiiet initij post perfectionem earum et destructionem nexus earum. Nam per accidentia bellorum et similium fit diminutio summitatum et extremorum." Et ex his ergo apparet quod extractio "significationum individuorum circularium non accipitur nisi a motibus naturalibus eo quod sint sensui propriores (*lege* propiores) significationibus individuorum superiorum. Cum ergo motus naturalis non excedat tres istas divisiones superexpressas, consideratus estordo per partitiones planetarum et per proprietates motus eorum volubilium. Ergo ille dividuntur in tres divisiones, quarum prima est planetarum altiorum ordinatorum super luminare maius et secunda est luminaris minoris (*lege* maioris), tertia vero est planetarum inferiorum qui sunt positi infra luminare maius"' (*Laurentij Bonincontri Miniatensis super centiloquio Ptolomei*, ms. Florence Bibl., Laur. Med., pluteus 29,3 fols 46v–47r). Cf. William of Aragon, *Centiloquium cum commento Haly Eben Rodan et glosa sive commento edita a magistro Willhelmo de Arragonia*, ms. Paris, BNF, lat. 7480, fols 85r–85v: 'Et ideo tribus superioribus dederunt motum primum et res diuturna et prolixi temporis, dando Saturno principia divinitus quia divinacio dicitur administrare, Iovi fines vel perfectiones, marti occasiones vel adversitates que ex diversis perfectionibus et principiis veniunt; unde Saturnus est sicut Mars movens, Iupiter ut speciem tribuens, Mars vero ut operaciones controversiones specierum explicans; secundo motui proporcionatur luminare maius et per motum et per virtutem: non enim exorbitat, sed recte movetur sub linea una semper et omnia movet ad regimen vite'.

[26] Ristori, *Lectura super Ptolomei quadripartitum*, Lectio LIIII, fol. 220v.

[27] Ibid., Lectio XLIII, fol. 185r: 'Habemus hic cristallum in magna copia et habemus adamantem parvum: in cristallo est plus de quanto et de virtute, non tamen est tantæ

Ristori concludes: 'I affirm that the greatest *constellatio* is the solar eclipse with the conjunction of the three superior planets in the same term and decan. That is to say: at the time of an eclipse of the Sun, the three superior planets are conjunct in one term and in one decan, and are in a quartile or opposite aspect to the Sun or they are at least near their stations'.[28] This seems a compromise between two doctrines but it reveals, in fact, the predominance of the container theory. The greater the conjunction, says Kepler, the greater the disturbance exerted on the natural world; therefore, the greatest conjunctions are those of Saturn and Jupiter, not of the Sun and the Moon.[29]

'Container theory' is Grant's well-chosen expression.[30] We find it well defined in Albertus Magnus' *Metaphysics*:

> ...superioris autem motus est magis universalis et formalis et contentivus...[31]

That is to say that the orbs of the superior planets, since they hold and include within their area those of the inferior ones, are more perfect because their formal principles are more universal. But Albertus carries his thoughts further: the astrologers demonstrate that the inferior planets apply to the superior ones, and

---

efficaciæ sicut adamas'.

[28] Ibid., Lectio XLI, fol. 176v: 'Dico quod maxima constellatio est quæ fit ex deliquio Solis et coniunctione trium superiorum in uno termino et una facie, sic quod eo tempore quo fit Solis eclipsis fiat coniunctio trium superiorum in uno termino et una facie et quadrangulentur Soli aut diametrentur eo et si sint saltem propter stationes suas'.

[29] Johannes Kepler, *De stella nova in pede Serpentarii, et qui sub ejus exortum de novo iniit, Trigono Igneo* (Prague, 1606), p. 35 [= J. Kepler, *Gesammelte Werke*, vol. 1 (Mysterium Cosmographicum, De stella nova), ed. Max Caspar (Munich: C. H. Beck, 1938), p. 188.13–16]: 'Itaque quanta coniunctio, tanta naturæ commotio; si coniunctio diuturna, si rara, magna quoque et insolens est commotio ac perinde maior commotio a coniunctione Saturni et Iovis, quam a Solis et Lunæ; see also *Kepler's Astrology*, ed. Dorian Greenbaum, trans. Patrick Boner, *Culture and Cosmos*, 14 (2010), p. 223.

[30] Grant, *Planets, Stars*, pp. 220ff.

[31] Albertus Magnus, *Metaphysica* XI, 2, 32; cf. *Divi Alberti Magni summi in via peripathetica philosophi Theologique profundissimi naturalia ac supranaturalia opera per Marcum Antonium Zimaram ...*, Venice, 1518, p. 160rb. Cf. XI, 2, 28 (p. 159rb): 'Superiores planete Saturnus et Iupiter quando coniunguntur de circulo in circulum vel de triplicitate in triplicitatem accipiunt a spheris superioribus formas universales que signant res maiores que accidunt in mundo, sicut dicunt sapientes astrorum'.

through this application they receive the guidance of their actions. In fact, the conjunction of two planets consists of two parts: application and separation. The first demonstrates the form, the second the action that proceeds as a consequence. This process is a series of progressive and interdependent steps by which a result is attained, and it evolves by means of the continuous emanation of *planetarum virtutes*. And the virtues take effect in the world like the *virtutes naturales* in the human body; they flow from the outermost spheres to the interior ones, like the *virtutes naturales* flow from the brain to the heart, from the heart to the liver, from the liver to the testicles.[32] Moreover, since these virtues act on matter, the actions that follow them are physical: the sphere of Saturn engenders coldness and dryness, the sphere of Jupiter heat and moisture. Therefore, the two superior planets are able to cause great changes in the world.[33]

The power of the luminaries

Agostino Nifo (b. ca. 1473) and Pedro Ciruelo (1470–1548) contradict these arguments. In the fourth chapter of *De nostrarum calamitatum causis*, Nifo protests that those who follow Abū Ma‘shar are ignorant of philosophy,

---

[32] Cf. *Alberti Magni philosophie totius dilucidatoris doctissimi Opus nobile de causis proprietatum elementorum* (Magdeburg, 1506), I, 2, 9, sig. Ciiv (ed. Borgnet IX, p. 620a): 'Et huius simile videri possumus in corpore humano, ubi unum membrum transmittit aliis spiritum et humorem, et tamen membrum recipiens informat illa secundum naturam suam et virtutem quemadmodum cerebrum ipsum spiritum et humorem sibi a corde et epate missos informat ad virtutem et operationem animalem et testiculi spiritum et humorem eis missum informant ad virtutem generativam et formativam speciei: ita facit quilibet planeta qui recipit lumen ab alio'. This is not a simple figure of speech, but a clear explanation of the astrological topic of the application and separation between the planets; cf. Giuseppe Bezza, *Commento al primo libro della Tetrabiblos di Claudio Tolemeo* (1990; repr. Milan: Nuovo Orizzonti, 1992), pp. 375–78.

[33] Cf. Albertus Magnus, *De causis*, I, 2, 9 sig. Ciira (cf. Borgnet IX, p. 620b): 'Oportet quod illud quod universaliter est in superiori determinetur per inferiora, et illud quod primum determinat ad figuram et speciem est circulus stellatus. Prima autem ad complexionem ducentia sunt Saturnus et Iupiter, eo quod unus movet frigidum et siccum, et alter calidum et humidum; et cum ista conveniunt in ea triplicitate signi ex qua confortari habent et influentiam accipere, oportet quod per illas duas stellas totius mundi dispositio infundatur. Permutatio autem triplicitatis dicit permutationem primarum qualitatum elementalium universaliter'.

astrology and theology. Since virtue lies in the middle and the beginning, and the Sun lies in the middle and the Moon is at the point of time where everything begins, the luminaries are the first and the commanders, the others ministers and officers. In fact, the Sun regulates the motions of all the planets, whose powers depend on their relationships with the Sun. And if someone says that the superior spheres surpass the inferior ones, Nifo replies that it may be right for one reason, but wrong for many others; the horse, for example, is superior to the human being in carrying weights, but the human being is superior to the horse in many other things.[34]

Ciruelo determines ten rules about the powers of the celestial spheres.[35] The first says, *in maiore corpore maior virtus*, power is related to the magnitude of the body; the second, *omne agens fortius agit in propinquo*, everything that acts acts more strongly on what is close (i.e., in this instance, on the earth); the third, *qui tardius moventur ad maiora tempora effectus suos ostendunt*, what moves more slowly shows its effects over a longer time (i.e., larger the orbit, the greater the time in which effects are felt). The other seven rules proceed as a consequence from the first three,[36] and Ciruelo concludes that the greatest power is in the

---

[34] Euthici Augustini Niphi Philotei Suessani, *de nostrarum calamitatum causis liber ad Oliverium Carafam Cardlinalium maximum* (Venice, 1505), fols 31b–32a.

[35] Pedro Ciruelo, *Apotelesmata astrologiæ christianæ nuper edita a magistro Petro Ciruelo Darocensi super duabus tantum iudiciorum partibus, hoc est de mutationibus temporum et de genituris hominum, reiectis omnino interrogationibus et vanis electionibus falsorum astrologorum. Petri Cirueli D. Centilogium resolutorium sue artis iudiciariæ. Responsiones* (Alcalà, 1521), I, 3, sig. eviii^v.

[36] Ibid. The other rules: fourth, 'sol est maxime virtutis et potentie super universa astra celorum omnium'; fifth, 'post solem maioris virtutis et potentie super nos est luna simpliciter quam omnes alie stelle totius celi'; sixth, 'post duo luminaria magna celi tertium gradum in potentia activa ad nos habent tres planete superiores sole, quartum gradum habent inferiores et ultimum locum stelle fixe omnes'; seventh, 'in stellis fixis eiusdem magnitudinis ille que sunt magis elevate super nostrum hemisperium ut quando sunt in circulo meridiano, sunt maioris virtutis active super nos quam ille que minus elevantur; et septentrionales ab ecliptica magis quam meridionales etc. Probatio clara est quia fortius irradiant super nos. Eadem ratio est de planetis qui moventur ad diversa latera zodiaci: nam variat unusquisque eorum virtutem suam secundum quod magis vel minus elevatur secundum latitudinem zodiaci'; eighth, 'secundum excellentiam vel deffectum planetarum in virtute activa erga nos est significatio eorum in rebus magnis aut parvis huius seculi: probatur quia maiori virtuti active maior et dignior effectus est

luminaries, then in the three superior planets, then in the two inferior ones, and lastly in the fixed stars. Nevertheless, with regard to their *perfectio essentialis*, we can say that the superior spheres are nobler and therefore Saturn, Jupiter and Mars surpass the Sun. That is what Thomas affirms in his commentaries on Aristotle's *Metaphysics*. However, Ciruelo remarks that it is not the task of an astrologer to present reasons for or against the form of the stars. This is the task of the philosopher, while the astrologer deals with the *activa virtus*, the effects. So, the error of *Albumazar mahumeteus* was to mingle form and action together.[37]

Nifo and Ciruelo tried to follow the true Ptolemaic tradition: Nifo wrote one commentary on the first book of Ptolemy's *Quadripartitum* and another on the second book;[38] Ciruelo tried to expurgate the *Quadripartitum* itself from falsities and frivolities, above all those of Arabic origin. Guido Bonatti, Abū Ma'shar, Ibn Ezra and astrologers generally mix together superstitious elements and natural things. In this way they weave a fabric with threads of different kinds. This, says

---

attribuendus'; ninth: 'cum qualitates duorum luminarium sint manifestissime ad experientiam, aliorum planetarum complexiones ex comparatione eorum ad duo luminaria penes convenientiam et differentiam determinande sunt'; tenth, 'sicut omnium stellarum motus tanquam regulam habent motum ordinatissimum solis, sic etiam omnes stelle respiciunt motum lune tanquam omnibus eis familiarem et subsequentem'. Consequently, Ciruelo concludes: 'Ex omnibus his decem regulis elucet quanta dignitatis preminentia sint efferenda duo celi luminaria magna in hac scientia ... a qua sententia neque per unum iota discrepavit Ptolemeus, putans quod alie stelle celi sine testimonio luminarium nihil aut parum efficere valent in mundo, unde in omnibus figuris astrologicis maxime in illis que ad sciendas mutationes temporum formantur, ante omnia dicit inspiciendam esse coniunctionem aut oppositionem luminarium que precesserat, non sic Albumazar mahumeteus qui maiorem vim attribuit superioribus planetis quam luminarium et male'.

37 Ibid. 'Cum his tamen regulis stat quod si celi differant specie inter se, forte maior est perfectio essentialis stellarum superiorum quam inferiorum, ut saturni quam solis et cetera. Hoc tenet sanctus Thomas in commentario suo super duodecimo libro metaphisice. Sed de tali perfectione iam non est astrologi disputare, sed solius primi philosophi: nunc autem solum de activa virtute stellarum ad hec inferora intendimus'.

38 *Ad Sylvium Pandonium Boviani Episcopum Eutichi Augustini Niphi Philotei Suessani ad Apotelesmata Ptolemæi eruditiones* (Naples, 1513); Eutichi Augustini Niphi Ph. S., *de nostrarum calamitatum causis liber ad Oliverium Carafam Cardinalium maximum* (Venice, 1505).

Ciruelo, is what I mean to avoid, according to Holy Scripture:[39] do not plant your field with two different kinds of seed.[40]

The Centiloquium and Saturn–Jupiter conjunctions

Ciruelo's criticism of Ptolemy is based on the *Centiloquium*'s attribution to him, where a few aphorisms relating to conjunctionist theory are presented. In fact, until the middle of the sixteenth century, the *Centiloquium* was judged to be a genuine treatise of Ptolemy. One of the few exceptions to this view was that of Pontus de Tyard who, some centuries before Richard Lemay, considered the hundred aphorisms to be the forgery of the commentator himself.[41] Therefore, we can understand why one of the commentators in the first half of the sixteenth century, Giuliano Ristori, praises great conjunctions so much. In fact, Ristori, who often quotes from the *Centiloquium*, remarks that Ptolemy, in his aphorisms, extolled the conjunctions of the superior planets; then, addressing himself to his students, he says: you must always trust in the aphorisms; they are reliable, because they come from observations.[42]

Ristori was one of the many astrologers who thought Abū Maʻshar's doctrine an important contribution, capable of improving the proficiency of astrological interpretation. Against this view, we see one of the last commentators on Ptolemy, Valentin Naibod, quoting the text of *Quadripartitum* II, 4: 'The first and most potent cause of such events lies in the conjunctions of the Sun and Moon at eclipse and the transits of the stars at the time', and commenting:

> Someone could say that this passage of Ptolemy does not do away with the doctrine of the great conjunctions, but gives it praise and support, since one gives the power to cause great and general events not only to the eclipses of the luminaries, but also to the transits of the wandering stars. I reply: although Ptolemy, like all the other astrologers, ascribes to the superior planets the power to cause general events, nevertheless he does not agree with them concerning the degree of their power. The other astrologers, indeed, above all observe, in their enquiries concerning the time and place of general events, the conjunctions of

---

[39] Ciruelo, *Apotelesmata,* sig. aiiiv.

[40] *Leviticus* 19:19: 'Agrum tuum non seres diverso semine. Veste, quæ ex duobus texta est, non indueris'.

[41] Pontus de Tyard, *Mantice ou Discours de la verité de Divination par Astrologie* (Lyon, 1558), p. 13: 'Haly faussaire de son Ptolomee en cent endrois'.

[42] Ristori, *Lectura super Ptolomei quadripartitum,* Lectio XLIII, fol. 184v–185r.

Jupiter and Saturn, and extend their effects to many centuries. On the contrary, Ptolemy collects the time and place of the effects only from the eclipses of the luminaries.[43]

It is not surprising that medieval astrologers made Ptolemy and Abū Maʿshar compatible with each other, without any apparent contradiction, if we bear in mind that, as we have said, the *Centiloquium* was unanimously reckoned as a genuine work of Ptolemy. For instance, in the *Dialogus* of Giovanni Abbiosi it is Ptolemy, not Abū Maʿshar, who replies, quoting from the *Centiloquium* as his own work, to the *sophista* about the great conjunctions and the revolutions.[44] The astrological views of Abbiosi are typical of many astrologers of his time—those that, to repeat the words of Thorndike, 'hold that many things have been discovered since Ptolemy, whom the Arabic authors have both elucidated and added to'.[45] In the *Centiloquium* there are a few aphorisms that deal clearly with conjunctions and revolutions. The astrologers who wanted to follow the pure doctrine of the *Quadripartitum* tried to explain these aphorisms in a different way.[46]

---

[43] Naibod, *Enarratio*, pp. 355–56: 'Sed dicat aliquis, hoc textu Ptolemæi potius extolli atque communiri de magnis coniunctionibus doctrinam, quam tolli: siquidem non tantum defectibus luminum, sed et meantium stellarum transitibus vis magnos et generales eventus efficiendi tribuitur? Respondeo, quamvis Ptolemæus in generalibus mutationibus planetis superioribus æque atque reliqua astrologorum multitudo vim tribuat, non tamen tantum, neque sic quemadmodum ipsi de potentia illorum sentit. Etenim ipsi pro magnorum eventuum temporibus et locis eruendis, Iovis et Saturni coniunctiones potissimum observant, atque earundem effectum ad multa secula extendunt. At Ptolemæus econtrario tempora et loca effectuum ex solis luminarium defectibus colligit.'

[44] Giovanni Abbiosi, *Dialogus in Astrologie defensionem cum Vaticinio a diluvio usque ad Christi annos 1702* (Venice, 1494).

[45] Lynn Thorndike, *A History of Magic and Experimental Science*, V (New York: Columbia University Press, 1941), p. 221.

[46] The best examples are Aphorisms 58 and 64. The first presents, in the medieval manuscripts, the word 'alkirem', which is a transliteration of Arabic *al-qirān* ('conjunction'). But those readers, like George of Trebizond and Giovanni Gioviano Pontano, who had at hand the Greek text of Καρπός, read σύνοδος, and they thought Ptolemy referred here to the conjunction of the Sun and Moon. The second aphorism deals with the greater, middle and minor conjunctions of the superior planets. Pontano (*Commentariorum in centum Claudij Ptolemæi sententias, libri duo* [Basel 1531], p. 114) admits

Ibn Riḍwān and Saturn–Jupiter Conjunctions

One of the first commentators on Ptolemy's *Quadripartitum*, the Egyptian physician 'Alī ibn Riḍwān, affirms that the *Centiloquium* is a Hermetic writing. Ibn Riḍwān makes five sharp attacks on Abū Ma'shar, all of them with the intent of demonstrating his ignorance, or at least his imperfect understanding, of astronomical matters and the superstitious elements of his doctrine. In the commentary on the second chapter of the first book, he says that Abū Ma'shar and his followers eagerly applied themselves to the knowledge of what is impossible, like the millennia and the centuries. Ibn Riḍwān alludes here to the *tasyīrāt* and the *intihā'āt*, the regular progressions and profections utilized by Abū Ma'shar in the *Kitāb al-ulūf*,[47] the *Liber millenarius* now lost in both Arabic and in Latin, but known to some Latin astrologers of the Middle Ages.[48]

---

his trouble here: 'Verba ipsa magnopere me addubitare faciunt propter obscuritatem', in the same way as George of Trebizond (*Claudij Ptolemæi Alexandrini Astronomorum Principis Centum sententiæ interprete Georgio Trapezuntio...* [Rome, 1540], sig. Kii^{r}). In his critique of the conjunctionist doctrine, Cornelius Scepper quotes both Pontano and George of Trebizond (*Assertionis fidei adversus astrologos, sive de significationibus coniunctionum superiorum planetarum anni millesimi quingentesimi vicesimi quarti* [Antwerp, 1523], fols 14v; 120v–121r). Only Francesco Cigalini, *Coelum sydereum*, Book VII, pp. 407–10, tried to give a 'true Ptolemaic meaning' to the second aphorism: assuming that the three conjunctions are conjunctions of the luminaries, the greater is a *defective* conjunction, that is, an eclipse; the middle, the conjunction that precedes each season; the minor the monthly conjunction. Pedro Ciruelo offers a slightly different interpretation: 'Ergo volentes in hoc capitulo modum precedentis observare in divisione maiorum constellationum per medias et istarum per minores, anni principium in equinoctio vernali mensis martij et in principio signi arietis ponimus, existimantes figuram principij veris esse velut unam magnam coniunctionem sub qua tres alie medie ipsam dividentes erunt figure principiorum estatis, autumni et hyemis et sub qualibet earum lunationes mensium erunt quasi minores coniunctiones, medias et maiores dividentes; sed has figuras omnes, more Ptholemei, figuras coniunctionum vel oppositionum solis et lune facere intendimus, utpote quia in eis est maior certitudo' (*Apotelesmata*, II, 3, sig. hv^{v}).

47 Cf. Edward S. Kennedy, 'Ramifications of the World-Year Concept in Islamic Astrology', in *Actes du Dixième Congrès International d'Histoire des Sciences, Ithaca 26 VIII 1962 – 2 IX 1962*, 2 vols (Paris: Hermann, 1964), I, pp. 23–43; David Pingree, *The Thousands of Abū Ma'shar* (London: Warburg Institute, 1968), pp. 57ff.

48 Cf. Guido Bonatti, *Decem continens tractatus de astronomia* (Augsburg, 1491). In ch. 117 of Book VIII Bonatti quotes the long judgement that Abū Ma'shar presents about the succession to the caliphate, founded on the *introitus solis in Arietem* of the year 656 (16

Nevertheless, if Ibn Riḍwān criticizes Abū Ma'shar's doctrine on the whole,[49] he

---

Ramadan 35H). This is a quotation from Abū Ma'shar's *Liber millenarius*. Cf. sig. Z3v: *Qualiter sit procedendum super significatores regis et rusticorum secundum Albumasar.* It is the year in which 'Uthmān ibn 'Affān was murdered and 'Alī ibn Abī Ṭālib ascended the throne'. This horoscope is quoted in the *Kitāb al-qirānāt wa taḥāwīl sinī al-'ālam* of al-Sijzī, who wrote, in the 10th century, a compendium, *mujmal*, of the *Kitāb al-ulūf* of Abū Ma'shar; cf. Pingree, *The Thousands of Abū Ma'shar*, pp. 99–100. We can find also this horoscope in Māshā'allāh, *Fī qiyām al-khulafā' wa ma'rifa qiyām kull malik*; cf. Edward S. Kennedy and David Pingree, *The Astrological History of Māshā'allāh* (Cambridge, MA: Harvard University Press, 1971), p. 133; and in Mūsā ibn Nawbakht, cf. *Al-Kitāb al-Kāmil, Horóscopos históricos*, ed. and trans. Ana Labarta (Madrid: Instituto Hispano-Árabe de Cultura, 1982), p. 86. On the knowledge of the *Kitāb al-ulūf* in the Latin Middle Ages, cf. Hermann of Carinthia, *De essentiis*, ed. Charles Burnett, (Leiden: E. J. Brill, 1982), p. 140; 164 (Abumaixar in Libro millenario), cf. Charles Burnett, 'The Legend of three Hermes and Abū Ma'shar's *Kitāb al-ulūf*', *Journal of the Warburg and Courtauld Institutes* 39 (1976): pp. 231–34.

[49] In his commentary on the *Quadripartitum*, Ibn Riḍwān makes some sharp attacks on Abū Ma'shar and his conception of astrology, accusing him of superstition and errors; cf. especially the critique against the doctrine of the hundreds and the thousands and, in general, against historical cycles: *Liber quadripartiti Ptholemei, idest quatuor tractatuum, in radicanti discretione per stellas de futuris et in hoc mundo constructionis et destructionis contingentibus cum commento Haly Heben Rodan* (Venice, 1493), fol. 6rb: 'vidi nam ex illis qui studebant in libris miliariorum et centenariorum et decennariorum et credebant certum et verum esse quicquid locutus fuit ibi Albumasar et similes et voluerunt hoc experiri in rebus preteritis et ibi nullam certitudinem invenerunt. Et ego dixi: magnum mirum est de vobis qui dimitt<it>is inspicere motus stellarum et coniunctiones magnas et vultis scire ea que futura sunt per numerum annorum, quia si hoc verum esset ars astronomie et ea que per stellas scire possumus de eo quod futurum est nihil esset'. Cf. J.A. Seymore, 'The Life of Ibn Riḍwān and His Commentary on Ptolemy's *Tetrabiblos*', (PhD Dissertation, Columbia University, 2001), pp. 115ff. In his paraphrase of Ibn Riḍwān's commentary, Conrad Heingarter repeats this critique in a slightly different way: 'Aliqui ut se sapientes ostendant libros fecerunt et nos multis verbis turbaverunt et vias multas quarum nulla recta dederunt. Quare tibi consulo ut non velis laborare in illis libris et applices mentem et tuum studium ad libros solummodo Ptholomei, quoniam in eis reperies viam certam et res certificatas et ratione et experientia probatas et dimittemus sophisticationes et vanitates de quibus Albumasar in libris millenariorum, centenariorum et decanorum (sic) loquitur, et alij complures. Nam sunt ipsi truffe et vanitates, nec est sapiens qui eis consentiat' (ms. Paris, BNF, lat. 7432 fol. 8v; cf. ms. Paris, BNF, lat 7305, fol. 20r–v).

accepts the apotelesmatic effects that the conjunction of the superior planets has in itself. In the commentary on the fourth chapter of the second book of the *Quadripartitum,* he combines eclipses and Saturn–Jupiter conjunctions. Then, in his exposition of the cycles of these conjunctions, he goes beyond the cycle of 960 years. In fact, in this space of time, Saturn and Jupiter make four middle conjunctions, one in each triplicity of the zodiac, as a result of four *intiqālāt,* transitions of the conjunction from one triplicity to the next (i.e., 240 years times 4). In 2880 years we have 12 *intiqālāt,* namely 240 times 12, and 144 conjunctions of Saturn and Jupiter (144 times 12 = 2880). Finally, if you multiply the 144 conjunctions by the twelve zodiacal signs, we have 1728 conjunctions which will happen over the course of 34,560 years. This figure is very close to the complete revolution of the fixed stars.[50] For this reason, Ibn Riḍwān concludes, the conjunctions of Saturn and Jupiter have great effectiveness in signifying the changes of kingdoms and religions and the migrations of the peoples from one place to another.

---

[50] *Liber quadripartiti Ptholemei,* fol. 37va. I quote here the paraphrase of Conrad Heingarter (ms. Paris, BNF, lat. 7305 fol. 132v) with the variants of the Latin text of Ibn Riḍwān: 'Et postquam Saturnus et Iupiter coniunguntur vice una omnibus 20 annis vel circa duodecies in quolibet trigono, in 240 anni vel circa stabunt in uno trigono antequam de trigono illo ad alium mutentur. Aliquando accidit quod 13 coniunctiones fiunt in uno trigono antequam de trigono illo ad alium mutentur, ut per tabulas motuum patet quas in scientia quadriviali composuimus ad eram Johannis Borbonij atque Alvernie ducis illustrissimi; et certum est quod coniunguntur in quolibet signo quater et erunt anni 960. Et eorum coniunctio semper mutatur de uno trigono ad alium trigonum sequentem et de signo ad signum sequens. Verbi gratia, quando fit mutatio coniunctionis a capite Arietis in 240 annis perveniet ad signum Tauri. Postmodum secundum hoc convenit ut fit hec mutatio post 960 anni quod iterum redeat ad caput Arietis quoniam in tot annis erunt coniuncti in quolibet signo quater. Et redibit mutatio ad aliquod signum ad caput de 1920 annis. Et redibit ad primum signum ad caput 2896 [2880] annis et in tot annis essent coniuncti 144 vicibus. Et quando multiplicabimus numerum coniunctionum per numerum signorum erunt coniunctiones 1628 [1728] et erunt anni [circa de] 34,000. Et hoc est circa numerum annorum quibus stelle fixe complent circulum suum per totam spheram. Et in tanto tempore revertitur principium mutationis ad quodlibet <signum> duodecies, tantum quantum est numerus signorum. Et propter hec coniunctio Saturni et Iovis habet virtutem magnam valde in regnis et sectis mutandis et habitationibus de uno loco ad alium, quia uterque planetarum est supremus et virtutis magne'.

	years	*coniunctiones minimae*	*coniunctiones mediae*	ratio between *minimae* and *mediae*
coniunctio minima	20	1		
coniunctio media	240	12	1	12:1
coniunctio maxima	960	48	4	48:4 = 12:1
complete cycle	2880	144	12	144:12 = 12:1
Perfect cycle	34,560	1728	144	1728:144 = 12:1

Fig. 3: Ibn Riḍwān's great year.

In this passage we have one of the first associations of the two distinct traditions: that of the cycles of Saturn–Jupiter conjunctions and that of the revolution of the eighth sphere. The value of 36,000 years is also present, but in the form of an imaginary cycle of the regular progressions, *tasyīrāt*, of conjunctionist astrologers, for example Abū Ma'shar[51] and Mūsā ibn Nawbakht.[52] On the contrary, here Ibn Riḍwān proposes a figure of the great year measured by the value of Ptolomy's precession of 1 degree every 100 years.

According to Abū Ma'shar, Saturn and Jupiter form a conjunction every 20 years and this conjunction is called *minor*.[53] Then, the two planets form 12 or 13 *minores* conjunctions in signs of the same triplicity; they pass to the sign of the next triplicity after 240 years. This conjunction is called *maior* or *media*. Thus, when they perform four conjunctions in the four different triplicities, they return to the starting point after 960 years. This conjunction is called *maxima*. Note that the terms 'magna', 'media/maior', 'maxima' are not used by Abū Ma'shar but by later Latin writers, such as Roger Bacon.[54] The intervals between these

[51] Cf. Pingree, *The Thousands…, loc. cit.*

[52] Cf. *Kitāb al-azmina wa-l-duhūr, Tratado de Astrología mundial,* ed. Ana Labarta, comm. Ángel Mestres (Valencia: Universidad de Valencia. Área de Estudios Árabes e Islámicos, 2005), p. 23.

[53] Described in Abū Ma'shar, *On Historical Astrology,* I, 1 [12–17], vol. I, pp. 10–17.

[54] See, e.g., Roger Bacon, *Opus maius,* ed. John Henry Bridges (Oxford: Clarendon Press, 1897), I: p. 263: 'Therefore Albumazar, in his Book of Conjunctions, and other astronomers determine that there are three kinds of Saturn-Jupiter conjunctions: great,

conjunctions are computed on the basis of the mean motions of the planets. The computation is as follows: the mean diurnal motion of the mean centre of the epicycle of the slower planet must be subtracted from that of the faster one. Then, one must divide the whole circle of 360 degrees by the difference of the above-mentioned mean planetary motions; the result is the interval between the

---

greater and greatest. A great conjunction is when it is conjoined every twenty years in whatever sign it may be. For Jupiter completes its orbit in twelve years, and Saturn in about thirty years, and so it happens that after twenty years they are joined in the ninth sign from that in which they were first joined; and after another twenty years in the fifth from the first sign; and after a third twenty years again in that first one. And this is a great conjunction, which happens in this triplicity twelve times or sometimes thirteen. For the first, fifth and ninth signs make a triplicity. And this conjunction is said to signify frequently the elevation of kings and the powerful, and dearness in the price of food, and the rise of prophets. And after they have been conjunct in this triplicity so many times, they are changed to another, and then the conjunction is called 'greater'. And this happens every two hundred forty years or thereabouts, and signifies a sect and its change in certain regions. And when the conjunction has changed from that triplicity into another, as from the end of Cancer to the beginning of Aries, then it is said to be 'greatest', through the revolution of Saturn thirty-two times, and this happens every nine hundred sixty years, and signifies changes of empires and kingdoms, and fiery impressions in air, and floods, and earthquakes and dearness in the price of food.' 'Albumazar igitur in libro conjunctionum et caeteri astronomi determinant tres esse Saturni et Jovis conjunctiones, magnam scilicet, majorem et maximam. Magna est, qua conjungitur in omnibus viginti annis in quocunque signo hoc sit. Jupiter enim perficit suum cursum in duodecim annis, et Saturnus quasi in triginta annis, et ideo fit ut post viginit annos junguntur in nono signo ab eo, in quo prius juncti fuerant; et post alios viginti in quinto a primo; et post tertio viginti iterum in illo primo. Et haec est conjunctio magna, quae fit in hac triplicitate duodecies, vel aliquando terdecies. Primum enim signum, quintum et nonum faciunt triplicitatem. Et haec conjunctio dicitur significare pluries super sublimationem regum et potentum, et super gravitatem annonae, et super ortus prophetarum. Et postquam totiens in ista triplicitate conjuncti fuerint, ut ad aliam mutentur, tunc vocatur conjunctio major. Et hoc fit in omnibus ducentis quadraginta annis vel circiter, et significat super sectam et mutationem ejus in quibusdam regionibus. Et quando mutata fuerit conjunctio ab ista triplicitate in aliam, ut a fine Cancri ad initium Arietis, tunc dicitur maxima, per revolutionem Saturni triginta duabus vicibus, et fit omnibus nongentis sexaginta annis, et significat super mutationes imperiorum et regnorum, et super impressiones ignitas in aere, et super diluvium, et super terrae motum et gravitatem annonae.'

two conjunctions expressed in the number of days.

Key
C = centre of the world
A = centre of the deferent of the epicycle
V, X, Z = centres of epicycles
P = planet traversing the epicycle
M = mean apogee of the epicycle
N = true apogee of the epicycle
CS = line of mean motion of the epicycle, or planet, from the centre of the world to the zodiac, parallel to lines AVM and AXM
CVN = line of true motion of the centre of the epicycle
CPF = line of true and apparent motion of the planet

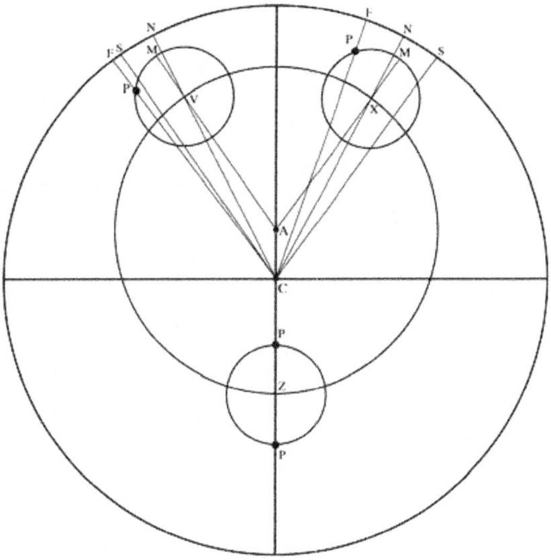

Fig. 4: Diagram of Mean and True Motions.

coniunctiones	*Auctores*	*anni, dies, horae, min., sec.*
minor	Albumasar, Alchabitius, etc.	20, 0, 0, 0
	Cardanus, Naiboda	19, 315, 19, 0, 0
	Reinhold, Magini, Origanus	19, 314, 12, 59, 23
	Keplerus	20 *fere*
media	Albumasar, Alchabitius, etc.	240, 0, 0, 0, 0
	Cardanus, Naiboda	198, 236, 0, 0, 0
	Reinhold, Magini, Origanus	198, 216, 9, 53, 52
	Keplerus	200 *fere*
maxima	Albumasar, Alchabitius, etc.	960, 0, 0, 0, 0
	Cardanus, Naiboda	794, 214, 0, 0, 0
	Reinhold, Magini, Origanus	794, 133, 15, 35, 28
	Keplerus	794 *fere*

Fig. 5: The Intervals of Saturn–Jupiter Conjunctions in Julian Years.
G. B. Riccioli, Almagestum novum, *Bologna, 1651, p. 674.*

Mean or true motion?

Nevertheless, the intervals of Abū Ma'shar, as well as of all Arabic authorities, were larger than those introduced by the Alphonsine Tables, since the diurnal motions of the planets were different. In spite of this fact, the first European scholars, who enthusiastically received the conjunctionist doctrine, from Roger Bacon to Pierre d'Ailly, accepted unquestioningly the larger intervals of the Arabic theory. Heinrich von Langenstein, a contemporary of Pierre d'Ailly, pointed out the mistakes of Abū Ma'shar, for the mean motions defined by the Alphonsine Tables are correct.[55] The anonymous of Cracow who, in the second half of the fifteenth century, wrote a commentary on Ptolemy's *Quadripartitum*, supposed that in the time of Abū Ma'shar the values for planetary mean motion had not yet been ascertained. Moreover, he wondered how many distinguished scholars, following like sheep, accepted Abū Ma'shar's mean planetary motions.[56]

---

55 Cf. Hubert Pruckner, *Studien zu den astrologischen Schriften des Heinrich von Langenstein* (Leipzig-Berlin: Teubner, 1933), pp. 142–43; the same statement in Ciruelo, *Apotelesmata*, II, 2, sig. gviii: 'loquendo de medijs coniunctionibus per tabulas Alfonsi regis que aliarum omnium sunt certissime'.

56 Anonymous of Cracow, *Ad Tabulam quadripartiti Ptolemaei explanationes et commentationes, accedit capitulum de dominio anni.* ms. Florence, Bibl. Laur. Med., Ashb. 202, fol. 37v: 'Credo quod temporibus Albumazar nondum fuit habita vera quantitas mediorum motuum Saturni et Iovis et merito ipse dominus Albumazar erravit. Sed miror quod tot et tanti viri secuti sunt eum usque ad nostra tempora, videlicet Abraham Averre, Haly Abenragel, Guido Bonati, auctor *summe anglicane,* Cameracensis et alij. Cuius causa non puto aliam nisi quod sicut ovis unus sequebatur alium, nec aliquis curavit ad praxim predictam quantitatem tam temporis quam motus reponere, quare ad magnos devenerunt errores'.

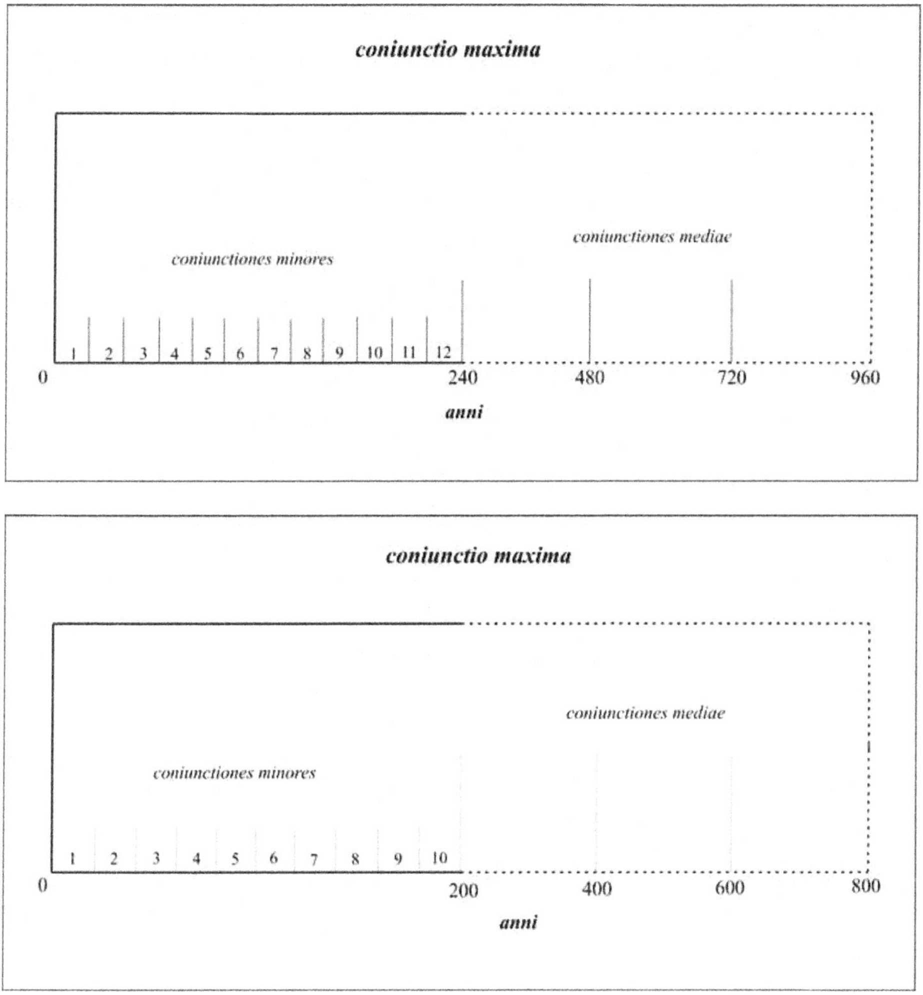

Fig. 6: The Intervals of Saturn–Jupiter Conjunctions according to Followers of Abū Ma'shar and according to the Moderns.

But the conjunctionist doctrine of Abū Ma'shar was vulnerable to another criticism; conjunctions were calculated according to the mean motions of the planets and mean conjunctions, says Ciruelo, are fictitious and cannot produce any effect in the world.[57] Mean and true conjunctions only coincide when the two planets are at the apogee or perigee of the epicycle or the eccentric.[58] Medieval astrologers were aware that the true, not the mean conjunctions, were influential.[59] For this reason the anonymous of Cracow says that Abū Ma'shar, a man of great knowledge, founded his judgements on the true conjunctions.[60] Furthermore, for the Medieval astrologers there is no question of the exact time of the true conjunction, because the judicial decision was dependent on another moment of time: the entrance of the Sun into the first degree of Aries. On the other hand, since the exact time of the true conjunctions constitutes a critical moment of decisive importance with respect to the outcome, the astrologers never ceased to argue about this. In the commentary on the second chapter of the first book of the *Quadripartitum*, where Ptolemy explains what the proper actions of the Sun, Moon and planets are, Cardano says that it is impossible to know not only the hour, but also the day of the conjunction of the superior planets. Thus, he concludes, everybody can easily understand how this doctrine (that is, the conjunctionist theory) is uncertain.[61] The same Cardano is the author

---

[57] Ciruelo, *op. cit.*, I, 2, sig. gviiiv: 'Albumazar solas medias coniunctiones superiorum planetarum curavit, que sunt pure imaginarie et nullum effectum faciunt in mundo'. Cf. Lucio Bellanti, *De astrologica veritate* (Florence, 1498), XI, 3; Georg Tannstetter, *Libellus consolatorius* (Vienna, 1523), sig. biiir. It would take too long to review all the opinions about this question; Giovanni Battista Riccioli, *Almagestum novum* (Bologna, 1651), p. 672 and Giuseppe Cervi, *Anergica magnarum coniunctionum panurgia. Problema Physico-Theologico-Astrologicum* (Parma, 1683), pp. 11–12, give a survey of the various opinions.

[58] Cf. Pierre d'Ailly, *Elucidarium,*, c. 26, sig. f6r: 'Et aliquando vera cum media concordat in tempore, sed hoc contingit rarissime, videlicet quando ipsi planete sunt in auge vel opposito augis ecentrici vel epicicli'.

[59] Ibid., c. 13, sig. f1r: 'Sed tamen astronomi iudicant secundum coniunctiones veras, quia autores volunt influentias planetarum magis habere processum in coniunctionibus veris quam in medijs. Unde secundum Alkindum in effectibus magnis provenientibus ex magnis coniunctionibus saturni et iovis non debemus habere respectum ad eorum motus medios, sed ad veros et ad veram eorum coniunctionem, licet Albumasar secundum medios motus eorum processerit'.

[60] Anonymous of Cracow, *Ad tabulam*, fol. 38r: 'Et ego tamen credo dominum Albumazar fuisse magne sapiencie virum et iudicia sua super certissimis fundasse radicibus et super coniunctionibus veris, sed de medijs mencionem facit more antiquorum sapientum'.

[61] Girolamo Cardano, *Opera Omnia*, V (Lyon, 1663), p. 173b: 'Igitur nec certa dies, nedum hora, aut cœli figura et status, haberi possunt ... Hanc ob causam scientiam talium

of a terse saying which the astrologers who came after him were fond of quoting: 'The true motions perform the actions, while the mean ones are like their models.'[62]

Francesco Levera, in his long chapter *De motibus secundorum mobilium æqualibus vulgo medijs, ac simplicibus, eorumque viribus, ac virtutibus,* quotes this aphorism of Cardano and tries to make a distinction between the mean and true planetary motions. In the former there are *unitas et simplicitas et integra virtus, ordo et perfectio, nullusque excessus neque defectus*; in the latter there are *accidentales* conditions, *minime autem essentiales.* He relied on the authority of Aristotle, especially in the *Physics,* where the philosopher affirms that, although a part of circular motion (περιφορά) is a portion of time, it certainly is not a circular motion; for what is taken is only a part of circular motion, not the circular motion as a whole.[63] For Levera, the part of circular motion is the *motus inæqualis* and the circular motion itself is the *motus aequalis,* which is well-ordered and regular.[64] For the planets, the beginning of their circular motion and, so to speak, their critical moments, are when they are joined with the Sun or are opposite to it, at the apogee or perigee of the eccentric circle, since there is no difference between the mean and true motions at those times. These positions are critical because they are, for the planets, what the two syzygies are for the Moon. In the other steps of their circular motion, the mean and true positions diverge because of the distance of the planets with respect to the Sun and the earth. Thus, Levera concludes that, according to nature, the mean motions are the first: they precede all the irregular ones and, for this reason, they act on the sublunar world.[65]

---

coniunctionum quæ ad hanc usque diem celebrata fuit, quam parvi sit momenti, clare quisque intelligit'. Cf. Naibod, *Enarratio,* p. 357.

62 'Veri motus actiones perficiunt, medij autem sunt ut illorum exempla.' *Aphorismorum astronomicorum segmenta septem,* in: Cardano, *Opera Omnia,* V, VI, 9, p. 68°.

63 Aristotle, *Physics,* iv, 10; 218b1.

64 Francesco Levera, *Prodromus Universæ Astronomiæ restitutæ ...* (Rome, 1663), p. 78: 'Simplices enim et æquales motus cælestium corporum, eorumque coniunctiones per motus eorundem æquales, considerabiles etiam admodum fiunt propter harmoniam, relationem, et proportionem continuatam, et perpetuam, quam habent ad partes omnes sui motus, necnon ad reliquas coniunctiones invicem æquales lege naturæ, tam præcedentes, quam sequentes in cunctis seculis: tum etiam quia æquales, seu medij motus tantum, minime autem inæquales, habent harmonia, proportionem, et analogiam in cunctis partibus sui motus cum vera, et tota periodo eiusdem motus'.

65 Ibid., pp. 69ss.; cf. p. 77–78: 'Nam licet tunc non appareant nobis coniuncti respectu

In consequence of these arguments, Levera agrees with the hypothetical conclusion suggested by Riccioli that, by their true motions, Saturn and Jupiter stay in conjunction for three or four days, while the conjunction of the centres of their epicycles occurs in an instant. For this reason we must make use of the mean motions and of the mean conjunction, instead of the true.[66] Only with the mean conjunction is it possible to establish the minute of time, the horoscope.[67]

Practicing conjunctionist astrology

For medieval astrologers this question is meaningless. If the Renaissance astrologers accepted, more or less, the conjunctionist doctrine, they gave up some requisite elements. William of Aragon, in his commentary on Aphorism 64 of the *Centiloquium*, explains clearly that the elements of the judgement depend, in descending order, on the conjunction of the superior planets, since the conjunctions are the principle, the rule and the measure of all things

---

terræ, quam habitamus, tamen coniuncti sunt respectu aliorum centrorum, quæ in Universo habent; et in hæc inferiora, quamvis non influant directe sic coniuncti, tamen influunt reflexe, et per consensum partium, ut supra diximus. Quin immo influxus, et actiones cælestium corporum digniores, et nobiliores, sunt magis ab æqualibus, et in sua æqualitate semper perseverantibus motibus et circulationibus'.

66 Riccioli, *Almagestum novum*, p. 672. In the chapter *Mediæ an veræ coniunctiones sint considerandæ cum de magnis aut maximis agitur?* Riccioli presents an astrological point of view: if the mean conjunctions precede the true, the former open the latter; if they follow the true conjunctions, they hold something of the impression. In the first case, it is like the astrological topic of the application of the fast planet to a slow one, in the second, of the separation. This argumentation is quoted by Levera, *op. cit.*, p. 67 and is presented by Cervi, *Anergica magnarum coniunctionum*, pp. 11–12, as his own.

67 Cf. A. Zoboli, *Asicometologia. Discorso del Sig. Dottore Alfonso Zoboli Reggiano intorno all'apparizione della nuova Stella, et del corpo metheorologico, che si viddero circa alla fine dell'Anno MDCXVIII* (Bologna, 1619), p. 73: 'Io sto in forse di credere se la congiontione presa con li mezi moti de' pianeti sia di ugual'efficacia con la congiontione vera, il che se non assolutamente si dovesse affermare, crederei però che fosse di forze poco inferiore, alla qual cosa mi esorta l'esperienza delle Sisige de' luminari, nelle quali sovente si vedono precedere o seguirne effetti, che non sono punto accennati nella congiontione vera, ma di questo in altro luogo. Ho voluto di ciò far mentione con l'occasione che chi si volesse valere della congiontione de' superiori presa secondo questi mezi moti per trovare l'ascendente di tal congiontione, sappia che più esattamente potrà trovarlo che per il moto vero'.

('coniunctiones enim sunt principium et regula et mensura omnium'):[68]

> The minor conjunction contains 20 revolutions of the year and every revolution contains the quarters of the year and every quarter contains at least 3 conjunctions and three oppositions <of the Sun and the Moon> and 6 quartiles and every quartile contains 7 days, and the day is the indivisible revolution, which measures all the aforesaid revolutions.[69]

For the most part, the annual *prognostica*—from the Middle Ages until well after the Renaissance—show, in a well-ordered manner, all the elements of Arabic general astrology. At the beginning of his first prognosticon for the year 1484, Domenico Maria Novara explains clearly the two methods on which the *prognosticationes* are founded: that of Ptolemy and that of Abū Ma'shar. But the Ptolemy of Domenico Maria, as well of the majority of the Medieval and Renaissance astrologers, is the author not only of the *Quadripartitum*, but also of the *Centiloquium*:

> You must know that the revolutions of the years of the world, which indicate certainty of judgement in prognostication, are composed of three main parts. The first and more effective one is taken from the degrees of the great conjunctions, on the progression of their places and on the application of the place of the division. The second lies in the eclipses of the Sun and the Moon and the quantity of their obscuration. That is the way followed by Ptolemy in the second book of the *Quadripartitum*. Another way is handed down by Geophar in his book *De magnis coniunctionibus*, and some follow both these principles: and this is the way that Albumasar seems to favour in the aforesaid treatise. The third, and the last one, is brought about by the entrance of the Sun into the point of the vernal equinox and on the conjunction or opposition of the luminaries together with the disposition of the stars. It is necessary for one making a forecast to think carefully about these three principles if he wants to know beforehand the quality of future events.[70]

---

[68] *Centiloquium*, fol. 84v.

[69] 'Minor coniunctio continet 20. revolutiones annorum et quelibet revolucio quartas anni et quelibet quarta ad minus 3. coniunctiones et 3. preventiones et 6. quadraturas et quelibet quadratura 7. dies, dies autem est indivisibilis revolucio, omnes predictas mensurans' (*Centiloquium*, fol. 109r).

[70] 'Scias quod revolutiones annorum mundi qui certitudinem iudicij in pronosticando demonstrant ex tribus potissimis partibus complentur. Et prima illarum que omnibus fortior existit sumitur a gradibus magnarum coniunctionum et a profectu ex locis

After this, Domenico Maria tells us the five elements that the astrologer must bear in mind if he wants to make a correct judgment about future events: 1) the time of the entrance of the Sun into the point of the vernal equinox; 2) the syzygy before that entrance; 3) the conjunctions of the superior planets that have already occurred; 4) the progressions of the places of the great conjunctions; 5) the reckoning of the *orbis magnus*, according to the teaching of Abū Ma'shar. These five elements are in agreement with the doctrine that Abū Ma'shar presents in the first chapter of the first book of *De magnis coniunctionibus*, where the Ptolemaic elements (eclipses and syzygies) are subordinate to the great cycles and to the conjunctions of the superior planets.

Since the branch of general astrology transmitted by the Arabs is modelled on the techniques of genethlialogy it was necessary to find, as in genethlialogy, a definite principle on which to establish a regular and uniform cycle of rulership of the signs and planets. This cycle of rulership was based on a sexagesimal model, analogous to what, in the doctrine of nativities, is the *profectio, intihā'*. As a rule, astrologers do not assume an alleged nativity of the world as the beginning, but the great conjunction of the two superior planets, Saturn and Jupiter, which occurred before the flood. Lucio Bellanti explains, in his reply to Pico,[71] the reason for that choice:

> If we knew the beginning of the world, certainly we would start the cycle from it. But, since the world had been in some way renewed by the flood, and the cause of this renovation was Saturn, the highest planet, and the sign of Cancer is the most

---

ipsarum cum applicatione loci divisionis. Secunda vero sumitur ex eclipsibus que accidunt in sole et luna in quantitate tenebrarum. Hanc autem viam insequitur Ptholomeus in secundo quadrupartiti. Aliam vero tradit Geophar in libro de magnis coniunctionibus et quidam revolvunt super hec duo principia sicut Albumasar tractatu preallegato videtur annuere. Tertia vero et ultima ab introitu solis in puncto vernalis equinoctij et ab hora coniunctionis seu oppositionis luminarium cum dispositione stellarum perficitur. Necesse est igitur pronosticatorem super his tribus principijs considerare si qualitates futurorum effectuum prescire voluerit.' *Pronosticon magistri Dominici Marie de Ferraria anni domini 1484*, in F. Bónoli, Giuseppe Bezza, S. De Meis and C. Colavita, *I pronostici di Domenico Maria da Novara* (Florence: Leo S. Oschki, 2012), p. 133–34.

[71] Pico della Mirandola, *Adversus astrologos*, in *Opera* (Strasbourg, 1504), sig. 158v: 'Dicant igitur mihi si magni illi orbes sint statuendi an in ipsa prima mundi constitutione, cui omnes consentiunt, novi orbis exordium faciant an non faciant'.

> powerful of the four angles, which is the nearest to the zenith of that part of the earth, strength and power were assigned to both of them.[72]

This conjunction occurred 279 years before the flood, that is, in 3101 BCE; from that conjunction a cycle of 360 years begins, ruled by a planet and a zodiacal sign. This cycle is divided into twelve parts of 30 years each, each one ruled by a planet and a zodiacal sign. The Arabic term that denotes this cycle is *dawr*, which has several meanings in the astronomical lexicon: revolution, rotation, period, orb;[73] but medieval astrologers translated this word as *orbis*, and the *dawr* of 360 years stands for the *orbis magnus*.

In the *Prognosticon* of 1484, Domenico Maria Novara begins by noting the *orbis magnus* of his time: it is the fourteenth; its planetary ruler is the Moon, and its zodiacal sign is Leo. He quotes as his authority the author of the *Summa Anglicana*.[74] Its author, John of Ashenden, like John of Glogau, expounds some rules about the observation of *signum orbis magni*: one must estimate the condition of the sign and its ruler at the time of the syzygy that occurred before the vernal equinox and at the time of the entrance of the Sun into the first point of Aries.[75] Novara tells us, in the *Prognosticon* for the year 1500, that the first consideration in astrological judgements lies in the observation of the *orbis magnus*.[76] And because this sign, Leo, is corrupted by the two noxious planets in the revolution of the year (especially by the opposition of Mars), he can predict that Italy will be violently shaken by wars. Moreover, Novara, like many other

---

[72] 'Si mundi initium haberemus, proculdubio ab ipso ordinem susciperemus. Sed quoniam per diluvium mundus quodammodo innovatur eiusque innovationis causa fuit Saturnus, primus planetarum altior, signumque Cancri potentissimum ex quatuor cardinibus propius ad zenith partis terre, ideo his duobus vis et potestas tributa est'. Lucio Bellanti, *Responsiones in disputationes Iohannis Pici Mirand. Co. adversus astrologos* (Florence, 1498), sig. fv^{v}.

[73] Cf. Abū Ma'shar, *On Historical Astrology*, I, p. 587.

[74] John of Ashenden, *Summa astrologiæ*, I, 4, sig. 12rb.

[75] Ioannes Glogoviensis, *Tractatus preclarissimus in judicijs astrorum de mutationibus aeris cæterisque accidentibus singulis annis evenientibus iuxta priscorum sapientumque sententias*, (Cracow, 1514), cc. 2ra.

[76] This is a general rule, cf. Pierre d'Ailly, *Elucidarium*, ch. 19: 'Sciendum est ergo quod antiqui philosophi dixerunt et experientia docuit quod signa et planete dominantur orbibus successive idest unum signum et unus ;planeta regunt mundum universaliter per 360 annos et hoc temporis spacium vocant orbem magnum'.

astrologers, mixes together Arabic and Ptolemaic elements, since he follows the astrological chorography of Ptolemy, who placed Italy under the sign of Leo.

anni			*signa orbis magni*		*dominus orbis*	*signa divisionis*		*divisor*
a coniunction e diluvij significante	*post diluvium*	*Ante nativitatem Christi*	*signa*	*num.*		*signa*	*num .*	
		3380	Cancer	I	Saturnus			
anno 3101 ante Christum natum diluvium factum est								
360	80	3020	Leo	II	Iupiter			
720	440	2660	Virgo	III	Mars			
1080	800	2300	Libra	IV	Sol			
1440	1160	1940	Scorpio	V	Venus			
1800	1520	1580	Sagitarius	VI	Mercurius			
2160	1880	1220	Capricornus	VII	Luna			
2520	2240	860	Aquarius	VIII	Saturnus			
2880	2600	500	Pisces	IX	Iupiter			
3240	2960	140	Aries	X	Mars			
post nativitatem Christi								
3600	3320	220	Taurus	XI	Sol			
qīrān al-milla, id est coniunctio sectam Arabum significans								
3960	3680	580	Gemini	XII	Venus			
4320	4040	940	Cancer	XIII	Mercurius			
4680	4400	1300	Leo	XIV	Luna	Aries	I	Luna
		1330				Taurus	II	Saturnus
……								
		1450				Virgo	VI	Venus
		1480				Libra	VII	Mercurius
		1510				Scorpio	VIII	Luna

Fig. 7: Orbis magnus.

These kinds of judgments are not in Abū Maʻshar's book, but are elaborations by later Western astrologers. One of the best examples is the *iudicium* of Clemente Clementini for the year 1497. He begins his interpretation of future events with the more general causes, that is, by the consideration of the *orbis magnus*. Since the Moon is the ruler of the *orbis magnus*, the condition of human beings is weak and their lives are short. Leo, the sign of the *orbis magnus*, signifies proud and rapacious men. Mercury, who is the *divisor*, makes men ingenious and clever, and so on.[77]

After commenting on the sign and the planet which rule the *orbis magnus*, the astrologer deals with the conjunctions and the revolution of the year. The entrance of the Sun into the first point of Aries constitutes the chief element for making substantial judgments about the events of the year. In his commentary on the *Quadripartitum*, Ibn Riḍwān decisively criticizes this standard procedure, because of its absolute discordance with the doctrine of Ptolemy:

> Some people say that the significance of every season must be inferred from the hour of the entrance of the Sun into each of the four seasonal points. This opinion is defective for four reasons. The first: the complexion of the Sun and Moon is more powerful and has more than the power of the Sun joined with the power of that point. In fact, the sign, as a whole, has no power in itself, but only on account

---

[77] See for example Clementini, *Iudicium anni huius Mccccxcvii Clementini de Clementinis de Ameria artium et medicine doctoris* (Rome, s.d.): 'Ut rectum sapientis ordinem nature sequamur, primum a generalibus initium faciemus exinde gradatim disserendo proficiscemur ad specialia. Cum itaque hac tempestate universus orbis terrarum sub Luna domina magni orbis regatur, ideo genus hominum imbecillius: sumus enim vita breviores, magna paramus, sed nihil tandem laudabile perficimus, facili ratione sententiam mutamus, nimium ventri dediti sumus, frequentius in egritudines labimur. Et quamvis a veteribus omnia ad bene beateque vivendum accuratissime excogitata sint nobis relicta, attamen deteriores continue sumus et difficillime vivitur. Luna autem hec omnia ludibria et instabilia facit, quoniam incredibili velocitate suum peragit motum dispositionemque sue nature continue mutat atque inferior est ex materia crassiori compacta. Preterea Leo signum magni orbis superbos homines facit et rapaces, vi et dolo transgreditur iura, bella movet, imperia mutat, ad maiestatem domini suscipit tyrannos qui maxima cupiditatis avaritia sitiant aurum. Denique Leo una cum Luna societate coniuncti facit homines emulos, ambitiosos, superbos, qui sese inani gloria efferant et qui vincere ultra vires conantur et excellere. Sed Mercurius qui hoc anno est magni orbis divisor ingeniosa facinora excogitabit, ingenuos homines faciet, acutos et mercatores qui se ad omnia scient accommodare. Iuppiter autem dominus termini gradus divisionis auget facultatem honorum, religionem colit, pios et benivolos homines facit'.

of the Sun and this is even more true for one point of a sign. The second: the circumference does not have a starting point. The third: it is not possible to establish exactly the time of the entrance of the Sun into the beginning of Aries, due to the discrepancy of the tables: indeed we have no knowledge of the length of the year, which is necessary for this computation. For the conjunctions and oppositions the question is different, because we are able to compute them, as we can see in eclipses, and their ascendants agree in all the tables. The fourth: the signs are merely dwellings, but the virtues and operations belong to the stars; thus this point does not have a formal virtue which could exercise a directing influence over the whole year. Therefore, you can understand that the power of the conjunction and opposition (of the Sun and the Moon) is stronger than the time of the entrance of the Sun in that point.[78]

---

[78] I quote from the paraphrasis of Conrad Heingarter, ms. Paris, BNF lat. 7432 fol. 58v, cf. *Liber quadripartiti,* cc. 47v: 'Sunt tamen alij aliter dicentes quod significatio cuiuslibet temporis accipienda est ab hora introitus solis in aliquod quatuor punctorum. Et hec oppinio est quatuor rationibus defectiva, prima quia complexio solis et lune est forcior et maioris potencie quam virtus solis cum virtute illius puncti. Nam toti signo non est data virtus nisi propter solem et quanto magis uni puncto signi. Secunda quia circumferentia non habet principium. Tertia quia quando sol ingreditur in principium arietis certificari precise non potest propter diversitatem tabularum et quia quantitas anni precise numquam fuit inventa, que tamen necessaria ad hoc est, sed ita non sunt coniunctiones et oppositiones quia certificari possunt, ut patet in eclipsibus, quoniam eorum ascendentia concordant cum omnibus tabulis. Quarta ratio: signa Sunt mansiones tantum, sed virtutes et operationes Sunt stellarum, ideo huic puncto non inest formalis virtus que ab ea regatur totus annus. Per hoc enim intelliges quod virtus coniunctionis et oppositionis est maioris potencie quam quando sol ingreditur punctum illum'. The argument of Ibn Riḍwān is completely accepted by Domenico Maria Novara who, in his *iudicium* of the year 1496 affirms: 'Consideraremo le prevention de li dui luminari che precedano lo introito del sole ne li quattro puncti cardinali cum multe altre constellation pertinente ad esse. Affirmando anchora questo Haly Heben Rodoan suo commentatori nel secondo del quadrupartito nel capitolo decimo. Et dica li quelli che pongano el principio del anno da lo introito del sole in ariete errano in quattro modi etc. Sapiano anchora tali a faticarse circa quello che anchora non è trovato'. Cf. Heingarter, *Iudicium anni millesimi quadringentesimi septuagesimi sexti currentis,* ms. Paris, BNF, lat.7446 fol. 5r; Ciruelo, *Apotelesmata,* II, 3, sig. hiiiii^{v}; Francesco Cigalini, *Coelum sydereum,* Book V, pp. 299–302; Francesco Giuntini, *Speculum astrologiæ, universam mathematicam scientiam, in certas classes digestas, complectens* (Lyon, 1581), II, p. 1160b; Abbiosi, *Dialogus,* sig. diii^{r-v}; for the latest commentators on Ptolemy cf. Cardano, *Opera Omnia,* V, p. 122b; Naibod, *Enarratio,* pp. 357ff.; idem, *In Claudii Ptolemæi Quadripartitæ Constructionis Apotelesmata,* fol. 71v–72r:

The critique of Ibn Riḍwān rests on two arguments. One is astrological, namely the power of the luminaries *versus* the power of the signs; the other is astronomical, namely the impossibility of finding out precisely the time at which the Sun enters the first point of Aries. We can add another argument, to which an astrologer of the first half of the seventeenth century rightly draws attention, concerning the distinctive form of Ptolemy's doctrine: the logical manner of the procedure. Giovanni Bartolini points out that, according to custom, the astrologers make eight charts: four for the equinoxes and solstices, and four for the syzygies that precede these points. So, they establish a double principle for each season. This practice, Bartolini observes, is contrary to the mentality of Ptolemy, who always avoids the multiplicity of principles.[79] On the contrary, the main feature of general astrology in the West depends on the process of making consistent two theories which have two different principles. Therefore, each principle must have a distinct significance; from the syzygies, one can judge about the elements, from the revolution of the years of the world about the *elementata*, that is, the mixed bodies of the living beings that are composed of the elements. Thus, the significance of the first principle will be for the natural world that surrounds man and gives him his sustenance: the conditions of the

---

'Sed consideratione dignum est cur luminarium syzigias, quæ cardinalia puncta proxime antecedunt, examinare iubeat, et non potius Solis ad ipsa puncta cardinalia transitum, ut faciunt annuarum mundi revolutiones doctores, qui tantum Solis ad caput arietis restitutioni tribuunt, ut hoc in negotio syzygias luminarium negligunt, tantum abest ut eas proferant. Ad hanc hæsitationem respondemus breviter hunc procedendi ordinem requiri omnino in Ptolomæi methodo, ubi virtus potentior, competenti gradu semper antecedere debet anni imbecilliorem, atque luminarium per se magna potentia, quando per syzigiam unita quasi conduplicatur in maximam evadit potentiam, et ob id merito præferendam simplici Solis potestati, quam ad aliquod punctorum cardinalium solus absque Luna socia conscendens acquirit. Ergo memoratæ syzigiæ luminarium potiora et latius potentiora decernunt accidentia, quo efficitur, ut ea secundum artem per Solis in puncta cardinalia ingressum et per reliquorum planetarum inambulationes non tolli, sed potius intendi debeant remittique tanquam a causis inferioribus, quæ, cum ita sese habeant, manifestum est quod annuarum revolutionum mundi conditores, qui præter syzigiarum proximi signiferi quadrantes antecedentium etiam eclypsium decreta decretis a domino anni, ut vocant, factis subijciunt, non tantum ab autoritate Ptolomæi, verum etiam a validis eiusdem rationibus quam longissime recedant'.

[79] G. Bartolini, *Discorso astrologico delle mutationi de' tempi e delle quattro stagioni, col Pronostico dell'Anno, e dell'Eclisse Lunare* (Rome, 1611), p. 11.

weather, fertility and drought and so on. The significance of the second principle will be on the general condition of the life of humans, the changes that happen in society, governments and religions. The anonymous commentator of Cracow explains this distinction clearly:

> The heavenly power that comes from the time of the conjunction or opposition that precedes the entrance <of the Sun into the first point of Aries> is stronger than that which comes from the time of the entrance. This power prevails and rules the whole quarter, while the power of the entrance is secondary and follows that one, just-as the lesser power follows the greater one, and the greater changes the lesser and draws it towards it. Therefore, we need, in the first place, to observe the heavenly configuration at the time of the conjunction or opposition that precedes the entrance of the Sun into the first point of the quarter whose nature we seek, because that configuration is universal and concerns mainly the change of the elements. In the second place we observe the configuration at the time of the entrance, since it is related, properly and specifically, to the *elementata*; indeed, the heavenly power reaches the *elementata* through the elements. In this way we can attain an appropriate knowledge of the quarter.[80]

I quoted, at the beginning of this essay, the statement of John of Ashenden about the imperfection or even the incompletness of general astrology. We shall conclude with another, similar assertion. Tommaso Campanella, in the second book of his *Astrologicorum libri,* affirms that the doctrine of Ptolemy is unsatisfactory and defective because we cannot have knowledge of great events from eclipses, since eclipses signify events that do not extend more than thirty

---

[80] Anonymous of Cracow, *Ad tabulam quadripartiti Ptolemaei explanationes et commentationes, accedit capitulum de domino anni,* ms. Florence, Bibl. Laur. Med., Ashburnam 202, fols 56v–57r: 'Postquam igitur est quod virtus celestis forcior est illa que fit tempore coniunctionis aut oppositionis precedentis introitum quam illa que fit tempore introitus: est nam tanquam victrix et domina tocius quarti, et virtus introitalis est tanquam secundaria et sequens illam sicut virtus minor sequitur maiorem et forcior mutat minorem et reducit eam ad se. Necesse est in primis considerare configuracionem celestem tempore coniunctionis aut oppositionis precedentis introitum solis in punctum quarti cuius natura querimus et quoniam illa configuracio est universalis ad elementorum mutacionem principaliter relata. Deinde considerabitur configuracio tempore introitus tanquam particulariter ad elementata prope relata, quoniam virtus celestis non pervenit ad elementata nisi per elementa et ita debite complexio quarti cognoscetur'.

months. 'Therefore, we need greater causes, and Albumasar knew them, but his doctrine is imperfect'.[81] On the other hand, Cardano said that Ptolemy did not deal with events of longer duration, such as those that belong to the conjunctions of the three superior planets. Their effects are indeed too slow and not clear; therefore, they pertain to the prophets, not to the astrologers.[82] Nevertheless, in his commentary to the *Quadripartitum*, Cardano deals extensively with the doctrine of the *magnus annus* and tries to justify the conjunctionist theory based on true motions.[83] Naibod too tries to represent the cycle of the great conjunctions as a great year, where each season is like a middle conjunction. In this great year the predictive quality does not depend on the place of the conjunction itself, but on the regular sequence of the seasons. So, if we start from the greater conjunction of 1583, the first cycle—until 1782—will be like the spring of the year. And because the Sun and Jupiter are analogous to the nature of the spring, they signify the strength of kings, the restoration of kingdoms, the times of peace, and so on.[84]

---

[81] Campanella, *Astrologicorum libri VI, in quibus Astrologia, omni superstitione Arabum, et Iudæorum eliminata, physiologice tractatur* (Lyon, 1629), II, 3, 1, p. 66: 'Mancus est Ptolemæus in sua doctrina cum solis eclipsibus mutationes det, et initia rerum, cum enim Istæ sint parvæ durationis, non nisi super res parvi temporis indicationem habent (...) Oportet ergo causas potiores accipere, quod Albumasar cognovit, sed non perfecit'.

[82] Cardano, *Opera Omnia,* V, p. 195: 'Illud animadvertendum est quod de effectibus longioribus non tractat Ptolemæus, quæ spectant ad coniunctiones trium superiorum, maxime Saturni et Iovis, quia effectus tardiores sunt, et non adeo evidentes: qui potius ad prophetas pertinent quam ad astrologos'.

[83] Cardano, *Opera Omnia* V, ch. II, 9 (*de coloribus in deliquiis et crinitis ac huiusmodi aliis*), pp. 214–15.

[84] Naibod, *In Claudii Ptolemæi Quadripartitæ Constructionis Apotelesmata,* fol. 16r: 'Communiter qui annuos, status et mutationes iudicare volunt, sumunt initium ab ingressu Solis ad æquinoctij punctum vernale ob causas veritati consentaneas, quas supra memoravimus, similiter dici debet et intelligi longiora tempora ligari et dependere a coniunctionibus corporum cœlestium rarioribus, qualiter a Saturni et Jovis coniunctione ligantur anni viginti et huius coniunctionis restitutio ad æquinoctium vernale seu ad initium trizodiæ arietinæ igneæ requirit et continet annos 790, quod quidem curriculum habet instar cuiusdam anni magni, cuius quadrantes explentur annis ducentis proxime, debenturque Saturno et Jove coniunctioni in una trizodia persistentibus: vernali eius quadranti debetur trizodia arietina, æstivo taurina, autumnali Gemellorum et hyemali Cancrina trizodia. Vernale eius tempus nobis instat anno ab anno 1583 protensum ad

The scholars of the Renaissance who aimed to renew the purity of Ptolemaic prediction through astronomy, i.e., in a properly philosophical way, were unable to demolish the conjunctionist doctrine, although many of its elements lacked firm astronomical principles. Moreover, the Melanchthonian reform of the astrological art also had more success in regard to nativities than to revolutions of the years of the world. In fact, very few astrologers did not come under the spell of the conjunctionist doctrine or the idea of the great year. At the end of the seventeenth century, the Jesuit Giuseppe Cervi remarks that only a few people had discarded it.[85]

1782, cui communi imperio præsunt Sol et Jupiter, pacationem in mundo et collapsorum distractorumque imperiorum refectionem et monarchiarum restitutionem decernentes. Cumque ut cunctorum animalium ita etiam imperiorum sunt ætates, itaque ab hinc certum annis usque crescit monarchia et perveniet ad statum iuxta annum 1760 proxime, et quia Jupiter et Sol sunt præcipue cæli ornamenta, idcirco plurimos viros virtutibus clarissimos decernunt, addita aeris caliditate et calamitatibus popularibus ex siccitate provenire consuetis, hinc et syncera erga deum hominum pietas, addita rerum charitate. E contra vero quadranti æstivo decernuntur humiditates et exundationes, terræque grassationes ob Lunæ et Veneris apparitiones, excursiones vel potius excitationes cometarum frequenter in duobus maleficis, quæ in Capricorno dominantur; a quadrante autumnali decernitur monarchiæ arietinæ translatio, quia Saturnus cum Mercurio inimicantur Soli et Jovi, vigebitque ingeniorum acrimonia circa artes, fraus et vafritiæ, improbitas circa libidines, his adiungitur quoque commerciorum mercurialium frequentia; a quadrante ultimo hyemali cui Mars præest, et cujus causa iam viget decernuntur bella et præstantia artium mechanicarum, morbi venenosi et putridi, repentiaque ulcera et deparavatio synceræ religionis'.

85 Cervi, *Anergica magnarum coniunctionum*, p. 67: 'Non est opus authores huius sententiæ patronos recensere, qui post Albumasarem, et Alchabitium adeo pullularunt, ut perpaucissimi astrologorum ab ea non steterint'.

Appendix

From the commentary of the anonymous Greek commentator on the *Quadripartitum*, I, 2

Madrid, Bibl. Univ. n. 27 (*CCAG* XI, 2 n. 42) fol. 3r-v	editio H. Wolf, Basle, 1554, pp. 4–5 S: Escorial, T-I-14 (*CCAG* XI, 1 n. 6) fol. 385r-v
κατακρατούσης μὲν τῆς καθόλου ποιότητος	*Κατακρατούσης*[1] *μὲν τοῦ ἡλίου δυνάμεως*
εἰπὼν ἐν τοῖς ἀνωτέρω τὰς μεταβολὰς τῶν ὡρῶν ἐξ ἡλίου καὶ σελήνης γίνεσθαι, ἐπαγαγὼν δὲ ὅτι καὶ οἱ πέντε πλανώμενοι τρέπουσι τοῦ περιέχοντος τὴν κατάστασιν, ἵνα μὴ τις ἀπορήσας ζητήση τί μὲν ἥλιος δρᾷ εἰς τὴν μεταβολὴν τῶν ὡρῶν, τί δὲ οἱ πλανώμενοι· τοῦτό γε αὐτὸ νῦν ἐθέλει διακρίναι καὶ φησὶν ὅτι τὸ μὲν ἀεὶ δραστικὸν καὶ τὸ καθόλου τῆς ποιότητος τὸ ὑπὸ τοῦ ἡλίου περὶ τὰ τοῦ ἀέρος καταστήματα γινόμενον, ἀεὶ φυλάττεται καὶ οὐ δῦναται τὴν φύσιν μεταβαλείν· συνεργοῦσι δὲ ἢ ἀποσσυνεργοῦσι οἱ πλανόμενοι, τουτέστιν ἢ ἐντονωτέραν ποιοῦσι τὴν κρᾶσιν τῆς ὥρας τὴν ὑπὸ τοῦ ἡλίου γινομένην, ἢ ἀτονωτέραν, τῆς μὲν ἐντονωτέρας κράσεως διὰ τοῦ συνεργεῖσθαι δηλουμένης, τῆς δ' ἀτονωτέρας διὰ τοῦ ἀποσυνεργεῖσθαι.	εἰπὼν ἀνωτέρω τὰς μεταβολὰς τῶν ὡρῶν ἐξ ἡλίου καὶ σελήνης γίνεσθαι, ἐπαγαγὼν δὲ ὅτι καὶ οἱ πέντε πλανώμενοι τρέπουσι τοῦ περιέχοντος τὴν κατάστασιν, ἵνα μὴ τις ἀποροίη ὅτι ὁ μὲν ἄρης δρᾷ εἰς τὴν μεταβολὴν, οὐκ ἔτι δὲ οἱ πλανώμενοι· τοῦτό γε αυτον νῦν ἐθέλει διακρίναι καὶ φησὶν ὅτι εἰ καὶ δρῶσιν, ἀλλὰ καὶ τὸ καθόλου τῆς ποιότητος ἀεὶ φυλάττεται καὶ ου δύνατνται τὴν φύσιν μεταβάλλειν· τοῦτο δὲ ὑπὸ ἡλίου γίνεται. *ὑπὸ τῆς τῶν ἀστέρων σχηματογραφίας* καὶ ἑτέραν δὲ πρὸς τούτοις τίθεται διαφοράν, ὅτι αἱ μὲν διὰ τὸν ἥλιον γινόμεναι μεταβολαὶ δυναταὶ μὲν εἰσι καὶ χρονιώτεραι, αἱ δὲ ὑπὸ τῆς σελήνης καὶ συνεχεῖς καὶ μεγάλαι· αἱ δὲ τῶν ἄλλων ἀστέρων οὔτε ὡς αἱ τοῦ ἡλίου, οὔτε ὡς αἱ τῆς σελήνης εὔσημοι καὶ περιοδικαί, τουτέστι χρονιώτεραι καὶ ἄσημοι· τοῦτο δὲ τὸ
τῆς μὲν σελήνης ἐκφανέστερον καὶ	

συνεχέστερον καὶ ἑτέραν δὲ πρὸς τούτοις τίθεται διαφοράν, ὅτι αἱ μὲν διὰ τοῦ ἡλίου γινόμεναι μεταβολὰ διναταὶ μὲν εἰσι, πλὴν χρονιώτεραι, αἱ δ' ὑπὸ τῆς σελήνης συνεχέστεραι καὶ ἐμφαντικώτεραι· αἱ μέντοι τῶν ἄλλων ἀστέρων οὔτε ὡς αἱ τοῦ ἡλίου δραστικώταται, οὔτε ὡς αἱ τῆς σελήνης εὐσήμαντοι, ἀλλὰ περιοδικαί, τουτέστι χρονιώτεραί τε καὶ ἄσημοι· τοῦτο γὰρ δηλοῖ τὸ ἀνεπαίσθητον, οὐ τὸ παντάπασι λέγειν ἀνεπαίσθητον εἶναι τὴν τῶν πλανωμένων ἐνέργειαν, ἀλλὰ τὸ ἧττον τῇ αἰσθήσει ὑποπίπτον. πησὶ δὲ καὶ τοὺς καιροὺς καθ' οὓ μάλιστα ταῦτα συμβαίνει διὰ τωον σχηματισμῶν, οἷον ἐπὶ μὲν τοῦ ἡλίου κατὰ τὰς μεταβάσεις καὶ τῶν καιρῶν τὰς τροπάς, ἐπὶ δὲ τῆς σελήνης τὰς συνόδους καὶ τὰς πανσελήνους, ἐπὶ δὲ τῶν ἄλλων ἀστέρων τὰς φάσεις καὶ τὰς κρύψεις. λέγει δὲ φάσεις μὲν τὰς ἑῴας ἀνατολάς, διὰ τὸ τηνικαῦτα ἄρχεσθαι φαίνεσθαι, κρύψεις δ' ὡσαύτως τὰς δύσεις, προσνεύσεις δὲ φησι τὰς κατὰ πλάτος ἀπὸ τοῦ διὰ μέσον ἀποστάσεις.	περιοδικαὶ δηλοῖ τὸ ἀνεπαίσθητον, οὐ τὸ παντάπασιν ἀνεπαίσθητον, ἀλλὰ τὸ ἧττον τῇ αἰσθήσει ὑποπίπτον. φησὶ δὲ καὶ τοὺς καιροὺς καθ' οὓς μάλιστα ταῦτα συμβαίνει διὰ τῶν σχηματισμῶν, οἷον ἐπὶ μὲν τοῦ ἡλίου τὰς μεταβάσεις καὶ τῶν καιρῶν τὰς τροπάς, ἐπὶ δὲ τῆς σελήνης τὰς συνόδους καὶ πανσελήνους, ἐπὶ δὲ τῶν ἀστέρων τὰς φάσεις καὶ τὰς δύσεις. λέγει δὲ φάσεις τὰς ἀνατολάς, περὶ τὸ τότε φαίνεσθαι καὶ ἀνάφαυσιν γίνεσθαι, προσνεύσεις δὲ φησι τὰς κατὰ πλάτος κινήσεις. [1] S: καὶ πάλιν κατακρατούσας μὲν τῆς καθόλου ποιότητος [2] S: αὐτὸ
Latina translatio	Translatio H. Wolfij
Sole quidem virtute sua superante Cum in superioribus dixerit temporum mutationes ex sole fieri ac luna, illud quoque adducens quod quinque etiam planete statum aeris immutant, ne	*Prædominante Solis potentia* Cum supra dixerit, temporum mutationes a Sole et Luna solere fieri, atque adiecerit, etiam quinque planetas mutare statum aëris: nequis

quispiam dubitans per-quirerit quid sol efficiat ad temporum mutationem, quid etiam planete, hoc ipsum vult in presentia discurrere. Et ait quod efficientia illa continua et qualitatis universalitas quae a sole fit circa aeris status semper conservatur et non potest natura sua transmutare; cooperantur autem aut non cooperantur planete, hoc est aut intensiorem faciunt temporis complexionem que a sole est effecta aut minus intensam. Ex eo quod cooperantur, intensior complexio significatur, ex eo vero quod non cooperantur, minus intensam demonstrant esse complexionem.

Luna cum manifestius magisque continue

Alteram quoque praeter haec ponit differentiam quoniam mutationes quae per solem efficiuntur fortes quidem sunt, praeterquam diuturniores; quae vero a luna magis continuae, magisque manifestae. Eas vero quas faciunt reliquae stellae neque sunt ut illae solis efficacissimae, neque ut illae lunae manifestae, sed periodicae, hoc est diuturniores et obscurae, hoc autem significat insensibilem. Non quod omnino insensibilem esse dicit planetarum efficaciam, sed quod minus sub sensum cadat. Dicit etiam tempora in quibus haec praecipue ex figurationibus eveniunt: ut in sole quidem secundum transitus et temporum mutationes, in luna autem

dubitet, Martem quidem efficacem esse ad mutationes efficiendas, reliquos autem planetas non item: id ipsum nunc explicaturus ait, tametsi agant, tamen universalem qualitatem retineri, nec mutari naturam eius posse, id quod a Sole fit.

A descriptione figuræ astrorum

Aliud præter hæc discrimen ponit, mutationes quæ a Sole fiant, esse potentes et diuturniores; quæ a Luna et continentes et magnas; reliquorum autem planetarum, non tantam habere significationem, quantum vel Solis vel Lunæ, sed cito transire et obscuras esse. Verbum περιοδικαὶ; sciant id quod non quidem nulla ex parte sentitur, sed quod minus sub sensum cadit. Indicat et tempora quibus hæc maxime constringunt, ut in Sole, transitus, et anni temporum conversiones. In Luna, coniunctiones et plenilunia; in stellis, ortus et occasus. φάσεις enim ortum significat, quod tunc appareant et in conspectum veniant. appellat motus in latitudinem.

synodos et plenilunia, in alijs vero stellis ortus et occultationes; ortus autem dicit matutinas orientalitates, eo quod tunc apparere incipiant, occultationes eodem modo occasus vocat, declinationes vero distantias dicit a linea quae zodiacum secundum latitudinem per medium dividit.	

FROM BAGHDAD TO CIVITAS SOLIS: *HOROSCOPES OF FOUNDATIONS OF CITIES*

Jean-Patrice Boudet

In the Italian original version of *La Città del Sole,* composed by Tommaso Campanella whilst in jail in Naples in 1602, when the Hospitaler asks the Genoese what the *regimen* for the health of the Solarians and their life expectancy is, the Genoese begins his answer like this:

> They believe that first the whole of life should be examined and then its respective parts. Therefore, when they founded their city, they set the fixed signs at the four corners of the world – the Sun in the ascendant in Leo; Jupiter in Leo oriental to the Sun; Mercury and Venus in Cancer, but so close as to produce satellite influence; Mars in the ninth house in Aries looking out with benefic aspect upon the ascendant and the *apheta;* the Moon in Taurus looking upon Mercury and Venus with benefic aspect, but not at right angles to the Sun; Saturn entering the fourth house without casting a malefic aspect upon Mars and the Sun; Fortune with the Head of Medusa almost in the tenth house—from which circumstances they augur dominion, stability, and greatness for themselves. Being in a benefic aspect of Virgo, in the triplicity of its apsis and illuminated by the Moon, Mercury could not be harmful; but since their science [of the Solarians] is jovial and not beggarly, they were not concerned about Mercury's entering Virgo and the conjunction.[1]

[1] Tommaso Campanella, *La Città del Sole: Dialogo Poetico / The City of the Sun: A Poetical Dialogue,* translated with introduction and notes by Daniel J. Donno (Berkeley-Los Angeles-London: University of California Press, 1981), pp. 86–89; Campanella, *La Città del Sole/ Civitas Solis; Edizione complanare del manoscritto della prima redazione italiana (1602) e dell'ultima edizione a stampa (1637),* traduzione, apparati critici, note di commento e appendici a cura di Tonino Tornitore (Milan: Unicopli, 1998), pp. 80–82: 'Essi dicono che prima bisogna mirar la vita del tutto e poi delle parti; onde quando edificaro la città, posero I segni fissi nelli quattro angoli del mondo. Il Sole in ascendente in Leone, e Giove in Leone orientale dal Sole, e Mercurio e Venere in Cancro, ma vicini, che facean satellizio; Marte nella nona in Ariete, che mirava di sua casa con felice aspetto l'ascendente e l'afeta, e la Luna in Tauro, che mirava di buono aspetto Mercurio e Venere, e non facea aspetto quadrato al Sole. Stava Saturno entrando nella quarta, senza far mal aspetto a Marte e al Sole. La Fortuna con il Capo di Medusa in decima quasi era, onde

Figure 1 corresponds to the *figura coeli* of this Italian version: The four fixed signs of the zodiac, Taurus (at the mid-heaven), Leo (at the ascendant), Scorpio and Aquarius, are located in the four angles of the sky. The Sun is the aphetic planet because he is in the house of the ascendant, in Leo, his domicile, and in company of Jupiter, the most beneficent planet. Jupiter is in the first house, 'oriental to the Sun' in order not to be burnt by his rays (*sub radiis*). The Moon is in the tenth house in Taurus, sign of her exaltation. She beneficently looks upon Mercury and Venus with a sextile aspect (60°), without being in a bad square aspect (90°) with the Sun—indeed a delicate condition, which may be realized if the Sun is located in the middle or the end of the first house, while the Moon is at the beginning of the tenth. Mercury and Venus are in conjunction in Cancer, in the triplicity of water and in the twelfth house. Mercury is in a beneficent sextile aspect with Virgo, his domicile. Mercury is 'illuminated by the Moon' because it is in sextile aspect with her. Mars is in the ninth house, in Aries, sign of his domicile, and looks at the ascendant and the Sun with a benefic trine aspect (120°). Saturn is entering the fourth house, without being in opposition to Mars or in square aspect with the Sun. Fortuna (as the Lot of Fortune is called in Firmicus Maternus' *Mathesis*), and the Head of Medusa (*Caput Algol*), a star of first magnitude, are in conjunction 'almost in the tenth house', that is to say in the end of the ninth house.

---

essi s'augurano signoria, fermezza e grandezza. E Mercurio, sendo in buono aspetto di Vergine e nella triplicità dell'asside suo, illuminato dalla Luna, non può esser tristo; ma, sendo gioviale la scienza loro, non mendica, poco si curaro d'aspettarlo in Vergine e la congiunzione'.

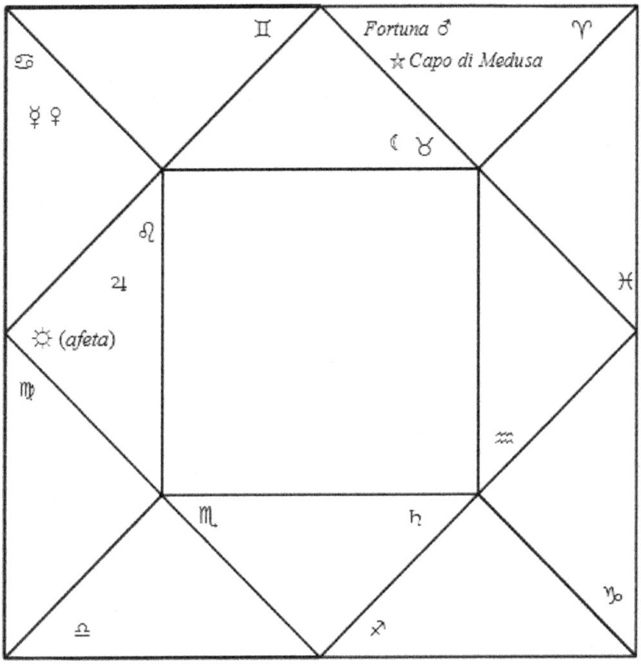

Key for all drawn figures: ♈ Aries ♉ Taurus ♊ Gemini ♋ Cancer ♌ Leo ♍ Virgo ♎ Libra ♏ Scorpio ♐ Sagittarius ♑ Capricorn ♒ Aquarius ♓ Pisces ☼ Sun ☾ Moon ♄ Saturn ♃ Jupiter ♂ Mars ☿ Mercury ♀ Venus ☋ Head ☊ Tail ☆ Star PF Pars fortunae

Fig. 1: Horoscope of the City of the Sun, Italian version (1602).

Campanella proposed some technical improvements to this horoscope in the Latin version of *Civitas Solis*, published in Paris in 1637, at a time when he was at the summit of his career at the French royal court, two years before his death (Fig. 2). Mars is now in the fifth house, in Sagittarius, Jupiter's domicile, in trine aspect with the ascendant, the Sun and Jupiter. The Lot of Fortune and the Head of Medusa now move into the tenth house, which is a better adaptation to the judgment according to which they 'augur dominion, stability, and greatness for themselves'.[2]

---

[2] Campanella, *La Città del Sole/ Civitas Solis*, ed. T. Tornitore (n. 1 above), pp. 80–82: 'Ipsi

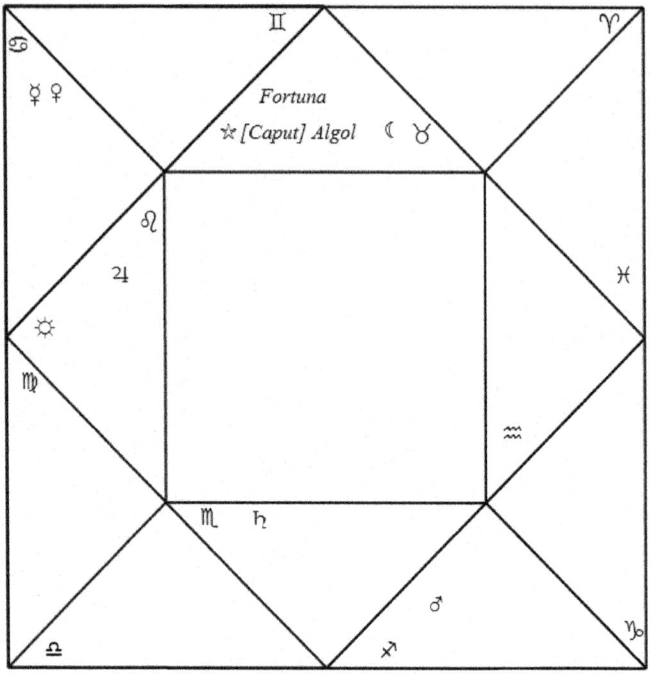

Fig. 2: Horoscope of the 'Civitas Solis', Latin version (1637).

Now if we look at the astrological literature on the subject, it seems clear that Campanella's horoscopes of the City of the Sun—notably the second one—fit quite well with the rules concerning elections for founding cities, especially, of course, if we read his own works. In the sixth book, entitled *De electionibus sideralibus* of his *Astrologorum Libri VII*, published in Lyons and Frankfurt in

---

docent prius consulendum esse vitae totius, deinde partium. Id circo quando civitatem extruxerunt signa fixa posuerunt in quatuor mundi angulis; in horoscopo Leonem et Iovem a Sole orientalem, Mercurium vero ac Venerem in Cancro, sed prope quod facerent satellitium; Martem in Sagittario in quinta, foelici aspectu aphetam et horoscopum roborantem; Lunam in Tauro, quae bene aspiciebat Mercurium et Venerem, nec tamen quadrato feriebat Solem. Saturnus quartam appetebat domum, nil tamen laedens Solem et Lunam sed stabiliens fundamenta erat. Fortuna cum Algol erat in decima, ex quo ipsi augurabantur sibi dominatus firmitatem et excellentiam. Porro et Mercurius in bono Virginis aspectu et absidis, a Luna illustratus, malus esse non potest; et cum iovialis sit, ipsorum scientia non mendicat; parum curant in Virgine ipsum praestolari et coniunctionem'.

1630, it is said that a man who wants to found a city must set the fixed signs at the four angles of the chart, Leo in the *medium coeli* or in the 'horoscope', i.e., in the ascendant (as in the two *figurae coeli* of the Solarian's City). The angles have to be in good aspects with the luminaries (the Sun is in the first house and the Moon is in the tenth house in the Solarian's City horoscopes). The Sun must be the *apheta* and the three superior planets must be in good places and have benefic aspects with the luminaries and the other planets, which is the general case in the two figures.[3]

However, Campanella adds some important parameters in these horoscopes, parameters which he got from other sources belonging to a very old astrological tradition.

First of all, in both versions, he indicates the position of the ascendant, the zodiacal signs, the Moon and the planets in accordance with the main Latin texts of medieval authorities on the matter, e.g., Hali Achmet Embrani's *De electionibus horarum*—unpublished but widely disseminated in manuscripts—[4]

---

[3] Campanella, *Astrologicorum Libri VII* (Frankfurt, 1630), VI:4, *De regnis et civitatibus et republica*, p. 220: '2. Civitatem potest homo fundare quando voluerit. Pone ergo signa fixa in 4 angulis, et Leone in M.C. vel in horoscopo, et angulorum dominos in bono aspectu luminarium, faciesque Solem aphetam, vel aliquam planetam ponderosum dominum temporis. 3. Optimus est Saturnus in bono situ, si et luminaria et planetae omnes applicant. Significat enim durationem maximam, et quod regum, et populorum, divitiae, honores et arma servient illi civitati. Iupiter consimiliter potens erit bonus. Omitte planetas leves, quoniam parvi temporis sunt iudices. Mars in bono situ cum satellitio, et dignitate, victoriosam faciet civitatem. Anomaliarum tarditas his favet rebus'.

[4] Hali, filius Achmeth Embrani [Alī ibn Aḥmad al-ʿImrānī, 10th century], *De electionibus horarum*, trans. Abraham bar Hiyya and Plato of Tivoli (1134), II:3. MS Paris, BnF, lat 16204, p. 522b (middle of the 13th century): '*Differencia 3a in edificatione urbium et castrorum.* Cum volueris edificare civitates vel castra, ponendum est ascendens signum fixum, terreum, et similiter signum in quo est Luna et dominus ascendentis. Sitque Luna aucta lumine et numero, iens ad exaltationem suam et ad coniunctionem fortune, fortunate in exaltatione sua vel exaltatione Lune recepta. Non tamen dominus esse nocivum si fuerit in signo aquatico, utile etiam est ut in declinatione septem tibi ascendenti. Sitque plusquam in medietate sui luminis crescens. Dixit Athabari: Ut sit in signis tortuosis eo quod significant augmentationem. Dixit Alkindi: Sitque pars fortune in aliquo angulo et anguli non sint remoti, Cauda in illorum, dominus vero coniunctionis vel preventionis, velox in motu suo, in dignitate sua, et hec futura bona est et autentica. Sed quandoque impossibile est hec omnia aptare, laudamus quoque si fuerit Luna sub terra et super terram, planete existenti iungatur, et aptemus Saturnum, significatorem edificationis urbium et populationis terrarum, et quod laudabiliter est in hoc est ut aspiciat

and the two major and famous treatises of Hali Abenragel[5] and Guido Bonatti,[6]

---

significatores aspectu trino cum receptione, licet aptemus planetam cuius exaltatio est ascendentem et dominum exaltationis loco Lune'. For the diffusion of this text, see Francis J. Carmody, *Arabic Astronomical and Astrological Sciences in Latin Translations. A Critical Bibliography* (Berkeley-Los Angeles: University of California Press, 1956), pp. 137-39.

[5] Albohazen Haly, filius Abenragel [Alī ibn Abi l-Rijāl, 11th century], *De iudiciis astrorum*, VII:20, trans. by Egidius of Thebaldis and Petrus of Regio (Basel, post 1254), ed. H. Petri (1551), pp. 309a–309b: '[...] Item, si potest, sit ascendens una domorum Iovis, sed si non potest fieri, sit alius una cum ascendente liber a Marte; sit etiam Mars cadens et remotus a Luna et ab ascendente et a domino horae initii et a domino termini ascendentis, et quod sit hic dominus termini ascendentis fortuna et directus in suo motus et crescens. Caveas etiam ne sit retrogradus, et quod sit dominus ascendentis in exaltatione sua vel gaudio praevide, et Sol in signo levi et directe ascensionis. Procura etiam ut pars fortunae et eius dominus sint in domibus fortunae, et quod pars aspiciat Lunam, quia a statu partis et eius domini, et a statu Lunae et aspectu eius cum parte, colligetur civitatis fertilitas et bonitas domini eius et suae gentis, et divitiae et bonum quod habebitur in ea, et lucra et profectus qui aliunde venient in civitatem. Remove etiam Martem a parte fortunae et adapta Saturnum quantum potes, et quia si quando Saturnus fuerit dominus partitionis domus, sicut diximus, et meliorem reddiderimus eum per coniunctionem Iovis vel per bonos aspectus eius, sicut diximus, significat durabilitatem civitatis longo tempore et quod erunt magna gens in ea et in multus populus, et quod habebunt inter eos pacem et convenientiam, et quod non depopulabitur. [. . .] Etiam si Mars applicuerit ad partem fortunae et eius dominum, et fuerit inter eos aliquis aspectus vel aliqua commixtio, significat caristatem annonae et diminutionem fertilitatis, et quod dominus qui ibi dominabitur semper erit pravus et iniquus suae genti. Bericus et alii sapientes antiqui cum eo dixerunt quod invenerunt civitatem quandam ceptam extrui in hora in qua Mars fuerat coniunctus Iovi et Veneri corporaliter, omnibus existentibus in succedenti ascendentis illius villae, unde per hunc locum damnavit Mars regem illius civitatis, et fecit eum malum, molestum, factorum malorum et multarum extorsionum a populo illius civitatis. Procura ergo quantum potes in inceptionibus civitatum ponere eum cadentem, et si non potes debilita eum in illo loco, et fortifica Iovem super eum et luminaria similiter et partem fortunae, quia si quando debilitatus fuerit in suo loco et Iuppiter fortificatus super eum et luminaria etiam fortificata et pars fortunae, non patietur civitas magnum damnum'.

[6] Guido Bonatus [Guido Bonatti († ca. 1297)], *De astronomia tractatus X* (Basel, 1550), pars II, 'De quarta domo, cap. 3, In aedificatione civitatum vel castrorum seu domorum et similium, et in populationibus terenum vel ficulnearum fixionibus', col. 434–435: 'Unde si volueris eligere alicui horam ut aedificet civitatem vel castrum, apta ascendens et dominus eius, Lunam quoque ac dominum signi in quo ipsa fuerit, et partem fortune similiter et eius dominum, et pone in ascendente aedificationis urbis vel castri aliquam ex illis stellis fixis, qua sunt de natura Iovis vel Solis vel Veneris aut Mercurii sive Saturni, si

published many times during the fifteenth and sixteenth centuries. In *Civitas Solis* the situation of Fortuna, the *pars fortunae,* in the tenth house and the localization of Mars in the fifth house, have been clearly modified in order to agree with Hali Abenragel and Bonatti.

But Fortuna is not alone in the two charts and Campanella gives great importance to the position of a fixed star in conjunction with Fortuna: the Head of Medusa, which was effectively located at 20° 40′ Taurus at the time of the composition of *La Città del Sole,* in August 1602. Guido Bonatti had already mentioned the augural role of a fixed star of the nature of Jupiter, Venus, the Sun, Mercury, or even Saturn, in his chapter *In aedificatione civitatum* of his *Liber introductorius ad iudicia stellarum* or *De astronomia*. The Head of Medusa, i.e., Caput Algol, is the third of the fifteen stars of great magnitude of the Hermetic *Liber de quindecim stellis*. According to this treatise, it is a very bright star, of the nature of Saturn and the complexion of Jupiter, 'one of the strongest of the whole firmament in nativities and conceptions of things'.[7] And I suspect that

---

Saturnus fuerit boni esse vel Lunae vel saltem de natura domini ascendentis illius horae. Ista enim significant prolongationem illius urbis vel castri et eius perpetuam durabilitatem, propter tardissimum motum earum atque ipsarum tardissimam mutabilitatem. Civitas enim et castrum debent esse res perpetuae durabilitatis, et hoc oportet fieri per successionem suorum individuorum quae sunt domus, que licet diu durent, non tamen perpetuantur nisi successive. Et visum est Hali quod sit aptandus Saturnus in aedificationibus urbium. Zael vero visus est non velle quod domus Saturno partem in aedificio, sed tamen non contradixerunt invicem, quoniam Hali intellexit de aedificationibus urbium, Zael vero intellexit de aedificationibus domorum. Et dixit Hali quod sit ascendens signum terreum, fixum, in aedificationibus, et dominus ascendentis et Luna similiter in signis terreis, fixis. Et dixit quod sit Luna aucta lumine et numero, iens ad exaltationem suam, et quod sit iuncta fortunae quae sit in exaltatione sua, vel in exaltatione Lunae, et sit recepta. Et dixit etiam Hali quod non videtur sibi conveniens ut sit Luna in signo aquatico, et quod est utile, si ipsa sit alias ascendens, et sit plusquam in medietate sui luminis. Et dixit Zael, cui videtur mihi satis conveniens assentire: fac Martem cadere ab omnibus significationibus aedificii, et nunquam des ei aliquam partem in aedificio. Et dixit quod si non potes facere quin des ei aliqua partem, in eo pone Venerem fortem in loco suo, et pone ei fortitudinem super Martem, et iurge eam sibi ex trino vel sextili aspectu, quoniam Mars non impedit rem Veneris, si receptio vel etiam aliquis bonus aspectus interveniat, trinus scilicet vel sextilis, propter multitudinem amicitatis eorum. Et dixit: fac cadere Saturnum a Venere pro posse tuo, propter inimicatem eius cum eo'.

[7] Louis Delatte, *Textes latins et vieux français relatifs aux Cyranides* (Liège-Paris: E. Droz, 1942), pp. 249–50: 'Tertia stella est Caput Algol; est namque stella lucida, rubea, clara.

one of the most authoritative texts that Campanella may have in mind here is Aphorism 36 of the *Centiloquium* (falsely ascribed to Ptolemy): 'Employ the fixed stars in the building of cities, and the planets in the building of houses. In all the cities founded when Mars is in the *medium coeli*, or any fixed star of the nature of Mars from the *beibenie*[8] is there, many princes will die by the sword'.[9] So I think we can better understand why Campanella decided, in the Latin edition of *Civitas Solis*, to put Mars in the fifth house, instead of the ninth house, near the *medium coeli* . . .

Moreover, Campanella may have in mind the third book of the *Tetrabiblos/Quadripartitum* and Ptolemy's theoretical preference for horoscopes of conception.[10] In the City of the Sun, the Solarians have sexual intercourse when

---

Permanet quoque in parte septentrionali distans per magnum spatium a via Solis. Cuius natura est natura Saturni et est eius complexio complexio Iovis. Sciendum quidem quod haec stella est una de fortioribus totius firmamenti in nativitatibus et in conceptionibus rerum'. The *Liber de quindecim stellis* is kept in more than thirty manuscripts from the thirteenth to the seventeenth century. See Paolo Lucentini and Vittoria Perrone Compagni, *I testi e i codici di Ermete nel Medioevo* (Florence: Edizioni Polistampa, 2001), pp. 44–47.

[8] In Arabic-Latin astrology, *stelle beibenie* are thirty bright stars of important magnitude: see the *De stellis beibeniis* ascribed to Hermes and published by Paul Kunitzsch in *Hermetis Trismegisti Astrologica et divinatoria*, eds. Gerrit R. Bos, et al. (Turnhout: Brepols, 2001 [CCCM, CXLIV, C, Hermes Latinus, IV.4]), pp. 3–81 (pp. 73–75 for *Caput Algol*).

[9] [Ps.-] Ptolemeus, *Centiloquium*, trans. Plato of Tivoli (1136), ed. B. Locatello (Venice, 1493), repr. by the heirs of O. Scoti, 1519, f. 110ra (with corrections from the best manuscripts suggested by Richard Lemay's edition, reviewed by Jean-Patrice Boudet, in progress): '*Verbum 36 in quibus edificationibus exerceri debent fixe et in quibus erratice*: Exerce stellas fixas in constructione urbium et planetas in constructione [compositione *ed.*] domorum. Omnes civitates fundate Marte existente in medio celi vel aliqua stella fixa ex albebenie [albemenia *ed.*] eius nature, morientur quamplures principes eius gladio'. [Commentary by 'Hali', i.e., Aḥmad ibn Yūsuf]: 'Intendit ut sint stelle fixe ex albebenie [albemenia *ed.*] que sunt ex complexione Iovis vel Veneris in ascendente constitutionis civitatis et in medio celi et in domo finis rerum [rei *ed.*] et in septima, et stelle erratice aspicientes illas vel coniuncte illis, quia almusteuli [from the Arabic *almustaulī*, 'the master of the moment'] in apparitione urbium ex stellis necesse est ut sint in maiori tarditate, ut prolongetur earum fixio et tardetur earum destructio. Stelle enim fixe maiorem significationem significant quam planete, unde stelle fixe civitatibus dantur, et planete domibus. Deinde dixit: Si fuerit Mars in medio celi, vel stella fixa cuius natura sit sicut Martis, plures principes eius peribunt gladio. Medium namque celum est ascendens principum eius, et Mars in tali loco terminat tempora eorum gladio'.

[10] Ptolemy, *Tetrabiblos*, ed. F.E. Robbins (Cambridge, MA, London: Harvard University

two magistrates, the Astrologer and the Physician, decide that it is a good moment to do so.[11] They have a perfect *regimen sanitatis,* and therefore their life expectancy 'is at least a hundred years, most of them reaching a hundred and seventy and a rare few reaching two hundred years'.[12] In his commentary of Sacrobosco's *De sphaera,* Cecco of Ascoli had already compared the foundation of a city with an individual's conception and concluded: 'the master of the ascendant at the moment when the foundation stone of a city is laid is its *significator,* as the soul is for the body of the individual'.[13] This is not exactly congruent with Christian dogma but Cecco's commentary was published at Venice in 1518 and Campanella may have read it. Following this kind of material, the second horoscope of the *City of the Sun* is a real masterpiece of utopian astrology and a noteworthy achievement of Medieval and Renaissance research on the ideal city.

Let us go back now to the earlier versions of this dream and try to reconstitute some of its experimentations.

Some indirect sources report astrological foundations of cities during Greek Antiquity, notably Alexandria, Seleucia and Constantinople,[14] but the most

---

Press, 1940), III:1, pp. 222–27.

11 Campanella, *La Città del Sole,* ed. Donno (n. 1 above), pp. 55–57: 'They sleep in separate neighboring cells until they are to have intercourse. At the proper time, the matron goes around and opens the cell doors. The exact hour when this must be done is determined by the Astrologer and the Physician, who always endeavour to choose a time when Mercury and Venus are oriental to the Sun in a benefic house and are seen by Jupiter, Saturn, and Mars with benefic aspect. So too by the Sun and the Moon that are often aphetic. Most frequently they seek a time when Virgo is in the ascendant, but they take great care to see that Saturn and Mars are not in the angles, because all four angles, with oppositions and quadratures, are harmful . . .'

12 Ibid., p. 89.

13 Lynn Thorndike, *The Sphere of Sacrobosco and its Commentators* (Chicago: University of Chicago Press, 1949), p. 375: 'Habet civitas significatorem edificationis. Nam (ut alias dixi vobis) simile est de edificatione civitatis quemadmodum est de conceptione individui. Nam sicut in proiectione vel in casu spermatis in matricem sumitur potentia infortunii et dignitatis illius, sic in primo lapide in civitate. Nam cum primis lapis proiicitur in fundamento sub tali ascendente, ille dominus ascendens indicat quid de civitate, et iste significator se habet ad civitatem sicut anima ad corpus [. . .]'

14 *Appian's Roman History,* English trans. by Horace White (London-Cambridge MA: Harvard University Press, 1962), II: pp. 214–17 (for Seleucia); E. Weinstock, 'Codices Britannici', in Franz Boll et al., *Catalogus codicum astrologorum graecorum,* IX–2 (Brussels: Henri Lamertin, 1953), pp. 176–79 (for Antioch, Alexandria, Gaza, Caesarea and

famous antique city about which we have quite important material on this subject is, of course, Rome. Cicero in his *De divinatione*, Plutarch in his *Life of Romulus* and, later, Solinus and John Lydus, gave some contradictory indications on the *dies natalis Romae* and its possible horoscope.[15] The little encyclopedia of Solinus, *Collectanea rerum memorabilium*, was very widely circulated during the Middle Ages and the Renaissance; Luca Gaurico refers to this text in his *Tractatus astrologicus*, published in Venice in 1552, where we find a collection of fourteen horoscopes of cities, the most important known to me.[16] Referring to Solinus and Tarutius (the author of the horoscope of Rome according to Cicero), quoting Manilius, Gaurico reproduces a first horoscope of Rome (Fig. 3) for 21 April 752 BCE at 5:00 P.M., a date which allows him to locate the ascendant in Libra, the sign of augural protection of Rome according to Manilius.[17]

Neapolis); Masudi, *Les Prairies d'or*, French trans. Charles Pellat (Paris: Société asiatique, 1965), p. 314, § 829; p. 316, § 834 (for Alexandria); David Pingree, 'The Horoscope of Constantinople', in *Πρίσματα. Festschrift für Willy Hartner* (Wiesbaden: Franz Steiner, 1977), pp. 305–15; Gilbert Dagron, *Constantinople imaginaire. Etudes sur le recueil des Patria* (Paris: Presses Universitaires de France, 1984), p. 119.

15 See Pierre Brind'Amour, *Le calendrier romain. Recherches chronologiques* (Ottawa: Editions de l'Université d'Ottawa, 1983), pp. 240–49; Anthony T. Grafton and Noel M. Swerdlow, 'The Horoscope of the Foundation of Rome', *Classical Philology* 81 (1986): pp. 148–53; Josephe-Henriette Abry, 'L'horoscope de Rome (Cicéron, *Div.*, II, 98–99)', in *Les astres. Actes du Colloque international de Montpellier (23–25 mars 1995)* (Montpellier: Université Paul Valéry, 1996), II: pp. 121–40; Stephan Heilen, 'Ancient Scholars on the Horoscope of Rome', *Culture and Cosmos* 11 (2007): pp. 43–68.

16 Lucius Gauricus, *Tractatus astrologicus, in quo agitur de praeteritis multorum hominum accidentibus, per proprias eorum genituras adunguem examinatis* (Venice, C.T. Navo, 1552), tractatus primus: 'Civitatum, et quorundam oppidorum figurae celestes, et earum eventus', fols. 1r–14r (horoscopes of Byzantium [2], Rome [2], Bologna [2], Florence, Venice [2], Pavia, Ferrara [3], Milan). First versions of the horoscopes of Venice, Bologna and Florence were already published by Gaurico in his *Praedictiones super omnibus futuris luminarium deliquiis* (Rome, 1539), fols. F1r–F2r.

17 Marcus Manilius, *Astronomica*, trans. and ed. G.P. Goold (Leipzig: Teubner, 1985), IV: vv. 773-777, p. 107. According to Tarutius, the Moon was in Libra when Romulus founded Rome, and Augustus' horoscope was very similar to Romulus', both of them being under the influence of Libra. See Auguste Bouché-Leclercq, *L'astrologie grecque* (Paris : E. Leroux, 1899), p. 369; Brind'Amour, *Le calendrier romain* (cit. n. 15), pp. 62–76; Patrizio Domenicucci, *Astra Caesarum: Astronomia, astrologia e catasterismo da Cesare a Domiziano* (Pisa: Edizioni ETS, 1996), pp. 111–38.

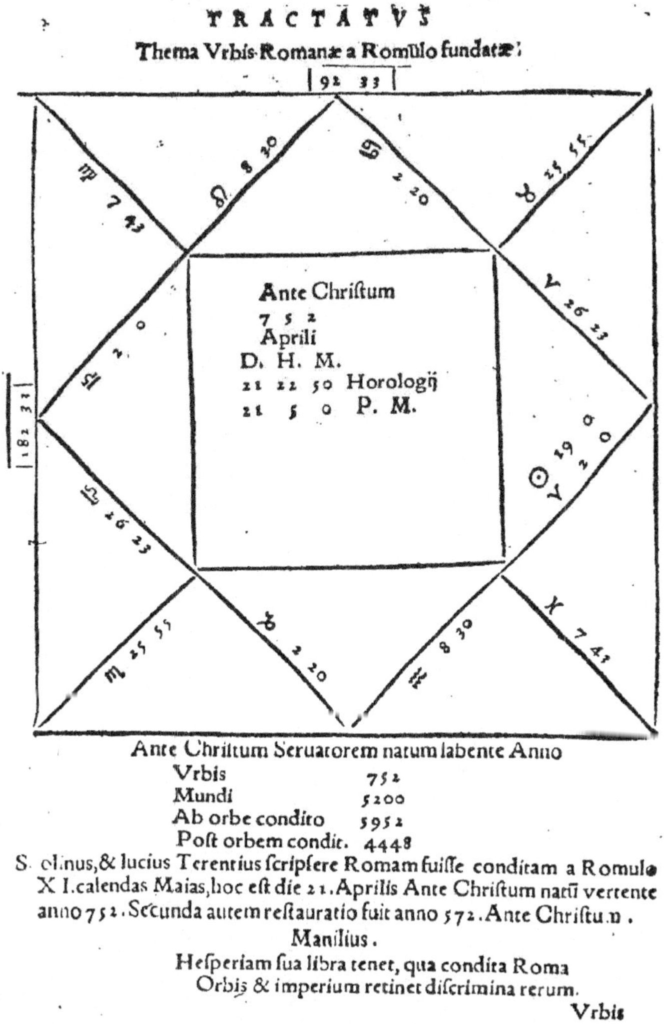

Fig. 3: Luca Gaurico, 'Thema Urbis Romanae, a Romulo fundatae', Tractatus astrologicus, *Venice, 1552, fol. 4v.*

But the position of the Sun at 19° Aries (the point of his exaltation) is not satisfying for him, probably because it was in the seventh house. Therefore he chooses another date for a hypothetical *Urbis secunda restauratio* (Fig. 4), 20 April 572 BCE [*sic*] at 0:49 P.M., which corresponds to a much better horoscope: Leo on the ascendant; the Sun in the ninth house and in his exaltation in Aries; the two beneficent planets, Jupiter and Venus, in conjunction with the Head of the Dragon at the *medium coeli* and in Taurus, the *domicilium* of Venus. With Mars in *casus* in Cancer (in the eleventh house, the house of friends) and Saturn in *detrimentum* in the same sign but in the twelfth house (the house of enemies), the two malefic planets seem to be impotent.

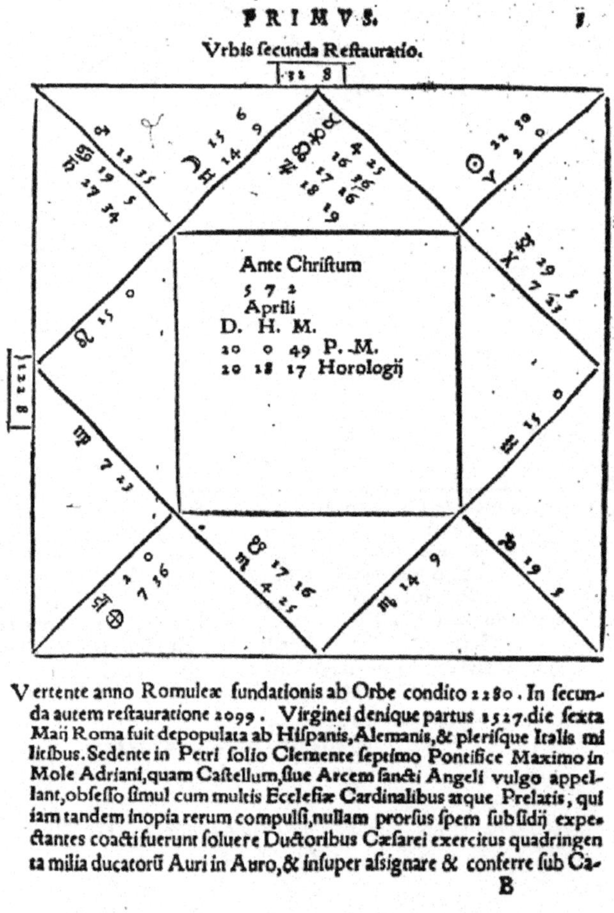
PRIMVS. I.

Vrbis ſecunda Reſtauratio.

Ante Chriſtum
5 7 2
Aprili
D. H. M.
20 0 49 P. M.
20 18 17 Horologij

Vertente anno Romuleæ fundationis ab Orbe condito 2180. In ſecunda autem reſtauratione 2099. Virginei denique partus 1527. die ſexta Maij Roma fuit depopulata ab Hiſpanis, Alemanis, & pleriſque Italis militibus. Sedente in Petri ſolio Clemente ſeptimo Pontifice Maximo in Mole Adriani, quam Caſtellum, ſiue Arcem ſancti Angeli vulgo appellant, obſeſſo ſimul cum multis Eccleſiæ Cardinalibus atque Prelatis, qui iam tandem inopia rerum compulſi, nullam prorſus ſpem ſubſidij expectantes coacti fuerunt ſoluere Ductoribus Cæſarei exercitus quadringenta milia ducatorũ Auri in Auro, & inſuper aſsignare & conferre ſub Ca-

B

Fig. 4: Luca Gaurico, 'Urbis secunda Restauratio', Tractatus astrologicus, *Venice, 1552, fol. 5.*

This was perhaps reliable for Roman domination but not for modern times. That is why, Gaurico explains, Rome was sacked by the troops of Charles V and the

Constable of Bourbon in 1527![18]

Luca Gaurico also provides two horoscopes of the 'new' Rome, Constantinople (Figs 5 and 6). Both are curiously dated 1 May of the world year 5838, i.e., 638 CE, instead of the usual date, 330; Gaurico believes that the chronology of the Byzantines was the same as that of Eusebius and Isidorus (5200 years between the Creation and the birth of Christ).

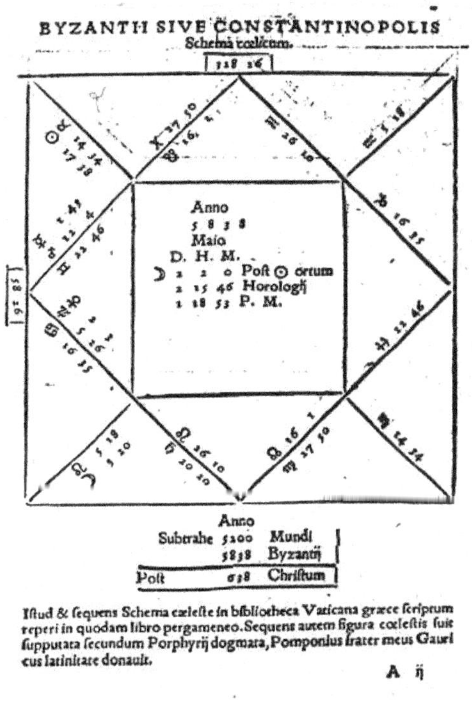

Fig. 5: Luca Gaurico, 'Byzantii sive Constantinopolis schema cœlicum', Tractatus astrologicus, *Venice, 1552, fol. 2.*

---

[18] For other examples of Gaurico's horoscopic manipulations, see Aby Warburg, 'Divinazione antica pagana in testi ed immagini dell' età di Lutero' (1920), repr. in Warburg, *La rinascita del paganesimo antico. Contributi alla studia della cultura* (Florence: La Nuova Italia, 1966), pp. 309–90; Mary Quinlan-McGrath, 'The Foundation Horoscope(s) for St. Peter's Basilica, Rome, 1506', *Isis* 92 (2001): pp. 716–41; Jean-Patrice Boudet, 'Manipuler le ciel: note sur les horoscopes d'Alexandre VI et de Jules II établis par Luca Gaurico', in *La fortuna dei Borgia*. Atti del convegno, Bologne, 29–31 ottobre 2000 (Rome: Roma nel Rinascimento, 2005), pp. 225–34.

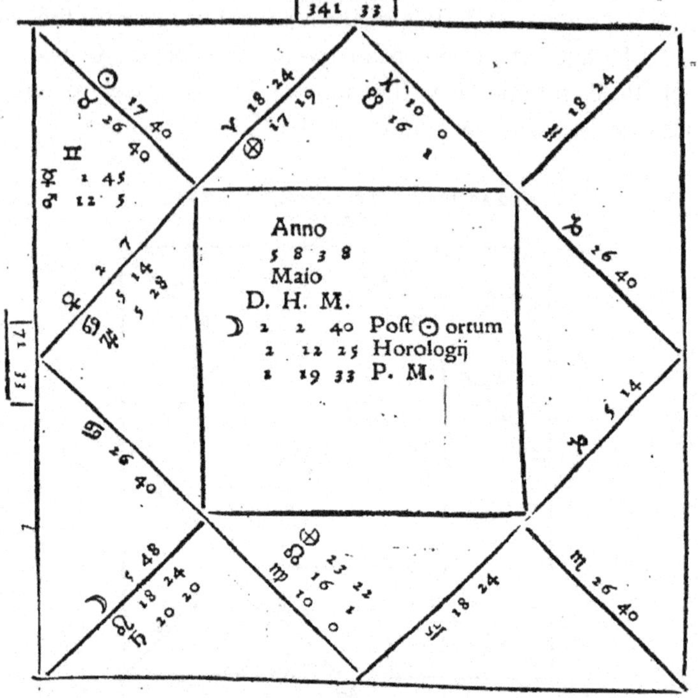
TRACTATVS

Bizantij thema.

Thema cœlicum vrbis Conſtantinopolitanæ, quæ olim Bizantium vocitabatur a Conſtantino Imperatore vltimo reſtaurata veluti in Bibliotheca vaticana reperit frater meus Pomponius Gauricus in libello Græci Aſtronomi epyſtographo. Fundamentum igitur Bizantij vtpote Cōſtantinopolitanæ vrbis quę noua Roma dicebatur iactum fuit Anno a prima Mundi origine 5838. id eſt quinquies milleſimo trigeſimo octauo poſt Chriſtum 638. die 2. Maij, hora 2. poſt ortum ☉ quippe ꝗ mane diem Græca gens incipit. Quod thema cœleſte erexit ſapientiſsimus ille vir Valens Antiochenus, erunt autem (aiebat ille) anni 766. ſeptingenti ſexaginta ſex circiter.

Fig. 6: Luca Gaurico, 'Byzantii thema', Tractatus astrologicus, *Venice, 1552, fol. 2v.*

But the two charts have different coordinates; Gaurico says that he found the first one in a Greek manuscript of the Vatican Library and that his brother Pomponio, professor of humanities in Naples, gave him the second one, which was cast according to the doctrine of Porphyry by the astrologer Vettius Valens.

This is a mistake because Valens, the author of the *Anthology*, flourished in the second century CE. But David Pingree edited a text which provides an explanation; most probably, this second horoscope was originally cast by the Byzantine astronomer Demophilus (ca. 990) and interpreted by him in accordance with rules found in the work of Vettius Valens. The real date corresponding to this chart is 11 May 330, the date of the 'feast of the dedication' of Constantinople, according to the Byzantine tradition.[19]

Another version of this chart is preserved in a Greek manuscript of the eleventh century where we find, on the same page, a *thema mundi* and six horoscopes of cities: Alexandria, Antioch, Constantinople, Caesarea, Neapolis and Gaza.[20] Except for Alexandria, founded in 330 BCE, the astronomical positions of these charts are highly problematic; but it is probable that they were originally cast in the seventh century, during the Arab conquest and the Byzantine loss of Palestine in 636. The horoscope of Gaza is rather fascinating (Fig. 7): Mars is in Aries (his domicile) in the twelfth house (of enemies); the Sun is in his exaltation in Aries, in the eleventh house; Jupiter is in his domicile in Pisces; the Moon is at the ascendant in Taurus, her sign of exaltation; Venus is in Taurus too, her sign of rulership; Saturn is in domicile in Aquarius. Mercury is the only planet badly placed, in detriment in Pisces, at the mid-heaven.

---

[19] Pingree, 'The Horoscope of Contantinople' (n. 14 above), pp. 206–08; Gilbert Dagron, *Naissance d'une capitale: Constantinople et ses institutions de 330 à 451* (Paris: Presses Universitaires de France, 1974), pp. 32–33.

[20] MS Leiden, BPG 78, fol. 2v. See E. Weinstock, 'Codices Britannici' (n. 14 above).

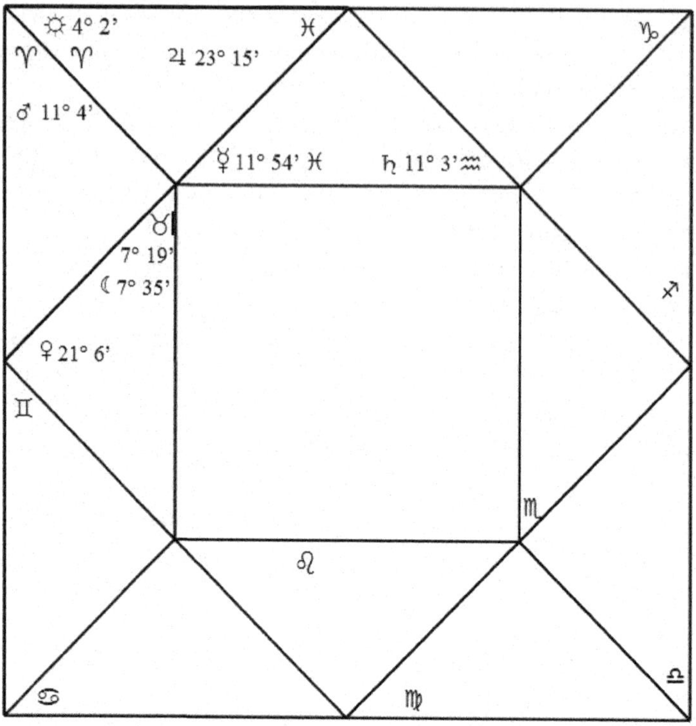

Fig. 7: Horoscope of Gaza, MS Leiden, BP, Graec. 78, fol. 2v (11th century).

It is clearly an ideal horoscope but I do not know if it was supposed to fit with a particular date. Anyway, the recent and too-real history of the town is especially cruel in this case.

In contrast, the best known medieval horoscope of a city seems much more realistic. I speak, of course, about the foundation chart of Baghdad (Fig. 8).

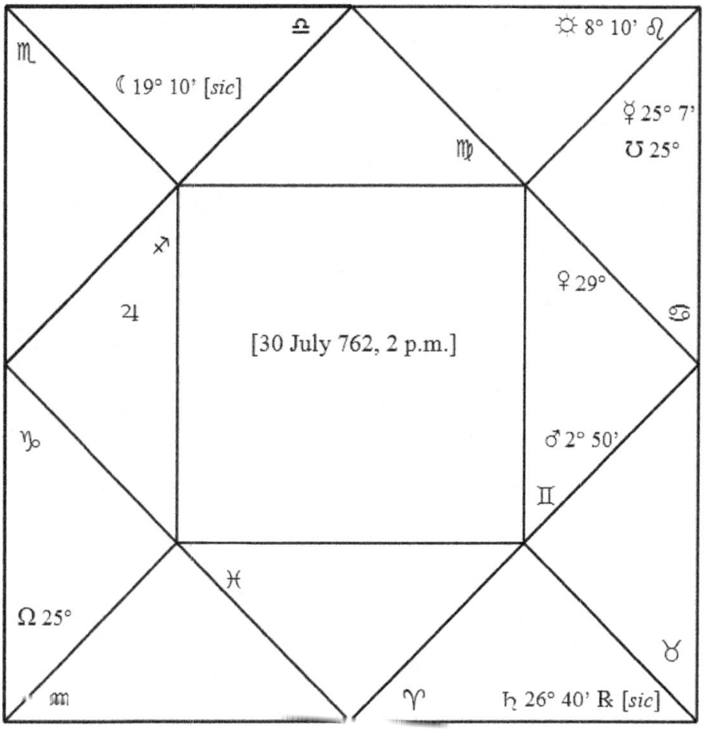

Fig. 8: Horoscope of Baghdad, according to Al-Bīrūnī.

At the end of the ninth century, the geographer Ya'qūbī says that the plans of the famous round city of the Abbasid Caliph al-Mansūr were prepared during the month of Rabi I of Hegira 141 (July-August 758), but that the real foundations were built later, at a moment chosen by Nawbakht the Persian, court astrologer of the Caliph, and by Māshā'allāh, a Jewish astrologer who became very famous in the Arabic and Latin Middle Ages.[21] Ya'qūbī does not indicate the precise date and the chart only adds that Nawbakht was present himself at the moment of the foundation, with two other astrologers and mathematicians: al-Fazārī and ['Umar ibn al-Farrukhān] al-Ṭabarī. This seems to be consistent with Al-Bīrūnī who says in his *Chronology of Ancient Nations* (ca. 1000) that it was Nawbakht who drew the chart and indicates the date: the year

[21] Ya'qūbī, *Kitāb al-buldān* (Leiden: Brill, 1892), pp. 238–42; Ya'qūbī, *Les Pays*, French trans. Gaston Wiet (Cairo: L'Institut Français d'Archéologie Orientale), pp. 11–15.

1074 of the Era of Alexander, i.e., 762 CE.[22] The astronomical positions of the chart actually correspond to 30 July 762 at 2:00 P.M. But as may be seen, this chart is not exceptionally favourable from an astrological point of view: Jupiter is at the ascendant in Sagittarius, his domicile, but seems to be in opposition with Mars in Gemini; the Sun is in Leo, his domicile, and in the ninth house, signifying religion, in trine aspect with the ascendant and Jupiter; Saturn is supposed to be impotent because he is retrograde at 26° 40′ Aries, in his *casus* and in the sign of exaltation of the Sun (actually, Saturn is direct and in the beginning of Taurus: I think it is a 'political' mistake to reassure the caliph making this malefic planet harmless). The angles are not in fixed signs, the chart does not include the *pars fortunae* or any fixed star and its astronomical positions seem to fit not too badly, for the Caliph, with an inaugural ceremony of entering into the round city. But it shows the difference between an ideal horoscope and an election of the better (or the less bad) moment to initiate a major political event.

We have some astrological indications about foundations of other cities in the Medieval Middle East. According to the geographer Mostawfi (fourteenth century) and to the *Shiraz nameh*, the Persian city of Shiraz was (re)built in 74 H/693 CE, when Virgo was in the ascendant.[23] According to the second version of the *Zafer nameh* (ca. 1425), Tamerlane used an astrological election to transform Kech, the desert place where he was born, into a real city; astrology holds an important place in Timurid political justification and propaganda.[24] In

---

[22] See Al-Bīrūnī, *The Chronology of Ancient Nations*, ed. Eduard Sachau (London: W. H. Allen and Co., 1879), pp. 270–71, trans. pp. 262–63; Carlo Alfonso Nallino, *Storia dell'astronomia presso gli Arabi nel Medio Evo*, in Nallino, *Raccolta di scritti editi e ineditti*, vol. V, *Astrologia-astronomia, geografia*, a cura di Maria Nallino (Rome: Istituto per l'Oriente, 1944), pp. 200–01; David Pingree, 'The Fragments of the Works of al-Fazārī', *Journal of Near Eastern Studies* 29 (1970): pp. 103–23 (104). See also Ibrahim Allawi, 'Some Evolutionary and Cosmological Aspects to Early Islamic Town Planning', in *Theories and Principles of Design in the Architecture of Islamic Societies*, ed. Margaret B. Sevcenko (Cambridge, MA: Aga Khan Program for Islamic Architecture, 1988d).

[23] *The Geographic Part of the Nuzhat al-Qulūb, composed by Hand-All'ah Mustafwī of Qazwīn in 740 (1340)*, trans. Guy LeStrange (Leiden: E. J. Brill, 1919), p. 113. I owe this reference to Anna Caiozzo.

[24] *Histoire de Timour-Bec, connu sous le nom de Tamerlan*, French trans. Alexandre L.M. Petis de La Croix (Paris: Antonin Deshayes, 1722), I: p. 308. See Anna Caiozzo, 'The Horoscope of Iskandar Sultān as a Cosmological Vision in the Islamic World', in *Horoscopes and Public Spheres. Essays on the History of Astrology*, ed. Günther Oestmann, H. Darrel Rutkin

the fifteenth century, the historian al-Makrīzī mentions an anonymous 'commentator' who said that the building of Cairo began when the two luminaries were in exaltation in two fixed signs, the Sun in Aries [*sic*, for Leo] and the Moon in Taurus.[25] Makrīzī also reports with others the famous and mythical story of Cairo which was supposed to have been accidentally built when Mars was in the ascendant, in July 969: a stupid crow woke up everybody in the middle of the night and the public works began at a very bad moment, considering the fact that, for the astrologers, Mars should not have any influence on the ascendant of a city and must be cadent from the angles of the sky in its birth horoscope.[26] Actually, this counter-example seems to have been inspired by the story of the foundation of Alexandria by Alexander the Great, reported by Masudi in the middle of the tenth century; however the etymological origin of the name Cairo (al-Qāhira, 'the Victorious') seems to have not much to do with the planet Mars.[27]

For the Latin Middle Ages, the available material is unfortunately rather poor, and no original horoscope of a city is preserved from this period. But we have some indirect evidence of it. According to the chronicler Rolandino Patavini, during the siege of Parma in 1247—when Frederick II tried to transform the military camp where he was living with his army into a true city adversary to Parma and gave it the name of Vittoria—he tried to put the ascendant in Aries (Fig. 9), domicile of Mars, because Mars is the god of war and Aries is the opposite sign to Libra, domicile of Venus, the dominant planet of Parma.

---

and Kocku von Stuckrad (Berlin, New York: Walter de Gruyter, 2005), pp. 115–44.

25 Maqrizi, *Description historique et topographquie de l'Egypte*, 4e partie, French. trans. Paul Casanova (Paris: E. Leroux, 1920), p. 69.

26 Compare with Alī ibn Abi l-Rijāl above, n. 5.

27 Janet L. Abu-Lughod, *Cairo, 1001 Years of the City Victorious* (Princeton: Princeton University Press, 1971), p. 18 and n. 13; Paul Kunitzsch, 'Zur Namengebung Kairos (al-Qāhir = Mars?)', *Der Islam* 52 (1975): pp. 209–25, repr. in Kunitzsch, *The Arabs and the Stars: Texts and Traditions on the Fixed Stars and their influence in Medieval Europe* (Northampton: Ashgate Variorum, 1989), n° XXV.

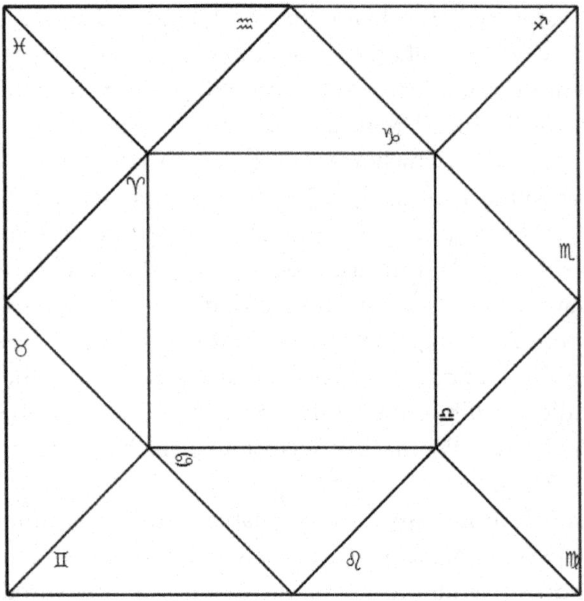

Fig. 9: Horoscope of Vittoria (1247), according to Rolandino Patavini.

But this turned into a disaster when the Parmesans destroyed Vittoria in February 1248. And Rolandino Patavini remarks that the emperor did not notice that in the election chart, the fourth house—signifying buildings, houses and cities—was in Cancer and that a city built under such unfavourable auspices could do nothing but *cancrizare*, i.e., walk crabwise . . .[28]

The astrology of elections and interrogations was criticized by the Church during the thirteenth century, and this caused trouble for Guido Bonatti. But the science of the stars became, in Late Medieval Italian cities, an important part of learned, lay and civic culture. One of the most interesting cases of this acculturation is that of Florence. Giovanni Villani, in his *Cronica* composed in the

28 Rolandino Patavini, *Cronica in factis et circa facta Marchie Trivixane*, ed. Antonio Bonardi (Città del Castello: S. Lapi, 1905), pp. 83–84: 'Tum quia signum est Martis, qui dicitur deus belli, tum quia erat Libre ascendenti contrarium in occasum, quod est signum Veneris, qui planeta Parme dicitur et esse fortuna ejus. Quasi per hoc forsitan cogitaret, quod Parmensium fortuna, qui opposita ei erat, tenderet in occasum. [...] Sed puto quod non notavit quartum ab ascendente fuisse Cancrum. Quartum enim hedificia, domos et civitates designat et sic civitas sub tali ascendente incepta cancrizare debebat'.

first half of the fourteenth century, says that Florence was founded by Julius Caesar, destroyed by Totila and rebuilt by Charlemagne and some Roman citizens at the beginning of April 801/802 (n.s.). These Roman citizens were helped by astrologers, Villani says, who chose for the ascendant the third degree of Aries, in the exaltation of the Sun, in a term of Jupiter and a decan of Mars, while Mercury was in conjunction with the Sun and Mars in a good aspect with the ascendant, which was important for the commercial and military prosperity of the city. Villani asserts that this astrological election is not at all incompatible with human free will and that it highlights 'the merits and sins of the Florentine people'.[29] Filippo Villani, Giovanni's nephew, in his *Liber de origine civitatis Florentie*, follows the same inspiration and adds that, 'almost by a miracle', the ascendant of Aries was the same for the foundation of Florence by Caesar and for the rebuilding of the city by Charlemagne. He also proposes a partly new

---

[29] Giovanni Villani, *Nuova cronica*, IV, 1, ed. Giuseppe Porta (Parma: U. Guanda, 1990), I: pp. 145–56, tries to show the opposition between the pagan consecration 'by nigromancy' of an augural statue of Mars erected at the head of the Ponte Vecchio to impart his regenerative virtue to Florence, and the more rational explanation of the destiny of the city provided by his horoscope: 'E dicesi che gli antichi aveano oppinione che di rifarla non s'ebbe podere, se prima non fu ritrovata e tratta d'Arno la imagine di marmo consecrata per gli primi edificatori pagani per nigromanzia a Marte, la quale era stata nel fiume d'Arno dalla distruzione di Firenze enfino a quello tempo; e ritrovata, la puosero in su uno piliere in su la riva del detto fiume, ov'è oggi il capo del ponte Vecchio. Questo nonn-affermiamo, né crediamo, però che ·cci pare oppinione di pagani e d'aguri, e non di ragione, ma grande simplicità, ch'una sì fatta pietra potesse ciò adoperare; ma volgarmente si dicea per gli antichi che mutandola convenia che ·lla città avesse grande mutazione. E dissesi ancora per gli antichi che' Romani per consiglio de' savi astrolagi, al cominciamento che rifondaron Firenze, presono l'ascendente di tre gradi del segno dell'Ariete, termine di Giovi e faccia di [Marti], essendo il Sole nel grado della sua esaltazione, e la pianeta di Mercurio congiunta a grado col Sole, e la pianeta di Marti in buono aspetto dell'ascendente, acciò che ·lla città multiplicasse per potenzia d'arme, e di cavalleria, e di popolo sollecito e procaccianti in arti, e in mercatantie e in ricchezze, e germinasse d'assai figliuoli e grande popolo. E in quegli tempi, secondo che ·ssi dice, gli antichi Romani, e tutti i Toscani, e gl'Italici, tutto fossero Cristiani battezzati, ancora teneano certe orlique a costume di pagani, e seguieno i loro cominciamenti secondo la costellazione; con tutto che questo non s'afermi per noi, però che costellazione nonn-è di nicessità, né può costrignere il libero albitrio degli uomini né 'l giudicio d'Iddio, ma secondo i meriti e peccati de' popoli. In alcuna operazione pare che ·ssi dimostra la 'nfruenza della costellazione detta, che ·lla città di Firenze è sempre in grandi mutazioni e dissimulazioni e in guerra, e talora in vittoria, e talora il contrario, e sono i cittadini di quella frequentati in mercatantie e in arti'.

astrological explanation for the talent of the Florentine people for commerce.[30]

Giovanni and Filippo Villani seem to refer to a real horoscope which could have been cast by Cecco of Ascoli, the only medieval astrologer who was burnt at the stake at Florence in 1327 because he was considered a relapsed heretic after a first condemnation by the Inquisition.[31] In his commentary on Alcabitius' *Liber introductorius*—the main handbook of astrology studied in medieval *studia* and universities—Cecco quotes Aphorism 36 of the *Centiloquium* and says that cities founded under the influence of fixed stars and fixed signs (there is an ambiguity here) have a better life expectancy than others.[32] It is clear for him that

---

[30] Filippo Villani, *De origine civitatis Florentie et de eiusdem famosis civibus*, ed. Giuliano Tanturli (Padua: Antenore, 1997), pp. 46–47: 'Quibus relatum est saliente Arietis singno super lineam circularem nostri orizzontis, quo cum tunc Mars atque Mercurius beningnissimis aliorum syderum aspectibus pariter ferebantur, manu Cesarem primum lapidem, coniecto prius calce, defossis specubus, coaptasse. Et quod est miraculo promixum, sine ulla celi dispositione previsa, reparante Karolo Mangno urbem nostram, que sub cineribus Attile per CCC aut circiter annos latuerat, eodem ascendente singno hisdemque comitantibus planetis et eadem ferme celi facie et figura restitui ac reparari iterum cepta sunt ampliora menia civitatis. Quam celi in urbis formatione et reformatione concordiam portendere mangna mathematici astrorum docti predixerunt, que postea sunt certissimis effectibus comprobata. Nam ut volunt periti syderum, aries animal est cornu belliger, sed vellere et omni re sua mercibus rurique et multis aliis hominum usibus atque utilitatibus commodissimus. Mars in fronte animalis mansueti potens, excitatus irritatusque temperata et ut plurimum ad defensionem bella conseruit. Mercurius in ceteris partibus animalis representantibus mercaturam Florentinos mercium cupiditate, per orbem terrarum dispertiendo eos, intequietis laboribus agitavit. Ceterum, cum celestis Aries, cum mundi specie creatus, quasi, matutinus consurgens, ex terra, que aspectui nostro continuatur, celi convexa scanderet, diuturne durationis mundi fecisse presagium videretur, ita et urbi nostre perpetuitatem perennem cum seculis perituram promisisse videtur veteribus astrologis placuisse. Quorum sententiam attestare videntur lictere que in marmoreo pavimento templi dudum Marti gentili stultitia dedicati, hodie christiana religione Iohanni Baptiste consecrati, scalpro fabrili sculte intexto nigro marmore perleguntur'. For the end of this text, see Luca Gatti, 'Il mito di Marte a Firenze e la "pietra scema". Memorie, riti e ascendenze', *Rinascimento* 35 (1995): pp. 201–30.

[31] See Giuseppe Boffito, 'Perché fu condannato al fuoco l'astrologo Cecco d'Ascoli?', *Studi e documenti di Storia e diritto* 20 (1899): pp. 357–82; Nicolas Weill-Parot, 'I demoni della Sfera: La "nigromanzia" cosmologico-astrologica di Cecco d'Ascoli', in *Cecco d'Ascoli: cultura, scienza e politica nell'Italia del Trecento*. Attti del convegno, Ascoli, 2–3 dicembre 2005, ed. Antonio Rigon (Rome: Istituto storico italiano per il medioevo, 2007), pp. 103–28.

[32] Giuseppe Boffitto, *Il commento di Cecco d'Ascoli all'Alcabizzo* (Florence: L.S. Olschki,

the main cities of Northern and Central Italy have a foundation horoscope, considered as a conception chart, which defines the personality of the city and has an influence upon its destiny; Bologna has Taurus for its ascendant, Ferrara has Scorpio, Florence has Aries. Some zodiacal signs such as Taurus, Bologna's ascendant, and Aries, the ascendant of Florence, are predisposed to luxury, and Venus has of course an influence upon female beauty, especially in Bologna and Siena, which was called *Civitas ydearum* by Cino da Pistoia.[33] And above all, these foundation charts have an influence on the city government: the Scorpio ascendant of Ferrara inclined its inhabitants to be governed by *nobiles* and *magnates*; by contrast, in Bologna, because it was built under Taurus, which is the exaltation of the Moon and the domicile of Venus, the *popolo* dominates, because the Moon signifies the *popolo* and because the ascendant of the Bolognese *nobiles* is Aquarius, domicile of Saturn, which was impeded during the building of Bologna.[34]

Girolamo Cardano, in his collection of 67 horoscopes published at Nuremberg in 1543, reproduces a rebuilt chart for Florence where the ascendant is 3° Aries, as Giovanni Villani said two hundred years earlier (Fig. 10).

1905), pp. 31-32: 'Nam ut civitas duret debemus signa fixa in edificatione eligere et actare planetas in compositione domorum, ut dicit Ptholomeus in *Centiloquio*, 36 verbo: "Exercere stellas fixas in constructione urbium et planetas in constructione domorum." Iuxta quod debetis intelligere quoc civitates que edificate sunt sub stellis fixis plus durant quam ille que edificate sunt sub aliis. Nam civitates que fundate sunt sub signis mobilibus parum multiplicantur et ex modica guerra destruuntur, ut patet in multis civitatibus destructis quia lapidum et murorum insignia videntur in locis desertis'.

33 Cecco defines his doctrine on this matter in his commentary of Sacrobosco's *De sphaera*, ed. Thorndike (cit. n. 13 above), pp. 374-75, and in his commentary on Alcabitius (cit. n. 32 above), pp. 50-51.

34 Ibid., p. 32: 'Et quia Bononia fuit edificata sub Tauro, qui est exaltatio Lune et domus Veneris, et sunt stelle fixe, idcirco hic populus regnat et regnabit in futurum, quia Luna significat populum et quia ascendens nobilium, scilicet medium celi, est Aquarius, domus Saturni, et Saturnus fuit impeditus in edificatione quod patet per effectus, idcirco nobiles sunt nullius valoris. Unde regnabit populus, deprimentur nobiles, vigebunt tripudia, luxuria, cantus, et nunquam destruetur Bononia sed marescet'.

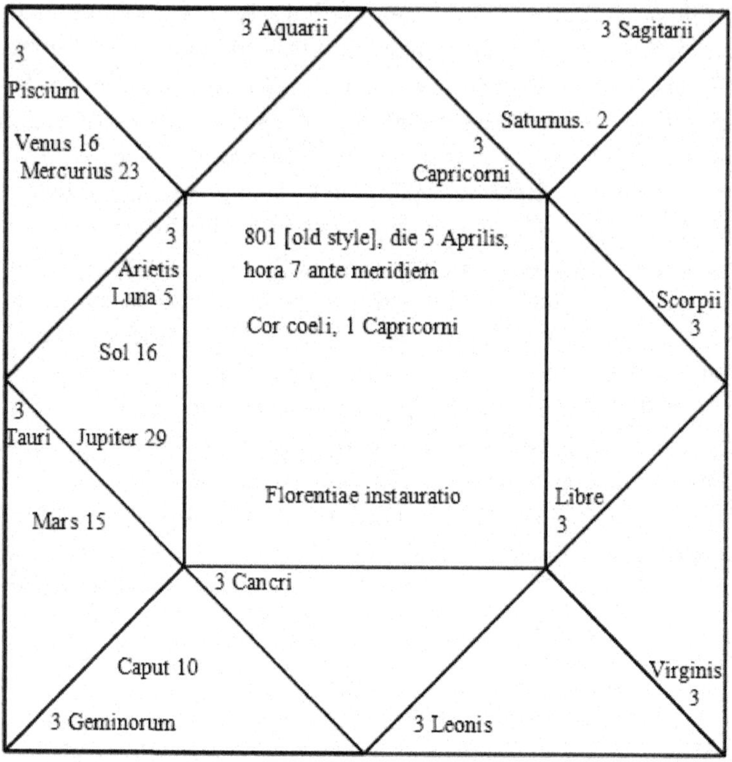

Fig. 10: Horoscope of Florence, according to Girolamo Cardano.

But Mars, instead of beneficently looking at the ascendant, is here located in Taurus, his *detrimentum*, which for Cardano explains the Florentine lack of talent for war. And Mercury, instead of being in conjunction with the Sun, is here at 23° west from the Sun, in the twelfth house and in Pisces, his *detrimentum*. That is why, Cardano says, Florentines are less literate that Milanese.[35] Of course, Cardano was born in Milan . . .

Moreover, Cardano adds that Saturn, in conjunction with the *medium coeli*, was in his domicile, and concludes that Florence is structurally subject to political mutations and social seditions. This was a scandalous judgment,

35 Hyeronimus Cardanus, *Supplementum Almanach, De restitutione temporum et motuum coelestium; Item, Geniturae LXVII insignes casibus et fortuna, cum expositione* (Nuremberg: J. Petri, 1543), fols. bb4v–cc1.

according to the Florentine astrologer Francesco Giuntini, author of the enormous and magnificent *Speculum astrologiae,* published in Lyons in 1581 and reprinted two years later.[36] Giuntini also used Giovanni Villani's *Cronica* but for another event: the building of the sixth surrounding wall of Florence on 29 November 1298 (Fig. 11).

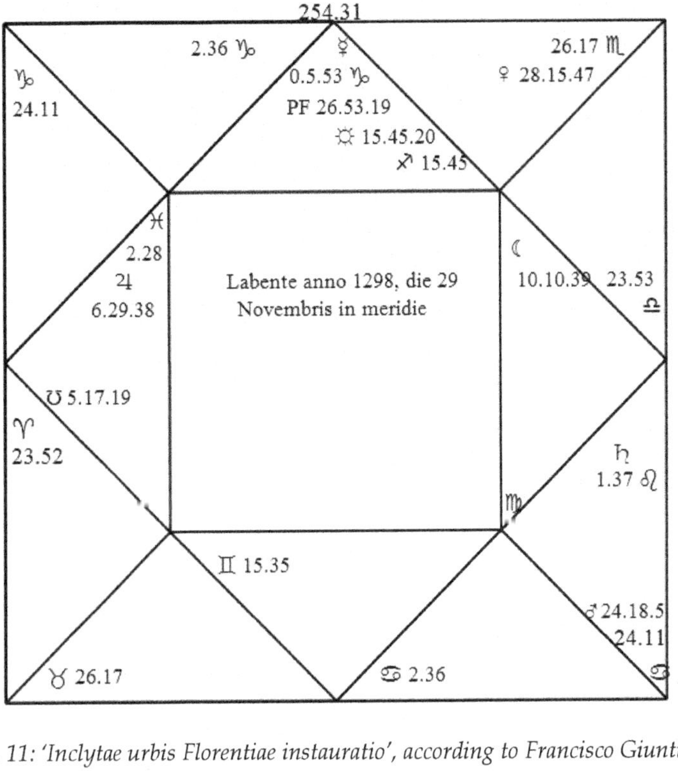

Fig. 11: 'Inclytae urbis Florentiae instauratio', according to Francisco Giuntini.

He chose the best hour and was able to get a very appropriate horoscope for it: Jupiter was in the first house (as for Baghdad), in domicile in Pisces—that is why the Florentines are rich and religious, because Venus was also in the ninth house, the *templum religionis*; Mercury was in the mid-heaven in Capricorn which signifies, according to Ptolemy, constancy, intelligence and an exceptional

36 Franciscus Iunctinus, *Speculum astrologiae*, ed. Symphorien Beraud, (Lyons, 1583), II: pp. 815–56.

capacity in liberal and mechanical arts; the Sun was in the mid-heaven in Sagittarius, in his triplicity and *bene dispositus* for the fame and glory of the city. Giuntini concludes with a critique of Cardano's judgement about the so-called inferiority of the Florentines in Literature and Art; he cites Dante, Petrarch, Bocaccio, Michelangelo, the jurist Francesco Accursio and a dozen famous physicians, astrologers and some sixteenth-century men of war.

Finally, Cardano's horoscope of Bologna (Fig. 12) seems to have been copied from a chart published by Gaurico in 1539. But his horoscope of Milan, which fits with the rebuilding of Milan in 1167 (Fig. 13), looks like an original one and a good occasion for a plea *pro domo*—with a final allusion, however, to the subordination of Milan to the king of France during the Italian wars.

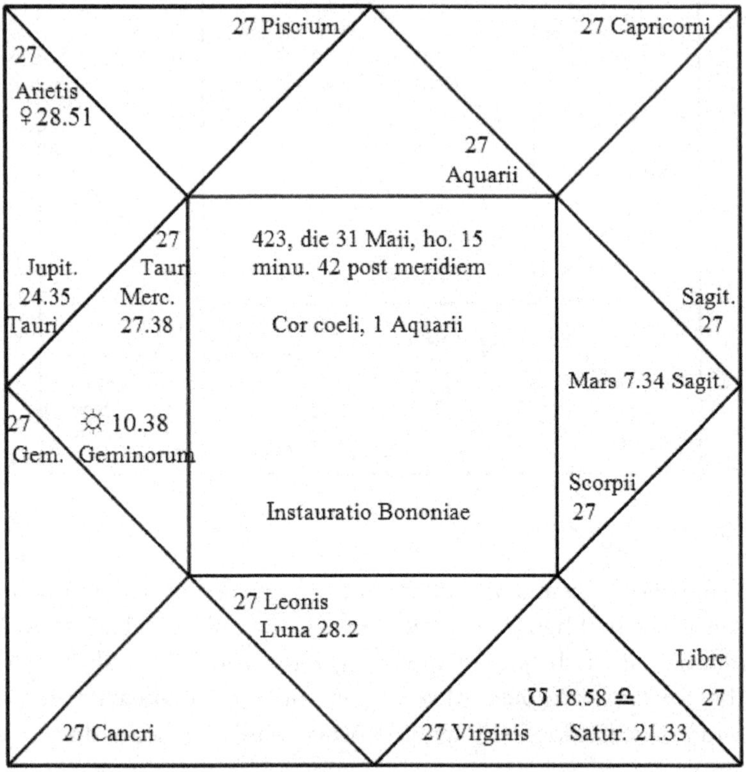

Fig. 12: Horoscope of Bologna, according to Girolamo Cardano.

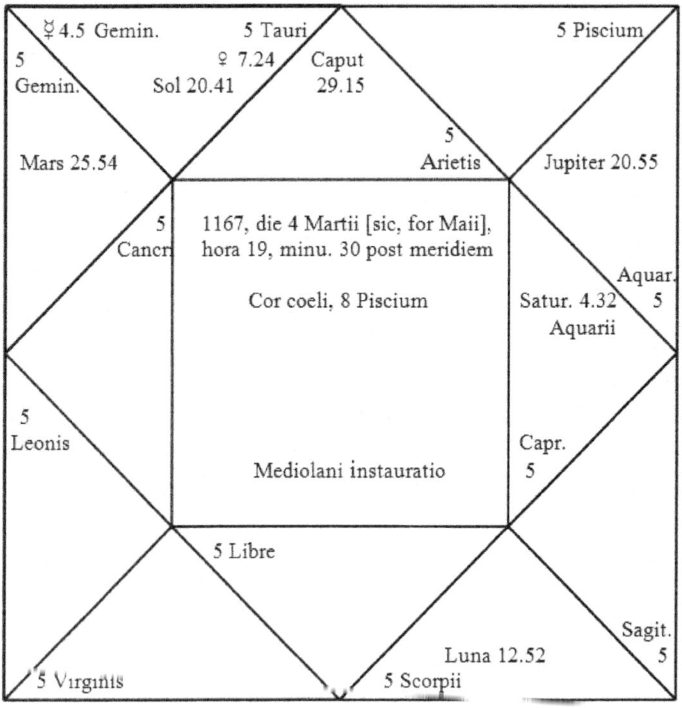

Fig. 13: Horoscope of Milan, according to Girolamo Cardano.

Gaurico in 1539 and 1552, Cardano in 1543 and Giuntini in 1581 also provided some *figurae coeli* and commentaries for the foundation of Venice, dated 25 March 421/422 (n.s.), with two different appreciations of the time, at 17:50 or 17:43 'horologii' according to Gaurico,[37] and for Pavia and Ferrara.[38] But Venice

[37] Gauricus, *Praedictiones* (cit. above n. 16), fol. F1; Cardanus, *Supplementum* (cit n. 35 above), f. bb3; Gauricus, *Tractatus astrologicus* (cit. above n. 16), fol. 9v–10; Iunctinus, *Speculum* (cit. n. 36 above), I: p. 816. Below his first horoscope for Venice in the *Tractatus*, Gaurico said: 'In Rivoalto fuit iactus primus lapis, ubi est ecclesia sive sacellum divi Iacobi. Quemadmodum ex auspicacissima atque foelicissima inclitae civitatis Venetiarum genitura a Patavinis fundata luce clarius elicitur. Sol apheta in suo trono et coelorum culmine partiliter supputatus, insinuat quatenus Venetiarum senatores dominii sceptra ministrabunt ad calcem usque Virginei partus 1880 anni vel circiter'. Another horoscope of Venice is conserved in MS Paris, BnF, lat. 7458, fol. 103 (16th century), with a

is probably the only European city to have been the subject of an entire treatise about her astrological birth, history and future. Dated 1607 and composed by Hilario Altobelli of Verona, this very interesting text, preserved in a single manuscript and based upon a horoscope calculated with both the Alfonsine and the Prutenic Tables, should be edited and studied.[39]

As far as I know, there is no occidental foundation chart for other cities outside Italy. The Italian Cinquecento may be considered as the golden age of the horoscopes of cities, with a remarkable competition between the main Italian urban states and their champions in this matter—Cardano, Gaurico and Giuntini—who copied and modified a largely common astrological practice with an important manipulation. Almost all of these horoscopes are not properly catarchic but try to explain, *a posteriori*, the major historical events of the cities. In this context, true horoscopes of election are recent and very rare. It seems, for example, to have been the case, in Gaurico's material of his *Tractatus astrologicus*, for the '*restauratio* of the new Ferrara' by Hercule I of Este, in August 1492, and its equivalent for Modena by Hercule II in August 1546.[40]

Between the two opposite exceptions of Baghdad and the City of the Sun, the great majority of foundation horoscopes I have studied seem to resemble attempts at retrospective analysis, and this is not very surprising. Astrology, as a type of Magic, seeks a kind of utopia in an ideal horoscope. In doing so it becomes not only an art dedicated to the knowledge of the future, but also a tool for historical analysis.

---

commentary founded upon the authority of Pietro of Abano.

[38] Gauricus, *Tractatus astologicus*, fol. 11–11v; Iunctinus, *Speculum*, I: p. 817. In the *Tractatus*, the horoscope of the 'Instauratio Patavii Antiqua' is dated 3 May 287 and followed by this commentary: 'Haec coelestis figura fuit ab aliis supputata. Multi hallucinantur fuisse Scorpionis signum in horoscopo [the ascendant is at 16° Leo in the figure], dicentes fuisse illam Antenoream civitatem ante Urbem Romuleam annis 465 vertentibus. Lucas Gauricus arbitraretur fore observandam vicinam Patavii restaurationem ab Dominis Venetis fundatam'. Below the horoscope of 'Ferraria Vetus', dated 8 September 413, Gaurico said: 'Istud schema coelitum supputavit Celius Calcagninus Ferrariensis, vir doctissimus, et Priscianus de Peregrnis, vel potius Ioannes Blanchinus Bononiensis', i.e., the humanist and scientist Celio Calcagnini (1479–1541), and two well-known scholars of the fifteenth century, the astrologer Pellegrino Prisciani († 1510) and the astronomer Giovanni Bianchini († ca. 1469).

[39] Paris, BnF, MS lat. 7452, fols. 1r–45r. I owe the reference of this codex to David Juste.

[40] Gauricus, *Tractatus astologicus*, fols. 12 and 14.

GALILEO'S ASTROLOGICAL PHILOSOPHY

Bernadette Brady

Introduction

In 1881 Antonio Favaro published the first works which discussed the judicial astrology of Galileo Galilei (1564–1642).[1] Since then Galileo's astrological papers have been the subject of different researches. Noel Swerdlow produced a detailed study of three of Galileo's charts drawn in his own hand in order to explore Galileo's date of birth as well as the accuracy of the ephemerides Galileo was using.[2] In 2003, Nicholas Campion and Nick Kollerstrom edited a collection of papers, *Galileo's Astrology* and, in an article I wrote for this collection, I built on Swerdlow's work and investigated Galileo's astrological techniques in four of his horoscopes.[3] In 2005 Darrel Rutkin published a consideration of Galileo's astrology with his primary focus being on Galileo's letters and some of the written text of Galileo's astrological notes.[4] This current work is, however, focused on the actual astrological techniques employed by Galileo and the philosophical implications of these techniques. Such an investigation aims to contribute to the question within the history of science on the origin of Galileo's philosophy of nature.

Galileo's approach to the natural world has been the cause of much debate. In 1936 Philip Wiener concluded '. . . that the innovations in the contents of his physical doctrines were made by Galileo within the framework of a Platonic conception of the physical world'.[5] Wiener based his claim of Platonism in Galileo's approach by Galileo's use of thought-experiments in his work.[6] Later in

---

[1] Antonio Favaro, 'Galileo, Astrologer', trans. Julianne Evans, in *Galileo's Astrology*, ed. Nicholas Campion and Nick Kollerstrom (Bristol, UK: Cinnabar Books, 2003), pp. 9–19.

[2] N.M. Swerdlow, 'Galileo's Horoscopes', *Journal for the History of Astronomy* 35 (2004): pp. 135–41.

[3] Bernadette Brady, 'Four Galilean Horoscopes: A Technical Analysis', in *Galileo's Astrology*, ed. Nick Kollerstrom and Nicholas Campion (Bristol, UK: Cinnabar Books, 2003), pp. 113–67.

[4] H. Darrel Rutkin, 'Galileo Astrologer: Astrology and Mathematical Practice in the Late-Sixteenth and Early-Seventeenth Centuries', *Galilaeana* II (2005), pp. 107–43.

[5] Philip Paul Wiener, 'The Tradition Behind Galileo's Methodology', *Osiris* 1 (1936): pp. 733–46 (p. 733).

[6] Ibid., pp. 738–39.

1943, Alexandre Koyré agreed and pointed out that Galileo needed a philosophical source for his famous utterance that the 'Book of Nature' was written in geometrical characters and this source was Plato's creation myth in the *Timaeus*.[7] In that same year, Leonardo Olschki disagreed with these arguments by pointing out that Platonism, although evident in Galileo's work in his attempt to find abstract mathematical concepts, was not evidenced by his desire to use these concepts to produce a 'functional, concrete, and measurable reality'.[8] Olschki concluded that there was indeed no philosophical background that supported Galileo's natural philosophy which 'developed into a science of quantities and relations' and that 'the epistemological value of mechanics had never been anticipated, much less proclaimed and taught, by any one of his precursors'.[9] Olschki resolved that there was no source in science or philosophy which provided the inspiration for Galileo to use the principles of the movement of the heavens as a source for the quantification of the natural world.[10] This conclusion appears to have silenced the questions around the source of Galileo's philosophy and from the second half of the twentieth century the debate shifted to the manner in which Galileo developed his ideas. The current scholarship therefore tends to focus on an examination of Galileo's notebooks in the attempt to understand the role that his experiments actually played in his final published works.[11] My work, however, returns to Olschki's conclusion and argues that there is a source for Galileo's philosophy and that this source can be observed in his astrological notebook, the *Astrologica nonnulla*.

Galileo's Cosmology

The cosmology born of Plato's tradition was of a world of divine perfection contained within the circular rotation of the heavens with the sublunar realm being a mere imperfect reflection of this divinity.[12] Aristotle's cosmology differed from Plato's by allowing for perfection within the sublunar realm; yet

---

[7] Alexandre Koyré, 'Galileo and Plato', *Journal of the History of Ideas* 4 (1943): pp. 400–28 (p. 419).

[8] Leonardo Olschki, 'Galileo's Philosophy of Science', *The Philosophical Review* 52 (1943): pp. 349–65 (p. 355).

[9] Ibid., pp. 355–56.

[10] Ibid., p. 357.

[11] See Ronald H. Naylor, 'Galileo's Method of Analysis and Synthesis', *Isis* 81 (1990): pp. 695–707; Joseph C. Pitt, 'Galileo, Rationality and Explanation', *Philosophy of Science* 55 (1988): pp. 87–103.

[12] Plato, *Timaeus*, ed. John M. Cooper, trans. Donald J. Zeyl, in *Plato Complete Works* (Cambridge: Hackett Publishing Company, 1997), pp. 28–29.

he still maintained a two-world theory, that of the perfect motion of the heavens and the corruptible and changing sublunar realm.[13] Previous to Galileo's work Aristotle's view was upheld and celestial motion was viewed as a ceaseless, circular and perfect cosmological phenomenon which occurred in the heavens. Aristotelian physics relied upon an ordered hierarchical system. At the top of this hierarchy was God, positioned as the primary cause; the planetary spheres and their movements provided additional secondary causes. The earth, with its sublunar position, received the commingling of both primary and planetary secondary causes. The perfect motion of the heavenly bodies therefore produced a temporary disturbance below the moon in all earthly objects. This temporary disturbance was believed to be an unwelcome influence on earthly objects, with the result that earthly objects sought to restore themselves to the perfect motion of the heavens. Movement in the sublunar world was, therefore, considered to be the pull towards this perfection by an object and was deemed to be a philosophical or even spiritual phenomenon rather than a natural concept.[14] To attempt to understand it through geometry or mathematics was, as Olschki pointed out, beyond the principles of Aristotelian cosmology.[15] Thus, within Aristotle's model, nature was not seen as autonomous; and thus consistent predictability in the sublunar realm was philosophically impossible.[16] As described by David Bostock, Aristotle did not seek an understanding in terms of predictable laws in his approach to nature, but rather sought an explanation through the nature of the thing itself: a *who* rather than a *what*.[17] Galileo, however, did not accept this dualist cosmology and viewed both worlds, the heavenly and the earthly, as being subject to the same influences of change and corruptibility.[18] This is the cosmology that he applied to his studies of motion in the sublunar world. Thus, rather than altering Aristotle's physics Galileo's approach to motion required that he totally dismantle Aristotle's physics.

---

[13] Aristotle, *Categories*, ed. Jonathan Barnes, trans. John L. Ackrill, in *The Complete Works of Aristotle* (Princeton, NJ: Princeton University Press, 1984), 4a, pp. 17–20.

[14] Aristotle, *On the Heavens*, ed. Jonathan Barnes, trans. J.L. Stocks, in *The Complete Works of Aristotle* (Princeton, NJ: Princeton University Press, 1984), IV: 3, p. 310a35; W. D. Ross, *Aristotle*, 6th ed., introduction by John L. Ackrill, ed. (London: Routledge, 1995), p. 77.

[15] Olschki, 'Galileo's Philosophy of Science', p. 351.

[16] See, for example, Aristotle, *Categories*, in *The Complete Works of Aristotle*, ed. Jonathan Barnes (Princeton, NJ: Princeton University Press, 1984), 3b, pp. 10–20.

[17] David Bostock, *Space, Time, Matter, and Form: Essays on Aristotle's Physics* (Oxford: Oxford University Press, 2006), p. 76.

[18] Galileo Galilei, *Dialogue on the Two Chief World Systems*, trans. Stillman Drake (Madison, WI: University of Wisconsin Press, 1967 [1632]), pp. 37–48.

Similarly Galileo also dismissed the Platonist/Pythagorean philosophy of the mystique of number by stating that numbers were about quantity and not quality. Galileo wrote, 'I feel no compulsion to grant that the number three is a perfect number, nor that it has a faculty of conferring perfection upon its possessors'.[19] In the *Assayer* he expanded this notion to geometry by stating:

> Before I proceed let me tell Sarsi that it is not I who want the sky to have the noblest shape because of its being the noblest body; it is Aristotle himself, against whose views Sig. Guiducci is arguing. For my own part, never having read the pedigrees and patents of nobility of shapes, I do not know which of them are more and which are less noble, nor do I know their rank in perfection. I believe that in a way all shapes are ancient and noble; or, to put it better, that none of them are noble and perfect, or ignoble and imperfect, except in so far as for building walls a square shape is more perfect than the circular, and for wagon wheels the circle is more perfect than the triangle.[20]

By demystifying number and shape (geometry) Galileo was free to use them as tools to understand the natural world. In his dialogue between Simplicio and Sagredo he wrote:

> Simplicio: But I still say, with Aristotle, that in physical (*naturali*) matters one need not always require a mathematical demonstration.
> Sagredo: Granted, where none is to be had; but when there is one at hand, why do you not wish to use it? [21]

With number thus freed from mysticism Galileo's methodology was to proceed in an axiomatic manner, bolting one concept or axiom to another, building up his solutions to dynamic problems to produce, eventually, theorems which in turn led to predictability in the sublunar world.[22] He was both mathematical and mechanical and, as T.R. Girill argued, once Galileo had devised a theorem he then used it for empirical predictions which, in turn, helped prove his original theory.[23] Galileo's use and application of number and geometry was unique. Previous to him, Robert Grosseteste (1175–1253) and Roger Bacon (d. 1294), in

---

[19] Ibid., p. 11.
[20] 'The Assayer', in *Discoveries and Opinions of Galileo* (New York: Doubleday & Co., 1957 [1623]), p. 263.
[21] *Dialogue on the Two Chief World Systems*, p. 14.
[22] See for example *Dialogues Concerning Two New Sciences*, trans. Henry Crew and Alfonso de Salvio (Buffalo, NY: Prometheus Books, 1991 [1638]), p. 153.
[23] T. R. Girill, 'Galileo and Platonistic Methodology', *Journal of the History of Ideas* 31 (1970): pp. 501–20 (p. 520).

their work in optics, had both made what A.C. Crombie stated was a 'quasi-quantitative account of Aristotle's explanation of colour as a mixture of light and darkness'.[24] Crombie concluded that until the time of Galileo there had been no attempt to use number to measure amounts of change except in matters of astronomical observation, astrology and navigation.[25] Galileo's genius was that he freed number from quality and then used it to actually *measure* qualities.

In returning to Olschki's argument of 1943 that there was no known source for Galileo's cosmological view there was, however, one such source. In early seventeenth-century Europe there was a body of philosophy that did support a link between the movement of the heavens and the quantification of that movement applied to the natural world. This pragmatic, predictive-seeking, axiomatic approach to the physical world was evident within astrological thought of that period. In commenting on Galileo's research methods, Girill pointed out that Galileo 'introduced figures, numbers and abstractions into his theories for the essentially practical reason that they aided him in organizing and explaining the flux of phenomena'.[26] This same approach is shown in Galileo's astrological papers where he used figures, numbers and abstract quantification as he worked with his astrological methodologies in his attempt to predict or explain the 'flux of phenomena' in the lives of his family, friends and associates.

Galileo and Astrology

Central to my investigation are Galileo's astrological notes and chart collection called the *Astrologica nonnulla*. These comprise some fifty pages of horoscopes and supporting astrological calculations in Galileo's own hand and form the first volume of the sixth part of Galileo's Manuscripts at the Biblioteca Nazionale in Florence.[27]

Galileo's encounter with astrology probably began around 1582, when at the age of seventeen he became a student of medicine at the University of Pisa. It was in Pisa therefore that he would have learnt, or consolidated, his astrology, for it formed a part of his medical training. The biographer James Reston wrote, 'Ironically, medicine came under the heading of the arts, and this was apt since the profession still contained a large element of faith and hocus-pocus'.[28] Reston's reference to astrology as 'hocus-pocus' is a twentieth-century opinion,

---

[24] A.C. Crombie, 'Quantification in Medieval Physics', *Isis* 52 (1961): pp. 143–60 (p. 148).
[25] Ibid., p. 149.
[26] Girill, 'Galileo and Platonistic Methodology', p. 520.
[27] This research has been conducted using photocopies and images of this material.
[28] James Reston, Jr., *Galileo: a Life* (New York: Harper Collins, 1994), p. 13.

yet in the early seventeenth century astrology was a respected subject within medical studies.[29] Nevertheless Galileo did not finish his medical training, but moved into the study of mathematics. By 1589, at the age of 24, he was appointed Professor of Mathematics at Pisa and, in 1592, to the same position at Padua University where he stayed until 1610. According to Favaro, Dava Sobel and Darrel Rutkin, one of the duties of this chair was to teach astrology to the medical students.[30] While holding the position of Professor of Mathematics at Padua, Galileo also undertook paid work as an astrologer. His own daily account books show that he recorded income received for astrological readings.[31] His reputation as an astrologer was well known and his services were called upon by the Grand Duchess Christina of Lorraine who implored him to find the true day of birth of the Duke by using judicial astrology.[32] His genuine interest in astrology is also revealed by his longstanding correspondence with Ottavio Brenzoni, a professional astrologer in Verona with whom he discussed charts and sought astrological opinions over the course of his eighteen years at Padua University.[33]

Independent of Galileo's own papers there are also the records of the Inquisition. In April 1604 Galileo was summoned and tried for being too fatalistic in his astrological forecasts for his clients. He was found to be a heretic and charged with 'living as a heretic' but his position at Padua University probably protected him from further prosecution.[34] The implications of this trial concerning the nature of Galileo's astrology will be discussed later in this paper.

It is during this time at Padua that Galileo compiled his collection of notes which he titled *Astrologica nonnulla*. These notes are, in fact, his personal collection of horoscopes of family members and friends which he maintained and annotated for his own use. They consist of twenty-seven/twenty-eight horoscopes, notes, drawings and random calculations. Of these horoscopes,

---

[29] Robert S. Westman, 'The Astronomer's Role in the Sixteenth Century: A Preliminary Study', *History of Science* 18 (1980): pp. 105–47 (p. 118).

[30] Favaro, 'Galileo, Astrologer', pp. 17–18; Dava Sobel, *Galileo's Daughter* (London, UK: Fourth Estate, 1999), p. 52; Rutkin, 'Galileo Astrologer: Astrology and Mathematical Practice', p. 112.

[31] Favaro, 'Galileo, Astrologer', pp. 13–14.

[32] Ibid., p. 11.

[33] See Grazia Mirti, 'Galileo's Correspondence', in *Galileo's Astrology*, ed. Nicholas Campion and Nick Kollerstrom (Bristol, UK: Cinnabar Books, 2003), pp. 73–84.

[34] See Antonino Poppi, 'On Trial for Astral Fatalism: Galileo Faces the Inquisition', in *Galileo's Astrology*, ed. Nicholas Campion and Nick Kollerstrom (Bristol, UK: Cinnabar Books, 2003), pp. 49–58.

nineteen consist of a single chart, with or without planetary calculations, and eight are charts accompanied by *Dominus Geniturae* tables, which are designed to reveal the planet which holds rulership over the individual's character. Of these eight charts, two have additional pages of predictive work. The dates of the charts range from 1505 to 1603, with one further chart constructed for the birth of a child named Augusta on 6 August (27 July OS) 1624 at 2:35 AM (LMT) for a location in northern Romania (48N00, 24E30).This chart was drawn up by Galileo when he was sixty years of age and suggests that he maintained his interest in astrology throughout his life.

What is revealed in these papers is an astrology which is predominantly Arabic. It contains the quantification of qualities known as almuten tables, an Arabic astrological technique which assigns a numerical value to a particular planet based on its horoscopic attributes. Additionally Galileo used *Dominus Geniturae* tables, which are a series of astrological axioms assigned a numerical value which is then added or subtracted to find the planet with the highest score in order to reveal the planet with the greatest astrological influence over the person's life.

Arabic Astrology and the Aristotelian Cosmology

Arabic astrology, the body of astrological works that had been written in Arabic within an Islamic cultural milieu, had been introduced into Europe through a series of translations into Latin made between the late tenth and the thirteenth centuries. For example, the *Great Introduction to Astrology* of the Iranian-Afghan astrologer Abū Maʿshar (787–886), was translated into Latin twice (in 1133 and 1140), and included a section on the usefulness of astrology for doctors.[35] The translation of these texts into the Latin was concurrent in Europe with the development of theoretical medicine, and the notion of the doctor acting in partnership with nature as a whole. According to Roger French, the medical texts used in Europe prior to the introduction of Arabic astrology were 'innocent of predictive astrology' and 'With the new Arabic mathematical astrology', he writes, 'came the notion that celestial causes were linked to mundane effects in a necessary way, which implied that once the rulers were known prediction was guaranteed'.[36] Such links between the human body in the sublunar realm with the heavenly movement of the divine world were expressed in the fifteenth

---

35 Charles Burnett, 'The Certitude of Astrology: The Scientific Methodology of Al-Qabīṣī and Abū Maʿshar', *Early Science and Medicine* 7 (2002): pp. 198–213 (p. 212); L. Thorndike, *The History of Magic and Experimental Science* (New York: MacMillan, 1923), II: p. 77.

36 Roger French, 'Foretelling the Future: Arabic Astrology and English Medicine in the Late Twelfth Century', *Isis* 87 (1996): pp. 453–80 (pp. 458–59).

century by Theophrastus Paracelsus (1493-1541) who commented, 'The physician must decidedly base his knowledge on the stars. He must define medicine in accordance with the stars, recognizing that the *astra* are both above and below. And since medicine can do nothing without the heavens, it must be guided by the heavens'.[37] In this way the doctor in treating his patient was required to join the sublunar elements with the movements of the heavenly bodies to, in fact, consider the body a microcosm within the macrocosm of the universe.[38]

Nevertheless, the use of the tool of Arabic astrology with its quest for empirical prediction in the sublunar world presented challenges to European Christian-Aristotelian cosmology. By the early fourteenth century Aristotle's cosmology had been adopted into Christian theology through the work of Saint Thomas Aquinas (c. 1225–1274); as a result, French comments that consistent predictability in the sublunar world was not only thought to be outside Aristotle's physics but was also heretical.[39]

Within Islam, however, Aristotle's cosmology had varying levels of acceptance. The Persian philosopher Avicenna (c. 980–1037) described God as being concerned with universals rather than particulars, and God knew of particulars only in a universal way. For Avicenna there was a fine theological distinction concerning the nature of universal knowledge as distinct from knowledge of particulars. Avicenna's position actually allowed for an element of free will within the sublunar world and supported an Aristotelian cosmology of primary cause and the commingling of secondary causes.[40] But Avicenna's views were not universally accepted. From as early as the ninth century opponents of causality within Ash'arite Sunnism promoted the doctrine that God was the sole cause of all events, thereby denying the existence of any secondary causes.[41] These views were supported by al-Ghazālī (1058–1111) when he attacked Avicenna's philosophy and challenged the principle of causation, stating that Avicenna's God who knew *only* universals knew neither individual men nor their individual acts.[42] The Ash'arite doctrine of a world of

---

[37] Andrew Weeks, ed. *Paracelsus (Theophrastus Bombastus Von Hohenheim, 1493–1541) : Essential Theoretical Writings* (Leiden; Boston: Brill, 2008), H2: pp. 63–64.
[38] Ibid., H2: p. 24.
[39] French, 'Foretelling the Future', pp. 458, 475, 479.
[40] See Michael E. Marmura, 'Some Aspects of Avicenna's Theory of God's Knowledge of Particulars', *Journal of the American Oriental Society* 82 (1962): pp. 299–312.
[41] Ilai Alon, 'Al-Ghazālī on Causality', *Journal of the American Oriental Society* 100 (1980): pp. 397–405 (p. 399).
[42] Michael E. Marmura, 'Aspects of Avicenna's Theory', p. 312.

no causation was further supported by al-Ghazālī's condemnation of the works of Plato and Aristotle in *The Incoherence of the Philosophers*.[43] Al Ghazālī's position, which became known as Islamic occasionalism, stated that God was the sole reason for the existence of all things and that there was, in fact, no causation.[44]

In parallel with these theological debates a development occurred within Arabic astrology that separated it, in techniques at least, from its Aristotelian/Ptolemaic foundation. Patrick Curry makes the case that the nature of astrological practice tends to be a reflection of its surrounding culture.[45] Hence it is difficult to think that the changes in Arabic astrology in the ninth century were in isolation and separate from the emerging philosophical or theological milieu of the period. The new developments appeared in the astrology of Omar of Tabaristan ('Umar ibn al-Farrukhan al-Tabari; died c. 816 CE) as an increasing emphasis on the idea of the *al-mubtazz*, known in Latin as almuten. This was the practice of assigning quantitative values to the qualities of planets in terms of their horoscopic and zodiacal position.[46] For example, a house cusp in a horoscope may be in the sign of Libra. Venus, which rules Libra would, in this technique, be assigned a value of 5 points. Saturn, however, as the exalted ruler of Libra, would gain 4 points while also gaining an additional 3 points for its triplicity rulership of that sign. Thus, Saturn with 7 points and not Venus with 5 points would be considered the stronger planet governing the affairs of the house.

There were other changes in Arabic astrology in this period which, according to Robert Hand, were the application of orbs, different aspect theory and quadrant houses.[47] It is the Islamic use of the technique of *al-mubtazz*, however, which suggests a form of astrology reflective of the spirit of the ninth century Ash'arite doctrine. For the *al-mubtazz* reductionist approach to the relationship between planets and chart required that the influences of the comminglings of secondary causes were either greatly simplified or totally removed. Indeed, Abū Ma'shar shows sympathy toward the Ash'arite doctrine in his *Great Introduction*

---

43 Ibid.

44 Al-Ghazālī, *The Incoherence of the Philosophers: A Parallel English-Arabic Text*, trans. Michael E. Marmura (Provo, UT: Brigham Young University Press, 1997), Discussion 1, pp. 10–25; Alon, 'Al-Ghazālī on Causality'.

45 See Roy Willis and Patrick Curry, *Astrology Science and Culture, Pulling Down the Moon* (New York: Berg, 2004), pp. 77–86.

46 Omar of Tiberias, *Three Books on Nativities*, trans. Robert Hand (Berkeley Springs, WV: Golden Hind Press, 1997), p. 13.

47 Robert Hand, 'Introduction' in Omar, *Three Books on Nativities*, p. ii.

when he responds to the second criticism against astrology which is that planets indicate universal things, but not particular things such as the lives of individuals. Abū Ma'shar refutes this by stating:

> 1. Genus, species, the four elements and coming-to-be and passing-away are found in every individual. 2. The planets indicate the genus, species, the four elements and coming-to-be and passing-away. 3. Therefore, the planets indicate separate individuals.[48]

Charles Burnett suggests that in this passage Abū Ma'shar was rejecting the existence of genera and species as Platonic forms; thus when a planet indicated a universal it also indicated the individual or particular.[49] This is reflected in Abū Ma'shar's views on predictability when he wrote 'although men have free choice and can deliberate and ask advice, their decisions are still determined by the stars, which have indications for their animal and rational souls as well as over their bodies'.[50] Therefore, for Abū Ma'shar, God knew of the particulars of an individual life and these particulars could be pursued within the horoscope. Hence, one could extend Burnett's argument of Abū Ma'shar's rejection of Platonism and suggest that in practice the astrology being developed in this period, with its concepts of quantifiable almutens, demonstrated an astrology based more on a type of non-causal (or divine causal) atomism than Aristotelianism.

The theological environment within Islam at this time therefore created the breathing space for these new astrological techniques to emerge. For if there was no causation, then God knew particulars and astrology could explore, in practice at least, the direct link between the heavens and the individual without the interference of Aristotelian secondary commingling. Thus, astrologers could pursue a quantifiable analysis of the horoscope which provided repeatability and consistency from one horoscope to the next. Campion notes that in the eleventh and twelfth centuries Arabic astrology 'held out [to the Christian world] the seductive prospect of control over a natural world which was otherwise chaotic and threatening'.[51] It is this form of astrology, as previously

---

48 Requoted from Charles Burnett, 'The Certitude of Astrology: The Scientific Methodology of Al-Qabīṣī and Abū Ma'shar', p. 207. The translation of the 'Great Introduction' had not yet been published at the time of writing this paper.

49 Burnett, 'The Certitude of Astrology', p. 207.

50 Ibid., p. 208.

51 Nicholas Campion, 'The Concept of Destiny in Islamic Astrology and Its Impact on Medieval European Thought', *ARAM* 1 (1989): pp. 281–89 (p. 288).

stated, that reached Europe in the twelfth century, principally through the translations of Abū Ma'shar, Māshā'allāh and Al-Qabīṣī (Alcabitius) and was adopted into the study of medicine. Thus, roughly four hundred years later, this is the astrology linked to medicine in Padua in Galileo's time, and this is the style of astrology seen in his astrological papers.

It is from Galileo's trial by the Inquisition in 1604 that one can also glimpse Galileo's astrological philosophy as he used this quantifiable style of astrology. At that trial he was accused and found guilty, not of the charge of practicing astrology but, rather, the charge that his astrology was seeking exact prediction in the sublunar realm.

> Q: [From the Inquisitor] You said before that in the nativities that this Galileo makes, he calls his predictions certain; this is heresy...'
> A: [From the person bearing witness against Galileo] I know that he said that and that he calls his predictions from the nativities certain, but I am not aware that this has been declared heresy.[52]

For Galileo, as for any astrologer, the chart with its planets, zodiac signs, houses and aspects was a complex web of relationships. However, as already demonstrated, the use of the technique of *al-mubtazz* allowed the astrologer to reduce the quality of a feature of the chart to a numerical value. The actual scores allocated by Galileo were 5 points for the house (*domus*) ruler, 4 points for the exalted ruler, 3 points for the triplicity ruler/s, 2 points for the term ruler and 1 point for the face ruler. These individual planetary or house cusp almutens were also added together to form compound almutens in order to find the planet with rulership over a particular subject matter. For example, a person's 'faith' could be discovered or predicted, according to Omar of Tabaristan, by adding together the following list of individual almutens: the 9th house cusp, the lord of the 9th house, the term ruler of the 9th house lord, any planets in the 9th house and the Part of Faith.[53] By the time of Guido Bonatti (d. ca. 1296) these tables had become quite complex and in his *Second Tractatus* he discussed what he labeled as the *Almudebit*,[54] which was used to find the planet that ruled over the person's life-force and contained the combined almutens of 27 natal points and/or planets.[55] Apart from creating new compound almutens

---

52 Requoted from Poppi, 'On Trial for Astral Fatalism: Galileo Faces the Inquisition', p. 54.
53 Omar of Tabaristan does not actually list his scoring system, only the points required to make the compound almuten.
54 Possibly *al-mudabbir*, 'dispositor'. I thank Charles Burnett for this suggestion.
55 Guido Bonatti, *Liber Astronomiae Part II*, trans. Robert Zoller (Berkeley Springs, WV:

focused on a particular subject astrologers would, from time to time, add personal nuances to an already established formula. In the twelfth century, Abraham Ibn Ezra expanded the compound almuten for the Lord of the Nativity by including the natal houses of the planets and the phasing of the superior planets in relationship to the Sun.[56] Such nuances provided insights into the astrologer's thinking concerning the level of importance of certain horoscopic or celestial features in their final prognosis.

Galileo's Thinking in the Astrologica nonnulla

In turning now to consider the evidence of the *Astrologica nonnulla,* insights into Galileo's methodology and his exploration of motion are both evident. Galileo, like other astrologers of his time, used an almuten-like approach by taking one astrological component, e.g., the number value of a planet's zodiac sign, and then joined this, for example, to the number value assigned to the phase between a planet and the sun. In considering Galileo's own horoscope, he lists his natal Venus as exalted in Pisces (see Fig. 1) and assigns the value of 4 points. With the quality of Venus' exaltation reduced to a number, Galileo could then add to (or subtract from) this number other astrological features of his Venus. Galileo used, in varying ways, another nine to thirteen astrological features of the planet. He followed this procedure of adding or subtracting astrological axioms for each planet, allowing him to eventually compare their final totals and thereby determine the planet which had governorship over the subject of the enquiry. Through such astrological axioms number was functional, not mystical, and used to assign a value to a celestial quality in order for a more complex position to be understood; quality became quantity with this style of astrology.

Galileo constructed these Arabic-informed astrological tables and, in a similar way to Abraham Ibn Ezra, adjusted his tables in scoring as well as content to fit his thinking at the time. He used single almutens to explore the different house cusps and astrological axioms to search for the *Dominus Geniturae* (Lord of the Nativity). Once these had been calculated Galileo could use these to aid his predictive work, or predict character in the case of his *Dominus Geniturae* tables. In all, Galileo's notes have calculations for eight *Domini Geniturae*.

The following tables are three of Galileo's *Dominus Geniturae* tables. It is not known when he constructed these actual tables (they could have been redrawn

---

Golden Hind Press, 1994), pp. 105–06.

[56] Rabbi Avraham Ibn Ezra, *The Book of Nativities and Revolutions*, trans. Meira B. Epstein (USA: ARHAT Publications, 2008), pp. 13–14.

from earlier notes). Fig. 1 is the table for his own chart (16 February 1564, Pisa, for a time of 15:43 LMT).[57] Figure 2 is the table for a chart drawn for 1 April 1505, Padua, for a time of 19:44 LMT; given its presence in his personal papers, it shows his interest in a historical figure born some hundred years before Galileo is casting the chart or event. Figure 3 is the table for Giovanfrancesco Sagredo (20 June 1571, Padua, 00:46 LMT), his close friend while he was working in Padua. All of Galileo's *Dominus Geniturae* tables are an expression of his use of an astrological axiomatic technique.

Galileo began his *Dominus Geniturae* tables in the conventional manner by listing the planets and then allocating the scores, as previously described, for their different essential dignities. He then appeared to follow the method of Johannes Schoener (1477–1547) by including the speed of a planet as well as its direct or retrograde movement.[58] Schoener listed 33 ways, with scores, on how a planet could be strengthened (gain a positive score) and 34 ways that a planet could be weakened (gain a negative score). Galileo did not use all of these points but does follow Schoener's suggested scoring.[59] Within this system there was a strong bias in favour of motion. Direct or fast motion of a planet gained it far

---

57 This is the modern dating and timing of the second horoscope listed on fol. 7r. This horoscope with an ascendant of 14° 33′ Leo shows the Part of Fortune (a combination of the zodiacal positions of the ascendant, sun and moon), correctly calculated at 12° 31′ Libra. The other horoscope maintains the ascendant in Leo but has moved the rising degree to match the degree and minute of the natal Venus, another way to explore a natal horoscope in that period.

58 Antonio Favaro recorded Galileo's library in detail and listed among his astrological works a work of Filippo Melantone. Filippo Melantone is the Italian form of Philipp Melanchthon, the famous Lutheran scholar, who defended astrology on Christian grounds. He wrote an introduction to Johannes Schoener's astrological work *Opusculum Astrologicum* which was published with the work of Antonius de Montulmo *On the Judgement of Nativities* (1390). Schoener's work is a compendium of astrology, whereas Montulmo's is an approach to delineation. Johannes Schoener was also responsible for bringing to prominence the work of the German astronomer Regiomontanus (Johannes Müller von Königsberg, 1436–1476) who developed the house system used by Galileo. Furthermore, Schoener was active in astronomical circles as he was one of the people who urged Copernicus to publish his work on heliocentric astronomy. It would be difficult, therefore, to imagine that Galileo had not encountered the work of Schoener, directly or indirectly, given his involvement in the world of astronomy and the presence in his library of a work by Filippo Melantone.

59 Johannes Schoener, *Opusculum Astrologicum*, trans. Robert Hand (Berkeley Springs, WV: Golden Hind Press, 1994), p. 60.

more advantage over slower or retrograde planets. For example, in Fig. 1 the final scores for each planet, although not tallied by Galileo, were:

Sun	Moon	Saturn	Jupiter	Mars	Venus	Mercury
2	11	-3	8	8	9	-7

The values ranged from -7 to +11 and a planet's position on this scale was dependent upon (as already noted) the consideration of nine to thirteen different horoscopic points.[60] Following Schoener's work, Galileo allocated 4 points for direct motion (see Fig. 1, Mars, Venus and Mercury columns). However, if a planet was retrograde, Schoener suggested subtracting 5 points (see Fig. 1, Saturn and Jupiter columns). Therefore, any retrograde planet was automatically 9 points behind any planet that was direct. For instance, ignoring the Moon with 11 points (as it can never be retrograde) Venus is the highest-scoring planet at 9 points. If retrograde, Venus would lose the 4 points for direct motion and then another 5 points for being retrograde, so its tally on the scale would be zero. Although Galileo had not devised these individual scores he would have undoubtedly noticed their bias. He maintained this bias of motion being the single most important attribute of a planet throughout all his *Dominus Geniturae* tables and extended it to the luminaries. If the Sun or the Moon were moving fast he allocated a score of 2 points. The penalty for slow movement, however, was -2 points, so a fast-moving luminary had an advantage of 4 points. This he was double the emphasis allocated by Schoener, who gave -1 for slow and 1 for fast moment.

Furthermore, each of the three *Dominus Geniturae* tables shown display small alterations in their construction. In Figure 2 Galileo allocates only 1 point for a planet being in its own terms instead of 2 points (see Fig. 2, Mars and Mercury columns). In Fig. 3 Galileo has included a greater number of objects within his calculations. He adds points for aspecting and house position, as well as a fixed star aspect. The Jupiter column in Fig. 3 is a good example of where values are gained and lost for aspects, as well as deducted for Jupiter's position in the 12th house of the natal chart. This more complex table as shown in Fig. 3 is also repeated for the tables (not shown in this paper) drawn up by Galileo for his two

---

60 In Galileo's own table these points are 1) house rulership, 2) exaltation, 3) triplicity rulership, 4) term rulership, 5) face rulership, 6) its orb with regard to the Sun, 7) its orientation to the Sun, 8) speed and 9) mutual reception. However, in the other two tables additional points are considered, such as 10) aspecting, 11) fixed stars, 12) Joys of the planets and even 13) the Almuguea.

daughters and Cesare Galli. Whether he was developing these more complex tables or whether he was simplifying these complex tables to the reduced versions seen in Figs 1 and 2 is unanswerable. Indeed, no two of his tables are identical in either the chart points used, the nature of the essential dignities employed, or the quantitative values assigned to these points. Galileo was either a highly inconsistent individual or, more likely, was working with different astrological axioms in his efforts to attain greater predictability.

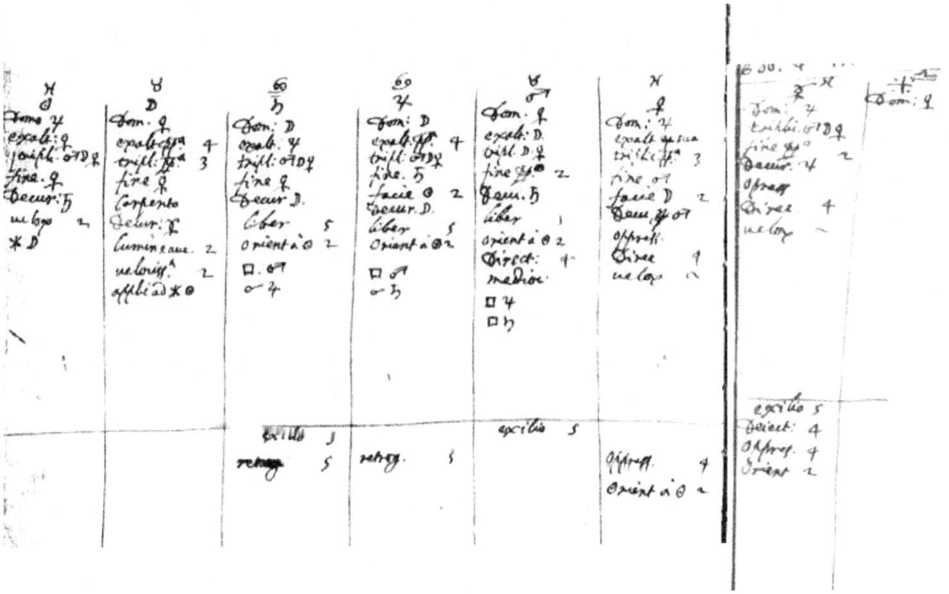

Fig. 1: Galileo's Dominus Geniturae *table for his own horoscope. (16 February 1564, Pisa at a time, according to his calculated chart, of 15:42* LMT*), fols 12v, 7r. All images from the* Astrologica nonnulla, *Ms. Gal. 81, reproduced with permission from the Biblioteca Nazionale Centrale, Florence. The table is reproduced below with the astrology clarified.*

Sun Pisces Ruled by Jupiter Exaltation: Venus Triplicity rulers: Mars, Moon, Venus Terms of Venus 'decur' [division of ten] Face of Saturn Fast moving = 2 Sextile Moon	*Moon Taurus* Ruled by Venus Its own exaltation = 4 Its own Trip. ruler = 3 Terms of Venus 'corpento' [unknown meaning] 'decur' [division of ten] Face of Mercury Waxing = 2 Fast moving = 2 Applying sextile to Sun	*Saturn Cancer* Ruled by the Moon Exaltation: Jupiter Triplicity rulers: Mars, Moon, Venus Terms of Venus 'decur' [division of ten] Face of Moon Free from the Sun = 5 Oriental of the Sun, = 2 Square Mars Conjunct Jupiter	*Jupiter Cancer* Ruled by the Moon Its own exaltation = 4 Trip. rulers: Mars, Moon and Venus Terms of Saturn 'facie' [Seeing] Reception with the Sun = 2 'decur' [division of ten] Face of Moon Free of the Sun = 5 Oriental of the Sun = 2 Square Mars Conjunct Saturn	*Mars Taurus* Ruled by Venus Exaltation: Moon Triplicity rulers: Moon and Venus In his own Terms = 2 'decur' [division of ten] Face of Saturn Free of the Sun = 5 Oriental of Sun = 2. Direct = 4: Average Square Jupiter and Saturn	*Venus Pisces* Ruled by Jupiter Its own exaltation = 4 Its own Trip. = 3 Terms of Mars Reception with the Moon = 2 'decur' [division of ten] Face of Mars Not free of the Sun Direct in motion = 4 Fast moving = 2	*Mercury Pisces* Ruled by Jupiter Triplicity rulers: Mars, Moon and Venus In its own Terms = 2 'decur' [division of ten] Face of Jupiter Not free of the Sun Direct = 4 Fast moving = 2
		In detriment = -5 Retrograde = -5	Retrograde = -5	In detriment = -5	Under the Sun = -4 Oriental of Sun = -2	In detriment = -5 In fall = -4 Under the Sun = -4 Oriental = -2

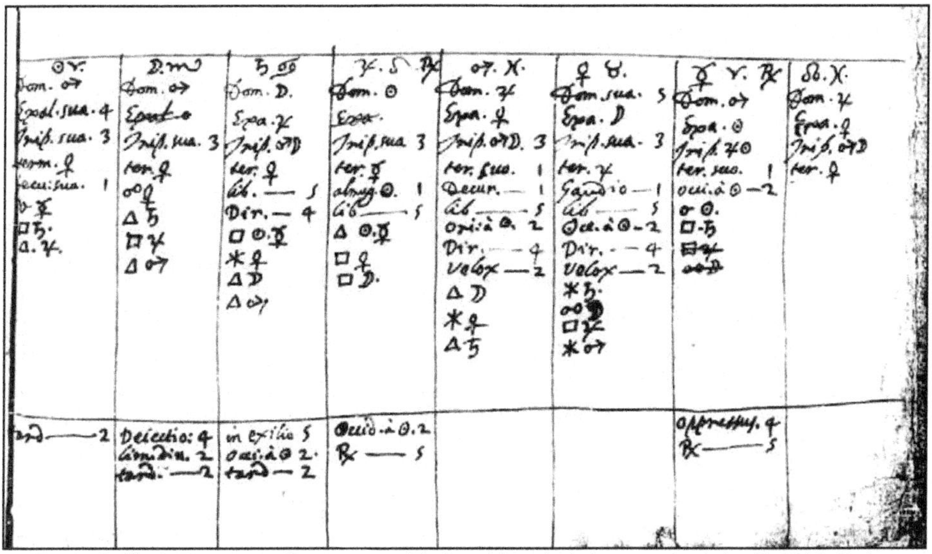

Fig. 2: Galileo's Dominus Geniturae *table for a historical chart set for 1 April, 1505, Padua, 19:44* LMT. Astrologica nonnulla, *fol. 14r, from the Biblioteca Nazionale Centrale, Florence. Below the table is reproduced with the astrology clarified.*

Sun Aries Ruled by Mars Its own exaltation = 4 Its own Trip. ruler = 3 Terms: Venus Its own Face =1 Conj. Mercury Square Saturn Trine Jupiter	*Moon Scorpio* Ruled by Mars Exalted: nil Its own Trip. ruler = 3 Terms: Venus Opposite Venus Trine Saturn Square Jupiter Trine Mars	*Saturn Cancer* Ruled by the Moon Exalted: Jupiter Trip. rulers: Mars, Moon Terms: Venus Free of the Sun = 5 Direct = 4 Square Sun & Mercury Sextile Venus Trine Moon Trine Mars	*Jupiter Leo Retrograde* Ruled by the Sun Exalted: nil Its own Trip. ruler = 3 Terms: Mercury Almuguea of Sun = 1 Free of the Sun = 5 Trine Sun Mercury Square Venus Square Moon	*Mars Pisces* Ruled by Jupiter Exaltation: Venus Trip. rulers: Mars and Moon = 3 Own terms = 1 Own face = 1 Free of the Sun = 5 Oriental of Sun = 2 Direct = 4 Fast in motion = 2 Trine Moon, Sextile Venus, Trine Saturn	*Venus Taurus* In its own rulership = 5 Exaltation: Moon Its own Trip ruler = 3 Terms: Jupiter In its own Joy = 1 Free of the Sun = 5 Occidental = 2 Direct in motion = 4 Fast in motion = 2 Sextile Saturn, Opp. Moon, Square Jupiter, Sextile Mars.	*Mercury Aries Retrograde* Ruled by Mars Exaltation: Sun Trip. rulers: Jupiter, Sun In its own terms = 1 Occidental = 2 Conjunct Sun Square Saturn	*Node Pisces* Ruled by Jupiter Exaltation: Venus Trip. rulers: Mars, Moon Terms: Venus
Slow in motion = -2	In fall = -4 Waning = -2 Slow in motion = -2	In Detr. = -5 Occidental = -2 Slow in motion = -2	Occidental = -2 Retrograde = -5			Under the Sun = -4 Retrograde = -5	

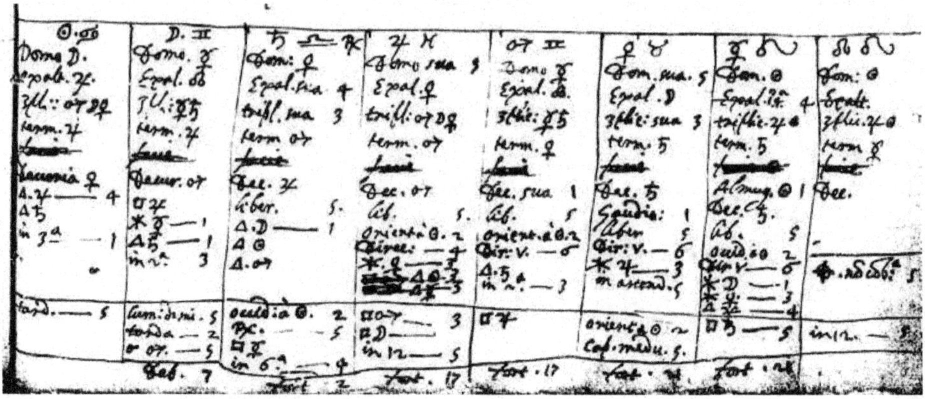

Fig. 3: Galileo's Dominus Geniturae *table for Sagredo, chart constructed for 20 June, 1571 at 00:46* LMT, *Venice.* Astrologica nonnulla, *fol. 13r, from the Biblioteca Nazionale Centrale, Florence. Below the table has been reproduced with the astrology clarified.*

Sun Cancer Ruled by Moon Exalted: Jupiter Trip. rulers: Mars, Moon, Venus Terms of Jupiter Face: Venus Trine Jupiter = 4 Trine Saturn In the 3rd house = 1	*Moon Gemini* Ruled by Mercury Exalted: Node Trip. rulers: Mercury, Saturn Terms of Jupiter Face: Mars Square Jupiter Sextile Mercury = 1 Trine Saturn = 1 In the 2nd house = 3	*Saturn Libra, Retrograde* Ruled by Venus In its own exaltation = 4 In its own Trip. = 3 Terms of Mars Face: Jupiter Free from the Sun = 5 Trine Moon =1 Trine Sun Trine Mars	*Jupiter Pisces* In own rulership = 5 Exalted: Venus Trip. rulers: Mars, Moon, Venus Terms of Mars Face: Mars Free of the Sun = 5 Oriental of the Sun = 2 Direct = 4 Sextile Venus = 3 Trine Sun = 3 Trine Mercury = 3	*Mars Gemini* Ruled by Mercury Exalted: Node Trip. rulers: Mercury, Saturn Terms of Venus In its own face = 1 Free of the Sun = 5 Orient of Sun = 2 Direct, and fast = 6 Trine Saturn In 2nd house = 3	*Venus Taurus* In its own rulership = 5 Exalted: Moon In its own Trip. = 3 Terms of Saturn Face: Saturn Free of the Sun = 5 In its own Joy = 1 Direct in motion, and fast = 6 Sextile Jupiter = 3 In the 1st house = 5	*Mercury Leo* Ruled by Sun ?? = 4 Trip. rulers: Jupiter, Sun Terms of Saturn Almuguea of Sun = 1 Face: Saturn Free of the Sun = 5 Occidental = 2 Direct and fast = 6 Sextile Moon = 1 Sextile Venus = 3 Trine Jupiter = 4	*Node Leo* Ruled by Sun Trip. rulers: Jupiter, Sun Terms of Mercury Face… Part of Fortune Not combust = 5
Slow moving = -2	Waning = -5 Slow moving = -2 Conjunct Mars = -5	Occident. = -2 Retrogr. = -5 Square Mercury In 6th house = -4	Square Mars = -3 Square Moon In 12th house = -5	Square Jupiter	Oriental of Sun = -2 Conjunct Algol = -5	Square Saturn = -5	In 12th house = -5
	-7	**2**	**17**	**17**	**21**	**21**	

Time, Motion and Measurement

A general feature of astrology, both in Galileo's time as well as today, is the philosophy that time is linked to the velocity of a planet and both need to be measured in order to produce a prognosis. The planets are seen as dynamic and their relationship to one another undergoes changes via their different speeds. Questions of how fast a planet was moving and how long it would take to move through a combust (close to the sun) situation, or in or out of aspect, were all key points for reading the horoscopes.[61] Galileo saw these changing relationships as different quantitative values assigned to the planets within his tables. For instance, a planet was either free from the sun's influence or it was 'oppressed'; this judgement greatly altered the score of the planet, as it could change its score by 9 points (see, for example Fig. 2, Venus and Mercury columns). Additionally, when considering aspects, a faster-moving planet could move into the orb of a slower-moving planet and gain a score reflecting its increase or decrease in effectiveness (see for example Fig. 3, Jupiter).

These planetary dynamics were also the principles of some astrological predictive techniques. The astrologer would apply a variable or fixed velocity to all, or part, of the horoscope in order to draw parallels between arcs of planetary or point movement, velocity of that movement, and the time as to when the alignment to a natal point would become exact. These parallels would then be equated, forming a combined prognosis of quality and time. For example, Fig. 4 contains Galileo's calculations of primary directions for Sagredo. Briefly, the method of primary directions moved a point or planet forward in a way which was reflective of the rotation of the earth in the first six or so hours after birth. This movement was in degrees of right ascension at the rate of 1° per year of the person's life.[62] The dynamic point or planet was observed as it travelled through the initial geometrical pattern (natal chart). As it encountered places in the geometry that were linked to other qualities (planets) then an event could be predicted, both in quality as well as timing. Thus the speed of the moving point was directly related to when the event would occur and how long it would last.[63] Galileo was using an established technique discussed by Ptolemy in the

[61] See Māshā'allāh, *On Reception*, trans. Robert Hand (USA: ARHAT Publications, 1998), p. 5; Ibn Ezra, *The Beginning of Wisdom*, pp. 116–26; Abū Ma'shar, *The Abbreviation of the Introduction to Astrology*, trans. Keiji Yamamoto, Michio Yano and Charles Burnett (New York: Brill, 1994), p. 24.

[62] At other times an astrologer may use degrees of the ecliptic or oblique ascension or indeed any other movements within the celestial sphere.

[63] For more information on this subject see Martin Gansten, *Primary Directions, Astrology's Old Master Technique* (Bournemouth, UK: Wessex Astrologer, 2009).

Tetrabiblos, Book II, chapter XIII, although Ptolemy recorded this in such an obscure manner as to cause constant debate amongst subsequent generations of astrologers.

The three columns in Fig. 4 represent Galileo directing Sagredo's horoscope. The ascending degree of 4°45′ Taurus is the left-hand column. The middle column is the directing of his Midheaven at 17°20′ Capricorn and the set of figures on the right are for the directing of his natal moon. In considering Sagredo's primary-directed Ascendant listed in the left-hand column it can be seen to move from a sextile (a 60° arc of separation) to Jupiter to form a new sextile to Venus (highlighted in Figure 4) which is a distance of 8°. Galileo calculated this to take 8 years and 9 months and to be effective in Sagredo's life when he was 19 years and 4 months old. The length of time this celestial geometry was in effect, which may have been given an orb of a month before and after, would have been a factor of the measurement of the velocity of the directed Ascendant and what orbs Galileo considered were required.

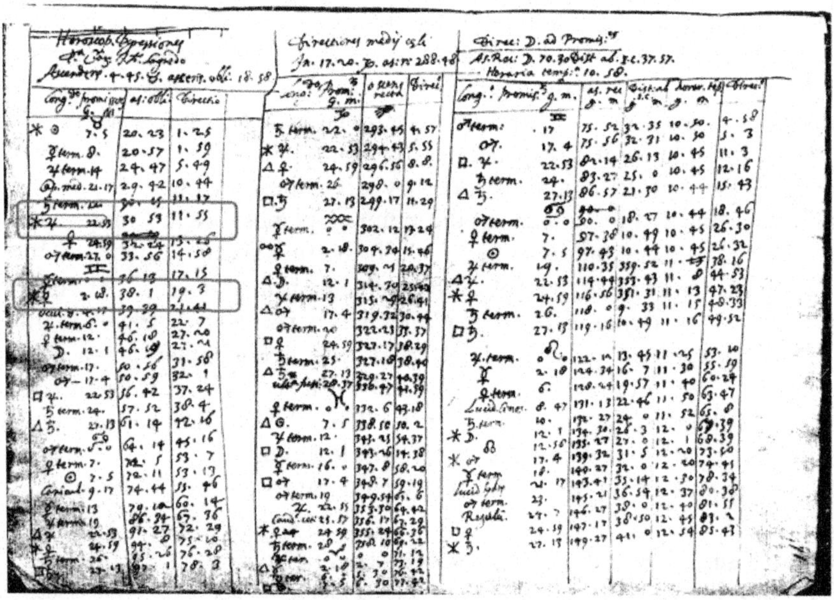

Fig. 4: Galileo's calculations of Primary directions for Sagredo. Astrologica nonnulla, *fol. 11r, from the Biblioteca Nazionale Centrale, Florence. It can been seen that Galileo has directed Sagredo's Ascendant (left-hand column) to a sextile to his natal Jupiter (first boxed set of figures) showing the degrees of the directed Ascendant as 30° 53′at 11.55 years old; later, the directed Ascendant forms a sextile to Venus, (second boxed set of figures) and Galileo shows the directed Ascendant at 38° 01′ when Sagredo was aged 19.3 years.*

If Fig. 4 was simplified by removing all the astrological symbols it is, in fact, a table showing an object in motion with its progress, or distance covered, shown both in degrees and in time. This measurement of time and distance which leads to the idea of velocity was not a part of the physics of that period. Plato's view of time was as circular motion and it belonged in the heavens. Aristotle concurred and linked time to life cycles, a coming into being and a passing away.[64] Time was circular and seen more as a quality of life rather than as an independent quantity. By the fourteenth century, mathematicians like Jean Buridan (1295–1358) with his concept of *impetus*, and Thomas Bradwardine (1290–1349) who defined speed as a magnitude determined by the ratio between two 'unlike' quantities, distance and time, did not consider that there was any need to take experimental measurements to see if these ideas really described the actual observed motion.[65] Time in the sublunar world was not automatically assigned to motion.

Indeed, René Descartes (1596–1650) criticised Galileo's experimentation by saying 'Everything Galileo says about the philosophy of objects falling in empty space is built without foundation: he ought first to have established the nature of weight'.[66] The problem for Descartes was that Galileo linked time to motion and then used it to measure motion. Descartes, however, was pursuing his own philosophy of motion and he defined motion thus:

> But motion (that is, local motion, for no other occurs to my thinking, nor, therefore, do I think that any other should be established in the nature of things), motion, I say, as it is commonly taken, is nothing other than the *action by which some body is transferred from one place to another*.[67]

The key statement in Descartes' words is that motion is 'nothing other' than the movement from one place to another and therefore does not require or warrant measurement. However, Galileo differed.

In his treatment of free fall, Galileo produced diagrams published in the Third Day of his *Two New Sciences* which linked time, space and velocity and allowed for measurement. Using Galileo's graphs or tables one could measure

---

64 Aristotle, *Physics*, iv 223b, pp. 13–30.

65 Crombie, 'Quantification in Medieval Physics', p. 152.

66 Requoted from E.N. da C. Andrade, 'Galileo', *Notes and Records of the Royal Society of London* 19 no. 2 (1964): p. 121.

67 René Descartes, *Principles of Philosophy*, trans. Valentine Rodger Miller and Reese P. Miller (New York: Springer, 1984 [1644]), Part II, Paragraph 24.

the movement and one could also measure the time taken by this movement.[68] Galileo's thinking on time and measurement had, according to Grosholz, 'wrested geometry from the geometer's preoccupation with extension, and put it in the service of the essentially temporal processes of physics'.[69] Such diagrams, Grosholz argued, had no counterpart in Descartes' geometry. For Descartes, the temporal and dynamic dimensions of the subject matter of free-falling bodies were irrelevant.[70] Greek scientific thinking believed that Ptolemy's mathematical astronomy could predict celestial motions (via epicycles) but could not explain *why* the planets moved. Aristotle's physics explained the quality of motion in the sublunar world but could not predict it. Crombie points out that Aristotle's physics was a distinctly separate field of enquiry from Ptolemy's astronomy.[71] What was valid in one field could not be applied to the other. Galileo disagreed with this argument.[72] So, too, did the practice of Arabic astrology.

To the astrologer, the heavens *were* a constantly changing canvas. The orbits were supposed to be perfect and circular, making them predictable, but the astrologer was aware of daily changes. Planets varied in speed and direction; the movement of the sky around the earth varied throughout the day. There were constant changes in the astrological quality of the planets, with shifts of power and expression through the essential dignities. Arabic astrology emphasised these changes, scoring and tabulating them so none would be overlooked. Thus the practitioner of Arabic astrology noted and measured such heavenly changes and although the astrologer may have believed in the perfection of the heavens, and that such changes were the result of the planet's influence on the sublunar world, this passage from Guido Bonatti suggests otherwise:

> Saturn, Jupiter and Mars after they go out from under the rays of the Sun . . . are said to be increased in strength up until they are then elongated from the Sun . . . just as a sick man who after a crisis, is increased in his strength and full health, until he resumes his former vigor . . .[73]

Bonatti's use of metaphor implied that it was the planets themselves which were

[68] Galilei, *Dialogues Concerning Two New Sciences*, pp. 173–74.
[69] Emily R. Grosholz, 'Geometry, Time and Force in the Diagrams of Descartes, Galileo, Torricelli and Newton', *PSA: Proceedings of the biennial meeting of the Philosophy of Science Association* 1988 (1988): p. 242.
[70] Ibid., pp. 242–45.
[71] Crombie, 'Quantification in Medieval Physics', p. 146.
[72] See, for example, Galilei, *Dialogue Concerning the Two Chief World Systems*, Day One.
[73] Guido Bonatti, *Book of Astronomy*, trans. Benjamin N. Dykes (Golden Valley, MN: The Cazimi Press, 2007), pp. 207–08.

changing rather than their influence on the sublunar world. This suggests, even if only at the vernacular level, that the practice of this style of astrology, was a challenge to the Platonistic position of the perfect unchanging heavens and the imperfect, unknowable, sublunar world. Hence the practice of Arabic astrology removed for the astrologer the intellectual limitation of the notion of an unchangeable heaven. With this limitation removed, even if not acknowledged, astrologers were free to consider how the changes in the heavens could be applied to the vagaries of life in the sublunar world. Thus for the astrologer both worlds were seen as linked, and in this union the velocity of planetary movement was translated into a measurement of time in a person's life. All of this could be calculated, measured and tabulated.

Weiner and Koyré both place Galileo within a Platonist philosophy primarily because he was not Aristotelian. Olschki argued that Galileo did not have Aristotelian or Platonist credentials because of his denial of the split between the super- and sublunar worlds and his use of number to quantify his natural philosophy. Yet Olschki could offer no explanation as to a source of Galileo's thinking about time, motion and velocity which would allow him to apply the mechanics of the heavens to his natural philosophy. Additionally, Mario Biagioli suggested that Galileo was a great bricoleur, being able to use whatever was available to gain what he needed. Biagioli used this term disparagingly, suggesting that Galileo's method of securing the patronage of the Medici family pandered to the Medici family's sense of divine destiny and their believed link to the planet Jupiter.[74] Yet within Galileo's astrological notes are drawings of spheres with arcs of movement for projectiles, and within his original drawings of the surface of the Moon made for the *Sidereus Nuncius* he also drew two rough horoscopes for Cosimo II de' Medici.[75] So Biagioli's label of 'bricoleur' may be apt, not in questioning Galileo's ethics, but rather in showing him as a man who knew no boundaries in his thinking.

Galileo's Arabic astrology is not evident in his writings within his mathematical methodologies, for there is no evidence of any of his astrology in his mathematical publications. Nevertheless this paper suggests that his astrology provided him with a different place to think. It was a subject which, for Galileo, contained the quantifying of qualities, the implication of a changeable heaven, and an expectation of exact prediction in the sublunar

---

74 Mario Biagioli, 'Galileo the Emblem Maker', *Isis* 81 (1990): pp. 230–58 (p. 258).

75 Guglielmo Righini, 'L'oroscopo Galileiano Di Cosimo II De Medici', *Annali dell' Instituto e Museo di Storia della Scienzia di Firenze* 1 (1976): pp. 28–36, trans. Julianne Evans as 'Galileo's Horoscope for Cosimo II De Medici' in *Galileo's Astrology*, ed. Nicholas Campion and Nick Kollerstrom, (Bristol, UK: Cinnabar Books, 2003), pp. 59–64 (p. 60).

world, as well as the concept of motion being associated with time through velocity.

As Galileo shifted between his astrological work and his study of motion in the sublunar world it is reasonable to assume that his mathematical mind carried his astrological philosophy into his physics, providing breathing-space for his thoughts and colouring his creative dreaming.

INTERPRETING INTERPRETATIONS: THE APHORISM IN THE PRACTICE OF THE RENAISSANCE ASTROLOGERS

Geoffrey Cornelius

Recent studies of the practice of renaissance and early modern astrologers have brought to light a substantial difference of opinion as to how the historian might interpret the astrologers' interpretations. This involves competing approaches to the wider question of the definition of astrology. In brief, the difference emerges in the consideration of judicial astrology (astrology's practical application in particular judgements) as a mode of *divination* rather than as an expression of what we now understand as *science*.[1] In support of the divinatory interpretation we cite a pioneering advance into the mode of thought of astrologers at the origins of our western astrological tradition, undertaken by Dorian Gieseler Greenbaum, whose work on the 'divinatory stochastic' is referred to below.[2] It is suggested that, even in a preliminary investigation, a view of the topic in the light of what may be broadly termed 'divination' yields a more satisfactory interpretation of principal elements of astrological practice than has so far been attained within the boundary-definition of the history of science.

The present discussion develops this argument by focusing on the use of the practical aphorism in astrological interpretation, taking a horoscope case study by Girolamo Cardano as an example. The intellectual scope of this sixteenth-century polymath, coupled with his fame and influence across several disciplines from medicine to philosophy and mathematics, lends weight to the significance of his lifelong project to illuminate astrology and reform the practice of his day. Anthony Grafton has marked out the ground for the modern

---

1 The difference in approach is highlighted in several papers in *Horoscopes and Public Spheres: Essays on the History of Astrology*, eds. Günther Oestmann, H. Darrel Rutkin, and Kocku von Stuckrad (Berlin: Walter de Gruyter, 2005). In particular I refer to the divinatory position suggested by Patrick Curry, 'The Historiography of Astrology: A Diagnosis and a Prescription', and the opposing view from Steven Vanden Broecke, 'Evidence and Conjecture in Cardano's Horoscope Collections'.

2 Dorian Gieseler Greenbaum, 'Arrows, Aiming and Divination: Astrology as a Stochastic Art' in *Divination: Perspectives for a New Millennium*, ed. Patrick Curry (Farnham, Surrey & Burlington, VT: Ashgate, 2010), pp. 179–210.

scholarly interpretation of Cardano's astrology in *Cardano's Cosmos*; a critique of Grafton's approach is a point of departure for the current discussion.[3] This centres on the nature of the aphorism, and illustrates the dilemma faced by modern historians when interpreting interpretations of the astrologers.

In the context of astrology the word 'aphorism' commonly refers to a maxim, often pithy, used as a guide to interpretation. Given its status in late medieval and renaissance astrology, the pseudo-Ptolemaic *Centiloquium* provides an ideal starting point.[4] This set of one hundred observations appended to Ptolemy's *Tetrabiblos* allows the discrimination of several distinct types of expression under the heading of 'aphorism'. For the purpose of the current discussion, I distinguish three categories of these expressions, namely philosophical, methodological, and practical. The *Centiloquium* commences with a group of significant maxims that are foundational in nature, suggesting a coherent philosophy of astrology and its practice. These initial *philosophical aphorisms* are clearly distinctive when compared to the practical and technical nature of the aphorisms that follow. There is a small collection of these foundational statements in the *Centiloquium* and all occur within the first twelve aphorisms. The remainder, which comprise the main body of the text, are concerned with practical interpretation and its working methodology. *Methodological aphorisms* are general guides to interpretation; they are rules for prioritising or weighing interpretations, for instance in assessing planetary strength and assessing the relative status of factors, such as the role of fixed stars. They may be distinguished from *practical aphorisms*, which provide concrete and detailed judgements. The characteristic form of this latter category is a definitive and singular worldly interpretation or judgement for the particular symbolism to which it refers, being applicable only to a single horoscope in which that symbolism is found. As is common with taxonomies, there are ambiguous or compound cases that fall on either side, or on both sides, of a definition, and depending on how we might distinguish 'philosophical' from 'methodological',

---

[3] Anthony Grafton, *Cardano's Cosmos: The Worlds and Works of a Renaissance Astrologer* (Cambridge, MA: Harvard University Press, 1999). Criticisms of Grafton's work have been published in Geoffrey Cornelius, 'Cardano Incognito', *Culture and Cosmos* 9, no. 1 (2005): pp. 99–111.

[4] The translation of the pseudo-Ptolemy *Centiloquium* cited here is that of James Holden, *Five Medieval Astrologers* (Tempe, AZ: American Federation of Astrologers, 2008), pp. 71–87, from the Greek text *Ptolemeus III – 2 Karpos*, 2nd ed. rev., ed. Emilie Boer (Leipzig: B.G. Teubner, 1961). In addition I have referred to the well-known English translation of Ashmand (originally published 1822) given as an appendix to *Ptolemy's Tetrabiblos or Quadripartite*, trans. J.M. Ashmand (London: Foulsham, 1917).

and both of these from 'practical', we will arrive at marginally different counts for each type. [5] However we differentiate them, a striking feature of these lists is that they appear to be a haphazard jumble of isolated anecdotal interpretations. This impression may mislead us. The lack of apparent consistency or theme obscures a significant function of both methodological and practical aphorisms. It is the purpose of the current discussion to clarify this function, particularly with respect to the practical aphorism, which is my focus of attention here.

The most common form of the practical aphorism combines universal interpretations for at least two symbolic factors, or alternatively distinguishes one of at least two phases or modes of appearance of a single factor such as the Moon, in an exemplary concrete and specific manifestation in the world. Aphorisms of this practical type are ubiquitous throughout the tradition of astrology. They occupy a vast middle ground between universal theory and worldly interpretation, standing subordinate to canonical and universal principles such as the doctrine of essential dignities, which lays out the relationship of planets and zodiacal signs. They also stand subordinate to the *symbolic arrays* of meaning attributed to symbols such as planets or zodiac signs. These arrays appear as lists of various worldly attributions, professions, affections, events, herbs, infirmities, colours, and sundry other items, given to each macrocosmic symbol. Practical aphorisms perform an intermediating role in judgement by specifying combinations or partial selections drawn from symbolic arrays, allowing a distinct interpretation for a specific nativity or event. In turn, aphorisms may be invoked to lend authority to an astrologer's interpretation where the specific configuration described in an aphorism occurs in a particular horoscope under consideration.

The style of the practical aphorism may be illustrated by an example given in the century after Cardano in Lilly's *Christian Astrology*. It appears in the section

---

[5] Of the opening twelve aphorisms seven may be considered unambiguously philosophical (1, 2, 4, 5, 8, 9, 12); the remainder of the twelve are more or less methodological. Ambiguity of definition arises because methodological statements express philosophical foundations and are engaged in practical outcomes, and for this reason different readers might produce marginally different counts. My best estimate is that the *Centiloquium* may be considered to be distributed between seven philosophical, fifty methodological, and forty-three practical aphorisms. Of these forty-three, the majority fit the simple definition given in this current discussion, of an interpretation involving at least two factors, or alternatively distinguishing between at least two phases of appearance of a single factor. A minority of the practical aphorisms are compounds, in effect combining several individual practical aphorisms that, taken singly, would match the simple definition.

on the tenth house in nativities:

> The *Significators* within distance of five degrees forward or backward, joyned with fixed Starres of Kingly signification, and of the first and second magnitude, and of those especially who are neer the Ecliptick, such a positure discernes admirable Preferment, great Honours, &c.[6]

Lilly lists six kingly stars, including the preeminent *α Leonis*, known by the names 'heart of the lion' and Regulus. The root concepts combined to create this aphorism are therefore royal stars and significators, which are principal horoscopic factors understood to govern character and destiny, such as the Lord of the Ascendant or the Midheaven. Cardano gives an abbreviated equivalent of this same aphorism, invoking Regulus, in the case below. The symbolism of Regulus recurs throughout western astrology, as in the textbook of Firmicus Maternus over a millennium earlier.[7]

In Lilly's presentation the horoscope house (the tenth) provides the ordering theme. However, within that remit there is no sense of completeness of interpretation, which Lilly makes plain by a carefully qualified discussion. This is not the only possible signification in a nativity for the attainment of honour and preferment; neither need this condition of the native be the only possible correlate of such a signification. It becomes apparent that this particular aphorism is brought forward not from the need for exhaustive analysis, but because the symbolism and the speculative interpretation derived from it are considered *exemplary*—that is, conducive to discernment and to the possibility of useful prediction.

The Implicit Coherence of the Aphorism

The practical aphorism typically points beyond itself to a larger implicit body of similar interpretations with which it belongs. In some instances aphorisms may remain isolated, perhaps dislocated fragments of tradition, or a single astrologer's noteworthy and non-thematised empirical observations. Apart from these few exceptions, the principle of implicit coherence generally holds. This may not be obvious to observation that does not look beyond the anecdotal and haphazard presentation of most aphorisms. How, then, may we infer an 'implicit' coherence? This suggestion becomes credible when we turn away from

---

[6] William Lilly, *Christian Astrology* (London, 1647) ch. 144, p. 616.

[7] Julius Firmicus Maternus, *Mathesis*, 6:2. (English translation in Jean Rhys Bram, *Ancient Astrology: Theory and Practice, Matheseos Libri VIII by Firmicus Maternus* (Park Ridge, NJ:Noyes Press, 1975).

individual aphorisms and examine the structure of texts that explicitly organise interpretations, either around a universal symbol (e.g., a single planet), or around a particular empirical theme such as marriage, honours or the nature of the native's death. As a model of organised and thematised interpretations we may observe Ptolemy's discussion of horoscope interpretation, as in Books III and IV of *Tetrabiblos*. To take just one sentence out of many that would equally serve the current discussion, Ptolemy states that '...when the moon is setting or declining from the angles, she portends journeys abroad or changes of place'.[8] In Ptolemy's text this statement does not stand alone, but is embedded in a thematic and extended discussion of significations for the circumstances of foreign travel. Yet taken up as a single observation this could be excised and transplanted into a list of dissimilar practical aphorisms after the fashion of the *Centiloquium*, where it would be no different in mode from dozens of other apparently haphazard observations.

The same principle is inferred from the other direction. In the majority of cases it would be a relatively simple task for the experienced astrologer to take a stand-alone practical aphorism and envisage a thematic discussion of the various combinations of those factors that have been employed in the singular instance of that particular aphorism. As an example, in the *Centiloquium* the astrologer is instructed to judge the grandfather's affairs from the seventh house, the uncle's affairs from the sixth. In the whole one hundred, this is one of only two identifiable references to the tradition of 'derived houses'.[9] It is evident that a complete and coherent doctrine of such secondary interpretations of horoscope houses could be readily extrapolated from these two aphorisms

8 δύνουσα γὰρ ἡ ἀποκεκλικυῖα τῶν κέντρων ξενιτείας καὶ τόπων μεταβολὰς ποιεῖ (Claudius Ptolemy, *Tetrabiblos*, ed. and trans. F. E. Robbins (Cambridge, MA: Harvard University Press, 1940, repr. 1994), IV.8 (195), pp. 422–23.

9 'Derived houses' is a modern term for a manipulation of the symbolism of the twelve houses of the diurnal rotation counting from the ascendant as the cusp of house I. In this manipulation one of the other eleven cusps, most frequently an angle (cusps of the 7th, 10th, 4th), is taken as a pseudo-ascendant with twelve secondary or derived houses measured from it. A common device in regular practice is to derive the 8th house as 2nd house from the 7th, hence a wife's or partner's (7th) money or moveable assets (2nd). In the *Centiloquium* the aphorisms indicating derived houses are nos. 89 (concerning the grandfather's and uncle's affairs) and, less obviously, 39. The reasoning in the 89th aphorism is that the father's father is shown by the derived 4th house (the father) from the 4th house in the natal horoscope, hence the 7th house of the original horoscope. The 3rd house (brother) from the 4th house (father) is the 6th house, showing the paternal uncle. The concept of derived houses appears as early as the 2nd century CE in Vettius Valens, *Anthology*, IX, 3 (thanks to Dorian Greenbaum for this information).

alone, and compiled to form a thematic and substantial chapter in a textbook.

This leads to the recognition that there is no essential distinction between the aphorism appearing singly and the aphorism gathered together with several others in order to express various possibilities around a common theme. This also allows us to infer that even where aphoristic statements are assembled together, and however comprehensive that assemblage is, the resulting interpretations remain examples conducive to discernment rather than being definitive or exhaustive.[10]

To infer thematic coherence underlying the aphorism is not to suggest that all aspects of astrological judgement are consistent and rational, nor is it to deny the possibility of fragmentation. Rather, it is to affirm that a substantial part of astrological practice may be considered to be shaped by its practitioners towards a coherent and communicable expression of symbolism. This is a significant suggestion but it is no more than a starting point. It does, however, provide a secure footing for the step of theory that is required in order to elucidate the judgements of astrologers. This takes us into an investigation of the semantics of the practical aphorism.

Signification in Judicial Astrology

Judicial astrology infers judgements on things in the world, including human temperament and actions, from heavenly significations. The astrologer starts with the world, or the life of the native under consideration, and determines details that are deemed worthy of note and capable of signification. These details are *microcosmic,* belonging to events in the world below the heavens, or to the 'little world' of the human body and soul. The astrologer takes up the horoscope and brings forward a number of configurations that are considered to be *potential significations,* in the general sense of 'having the possibility of signification'. The configurations, which may be simple or compound, are *macrocosmic,* belonging to signs or causes in the heavens.

As has already been suggested, it is an ubiquitous practice to express individual significations in the form of practical aphorisms rooted in an implicit thematic consistency. There are, however, several semantic possibilities for the aphorism. These have been abstracted for convenience in the table below, which is followed by an extensive explanation:

---

[10] This appears as the polyscopic (multiple) nature of significations indicated in Case 3 in the Table of Modes of Signification, consistent with Lilly's discussion on aphorisms of 'kingly signification' cited above.

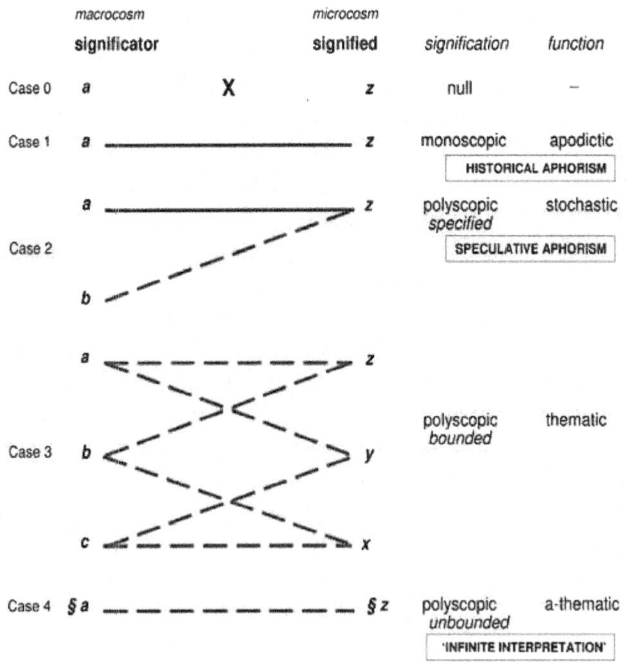

A broken line connecting significator to signified indicates a *potential for signification,* validated according to the conventions of astrology. Where interpretations are *thematic* (Case 3) then not all combinations of significator and signified are considered valid (heavenly *a* is not considered to potentially signify worldly *x*). An unbroken line indicates a specific interpretation actually made, but shown in two distinct modes – heavenly *a* **portends** worldly *z* (Case 2, speculative) **or is declared to have portended** worldly *z* (Case 1, historical).

Table 1: Modes of Signification.

This table is best approached by starting with the null case, Case 0. Here the astrologer considers there is no connection between a particular celestial configuration, '*a*', and a particular event or thing-in-the-world, '*z*'. The astrologer takes as given that there are various other matches, and sets out to discover them. This may be described as a search for potential matches among an array of celestial configurations (significators) for an even larger array of worldly or natal events and characteristics signified by these configurations

(Case 3). These potential significations are gathered and *thematised* by the traditional conventions of symbolism (e.g., the MC may signify some things, but does not signify other things). Case 3 is the corollary of the null case—Case 0—by showing that there are implicit *boundaries* to potential interpretation. From a consideration of potential significations, which in practice are usually quite limited and self-evident, the astrologer moves from Case 3 to a speculative judgement (e.g., a prediction), in Case 2.

The contrast now emerges with the situation at the other end of the spectrum, Case 4. The theoretical polyscopic universe of multiple possible significations is indicated by §*a* signifying §*z* (a large number of significators in multiple relationships with a large number of things signified). Although themes may be discovered within the material, the possibility or impossibility of a particular signification is not consistently predicated on its inclusion in, or exclusion from, one or another theme. Case 4 matches what is sometimes described as *infinite interpretation*.[11] The astrologer is envisaged as leaping spontaneously from Case 4 to Case 1, creating a specific and definitive interpretation of *a–z* largely unassisted by thematisation. This approach assumes that even if the astrologer does not hold all potential significations to be operative, interpretation is for practical purposes *unbounded*, with no obvious limit to the interpretations available in any particular instance. Under these conditions judicial astrology appears inaccessible to analysis. Even where the astrologer succeeds with a prediction *a–z*, he or she will be unable to demonstrate the logic of the symbolism, except by an essentially arbitrary or anecdotal explanation.[12] Here is the idea behind Grafton's assertion that horoscope interpretation involves an 'inexpressibly complex' balancing of factors.[13] He notes Tamsyn Barton's similar view, derived from her study of early authorities, of 'the labyrinthine technical complexity of ancient astrology—its emphasis on the multiple intersection of

---

[11] *Infinite interpretation* – the categorisation (and criticism) of a certain type of astrological interpretation as unbounded and infinite goes back to Ptolemy *Tetrabiblos* III.1 107; see below, n.18.

[12] A type of anecdote that is relevant to Case 4 'infinite interpretation' is the assumption of signification from a recurring pattern, e.g., Mars was at 23° Virgo when an event happened, now when Mars returns to 23° Virgo I predict that a similar event will happen. From antiquity it has been argued that recurrences over long historical periods may have provided an early empirical basis for astrology, prior to thematic symbolic interpretation, and it is possible that Ptolemy has this in mind in his criticism of ancient astrology. From the standpoint of the analysis undertaken here, this remains a-thematic if the *symbolism* of that pattern is not interpreted.

[13] Grafton, *Cardano's Cosmos*, p. 121.

stellar and planetary influences, impossible to analyze fully in any written text'.[14] Described in this way, judgement is understood to depend solely on the intuition, luck and cunning of the astrologer, making the supposed discipline of astrology well-nigh impossible to transmit or to learn.

Thematic Interpretation

However, a proper study of astrology and of the methods of astrologers through the classical tradition and into modern times dispels the notion that Case 4 is an adequate description. Although an ineradicable substratum of unbounded interpretation is seen in its folds and is sometimes revealed in moments of artistry, judicial astrology generally proceeds along the lines of thematic and bounded interpretation. Further, it does so in a relatively simple and logical manner, with no great mystery attaching to the operation. This possibility is indicated in Case 3, showing a consistent, even if not exhaustive, employment of *themes*. These abound in astrology texts, where the significations (*a*) of various worldly things or human characteristics are categorised under each of the planets, or each of the zodiacal signs and houses. Alternatively, there is a thematisation of things signified (*z*), where various celestial combinations are gathered as possible significators for a given microcosmic event or fact, such as fame or marriage. Significations are multiple, since there is more than one potential signified for every significator, and more than one potential significator for every potential signified. However, their groupings imply boundaries that render themes more or less distinct and recognisable. Various potential significations are unambiguously excluded; both *a* and *b* may signify *z*, but *c* does not do so. An interpretation *c* – *z* or *a* – *x* does not fit; it sounds a wrong note and threatens unsound judgement. Some significations may be in a middling area of 'not quite or only perhaps'; there will be differences in nuance and detail between different astrologers and different schools, and there may be

[14] Ibid, p. 145. Tamsyn Barton's work illustrates the gap in comprehension between some contemporary historians of astrology and their chosen subject. She offers a Foucault-style analysis of the master-astrologer's authority, based on the impossibility for an amateur to attain 'the jewel at the center of the maze' of such complexity. Her main work is *Power and Knowledge: astrology, physiognomics, and medicine under the Roman Empire* (Ann Arbor: University of Michigan Press, 1994). Her companion volume *Ancient Astrology* (London and New York: Routledge, 1994) attempts to demonstrate classical astrology at work by indiscriminately applying aphorisms from Firmicus Maternus and Dorotheus to the horoscope of Prince Charles (pp. 115–31). By conflating the categories of the aphorism discussed here, absurd contradictions are produced in a parody of astrological interpretation.

complete contradictions. These conditions are not represented in the table above, but they have their place in practical interpretation in alerting the astrologer to ambiguity and putting a question mark against a judgement. By corollary, for a decisive judgement in a matter of importance the astrologer will attempt to bring together convincing thematic confirmations from independent significators. In the table above, the Case 2 interpretation *b* – *z* is a 'testimony' to *a* – *z*, and goes some way to assuring the astrologer that z may indeed be true or come to pass.

Integral with the bounded nature of Case 3 interpretation, and characteristic of the tradition that comes down to us from Ptolemy to Cardano and beyond, is the fact that not only are interpretations thematised, they are also prioritised. This brings us into the realm of the methodological aphorism, where potential significations are effectively discriminated and ranked in the scope of their interpretation, their duration of effect, and their overall salience. The tradition of 'accidental dignities', which gives greater weight to planets in angular houses or on the angles themselves, is an example of this methodological principle.[15]

Gathering into themes is a self-evidently practical way of proceeding, and is the basis for the methodical explication of natal horoscope analysis given throughout the tradition. An important feature of bounded-thematic interpretation is that themes become more distinct as the signified becomes more fully described. This may be observed in Ptolemy's discussion of the influence on character of various combinations of planets; as his character description develops over an array of possible 'signifieds' for a given planetary combination, such as Mars and Mercury, the reader will less and less confuse this description with that for Saturn allied with Jupiter, or Jupiter in combination with Venus.[16] As a further example, in an extensive listing of seemingly disparate psychological attributes of Venus, Abū Ma'shar mentions 'much love-making' and 'arrogance'; among the attributes of Mars are listed 'indulgence in love-making' and 'haughtiness'. There is an overlap of meaning, and while interpretation stays in the overlap there appears to be no distinction of Venus from Mars. However, on moving through the two lists an interpretive distinction soon begins to form, as 'piety' and 'arrangement of garlands' are given to Venus while 'killing', 'little piety' and 'abortion' are given to Mars.[17] A modern astrologer might query this or that single item in a list, such as the

---

[15] *Tetrabiblos* III.3, 112–13.

[16] *Tetrabiblos* III.13, 164–65 Mars-Mercury; 158 Saturn-Jupiter; 162–63 Jupiter-Venus.

[17] Abū Ma'shar, *Abbreviation of the Introduction to Astrology*, ed. and trans. Charles Burnett, Keiji Yamamoto, Michio Yano (Leiden: Brill, 1994) V: pp. 12–13, 21–23.

reading of Venus and arrogance; debate on such points is a necessary and endlessly intriguing part of astrological discourse. However, the recognition of interpretive latitude is subsidiary to the fact that, taken overall, the readings of Venus show enduring threads of consistency across the classical tradition, from Greek antiquity to modernity. By virtue of thematic interpretation, and by virtue of broadly stable canons of prioritisation of significators, the modern astrologer is able to aesthetically engage and 'read' Ptolemy, Abū Ma'shar, Cardano and Lilly, just as these artists would be able to 'read' each other and a modern astrologer. This testifies to the remarkable durability of astrology's essential symbolism, showing a vitality that shines through the dense mesh of technique and is sensed above all in the interpretation of the planets.

Drawing a distinction between bounded-thematic and unbounded signification would seem to match Ptolemy's intention in differentiating his approach from that of 'the ancients'. Their method of prediction 'is manifold and well-nigh infinite . . . [and] depends much more on the particular attempts of those who make their inquiries directly from nature than of those who can theorise on the basis of their traditions'.[18] This suggests that he treats ancient astrology as matching Case 4 in our table. This would imply that its interpretations are leaps from the unbounded, at most only inconsistently thematised. Whether or not this is a reliable assessment is not the concern here. What is important for the present discussion is the contrast Ptolemy draws and, therefore, the characterisation he makes of his own intellectual project, where a major component in 'theorising on the basis of their traditions' would appear to be none other than thematising interpretations, along the lines already described.[19]

The Divinatory Stochastic

The interpretations so far discussed have been universal and potential rather than particular and actual. Cases 1 and 2 bring into view specific and concrete instances of interpretation. Here is the world of judicial astrology in practice. Instead of the theoretical possibility that *a* might signify *z*, we find the classic

---

18 πολύχουν τε ὄντα καὶ σχεδὸν ἄπειρον... ...καὶ μᾶλλον ἐν ταῖς κατὰ μέρος ἐπιβολαῖς τῶν φυσικῶς ἐπισκεπτομένων ἢ ἐν ταῖς παραδόσεσι ἀναθεωρεῖσθαι δυναμένων (*Tetrabiblos*, trans. Robbins, III.1, 107).

19 Vanden Broecke ('Evidence and Conjecture', p. 209) comments on Cardano's distinguishing of his method from that of the Egyptians and Arabs, which he considered to be characterised by 'infinite interpretation'. As with Ptolemy, such an observation is most significant for the characterisation it allows Cardano to declare for his own approach.

affirmative of *protasis/apodosis* defining the practical aphorism, 'as *a*, so *z*'. However, this simple syntax hides a logical trap for tyro and non-practising scholar alike, and the table of significations makes this clear. This is the point of departure between proto-scientific and divinatory interpretations of judicial astrology. Both cases show single stand-alone aphorisms, and in both cases configuration *a* is delimited to a single signification for *z*, yet they have distinct applications in practice. In Case 2, the mode of interpretation remains polyscopic, and the astrologer understands that from the point of view of theory no single signification within this mode is exhaustively definitive. Establishing *a* as significator to *z* as signified does not preclude the significatory potential of *b* to *z*. This necessarily follows from the observation already argued, that aphorisms imply themes and themes may be expressed in aphorisms. Case 2 is a single specific expression of the thematised interpretations of Case 3. Put another way, Case 3 establishes a bounded, rule-based, speculative framework out of which the 'best shot', Case 2, can be taken to hit a desired target in prediction or judgement. The *linguistic mood* in which this attempt is understood is *subjunctive*. It is a 'wish', a supposition that the subject shall be discerned in its fit signification, that the arrow may hit the target; a gambit that a signification *might be* so, not a declaration that it *is* so.[20]

The metaphor of targets, shooting and arrows reveals the most important function of the Case 2 aphorism in guiding the astrologer's prediction, or judgement upon unknown things. The fruitfulness of the ancient archery metaphor has been demonstrated in a seminal study by Dorian Gieseler Greenbaum. She argues that astrology was understood by its early practitioners, including Ptolemy, as a *stochastic art*,[21] aiming for a result in the same manner as an archer. The term 'stochastic' comes from the Greek for aiming at a target, as well as 'conjecture' or 'guess'. For the astrologer this is intelligent guessing,

[20] This is strictly the *optative*, a form of the subjunctive expressing *wishing that*. The optative mood is appropriate to the taking of oracles (an idea that is developed in Plutarch, *The E at Delphi 386c, d*). We find the similarity in some modern languages, as in the use of the subjunctive with the Arabic *inshallah*, 'God willing'. For astrology this may be heard as 'by the will of the heavens'. The distinction of optative and indicative in prophecy and divination is a complex issue, and particularly in literary treatments; from Homer onwards, there tends to be an elision of categories by virtue of an *ex post facto* stance. I suggest that the distinction is crucial in all forms of 'inductive divination' (divination by art, according to the classical description).

[21] Greenbaum notes that Joanna Komorowska has also written on this view of Ptolemy's: see Joanna Komorowska, 'Astrology, Ptolemy and *technai stochastikai*', in *MHNH* 9 (2009): pp. 191–203, although with different objectives than her own.

guided by the best estimate of significators and signified. Such conjecture is not predicated on certain knowledge of *a* – *z* before the event: 'the stochastic arts involve learning technique (or 'rules'), being able to apply those rules based on an intuition guided by experience and taking into account that particular situations will require a particular, not general, application of the technique'.[22] 'Rules' here refer to the thematisation and prioritisation already discussed, as well as the conventional techniques by which configurations are brought into consideration.

Greenbaum observes that historians have commonly brought astrological interpretation under the concept of science or production, but this is misleading. We are on firmer ground by seeing a relationship with metaphorical interpretation, with poetry and with divination. Productive art proceeds in a fixed manner towards a well-defined and secure result, as in weaving or basket-making. A stochastic art has no guarantee about its results; its methods must adapt to each particular case in order to hit as close as it can to its goal. This establishes a 'divinatory stochastic' mode as fundamental to astrological speculation and prediction. Coming back to the epistemological error mentioned earlier, it is unsustainable to argue that an experienced astrologer laying out an aphorism 'as *a* so *z*' or 'if *a* then *z*' suffers a crisis of interpretation or imagines that the rules of the art are broken if in a particular case *a* should not produce *z*. In that particular case *z* might have been produced from *b*, even if the astrologer's attempt to hit *z* from *a* was the 'best shot', the best that could reasonably be inferred in the circumstances. It is a common error, most frequently but not exclusively found in outsiders to astrology, to seize upon the practical aphorism *a* – *z* as if the astrologer intends a 'universal affirmative proposition' capable, without further qualification, of reduction to the Aristotelian logic of the syllogism.[23] In terms of the table of significations this is to mistake the astrologer's speculative interpretation that, in a given context *a* – *z*, and imagine that he or she asserts as an incontrovertible universal 'if *a* then *z*'. It should be observed in passing that the exact form and syntax of an aphorism gives no clue; the astrologer may say indifferently 'if *a* then *z*' or 'as *a* so *z*' or 'see *a*, see *z*'; the outcome in practical interpretation remains the same.[24]

---

22 Dorian Gieseler Greenbaum, 'Arrows', p. 179ff.

23 This reduction is sometimes found in astrologers who attempt a strict Aristotelian interpretation of astrology. See Vanden Broecke, 'Evidence and Conjecture', pp. 214–15.

24 It is recognised in linguistics that verb inflection does not necessarily reflect mood, as in modern English where the subjunctive is commonly not denoted in the inflection of the verb. It is not suggested that astrologers, renaissance or modern, will readily theorise about their judgements in the manner proposed above, since Arabic and European

The Historical Aphorism

The stochastic interpretation suggested above brings into clear view the distinctive nature of the monoscopic mode of the aphorism, namely the single definitive interpretation of *a* – *z*, presented without qualification. The key to understanding this interpretation is its utter historicality. It is a statement of fact recorded as a unique historical event, and is only ever found as an actual case reported. This suggests that temporality and context are the twin pillars of the historical circumstance in which any specific and concrete astrological signification occurs.

It appears in the identical 'as *a* so *z*' form of the speculative aphorism of Case 2, but now the circumstance entirely dictates both the signification and its linguistic mood, which is the *indicative*. The aphorism, treated monoscopically, refers to something actually seen where the signified is referred back to the significator as a statement of astrological fact, a given datum. This observation matches Cardano's interpretation of Poliziano, discussed below. The interpretation is *apodictic*, in that the astrologer asserts that exactly this is the meaningful connection, with no other condition to prevail over it or to be argued about, no *b* needed to give *z*. We are given *z* and given *a*. This is our datum. All else is mere speculation about other theoretical cases, but not this actual case where its signification has been seen for what it is and decisively declared.[25]

The temporality of interpretation determines how signification is declared. In the *historical* the astrologer establishes a completed and determinate singular reference of significator and signified. But in the *future*, '*a* so *z*' is stochastic. From its origin in Case 3 the astrologer will have had to weigh and balance other significators and other signifieds, and taken account of the balance of testimonies, before arriving at a judgement. A firm judgement when found to be predictively correct can then be stated monoscopically and with flourish, 'as *a* so *z*'. A comment from Anthony Grafton bears out this supposition:

> Here and there in the *Aphorisms*... Cardano flavored his bare, oracular statements

---

astrological *theory* has, from late antiquity, been conformed to the indicative mood of Aristotelian metaphysics and science. This remains the case in modern astrology. The suggestion is that, closely examined, astrological *practices and attitudes* are found to be informed by the historicality of judgement.

[25] The apodictic aphorism is an exercise in 'realised interpretation', in contradistinction to 'speculative interpretation' – see Geoffrey Cornelius, *The Moment of Astrology – origins in divination* (London: Penguin/Arkana, 1994), pp. 282–83; rev. ed. (Bournemouth: Wessex Astrologer, 2003), pp. 292–93.

> with individual genitures and anecdotes. When he did so, he adopted an assertive, dogmatic tone - more that of the prophet who had a direct link to a divine source than that of the astrologer struggling to take all the factors into account.[26]

I infer that Grafton has unwittingly recorded for us the distinctive change of voice between the stochastic and apodictic (historical) aphorism. The 'bare, oracular statements' are speculative and stochastic. Rather than seeing Cardano's 'assertive' tone as a self-aggrandising conceit, there is no good reason to suppose that it is other than the emphatic declaration that characterises an astrologer's recognition of fit signification in the historical case. This declaration is *indicative*—look, see, there! It expresses the delight that every symbolist experiences in symbolism—which is all the more delightful for the predictive astrologer who has happened to aim truly at this target in advance.

The fact that the casebook demonstration of the aphorism is linguistically in the indicative mood, and must in addition always be *ex post facto,* does not imply that the astrologer naïvely assumes a fixed determination before the event between *a* and *z*. '*Non cogunt*' says Lilly.[27] This recognition affirms that astrology is judicial, capable of concrete and specific judgement, yet non-determinate. The astrologer may hit the target many times with authentic and validated predictions, yet there is nothing in this to suggest that in practice astrology is determined, or deterministic.

There is a further point about the historical aphorism and why this should be so important in teaching astrology: the casebook approach to demonstrating astrology gives clear examples where the signified is referred back to the stars, since this is fundamental to the logic of astrological interpretation. The aphorism appearing interspersed with judgements in casebook form complements stochastic with apodictic aphorisms, illuminating Cardano's claim that this is a distinctive development in transmitting the tradition.[28]

---

26 Grafton, *Cardano's Cosmos*, p. 94.

27 *non cogunt*: Given the concrete nature of many of Lilly's published judgements, his declaration in the frontispiece illustration in *Christian Astrology* that the stars are 'not pushing' would be absurd unless we recognise that *in practice* Lilly follows the distinctions brought out here. I suggest this will be found to be the case with most experienced and successful astrologers.

28 Cardano's claim to originality: see Vanden Broecke ('Evidence and Conjecture', pp. 210–11). Vanden Broecke recognises that Cardano distinguishes the unique case interpretation as an 'empirical singular', to be contrasted with conjecture (see, for instance, pp. 215, 219) but does not adequately carry this through to a description of Cardano's praxis. This emerges in discussing the interpretation of the execution of a heretic, Laurentius of Louvain. Vanden Broecke suggests that Cardano faces a 'riddle'

These theoretical considerations are best examined in instances of practical interpretation. Cardano's treatment of the natal horoscope of Angelo Poliziano is a fitting example, particularly in light of the focus placed on it in Anthony Grafton's study. The story Cardano tells may be based on a faulty historical account, and the precise time given for birth appears to be the result of an undeclared astrological rectification, but notwithstanding these reservations, this stands as a good illustration of the nature of astrological judgement.

Cardano on Poliziano

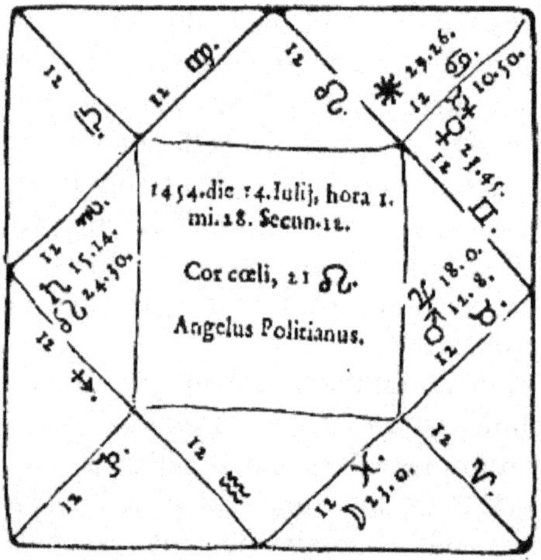

Fig. 1: Poliziano's Horoscope as cast by Cardano.

---

which is 'difficult to reconcile' with Ptolemy's aphorism that death by 'being set up on the stakes' (i.e., crucifixion) will occur 'if Mars is in quartile or in opposition to the sun or the moon, [. . .] at mid-heaven or the opposite point'. (*Tetrabiblos* IV 9 201). Laurentius was burnt alive under appropriate astrological directions of timing but his natal horoscope, while showing Mars quartile the Sun, places the malefic 'in the first house, not the tenth or fourth houses as required by Ptolemy's rule' (ibid. p. 212). Vanden Broecke describes Ptolemy's aphorism as 'apodictic', implying a firm 'rule'; but this misconstrues Ptolemy and exaggerates the task facing Cardano. Firstly, Ptolemy's aphorism is properly to be understood as stochastic (speculative) and is therefore exemplary rather than definitive, whereas Cardano's own analysis is apodictic (historical). Secondly, Cardano is applying an appropriate interpretive latitude, so that both his interpretation and Ptolemy's symbolism fall within the acceptable range of thematic consistency, which I suggest will be recognised by any competent practitioner.

Angelo Poliziano

Here Regulus was in the midheaven, and on account of it he was famous in his own time.

Saturn in the ascendant with the dragon's head bestowed perseverance in his studies, whence he became a famous orator, mellifluous poet, most eloquent writer, to contend with Pliny the Younger in his own writings.

Mars lord of the ascendant with Jupiter, in the 7th, decrees a happy and lasting sojourn outside one's native land.

Mercury was very well placed, in trine to the ascendant and sextile its lord, the Moon also in sextile to Jupiter and trine to the Sun.

Also the Sun sextile Jupiter and Moon trine Saturn, all in water signs, each one responsible for some degree of fame, both in life and after death, while the great conjunction is in water signs, and on account of this they raise him up among princes; however it would be astonishing if he had not suffered from a disease of the joints.

He died in the year 1509, on the 24th day of September.[29]

The narrative taken as a whole concerns three main topics, and primary amongst these is the signification of Poliziano's *fame*; such is the import of the opening statement concerning the potent placing of Regulus in the Midheaven. Following the logic we have already discussed, the statement concerning Regulus is monoscopic and apodictic, requiring no qualification and no further 'proof' than its self-evident appearance. Cardano in effect asserts that, whatever the placing of Regulus might or might not mean by way of speculation in any other horoscope, *this* stellar indication is decisive given the historical fact of *this* case, namely that Poliziano was indeed 'famous in his own time'.

---

29 *XCIV* 'Angelus Politianus. Hic Regulum habuit in corde coeli, et ob id clarissimus fuit temporibus suis. Saturnus in ascendente, pertinaciam cum draconis capite dedit in studendo, unde clarus orator, melifluus poeta, eloquentissimus scriptor evasit, ut cum Plinio secundo Caecilio, epistolis suis foeliciter decertet. Mars dominus ascendentis, cum Iove, in septima, foelicem ac perpetuam moram extra patriam decernit. Mercurius optime positus erat in trino ascendentis, et sextili domine illius, Luna etiam in sextili Iovis, in trinoque Solis. Sol etiam in sextili Iovis, et Luna in trino Saturni, omnesque in aqueis signis, gloriam quantam quisque alius, et in vita, et post mortem, donec magna coniunctio in aqueis signis, praestant, gratiaque illum apud Principes evehunt, mirum tamen est, si articulari morbo non laboravit. Mortuum est anno 1509, die 24 Septembris.' Source: Cardanus, *Opera Omnia* (1663), (Stuttgart-Bad Cannstatt: Friedrich Fromann Verlag, 1966/7), V, p. 500. I acknowledge the kind help of Graeme Tobyn in this translation. The year of death is wrongly recorded; Poliziano died 24 September 1494.

The second main topic, Poliziano's accomplishments, and the third topic, his abode, require more artful and nuanced treatment. It should be noted that with both these topics, Cardano follows a conventional path through the horoscope, giving priority to the condition of the ascendant and its ruler. He then reaffirms his interpretations of all three topics by the use of testimonies, subsidiary indications that strengthen the case for the principal symbolism.

The second topic concerns the literary accomplishments by virtue of which Poliziano became famous. On first reading this is the least secure major element in the judgement, although we may allow that Cardano sufficiently supports his interpretation with testimonies, discussed below. The horoscope shows 'literary accomplishment' much less obviously than the simple showing of 'fame'. Rather than avoid the issue of the possibly baneful signification of Saturn rising, he assigns its wearisome limitations to the *perseverance* of Poliziano's studies, which assertion he can immediately augment with the arguably more favourable indication of the Dragon's Head, also in the first house. Without further testimonies it is difficult to read these factors on their own as suggesting the 'mellifluous poet' and the 'eloquent writer'. However, Cardano stays faithful to the tradition of astrology by *not* ducking the issue of Saturn. Had he avoided the issue, the interpretation as a whole would be at risk of appearing unconvincing to experienced astrologers, whether classical, renaissance or modern.

The third main topic is Poliziano's life 'outside [his] native land'. This most likely refers to the fact that he was a native of Montepulciano but was always associated with Florence where he studied and worked for over thirty years. There is a curious double reference here, in that he was exiled from Florence for a brief but poetically fertile time.[30] But to return to our most likely interpretation, Cardano achieves an elegant and appropriate expression of symbolism in the

---

30 Poliziano was under the patronage of Lorenzo di Piero de' Medici, but in May 1479 he was expelled from the Medici household after a quarrel with Lorenzo's wife. In December of that year, instead of accompanying Lorenzo on a diplomatic mission, he went on his own travels in northern Italy and found patronage at the Gonzaga court in Mantua. However, the poet repeatedly appealed to be recalled to Florence, which request was granted by Lorenzo in August 1480. From the text it seems unlikely that Cardano intends this second reading of the fortunate exile theme despite its great significance for Poliziano, who compared his plight with that of Ovid, banished by Augustus from Rome. It is an apt symbolic expression for a well-placed natal Jupiter in Taurus that this second patron was a worldly but benevolent Cardinal, Francesco Gonzaga. The serendipity of this astrological match affirms the efficacy of Cardano's judgement and is characteristic of symbolism coming to life (cf. n. 31, Curry's defence of 'the truth of astrology in action').

phrase 'a happy and lasting sojourn outside one's native land'. The logic of this interpretation rests on Mars as lord of the Scorpio ascendant, representing the subject of this natal horoscope. Mars is in its sign of detriment, Taurus, exiled by being opposite its own sign, (therefore out of its own home) and furthermore opposing the ascendant. On its own this would be a difficult and even threatening configuration; however, Mars is with the benefic Jupiter in the steady and enduring sign of Taurus, which is why the sojourn is both happy and long-lasting.

The remaining significations bring up corroborative testimonies to the three principal symbolisms discussed above. The favourable aspects of Mercury—to the trine of the ascendant and to the sextile of Mars, lord of the ascendant—are undoubtedly intended by Cardano to be seen with respect to Poliziano's literary gifts. He does not need to make this explicit since the signification of Mercury for such gifts is self-evident to any astrologer. Likewise, the beneficent aspect of the Moon to Jupiter underscores and renders fully convincing the 'happy sojourn' theme.

In its closing section the text brings us back to the theme with which it opened, giving supporting testimonies that each add 'some degree of fame'. On their own, these would be inconsequential observations, but in the service of the principal significations they add fibre to the reading. A symbolism that has not survived into modern astrology is the use of the Jupiter-Saturn conjunction as a marker in an individual nativity; this fell in the water triplicity from 1425 on: thus, according to Cardano, adding to the power of these signs.[31] The closing note on diseased joints belongs in his medical casebooks, and I will not attempt to interpret it.

A couple of points are worth making here. Cardano has limited his interpretation to a few major facets of Poliziano's life, but within that limitation his text is consistent and integrated. The particular interpretation given to each factor employs conventional symbolism, even if the artful manner in which those themes are employed produces distinctive interpretations to match the unique historical circumstances of Poliziano. The important conclusion to be drawn is that there is nothing here that is especially mysterious, 'inexpressibly complex' or 'impossible to analyze fully'; the judgement is ordered, thematic and quite logical in its approach to the questions it has set itself. A distinction does, however, emerge between a few elements that seem very apt, as opposed to secondary factors whose relevance is more opaque. The assessment that we

31 On the topic of Jupiter-Saturn conjunctions, see the articles by Bezza and Heilen elsewhere in this volume.

make here is aesthetic, rather than scientific, and about such assessments there will always be variations of opinion; but in my view the signification for *foelicem ac perpetuam moram extra patriam*—a happy sojourn away from one's native land—is especially effective in its symbolism, and I imagine it will appeal to most astrologers. It must be remembered, however, that this belongs to a unique case of interpretation—that is, it is the exact fittingness that Cardano has observed in Poliziano's horoscope, and no other. It is this that makes it apodictic, a single-meaning historical aphorism. Since it is thematically well-grounded it could, in principle, be excised from its context and dropped into a collection of aphorisms; but in that case it would become stochastic and speculative in nature, carrying its themes into possible, but not definitive, meanings.

Misreading Judicial Astrology

This brings us to a possibility of profound misunderstanding where the reader, however conscientious, lacks an educated aesthetic sense of symbolic interpretation.[32] This emerges in Anthony Grafton's treatment of the Poliziano interpretation. He notes the frustration of some students on encountering Cardano's practices:

> One of these ... consisted of using one or two aphoristic statements about the powers and effects of individual planets and configurations to identify the central features of a geniture, without explaining what criteria defined the aphorisms in question as the most relevant ones to the case in question.[33]

---

[32] Cf. the radical prescription for scholarship advocated by Patrick Curry to counter the devaluation of both the historical practice of astrology and the intellect of its practitioners ('Historiography of Astrology', pp. 267–68): 'The historian should have experienced, for him- or herself, the truth of astrology in action, in practice, and without any *post hoc* "reaching after fact or reason" to disqualify such an experience as metaphysically, ideologically or personally unacceptable [. . .] Failing this, he or she should have recourse to some equivalent experience and a principled habit of accommodating it'. Such a view concerning the historian's own aesthetic experience would be uncontroversial if we were debating scholarly studies of poetry or the history of art and music—when it comes to symbolic and divinatory interpretation in general, and astrology in particular, it appears shocking. As a small defence of past scholarship, I would note that although modern astrology maintains an effective practice tradition, its theoretical discourse has not, in the main, been illuminating, so it is unsurprising that historians have fallen into inadequate interpretations.

[33] Grafton, *Cardano's Cosmos*, p. 89.

He describes marginalia criticisms made by a contemporary reader who observed conflicting interpretations by Cardano in different texts. In one of his texts Cardano noted that Mars, when it appeared in a prominent position in a geniture, tended to cause a violent death. Yet in the horoscope of Poliziano, he gave a quite different indication for Mars, with no mention of a death by violence. 'Gradually', comments Grafton, 'this reader came to see methodological incoherence as characteristic of Cardano's work'. However, from the analysis undertaken here, we can see that the confusion resides not in Cardano but in the failure to distinguish the apodictic-historical (Case 1), and the obscuring of the role of temporality and context at the heart of astrological interpretation.

Confusion also arises by interpreting the interpretations of astrologers as 'scientific' in the sense of hypothesising universal relationships between things independent of temporality and context. This is why astrological *judgement*—as opposed to astrological rationalisation and *theory*—may not be directly assimilated to the idea of universal causes and their effects, nor is it appropriately assimilated to the logic of the syllogism. For this reason, it is misleading to take 'celestial influence' as the fundamental tenet of astrology.[34] The major premise of astrology is that the heavens give us signs. How such signification comes to pass is a matter of theory and rationalisation in accord with the culture and science of the age; but the *how* is—by a whole order of concern—less significant for both astrologer and client than the perception, nurtured by tradition, *that* such signification continually arises. What survives is a remarkable divinatory and poetic practice-tradition that has learned to convey those signs.

[34] J.D. North, 'Celestial Influence—the Major Premiss of Astrology', essay 18 in *Stars, Minds and Fate: Essays in Ancient and Medieval Cosmology* (London: Hambledon, 1989).

CURRICULUM BY DESIGN: ABRAHAM IBN EZRA'S ASTROLOGICAL TEXTS

Meira B. Epstein

Introduction

Ibn Ezra's astrological works stand out as an integrated corpus of writing that covers all disciplines of the astrological doctrine, from the fundamental to the advanced. While working with the text, it is hard to escape a strong impression that it is not only intended as a transmission and recording of knowledge, but also as a teaching text. I call it 'impression' since nowhere is it clearly described as a textbook for students. Yet the structure, the contents and, most of all, the language support this thesis. Another indirect, yet strong, support for such a thesis comes from the time and place where this corpus was written: twelfth-century Provence, where the new Jewish mysticism of Kabbalah appeared, alongside great interest in astrology among the Jews, as is evident in *The Correspondence Between the Rabbis of Southern France and Maimonides about Astrology* (1194).[1]

Throughout his wandering years, especially in Europe, from the age of 50 to the end of his life at 75, Ibn Ezra depended on the good will of Jewish communities and benevolent patrons for support, food and shelter. In some places he was received with great honour while in others he just passed through. Many of his works are dedicated to those patrons;[2] thus it stands to reason that he also acted as a teacher in the household where he stayed, or for the patron himself.

[1] *The Correspondence between the Rabbis of Southern France and Maimonides about Astrology*, trans. and annot. Meira B. Epstein (Reston, VA: ARHAT, 1998), from the Alexander Marx critical edition (New York: Jewish Theological Seminary, 1926), based on manuscripts from the British Museum, the Library of Munich and the library of the Jewish Theological Seminary. Also see Shlomo Sela, 'Queries on Astrology sent from Southern France to Maimonides: Critical Edition of the Hebrew Text, Translation, and Commentary', *Aleph* 4 (2004): pp. 89–190.

[2] Israel Levin, *Abraham Ibn Ezra Reader*, annotated texts with introduction and commentaries (Hebrew) (New York, Tel Aviv: Israel Matz Pub., 1985), pp. 11–16.

Throughout all the books, in places too numerous to list here, Ibn Ezra conveys a strong personal presence by mentioning himself in the first person and addressing the student/reader authoritatively in the second person. It is clearly the style of a teacher instructing and speaking to the student directly. The art and skill of teaching include not only imparting information but caring about the student, understanding where difficulties may lie, anticipating confusion and providing effective methods of learning. Ibn Ezra demonstrates all that throughout his writings. My goal here is to point out and highlight such instances and show how their cumulative effect proves the teaching agenda behind them.

I have examined Ibn Ezra's astrological books in the original Hebrew, both published editions and manuscripts, listed here in the order in which they were written. This order itself is also meaningful in the context of Ibn Ezra's teaching plan, as we shall see later:[3]

Book of the Astrolabe [hereafter *Astrolabe*][4]
The Beginning of Wisdom [hereafter *Wisdom*][5]
The Book of Reasons, version 1 [hereafter *Reasons-1*][6]
The Book of Reasons, version 2, [hereafter *Reasons-2*][7]

---

[3] For chronology see: Shlomo Sela and Gad Freudenthal, 'Abraham Ibn Ezra's Scholarly Writings: A Chronological Listing', *Aleph* 6 (2006): pp. 13–55.

[4] Abraham Ibn Ezra, *Book of the Astrolabe* (כלי הנחשת *Kli Ha'Ne'hoshet*), Hebrew (Jerusalem: Meir Ben Yzhak Bakal, 1971, from a publication in Königsberg, Prussia, 1845).

[5] Abraham Ibn Ezra, *The Beginning of Wisdom* (ראשית חכמה *Re'shit Hokhma*), trans. and annotation Meira B. Epstein (Reston, VA: ARHAT, 1998); Hebrew text from Raphael Levy & Francisco Cantera's edition (Baltimore, MD: John Hopkins Press, 1939). Shlomo Sela proposes a possibility that Ibn Ezra wrote another introduction to astrology under the same name. This hypothesis is based on analysis and comparison of *Reasons-1* and *Reasons-2*. See Shlomo Sela, 'A Fragment From an Unknown Redaction of Re᾽šit Ḥokmah by Abraham Ibn Ezra', *Aleph* 10 (2010): pp. 42–66, Indiana University Press. Also discussed by Sela in *Reasons-1*, pp. 6–8, 359–64.

[6] Abraham Ibn Ezra, *The Book of Reasons* (ספר הטעמים *Sefer Ha'te'amim*) a parallel Hebrew-English critical edition of the two versions of the text, trans. Shlomo Sela (Leiden, Boston: Brill, 2007).

[7] Abraham Ibn Ezra, *The Book of Reasons* (ספר הטעמים *Sefer Ha'te'amim*), version 2, trans. and annotation Meira B. Epstein (from Naphtali Ben Menahem edition, Jerusalem 1941)

The Book of Nativities and Revolutions [hereafter *Nativities*][8]
The Book of the Luminaries [hereafter *Luminaries*][9]
The Book of Elections, versions 1 and 2 [hereafter *Elections-1, Elections-2*][10]
The Book of Interrogations, versions 1 and 2 [hereafter *Interrogations-1, Interrogations-2*][11]
The Book of the World, versions 1 and 2 [hereafter *World-1, World-2*][12]
Judgment for a Newborn [hereafter *Horoscope*][13]

(Original pub. Berkeley Springs, WV: Project Hindsight publication, 1994; currently: New York, http://bear-star.com). Also see Shlomo Sela, ibid.

[8] Abraham Ibn Ezra, *The Book of Nativities and Revolutions,* (ספר המולדות והתקופות *Sefer Ha'moladot ve'HaTkufot*) trans. and annotation Meira B. Epstein (Reston, VA: ARHAT, 2008).

[9] References and translation of the *Luminaries* text in this paper are based on manuscripts. Also, see *Abraham Ibn Ezra on Elections, Interrogations, and Medical Astrology,* a parallel Hebrew-English critical edition of the Book *of Elections, the Book of Interrogations, and The Book of the Luminaries,* trans. Shlomo Sela (Leiden, Boston: Brill, 2011). (Hebrew names respectively: ספר המבחרים *Sefer Ha'Mivkharim,* ספר השאלות *Sefer Ha'She'elot,* ספר המאורות *Sefer Ha'Me'orot*).

[10] Abraham Ibn Ezra, *The Book of Elections* (ספר המבחרים *Sefer Ha'Mivkharim*) version1 and version 2, trans. and annotation Meira B. Epstein, a critical edition currently in preparation from MSS on microfilm. See citation in Appendix for abbreviations used here. Version-1: BAV47, BAV390, BAV477, BER679, CAM1501, DRE384, JTS2623, MAD7, MUN45, MUN202, PAR189, PAR1045, PAR1056, PAR1057, WAR255. Version-2: BAV47, BER679, CAM481, CAM1517, MAD7, MOS421, MUN202, PAR1044, PAR1058, STP245, STP447.

[11] Abraham Ibn Ezra, *The Book of Interrogations* (ספר השאלות *Sefer Ha'She'elot*) version 1 and version 2, trans. and annot. Meira B. Epstein, currently in preparation from MSS on microfilm. See citation in Appendix for abbreviations used here. Version-1: BAV47, BA390, CAM1501, CAM1517, DRE384, MUN202, PAR1055, PAR1045, PAR1056. Version-2: BAV47, CAM481, FIR36, JTS2631, MAD7, MOS421, PAR1051, PAR1058, STP245.

[12] Abraham Ibn Ezra, *The Book of the World* (ספר העולם *Sefer Ha'Olam*), trans. Shlomo Sela, (Leiden, Boston: Brill, 2010).

[13] Abraham Ibn Ezra, *Judgment for a Newborn* (משפטי הנולד *Mishpa'tei Ha'Nolad*). See citation in Appendix for abbreviations used here: BAV47, CAM1517, DRE384, JTS2636, MUN202, PAR1057, STP447, WAR255. Also: Hebrew (Jerusalem: Meir Ben Yzhak Bakal, 1971).

Ibn Ezra's Audience

Ibn Ezra's astrological sources are Arabic; the fact that his work was written in Hebrew testifies to the fact that there was a non-Arabic-speaking Jewish audience who were seeking out this knowledge. Such an audience was found in the Languedoc region of Provence in the twelfth century, where Jewish scholarship and mysticism were thriving. It was this area where the *Kabbalah*, as we know it now, made its public appearance in the thirteenth century. The *Kabbalah* itself, as well as one of its predecessor books—*Sefer Yetzirah*[14]—also contains mystical, cosmological-astrological concepts. The Languedoc region was also home to the heretical gnostic Christian Cathar communities among whom the Jews lived; as Gershom Scholem points out, they most likely cross-influenced each other in ascetic practices and other mystical spiritual matters.[15] The Cathars also incorporated Gnostic esoteric astrological elements into their beliefs. It was the perfect milieu for astrology.

Ibn Ezra wrote almost all his astrological texts in a burst of productivity in the latter half of 1148, in the towns of Béziers and Narbonne in that region, where he was received with great honour by the Jewish communities.[16] There was a ready-made audience for this material, eager to learn everything there was to know about astrology, as is evident from the famous letter *The Correspondence between The Rabbis of Southern France and Maimonides about Astrology* (1194). This unique and intriguing document, which contains practical questions about astrology, its validity and its philosophical and theological implications, is addressed to Maimonides (1135–1204) and is published together with his response to them. The Rabbis' words convey intense preoccupation

---

[14] Anonymous, *Sefer Yetzirah* ספר יצירה (*The Book of Formation*), trans. and annotation by Meira B. Epstein (Las Vegas: ARHAT Publications, in press). The origins of *Yetzirah* are shrouded in mystery and the dating by scholars ranges from about the 2nd century BCE to 6th or 7th century CE. *Yetzirah* is a brief and concise mystical text that describes how God created the primary components of the world: Physical Space—spheres, elemental matter, planets and signs; Time—calendar, months and days; the Human Body—organs and functions; Life—conditions and tensions. The 22 letters of the Hebrew alphabet were the *Prima Materia* in this creation. *Yetzirah* also stands out as the first text where the *Ten Sefirot* appear.

[15] Gershom Scholem, *Origins of the Kabbalah*, trans. Allan Arkush, copyright The Jewish Publication Society (Princeton: Princeton University Press, 1987).

[16] See *Chronology*.

with astrology and a spiritual anxiety that was taking over their intellectual as well as personal lives, while the specific questions demonstrate extensive knowledge of astrological disciplines and techniques. They mention their sources only in a general way, but some of the text appears to be taken verbatim from Ibn Ezra's writing, as is easy to see in the Hebrew texts below.[17] Additional textual similarity can be found between *Correspondence* §3 and *Nativities* Introduction,[18] as well as between *Correspondence* §24 and *Nativities*, chapter 1.[19] It is evident that the Provençal scholars had access to Ibn Ezra's books.

---

17 Regarding the validity of the doctrine of interrogations, compare:
Correspondence, §15 - **וגם שמענו שיש מחכמי המזלות שידינו על פי שאלת אדם אע"פ שלא ידעו מולדו ויש מן החכמים שאמרו כי השאלות אין בהן ממש. וזה טעמם כי כל מה שיקרה בתחתונים הוא בעבור תנועות העליונים על הנבראים כפי תולדותם. ובעבור שנשמת האדם עליונה יוכל להשמר ולהוסיף וגם לגרוע על כן לא יורו העליונים על כל השאלות שתעלה על לב האדם. ויש חכמים אחרים שאמרו כי דיני השאלות בכוכבים ויש בהם ממש וזה טעמם כי מחשבות הנפש תשתנה כפי השתנות תולדות הגוף. והנה כח הנשמה יתהפך כפי התהפך כח הגוף ואחר שהכוכבים יורו על תולדות הגוף והתהפכו הנה נוכל לדעת המחשבות והשאלות.**
Interrogations-1 (translation tentative) - **חכמי המזלות נחלקו בשאלות לשתי תורות גדולות. התורה האחת חנוך ובטלמיוס וקדמונים רבים עמהם וכולם אומרים כי דיני המולדות הם ברורים ונכונים בדברי העולם ובנולדים רק השאלות אין בהם ממש וטעמם ידוע כי כל מה שיקרה בתחתונים הוא בעבור תנועות העליונים וישתנו כפי השתנות מערכתם זה אל זה. והנה זה דרך התולדת נכון שיורו העליונים על כל הנבראים כפי תולדתם ובעבור שנשמת האדם עליונה יוכל להשמר ולהוסיף גם לגרוע, על כן לא יורו העליונים על כל השאלות שתעלינה על לב האדם, ואלה היו חכמים גדולים בדעות הגלגלים. והתורה השנית ראשם דורוניוס וחכמי הודו וחכמי פרס וחכמי מצרים וכל חכמי המזלות שהם קרובים אלינו, וכלם מודים כי דיני השאלות נכונים כדיני המולדות, וזה טעמם ידוע הוא בחכמת התולדות כי מחשבות הנפש תשתנינה כפי השתנות תולדת הגוף והנה כח הנשמה יתהפך כפי התהפך כח הגוף, ואחר שהכוכבים יורו על תולדת הגוף והתהפכו הנה נוכל לדעת המחשבות והשאלות.**

18 Regarding predetermination in harmful situations, compare:
Correspondence, §3 - **וכן ראינו בתשובת הגאונים ז"ל אשר הזכרנו לפני רבי' וכלשונה נאמרה. ויש מתחכמים בדבר ואומ' בדברי הגאונים ז"ל ולא נאמרו אלא במי שראוי לבוא עליו חולי חם בזמן ידוע כפי מערכת כוכבי מולדו ויכול קודם לכן להשמר ולשתות משקיות קרים לצנן ולישר תולדות גופו. אבל מי שנגזרה עליו מיתה ביום ידוע כפי מערכת כוכבי מולדו לא תועיל שמירה קודם לכן.**
Nativities, Introduction - **כי אם היה הנולד חכם בחכמת המזלות וראה בתקופת שנתו כי יקרנו חולי מחום בזמן ידוע בהכנס מאדים אל מעלתו הצומחת, והנה אם ישמר הוא קודם בוא החולי מכל מאכל חם וישתה משקיות לקרר גופו הנה תתישר תולדת גופו בהכנס מאדים במעלתו הצומחת.**

19 Regarding ascertaining the rising degree of the nativity:
Correspondence, §24 has the exact wording of *Nativities* in chapter 1, p. 8, yet no mention of the source, only 'and so they said'. Ibn Ezra himself quotes Enoch (Hermes) -
וכן אמרו: לעולם במולד אדם מקום הלבנה ברגע המולד היא המעלה הצומחת ברגע רדת הטפה ברחם. והמעלה הצומחת ברגע המולד שם היתה הלבנה ברגע הטפה. על כן, לו ידענו רגע הטפה נוכל לדעת רגע המולד ואם ידענו רגע המולד נוכל לדעת מתי היה רגע הטפה.

Ibn Ezra's *Judgment for a Newborn* born in Narbonne is also written more as a scholarly treatise than as an interpretation of a child's horoscope for the doting parents. As a matter of fact, it reads as a supplement or illustration for topics covered in *Nativities*.

My conclusion is that Ibn Ezra wrote his astrological corpus precisely for the Provençal Jewish scholars in that milieu, possibly upon request.

The Books – Evidence for Teaching

Wisdom is where the astrological doctrines begin.[20] It is written as a typical astrological text, covering the fundamentals in the traditional style which I call 'non-integrated': for the most part describing the separate components of signs, planets, aspects and houses, using aphorism-like statements. Ibn Ezra is well versed in the various sources and the prevailing disagreements among some of his predecessors and wishes to remove confusion and facilitate study, as well as provide one complete and coherent source. In *Wisdom*, chapter 1, page 12, he says:

> In this book I will mention to you all that was agreed upon by the ancient Babylonians, the Persians, the Hindus, and the Greeks, whose chief was Ptolemy. I will mention the 'nines' and the 'twelves', and the bright and dark degrees, and the empty ones, the masculine and the feminine, and the pitted degrees, the degrees that increase grace and honour, and the place of the numerous [fixed] stars that are in the zodiac, their longitude and latitude, and the nature of the greater ones among them, *until my book is complete; and you will not need another book beside it for the beginning of this wisdom.*[21] (my italics)

As he is laying the initial ground he already recognizes a need for a deeper level of understanding of these basics. Right at the outset in *Wisdom*, page 1, he refers

---

[20] See *Chronology*. The series actually begins with *The Astronomical Tables* (*Lu'hot* I לוחות) (Lucca, 1142–45), and *Astrolabe* I (Mantua, 1146). For my thesis here, *Wisdom* is the logical place to begin.

[21] *Wisdom-LC*, p. viii: ואני אזכיר לך בספר הזה כל מה שהסכימה עליו דעת הקדמונים מן הבבליים וחכמי פרס והודו ויון שראשם בטלמיוס ואזכיר התשיעיות ושנים עשר והמעלות המאירות והחשוכות ואשר אין בהם כלום והזכרים והנקבות ומעלות בורות הכוכבים והמעלות המוסיפות חן וכבוד ומקום הכוכבים הרבים שהם בגלגל המזלות וארכם ורחבם וממסך הגדולים שבהם עד שיהיה ספרי שלם ולא תצטרך לספר אחר עמו בראשית החכמה הזאת.

to *Reasons*, promising to follow up with a book that will provide further explanations:

> So, here I shall begin to interpret the laws of the heavens according to the rules as practiced by the ancients, generation after generation, and after I complete this book I shall compose a book of interpretation of the reasons, and to God I shall pray for help, Amen.[22]

As the title indicates, *Reasons* represents the teaching aspect of his work, aiming to elaborate and elucidate astrological tenets by showing the underlying principles and astrological reasoning.

In both *Reasons* 1 & 2 we see concepts from *Wisdom*[23] frequently followed by 'and the reason is . . .', or beginning a sentence with 'the reason for . . . is . . .' Such instances either further break down an astrological theorem, or show the unified underlying astrological principle for facts listed separately, or add mathematical or natural explanations. In these instances Ibn Ezra also reveals the workings of his own mind as he looks for consistency and internal coherence. It is clearly not only the transmission and copying of predecessors' works, but the product of investigative motivation and the work of a scholar who cares about the understanding of the reader/student. In *Nativities*, page 4, following the introduction, he writes:

> After having said these things I shall mention what the ancients have tried, and because there are numerous books in the science of the signs and [in them] there are things that reason will refute, and there is a dispute in the judgments of the signs, *I must mention in this book every clear thing that the ancients agreed on and [which] I have tried many times.*[24] (my italics)

He then proceeds to discuss in great technical detail the critical issue of how to ascertain the exact rising degree of the nativity. This topic is also the first one in

---

22 *Wisdom-LC*, p. v: והנה אחל לפרש חקות שמים בדרך המשפטים כאשר נסו הקדמונים דור אחר דור ואחר שאשלים זה הספר אחבר ספר בפירוש הטעמים ואל השם אתחנן (לעזרני אמן).

23 Shlomo Sela proposes that Reasons-2 is the companion book for *Wisdom-Fragment*.

24 *Nativities*: ואחרי שהזכרתי אלה הדברים אזכיר מה שנסו הקדמונים, ובעבור שימצאו ספרים רבים אין קץ להם בחכמת דיני המזלות ויש שם דברים שהדעת תכחישם ויש מחלוקת בין דיני המזלות, הוצרכתי להזכיר לך בספר הזה כל דבר ברור שהסכימה דעת הקדמונים עליו גם נסיתי פעמים רבות.

Ptolemy's *Tetrabiblos*, whom Ibn Ezra often quotes or refutes. The *Tetrabiblos* is organized topically and hierarchically from the general to the particular. In Book III, following the mundane chapters, it addresses the individual nativity according to the natural sequence of life from birth to death, starting by comparing conception and birth, followed by the determination of the ascending degree. At this point Ibn Ezra decides to depart from Ptolemy's topical format and follow the familiar sequence of the houses, which are also topical divisions of life. He has the reader/student on his mind as he explicitly says (*Nativities* page 12):

> . . . therefore we have no need for the rising degree at the moment of the dripping, and *in order to make it easier for the students,* have followed the [other] astrologers in explaining the matters of nativities according to the twelve houses.[25] (my italics)

Luminaries is a natural follow-up for *Nativities,* as it deals with medical astrology, i.e., pertaining to the health of the individual. Unlike what the name implies, the focus is on the role and primacy of the Moon and the aspects made by it in prognosticating the progress of a disease, as well as the crisis days from the time of its onset. Such observations were an indispensable part of medieval medicine, and a must for the practitioner; this book is written with much practical detail that can be used for this purpose. Its placement in the series is an indication for the logical course of studies that the student needs to follow.

Elections (1 & 2) is written as instructions for the practitioner who needs to advise clients about the best time to start an undertaking. It incorporates and integrates all the astrological tenets from *Wisdom, Reasons* and *Nativities* into consistent and logical sets of instructions for specific topical situations. It addresses the student directly and imperatively, in the second person, usually providing several options for the situation at hand. Almost every sentence begins with verbs or phrases like 'For one who wishes to . . . place the ruler of . . . in . . .', 'If you wish to . . . do it in such a way that . . .', 'If you cannot do this, then . . .', 'And beware that . . .'.

Interrogations (1 & 2) is also instructions for the practitioner. But unlike the doctrine of Elections, which assumes active choice of timing for the start of an enterprise, Interrogations—now known to modern astrologers as horary

---

25 *Nativities:* על כן איו לנו צרך במעלה הצומחת ברגע הטפה ובעבור הקל על התלמידים הלכתי בעקבות בעלי המזלות לבאר דברי הנולדים על דרך הבתים השנים עשר.

astrology—simply looks at the horoscope of a given moment in time when a question is asked about a potential undertaking in order to judge the possible outcome, or about an event that has already taken place. There is no manipulation of chart timing on the part of the astrologer, only analysis and observation. Therefore, the phrasing, also styled as second-person imperatives, mostly begins with 'Look to see whether . . .'

Elections and *Interrogations* are sets of clear, unambiguous instructions founded on the same basic tenets laid out in the first three books; occasionally the boundary between the two is blurred when phrases like 'If you wish to do something, look to see whether . . .' could be used both in the analysis of an inquiry regarding a potential action, or to determine the best time to carry it out. Both disciplines look at the outcome of an action, one as 'What will happen if you were to do it . . .' and the other is 'Do it in such a way to maximize the outcome'.

World (1 & 2) is about mundane astrology, a field without which no celestial study is complete. In this endeavour the astrologer looks at changes and cycles in the world in general on physical, economic, social and historical levels. The book contains a survey of the mundane techniques and the style is still didactic, but at this point knowledge of all the prior material is assumed and referenced. With this book the circle, as in the word 'encyclopedia', is complete.

Backward and Forward Reference

The contents of the books themselves are also integrated as a continuum of material and thought. Written in the span of about 6 months, it is obvious that the whole project was all laid out in his mind from the start. In *Wisdom,* at the outset, he says he will provide more explanations in *Reasons,* and in *Wisdom,* chapter 7, he promises to resolve a controversy regarding 'out of sign' conjunctions in *Nativities* (which will come after *Reasons*); in *Reasons-2,* chapters 1, 8 and 10, he says he will provide more explanations in *Nativities;* in chapters 2, 6 and 10 he mentions *World* as a future book; in *Nativities* he mentions *Luminaries*. *Elections* and *Interrogations* which follow are not mentioned as future books, but they are a most natural continuation for *Nativities*. *Nativities* focuses on the astrological houses, and the doctrines of Elections and Interrogations depend on accurate identification of significators for the matter at hand—a process that is primarily based on the houses and their rulers.

Such forward references serve to assure the student that further necessary explanations and study will be available. In the backward references Ibn Ezra reminds the student that the topic was already covered, specifying books and contents, using phrases like: '. . . as I have mentioned in the book of . . .'; '. . . as I have shown you in . . .'; '. . . as I have explained to you in . . .'; '. . . as I shall explain in . . .'

In *Reasons-1*, chapter 1, page 34, under the topic of the elemental nature of the planets as taken from Ptolemy's *Tetrabiblos*, he refers to *Nativities*:

> and I Abraham the author say that this book (*The Four Chapters*, mentioned earlier in the text) was not composed by Ptolemy, for there are many things there that are invalid by reason and experience, as I shall explain in *Nativities*.[26]

This comment on 'invalid things' most likely refers to the discussion on the Degree of the Nativity, quoted below under the heading 'Dispute, Resolution and Testing'.

In *Reasons-1*, chapter 7, page 86, he promises to explain the lunar mansions in *World*—a topic already discussed in *Astrolabe*. In chapter 8, page 90, under the topic of the testimonies of the planets, he refers to *Nativities*, First House chapter, under the topic of what should be taken as proper testimony. In chapter 10, page 102, under computation of temporal hours, he refers back to *Astrolabe* and to future *Nativities*.

In *Elections-1*, Second House chapter, under a discussion on buying commodities, he refers the reader/student back to *Wisdom*:

> I have already explained to you in the book *The Beginning of Wisdom* all the things that are signified by each one of the planets. Therefore, observe the nature of the commodity you wish to buy, whether of plants or metals, or anything [else], and know which planet signifies it, and if you find the planet combust or retrograde do not buy it.

In *Nativities*, First House chapter, page 15, under appearance of the native, he refers back to *Wisdom*:

---

26 *Reasons-1*: **ואני אברהם המחבר אומר כי זה הספר לא חברו בטלמיוס כי יש שם דברים רבים בטלים משקול הדעת והנסיון, כאשר אפרש בספר המולדות.**

> I have already explained in the book *The Beginning of Wisdom* the nature of every sign and all that it indicates [for] one who is born in [each] of the faces.[27]

In its last chapter, *Luminaries* refers back to *Wisdom* when discussing the arrival of the Moon or the Sun at a degree that is 'similar' to its original place:

> If the illness has [not?] passed until (*by the time?*) the Moon has returned to its [first] place, and there has not been a completely good or bad critical day, you must look to the place of the Sun at the onset of the illness, and observe those of the planets or of the superior ones (*fixed stars*) that conjoin or aspect it and that is by the square aspects and by the opposition aspect, and when it (*the sun*) arrives at the degrees that are similar in the wheel. And the reason is that they (*the similar degrees*) are equally distant from the equator in the north or in the south, or a degree that has the same diurnal [temporal] hour as the nocturnal [temporal] hour of the other degree, as is written in the book of *Beginning of Wisdom*.[28]

In *Interrogation-1*, Introduction, in identifying the type of question based on the placement of the ruling planet, he refers back to *Nativities*:

---

27 *Nativities*: וכבר פירשתי בספר ראשית החכמה תולדת כל מזל ומזל וכל מה שיורה מי שיולד באחד הפנים.

28 These conditions are known as 'parallel' and 'contra-parallel', 'antiscia' and 'contra-antiscia', which appear in *Wisdom*, chapter 3, pp. 82–83. Contra-parallel degrees are equidistant from the equator, one north and one south, forming a symmetry along the equatorial axis. Examples: 10° Aries is contra-parallel 20° Pisces; 5° Taurus is contra-parallel 25° Aquarius; 17° Virgo is contra-parallel 13° Libra. Such sign pairs have the same ascensional times. Similarly, degrees that are in antiscia form a symmetry along the axis of 0° of Capricorn and Cancer (the Solstice points). These have the same length of day and night (i.e., same length of temporal hours, when the sun arrives there). Examples: 5° Sagittarius is in antiscia with 25° Capricorn. Degrees that are in contra-antiscia mirror that length reversing day and night. Examples: 20° Sagittarius and 10° Cancer; 28° Scorpio and 2° Aquarius. In *Wisdom* chapter 2, p. 14, Ibn Ezra provides information for each sign about the ascensional time and the length of the temporal hours.
Luminaries: אם עבר החלי עד שוב הלבנה אל מקומה ולא היה גבול טוב או רע גמור, יש לך להסתכל אל מקום השמש בתחלת החלי והבט אל המתחברים עמה או המביטים אליה מהמשרתים או העליונים, וככה במבטים המרובעים ובמבט הנכח ובגעתה אל המעלות שהם דומות בגלגל, והטעם שהם רחוקות מהקו השוה או בצפון או בדרום מרחק שוה, או מעלה שידמו זמני שעתה ביום כזמני שעה האחרת בלילה, ככתוב בספר ראשית החכמה כי כח גדול יש להם.

> and I shall give you a rule: if you find the ruler in the seventh house, and I have already mentioned in the book of *Nativities* that the seventh house is the house of women (wives), wars and partnership, so you have to co-mix the nature of the planet as written in the *Beginning of Wisdom,* with the house it is in.

In *World-1,* page 74, under the discussion on indications of war in the annual revolution for a country, he refers back to *Elections,* which contains clear rules for which side will have the upper hand and for the outcome of the conflict. Also in *World-1,* page 94, in evaluating conjunctions he refers the reader/student back to *Wisdom* for the essential nature of the planets:

> And I shall give you a rule. You should always observe the one hundred and twenty conjunctions which are the conjunctions of the planets with the luminaries, and as you have known (found out) in the book The Beginning of the Wisdom the nature of each star (planet), so you will judge...[29]

In *World-2,* page 170, in evaluating benefic and malefic planets at the annual revolution of the year of the conjunction (most likely Jupiter & Saturn) *Wisdom* is referred to for information on the 'power of the twelves'.[30] Also on page 170, in evaluating annual periods, he instructs the student to observe the current profection place, as he has shown in *Nativities.*[31] And on page 184, in a discussion on the moon and the lunar mansions in relation to rainfall, he fulfills his promise from *Reasons-1,* referring the student back to *Astrolabe* for computation of the lunar mansions using the position of the sun, and to *Reasons* for the figures contained in them, reminding the student to subtract 9 degrees of

---

[29] *World-1:* והנה כלל אדבר לך. יש לך להסתכל לעולם אל המאה ועשרים מחברות שהם מחברות הכוכבים המשרתים עם המאורות. ואחר שידעת בספר ראשית החכמה ממסך כל כוכב ככה תדין...

[30] *World-2:* ויש לך להסתכל אל מקום הכוכבים הטובים והרעים בתחלת שנת המחברת, ודע באי זה מזל הוא כח השנים עשר, כמו שפירשתי בספר ראשית חכמה. ומזה תוכל לדעת כל טוב וכל רע שיקרה לכל מדינה ומדינה.

However, in *World-1* he does provide a brief explanation and an example for this concept—evaluating the position of a planet in a twelvefold subdivision of the sign, corresponding to the sequence of the zodiac, beginning from sign itself. A full description is found in *Wisdom,* p. 24.

[31] *World-2:* גם יסתכלו בית הסוף בדרך תקופת המולד כאשר פרשתי בספר המולדות.

precession from the sun in the tables, in order to find the Hindu sun (sidereal zodiac), on which the figures are based.[32]

Reasoning, Analysis and General Rules

Ibn Ezra is aware of the need to simplify and unify a number of separate statements into a clear underlying rule, especially in cases of controversy. A detailed analysis may be followed by '. . . and so I shall give you a [general] rule . . .'

Example: Progression of a concept from a simple statement to a sophisticated explanation – On the planets' elemental nature.

In *Wisdom*, chapter 4, page 91, Saturn is simply described as 'cold and dry'. In *Reasons-1* chapter 1, page 32, we find a detailed discussion on the sub-elements of the signs and the planets: hot-cold, wet-dry. He says 'the reason for the nature of the planets is difficult [to explain]'. He proceeds to list Ptolemy's natural explanations, such as 'Mars is burning hot because it is near the Sun and its heat (the Sun's) rises to it', or 'Saturn is cold because it is far from the Sun', Jupiter is moderate because it is between the heat of Mars and the cold of Saturn, etc. Then he says 'others say that these qualities are known by way of experience, and the truth is that there is no planet or superior (fixed) star that is cold or hot, for they are of a fifth element, as Aristotle explained in complete evidence'. Also in *Reasons-1* chapter 2, page 46, he explains why Saturn participates in the rulership of the fiery triplicity:

> . . . and they assigned Saturn as participating for it is cold and [in] the hot sign its (*Saturn's*) nature will be tempered. You should know that what I said about cold and hot refers to the thing produced (*by the planets' motions, not to the planet itself*), [but] *in order to make it easy for the students it is said that way*.[33] (my italics)

---

[32] *World-2*: וחשבון המחברות תדענו כאשר הראיתיך בספר כלי הנחשת, ממקום השמש. רק תחסר ממקום השמש, שתמצאנה בספר הלוחות, תשע מעלות. ואז תמצא מקום השמש של הודו, שהוא כנגד הצורות כאשר פרשתי בספר הטעמים.

[33] *Reasons-1*: ושמו השותף שבתי בעבור היותו קר והמזל חם תתישר תולדתו. ויש לך לדעת כי זה שאמרתי קר וחם איננו אלא על הדבר שיולידו, ולהקל על התלמידים יאמר ככה.

In *Reasons-2*, page 4, in the entry on fire signs, he repeats the Aristotelian physics and adds a general rule:

> The philosophers explained that the signs are not composed of the four elements but are a fifth element by themselves. And so the Sun is not hot but is called so for he gives heat. *All the stars give heat, but whichever gives less heat than the temperament of man, who is even in his temperament, is called cold, like the flesh of the bull and the goat, since all flesh is warm.*[34] (my italics)

Example: Refutation of Māshā'allāh's statement on travel, based on Ibn Ezra's doctrine regarding the 'general and the particular'. Even though it is not explicitly mentioned here, this doctrine is presented in detail in *Nativities*, under 'Introductory Matters'. The question here is 'can the astrologer tell how long one will stay in a country, judging from the moment of entry?' In *Elections-1*, Third House chapter:

> . . . and I wonder about Mashallah who said that one could know from the rising sign at the time of entry into the country how many days he will stay there, and he (*Mashallah*) gave many examples for this. And this is a great error, for a hundred people [may] enter a country all at once, whether in a group (*meaning all at the same moment*) or in a convoy (*meaning one after another so the entry moment slightly changes*), and one [of them] stayed, and one passed through and one stayed overnight and one died and one is delayed, and this [eventuality] will happen according to what is indicated in the nativity of each one [individually], not depending on the influence of the sign under which they entered.[35]

However, it must be noted here that Ibn Ezra does advocate electing a time for the start of the travel itself. See *Elections-1*, here, and *Elections-2* on the Third House & Ninth House.

---

34 *Reasons*-2: חכמי התכונה נתנו ראיה כי המזלות אינם מורכבים מן המוסדים הארבעה והם תולדת חמישית בפני עצמם. וככה השמש איננה חמה רק נקראת כן בעבור שתוליד חום. וכל הכוכבים יולידו חום, רק המוליד חום מעט כנגד ממסך האדם הישר בממסכו נקרא קר, כבשר השור והעז, כי כל בשר הוא חם.

35 *Elections*-1: ואני תמה על מאשאללה שאמר שיוכל אדם לדעת מהמזל הצומח בשעת הכניסה למדינה כמה ימים יעמוד שם, ונתן דמיונות רבים לדבר. וזה טעות גדולה, כי מאה אנשים יכנסו בבת אחת למדינה בין בגדוד בין בשירה ואחד עמד ואחד עבר ואחד לן ואחד מת ואחד מתעכב. וזה יקרה כפי מולד כל אחד שיורה מולדו לא תלוי בכח המזל שנכנסו בו.

Dispute, Resolution and Testing

Ibn Ezra sets an example of intellectual rigor in many places where he lists known astrological techniques from various sources, adding '. . . and I have tried it and succeeded' or '. . . not succeeded', often concluding by saying to the student '. . . and you should do as I have shown you . . .'

Example: Obtaining the correct rising degree of the nativity is critical for the practicing astrologer, and the available techniques are often in dispute. This question is not mentioned at all in *Wisdom*; but in later books, where the application gets more sophisticated, Ibn Ezra tackles it in his typical decisive way by refuting Ptolemy's method (*Tetrabiblos*, III), later known as the *Animodar*, and then elaborating the one he supports. In *Reasons-2*, page 35, under 'The Degree of the Nativity', he writes:

> Ptolemy said that the number of degrees of the ruler of the conjunction (*new Moon*) or the opposition (*full Moon*) will be the number of degrees of the Ascendant. I have tried [it] many times when I took the number of the degree of the Sun at the time of birth, with the minutes and seconds and fixed the positions of the planets in the Tables of India and the Tables of Ptolemy and the Tables of Persia, and the Tables of Apparent [position], and I have not found the degrees of the Ascendant from the number of the ruler of the New or Full Moon. What Enoch said is true and has been tested and that is the nature of births.[36]

In *Nativities*, in the introduction section under the heading of 'The Equation of the Nativity', he first details Ptolemy's method and refutes it, then spells out the exact computation (not quoted here) that is derived from the position of the Moon in the wheel at conception and at birth, which he states to be the correct one (*Nativities*, page 7):

> Those that came after him confused it even more; for some say that we shall always take the degree of the Moon whether it is above or below the earth at

[36] *Reasons-2*: ותלמי אמר כי כמספר מעלות הממונה על מקום המחברת או הנוכח ככה יהיה מספר א' היתדות. והנה אנכי נסיתי פעמים רבות, שלקחתי מעלות גבהות השמש בשעת הלידה עם החלקים ורובי השנים, תקנתי מקום הכוכבים בלוחות הודו ולוחות תלמי ולוחות פרס והלוחות שהם אמת למראית העין ולא מצאתי א' היתדות ממספר א' הכוכבים. כלל – מה שהזכיר חנוך הוא אמת ומנוסה והוא דרך התולדות.

the moment of the opposition, and others say that we shall always take the degree of the luminary that is above the earth at the moment of birth. Ptolemy also said that the two luminaries rule over man, and therefore this is found (*applies*) only in the nativity of a person and not in the nativity of animals and birds. Others said that we should always take the number of one of the pivots (*i.e. angles*) according to the number of the degree of the ruler, and we shall do it thus: We should always look to see which one is close[er] to the moment of birth and according to its number we shall assign to [the number of degrees of] one of the pivots the number of degrees of that ruler. These are the equations that the practitioners of the judgements of the signs relied on, and they are false equations as I have tried them many times with a perfect astrolabe, reckoned the exact moment of birth, and have not found the degree of one of the pivots [to be the same] as the number of the degrees of the ruler (*of the prenatal lunation*). Then I thought the error might be in the determination of the ruler; so I reckoned the [place of the] rest of the planets and I did not find [among] the luminaries nor the planets [one] whose degree is like that of one of the pivots, except when there is an error in the time of birth of more than one third of an hour. Therefore, it became clear to me that these equations are nonsense. A Hindu astrologer mentioned three other equations, and they are all useless. The truth is [to be found in] the equations of Enoch, except that they need two corrections, for I have tried them in this way many times.[37]

The astrologers who came after Enoch concurred with him about these equations, and I have also tried [it] and succeeded, except that there are times

---

[37] *Nativities*: והנה החכמים הבאים אחריו נשתבשו כי יש אומרים כי אם השליט קרוב אל הבית העשירי יותר מהמעלה הצומחת נשים תחילת קו חצי השמים כמספר מעלותיו וממנו נוכל להוציא המעלה הצומחת כאשר מפורש בספר הלוחות, וככה אם היה קרוב יותר אל היתד הראשון או אל היתד הדומה שהוא תחילת הבית השביעי אז נשים מספר המעלה הצומחת כמספר מעלות השליט, ואם היה הנולד בין זמן הנכח ובין זמן המחברת נוציא מעלת הנכח בדקדוק יפה ונסתכל השליט על המעלה ונעשה כמשפט הכתוב. והנה נשתבשו עוד, כי הבאים אחריו יש אומרים לעולם נקח מעלת הלבנה בין שתהיה למעלה מן הארץ ובין שתהיה למטה ממנה ברגע הנכח, ואחרים אמרו לעולם נקח מעלת המאור ההווה למעלה ברגע הנכח, ואחרים אמרו לעולם נקח מעלת המאור ההווה למעלה מהארץ ברגע המולד. ועד אמר בטלמיוס כי שני המאורות פקידים על האדם ובעבור זה ימצא ככה במולד האדם לבדו ולא במולד הבהמות והעופות. ואחרים אמרו כי לעולם נקח מספר אחת היתדות כמספר מעלת השליט וככה נעשה לעולם נסתכל אי זהו קרוב לרגע המולד וכמספרו נשים אחת היתדות.
ואלה המאזנים סמכו עליהם דיני המזלות והם מאזני שקר כי אני ניסיתים פעמים רבות בכלי נחשת שלם שדקדקתי רגע המולד ולא מצאתי מעלת אחת היתדות כמספר מעלת השליט, וחשבתי בלבי שמא הטעות הוא בדעת השליט והנה תקנתי שאר המשרתים ולא מצאתי מאורות גם במשרתים שתהיה מעלתו כמעלת אחת היתדות רק שיהיה ברגע המולד טעות יותר משלישית שעה. על כן התברר לי כי אלו המאזנים הבל המה. גם הזכיר חכם הודו שלשה מאזנים אחרים ואת כולם ישא רוח, והאמת הם מאזני חנוך רק הם צריכים שני תקונים כי ככה נסיתים פעמים רבות.

> when it requires one of two corrections.[38]

These two corrections involve Mercury, Venus or Mars as additional triggers for parturition.

Example: The methodology needed to determine the parents' significators in the nativity and differentiate between the mother and the father. Traditionally, the fourth house indicates the father and the tenth the mother, but this assignment has occasionally been questioned, even today. The Sun and Saturn, the Moon and Venus also respectively signify the father and the mother. In the context of the longevity of the parents, Ibn Ezra suggests a logical way to clarify all that. He does not just state it axiomatically, but identifies the weak points and establishes a rational methodology to resolve the issue. In doing so, he compels the reader/student to engage all the relevant techniques and principles hitherto presented.

In *Wisdom*, pages 87 and 89, he simply states: 'the fourth house signifies the father' and 'the tenth house signifies the mother'. In *Reasons-1*, chapter 3, page 66, he gives another descriptive reason for assigning the tenth house to the mother:

> The ancients said that the fourth house indicates the father and the tenth the mother and Ptolemy says the opposite,[39] but the [correct] judgement is with the ancients, *for it is proper for the sign (house) that indicates the mother to be visible.*[40] (my italics)

Reasons-2, page 15, under The Houses, has a similar quotation, including Ptolemy's attribution of the tenth house to the father and the fourth to the mother. Why would the sign indicating the mother need to be visible? I suggest that Ibn Ezra's argument about the visibility of the tenth house is a 'Jewish touch' and harks back to Jewish law, which stipulates that a person is considered Jewish if born to a Jewish mother (even if the father is not). One

---

38 *Nativities*: והחכמים הבאים אחרי חנוך הודו לו באלה המאזנים גם אני נסיתי ועלה בידי, רק יש פעמים שהוא צריך לאחד משנים תקונים.

39 This most likely comes from a pseudo-Ptolemy.

40 *Reasons*-1: והקדמונים אמרו כי הבית הרביעי הוא יורה על האב והעשירי יורה על האם ובטלמיוס אומר הפך הדבר. והדין עם הקדמונים, כי ראוי להיות המזל שיורה על האם הוא הנראה לעין.

reason is that the biological mother is a visible, unmistakable fact; the tenth house is the most elevated and most visible place in the chart.

In *Nativities*, under the Fourth House chapter, he sorts out the confusion that may arise between the native, the mother and the father when determining the time of a health crisis, and suggests a logical approach. First, he instructs one to direct all four indicators of the father (Sun, Saturn, the cusp of the Fourth House, the Lot of the Father) to an abscission place according to the rules for directions. If the Sun cannot be used, then use Saturn, the Lot of the Father and the cusp of the Fourth House, in this order. At the time when two testimonies coincide, then the father will die. When only one testimony is found, it indicates sickness and harm that will come to the father according to the nature of the abscissor planet.

Which Houses Signify the Parents? (*Nativities*, page 41):

> Know that there is a controversy between Ptolemy and [other] astrologers, for he says that the tenth house signifies the father and the fourth house signifies the mother, and the other astrologers say the opposite.[41]

With a keen eye for logic, Ibn Ezra explains the confusion caused by concurrent indicators:

> The truth is what the other astrologers say, and here is the principal reason for this controversy. When we direct the Fourth House to an abscission place, at the same time the Tenth House will [also] reach an abscission place. If we can know the measure of the father's life only from the fourth house, and if we can know the measure of the mother's life only from the tenth house, then the father and the mother should die at the same time. And this is the reason for the controversy.
>
> Similarly, if we take the measure of the native's life from the Sun as well as the father's life, it is possible for the Sun to come to an abscission place and at the same time one of the [other] four places of life of the native [comes] to an abscission place, and so does the degree of the fourth house or the Lot of the

---

[41] *Nativities*: Also see previous footnote regarding Ptolemy and the parents.
ודע כי מחלוקת בין בטלמיוס ובין חכמי המזלות, כי הוא אומר כי הבית העשירי יורה על האב והבית הרביעי יורה על האם והחכמים אומרים הפך הדבר.

Father or the place of Saturn; then the father and the son (*the native*) will die on the same day.

Likewise, if two of the places of life of the native reach an abscission place, and at the same time the place of the Moon by night and also by day if she qualifies [as an indicator] to know the measure of life from, and at the same time if Venus, or the degree of the tenth house, or the Lot of the Mother reaches an abscission place, [then] the native and his mother will die in one day.[42]

The key to the differentiation is the requirement of two (or more) testimonies for the crisis, since any combination of the four indicators will be unique for the specific parent.

Application – From Theory to Practice

An astrological concept becomes viable when it is taken from an aphorism to practical application. As examples, I have selected some of the less familiar ones: in the nativity, in prognostication, elections and interrogations.

Example: Reading the chart based on built-in house relationships through planetary sign rulership.

It is common knowledge in astrological interpretation that the indications of the astrological house are modified and qualified by the planet that rules the sign on the cusp of that house. Standard basic interpretation of the chart requires analysis of the condition of that planet to know whether the affairs of that house manifest positively or negatively. Ibn Ezra shows us how to evaluate the houses without resorting to the planet, using only the rulership

---

42 *Nativities:* והנכון דברי החכמים והנה עקר זה המחלוקת כי כאשר נבהג הבית הרביעי אל מקום כרת באותו זמן יגיע הבית העשירי אל מקום כרת, והנה אם לא יכולנו לדעת מדת חיי האב מהשמש או משבתי ולא מגורל האב כי אם מהבית הרביעי גם לא יכלנו לדעת מדת חיי האם מנגה ולא מהלבנה ולא מגורל האם רק מן הבית העשירי אז ימות האב והאם בזמן אחד, ובעבור זה באה המחלוקת. וככה אם לקחנו מדת חיי הנולד מהשמש גם חיי האב ממנה ויתכן שיגיע השמש אל מקום כרת וככה מעלת הבית הרביעי או גורל האב או מקום שבתי אז ימות האב והבן ביום אחד, וככה אם יגיעו שנים ממקום החיים של נולד אל מקום כרת ויגיע באותו הרגע מקום הלבנה בלילה גם ביום אם היתה ראויה לדעת ממנה כמה מדת החיים, גם באותו הרגע יגיע נגה או מעלת הבית העשירי או גורל האם אל מקום כרת ימות הנולד ואמו ביום אחד.

scheme,[43] since two houses ruled by the same planet have an inherent connection between them. Such a connection can be of the nature of the square aspect—Mercury's houses and Jupiter's houses, a first-house to tenth-house connection—or of an inconjunct, Venus' houses and Mars' houses, a sixth-house or an eighth-house connection. Saturn's houses and the Luminaries' houses are adjacent to each other and create a twelfth-house or second-house connection.

In *Nativities*, chapter 3, page 35, Ibn Ezra, with a keen eye for patterns, lists some of the manifestations of such connections:

> Doroneus (*Dorotheus*) said that if the rising sign is Capricorn or Cancer, then the native will have quarrels with siblings. The reason for this is known since the ruler of the third house is [also] the ruler of the twelfth house which indicates quarrels.[44] In the same way you will figure all the signs, for if the rising sign is Aries or Libra, the native will cause his own death[45] and will have money from women, and he will have a chronic illness in one of his limbs, and he will rejoice with his father for the nature of the Moon and the Sun is the same,[46] and he will have arguments in a foreign country or with inn keepers

---

43 Sun - Leo; Mercury - Gemini and Virgo; Jupiter - Sagittarius and Pisces; Moon - Cancer; Venus - Taurus and Libra; Saturn - Capricorn and Aquarius; Mars - Aries and Scorpio.

44 Footnote from *Nativities*, p. 35: 'Capricorn on the ascendant puts the domiciles of Jupiter (Sagittarius & Pisces which are in a square to each other) on the cusps of the 12th and the 3rd houses. When Cancer is rising, the domiciles of Mercury (Gemini & Virgo) create the same condition. Here, and in the text that follows, Ibn Ezra draws attention to an interpretation principle derived from the fact that each planet rules two signs. Such pairs are known as Same Engirdling [sic] signs.'

45 Footnote from *Nativities*, p. 35: 'With Aries rising Mars also rules Scorpio on the 8th house cusp, and with Libra rising Venus also rules Taurus on the 8th house cusp. This creates what can be called a union between these houses. Only Mars and Venus can do that because they rule signs in quincunx (150° apart). This also creates a connection between the ascendant and the 6th house when Taurus or Scorpio are rising. Note that both Jupiter and Mercury rule square signs, and can thus create a union between angles, which is a very desirable condition'.

46 Footnote from *Nativities*, p. 35: 'This may be derived from the fact that elsewhere Ibn Ezra says that the Sun and the Moon always receive each other, which means that they have power in each other's domicile. Reception also creates a union. A possible interpretation is: With Aries rising the Moon rules Cancer in the 4th house of fathers and

> [variant text: 'or with learned people']. If the rising sign is Taurus or Scorpio, the native will bring illnesses on himself; he will have quarrels with women, and money from land, and most of his friends will die. If the rising sign is Gemini or Sagittarius, his siblings will destroy his money, and [he] will make money from things that are laid away as treasures; most of his children will become his enemies. These things do not require explanations for they are taken from the relationship between the houses that belong to a single planet. In the same way [you should] derive the rest of the rules [for the signs] that I did not mention.[47]

Example: Evolution of meaning for one of the least-known indications of the second house: 'household assistants'.

Wisdom, chapter 3, page 86:

> The Second House denotes money and possessions, and trading, and food, *and one's assistants, and those who obey one's command.*[48] (my italics)

In *Reasons-1*, chapter 3, page 66, a further explanation is added:

> Since the second house is adjacent to the first pivot, which indicates life, therefore they said that it is the house of wealth and the house of those who assist the native.[49]

---

the Sun, which has dignity of exaltation in the ascendant, also rules Leo in the 5th house—the house of pleasure and enjoyment, which trines the ascendant. With Libra rising we have Saturn ruling Capricorn on the 4th cusp and Aquarius on the 5th trine the Libra ascendant where Saturn is dignified by exaltation'.

47 *Nativities*: אמר דורוניאוס אם היה המזל הצומח גדי או סרטן יהיה לנולד מריבות עם האחים, וטעם זה הדבר ידוע בעבור היות בעל הבית השלישי הוא בעל בית שנים עשר שיורה על המריבות, ומזה הדרך תלמוד לכל המזלות, כי אם היה המזל הצומח טלה או מאזנים יסבב סבות הוא בעצמו למיתתו, ויהיה לו ממון מן הנשים, ויהיה חלי קבוע באחד מאחיו, וישמח עם אביו, בעבור כי תולדת הלבנה והשמש שוה, ויתחדשו לו מריבות בארץ נכריה או עם אנשים אכסנאין. ואם המזל העולה שור או עקרב יסבב על נפשו חלאים, ותהיין לו מריבות עם האנשים וממון קרקעות, וימותו רובי אוהביו. ואם המזל העולה תאומים או קשת ישחיתו אחיו ממונו, ויקנה ממון מדברים שהם נאצרים, ורובי בניו יתהפכו לו לאויבים. ואלה הדברים אין צריכים לפרש טעמיהם כי הם לקוחים מערך הבתים שהם לכוכב אחד, ועל זה הדרך להוציא שאר הדינין שלא הזכרתי.

48 *Wisdom*-LC, p. xli: הבית השני יורה על הממון והקנין ומשא ומתן ומאכל והעוזרים אותו והסרים למשמעתו.

49 *Reasons*-1: ובעבור היות הבית השני סמוך אל היתד הראשון שיורה על החיים, על כן אמרו שהוא

Nativities is silent on this particular indication but later on, in *Elections-1* this meaning is employed as one's army ('those who obey one's command'). *Elections-1*, Seventh House chapter on waging war:

> This house indicates three things – wars, wives and partners. So if you wish to wage war or send out a military commander by land, place the rising sign in one of the domiciles of the superior planets, and if they are those of Mars it is even better, except that Mars should not be combust, nor retrograde, nor in the second house, for (if in the second house) he will destroy his troops by his own hand, since the second house indicates [one's] army.
> . . . and beware that the ruler of the second house should not be in a square or opposition aspect with the rising sign or its ruler, for that indicates that his troops will conspire against him and will not obey his orders.
> . . . Abū Ma'shar said: if many planets aspect the rising sign then he will have many helpers, and if the ruler of the eighth house beholds it in a good aspect the enemy's troops will defect to his camp.[50]

The eighth house in this context is the second from the seventh, hence the 'assistants' of the opponent.

Astronomy and Computations
The study of astrology is not complete without learning the necessary computations for the nativity, planetary aspects, directions, the annual solar revolution, divisions of time and planetary conjunctions and cycles. These are found throughout the books as part of the plan to provide one complete source of study. The text on these subjects is too involved to quote so only brief description is provided here, aiming to show how the scientific material, both

---

בית העושר ובית העוזרים את הנולד.

[50] *Elections-1*, Seventh House chapter: זה הבית יורה על שלשה דברים - על המלחמות ועל הנשים ועל השותפים. והנה אם רצית לבחור לצאת למלחמה או להוציא שר גדוד ביבשה, שים המזל הצומח מאחד בתי הכוכבים העליונים, ואם היו בתי מאדים הם יותר טובים, על מנת שלא יהא מאדים נשרף ולא שב אחורנית ולא יהיה בבית השני, כי הוא בעצמו ישחית מחנהו כי הבית השני יורה על הגדוד.
... והשמר שלא יהיה בעל הבית השני על מבט רביעית או נכח עם המזל הצומח או עם בעליו, כי אז יורה כי יקשור גדודו עליו ולא יסור אל משמעתו.
...אמר אבו מעשר -אם יביטו כוכבים רבים אל המזל הצומח יהיו לו עוזרים רבים, ואם בעל הבית השמיני יביט אליו מבט טוב יברח מגדוד האויב אליו.

astronomical and mathematical computations, progresses from the fundamental to the complex.

The fact that *The Book of the Astrolabe* is the first in Ibn Ezra's astrological corpus substantiates the thesis of a systematic teaching agenda that underlies these texts. The student's first astrological task is drawing up the nativity, which requires basic knowledge of astronomical computations, followed by more advanced astronomy, calendar considerations and other computations—all of which are not possible without the knowledge and skill of using this tool. *Astrolabe* covers the structure and use of the astrolabe, computation of a complete chart—angles and intermediate house cusps, planetary positions and the fixed stars, the lunar mansions—and also computing the height of objects.

In *Wisdom,* chapter 10, Ibn Ezra provides a brief overview of directions in the nativity and in affairs of the world.[51] In regard to the nativity he mentions some guidelines and settles a dispute regarding direction by zodiacal degrees versus ascensional times. He also lists the method of a sign-house per year[52] and the *Firdar* method. Regarding mundane directions we find the standard Jupiter–Saturn cycle, as well as the scale of one hundred or one thousand years per sign.

In *Reasons-1,* chapter 10, we find a detailed exposition on the issue of aspects computed in zodiacal degrees versus aspects in the mundane sphere where logical distortions may occur. This is followed by instruction on intermediate house computations, as well as a mention of the already-written *Astrolabe* and of further instructions in the future *Nativities.* Instructions are given for computation of aspects in the mundane sphere using temporal hours and ascension tables. The directions are mentioned briefly again, with approval of the *profection* and the *firdar* methods, as well as a comment on the 'great mutation' of the Jupiter–Saturn cycle. This comment is concluded by a promise to further explain this in *World.*

In *Reasons-2,* the End of the Book chapter, we find a brief discussion regarding the tropical versus sidereal zodiac, with interesting observations as follows: the specific degrees that are known as the dark, bright or pitted must be

51 'Directions' refers to symbolic methods by which astrological forecasting is done. They are symbolic since they are based on equating astronomical-geometrical units with time units as, for example, the popular 'degree for a year'. It can also be a house for a year, etc. In a nativity angular distances between planets are thus converted to the length of time that it would take for the planets to make contact and bring on an event.

52 In later literature known as Profections.

adjusted to the sidereal zodiac, since they correspond with fixed stars of this nature, while the domiciles (signs), the domiciles of exaltations (of the planets) and the bounds (terms) should be observed in the tropical zodiac. To determine whether a planet is in a human sign (or others, such as animal signs), adjustment to sidereal is also necessary since the constellations are based on forms.

In *Nativities* Part Two, on the Annual Revolution, we find a discussion on the length of the year and instructions for calculations of the chart for the solar revolution, accompanied by guidelines for interpretation of this annual event. A brief mention of Ptolemy's ages of life is followed by explanation of the *Firdar* system of periods and sub-periods, as well as some age-appropriate guidelines for interpretation. *Profection* is explained, counting years and months and days, topped off by instructions on finding the planetary ruler of the day and hour of the solar revolution chart.

World 1 & *2* contains both scientific and interpretive material. The scientific material has discussions on determining planetary conjunctions and cycles—specifically Jupiter–Saturn—and on computation of the equinoctial precession. Detailed attention is given to the issues involved in determining the Vernal Ingress which depends on accurate computation of the length of the year and the declination of the sun.

Summary and Conclusion

Good teachers are not made—they are born that way. They possess the instinct for what needs to be taught and the best way to do it, and it is clear that Ibn Ezra was such a teacher. The expression of this talent came out at the right time and place among the mystically-inclined Jewish communities in Southern France, whose eagerness to learn must have inspired him to write this complete corpus.

Throughout the books, in a consistent progressive way, he builds the foundation of the fundamental concepts, and then proceeds to integrate them into more coherent units of information, with an eye for a beginning student as well as the advanced practitioner. While the contents are mostly a logically-organised compilation of the sources, in the process he often examines the underlying rationale of conflicting doctrines and comes up with his own resolutions. By doing so he is also teaching the students to think critically, compare and judge for themselves.

Ibn Ezra's popularity and teaching lived on as his astrological works were quoted, translated and copied by generations of scribes for centuries to come.[53] In the Jewish world of the post-Maimonides era the mainstream study of astrology was pushed into a dark forbidden corner where it never recovered from the weight of the prohibition that Maimonides imposed on it. Yet Ibn Ezra's Biblical exegeses, which remain highly popular to this day and are still part of standard Jewish Biblical texts, include astrological concepts and explanations in many places. The learned Jews who tried to figure these out needed some minimum astrological explanations, which were readily found in Ibn Ezra's books, and further transmitted through the Rabbinical commentaries and super-commentaries that followed.

Scholars who have studied the works of Ibn Ezra call it encyclopedic, but here we may conclude that it is also pedagogical, as is evident when all the pieces are put together.

---

53 *Wisdom-LC*, Levy's introduction, pp. 13–14.

Appendix: Manuscripts Used

Source: Microfilms from IMHM – Institute of Microfilmed Hebrew Manuscripts, Jewish National and University Library, Jerusalem. Original library source abbreviated here in [ ]:

1. Berlin – Staatsbibliothek (Preussischer Kulturbesitz) Or. Qu. 679 [abbr. BER679]
2. Cambridge – University Library Add. Add. 481 [abbr. CAM481]
3. Cambridge – University Library Add. 1501 [abbr. CAM1501]
4. Cambridge – University Library Add. 1517 [abbr. CAM1517]
5. Dresden – Saechsische Landesbibliothek Eb 384 [abbr. DRE384]
6. Florence – Biblioteca Nazionale Centrale Magl. III.36 [abbr. FIR36]
7. Madrid – Biblioteca de la Real Academia de la Historia Hebr. 7 [abbr. MAD7]
8. Moscow – Russian State Library, Ms. Guenzburg 421 [abbr. MOS421]
9. Munich – Bayerische Staatsbibliothek, Cod. hebr. 45 [MUN45]
10. Munich – Bayerische Staatsbibliothek, Cod. hebr. 202 [abbr. MUN202]
11. New York – Jewish Theological Seminary Ms. 2623 [abbr. JTS2623]
12. New York – Jewish Theological Seminary Ms. 2631 [abbr. JTS263]
13. Paris – Bibliothèque Nationale heb. 189 [abbr. PAR189]
14. Paris – Bibliothèque Nationale heb. 1044 [abbr. PAR1044]
15. Paris – Bibliothèque Nationale heb. 1045[abbr. PAR1045]
16. Paris – Bibliothèque Nationale heb. 1051 [abbr. PAR1051]
17. Paris – Bibliothèque Nationale heb. 1055 [abbr. PAR1055]
18. Paris – Bibliothèque Nationale heb. 1056 [abbr. PAR1056]
19. Paris – Bibliothèque Nationale heb. 1058 [abbr. PAR1058]
20. St. Petersburg – Russian National Library Evr. II A 245 [abbr. STP245]
21. St. Petersburg – Inst. of Oriental Studies of the Russian Academy B 447 [abbr. STP447]
22. Vatican – Biblioteca Apostolica ebr. 390 [abbr. BAV390]
23. Vatican – Urbinati ebr. 47 [abbr. BAV47]
24. Vatican – Biblioteca Apostolica ebr. 477 [abbr. BAV477]
25. Warsaw – Zydowski Instytut Historyczny 255 [abbr. WAR255]

ASTROLOGY IN AL-ANDALUS DURING THE ELEVENTH AND TWELFTH CENTURIES: BETWEEN RELIGION AND PHILOSOPHY[*]

Miquel Forcada

Introduction

In general the quality of the astrological texts written in al-Andalus is not as high as that of other disciplines, and certainly far below that of the astrological works of Abbasid Baghdad between the eighth and tenth centuries. Nevertheless, the work of Andalusī astrologers was by no means insignificant and experienced something of a golden age during the eleventh century, coinciding with the flourishing of Andalusī mathematical astronomy.[1] Interestingly, as astrological production grew in quantity and quality, so did the anti-astrological literature written by religious scholars.

---

* The research for this paper has been funded by the Spanish Ministry of Economy, 'La evolución de la ciencia en la sociedad de al-Andalus desde la Alta Edad Media al pre-Renacimiento y su repercusión en las culturas europeas y árabes (siglos X-XV-2)', FFI2011-30092-C02-01.

1 Astrology in al-Andalus and the Maghrib has been thoroughly studied in the last decades from a mathematical point of view by Samsó and some of his disciples (cf. the volumes of collected essays by Julio Samsó, *Islamic Astronomy in Medieval Spain* [Aldershot-Brookfield: Ashgate Variorum, 1994] and *Astrometeorología y astrología medievales* [Barcelona: Publications i Edicions de la Universitat de Barcelona, 2008]; Josep Casulleras, *La astrología de los matemáticos. La matemática aplicada a la astrología a través de la obra de Ibn Muʿaḏ de Jaén* [Barcelona: Publications i Edicions de la Universitat de Barcelona, 2010]; Montserrat Díaz Fajardo, 'Tasyīr y proyección de rayos en textos astrológicos magrebíes' [unpublished PhD dissertation, University of Barcelona, 2007] and the additional bibliography given below). Other aspects of the question are treated in Marie G. Balty-Guesdon, 'Médecins et hommes de science en Espagne Musulmane (IIe/VIIe–Ve/XIe s.)' (PhD dissertation, [Université de la Sorbonne], Université de Lille III, 1992 [microfiche]); Julio Samsó, *Las ciencias de los antiguos en al-Andalus* (Almería: Fundación Ibn Tufayl de Estudios Árabes, 2011); Juan Vernet, *La cultura hispano-árabe en Oriente y Occidente* (Barcelona: Ariel, 1978) and *El islam de España* (Madrid: Mapfre Editorial S.A., 1993).

However, astrology's heyday lasted only about a century. The Almoravids, a pious (and therefore anti-astrological) dynasty came to power at the transition between the eleventh and twelfth centuries and so the political context that had encouraged astrology changed dramatically. Its problems did not end there. The turn of the century also saw the emergence of Andalusī philosophy, strongly influenced by an anti-astrological author, al-Fārābī. Though some philosophers were well-disposed towards astrology, Ibn Rushd's rejection of it and the influence of al-Fārābī (and, secondarily, the influence of Ibn Sīnā) on the major philosophical trend of al-Andalus (defined by the oeuvre of Ibn Bājja, Ibn Ṭufayl and Ibn Rushd) strongly suggest that philosophical circles of the twelfth century were, in the main, against the practice of astrology. Facing this three-tier alliance, Andalusī astrology almost died out during the twelfth century, although scientific activity flourished in this period. The presence of astrological materials in other sciences was fairly limited at that time, perhaps because of the delicate ground that Andalusī astrologers were obliged to tread. As far as I know there are no traces of astrological materials in the medical works of the eleventh and twelfth centuries. However, astrology is well represented in agronomy, the rising discipline of that period; to a certain extent, it may be considered that astrology found a refuge of sorts in earth sciences, particularly during the dark years of the Almoravid rule. The aim of the present paper is to survey the anti-astrological arguments of the religious scholars of the eleventh century that hastened astrology's decline, and their relationship with the anti-astrological discourse of the philosophers. The paper will also study the place of astrology in the scientific practices of this time and, most particularly, in agronomy.

First Rise and Fall: Astrology between the Eighth and Mid-Ninth Century

We have a reasonably good idea of the early stages of Andalusī astrology, which may be summarized as follows:[2]

---

[2] Cf. Miquel Forcada, 'Astronomy, Astrology and the Sciences of the Ancients in Early al-Andalus (2nd/8th–3rd/9th Centuries)', *Zeitschrift für Geschichte der Arabisch-Islamischen Wissenschaften* 16 (2004–2005): pp. 1–74; Julio Samsó, 'The Early Development of Astrology in al-Andalus', *Journal for the History of Arabic Science* 3 (1979): pp. 228–43 and 'Sobre el Astrólogo 'Abd al-Wāhid b. Ishāq al-Dabbī (fl. ca. 788–860)', *Anaquel de Estudios Árabes* 12 (2001): pp. 657–69.

i. Astrology exerted a deep influence on the Cordovan court due to the interest of kings, most particularly that of ʻAbd al-Raḥmān II (r. 822–852).

ii. The knowledge and practice of astrology is one of the many facets of the acculturation of the Abbasid civilization in the Umayyad court of Cordova. Andalusī astrology of that time was indebted to the astronomical and astrological textbooks brought from Baghdad, though it also included certain techniques that had survived from the Roman substrate of al-Andalus.

iii. For many years ʻAbd al-Raḥmān II sponsored a large and expensive circle of astrologers. Its members were knowledgeable in other disciplines of a heterodox bias.

iv. The religious scholars, mainly followers of the Mālikī rite, reacted against the members of this circle not only because of their astrological practices but also because of their opinions on theological issues. Paradoxically, the belief in free will seems to have spread in the circle.[3] The first anti-astrological treatise of Andalusī culture appears at that time, written by the *faqīh* ʻAbd al-Malik b. Ḥabīb (d. 853).

v. Though the astrologers remained at the service of the court for some time after the death of ʻAbd al-Raḥmān II, they were dismissed by the emir Muḥammad (r. 852–886). The reasons were mainly religious, though other factors cannot be ruled out (for example, the court's finances were not as healthy as they had been some years before).

For a long time afterwards, there are only passing references to the practice of astrology in courtly circles or elsewhere in Andalusī society. There was little room for astrology in a political context in which, on the one hand, the religious scholars provided much of the legitimacy that the Umayyad dynasty needed and, on the other, the rulers (most particularly ʻAbd al-Raḥmān III; r. 912–961)

---

[3] The problem of how an Arabo-islamic scholar of the ninth century who believed in human free will could be at the same time an astrologer is insightfully solved in Peter Adamson, 'Abū Maʻshar, al-Kindī and the Philosophical Defense of Astrology', *Recherches de Théologie et Philosophie Médiévales* 69 (2002): pp. 245–70.

had implemented a strict policy of persecuting heterodoxy.

The official position of religious authorities on astrology appears to have been expressed in the books by 'Abd al-Malik b. Ḥabīb mentioned above.[4] Although the treatise in which he refuted astrology has not come down to us, the core of his arguments is summarized in a book on Arabic folk astronomy entitled *Risāla fī l-nujūm* ('Treatise on Stars'). The author, who says that he is quoting the sayings about astronomy of Mālik b. Anas, the founder of Mālikism, puts forward two lines of argumentation against astrology that are very simple but effective, and will appear recurrently in the literature of this kind. On the one hand, he presents some examples of facts that contradict astrology, thus implicitly alluding to the argument of experience; on the other hand, he treats astrology as a deviant doctrine that diverges from the Koran and the opinion of religious authorities that complement the sayings of Mālik.

Against the astronomy and astrology of the Greek tradition, Ibn Ḥabīb places Arabic folk astronomy, which he combines with materials of a scientific kind such as the existence of lunar and solar zodiacs made by regular divisions of the ecliptic. Interestingly, Ibn Ḥabīb had a certain awareness of the fundamentals of the science that the Abbasid circles had begun to translate into Arabic from the Greek, Persian, and Sanskrit. Indeed, his treatises on scientific matters, the *Risāla fī l-nujūm* quoted above and the treatise on prophetic medicine (*Mukhtaṣar fī l-ṭibb*), prompt speculation that his aim was to Islamicise the rational sciences. Nevertheless, he did not accept any of the doctrines that might cast even the slightest shadow of doubt over his orthodoxy, such as the analogy between the macrocosmos and the microcosmos.

Underground Activity and Astrology's First Revival

Astrology led a largely clandestine life during a part of the tenth century, yet historical evidence suggests that some courtiers practised this discipline privately and were generally tolerated. On the other hand, we find the members of Ibn Masarra's circle—a focus of mysticism and esoteric knowledge—who were persecuted by the Umayyads. Fierro consistently argued some years ago

---

[4] Paul Kunitzsch, trans. and ed., ''Abd al-Malik b. Habīb's Book on the Stars', *Zeitschrift für Geschichte der Arabisch-Islamischen Wissenschaften* 9 (1994) and ''Abd al-Malik b. Habīb's Book on the Stars (Conclusion)', *Zeitschrift für Geschichte der Arabisch-Islamischen Wissenschaften* 11 (1997); cf. Balty-Guesdon, 'Médecins et hommes', pp. 135–39 and Forcada, 'Sciences of the Ancients', pp. 48–57.

that the *Ghāyat al-Ḥakīm* (the most famous treatise on magic, otherwise known as *Picatrix*) and *Rutbat al-Ḥakīm* (a treatise on alchemy) were written by Maslama b. Qāsim (d. 964), a disciple of Ibn Masarra.[5] Therefore, since at that time there were Andalusī scholars practising these esoteric disciplines which are closely akin to astrology, they would no doubt have had advanced astrological knowledge.[6] In addition, we have ample evidence of the fact that in the first third of the tenth century the Cordovan scholars were aware of the work of al-Kindī,[7] an author who wrote many treatises on astrology and related matters.

Astrology flourished once more during the caliphate of al-Ḥakam II (r. 961–975). Though there are no sources that state that the caliph showed a particular keenness, either for astrology or for any other science of the ancients, the most learned king that ever ruled al-Andalus had an astrologer in his service (Aḥmad b. Fāris), together with many other courtiers who practised scientific professions.[8] One of his maidservants could use the astrolabe and perform astronomical calculations;[9] his son, the caliph Hishām II, was an astrophile.[10] A treatise on paediatrics, apparently written in that era by the physician and courtier ʿArīb b. Saʿīd (d. 981), *K. Khalq al-janīn wa-tadbīr al-ḥabālā wa-l-mawlūdīn*, is one of the few medical books of al-Andalus that contains astrological materials.[11]

---

[5] Maribel Fierro, 'Bāṭinism in al-Andalus. Maslama b. Qāsim al-Qurṭubī (d. 353/964), author of the *Rutbat al-Ḥakīm* and the *Ġāyat al-Ḥakīm* (*Picatrix*)', *Studia Islamica* 84 (1996): pp. 87–112.

[6] It is worth noting in this regard that *Kitāb Ghāyat al-Ḥakīm* bears good evidence of the astrological knowledge of the time in which it was written inasmuch as its core issues are the techniques by which one may attract astral influences and employ them in the sublunary world (cf. *Kitāb Ghāyat al-Ḥakīm*, ed. Helmut Ritter (Leipzig: Teubner,1933), p. 54. and passim; the reader will find more references to the astrological and magical sources of the book in Helmut Ritter and Martin Plessner, *'Picatrix': Das Ziel des Weisen von Pseudo-Mağrīṭī* (London: Warburg Institute, 1962), introduction and index, and in David Pingree, 'Some of the Sources of the *Ghāyat al-Ḥakīm*', *Journal of the Warburg and Courtauld Institutes* 43 (1980): pp. 1–15.

[7] Forcada, 'Sciences of the Ancients', p. 28.

[8] Miquel Forcada, 'Astrology and Folk Astronomy in al-Andalus: the *Mukhtaṣar min al-Anwā'* of Aḥmad b. Fāris', *Suhayl* 1 (2000): pp. 108–13.

[9] Balty-Guesdon, 'Médecins et hommes', p. 405.

[10] Vernet, *El islam de España*, p. 180.

[11] ʿArīb b. Saʿīd, *Kitāb Khalq al-Janīn wa-tadbīr al-ḥabālā wa-l-mawlūdīn*', ed. Henri Jahier

Maslama al-Majrīṭī (d. ca. 398/1007),[12] the most important mathematician and astronomer of the Umayyad period, also appears to have flourished at this time, or slightly earlier. Though there is little historical evidence of his astrological activity,[13] the fact that he was probably the most important astrologer of his time is witnessed by his version of al-Khwārizmī's astronomical tables: he included a set of astrological tables in his own hand which contains, among several features, a procedure for the projection of rays that improved on al-Khwārizmī's original technique.[14] He also left a group of numerous disciples, among them some excellent astrologers.

In fact, the best evidence of the momentum of astrology during al-Ḥakam II's reign is an argument *a contrario*: the harsh persecution of astrology and philosophy imposed by al-Manṣūr (d. 1002) shortly after the caliph's death, which would never have occurred if astrology had not been widespread in courtly and scholarly circles. As is well known, the *ḥājib* (i.e., prime minister) al-Manṣūr usurped *de facto* the Umayyad throne taking advantage of the minority of its heir, Hishām II (r. 976–1009 and 1010–1013). In order to gain the legitimacy that could only be provided by religious scholars, he feigned strict religiosity and purged the royal library of the books that offended religious sensitivities—namely astrological and philosophical treatises—and persecuted several men of science.[15] Nonetheless, he himself had believed in astrology before this episode

---

and Abdelkader Noureddine (Algiers: Librairie Ferraris, 1956), pp. 57–60; about the astrological materials of the text, cf. Ron Barkaï, 'Médicine, astrologie et magie', in *À l'ombre d'Avicenne: la médecine au temps des caliphes,* coord. Éric Delpont (Paris: Institut du Monde Arabe, 1996), p. 190; on the author, Juan Castilla-Brazales, 'Ibn Sa'īd, 'Arīb', in *Biblioteca de al-Andalus,* ed. Jorge Lirola and José Miguel Puerta Vílchez, vol. 5 (Almería: Fundación Ibn Tufayl de Estudios Árabes, 2007), pp. 119–26.

[12] For a recent and complete synthesis about his life and astronomical/astrological works, cf. Casulleras, 'Majrīṭī: Abū l-Qāsim Maslama ibn Aḥmad al-Ḥāsib al-Faraḍī al-Majrīṭī', in *Biographical Encyclopedia of Astronomers,* ed. Thomas Hockey, et al., vol. 2 (New York: Springer, 2007).

[13] Vernet, *El islam de España,* pp. 184–85.

[14] This procedure is studied in Jan P. Hogendijk, 'The Mathematical Structure of Two Islamic Astrological Tables for "Casting the Rays"', *Centaurus* 32 (1989).

[15] About this story cf. Maribel Fierro, *La heterodoxia en al-Andalus durante el periodo omeya,* (Madrid: *Instituto Hispano-Árabe de Cultura,* 1987), p. 161, and Balty-Guesdon, 'Médecins et hommes', p. 234.

and continued to believe in it afterwards,[16] in much the same way as Hishām II, the caliph who ruled nominally. Luckily for Andalusī astrology, the regime of al-Manṣūr and his heirs ended in 1009 and, during the tempestuous years that saw the collapse of the Umayyad caliphate (the *fitna*, 1009–1031), astrology kept its place in the service of the Umayyad rulers and of the courtly circles. Maslama's disciple Ibn al-Khayyāṭ is credited with having been the astrologer of the caliph Sulaymān al-Musta'īn (r. 1009 and 1013–1016) and other princes of the period;[17] another disciple of Maslama, Ibn al-Kattānī (d. 1029), earned a large amount of money from the training and selling of maid-slave singers (the *qiyān*, the Arabic version of the gheishas), to whom he taught astrology and astronomy and other theoretical sciences (arithmetic, geometry, music, logic, philosophy and medicine).[18]

The Golden Age of Astrology: Astrology Tolerated

As is well known various dynasties shared out the political power left by Cordova after the Umayyad collapse. In the process, the cultural legacy of the Umayyad state spread throughout the Iberian Peninsula and created several foci of sciences and letters in which astrology again found a favourable environment. Even assuming that almost all medieval rulers had a natural fondness for astrology, a question remains to be answered: why did the attitude of the Andalusī petty kings towards astrology change so dramatically?

Though we lack precise studies on the issue, we might reasonably surmise that several favourable circumstances would have converged at one and the same time. First, a large number of astrologers had been trained during the epoch of al-Ḥakam II and were now ready to offer their services to the new rulers; second, the influence of religious scholars on political power seems to have diminished, at least momentarily; third, as the persecution of heterodoxy

---

16 Vernet, *El islam de España*, pp. 181–82.

17 Ṣā'id al-Andalusī, *Ṭabaqāt al-umam*, ed. Ḥayāt Bū 'Alwān (Beirut: Dār al-Talī'a, 1985), p. 199. It is worth remembering that there are ten Umayyad caliphs in al-Andalus between 1009 and 1031.

18 Manuela Marín, *Mujeres en al-Andalus: Estudios Onomástico-biográficos de al-Andalus* (Madrid: Consejo Superior de Investigaciones Científicas, 2000), pp. 642–44. On the author, cf. S. Sadiq and Jorge Lirola, 'Ibn al-Kattānī, Abū 'Abd Allāh', in *Biblioteca de al-Andalus*, ed. Jorge Lirola and José Miguel Puerta Vilchez, vol. 3 (Almería: Fundación Ibn Tufayl de Estudios Árabes, 2004), pp. 735–38.

was no longer a priority for the new dynasties, none of the kings had the need to take up the banner of pure religion.

Nevertheless, astrology was far from being accepted as a legal practice by the religious scholars and its practitioners were well aware that their discipline was, at best, tolerated. Two of the most conspicuous Andalusī 'astrolophiles' of this time bear witness to the ambivalent social attitude towards the discipline. The first is Ṣā'id al-Andalusī (d. 1070), the well-known judge-astronomer to whom we owe much of the progress made in mathematical astronomy and astrology during the eleventh century. His most famous bio-bibliographical treatise on science and scientists, *Kitāb Ṭabaqāt al-umam,* (written in 1068), which speaks at length of astrology and of the astrological works written by the Andalusīs, states that astrology is not permitted by the '[legal] schools of al-Andalus' (*madhāhib al-Andalus*).[19] The other 'astrolophile' is the Zirid king of Granada, 'Abd Allāh b. Buluggīn (r. 1075–1090). His memoirs (*Tibyān 'an al-ḥāditha al-kā'ina bi-dawlat Banī Zīrī fi Gharnaṭa*) are not only one of the most useful sources for the period but also the best testimony of the contradictory feelings that astrology aroused in the soul of a Muslim ruler (albeit not a particularly pious one). Perhaps it was because of his guilty conscience that such a large part of the book is devoted to astrology,[20] which appears, interestingly enough, in a section that deals with drinking wine, yet another sinful habit. The king's belief in astrology is crystal clear from the outset ('everything is stamped at birth and in one's early life', he says), as is the need he feels to justify his belief. For this reason, he presents a complete case study of astrology that includes:

i. A thorough description of his natal horoscope (which means, of course, that he was brought up in a family that also believed in astrology).[21]

ii. General notions of astrology which are mentioned somewhat haphazardly.

---

[19] Ṣā'id al-Andalusī, *Ṭabaqāt al-umam,* p. 163, lines 13–14.

[20] 'Abd Allāh b. Buluggīn, *Tibyān,* English trans. Amin T. Tibi (Leiden: E.J. Brill, 1986), p. 181.

[21] For a study of this horoscope, cf. Julio Samsó, 'Sobre el horóscopo y la fecha de nacimiento de 'Abd Allāh, último rey zirí de Granada', *Boletín de la Real Academia de la Historia* 187 (1990): pp. 209–15.

iii. An apology for astrology.

Since this is the only text of this class that has come down to us from an Andalusī source of that period, we will examine it in more detail. The apology takes the shape of a reply (purportedly) made by one of the king's astrologers, whose name is not mentioned, to a criticism of astrology (purportedly) made by the king himself. The astrologer puts forward the following reasons to defend his discipline:

i. There is an interconnection between the upper and sublunary worlds.

ii. The astrological effects of the stars are of the same nature as the physical effects that one may verify empirically (viz. the light of the Sun).

iii. All these causes and effects have been planned by God.

iv. The stars are not the real agents of the events; rather they exert an influence on them.

v. Following on from the above point, the astrologer does not say what will happen but what the stars indicate will happen; therefore, astrology does not deny the Koranic assertion that only God knows the unknown.

vi. The general characters that stars imprint on humankind are borne out by experience: Muslims, who are governed by Venus, share with it the characters of being clean, virtuous, faithful and so on; by the same token, Christians are white and tend to celibacy because of the Sun, and Jews are miserly and wicked because of Saturn. There is also a strong correlation between planets and the horoscope and the calendar of these communities: Friday is the Muslims' day because it is Venus' day, and similar relationships apply in the case of Christians (Sun and Sunday) and Jews (Saturn and Saturday). Furthermore, the eighth, ninth and tenth houses of the zodiac correspond with the same months of the Muslim calendar.

As a conclusion, he says that not only is the astrologer by no means a heretic, but astrology is a form of genuine worship.[22] The apology contains some of the rationales that underlie Muslim science's most authoritative work on the matter, the first sections of Abū Ma'shar's *Mudkhal*,[23] yet the two texts differ considerably in many ways, not least that, unlike Abū Ma'shar, 'Abd Allāh's astrologer conveys his arguments to a public that is not trained in either scientific or theological speculation. His addressees (here represented by the king) are what we might call 'average members of the Andalusī upper class', who needed arguments to challenge the anti-astrological position of their religious leaders. Though 'Abd Allāh's astrologer is not as subtle and scientifically informed as Abū Ma'shar, he produces a convincing apology able to reassure a Muslim soul, provided that this soul has a previous bias towards astrology.

Astrology's Detractors: Religious Scholars against Astrology

Though the huge mass of legal and religious treatises that have come down to us from this period may contain a great deal of anti-astrological materials not yet discovered, there is evidence to state that the religious scholars of that period revitalized the old genre of anti-astrological literature in order to counter the flourishing of the practice in the eleventh century. In what follows, we shall survey the anti-astrological arguments contained in the œuvre of three of the most outstanding religious scholars of the period: Ibn 'Abd al-Barr (978–1071), Abū l-Walīd al-Bājī (1012–1081), and Ibn Ḥazm (991–1064).[24] To give an idea of

---

[22] 'Abd Allāh b. Buluggīn, *Tibyān*, trans. Tibi, pp. 182–83.

[23] Abū Ma'shar al-Balkhī, *Kitāb al-Mudkhal al-kabīr*, ed. Richard Lemay (Naples: Istituto Universitario Orientale, 1995), II: p. 30. It is worth noting that a disciple of Ṣā'id al-Andalusī, Abū Marwān al-Istījī, included scientific and philosophical arguments in favour of astrology in his *Epistle on Tasyīr* (cf. Julio Samsó and Hamid Berrani, 'The Epistle on *Tasyīr* and the projection of rays by Abū Marwān al-Istīji', *Suhayl* 5 (2005): pp. 170 and 177–82). Their study and comparison with Abū Ma'shar's argumentation is out of the scope of the present article.

[24] For a thorough and recent biobibliography of these authors, cf. respectively, Maribel Fierro, 'Ibn 'Abd al-Barr, Abū Umar' and 'Al-Bājī, Abū l-Walīd', in *Enciclopedia de al-Andalus, Diccionario de Autores y obras andalusíes*, eds. Jorge Lirola and José Miguel Puerta Vílchez (Granada: Fundación El Legado Andalusí, 2002), pp. 287–92 and 118–23, and José Miguel Puerta Vílchez and Rafael Ramón Guerrero, 'Ibn Ḥazm, Abū Muḥammad', in Jorge Lirola Delgado and José Miguel Puerta Vílchez, (eds.), *Biblioteca de al-Andalus, 3* (Almería: Fundación Ibn Tufayl de Estudios Árabes, 2004), pp. 392–443.

the importance of their anti-astrological works, it suffices to say that the two first appear to have been the most influential scholars of Andalusī Mālikism; and that the third, as is well known, was the finest thinker of the period in many fields, and particularly in law (according to Ẓāhirite rite) and theology. Therefore, in the case of Ibn Ḥazm, one must consider first and foremost the quality of his arguments against astrology, whereas in the case of Ibn ʻAbd al-Barr and al-Bājī, it is the quantitative impact of their anti-astrological works that is important, since these authors had a large audience among Andalusī Muslims.

Their texts are more sophisticated than the work of their forerunner Ibn Ḥabīb, mentioned above. Unlike Ibn Ḥabīb, they do not refute Greek astronomy *in toto* because, at that time, Ptolemaic astronomy was widespread among learned elites; thus, religious scholars were obliged to regard it as a serious, even worthy, science and to differentiate it from astrology. In Abū l-Walīd al-Bājī's *Waṣiyya* (testament) the author plainly deemed astronomy and astrology to be important matters, as he provides some guidance for his heirs, warning them, first of all and without argumentation, that the believer in astrology is an apostate. He goes on to extol the usefulness of astronomy in religious worship (for the determination of *qibla* and prayer times). The use of the expression *taʻdīl al-kawākib* ('computation with astronomical data') strongly suggests that the author had in mind mathematical astronomy rather than Arabic folk astronomy. The text reads as follows:[25]

> Beware the judgements of the stars and prediction, for this to the believer means leaving religion and entering the group of the apostates. But the computation of the positions of celestial bodies (*taʻdīl al-kawākib*), the explanation of their characters, the knowledge of their risings and settings, the specification of their mansions and signs, and of the moments in which the Sun and Moon occupy them, the arrangement of their degrees in order to be guided by them, the knowledge of *qibla* direction, the hour divisions, prayer times according to shadows or to it [the stars], all this is something good which is attained by means of a known method of calculation and an intelligible aim of rightness. God the Sublime said: 'It is He who has appointed for you the stars, that by them you might be guided in the shadows of land and sea', and also: 'It is He who made the Sun a radiance, and the Moon a light, and determined it by stations, that you might know the number of years and the reckoning. God created that not save with the truth, distinguishing the signs to a

[25] Abū l-Walīd al-Bājī, *Waṣiyya*, ed. ʻAbd al-Raḥmān Hilāl (1955): p. 39.

people who know.

The second author, Ibn ‘Abd al-Barr, is of more interest to us since his anti-astrogical discourse appears in a treatise on religious knowledge (*Jāmī‘ bayān al-‘ilm wa-faḍlihi*), included in a classification of the sciences that the author sketches so as to define the relationship between religious and secular sciences.[26] His classification is three-tiered and distinguishes between major sciences (religious sciences), minor sciences (arts, crafts and elementary teachings such as reading and writing), and intermediate sciences, in which category, he includes arithmetic (actually, arithmetic and geometry), astronomy, medicine and music. After saying that no religion would admit the science of music and describing the disciplines that are included in 'arithmetic', he makes some further comments on astronomy:[27]

> As for astronomy (*tanjīm*), its benefit and usefulness, according to all religions, consists of [knowing] the course of the heaven; the path of the planets and the rising times of stars; day and night hours and the nocturnal and diurnal arc for any date and place; the distance of any place that lies between the equator and the North Pole and the eastern and western horizons; the appearance of the crescent; the rising time of the stars involved in *anwā'* and other stars as well, together with their path [...] and their longitude and latitude; the lunar and solar eclipses and their time and magnitude for any place; the periods of Sun, Moon and stars.
>
> Among the scholars, there are some who disapprove that one might know of some of these issues on account that no one must know anything that belongs to the hidden by means of astrology [*nijāma*], and that no one may attain a sound knowledge of these issues except the prophets, who are endowed by God with the awareness of what is impossible [for a human mind] to grasp.
>
> [These scholars] say: 'Nowadays, no one seeks to know the hidden except the ignorant, the gullible and the mendacious, for they are only able to talk, over and over again until the day we die, of that which refutes the knowledge they feign to possess. Those who cheat by means of astrology are like those who cheat by means

---

[26] On Ibn ‘Abd al-Barr's classification, cf. Anwar G. Chejne, *Ibn Ḥazm* (Chicago: Kazi Publications, 1982), pp. 88–92, Balty-Guesdon, 'Médecins et hommes', pp. 471–72 and Forcada, 'Ibn Bājja and the Classification of the Sciences in al-Andalus', *Arabic Sciences and Philosophy* 16, (2006): pp. 289–91.

[27] Ibn ‘Abd al-Barr, *Jāmī‘ bayān al-‘ilm wa-faḍli-hi* (Beirut, s.a.), 2nd part, p. 38, lines 9–22.

of omen, ornithomancy, chiromancy, scapulomancy, inspecting places bitten by mice, maculomancy, healing by mind, possession of *jinns*, and all that resembles these practices that no intelligence would admit because they bear no demonstration. There is nothing right in these issues because all that they manage to understand of them is precisely all in which they err (…). There is nothing right about truth anywhere but in the messages of the prophets'...

[This text is followed by a page that contains several sayings of the prophet against astrology, some of which speak of the danger of astrolatry.]

Several points of interest emerge from this text. First, as we will see in a moment, it is a precedent of the most famous epistle on the classification of the sciences written by Ibn Ḥazm under the title *Marātib al-'Ulūm*. Second, the text shows that some religious scholars like Ibn 'Abd al-Barr, growing up in Cordova during the second flourishing of astronomy and astrology described above, have accepted Ptolemaic astronomy as an orthodox science, whereas others remained very reluctant to do so. In spite of the fact that the anti-astrological section is attributed by the author to the group that also adopts a hostile stance towards astronomy, there is no doubt that both the pro- and contra-astronomy parties held the same opinion of astrology. Third, there are few arguments against astrology because its inconsistency is considered self-evident and is therefore taken for granted. Astrology is compared with the magical techniques of the charlatans and fortune tellers. Interestingly, the author is not particularly critical of the latter or of astrologers because he treats them as stupid rather than heretical; obviously, one does not sentence a fool to death. The main argument that Ibn 'Abd al-Barr puts forward against astrology is religious (no one can know the hidden save the prophets). Yet he does not develop it in detail since the prophetic sayings that are quoted refer to other aspects of the problem (i.e., astrology is like magic; it involves a belief in stars); the secondary argument that he uses (i.e., it is an irrational practice) suggests that the author has in mind the objections of the philosophers (i.e., its conclusions cannot be demonstrated); or, as we shall see in a moment, that he knew Abū Ma'shar's work.

Ibn Ḥazm proceeded along much the same lines as his master Ibn 'Abd al-Barr. Like the latter, he appreciated the benefits of mathematical astronomy as much as he despised astrology. He wrote against astrology on many occasions.

Although two of these texts have been the object of some study,[28] we still lack a full survey of his anti-astrological discourse. Here we explore the topic through an analysis of his *K. al-Fiṣal, Marātib al-'ulūm* and *Risālat al-Tawqīf 'alā shāri' al-najāt bi-ikhtiṣār al-ṭarīq*.

As is well known, Ibn Ḥazm was neither a scientist nor a true philosopher. Nevertheless, he had a thorough knowledge of the sciences of the Greek tradition. As for the sciences proper, there is little evidence of his proficiency but it is worth noting that he had a good awareness of Galenic[29] medicine and that, when he spoke about astrology, he showed some familiarity with its technical terminology and procedures.[30] What is more, he says in *Marātib al-'ulūm* that 'one has to be acquainted with astrology in order to realize its falsity for wrong cannot be known from right without a knowledge of astrology'.[31] He was above all a good logician, and we know by his own testimony that he owed much of his training in that discipline to the above-mentioned Ibn al-Kattānī, a multifaceted scientist who may also have taught him philosophy, medicine, mathematics, astronomy and astrology.[32] However, Ibn Ḥazm subordinated scientific knowledge to prophetical revelation and believed that only religious sciences led to salvation. The other sciences were, like language, divine gifts which served only for worldly purposes (namely earning money and preserving health).[33] Hence, he put all his scientific training at the service of religion; he used logic to provide a solid basis for his legal and theological doctrines, and philosophy to refute deviant doctrines (see, for example, his refutation of al-

[28] Chejne, *Ibn Ḥazm*, pp. 180–84 and Balty-Guesdon, 'Médecins et hommes', pp. 421–23, *apud* Ibn Ḥazm, *Kitāb al-Fiṣal* and *Marātib al-'ulūm*.

[29] Emilio García Gómez, 'El *collar de la paloma* y medicina occidental' in *Homenaje a Millás Vallicrosa*, vol. 1 (Madrid: Consejo Superior de Investigaciones Científicas, 1954) and Julio Samsó, 'En torno al *Collar de la Paloma* y la medicina', *Al-Andalus* 40 (1975): pp. 213–19.

[30] Ibn Ḥazm, *Marātib al-'ulūm*, ed. Iḥsān 'Abbās (Beirut: Al-Mu'assasa al-'Arabiyya li-l-Dirasāt wa-l-Nashr, 1987), 4: p. 71, lines 3.

[31] Ibn Ḥazm, ibid., p. 83, lines 4–6; trans. borrowed from Chejne, *Ibn Ḥazm*, p. 208. One must consider, moreover, that it is highly improbable that a young member of the Cordovan educated elite growing up after al-Manṣūr's death would have had no astrological training at all; in an autobiographical paragraph from his most famous work, *Ṭawq al-Ḥamāma*, Ibn Ḥazm himself intimates that someone cast his natal horoscope.

[32] Rafael Ramón Guerrero, 'El pensamiento griego en la obra de Ibn Ḥazm. Su *Kitāb al-Taqrīb*', *Anales del Seminario de Historia de la Filosofía* 19 (2002): pp. 37–38.

[33] Ibn Ḥazm, *Marātib al-'ulūm*, 4: p. 63, lines 3–5.

Kindī on the issue of God's causation).[34] He treated astronomy and astrology in much the same way, subscribing to the anti-astrological arguments already sketched by his master Ibn 'Abd al-Barr, and extolling at the same time the theoretical and practical value of Ptolemaic astronomy.[35]

His anti-astrological doctrines contain an original argument which stems from his ideas about the place that the 'worldly sciences' occupy in the scale of wisdom and their role in providing salvation: it does not matter whether astrology is right or wrong; even if it were right, it would still be useless. What is the benefit of knowing something that would happen anyway, besides anticipating pain and sorrow?[36]

> Occupation with astrology is meaningless. It is inescapable that what is said about the influence of the stars is either right or wrong, and there is no third alternative. If the influence of the stars is right, it has no usefulness except hastening anxiety, grief, misfortune, and trouble such as the occurrence of illness, tragedies, death of beloved ones, shortening of life, and the knowledge of offspring's corruptibility. If the advocates of astrology maintain that it is possible to repel all that, they will then contradict themselves in that astrology will have no reality of is own, for indeed, there is no way of rescinding the decreed truth. And if astrology is wrong, there is no point in occupying oneself with it.

It is worth noting that, in spite of his harshness against astrology, Ibn Ḥazm does not preclude all possibility of its being a science. Besides this consideration, his main argument against astrology is methodological (therefore philosophical) in nature: astrology is by no means a demonstrative science:[37]

> Judging by means of stars is false because it lacks demonstration. It is merely a

---

[34] On this question cf. Hans Daiber, 'Al-Kindī in al-Andalus. Ibn Ḥazm's Critique of his Metaphysics', *Actas del XII Congresso de la U.E.A.I.* (Madrid: Union Européenne d'Arabisants et d'Islamisants, 1986).

[35] Ibn Ḥazm, *Risālat al-Tawqīf 'alà shāri' al-najāt bi-ikhtiṣār al-ṭarīq*, ed. Iḥsān 'Abbās (1987), 3: pp. 132 i.f.–133, line 5; *Marātib al-'Ulūm*, 4: p. 69, lines 18–70, line 1 and 82, lines 15–16; *Kitāb al-Fiṣal*, 5: p. 37, lines 11–19. Ibn Ḥazm's arguments are: astronomy is a demonstrative science; it is a sign for man of God's creation; it is useful for religious time-keeping and for determining the *qibla*.

[36] Ibn Ḥazm, *Marātib al-'ulūm*, 4: p. 69, lines 9–15; trans. Chejne, *Ibn Ḥazm*, p. 197.

[37] Ibn Ḥazm, *Risālat al-Tawqīf*, 3: p. 133, lines 6–8.

> [groundless] claim. I cannot count how many times I have found verified the falsity of an astrologer's judgement, and if you want to realize this, you only have to try it out yourself. You will find that the falsity of astrologers is much greater than their truth, as happens with the warlock and the fortune-teller; indeed there is nothing to distinguish between them.

This text summarizes a longer case study that Ibn Ḥazm includes in *Marātib al-'ulūm*[38] whose main argument is drawn, not surprisingly, from Abū Ma'shar's *Mudkhal*, though Ibn Ḥazm does not mention him. As is well known, this treatise contains a long section devoted to refuting astrology's refuters, which addresses several arguments. The fifth chapter[39] criticizes those who say that astrology is not supported by sound experience: since any given set of stars will return to any given position only thousands of years later, there cannot be human experience of the effects produced by that particular position. The rationale underlying this argument is purely Aristotelian and shows that neither the unknown authors who were thinking about it for the first time nor Ibn Ḥazm were bad logicians: since scientific demonstration is based on irrefutable and universal premises which are brought forth by experience, and the empirical data about astrology are patently insufficient, there is no demonstration in astrology; therefore astrology is not a science. Abu Ma'shar objects that this is not true, for the astronomers inherit the experience of their predecessors; aware of this rejoinder, Ibn Ḥazm says that the civilizations whose history is well known (Sassanid or Greek) did not last enough to acquire the necessary experience, and that others (Syrian, Coptic, Chinese and so on) which might have had it, left few traces, if any, of their astronomical practice.[40]

From this first argument follows a second one:[41] a horoscope contains so many elements that an astrologer cannot calculate them all exactly; no one can calculate accurately enough the position occupied by several planets at the same time because, when we have obtained a value for a given planet, the others will have already moved a certain amount and so the following values will not correspond to the same moment. However fallacious this argument may seem, it makes it clear that to cast a horoscope is as humanly impossible as to gather

[38] Ibn Ḥazm, *Marātib al-'ulūm,* 4: p. 70. lines 3; cf. also *Kitāb al-Fiṣal,* 5: p. 38, lines 10.
[39] Abū Ma'shar al-Balkhī, *Kitāb al-Mudkhal al-kabīr,* 2: pp. 39–51.
[40] Ibn Ḥazm, *Marātib al-'ulūm,* 4: p. 70, lines 12–71, line 2.
[41] Ibn Ḥazm, ibid., p. 71. lines 2–7; cf. also *Kitāb al-Fiṣal,* 5: p. 38, lines 16–20.

sufficient experience on the interrelation between the stars and the sublunary world.[42]

According to Ibn Ḥazm, experience does not provide good evidence in favour of astrology but, in fact, refutes it in many instances. His arguments may be summarized as follows:[43]

i. According to astrology, the planets assign to some individuals a violent death and to others a natural death; however, the fate of domestic animals refutes this assumption since some (hens, cows and so on) are usually slaughtered whereas others (mules, horses and so on) usually die a natural death, regardless of the planets under which they were born. [This is followed by a similar example focused on the prevalence of castration among people who live in certain climates, but here Ibn Ḥazm's reasoning is much weaker.]

ii. Experience shows that one may overcome the 'judgement of stars', yet if they were true and irrevocable no one could alter them.

iii. Experience shows that astrologers are wrong far more often than they are right

The experiential and methodological arguments are complemented with yet another reason which also belongs to the sphere of philosophy (physics):[44] there cannot be a true interconnection between the stars and the sublunary world, for neither can an accident exceed the substance in which it inheres, nor can a substance go beyond the place marked out for it by God. Accordingly, the planets cannot convey their qualities (heat, cold and so on) to sublunary bodies. On the basis of this second argument, Ibn Ḥazm says that the assignment of the climates of the earth or the parts of the human body to the influence of a planet

---

42 Obviously, an astrologer who uses astronomical tables and instruments may calculate any planetary position whenever and wherever he wants. Since it is difficult to believe that Ibn Ḥazm was unaware of the endless capacity for calculation of medieval astronomers, one must assume that he did not trust in the efficacy of astronomers' tools, for the reasons mentioned above.

43 Ibn Ḥazm, *Kitāb al-Fiṣal*, 5: p. 39, lines 3–20.

44 Ibn Ḥazm, ibid., p. 38, lines 20–23.

is nonsense.[45] On the basis of both arguments, the author criticizes the parallelism that astrologers draw between astrological influences and human experience of celestial influences (tides, the growth of plants and so on). Nobody can deny that these phenomena exist, yet they are brought forth by certain faculties that God has created in the planets and cannot be compared to the purported effects of astrological influences.[46]

One of the conclusions that Ibn Ḥazm reaches on the basis of rational arguments is that astrology corresponds to the magic that foretells the future by dubious means like the use of scapulae or pebbles.[47] This assumption leads to another line of reasoning that is religious in character. Its core issue is the extent to which it is possible for a human being to know the hidden. Obviously, Ibn Ḥazm says that only the prophets can do this, but he also makes an interesting point about the difference between a prophet's awareness of the hidden and divination.[48] The prophet does not use any technique to gain his knowledge, which is miraculous and infallible; the fortune-teller, although he does not know the hidden, may be right when he uses his divinatory technique. What is more, Ibn Ḥazm holds that true divination existed until the advent of Muḥammad, and that the extinction of divination was one of the signs of his advent.[49] Put another way, Ibn Ḥazm accepts the very existence of divination in much the same way as he concedes that the basic theory of astrology may not be totally wrong, yet both are out of human reach.

In this way, Ibn Ḥazm differentiates between two kinds of believers in

---

[45] Ibn Ḥazm, ibid., p. 38, lines 25–39, line 3.

[46] Ibn Ḥazm, ibid., p. 38, lines 2–10.

[47] Ibn Ḥazm, ibid., p. 39, lines 17–20.

[48] Ibn Ḥazm, ibid., p. 39, lines 22–40, line 1.

[49] It is interesting to note that the early Christians say something similar about the advent of Christianity, i.e., that after Christianity, astrology is no longer effective (Tertullian, *De idol.* 9.4) and that until baptism, Fate is true but after it astrologers can no longer arrive at the truth (Theodotus, 78.1). I owe this information to Dorian Greenbaum, whom I thank for it. As is well known, Ibn Ḥazm had a good knowledge of Christian religion, which he criticized in many works, among them *Kitāb al-Fisal* quoted above. We know by his own witness that he discussed with Christians, although he does not mention their names (cf. Abdeliah Ljamai, *Ibn Hazm et la Polémique islamo-chrétienne dans l'histoire de l'islam* (Leiden: Brill, 2003), pp. 37–42).

astrology:[50] on the one hand, those who think that planets and stars are endowed with senses, soul and will, and intervene voluntarily in the sublunary world; on the other, those who think that planets and stars are mere indicators of future events. The former profess astrolatry and therefore deserve to be considered as heretics and punished accordingly (death and confiscation of their property), whereas the latter are merely mistaken people who cannot be regarded as either heretics or infidels. Accordingly, the king, ʻAbd Allāh, and his astrologer come under the second category, like most other Andalusīs.

Philosophers against Astrology

Two major trends concerning astrology emerged among the Islamic philosophers. On the one hand were the followers of al-Kindī (among them Abū Maʻshar), who fully accepted the discipline once they were able to resolve the contradiction between astrological determinism and free will.[51] On the other were the followers of al-Fārābī (among them Ibn Sīnā), who flatly rejected it on the basis of the methodological arguments already discussed and because al-Fārābī thought that celestial influences were not powerful enough to determine human volition.[52]

It is worth noting that two of the main topics found in Ibn ʻAbd al-Barr's and Ibn Ḥazm's refutations (the methodological argument and the comparison of astrologers to fortune-tellers) appear as well in al-Fārābī's *Nukat fī mā yaṣiḥḥū wa-la yaṣṣiḥu min aḥkām al-nujūm*. This suggests that the religious scholars of the Andalusī knew this treatise and used it together with Abū Maʻshar's *Mudkhal*. Interestingly enough, it seems that both Ibn ʻAbd al-Barr and Ibn Ḥazm were more in tune with al-Fārābī than Andalusī philosophers, who seem to have

---

[50] Ibn Ḥazm, ibid., p. 37, line 20–38, line 2.

[51] Cf. above, n. 3.

[52] Cf. particularly al-Fārābī's *Nukat fī mā yaṣiḥḥū wa-la yaṣṣiḥu min aḥkām al-nujūm*, ed. Friedrich Dieterici (1890), pp. 104–13; on the anti-astrological writings of al-Fārābī, cf. Thérèse-Ann Druart, 'Astronomie et astrologie selon al-Fārābi', *Bulletin de Philosophie medievale* 20 (1978) and 'Le second traité de Fārābi sur la validité des affirmations basées sur la position des étoiles', *Bulletin de Philosophie medievale* 21 (1979); cf. also Yahya Michot, *Avicenne: Réfutation de l'astrologie* (Beirut: Les editions al-Bouraq, 2006), which contains the edition and study of *Ishārāt ilā fasād aḥkām al-nujūm*. For an overview of the philosopher's attitude towards astrology, cf. George Saliba, 'The Role of the Astrologer in Medieval Islamic Society', *Bulletin d'Études Orientales*, 44 (1992): pp. 46–47.

taken al-Kindī's lead during the eleventh and early twelfth centuries. The main centre of Andalusī philosophy in the eleventh century, the kingdom of Saragossa, is closely associated with the practice of astrology. First, the above-mentioned Ibn al-Kattānī and al-Kirmānī, two notable scholars trained in Cordova by Maslama al-Majrīṭī who were knowledgeable of philosophy, astronomy and astrology, lived and taught in Saragossa in the first half of the century.[53] Second, the most important sponsor of that philosophic and scientific circle, the king al-Mu'taman b. Hūd (d. 1085), is credited with being one of the best philosophers of his time and a firm believer in astrology as well.[54] Third, the library of the Saragossan kings is a treasure trove of astrological and magical texts that the Latin translators of the twelfth century were to exploit intensively.[55] Fourth, another of the rare treatises on magic written in al-Andalus issued from the hand of a Saragossan author, Abū Aflaḥ al-Saraqusṭī.

The evidence of belief in astrology among the main thinkers active during the first half of the twelfth century is contradictory. It is possible that the philosopher and linguist Ibn al-Sīd al-Baṭalyawsī, who was not from Saragossa but lived there for some time, believed in astrology; we know from one of his short tracts that he believed in alchemy, and he was also influenced by the epistles of the Brethren of Purity.[56] Abū l-Ṣalt al-Dānī, one of the rare philosophers of that period who had no links with the Saragossan circles, wrote a short anti-astrological poem;[57] but, as an expert on mathematical astronomy, he also composed a treatise on the equatorium, which is a useful instrument for an astrologer since it presents the position of the planets.[58]

---

[53]As for al-Kirmānī, we must remember that he brought to Saragossa the most famous *Epistles* of the Ikhwān al-Ṣafā' (Brethren of Purity), in which astrology plays an important part.

[54] The source is highly credible: 'Abd Allāh's memoirs, in which he quotes the testimony of one of al-Mu'taman's generals (cf. *Tibyān*, trans. Tibi, p. 94).

[55] Charles Burnett, 'The Translating Activity in Medieval Spain', in *The Legacy of Muslim Spain*, ed. Salma Khadra Jayyusi (Leiden: E.J. Brill, 1992), pp. 1040–41.

[56] Emilio Tornero, 'Las cuestiones filosóficas del *Kitāb al-Masā'il* de Ibn al-Sīd de Badajoz', *al-Qanṭara* 5 (1984): pp. 22, 28.

[57] Vernet, *el Islam de España*, p. 189.

[58] On Abū l-Ṣalt's astronomical works, cf. Mercé Comes, 'Ibn Abī l-Ṣalt al-Dānī Umayya', in *Enciclopedia de al-Andalus* (Granada: Fundación El Legado Andalusí, 2002), nos. 3, 4, 12, 18 and 21. He wrote moreover a treatise entitled *On Medicine, Astrology and Harmony*

Paradoxically, the apparent rejection of astrology seems to have had its roots in the Saragossan circles. Although again the evidence is indirect, one cannot dismiss the fact that al-Fārābī exerted a heavy influence on the first major Andalusī philosopher, the Saragossan Ibn Bājja (d. 1139), and that this influence was particularly intense in the field of scientific method. Ibn Bājja learned the *Organon* via al-Fārābī's epitomes and introductory works to logic, and much of his work is devoted to reconsidering scientific practices on the grounds of the Aristotelian scientific method. Though there is no direct evidence that Ibn Bājja was acquainted with the anti-astrological works by al-Fārābī (or by Ibn Sīnā, though this is fairly improbable), it is more than likely that he knew them; indeed, in all probability he came to the same conclusion as al-Fārābī after reading the latter's works that dealt in one way or another with the scientific method.[59] For this reason, he compared a doctrine of Galen that he judged as false with 'alchemy and astrology'.[60]

Besides this assertion, the textual evidences that we have of this Farabian line of criticism are scanty sentences in Ibn Rushd's works. The most famous of them appears in *Tahāfut al-tahāfut* and echoes what we can call 'the divination argument': 'astrology is not among them [the sciences], rather it is a foreknowledge of future events and thus is a kind of divination and augury'.[61] Needless to say, this sentence would require that Ibn Rushd, and seemingly his vast group of followers, espoused all that al-Fārābī and Ibn Sīnā had said about the inconsistency of astrology. It is therefore no surprise that in the courtly circles of the Almohads (the dynasty that ruled al-Andalus from the mid-twelfth century onwards), astrology was not practised at all; it had been banished not only by the religious ideology of the rulers, but also by the criticism of the philosophers who played prominent roles in the Almohad court as physicians,

---

which unfortunately has not come down to us.

59 Remember in this connection that Ibn Bājja criticized Ptolemaic astronomy because it was inconsistent with scientific method (cf. Miquel Forcada, 'Ibn Bājja', in *Medieval Science Technology and Medicine: An Encyclopedia*, eds. Thomas Glick, et al. [New York, London: Taylor & Francis Group, 2005]).

60 Ibn Bājja, *Tadbīr al-mutawaḥḥid*, ed. Mājid Fakhrī (Beirut, Dār al-Nahār, 1968), p. 44, line 1.

61 Ibn Rushd, *Tahāfut al-tahāfut*, ed. Sālim Dunyā (Cairo, Dār al-Ma`ārif, 1964), 2: p. 768, lines 12–14; English trans., Saliba, 'The Role of the Astrologer', p. 46, n. 9.

theologians and jurists.[62] Even the learned caliph Abū Ya'qūb Yūsuf could hardly allow himself to study astrology, in spite of his interest; when he heard that a Sevillian subject had a fine library on astrology in his home, the caliph had it confiscated and no one knows what happened to it.

Astrology in other Sciences

The presence of astrological materials in disciplines other than astrology is rare during the eleventh and twelfth centuries. There are few treatises on alchemy and the occult sciences – the fields most akin to astrology, especially, as we said above, after the *Ghāyat al-Ḥakīm* and *Rutbat al-Ḥakīm,* written in the mid tenth century. The references to astrology in the medical texts from the time of *K. al-Ḥabālā wa-l-mawlūdīn* by 'Arīb b. Sa'īd, written in the second half of the tenth century, are few and scanty. What is more, one of the rare medical treatises written in Arabic in the medieval Iberian Peninsula that contains astrological features, apart from 'Arīb's work, is a book written by a scholar who was neither Muslim nor Andalusī, the *K. al-Ṭibb al-qashṭālī al-malūkī,* written ca. 1312 by a virtually unknown Jewish physician in Castile.[63] One may add to these books the treatise on astrological obstetrics written by Ibn al-Kammād (fl. early twelfth century), *Kalām fī l-naymudār li-tasḥīḥ ṭawāli' al-mawālid,*[64] with the caveat that it is

---

[62] Miquel Forcada, 'Síntesis y contexto de las ciencias de los antiguos en época almohade', in *Los almohades: problemas y perspectivas,* eds. Patrice Cressier, Maribel Fierro and Luis Molina (Madrid: Consejo Superior de Investigaciones Científicas, 2005), 2, pp. 1107–10.

[63] Anonymous, *Kitāb al-Ṭibb al-qashṭālī al-malūkī,* ed. María de la Concepción Vázquez de Benito, 'El *Kitab al-ṭibb al-qašṭalī al-malūkī* (*Libro de medicina castellana regia*) (c. 1312)', in Expiración García Sánchez and Camilo Álvarez de Morales (eds.), *Ciencias de la naturaleza en al-Andalus. Textos y estudios, VII* (Granada: Consejo Superior de Investigaciones Científicas, 2004), pp. 32 and 71–73. The fragments deal with the planetary influence on the human body in general terms. The second fragment is particularly interesting. It says that since the motion of the planets varies in the course of time, and this motion influences the sublunar world, we may soundly believe that the size of human body has diminished since Galen's time; the author takes for granted that the bones of his predecessors are bigger than the bones of his contemporaries because many people have verified this fact for themselves.

[64] For a study and Catalan translation of this book, see Juan Vernet, 'Un tractat d'obstètrica', *Boletín de la Real Academia de Buenas Letras* 22 (1949); about the author, one of the rare astrologers in twelfth-century al-Andalus, see Comes, 'Ibn al-Kammād', *Biblioteca de al-Andalus,* eds. Jorge Lirola and José Miguel Puerta Vílchez, vol. 3 (Almería:

an astrological treatise on a medical subject rather than a medical book that contains astrology. To a large extent, it seems that the Andalusī physicians were still more reluctant to accept astrology than their Islamic colleagues,[65] not to mention Jewish and Christian physicians, perhaps on account of the adverse attitudes that we have mentioned earlier. The same would apply to magic remedies and doctrines, which are conspicuous by their little presence in the medical and pharmacological books of al-Andalus.[66]

Nevertheless, it is hard to believe that Andalusī physicians had no recourse at all to astrology – especially those who worked in courts that favoured it – or that they were not trained in this matter. In fact quite the opposite is true; insofar as astronomy and astrology were disciplines that had been regularly taught to future physicians since Antiquity, the biobibliographical sources[67] suggest that a considerable number of physicians were knowledgeable in medicine and astronomy (and therefore in astrology, though the biographical sources tend to be elusive on this matter); what is more, one of them appears as a professional astrologer.[68] So although the Andalusī physicians did not use astrology in their medical treatises, they did not overlook it completely.

A genre which is heavily indebted to medical science and which also contains

Fundación Ibn Tufayl de Estudios Árabes, 2004), pp. 732–34.

[65] Barkaï, 'Médecine', p. 189, states that astrology occupies a lesser place in Islamic medicine than in Latin and Jewish medicine.

[66] There are, however some references to non-scientific remedies of this kind. Cf., for instance, Fernando Girón Irueste, 'Estudio de algunas prácticas terapéuticas de tipo empírico-creencial contenidas en el *K. al-Jāmi'* de Ibn al-Bayṭār', in *Actas del XII Congreso de la U.E.A.I.* (Madrid: Union Européenne d'Arabisants et d'Islamisants, 1986), on Ibn al-Bayṭār (d. 1248); some other elements are noted in passing by Camilo Álvarez de Morales and Julia Carabaza in *Kitāb al-Adwiya al-mufrada* of Ibn Wāfid, d. 1075 (cf. *Biblioteca de al-Andalus*, ed. Jorge Lirola, vol. 5 (Almería: Fundación Ibn Tufayl de Estudios Árabes, 2007), pp. 565–69, at p. 566).

[67] The reader will find references to them in the bibliography given in n. 1 and in Miquel Forcada, 'Las ciencias de los antiguos en al-Andalus durante el periodo almohade: una aproximación biográfica', in *Estudios onomástico-biográficos de al-Andalus*, ed. M. L. Ávila and Maribel Fierro, vol. X (Madrid-Granada: Consejo Superior de Investigaciones Científicas, 2000), pp. 359–411.

[68] Ibn al-Khayyāt (d. 1055–1056), on whom see Julio Samsó and Jorge Lirola, 'Ibn al-Jayyāṭ', *Biblioteca de al-Andalus*, eds. Jorge Lirola and José Miguel Puerta Vílchez, vol. 3 (Almería: Fundación Ibn Tufayl de Estudios Árabes, 2004), pp. 723–25.

a large number of astrological texts is the agronomical treatise.[69] Though Andalusī agronomy follows the geoponic traditions that flourished around the Mediterranean since time immemorial (Roman, Byzantine and Mesopotamian), it also presents several original contributions. Its innovative character stems, on the one hand, from the experience that Andalusī agronomists could add to what they had inherited from their forerunners, and on the other, from a theoretical approach to agronomy which is rooted in the principles and methods of the physicians who specialized in botany and pharmacology.[70] As astrology was an important element in medieval medicine and physics, it is no surprise that it appears sporadically, but by no means rarely, in Andalusī treatises, especially if one considers that Andalusī agronomy flourished during the eleventh century in circles that were highly favourable to the discipline (the Toledan court of the Banū Dhī l-Nūn and the Sevillian court of the ʻAbbādids). It is likewise not surprising that these astrological materials coincided with elements of a magical and superstitious kind[71] since not only are they frequent in agriculture, but one of the most authoritative sources for Andalusī agronomists was the *Nabatean Agriculture,* a treatise which was considered in its own right as a source for magical books such as the above quoted *K. Ghāyat al-Ḥakīm.*

With a single exception (Ibn Baṣṣāl's *K. al-Filāḥa*), all the treatises written between the eleventh and twelfth centuries contain astrological materials in one way or another:

i. The treatise by Ibn Wāfid (d. 1075), not preserved in Arabic, contains a chapter on the choice of the best moment for building houses according to the Moon and lunar mansions.[72]

---

[69] For an overview of Andalusī agronomy see Expiración García Sánchez, 'Agriculture in Muslim Spain', in *The Legacy of Muslim Spain,* pp. 987–99 and Samsó, *Las ciencias,* passim.

[70] Samsó, *Las ciencias,* pp. 290–91. On the theoretical basis of Andalusī agronomy, see Lucie Bolens, *Agronomes andalous du Moyen-Age,* (Genéve-Paris: Droz, 1981), p. 50.

[71] Cf. Camilo Álvarez de Morales, 'Magia y superstición en la literatura agrícola andalusí' in *Ciencias de la Naturaleza en al-Andalus: Textos y Estudios III,* ed. Expiración García Sánchez (Granada: Consejo Superior de Invesigaciones Científicas, 1994), pp. 391–402 and Toufic Fahd, 'Sciences naturelles et magie dans *Gāyat al-ḥakīm* du Pseudo-Majrīṭī', in *Ciencias de la Naturaleza en al-Andalus. Textos y Estudios I,* ed. Expiración García Sánchez (Granada: Consejo Superior de Invesigaciones Científicas, 1990), pp. 11–21.

[72] Ibn Wāfid, *Kitāb al-Filāḥa,* Alfonsine trans., ed. Cipriano Cuadrado Romero (Málaga:

ii. *Al-Muqniʿ fī l-filāḥa* by Ibn al-Ḥajjāj (fl. eleventh c.) contains the same chapter on the time for building houses (probably an interpolation from Ibn Wāfid's text) and an agricultural calendar that specifies several moments in which the Moon exerts its influence.[73]

iii. *Kitāb al-Filāḥa* by Abū l-Khayr (fl. eleventh c.) [54-55] contains a specific chapter on the influence of the Moon on the crops and agricultural work and a mention of talismans.[74]

iv. *K. Zuhrat al-bustān wa-nuzhat al-adhhān* by al-Ṭighnarī (fl. between the eleventh and twelfth centuries) has a long introduction that contains astrological materials which deserve further comment (see below).

v. *K. al-Filāḥa* by Ibn al-ʿAwwām (fl. between the twelfth and thirteenth centuries) contains two chapters based on *Nabatean Agriculture* on the subject of astrometeorology and of talismans crafted according to astrological specifications.[75]

It is difficult to evaluate the role that astrology plays in Andalusī agronomic books since the only text that has come down to us in an almost complete form (only one chapter is missing) is Ibn al-ʿAwwām's treatise, which possibly dates from the thirteenth century. The other book in a good state of conservation, though not as good as Ibn al-ʿAwwām's treatise, is al-Ṭighnarī's work. Interestingly, these two treatises are the ones that contain the most astrological materials. In contrast, Ibn Wāfid's book presents an incidental reference to astrology which has little to do with agronomy but is, however, true astrology; Abū l-Jayr's book has only one chapter in which he systematically explains several aspects of the Moon's effects that have little to do with astrology; in much the same way, Ibn al-Ḥajjāj's book only makes sporadic references to solar

Universidad de Málaga, 1997), p. 80.

73 Ibn al-Ḥajjāj, *al-Muqniʿ fī l-filāḥa,* ed. Jarrar and Abū Ṣafya (Amman: The Jordanian Academy of Arabic Language, 1982), pp. 8, 64.

74 Abū l-Khayr, *Kitāb al-Filāḥa,* ed. Julia Carabaza (Madrid: M.A.E., Agencia Española de Cooperacion Internacional, 1991), pp. 50, 54.

75 Ibn al-ʿAwwām, *Kitāb al-Filāḥa,* ed. Josef Antonio Banqueri (Madrid: La Imprenta Real, 1802), II: pp. 337–39; 449–57.

and lunar effects in a chapter on the agricultural calendar. Nevertheless, astrology appears in all three, albeit in a very primitive form or only in passing.

In the other two treatises, astrology occupies a significant part, most particularly in al-Ṭighnarī's *K. Zuhrat al-bustān wa-nuzhat al-adhhān*. This latter is probably the most interesting work for us, since it is well preserved and belongs to the main trend of Andalusī agronomy (Ibn al-ʿAwwām was not a member of the geoponic schools of Toledo and Seville). Accordingly, *K. Zuhrat al-bustān* may be considered as the best expression of the concerns and methods of the schools of Seville and Toledo in the eleventh century. The body of the book is preceded by two introductions. The first one, which has a pronounced religious motivation, was added by an author from the fourteenth century or later who seems to have objected to the second introduction because of its astrological contents. The second is a long prologue which was written by the author himself on the basis of the introduction to al-Masʿūdī's *K. al-Tanbīh*. Al-Ṭighnarī approaches agronomy in this second prologue with astrological theory in much the same way as a physician would consider the human body as a reflection of the upper world and draws a parallelism between the Earth and the body which reads as follows:[76]

> The months are divided according to the zodiacal signs (…); the week has seven days which are divided according to the seven planets; the nights are divided according to the lunar mansions; the seven climates are likewise divided according to seven planets. This is because [the parts] of the world are bound to one another like the meaning hangs from the word, the branch from the root and the fruit from the tree, and everything that needs the assistance of its Creator must obey His omnipotence and affirm His sovereignty, for there is no God besides Him, the wise and the knowing.
>
> It is said about the earth that, in spite of its being cold, dry and the farthest thing from spiritual entities, if you consider it as the last part of the world, you will find that it bears close resemblance with man. Its liver is its contents of red clay; its blood, that of red ochre; its spleen, that of black clay and mud; its gallbladder, that of sulphur and arsenic; its joints are the mountains; its bones, the marble; its lungs, its content of clay; its guts are the big rivers; its veins, the channels and irrigation canals; its soul, its content of noble salts; its spirit, its gold and silver mines; its brain, its contents of gypsum and lime; its hair are the comets;

[76] Al-Ṭighnarī, *Kitāb Zuhrat al-bustān wa-nuzhat al-adhhān*, ed. Expiración García Sánchez (Madrid: Consejo Superior de Investigaciones Científicas, 2006), pp. 29–30.

its face, the gardens, flowers and beautiful plants.

Apart from this fragment, which is entirely original, the prologue contains the following sections that deal with astrology, astronomy and magic:[77]

i. On the solar year.

ii. On the analogy between the earth and the human body.

iii. On astrological geography, in which the author quotes Ptolemy via al-Masʻūdī.

iv. On the beginning of the year according to several cultures, in which the author mentions the dates of the winter solstice according to Battānī and the Sind-Hind tables.

v. On winds.

vi. On the Earth (its measurements, its inhabited parts and so on).

vii. On *raʻdiyya*, a divinatory technique that foretells what will happen the following year by means of hearing of thunder on some specific days.

viii. A chapter that explains what will happen the following year according to the day of the week in which the year begins. The planet that rules this day seems to exert its influence on the full year.

ix. On the events that are foretold by the behaviour of animals.

Conclusion: Why in Agronomy and not in Medicine?

It would seem that an Andalusī scholar of the eleventh or twelfth century had little reason to believe in astrology, because the anti-astrological arguments of philosophers and religious scholars were strong and consistent. Clearly, many of them considered astrology as a scientific discipline in its own right but its

[77] Al-Ṭighnarī, ibid.: i, p. 26, lines 6–29, line 11; ii, p. 29, lines 11–30, line 7; iii, p. 30, lines 8–34, line 2; iv, p. 34, lines 3–38, line 4; v, p. 38, lines 5–39, i.f.; vi, p. 40, lines 1–48, line 7; vii, p. 49, lines 1–51, line 13; viii, p. 51, lines 14–53, i.f.; ix, p. 54, lines 1–56, line 8.

practice seems to have been confined to the narrow limits of the circles specifically devoted to it.

There may be several reasons for the presence in agronomical treatises of the astrological materials that are not found in medical books. One is the diffusion of the treatises. The addressees of medical treatises were a relatively large community of physicians, and so a book could attract a relatively broad readership. In the case of agronomical books, we cannot be sure who their readership was, but they were probably read by a very small but select group. There is evidence that the governmental concern for improving agricultural yields may have helped to establish agronomical studies in al-Andalus in the tenth century. We also know that the sponsorship of Toledan and Sevillian dynasties made a strong contribution to the flourishing of agricultural studies in the eleventh century. It is certainly possible that agricultural treatises were first and foremost addressed to court officers who were more concerned with efficiency than with what was politically (and religiously) correct. It is worth noting in this regard that Andalusī treatises on agronomy, in spite of their theoretical basis drawn from medicine, were eminently practical. For this reason, the Andalusī geoponist most liked to quote techniques and procedures that he believed were backed up by the 'experience' of his predecessors, regardless of their real nature. This 'practice' encompassed a wide array of matters, ranging from grafting techniques to talismans against plagues prepared under certain astrological conditions, which were included mainly because they were genuinely believed to be effective.

KEPLER'S PERSONAL ASTROLOGY: TWO LETTERS TO MICHAEL MAESTLIN

Dorian Gieseler Greenbaum

Introduction

The astronomical work of Johannes Kepler has been justly praised and analysed since its publication during Kepler's life. His great works, *Mysterium Cosmographicum*, *Astronomia nova* and *Harmonice Mundi*, have made an impact on science and the history of science and have been translated into several modern languages. Two editions of Kepler's collected works, the *Opera Omnia* edited by Christian Frisch, and the ongoing *Gesammelte Werke*, have gathered most of Kepler's writing into a series of volumes.[1]

However, there is one area in which Kepler research has been less extensive. Although a body of secondary scholarship exists on the topic, Kepler's practice of astrology has not received the same attention as his astronomical writings.[2] The popular conception of Kepler's astrology is that it was something he 'had to do' to make a living.[3] While it is certainly true that Kepler drew up horoscopes and wrote astrological calendars and weather predictions for pay, as well as being the Imperial Mathematician for Rudolf II (who sometimes paid him), it is

[1] Johannes Kepler, *Opera Omnia*, ed. Christian Frisch, 8 vols. (Frankfurt-am-Main: Heyder & Zimmer, 1858–1871): hereafter *OO*; Johannes Kepler, *Gesammelte Werke*, eds. Max Caspar, Franz Hammer, Volker Bialas, et al., 21 vols. (Munich: C. H. Beck, 1938–): hereafter *GW*. Vol. 21, 2.2 (ed. F. Boockmann and D. A. Di Liscia, published 2009) contains the extant horoscopes and some strictly astrological texts.

[2] I have recently edited (and co-translated) a volume devoted to Kepler's writings on astrology: Dorian G. Greenbaum, ed., *Kepler's Astrology*, in *Culture and Cosmos* 14, nos. 1 and 2 (2010).

[3] As just one example, see Dr David Whitehouse, 'Medieval Astronomer's Horoscope Discovered', Sci-Tech section, BBC News online, 3 March 1999, at http://news.bbc.co.uk/1/hi/sci/tech/289730.stm, which contains statements like 'Kepler may have been sceptical about horoscopes but they were a profitable sideline' and, quoting Edward S. Holden (first director of the Lick Observatory, in 1896), 'But nothing is more suitable to recall the personality of Kepler than this piece of astrology, by means of which he kept the wolf from the door, and purchased the strength and leisure for higher things.' In recent years, serious scholarship on Kepler (as opposed to the popular press) has acknowledged Kepler's practice of astrology as a fundamental part of his intellectual life, though less attention has been paid to his personal use of astrology.

equally true that he believed the planets influenced life on earth and used astrology in his personal life, as well as delineating the astrology of his friends and colleagues. He was also passionate about reforming astrology as a science. One does not try to 'reform' a subject which one believes has no value and substance.

The purpose of this article is to explore one piece of Kepler's approach to the astrology he used in his personal life. Without embarking on a major study of his personal astrology, which is beyond the scope of this essay, it is possible to gain insight into the way Kepler used astrology personally by examining a set of letters written between March and June of 1598, when the births of two children made an impact on Kepler's life and the life of his former teacher from Tübingen, Michael Maestlin. These children were Kepler's first-born son, Heinrich, and Maestlin's son August. In Kepler's letters, written in March and June of 1598, he makes an analysis of Maestlin's and his son August's chart, followed by an analysis of his own and his son Heinrich's chart. The letters plainly show Kepler's personal interest in using astrology.[4] In addition, these two letters illustrate some of the techniques Kepler used in horoscope analysis, including what modern astrologers call synastry, the comparison of two (or more) charts. It is clear from this synastric analysis that Kepler looked for similar patterns within the different charts of the same family; for example, he not only describes astrological similarities and connections between the two Maestlin charts, but also links them to other Maestlin family charts. Sadly for both Kepler and Maestlin, their sons died in infancy, and the second letter sends touching condolences to Maestlin and lets us see some of Kepler's own pain on the death of his little boy.

To set the stage for the discussion of the letters, it will be useful to give some background information on both Kepler and his teacher.

---

[4] These letters are not unique in this regard: many more instances can be found in other letters and documents where his knowledge and use of astrology for personal reasons is evident. See, e.g., his correspondence with David Fabricius, a fellow astronomer/astrologer; his discussions of his grandparents' and parents' charts; and his astrological delineation of his own chart, his 'Self-Characterization' (Franz Hammer and Esther Hammer, *Johannes Kepler. Selbstzeugnisse* (Stuttgart-Bad Cannstatt: Friedrich Frommann Verlag [Günther Holzboog]), 1971, pp. 16–30), among others. For a study of Kepler's astrology, see, among others, Heinz A. Strauß and Sigrid Strauß-Kloebe, *Die Astrologie des Johannes Kepler: Eine Auswahl aus seinem Schriften* (Munich/Berlin: K. Oldenbourg, 1926); Franz Hammer, 'Die Astrologie des Johannes Kepler', *Sudhoffs Archiv: Zeitschrift für Wissenschaftsgeschichte* 55 (1971): pp. 113–35; and the issue of *Culture and Cosmos* devoted to Kepler's astrology (see n. 2).

Biographical Sketch: Kepler

Kepler was born in Weil der Stadt, in southern Germany, on 27 December, 1571 OS (6 January 1572 NS). He was the first child of Heinrich and Katharina (Guldenmann) Kepler, and was premature (a 'seven-months' baby').[5] He was sickly as a child, and was picked on at his school in Adelberg.[6] After attending the convent school at Maulbronn (where due to his slight build, he was chosen to portray Mariamme in a winter play, and became sick because of it)[7] he matriculated at the University of Tübingen, where he was to meet one of the greatest influences on his life, Michael Maestlin. As Professor of Mathematics at Tübingen, Maestlin introduced Kepler to the ideas of Copernicus. Throughout his life Kepler kept up a long correspondence with Maestlin, of which our two letters form a small part. He received his Master of Arts at Tübingen in August of 1591,[8] and in 1594 was appointed to the position of mathematics teacher in Graz. It was in Graz that his first son, Heinrich, named after Kepler's father, was born. Two years before Heinrich's birth, Kepler had put the finishing touches on his first great work of astronomy, *Mysterium Cosmographicum* ('A Cosmographic Mystery').[9] He was already a skilful astrologer: while a student in Tübingen, he became known among his compatriots for his casting of charts,[10] and had solicited another astrologer, Helisaeus Röslin, to delineate his own chart in 1592.[11]

---

5 Max Caspar, *Kepler*, trans. and ed. C. Doris Hellman, introd. and refs Owen Gingerich (New York: Dover, 1959), repr. 1993, p. 34.

6 See Letter to David Fabricius, 1 October 1602; *OO*, I, p. 311; no. 226 in *GW*, XIV, p. 275.488–91 (translation in Greenbaum, ed., *Kepler's Astrology*, p. 46).

7 See Edward Rosen, 'Kepler's Attitude toward Astrology and Mysticism', in *Occult and Scientific Mentalities in the Renaissance*, ed. Brian Vickers (Cambridge/London/New York: Cambridge University Press, 1984), pp. 253–72, here pp. 253–54; Letter to David Fabricius, 1 October 1602, *OO*, I, p. 310; no. 226 in *GW*, XIV, p. 275.473–79 (translation in Greenbaum, ed., *Kepler's Astrology*, pp. 45–46).

8 *GW*, XIX, pp. 319–20, 7.11. On p. 320: 'Anno Domini M.D.XCI. die XI. Augusti, M. Erhardo Cellio primum Decano, Magisterij ascenderunt ad honores hoc ordine: [1] Johannes Hippolytus Brentius Tübingen; [2] Johannes Keplerus Vuilensis'.

9 In *GW*, I (translated into English, German and French as 'The Secret of the Universe': Johannes Kepler, *Mysterium Cosmographicum: The Secret of the Universe*, trans. A.M. Duncan, intro. and comm. E.J. Aiton (New York: Abaris Books, 1981); Johannes Kepler, *Mysterium Cosmographicum: Das Weltgeheimnis*, intro. and trans. Max Caspar (Augsburg: Dr. Benno Filser Verlag, 1923); Johannes Kepler, *Le Secret du Monde*, intro., trans. and annot. Alain Segonds (Paris: Les Belles Lettres, 1984).

10 Caspar, *Kepler*, p. 48.

11 *GW*, 19, pp. 320–21; *OO*, vol. 8, pp. 294–95 (note that *OO* gives the date as 1593).

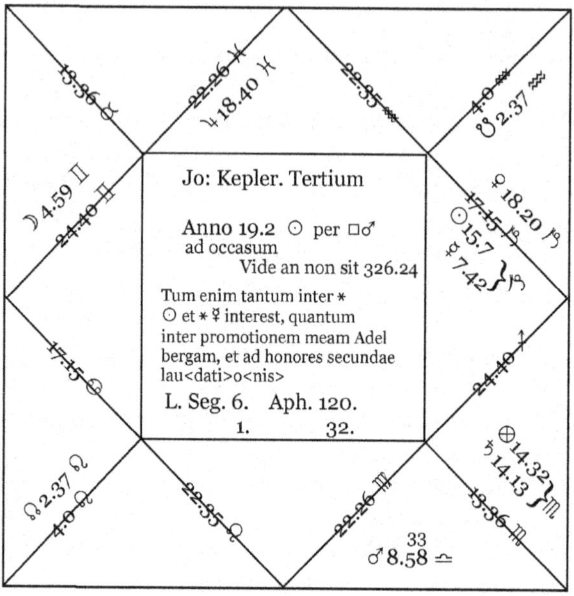
Jo: Kepler. Tertium
Anno 19.2 ☉ per □♂
ad occasum
Vide an non sit 326.24
Tum enim tantum inter ✱
☉ et ✱ ☿ interest, quantum
inter promotionem meam Adel
bergam, et ad honores secundae
lau<dati>o<nis>
L. Seg. 6. Aph. 120.
1. 32.
33
♂ 8.58 ♎

Fig. 1: Kepler's Birthchart transcribed from one in his own hand, corresponding to the positions sent to Röslin.[12]

While in Graz, Kepler began a courtship with the woman who was to become his first wife, Barbara Müller. After some difficulties with the courtship, the betrothal took place on 9 February, and he and Barbara were finally married on 27 April, 1597. In one of Kepler's letters to David Fabricius (a Lutheran pastor who was also an accomplished astronomer and astrologer), he makes the famous remark that he was married 'under a calamitous sky', and describes the unfortunate astrological circumstances: [transiting] Mars in opposition to Saturn, a Saturn which opposed his radix Jupiter, while [transiting] Jupiter opposed his radix Saturn.[13]

---

[12] Kepler drew up three versions of his birthchart, for the times of 1:00 PM, 1:30 PM and 2:30 PM. See *GW* XXI, 2.2, pp. 55–56, 70 for all three versions. The 2:30 chart, 'Tertium' (p. 70, Pulkowa XXI, 457v), pictured above, is what he used for his own work, and those positions were sent to Röslin.

[13] Letter to David Fabricius, 1 October 1602; *OO*, I, p. 311; *GW*, XIV, p. 276.522–23: 'Anno [15]97. ... 27 Aprilis nuptias celebravi calamitoso caelo. Erat ♂ in ☍♄ et ♄ in ☍♃ radicalis: contra ♃ in ☍♄ radicalis.' 'The year [15]97. On the 27th of April I celebrated my nuptials under a calamitous sky. Mars was in opposition to Saturn and Saturn was in opposition to radix Jupiter: against Jupiter in opposition to radix Saturn' (translation also

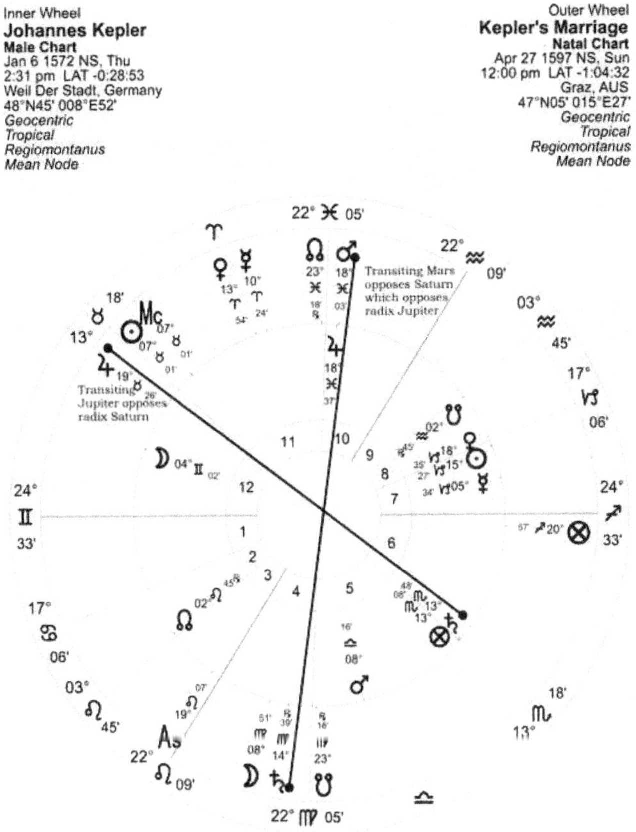

Fig. 2: Transiting planets for the marriage day compared with Kepler's chart[14]

In fact, the marriage was somewhat difficult[15] (perhaps foreshadowed by the problems with the courtship), and as early as 1599 Kepler even wrote

---

in Greenbaum, ed., *Kepler's Astrology*, pp. 49–50). Though Kepler mentions Jupiter in the 'radix', or natal chart, when he cites planets without a descriptor he means their position in the wedding, or 'transiting' chart (i.e., the planets moving in the sky at present) and their relationship to those in the radix. Transiting Mars is also conjoined (in about the same zodiacal longitude) to radix Jupiter, which Kepler does not mention.

14 For the purposes of the diagram, I have used a modern calculation programme (Solar Fire Gold) for Kepler's natal chart and the marriage; the modern calculations for Kepler's natal chart are close to, but not exactly the same as, his own computed positions.

15 See Caspar, *Kepler*, pp. 175–76.

disparagingly about his wife's characteristics in light of her birthchart:

> If you see a person in whose nativity the good planets Jupiter and Venus were not propitiously placed, you will see that such a person can be upright and wise and yet will lead a dismal and cheerless existence. Such a woman is known to me. She is praised throughout the city because of her virtue, modesty and humility. Yet she is simpleminded and fat. . . . Also she gives birth with difficulty.[16]

However, in the very early years of the marriage they were happier, especially when Barbara gave birth to their first son, Heinrich, in early February of 1598. Kepler wrote in his journal, which often included information on his solar returns, after he had cast his son's chart:

> Revolution of the year: The trine of Saturn and Jupiter in the radix signifies something great.[17] A son! A son, Heinrich Kepler, was born on 2 February. The stellar configurations bestow a noble disposition, nimble body, fingers and hands, suited for the mathematical and mechanical arts. The Moon in square to Saturn a strong imaginative power, diligence, though also mistrust and stinginess; from both [planets come] solicitude and deep thinking, devotion, compassion, sorrow – graceful. The Ascendant in square to the Sun supports those things, and with the brighter Libra southern in rising [*ortu*],[18] it signifies that he is stubborn and unruly, and admiring of greatness.[19]

---

[16] Letter to Herwart von Hohenburg, 9–10 April 1599, *GW*, XIII, no. 117, pp. 310.236–311.242: 'Videas hominem, in cuius genesi non commode siti sunt boni illi, Jupiter et Venus, . . . talem igitur hominem videas, quamvis probum et sapientem, invenustiori tamen et subtristi ut plurimum fortuna uti. Talis mihi nota faemina est. Laudatur tota urbe ob virtutem, pudorem, modestiam. Simplex tamen juxta est, et crasso corpore. . . . Etiam parit difficulter.' Translation of Caspar, *Kepler*, p. 76, slightly modified. See also Carola Baumgardt, *Johannes Kepler: Life and Letters* (New York: Philosophical Library, 1951 [London: Victor Gollancz Ltd, 1952, same pagination]), pp. 51–52.

[17] Although many of Kepler's personal solar returns (i.e., 'revolutions of the year') are extant, the one for 1598 does not appear in *GW*, 21,2.2. However, modern calculation of the return for 5 January 1598 NS in Graz does show a trine between Saturn (♎ 4°) and Jupiter (♊ 7°), as Kepler indicated.

[18] 'australi[s] in ortu'. This phrase is difficult, because Kepler often uses *ortus* for 'birth'. But if the Ascendant is Libra it is not, strictly speaking, 'southern' in the birth but eastern. If the Ascendant is Scorpio, then *ortus* could mean 'rising' here, in that Libra is rising in the southern quadrant toward the Midheaven in the south. The German version has 'südlich im Aufgang', so clearly Kepler does not mean the birth in general.

[19] *OO*, 8.2, p. 699: Revolutio anni: Trinus ♄ ♃ in radice significat aliquid magnum. En filium! Natus est filius Henricus Kepler d. 2 Februarii. Constellationes largiuntur ingenium nobile, corpus, digitos, manus agiles, mathematicis et mechanicis artibus

Unfortunately, any original diagram Kepler might have made of Heinrich's chart is not extant. We do possess a list of the planetary positions, Ascendant, Midheaven and Moon's nodes, culled from a comparison (entitled by him 'A Wonderful birth relationship' [*Mira cognatio*]) Kepler made between the charts of himself, his wife and the two eldest children, Regina (Barbara's daughter by her first marriage) and Heinrich.[20]

☉ ♒ 13.30°
☽ ♑ 2.0°
☿ ♒ 22.58°
♀ ♓ 28.3°
♂ ♊ 24.46°
♃ ♊ 5.54°
♄ ♎ 4.0°
☊ ♓ 8.10°; ☋ ♍ 8.10°
Ascendant ♎ 26; 7th house cusp ♈ 26°
Alternate Ascendant: ♏ 3°; 7th house cusp ♉ 3°
Midheaven ♌ 3°[21]

---

aptum. Luna in □♄ imaginativam vim fortem, industriam, suspicionem, tenacitatem; ex utraque curae, profundae cogitationes, devotio, miseratio, tristitia, – anmüetig. – Ascendens in □ ☉ adjuvat illa, et cum luminosiore ♎ australi[s] in ortu, pertinacem et indomitum significat et magna suscipientem. A very similar entry, in German, appears in J. Schmidt, *Johann Kepler: Sein Leben in Bildern und eigenen Berichten* (Linz: Rudolf Trauner Verlag, 1970), p. 227: 'Ein Sohn! Geboren ist der Sohn Heinrich Kepler am 2. Februar, die Stellungen der Gestirne verheißen edle Vernlagung, Körper, Finger, Hände beweglich, zu mathematischer und mechanischer Kunst befähigt. Der Mond in Quadratur zum Saturn verheißt starke Einbildungskraft, Fleiß, Argwohn, Geiz. Aus beiden Fürsorge, tiefes Denken, Frömmigkeit, Mitgefühl, Traurigkeit, Anmut. Der Aszendent in Quadratur zur Sonne unterstützt jene Eigenschaften and mit der lichtvolleren Waage südlich im Aufgang kennzeichnet einen Hartnäckigen, Ungebärdigen und das Große Bewundernden'.

20 *GW* XXI, 2.2, pp. 41–45: No. 73, 'Mira cognatio' ['A wonderful birth relationship'], astrological comparison of the birthcharts of Barbara Kepler, Regina Kepler, Johannes Kepler and Heinrich Kepler, Pulkova XXI, 429–32 (note that the transcription on p. 41 mistakenly lists a position for Jupiter, at ♎ 4.0°, but the glyph in the ms. is ♄, not ♃; Heinrich's actual Jupiter is given correctly as ♊ 5.54° on p. 42). Thanks to Peter Nockolds for inspecting and verifying the glyphs in the ms. (See a full translation of this text in Greenbaum, ed., *Kepler's Astrology*, pp. 55–63.)

21 Kepler gives a different position for Heinrich's Midheaven (♌ 23°) in his treatise *De directionibus* (1601), *OO*, vol. 8, p. 297; *GW*, 21.2.2, pp. 497–98 (see translation in

It is likely that a chart for Heinrich must have existed at one time, because the other charts in the comparison do exist,[22] and because of the further synastry mentioned in his letter to Maestlin (discussed below).

Biographical Sketch: Maestlin

While Kepler was celebrating his first-born son's birth in Graz, in Tübingen his old teacher Maestlin was also welcoming a son into the world, for his son August had been born about ten days earlier than Heinrich.

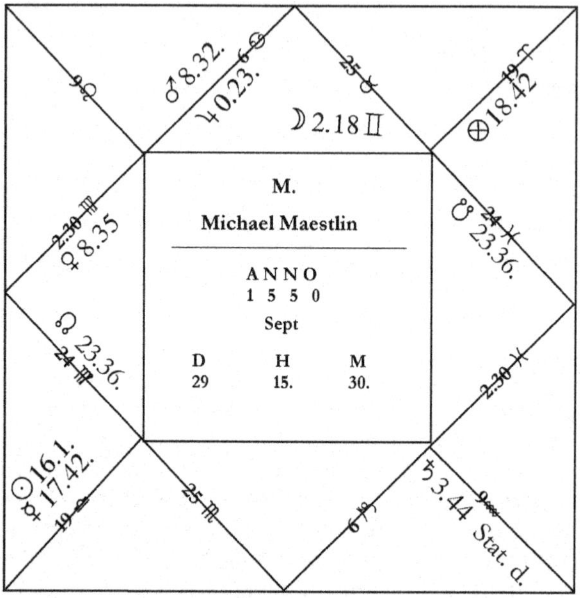

Fig. 3: Michael Maestlin's Birthchart transcribed from the one drawn by Kepler. (Pulkova, vol. 18, f. 223r)[23]

Michael Maestlin was born in 1550, but ended up outliving Kepler by one year. He had been the Professor of Mathematics and Astronomy at the University of Tübingen since 1583. He was, as Max Caspar declares, 'one of the most capable

Greenbaum, ed., *Kepler's Astrology*, pp. 242–43).

[22] See *GW* XXI, 2.2, pp. 41–45; Barbara's chart No. 59, p. 34; Regina's chart No. 60, pp. 34–35.

[23] See original image in Greenbaum, ed. *Kepler's Astrology*, Fig. 10, p. 325.

astronomers of the time and enjoyed great esteem in the learned world'.[24] He was a proficient observer of the heavens, the first to compute (though incorrectly) a comet's orbit, and also the first to calculate the golden section as a decimal, in a note written on one of Kepler's letters to him in 1597.[25]

Throughout his life, Kepler kept up his correspondence with Maestlin and treated him with great respect.[26] These letters included discussions of astrology on both a theoretical and personal level. Although Richard Jarrell, one of Maestlin's biographers, claimed he was against astrology and didn't even know how to cast a horoscope,[27] Charlotte Methuen has shown that Maestlin was not an opponent of astrology.[28] Certainly Kepler would not have written to Maestlin about the astrology of their two sons had he thought Maestlin was against it. Furthermore, these are not the only letters detailing the horoscopes of Maestlin's children: in his own hand, Maestlin also sent Kepler his newborn daughter Sabina's horoscope.[29]

In 1577 Maestlin married Margarethe Grüninger, the daughter of the mayor of Winnenden, with whom he had six children; she died in childbirth in 1588. He then married Margarete Burckhardt, daughter of another Tübingen professor, with whom he had eight children, one being the August mentioned in these letters. Maestlin wrote to Kepler on 2 May 1598, sadly informing him of August's death.

Kepler's Astrological Analysis: Michael and August Maestlin

Let us now turn to the letters themselves. (See the Appendix to this article for the letters and translation; page numbers in square brackets here refer to the Appendix.)

The excerpt from the first letter, which contains the astrological analysis, is

---

[24] Caspar, *Kepler*, p. 45.

[25] The calculation by Maestlin is found in a margin note on a letter Kepler sent to Maestlin at the beginning of October, 1597: *GW* XIII, pp. 140–44; the note (given on p. 144) refers to the figure on p. 142.

[26] Caspar, *Kepler*, p. 47.

[27] Richard A. Jarrell, 'Astrology at the University of Tübingen', in *Wissenschaftsgeschichte um Wilhem Schickard*, ed. Friedrich Seck (Tübingen: J.C.B. Mohr [Paul Siebeck], 1981), pp. 9–19, here p. 17.

[28] Charlotte Methuen, *Kepler's Tübingen: Stimulus to a Theological Mathematics* (Aldershot/Brookfield, VT/Singapore/Sydney: Ashgate, 1998), pp. 129 and n. 63, 130, 132.

[29] *GW*, XXI, 2.2, p. 413 (No. 1171) gives the chart; Maestlin's letter is in *GW* XIII, p. 368; and Kepler's reply in *GW*, XIV, p. 43.

part of a much longer letter to Maestlin about solar eclipses, and then about astrological theory. The first paragraph of the letter contains the famous quotation: 'I . . . am a Lutheran astrologer'.[30] Kepler was making an analogy with the Lutherans as reformers, namely those who keep the core and discard the frills. But this statement is extraneous to the real purpose of this section of the letter, which is for Kepler to make his astrological analyses of Maestlin's and his son's charts, and his own and his son's charts. The mechanism of comparison is set up in the first sentence of this section: 'A son, August, was born to you. . . . A son, Heinrich, was born to me. . . .'[31] (See Appendix, p. 196, paragraph 2, lines 1–2.)

Kepler's opening remarks point out August's Midheaven in Libra and his Ascendant in Sagittarius, and assert that the planetary configurations are 'extremely powerful' (*validissima*).[32] (See Appendix, p. 196, paragraph 2, line 8.) His next remarks concern comets and their relationships to planets, no doubt arising from his interest in mundane astrology and astro-meteorology.

The next section of the letter is, in my view, the most fruitful for understanding how Kepler approached chart delineation and comparison. Here Kepler makes his delineation using the synastry between Maestlin's chart and his son's. While the astrological technique of chart comparison has been known since antiquity,[33] this is an especially striking description of synastry written by an astrologer with a personal interest in the matter. In the letter to Maestlin, Kepler first notices similarities in aspect between Maestlin's and August's charts:[34]

- Both have Sun-Mercury conjunction (this, of course, is true of many charts, since the Sun and Mercury can never be more than 28 degrees from one another)
- Both have posterior Mercury[35]

---

[30] For a discussion of Kepler as a Lutheran astrologer, see J.V. Field, 'A Lutheran Astrologer: Johannes Kepler', *Archive for History of Exact Sciences* 31 (1984): pp. 189–272, esp. pp. 219–25.

[31] *GW*, XIII, p. 184.179–80: 'Natus tibi filius est Augustus. . . . Natus mihi est filius Henricus. . . .'

[32] Ibid., p. 184.183.

[33] Ptolemy (*Tetrabiblos*, IV, 5) and Hephaestio of Thebes (*Apotelesmatika*, II, 23) both describe methods for chart comparison, and the Tabula Bianchini, with its two sets of zodiac circles, seems set up to accommodate this practice.

[34] *GW*, XIII, p. 184.191–95 (see Appendix, p. 197, lines 1–13).

[35] In fact, the modern calculation of August's Mercury is 29° Capricorn, which will rise ahead of the Sun. But perhaps Kepler's calculation gave a different result (the position of

- Maestlin has a trine between Saturn and the Moon; August an approximate sextile
- Maestlin has an approximate trine between Saturn and the Sun; August also has a trine
- Maestlin's Jupiter and Mars are close; so are August's (but 18° apart)

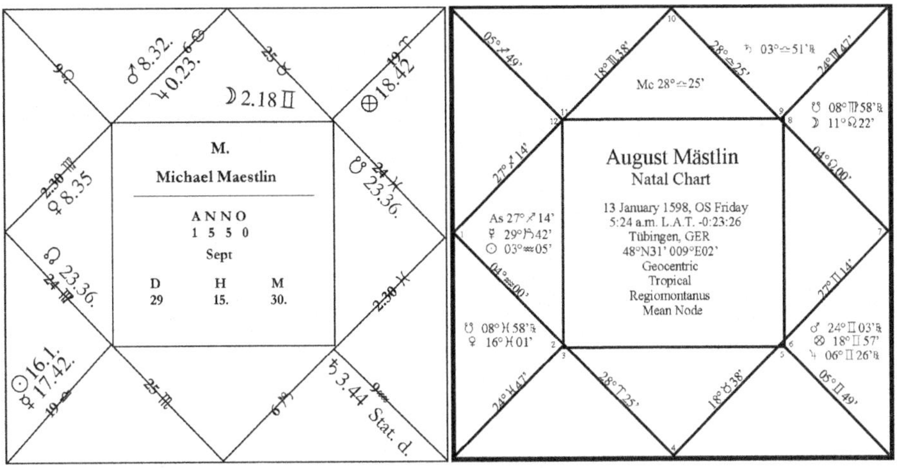

Fig. 4: Michael Maestlin's birthchart and August Maestlin's birthchart.[36]

Next, Kepler looks at the placement of planets vis-à-vis the other chart:[37]

- Maestlin's Saturn = August's Sun/Mercury
- Maestlin's Moon = August's Jupiter
- Maestlin's Venus = August's South Node
- Maestlin's Venus opposes August's Venus
- Maestlin's Jupiter (0° Cancer) ≈ August's Mars (24° Gemini)

Mercury is notoriously difficult to calculate). Michael Maestlin's Mercury, at 18° Libra, is posterior to the Sun at 16° Libra.

36 My transcription of Michael's nativity from Kepler's drawing. No chart for August has been found. I have used a modern calculation programme (Solar Fire Gold) for the birth date and time given in the letter. These positions probably do not exactly match the positions Kepler calculated.

37 *GW*, XIII, p. 184.193–95 (see Appendix, p. 197, lines 7–13).

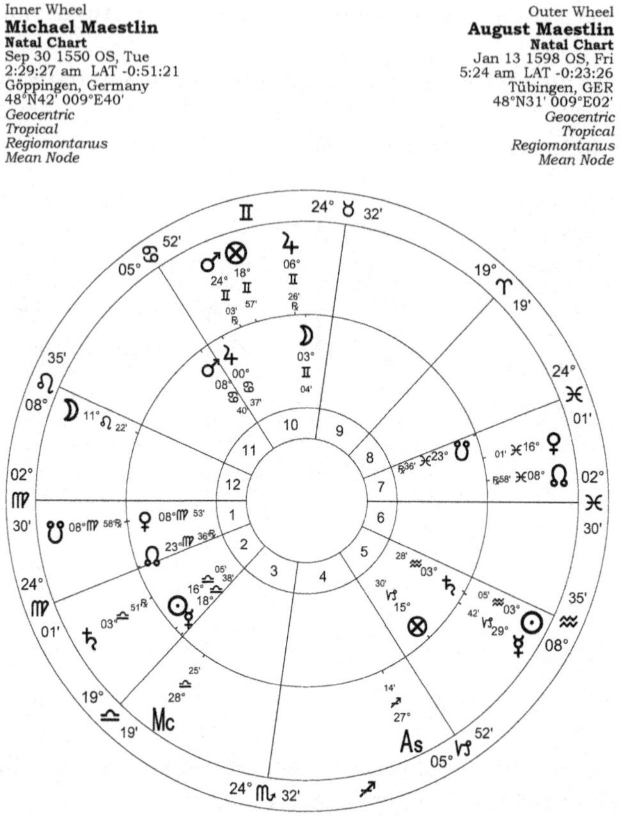

Fig. 5: Bi-wheel comparing Michael and August Maestlin's birthcharts.[38]

Kepler then makes an interesting comment about astrological family patterns, which he fears August has also inherited: 'Then I recall that most of your family have something bad in the seventh house. This is the case here as well. Mars is very close to the seventh'.[39] (Appendix, p. 197, lines 13–16.) As with the *Mira*

[38] This is a modern calculation (with the programme Solar Fire Gold) of the two charts, which results in slightly different longitudes for the planets, Sun and Moon. Michael Maestlin's ascendant of 2°30′ Virgo, as in Kepler's drawing, is used, whereas a chart cast for the given time of 15:30 hours from noon on 29 September (= 3:30 A.M., 30 September) would produce an ascendant of 13°30′ Virgo.

[39] *GW*, XIII, p. 184.195–197: 'Deinde, memini plerisque tuorum esse aliquid in septima mali. Hoc etiam hic est: Mars nempe prope 7mam.'

cognatio, this remark indicates that Kepler paid attention to astrological patterns in family charts (if not necessarily espousing astrological inheritance). The comment (perhaps unintentionally) also belies Kepler's own stated theoretical belief that houses were not important in astrology.[40] Is this an example of practice trumping theory?

Kepler ends his analysis of the charts by expressing his fear for the child's life and possible death by epilepsy, based on astrological aspects.[41] (Appendix, p. 197, lines 13–22, 30–32, 37–38; p. 198, lines 39–46.) He also delineates some features of the child's character from the planets: the trine of Mercury-Sun with Saturn making him thrifty and industrious; a good craftsman but also quarrelsome because of Mars in Gemini;[42] and emphasizing the trine of Saturn and Jupiter with the Sun-Mercury, a most propitious aspect (even in modern astrology). He closes by again expressing his fears about the child's survival based on aspects which form certain weather conditions.

Kepler's fears, sadly, were realised, for August did indeed die of epilepsy on 16 February 1598, his little body wracked with spasms.[43] Maestlin wrote to Kepler on 2 May 1598 with the news, and almost three months after his death

---

40 E.g., later in this letter he says: 'From this you will see that I do not reject anything from astrology, except for the useless instruments of the number-houses. . . .' *OO*, I, p. 299; *GW* XIII, p. 185.235–37); also his Letter to Thomas Harriot, 2 October 1606: 'For ten years I have rejected all these things – the division into 12 equal [signs], houses, rulerships, triplicities, etc. . . .' 'Ego iam a decennio divisionem in 12 aequalia, domus, dominationes, triplicitates etc. omnia rejicio. . . . *GW* XV, p. 349.74–76. (The same quotation in David Juste, 'Musical Theory and Astrological Foundations in Kepler: The Making of the New Aspects', in *Music and Esotericism*, ed. Laurence Wuidar [Leiden: Brill, 2010], pp. 178–79 and n. 5. I thank David Juste for bringing the quotation to my attention.)

41 *GW*, XIII, p. 184.197–200, 205, 208–09; p. 185.210–13. The canard that Kepler had predicted only good fortune for both his son and Maestlin's seems to have originated with Norbert Herz, *Keplers Astrologie* (Vienna: Carl Gerolds Sohn, 1895), p. 7: 'Beiden hatte er bei der Geburt die günstigen Prognosen gestellt – beide starben schon im ersten Lebensjahre.' The actual text, however, does not bear out this opinion.

42 Note that Kepler points out the sign of Mars and delineates from it, though he claims that zodiac signs are also to be rejected (see n. 40 above).

43 *GW*, XIII, Letter from Michael Maestlin to Kepler on 2 May 1598: p. 209.12–14: 'Etenim die ☿, qui fuit 15. Febr. epilepsia laborare cepit, hora noctis 8. Inde sequente die ♃ continuis paroxismis totum corpusculum enervatum fuit, ut hora noctis 10. postremum exhalaverit spiritum.' 'For on Wednesday, which was the 15th of February, he began to suffer from epilepsy, at the 8th hour of the night. Then on the following day, Thursday, his whole little body was weakened with continual paroxysms, so that at 10 o'clock at night he breathed his last.'

Maestlin's pain is yet unabated:

> Ah, where is my hope? my joy? those congratulations? They all ended in sorrow, tears and insurmountable sadness. . . . The Lord gave, the Lord took away, may God's name be blessed (ah, how painfully these things burst forth from my troubled heart). Yet may thy will be done, Lord. I cannot write more.[44]

Kepler's Astrological Analysis: Johannes and Heinrich Kepler
Kepler now turns to his own son's chart to perform the same kind of analysis. The comparison of Heinrich's and Johannes's charts detailed in the letter to Maestlin echoes parts of the *Mira cognatio* synastry where Kepler compared Heinrich's chart not only to his own chart, but to his wife's and stepdaughter's.[45] Kepler's synastric analysis included both similarity of planetary aspects and similarity of planetary postions. In fact, every common aspect or planetary position outlined in the letter to Maestlin can be found as well in the *Mira cognatio*.

Common Aspects

- Both have Jupiter trine Saturn
- Kepler has an 'almost partile' Mars-Mercury square; Heinrich has an 'almost partile Mars-Mercury trine

---

[44] Ibid., p. 209.14–16, 29–32: 'Ah ubi mea illa spes? meum gaudium? illae gratulationes? in maestitiam, lachrymas, et insuperabilem tristitiam omnia sunt resoluta. . . . Dominus dedit Dominus abstulit, Sit nomen Domini (·ah quam aegre haec ex perturbato corde prorumpunt·) benedictum. Verum fiat voluntas tua Domine. Plura scribere non possum.'
[45] See n. 21 for citation.

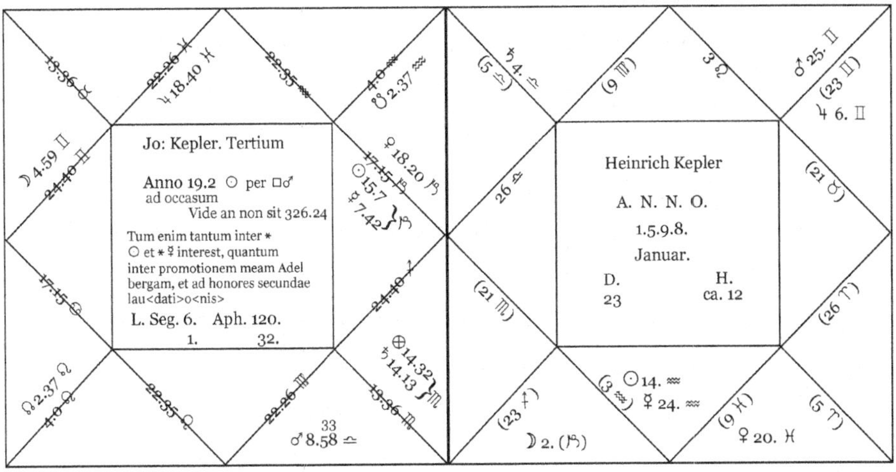
Jo: Kepler. Tertium
Anno 19.2 ☉ per □♂ ad occasum
Vide an non sit 326.24
Tum enim tantum inter * ☉ et * ☿ interest, quantum inter promotionem meam Adel bergam, et ad honores secundae lau<dati>o<nis>
L. Seg. 6. Aph. 120.
1. 32.
Heinrich Kepler
A. N. N. O.
1.5.9.8.
Januar.
D. 23
H. ca. 12

Fig. 6: Kepler's and Heinrich's charts.[46]

Placement of Planets

- Kepler's Ascendant = Heinrich's Mars
- Kepler's Moon = Heinrich's Jupiter
- Kepler's Mars = Heinrich's Saturn
- Kepler's Midheaven = Heinrich's Mercury

[46] Kepler's chart reproduces the style and positions of the diagram in his own hand which appears in Pulkowa XXI, folio 457v (see also in Fig. 1). Heinrich's chart is drawn in the square style Kepler used, incorporating the positions from *Mira cognatio* (calculations for Regiomontanus house cusps—not given in *Mira cognatio,* placed in parentheses—were made by a modern calculation programme, Solar Fire Gold). The bi-wheel of Figure 7, given for easier viewing of the comparison, uses the modern calculated positions.

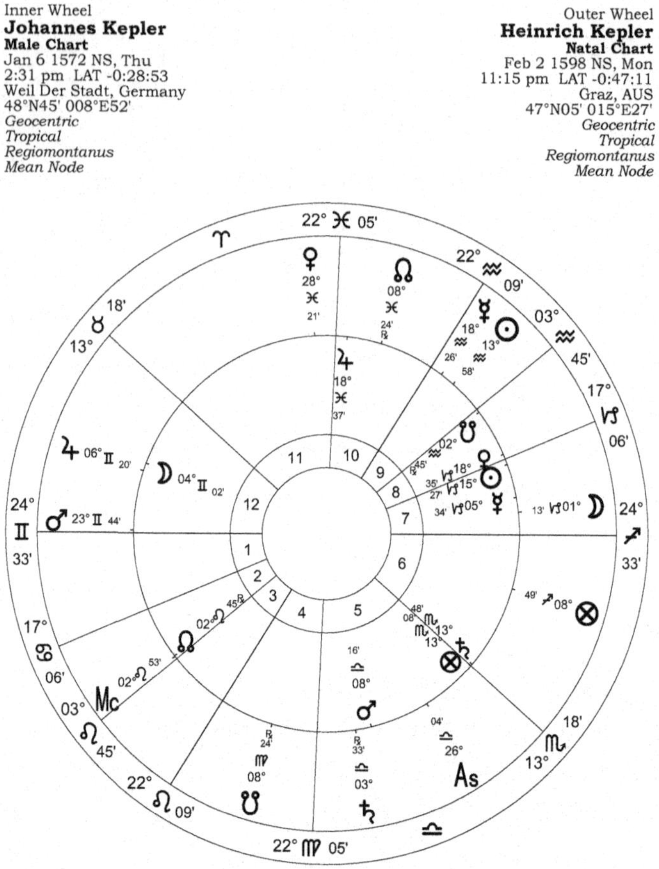

Fig. 7: Bi-wheel comparing Johannes and Heinrich Kepler's Charts

Again, as he did with Maestlin's son, Kepler delineates the child's character from the planets: Moon going from the opposition with Mars to a square with Saturn, Venus going from a square with Mars to opposition with Saturn, and Mercury trine Mars signify the child's insensitivity (as Kepler says, the malefics form aspects with the planets ruling the emotions, Venus and the Moon).[47] (Appendix, p. 198, second paragraph, lines 9–14.) Yet Mercury in Aquarius in the fourth house also 'makes him careless, popular and easy-going'.[48] But Kepler

47 *GW*, XIII, p. 185.219–21.

48 Ibid. p. 185.229–31: 'Facit et temerarium et populariter bonum atque facilem.' Again,

worries about eye damage and falls.[49] (Appendix, p. 198, second paragraph, lines 14–16.)

A strange comment stems from the affliction of Venus and the Moon by the malefics:

> And since Venus and the Moon are oppressed, he was therefore born monstrous. For the penis, signified by Venus and the Moon, is uncovered after Jewish custom, twisted back, and below the penis, next to the scrotum, he has another way for urine than other men have. The whole arrangement has the form of a cooked turtle in its shell, which is a favourite of my wife.[50]

Apparently Kepler associated a pregnant woman's diet with the physical features of her child.[51] In this case Kepler's wife, Barbara, was fond of turtle which, along with the Venus and Moon afflictions, caused Heinrich's genitals to be deformed! In this way we can see that Kepler did not depend entirely on the heavenly configuration of the birth chart to make his delineation, but also on other physical circumstances that (however foolish they may seem today) were deemed important as influences.

Kepler ends his analysis by pointing out other troubles from Heinrich's aspects, including impetuosity, carelessness, irascibility and 'of despicable manners'.[52] But the Mercury-Mars trine also makes him agile and fast[53] (Appendix, p. 199, lines 10–17.) (Kepler has already made similar remarks about these traits in his journal).[54] Finally, he worries about a bad solar revolution in

---

going against his theoretical principles, Kepler invokes the sign of the planet and its house in his delineation.

49 Ibid., p. 185.221–22.

50 Ibid., p. 185.223-27: 'Et quia Venus et ☽ laborant, ideo natus est monstrosus. Membrum enim virile, a ♀ et ☽ significatum, est instar Judaei retectum, retortum, et infra agnatum scroto, meatus urinae alius, quam ceteris hominibus. Totum compositum habet formam testudinis coctae in domuncula, quae sunt uxoris meae deliciae'.

51 Was this a common notion at the time? In his *Tertius Interveniens* (GW, IV), Kepler comments on the influence of a mother on her child 'through the imagination of the mother before birth and through rearing after birth'. (*Tertius Interveniens*, in *GW*, IV, p. 209–10, Thesis LXV: '. . . durch der Mutter Ennbildungen vor der Geburt / und durch die Auffzucht nach der Geburt', quoted and translated in Sheila J. Rabin, 'Two Renaissance Views of Astrology: Pico and Kepler' [PhD Thesis, The City University of New York, 1987], p. 176.)

52 *GW*, XIII, p. 185.232–233: 'contemptis moribus'.

53 Ibid., p. 185.229.

54 See p. 182 and n. 19.

1601, 'which will either take me or him away'.[55] (Appendix, p. 199, line 21.) Alas, poor Heinrich never made it to his 1601 solar return, but passed away on 3 April 1598, probably from meningitis (Kepler calls it an *apostema capitis*, an abscess in the head).[56]

Kepler, no less than his wife, was devastated. His letter of 11 June 1598 to Maestlin, after Maestlin's August had also died, is poignant and very touching: (Appendix, p. 200, lines 1–6.)

> I send my utmost condolences on the death of your little son. I can well imagine how great your pain was because of my own, as the highest and best God likewise called my little son Heinrich away from life at that very time which, as I wrote to you, I had feared.[57]

At this point, astrology is no solace, and Kepler can only mourn his son and the pointlessness of existence: 'Vanity of Vanities, all is Vanity' (Eccl. 1:2).[58] (Appendix, p. 200, lines 12–13.) His earlier analysis, almost clinical in its style, gives way to the pure emotion of loss.

Conclusions

What can we learn from Kepler's delineation of these charts? First and foremost, that Kepler took his astrology seriously, both in his personal and his professional life. Second, that he closely followed the astrology not only of his own family, but that of his friends as well. Third, that this was not a dilatory pastime; Kepler clearly spent many hours constructing both natal charts and subsidiary charts like solar returns for himself, his friends and their children.[59] It is also clear, even from looking at the few examples from these letters, that Kepler relied as well on rectification of charts to better match astrological circumstances with events and with chart comparison.[60]

---

[55] *GW*, XIII, p. 185.234–235: '. . . quae aut me aut ipsum tollet . . .'.

[56] See Caspar, *Kepler*, p. 77.

[57] *GW*, XIII, p. 228.360–63. Kepler did not exactly say this in his earlier letter, but referred to a period of danger in three years' time. Was he fudging his prediction, or had he forgotten the date?

[58] Ibid., p. 228.367: 'Vanitas Vanitatum et omnia Vanitas.'

[59] There are 1170 discrete charts (some partial charts), applying to 850 people in the new *GW* volume (21, 2.2) of Astrologica. These included many charts of his family members, as well as friends and clients.

[60] Rectification is an astrological technique which uses events in a person's life to try to find connections between the astrological positions for those events to the positions in the birth chart, thus pinpointing the most accurate moment of a birth. Note that Kepler has

We may draw as a fourth conclusion that Kepler considered synastry a necessary tool of analysis for members of the same family; and that he looked at similar aspects, placement of planets within the charts, and even family patterns to make this analysis. Kepler also used aspects between planets for a psychological analysis of character and temperament. In this he actually foreshadows modern psychological astrology, which is not dissimilar in this regard.[61]

In addition, in considering these letters we must compare the work of Kepler, the practising astrologer, to that of Kepler, the theoretician and self-proclaimed reformer of astrology. Certainly Kepler's commitment to reforming astrology included taking out what he calls 'frills' like houses and zodiac signs. However, his use of them in actual practice, as these letters demonstrate, shows that this elimination may have been easier said than done. Finally, far from considering astrology as just a paycheck, or even just as a theoretical exercise these letters, as examples of his practice, show how integral astrology was to the way that Kepler conducted his life both professionally and personally.

---

three versions of his own birth chart (he used the third, final version in his chart comparison), and that he proposed two different Ascendants and Midheavens for Heinrich.

61 See, e.g., Charles E.O. Carter, *The Astrological Aspects* (Romford, Essex: L.N. Fowler & Co., Ltd., 1967 [1930]) or Sue Tompkins, *Aspects in Astrology* (Longmead: Element Books, 1989).

Appendix: Kepler's Two Letters to Michael Maestlin
Translation by Cornelia Linde and Dorian Greenbaum: from the Latin text of the *Gesammelte Werke*, vol. 13, pp. 184–85, 228

Letter No. 1: 15 March 1598 (p. 184.173–179)
Optime praeceptor, an non | recte ago, si operam do, ut doctis et philosophis etiam operationem | caeli persuadeam distinctam? Ago itaque ut Jesuitae: qui multa emen | dant, ut homines catholicos [sic] faciant. Imo non ita ago, nam qui omnes | nugas defendunt, sunt Jesuitis similes, ego sum Lutheranus astrologus, | qui nugis abjectis retineo nucleum. Sed ecce non tantum volebam di | cere. Ad exemplum itaque venio.

O best of teachers, am I not acting correctly if I commit myself to convince the learned and the philosophers that the activity of the sky is properly established? I act therefore as the Jesuits do: they improve many things, in order to make men Catholics. Rather, I do not act like that, for those who defend all frills are like the Jesuits; I, who I retain the core after having discarded the frills, am a Lutheran astrologer. But look, I did not want to say that much. Therefore I will get to my example.

p. 184.179–191
Natus tibi filius est Augustus 13. Jan. | St. V. hor. 5.24 ante m. Natus mihi est filius Henricus diem inter 23 | et 24. Jan. St. V., paulo post h. 12 nocturnam. Sed de tuo. M.C. 28 ♎, Asc. | 27 ♐; ♂ ante 7mam, forte etiam in VII, ut paulo maturius acciderit. Constellatio validissima est. Aiunt cometam videri jam per 3 septi | manas. Id si est, non enim vidi, non dubito, quin ab illis 3 planetis | stantibus, ♃, ♂ in propinquo, △♃ ♄ diuturno, □♄, ♂ platico. Sum | enim in ea opinione, etsi cometa aliquis vel ipsa terra major sit, et altis | simus etiam, dummodo currat, terrae sobolem esse. Cur? Quia semper, | quotiescunque sunt cometae, praecessit paulo ante valida ♄, ♃ con | figuratio, aut aequipollens, ut cum ♂ est stationarius, tum enim vires | habet ut superior, re vera tardus. Configuratio autem, ut nosti, et aspectus | est in terra, non in caelo alibi.

A son, August, was born to you on 13 January (Old Style) at 5:24 a.m. A son, Heinrich, was born to me between 23 and 24 January (Old Style), a bit after midnight. But about your son. His Midheaven is 28° Libra, Ascendant 27° Sagittarius; Mars is just before the seventh house, perhaps even in the 7th, as if [the birth] had happened a bit earlier. The planetary configuration of the chart is extremely powerful. They say that a comet has been seen now for three weeks. If that is so, for I have not seen it, I do not doubt that from those three planets, Jupiter and Mars stationing near each other, Jupiter trining Saturn for a long while and Mars in platic square to Saturn.[62] I am of the opinion that even if a comet itself is bigger than the earth and also extremely high, even though it is running [through the sky], it is an offspring of the earth. Why? Because always, whenever there are comets, a a strong configuration of Saturn and Jupiter has occurred shortly before or, equally strong, that when Mars is stationary, it then has the same powers, as it is superior and, indeed, is slow. But the configuration, as you know, and the aspect, are on Earth, not elsewhere in the sky.

62 Jupiter went into trine, and Mars into square, with Saturn by sign in November of 1597. Mars separated from its square with Saturn in January of 1598, when it retrograded into Gemini. ('Platic' means an aspect which is not exact.)

p. 184.191–209

Vide autem cognationem thematum. Habes | tu ☌☉ ☿, habet et ille uterque ☿ posteriorem, habes tu △♄ ☽, habet et | ille fere ✶♄ ☽, habes tu fere △♄ ☉, habet et ille. Ubi tibi ♄, ipsi | ☉, ☿, ubi tibi ☽, ipsi ♃, ubi tibi ♀, ipsi ☋. Sunt vobis ♀ oppositae. Habes | tu ♃, ♂ vicinos, et ille. Ubi tibi ♃, fere illi ♂. Deinde, memini plerisque | tuorum esse aliquid in septima mali. Hoc etiam hic est: Mars nempe | prope 7mam. Ex eo est nonnihil, quod illius vitae metuam. Nam Luna | plena, et via lactea ascendens et Mars in ejus opposito, et Sol tam prae | cise in triangulo Saturni, videntur cerebro et oculis nocituri et epilepti | cum significare. Faciunt etiam praecipitio obnoxium, aut gibbum. Sed | triangulus Solis omnia mitigat. Erit parcus, tenax, ex ☿ et ☉ in △♄, | egregii ingenii et profundi atque laboriosi, propter eundem aspectum. | Optimus artifex, ob ♂ in II et confinio solstitii in VII. Contentiosus et | factiosus ob id. [Tales sunt plerumque bombardarum | studiosi.]* Sed victurus ne sit, dubito, propter id ipsum. Si tamen vivat, | magnus evadet vere. Habet enim triangulum ♄ ♃ ☉ ☿, qui sunt fortis | simi aspectus. Itaque vide, quid futurus December sit allaturus, cum post | humectationem a ♃ transeunte per 7, ☉ et ♂ ferventes succedunt. Si | nebulae erunt, ut credo, vix infans ab epilepsia liber erit,

But have a look at the relationship between the charts. You have a conjunction of Sun and Mercury and he has that as well. You both have a posterior Mercury.[63] You have a trine of Saturn and the Moon, and he has an approximate sextile of Saturn and the Moon. You have an approximate trine of Saturn and the Sun, and he has that as well. Where you have Saturn, he has the Sun and Mercury, where you have the Moon, he has Jupiter, where you have Venus he has the South Node. Your Venuses are opposed. You have Jupiter and Mars near each other; he has that as well. Where you have Jupiter, he has Mars, approximately. Then, I recall that most of your family have something bad in the seventh house. This is the case here as well: Mars is very close to the seventh. There is a certain amount to be deduced from that which causes me to fear for his life. For the full Moon, the Milky Way ascending and Mars opposite to it, and the Sun so precisely in trine to Saturn seem to signify that they will be hurtful to the brain and the eyes, that he will be epileptic. They also cause him to be liable to falling, or hunch-backed. But the trine of the Sun mitigates all this. He will be thrifty and steadfast due to Mercury and the Sun in trine with Saturn, of outstanding, profound and industrious nature because of the same aspect. The best craftsman, due to Mars in Gemini and the closeness of the solstice [degree] in the 7th. He will be quarrelsome and domineering because of that. Such people are often experts on fire arms. But for the same reason I doubt whether he will be victorious. However, if he lives, he truly will come out great. For he has a [grand] trine of Saturn, Jupiter, Sun and Mercury, which are extremely strong aspects. Therefore see what the coming December will bring when, after the moisture from Jupiter transiting the 7th, hot Sun and Mars follow. If there are fogs, as I believe, the little child will hardly

63 In fact, the modern calculation of August's Mercury is 29° Capricorn, which will rise ahead of the Sun. But perhaps Kepler's calculation was different. Michael Maestlin's Mercury at 18° Libra is posterior to the Sun (15° Libra).

p. 184.209–185.214
sunt enim haec | analoga. Sane Jovis situs non bonus est, non quidem propter II tanquam | suum casum: nam illustres cum ipso fixae sunt, unde propter hoc po | tens est; sed propterea, quia decidit ab angulo et opprimitur a ♄ alto | triangulo brevi, quod aequipollet quadrato. Haec et hujusmodi bona et | naturali ratione dicuntur, etsi non in specie quicquam dicitur.

be free from epilepsy; for these are analogous.[64] Certainly the position of Jupiter is not good, not because of Gemini inasmuch as it is its fall[65] (for bright fixed stars are with it, on account of which it is powerful);[66] but for the reason that he [Jupiter] has declined from the angle and is oppressed by Saturn [♄] from a superior trine in short ascension, which is equal in power to the square.[67] These and things of this kind are also explained through a good and natural reason, even if something is not explained in outward appearance.

p. 185.214–223
Aliud | exemplum mei filioli. Est in mea et ipsius nativitate triangulus Jovis | et Saturni, Jove posterioribus in gradibus. Ubi mihi asc: illi Mars, ubi | mihi Luna, illi Jupiter, ubi mihi Mars, illi ♄; ubi mihi M.C. ipsi ☿. Ego habeo | □♂ ☿ fere partilem, ille habet △♂ ☿ fere partilem. Plura reperiri | possunt hujusmodi. Itaque Luna in quadrato Saturni, post ☍♂, Venus | inter □♂ et ☍♄, Mercurius in trino ♂ hominem durum significant, | cum qui affectus denotant planetae, omnes sint in aspectu malorum. | Metuo etiam ipsius oculis ob ☽, metuo a praecipitibus casibus ob stantes | tres planetas.

Another example, that of my little son. His nativity and mine both have a trine between Jupiter and Saturn, with Jupiter in later degrees. Where I have the Ascendant, he has Mars; where I have the Moon, he has Jupiter; where I have Mars, he has Saturn; where I have the Midheaven, he has Mercury. I have an almost partile[68] Mars-Mercury square; he has an almost partile Mars-Mercury trine. More can be investigated in this way. And so the Moon in square to Saturn, after an opposition with Mars;[69] Venus between a square with Mars and an opposition with Saturn;[70] and Mercury in trine with Mars signify an insensitive person, because the planets which denote emotions are all in aspect to malefics. I fear for his eyes because of the Moon, and am afraid of dangerous falls because of the three stationary planets.

64 That is, fogs and epilepsy. I am not aware of other instances where this analogy is made.
65 Actually, Jupiter is in its detriment in Gemini, not fall.
66 Kepler is referring to the bright fixed stars in Gemini.
67 Saturn trines from the ninth house, above Jupiter in the sixth; because Gemini is a sign of short ascension, even though the aspect is a trine, it is a square 'in mundo'.
68 I.e., both planets in the same degree number.
69 The Moon's next aspect is the square to Saturn; it opposed Mars when it was in Sagittarius.
70 Venus at 28° Pisces has separated from her square with Mars at 23° Gemini, and when she gets to 3° Aries she will oppose Saturn.

p. 185.223–241

Et quia Venus et ☽ laborant, ideo natus est monstrosus. | Membrum enim virile, a ♀ et ☽ significatum, est instar Judaei retectum, | retortum, et infra agnatum scroto, meatus urinae alius, quam ceteris | hominibus. Totum compositum habet formam testudinis coctae in do | muncula, quae sunt uxoris meae deliciae. Sed plura ipsi incommoda | circa illa loca evenient. ♀ in □♂ impetuosum et indomitum significat, | ☿ in △♂ agilimum, celerrimum et ingeniosum. Est enim ☿ in illustri | constellatione ♒ et in domo quarta. Facit et temerarium et populariter | bonum atque facilem. Utrumque hoc valde iracundum denotat. ☽ in | □♄ laboriosum, invidum, avarum. Et propter hunc aspectum con | temptis erit moribus. Nisi quod hic quadratus brevis est, sextili aequi | pollens. Atque etiam illi anno 1601 pessima revolutio illucescet, quae | aut me aut ipsum tollet (significando naturaliter). Ex quibus vides, me | nihil rejicere ex astrologia, praeter inutilia domuum numeralium instru | menta, et illam arrogantem praesumptionem de speciali praedictione, | quasi quem suspensum iri dicamus, ei non aeque caelum generali sub com | plexu aquarum pericula denotare possit: aut quasi erraverimus, mortem | alicui praedicentes, qui eo tempore periculoso ex morbo vix evasit. | Vides haec non ad contemptum, sed honorem nostri ordinis pertinere. …

And since Venus and the Moon are oppressed, he is therefore born monstrous. For the penis, signified by Venus and the Moon, is uncovered after Jewish custom, twisted back, and below the penis, next to the scrotum, he has another way for urine than other men have. The whole arrangement has the form of a cooked turtle in its shell, which is a favourite of my wife. But more troubles will arise for him from these positions. Venus in square with Mars means that he is impetuous and uncontrolled, Mercury in trine with Mars means that he is extremely agile, fast and gifted. For Mercury is in the bright constellation Aquarius and in the fourth house. It makes him careless, popular and easy-going. Both make him very irascible. Moon in square with Saturn marks him as industrious, envious and greedy – and because of this aspect, of despicable manners. Except, because this square is of short ascension, it is of equal power to the sextile.[71] And an extremely bad solar revolution is awaiting him as well in the year 1601, which will either take me or him away (meaning in the natural sense).[72] From this you see that I do not reject anything from astrology, except for the useless instruments of the number-houses, and that arrogant presumption about specific prediction, such as if we say someone will be hung, to whom the sky could not equally mark dangers of water under the general complexion: or if we err in predicting death to somebody who at the time has barely escaped from a dangerous disease. You see that this[73] leads not to the contempt, but to the honour of our rank.

---

[71] The Moon in Capricorn is in a sign of short ascension.

[72] Heinrich Kepler's Solar Return for 1601 shows Leo rising. In traditional astrological practice one would notice its lord, the Sun, in the 6th house (illness) conjunct the Moon and Mars; and all three of these planets in square to Saturn in Scorpio on the cusp of the I.C., traditionally the 'end of the matter' and death. The 4th is also the house of the father, which perhaps is why Kepler said it could be 'me or him'. However, it is all moot, because Heinrich died in April of 1598.

[73] Kepler's new methods.

Letter No. 2: 11 June 1598

p. 228.360–368

De morte filioli tui tanto tibi vehementius condoleo, quod, quantus | dolor tuus fuerit, ex meo ipsius conjecturam facio, cui itidem Deus | Opt. Max. filiolum Henricum eo ipso tempore ex hac vita evocavit, | quo ipsi me metuere tibi scripsi. Nam die 1. Aprilis St. N. aegrotare | caepit, die 3. ejusdem hora 12 meridiana mortuus est, dies natus sexa | ginta dimidio minus. Ex pallore cadaveris in lateribus collegerunt, | apostemate capitis extinctum esse. Desiderium ejus uxori meae nulla | dies leniet; mihi illud cordi est: Vanitas Vanitatum, et omnia Vanitas. | Faxit Deus, ut faustae tuae precationes aliis in rebus meis ratae sint.

I send my utmost condolences on the death of your little son. I can well imagine how great your pain was because of my own, as the highest and best God likewise called my little son Heinrich away from life at that very time which, as I wrote to you, I had feared.[74] For on the 1st of April (New Style) his illness began, and on the 3rd of the same month, at noon, he was dead, sixty days less a half after his birth. From the paleness of the corpse they deduced that he had died because of an abscess in the head. No day alleviates my wife's longing for him. These words are in my heart: Vanity of Vanities, all is Vanity.[75] May God grant that your favourable invocations in my other matters are valid.

[74] Kepler did not exactly say this in his earlier letter.
[75] Ecclesiastes 1:2.

EVIDENCE IN BONATTI FOR THE PRACTICAL APPLICATION OF CERTAIN ASTROLOGICAL TECHNIQUES

Robert Hand

It is clear from the historical evidence of chronicles that patrons of astrology in late medieval and early modern Italy employed astrologers to predict the outcomes of military actions and to advise on military strategy.[1] As a result of this demand the existing material, as it was received from astrologers of the Arabic world, was elaborated and amplified. However, my intention is not to 'prove' that military astrology was or was not a significant factor in the military strategy of late medieval Italy. We know that it was, although it is not clear to what extent. The question I ask is whether the elaboration and amplification of astrological technique is closely correlated with the demand for the use of astrology in military matters. If so, it suggests that close readings and comparisons of the astrological texts during and after the medieval Italian period, with respect to the material received from Arabic sources, can be used by historians to show which applications of astrology described in the texts were actually employed. As mentioned before, I intend to demonstrate the method of textual analysis with regard to the area of war and conflict, and from this demonstrate further how it can be applied to other possible applications of astrology.

Why is this an issue? While it is generally agreed among more recent scholars that the influence and application of astrology in the Middle Ages was wide-

[1] For Bonatti's role in this respect see Filippo Villani, *Philippi Villani De Origine Civitatis Florentie Et De Eiusdem Famosis Civibus*, ed. Giuliano Tanturli (Padua: In ædibus Antenoreis, 1997), pp. 403–06. This was a part of Filippo's continuation of previous Villani chronicles of Florence. According to Talbot Selby, Villani's account may be derived from a source nearly contemporary with Dante, hence also nearly contemporary with Bonatti. This is Benvenuto de Rambaldi's commentary on Dante. See n. 23 below for the Rambaldi reference. For Selby, see Talbot R. Selby, 'Filippo Villani and His Vita of Guido Bonatti', *Renaissance News* 1, no. 11 (Winter 1958): pp. 243–48. For another example of the use of astrology in planning military campaigns in Italy see Rolandino, *The Chronicles of the Trevisan March*, trans. Joseph R. Berrigan (Lawrence, KS: Coronado Press, 1980), pp. 64–65, 84–85, 142, 180. For the Latin see the Rolandinus entry in the bibliography. More such examples will be presented in my later work.

spread,[2] what it was used for is not always exactly clear. We do know that it was used as an adjunct to medical practice and that, in the early modern period, almanacs making astrological predictions for the year ahead were a com-mon form of popular literature. But when one examines the actual medieval texts, both in Arabic and Latin, one finds that the described scope of astrology in these texts was truly vast. The subject areas covered nearly every aspect of daily life from such topics as choosing times, through having sexual intercourse for the conception of a male heir, to more arcane applications such as alchemy and magic. One can even find material on choosing times for taking baths, cutting one's hair, and placing children with tutors. When confronted with the variety of applications in the texts, the historian must wonder how much of this material was actually used at any given period, and how much of it was simply passed from author to author as part of the tradition, even though particular parts of the tradition may have ceased to be in use. (We know that some of the material falls into the latter category, as I will illustrate below). Also, we find that some topic areas—such as the astrology of marriage and relationships, elaborately worked out in ancient times—evolved little or not at all in the Middle Ages and early modern period, but had a new and unprecedented flourishing in the twentieth century. Obviously at some time or another all of the material in the texts was used, but the questions remain: how often, at what times and places, and under what circumstances.

An Overview of Change versus Tradition in Astrology

The historian of astrology must understand the conservatism of astrological texts. It has been stated more than once that 'astrology is largely unchanged since Ptolemy'.[3] Contrary to the spirit of modern research and scholarship, the

---

[2] Of course, the extent of the application of astrology varied from country to country and period to period. It was relatively light in medieval England, quite extensive in France in the reign of Charles V, and also in medieval Italy, at least from the thirteenth century on. For England see Hilary M. Carey, *Courting Disaster: Astrology at the English Court and University in the Later Middle Ages* (New York: St. Martin's Press, 1992), passim, and Theodore Otto Wedel, *The Medieval Attitude toward Astrology Particularly in England* (New Haven: Yale University Press, 1920), *passim*. For France see Jean-Patrice Boudet, *Entre science et nigromance: astrologie, divination et magie dans l'Occident médiéval (XIIe–XVe siècle)* (Paris: Publications de la Sorbonne, 2006), passim. For Italy the case is made throughout this paper. The material in the volumes on the twelfth through fifteenth centuries of Lynn Thorndike, *History of Magic and Experimental Science*, 8 vols. (New York: Columbia University Press, 1923–58), pertains to all these nations.

[3] See 'Views of modern philosophers. Mostly bad news for astrology' at http://www.rudolfhsmit.nl/p-view2.htm accessed 18 April 2010. This is an 'expanded

faithful transmission of the tradition was often (although not always, as we shall see) valued more highly than innovation or new discoveries. Ancient authorities were often cited to give material increased credibility. Material was also transmitted without attribution, although transmitted nonetheless in the same apparent spirit of preserving the tradition. Sometimes the transmissions were made with astonishing fidelity to the original texts, virtually *verbatim* quotations. Whole paragraphs complete with metaphors and imagery would move from author to author; little changed except for occasional copying errors.[4] This practice is found in both Hellenistic and medieval astrological works, as well as in works in the Hindu tradition.

Yet there was change and evolution. Contrary to assertions made by some, the astrology of the Latin Middle Ages and the astrology of Claudius Ptolemy are very different. There are times and authors in which we see a good deal of new material which seems to have no origin except from the experience of individual astrological authors. Looking at change in the texts overall we find four categories of evolution, which can be grouped into two major super-categories as outlined below.

I. Material Exhibiting Little Change.
   A. Material transmitted *verbatim* or nearly so.
   B. Material in which the basic outlines are unaltered but where changes have occurred. These changes are of two kinds.
      1. Elaboration or additional commentary on the original material but little that is truly new.
      2. Modifications introduced to account for changes in astrological

version of a summary from *Correlation* (1995) 14(02), pp. 33–34'. *Correlation* is an astrological journal of research which has at times taken an extremely critical attitude toward astrology, especially when Rudolf Smit was its editor. The passage in question is from Thomas H. Leahey and Grace E. Leahey, *Psychology's Occult Doubles: Psychology and the Problem of Pseudoscience* (Chicago: Nelson-Hall, 1983), pp. 41–42. The position stated here is neither unusual nor infrequent in literature critical of astrology.

[4] This is exemplified by the following work: Antonius de Montulmo, *On the Judgment of Nativities, Parts 1&2*, trans. Robert Hand (Berkeley Springs, WV: Golden Hind Press, 1995). The only version of the text we had was a very badly edited early modern printed edition. Parts were so corrupt that I could only correct them by referring to other texts which cited the same material verbatim. The edition in question is *Antonii de Montulmo, artium ac medicinae doctoris, de Iudiciis Nativitatum liber praeclarissimus* (Nuremberg: Johannes Petreius, 1540). It is bound together with Lucas Gauricus, *Tractatus astrologiae iudiciariae de nativitatibus virorum et mulierum*, printed in the same year and place.

theory.

II. Material Which Evolved.
   A. Material in which the basic outlines follow tradition but in which there is both significant alteration of details, and the addition of new material.
   B. Substantially new material.

I will briefly discuss each of these categories and mention some examples of each.

Material Exhibiting Little Change

Our first category, I.A., shows the highest degree of consistency from author to author. Clearly some, if not many, authors lifted material from earlier authors (often without attribution) simply to fill in the gaps in areas which were outside the range of the author's own experience. This is especially found in texts whose scope is encyclopedic, that is, which intended to cover every aspect of the tradition. Given the range of topics of the tradition no one could ever possibly have practised every part of the astrological art. So passages were taken from previous authors. Here is an example of this type of transmission, from Schöner's *Three Books on the Judgments of Nativities*, Book II:[5]

> In secunda, victus eius erit ratione servorum, aut pro dando bestias ad victoriam, et quod inde lucrabitur, modicum erit . . .
>
> <The ruler of the sixth house> . . . in the second house, his livelihood will be because of servants, or will have regard to providing beasts to victory (?), and what profit he makes from this will be modest.

From Haly Abenragel, the same passage.[6]

> . . . in secunda: victus nati erit ratione servorum: aut pro dando bestias ad victuram: et quod inde lucrabitur modicum erit . . .

The two passages are nearly identical except for the underlined words, *eius* – *nati* and *ad victoriam* – *ad victuram*. However the phrase in Schöner, 'ad

[5] Johannes Schöner, *De iudiciis nativitatum, libri tres* (Nuremberg: Johannes Montanus, 1545) fol. LXXXIVr.

[6] Haly Abenragel, *Liber completus in iudiciis stellarum quem composuit albohazen Hali filius abenragel* (Venice: Erhard Ratdolt, 1485), fol. 77v.

victoriam', makes no sense, where Haly has 'ad victuram' which also makes little sense because there is no root word for *victuram* which works in this context. However, another version of the Haly text[7] has *ad vecturam* which does make sense as *vectura* means 'hauling'. So while the Schöner passage reads 'dando bestias ad victoriam'—'providing beasts for victory'—with the correction from the later edition, Haly has 'providing beasts for haulage'. Since much of this portion of Book II in Schöner is lifted *verbatim* (but not always accurately) from the Latin translation of Haly's work this is a plausible correction to Schöner's text. It is also apparent that copying or editing in Schöner was done unintelligently, but deliberately, with *victoriam* as a mistaken 'correction' for the spelling *victuram*. While such wholesale copying, as we see in Schöner, is considered unacceptable in modern writing (since it amounts to plagiarism) this is merely an example of passing on the tradition. And we see here how it has the additional bonus of enabling the historian to repair damaged transmissions of text from one author to another.

The above example involved a technique which was clearly employed by medieval astrologers: namely the analysis of what it means when the ruler of one house is found in another house.[8] This kind of material is found in most, if not all, textbooks of medieval astrology and often the material is original. I have no clear evidence as to why Schöner only copied earlier material but, as we shall see, it may be a sign that he was not an active practitioner, merely a compiler.

Then there are the 'fossils', once-living parts of the astrological tradition that had, by the medieval Latin period, fallen out of use. Two examples of these are subdivisions of zodiacal signs, faithfully described in most of the medieval textbooks but never used either in actual examples of charts, or in descriptions of more advanced methods that might employ them. These are the divisions of the signs of 30° into nine equal parts of 3° 20', and into twelve equal parts of 2° 30'. In the form in which they appear in medieval astrology they appear to come from Hindu astrology where they are used, to this day, as a basic tool of Hindu astrological practice. They are known as *navamsas* and *dwadasamsas* respectively

---

7 Haly Abenragel, *Albohazen Haly filii Abenragel libri de iudiciis astrorum* (Basel: Henrichus Petrus, 1551), p. 205. This edition was substantially edited so as to bring the Latin into closer accord with the standards of humanistic Latin which often damages the meaning of the original Latin translation, but in this case the editing did improve the text.

8 The ruler of a house is a planet that has a strong relationship to the sign in the house. When a planet is in such a sign, it benefits and is said to be 'essentially dignified'. When it is not in such a sign, it still has an influence on the affairs represented by that house. Houses are a twelvefold division of the chart, usually distinct from the signs, which enable the astrologer to assign particular areas of the chart to particular areas of life.

in the Hindu texts and as *novenariae,* and *duodenariae* in medieval Latin astrology. The *duodenariae* do make a comeback in an older form, as found in Greek texts, where they are called in Latin by the name *dodecatemoria,* which is simply the Latinized form of the Greek word δωδεκατημορια (twelfth-parts). This reappearance of the technique in the early modern period in Schöner is probably due to the influx of Greek texts from Byzantium which may have made the technique, again, briefly fashionable. Yet the usage in Schöner is the only instance I have found.[9]

Now let us turn briefly to our second category, I.B. These texts contain material that is so much a part of basic astrological method as used in this period that it is also transmitted faithfully from author to author, but not *verbatim* and not unintelligently. The original source material is often amplified with commentary and explanation. There are frequent examples of chart interpretations which employ these methods to demonstrate their use (especially in early modern texts) and these examples are often from the author's own time. However, little or none of the material is genuinely new. There are, however, some changes, which may be due to a shift in the philosophical foundations of astrology that occurred as the result of the writing of Abū Ma'shar (d. 886). Abū Ma'shar (according to Richard Lemay)[10] made astrology *systematically* Aristotelian. Prior to his time astrology, insofar as it had a coherent philosophical basis, was a mixture of Pythagorean, Stoic, Platonic, Hermetic and Aristotelian principles derived from late classical philosophy. Ptolemy himself, although he is often characterized as an Aristotelian, exhibited exactly that same kind of mixture.[11] So Ptolemaic methods that depended on particular non-Aristotelian principles were modified somewhat to bring them into accord with

---

[9] In Schöner's *Three Books,* there is an introduction to the method which closely parallels the kind of material found in earlier medieval Latin texts. See fols. IVv and Vr. However, scattered through the text are aphorisms which actually employ this method. This is what is unusual in Schöner's presentation. Among several examples, here are two taken from Book I, fol. XIVv:

'Dodecathemorion Iovis in ascendente, significat nobilitatem parentum eius, et potentiam ipsorum'.

'Dodecathemorion Solis aut Lunae in Medio Coeli, significat nobilitatem patris et matris. Sed in duodecima, significat depressionem parentum, et negociorum suorum, et quod sint vilis progenei'.

[10] Richard Lemay, *Abu Ma'shar and Latin Aristotelianism in the Twelfth Century: The Recovery of Aristotle's Natural Philosophy through Arabic Astrology* (Beirut: American University of Beirut, 1962), passim, but especially the first part of the book.

[11] This is well described in Liba Chaia Taub, *Ptolemy's Universe: The Natural Philosophical and Ethical Foundations of Ptolemy's Astronomy* (Chicago: Open Court, 1993). See especially the early chapters.

Abū Ma'shar's Aristotelian 'reform'. Here is an example.

An important technique derived from Ptolemy is the one area of genethliacal astrology (also known as 'natal' astrology) which attempts to deal with an individual's psychology or personality, as opposed to destiny. Antonius de Montulmo, in his discussion of the medieval version of this technique, refers to it in the title of his chapter 'De natura, intellectu, sensu, ac moribus nati'.[12] Here he describes the traditional method for deriving the basic character traits of an individual from the birth chart. In Ptolemy's *Tetrabiblos*, Book III, the equivalent chapter is entitled (in Robbins' translation) 'Of the Quality of the Soul'.[13] 'Soul', as used here, means something more like what we would call 'mind'. The Latin reflects this. Montulmo's Latin title translates as 'On the Nature, Intellect, Sense and Character of the Native'. Although time and space in this paper do not permit an item-by-item comparison of the Montulmo with Ptolemy, three things are clear.[14] Firstly, Montulmo's text *is* derived from Ptolemy's. Secondly, a significant change has been made in the model of the soul employed in the analysis. Ptolemy's model of the soul has two levels: an irrational and a rational level. This reflects both Stoic and Hermetic psychology. Montulmo's model follows Aristotle in having three levels: the vegetable, animal and intellective. Thirdly, much explanatory material has been added to Ptolemy's rather terse account. In fact, if one examines the medieval textbooks and their discussions on 'soul', one does find considerable variation on the basic Ptolemaic method. Montulmo's, however, except for the tripartite division of the soul, is much closer than most to Ptolemy.

Before we leave the issue of conservatively transmitted texts, there is one area where we might expect to see evolution in astrological method, but in fact there is very little. This is in the astrology of marriage and sexual relations mentioned previously. The basic outline of the method is derived from Ptolemy's *Tetrabiblos*, Book IV chapter 5, 'On Marriage', in Robbins' translation.[15] As we go

---

[12] Montulmo, *Judgement of Nativities*, Ch. ix.

[13] Περὶ ποιότητος ψυχῆς. Book III, chapter 14: Ptolemy, *Tetrabiblos*, ed. and trans. F. E. Robbins (Cambridge, MA, and London: Harvard University Press and William Heinemann Ltd, 1980), pp. 362–72 = Ptolemy, *Apotelesmatika*, ed. W. Hübner (Stuttgart and Leipzig: Teubner, 1998), pp. 248–74.

[14] The dissertation contains such an item-by-item comparison.

[15] Περὶ συναρμογῶν in Greek. The second word means both 'wedlock' and 'combination'. Given the nature of some of the 'marriages' described in this chapter, Robbins would have been better off using the second rather than the first translation: Ptolemy, *Tetrabiblos*, ed. and trans. F. E. Robbins, p. 393 = Ptolemy, *Apotelesmatika*, ed. Hübner, p. 306.

forward through medieval astrology into early modern we find that the equivalent sections of later textbooks follow Ptolemy so closely that one gets the impression that no original work was done at all. Even as recently as 1911 A.J. Pearce in his *Textbook of Astrology* goes not one whit beyond Ptolemy.[16] His chapter is a paraphrase of Ptolemy as he had it from the translation by A.J. Ashmand in the early nineteenth century.[17]

Material which Evolved

Now we come to the second major category, first subcategory (II.A.). Here we see evolution to such a degree that we have to assume that the individual astrologers involved must have engaged with the material quite seriously and found it necessary to modify what the tradition had handed down to them, even while maintaining the basic structure. In this paper I will be using one chapter each from Sahl ibn Bishr and Bonatti to illustrate this. Bonatti, his other predecessors, and his relationship to them, has been covered more completely in the complete dissertation.

And finally, we come to the last category II.B: completely new material. This can be disposed of fairly simply. We do not find such material until the early modern period. By this time the decline of astrology and its influence in Western thought was already well under way. We see it in authors such as Brahe, Kepler, Placidus de Titis, Morinus, and Maginus. It comes about increasingly as astrologers attempt to deal with the criticisms of astrology leveled at it by its critics. It is arguably not the result of astrologers having to develop new material to deal with the demands of their patrons. It is the result of the breakdown of the tradition. However, this is a discussion best left to another time and place.

Having described general categories into which one may place astrological material transmitted from one astrological author to another, let us return to our category II.A. In doing so one might ask why I focus on Bonatti. There are several reasons.

Firstly, Bonatti's text (given various names but commonly called the *Liber Astronomiae*) is far and away the most encyclopedic text on the subject composed by a European in the Middle Ages. There are no texts of comparable scope and

---

16 Alfred J. Pearce, *The Textbook of Astrology* (London: Mackie and Company, 1911), pp. 155–59.

17 Claudius Ptolemy, *Ptolemy's Tetrabiblos*, trans. J.M. Ashmand (London: Davis and Dickson, 1822), pp. 190–96.

length until the sixteenth century.[18] In fact, the only other single text, even of the sixteenth century which compares to Bonatti, is the *Speculum* of Francesco Giuntini (1523–1590). Girolamo Cardano (1501–1576) also left behind a huge corpus of work in the sixteenth century—all of which taken together is equivalent to Bonatti's work in its coverage—but Cardano's is not an integrated work even if it is all taken together. It was written throughout his life; it evolved considerably from his early work to his later work; and it was not conceived and written as a single *opus* expounding a complete and integrated system. He changed methods and extensively revised his earlier ideas. In short, he wrote no final *summa* of his astrology. Bonatti and Giuntini's works were such *summae*. The only earlier work comparable to them is that of the North African Arabic author mentioned above, Haly Abenragel, whose similarly encyclopedic work was extremely influential, especially in the period after Bonatti.

Secondly, although little is known about Bonatti's personal life, he does appear as a personality from time to time in chronicles and other works, making an appearance in Dante's *Divine Comedy*—specifically in the *Inferno* as one of those whose heads were turned completely around, facing permanently backwards as punishment for spending a lifetime looking forward attempting to predict the future.[19] Bonatti was especially known for his employment by the tyrant Ezzelino da Romano and Guido, Duke of Montefeltro. In this connection Bonatti himself provides many details in the *Liber Astronomiae*. From references in his own and other works, we know that Bonatti was employed for his advice in military matters. Charts pertaining to military matters are provided in his own work and there are references in the chronicles, especially to Guido Montefeltro and his use of Bonatti's astrology for military planning. As far as we know, Bonatti was the only astrologer he ever employed.

Thirdly, Bonatti was unusual in that he cited his sources. It is typical of him in any discussion of an astrological point to cite the opinions of his Arabic predecessors, then give his own opinions, which frequently diverge.[20] While differing from predecessors is not peculiar to Bonatti, he is unique in the scrupulous way he mentions them by name. We have the works of the great majority

---

[18] The only other comparable work in the Middle Ages was Leopold of Austria's text, which has much the same coverage as Bonatti's but nowhere near the depth of explanation. It is, as its title suggests, a compilation. Leopold of Austria, *Compilatio Leupoldi dicatus Austrie filii de astrorum scientis Decem continens tractatus* (Augsburg: Erhard Ratdolt, 1489).

[19] Dante, *Inferno*, Canto XX, 118ff.

[20] He cites no other Latin authors but does cite some Greek sources as they came to him through Arabic intermediaries, notably Vettius Valens and Dorotheus of Sidon.

of these writers. Where we do not, it appears that Bonatti did not have them either, but knew them only through other Arabic writers who referred to them. Bonatti shows no evidence of reading or writing Arabic, and must have relied completely on Latin translations, which he sometimes cites nearly *verbatim* and at other times closely paraphrases. This enables us to compare Bonatti to his predecessors quite thoroughly. Bonatti's attitude is respectful but not exactly servile because, given the range and completeness of his knowledge, it would seem that he was uniquely qualified to state his own opinions.[21]

As to the choice of the chapter which I compare to Sahl, I can assure the reader that it is typical in its relationship to its predecessors. Many more examples can and will be analysed at a later date. But before I proceed there needs to be a brief word on Bonatti's particular sources in this area. The example to be presented below is from Bonatti's and Sahl's material on interrogations, a branch of astrology in which a question is asked of an astrologer and a chart is erected for the moment of the asking. The answer is then derived from an analysis of the astrological chart so erected. Among Arabic-era authors the texts that we have on this subject are from Māshā'allāh, Sahl ibn Bishr, al-Kindī, and Haly Abenragel. There is also a compendium of the opinions of nine different authors called the *Book of the Nine Judges* (*Liber novem iudicum*)[22] which gives the opinion of nine different authors in each branch of interrogations and the closely related branch of astrology known as inceptions.[23] Of these authors al-Kindī seems to have only been an indirect source.[24] Nor does Haly seem to have been a source for Bonatti in interrogations.[25] The complete argument is beyond the

[21] The fourteenth-century Italian commentator on Dante, Benvenuto Rambaldi, referred to Bonatti's work as follows: 'Nam Guido fecit opus pulcrum et magnum in astrologia, quod ego vidi, in quo tam clare tradit doctrinam de astrologia quod visus est velle docere feminas astrologiam'. 'For Guido <Bonatti> created a great and handsome work on astrology which I have seen. In this work he transmits the doctrine of astrology so clearly that he seemed to want to teach astrology to women'. See Benvenutus de Imola, *Comentum super Dantis Aldighierii comoediam*, tome II (Florence: J.P. Lacaita, 1887), p. 90.

[22] These authors are al-Kindī, 'Umar ibn al-Farrukhān al-Ṭabarī, Sahl ibn Bishr, 'Aristotle', Abū 'Alī al-Khayyāṭ, Jirjīs, Dorotheus, Māshā'allāh and Abū Ma'shar. It is not known for certain who 'Jirjīs' was. Aristotle was of course derived from a pseudonymous work, which has not been identified.

[23] This is the art of choosing times for beginning various enterprises according to favourable astrological influences.

[24] He is not cited.

[25] Haly may have been a source for Bonatti in electional astrology, the astrology of choosing favorable times, but it is not clear whether the 'Haly' referred to in that part of

scope of this paper, but there are two major reasons why I have come to this conclusion. Firstly, according to David Juste, the Latin text of Haly Abenragel was translated from the Old Castilian version made by Yehudā ben Moshe for Alfonso X in 1254;[26] while we do not have the exact date of Bonatti's work, the *Liber astronomiae* was written at about the same time as the translation of Haly. Bonatti lived in northern Italy; the Haly translation was done in Castile. It is not impossible that the text could have reached Bonatti before he compiled his own work, but it is not very likely. Secondly, Bonatti usually cites his sources. In the material on interrogations regarding war and conflict only one author is cited: Sahl ibn Bishr. For this reason we can eliminate Māshā'allāh as well. Besides, Māshā'allāh's text, traditionally entitled in its Latin translation, *De receptione,* is not a complete, encyclopedic text of interrogations as are Sahl, Bonatti, and Haly (which are the only *complete* medieval expositions on interrogations). General principles are indeed presented, but there is nothing like the completeness of the survey of the field that we find in our other authors. And again Bonatti cites only Sahl ibn Bishr, under the name Zael or Zahel.

Worked Example: Comparing Bonatti and Sahl

While the focus of the complete study is on all of the material on conflict and warfare presented in Bonatti, his sources and in later authors, the example here is from chapter 9: the material on the seventh house, tractatus 6, entitled in English, 'Concerning a Lawsuit or Controversy Which May Exist Between Certain Parties: Which Side Shall Prevail, Which Succumb, or Will They Settle Before the Dispute Begins?'[27] The equivalent chapter in Sahl is entitled in translation 'Concerning a Dispute Between Two Persons, Which of Them Will Win?'[28]

Before I begin, let me say that the two authors' sections on seventh house matters have the same question topics (albeit with different wording). A

Bonatti was Haly Abenragel. However, it is more likely that it was Haly Emrani.

[26] See *Bibliotheca Astrologica Numerica,* The Warburg Institute, s.v., 'Haly Abenragel, *De iudiciis astrorum*', by David Juste and Charles Burnett, accessed 10 April 2010, http://warburg.sas.ac.uk/mnemosyne/Orientation/Bibastro.htm#alb.

[27] Guido Bonatti, *Decem Continens Tractatus Astronomie* (Augsburg: Erhard Ratdolt, 1491), fol. 127v. This edition may be found online at http://mdz10.bib-bvb.de/~db/0002/bsb00025600/images/, courtesy of the Bayerische Staatsbibliothek, accessed 24 April 2010.

[28] Sahl Ibn Bishr, 'De Interrogationibus', in *Quadriparti. Ptolo., que in hoc volumine continentur haec sunt* . . . (Venetiis: mandato ac sumptibus heredum. . . Octauini Scoti. . . et socio[rum], 1519), fol. 118v. This edition is available online at http://fondosdigitales.us.es/fondos/libros/640/13/quadriparti-ptolo-que-in-hoc-volumine-continentur-haec-sunt/, accessed 24 April 2010.

superficial examination of the two texts would suggest that Bonatti's work is completely derivative from that of Sahl and that one is likely to find little that is different or original in Bonatti. However, one notices something else immediately. The material in Bonatti is much more extensive; the treatments are sim-ply longer. There are three reasons for this. Firstly, Bonatti is a much wordier writer. Secondly, Bonatti explains more. Thirdly, Bonatti has a good deal of ma-terial that is not in Sahl at all, and also does not appear to be in Haly or Māshā'allāh (so in this respect it is irrelevant whether or not he used the latter two authors as sources). If we were to look in terms of just the first two factors—Bonatti's wordiness and lengthier explanations—we could say that Bonatti's work falls into our second category, I.B., where the material is amplified solely by more ample commentary or explanation. But as we will see below, Bonatti has much new material.

The Bonatti text is based on the Ratdolt edition of 1491 cited above. The Latin is unedited, with the spelling and punctuation exactly as in the original edition. The same is true of the editing of the Sahl text taken from the 1519 edition (also cited above) which contains a translation of the *Tetrabiblos* and other works.

The comparison is made in the body of this paper in the English translations. These are not complete in that certain transitional material, as well as exemplifications that do not represent new material, is omitted in the English. The Latin of each passage is presented in full in the footnotes with material *omitted* in the English underlined in the Latin. In the English comparison of the two sets of texts from Sahl and Bonatti, the passages in Bonatti that have no counterpart in the Sahl are in *italics,* as well as an instance in Sahl of material that does not occur in Bonatti.

1. Sahl – Place the Ascendant and its lord and the Moon for the querent and the seventh and its lord for the opponent.[29]

   Bonatti – . . . for the querent look at the Ascendant and its lord at the time in which you were asked about this, and also at the significatrix, the Moon; for the adversary look at the seventh house and its lord.[30]

---

[29] 'Et si interrogatus fuerit de contentione que fuerit inter duos quis eorum vincet et obtinebit victoriam. Pone ascendens ac dominum eius et luna interroganti qui te interrogat et .7. ac dominum eius contentori'.

[30] 'Si de lite seu controversia que vertitur inter aliquos vel parata est verti aliqua ex partibus quis obtinere debeat a te certificari voluerit atque tibi super hoc moverit questionem: aspice ascendens hora qua fueris interrogatus ab eo qui de hoc tibi fecerit questionem et dominum eius et significatricem: videlicet lunam pro querente et

Commentary - As one can see the content of the two passages is identical. Only the wording and style are different.

2. Sahl - After these matters, look at both planets to see whether they are being joined by the sextile or trine aspect. <If so> the two sides will make peace before the suit.[31]

   Bonatti - . . . See if the lord of the Ascendant, *or the Moon,* is being joined with the lord of the seventh, or the lord of the seventh is being joined with either the lord of the Ascendant *or the Moon,* and this by a trine or sextile aspect *with mutual reception;* <if so> it is clear that the parties will come to an agreement among themselves *without the involvement of anyone else. But if one significator receives the other, and the received planet does not receive the receiving planet, they will <also> agree without the lawsuit but not without the involvement of others, and those others who involve themselves will for the most part be on the side of the party whose significator receives the other.*[32]

Commentary - Now we see significant variation between the two authors. The material is presented by both authors in exactly the same order but note the additional material in Bonatti. First, Bonatti explicitly mentions the Moon as a significator (planet which gives indications) for the querent. Sahl does not. However, the reference to the Moon is not peculiar to Bonatti and is found in most authors other than Sahl. But Bonatti is very different from Sahl in stressing not only the necessity of the benign angular relationship between the two sets of significators (trine 120°, sextile 60°) but also the presence of mutual reception for the best results. Reception exists when a planet [A] makes an aspect (significant angular relationship) with another planet [B] that rules the sign in which A is located as either the domicile or exaltation lord of A's sign.[33] A *mutual* reception

---

septimam et eius dominum pro adversario:'

31 'post hec aspice si ambo planete inuicem coniuncti fuerint a sextili aspectu vel trino pacificabuntur ante contentionem'.

32 '. . . et vide si dominus ascendentis vel luna iuncti fuerint cum domino septime vel ipse cum aliquo ipsorum a trino vel a sextili aspectu cum receptione mutua concordabunt simul inter se de plano sine alterius intromissione. Si vero unus receperit alterum et ille receptus non receperit recipientem concordabunt sine litigio: sed non sine intromissione alterius: et erunt illi qui se intromittunt ut multum ex parte illius cuius significator receperit alium'.

33 There is not enough room in this short paper for a complete explanation of all of these terms of art, but the reader is referred to John Christopher Eade, *The Forgotten Sky: A Guide to Astrology in English Literature* (Oxford: New York: Oxford University Press, 1984).

exists when the planets exchange rulerships, i.e., A is B's sign and B is in A's sign and they are in an aspect.

Note how Bonatti uses the different degrees and kinds of reception to indicate various possible outcomes. Nothing of this sort is found in Sahl. The concept of reception dates back to Ptolemy (although neither the term nor an equivalent appears in his work). However, the most elaborate discussion of this concept occurs in the previously mentioned work of Māshā'allāh on interrogations, which features the use of reception to such a degree that it came to be known in Latin as *De receptione, On Reception*. (But Māshā'allāh's work is, in fact, on interrogations in general). Bonatti was clearly fond of the use of reception and may have been influenced by Māshā'allāh in its use; but this particular question does not appear in Māshā'allāh.[34]

3. Sahl – If they are joined by the square or opposition aspect, they will not make peace except after strife and quarreling.[35]

   Bonatti – If the significators are joined by the square or opposition aspect *with reception, or the trine or sextile without reception,* the parties will agree but first they will sue *and agreement will always begin with the side whose significator is less slow and which commits its disposition to the other; it is better if each significator receives the other. If a swift planet is being joined to a slow one and it does not receive the slow one, but the slow planet receives the swift one, it signifies that the <side signified by the> receiving planet wishes to come to an agreement even if <the side signified by the> swift planet does not wish to do so, and that <other> side will not stand by the agreement.*[36]

This is an excellent summary of medieval astrology designed for scholars with little or no knowledge of astrology.

[34] For an English translation of this work see Māshā'allāh, *On Reception*, trans. Robert Hand (Reston, VA: ARHAT, 1998). There are various early modern printed editions of the Latin available on the internet. A website that references most of these editions is to be found at http://cura.free.fr/DIAL.html (April 2010). This is a comprehensive resource for anyone interested in the history of medieval astrology.

[35] '. . . et si fuerint iuncti a quarto aspectu vel ab oppositione non pacificabuntur nisi post guerram et contentionem'.

[36] 'Et si fuerint iuncti a quarto aspectu vel ab oppositione cum receptione vel a trino seu sextili sine receptione concordabunt sed prius litigabunt. et incipiet concordia semper ex parte illius cuius significator fuerit minus ponderosus: et qui commiserit dispositionem suam alteri: et eo melius si uterque significator receperit alterum. Si levis iungatur ponderoso et non recipiat eum sed ponderosus recepit levem significat quod recipiens velit concordare: etiam si levis non velit nec stabit per eum'.

Commentary - Again, note the significant use of reception in Bonatti. Also, the material on which side begins to sue for peace or an agreement is not present in Sahl.

The phrase 'commits its disposition to the other' refers to the following. In general, significant angular relationships (aspects) are formed when a faster moving planet moves toward the aspect position of the slower planet (called 'applying to an aspect'). In doing so the faster planet is the active partner in creating the aspect. However, this does not make it the senior partner, so to speak, in the transaction. It is the reverse. The slow planet acts as if it were a lord or patron that the faster moving planet approaches in the relationship of a client to a patron (in the ancient and medieval sense). In doing so the faster planet commits its affairs (commits disposition) to the slower planet. If each planet receives the other, then the agreement will be binding. If only the slow receives the faster, the side signified by the slow planet will try to compel an agreement, but the side signified by the faster moving planet will not keep the agreement. None of this subtlety is found in Sahl.

4. Sahl - If both significators come together in one sign, there will be peace between them without the involvement of another and without another person who would come between them for the sake of making peace.[37]

   Bonatti - *<In general, agreement is> more likely if the aspect is a trine or sextile and* if they are joined bodily in one sign such that their aspect or conjunction is not impeded by any other planet, <and this is so> *whether the aspect or conjunction is with or without reception.* They will even reach agreement without the involvement of any other.[38]

Commentary - Here Bonatti adds the trine (120°) and sextile (60°) aspect to the bodily conjunction (coming 'together in one sign'). And again Bonatti refers to, although in this instant does not require, reception.

5. Sahl - If the lord of the Midheaven aspects them and there is a joining together with it before one of them may be joined to the other, they will not

---

[37] '. . . et si vtrique conuenerint in vno signo erit inter eos pax absque immissione alterius et absque alio qui ingrediatur inter eos causa pacificandi'.

[38] '. . . et eo magis si fuerit aspectus trinus vel sextilis et si fuerint iuncti corporaliter in uno signo ita quod eorum coniunctio non impediatur ab aliquo sive cum receptione sive sine receptione concordabunt etiam sine alterius intromissione'.

make peace until they come before the king;[39]

Bonatti – After this look at the significator of the king, *podestá,*[40] or judge . . . the lord of the tenth house. If it aspects . . . one of the significators, . . . or if it is being joined bodily <to one of these>, *or if the lord of the Ascendant is endeavouring to be joined with the lord of the seventh, or the lord of the seventh with the lord of the Ascendant, and the lord of the tenth house cuts off their joining,* the parties will not agree unless first they litigate in the presence of the judge; *this will be because of the judge (or other person in authority). He will not permit them to settle, and he will cause them to litigate perhaps for the sake of extorting something from this.*[41]

Commentary – Here we see that Bonatti was a medieval northern Italian and therefore a product of the city-state culture of that region in which kings were not the normal chief executive officer of the state: hence, the reference to officials other than the king. This is not particularly remarkable, but Bonatti also adds considerable detail about the nature and behaviour of the judging official not found in Sahl. The phrase 'cuts off their joining', not found in the Sahl, means that the planet which indicates for the judge joins one of the planets which indicates for the two parties (significators) before the other such planet can do so.

6. Sahl – . . . and if the Moon transfers light between them, the beginning of peace will be at the hands of legates.[42]

Bonatti – Then look at the Moon and see if she transfers light between the lord of the Ascendant and the lord of the seventh; *and if the Moon does not*

[39] '. . . et si aspexerit eos dominus medii celi et fuerit cum eo coniunctio antequam vnus eorum iungatur alteri non pacificabuntur donec veniant coram rege:'

[40] The Latin is 'potestas' which in medieval Italian Latin meant a type of city officer called, in Italian, the *podestá*. Although the exact nature of the office varied from city to city, it was generally an executive office occupied by someone who was hired for the job. Unlike modern executive officers, they also served as judges.

[41] 'Post hoc aspice significatorem regis seu potestatis sive iudicis qui est dominus decime domus si aspexerit aliquem ex significatoribus dominum scilicet ascendentis vel dominum septime vel fuerit ei iunctus corporaliter: vel si dominus ascendentis voluerit iungi cum domino septime vel ipse cum eo et dominus decime domus absciderit coniunctionem eorum non concordabunt nisi primo litigent coram iudice: et hoc erit ex parte iudicis seu potestatis qui non permittet eos componere et faciet eos litigare forte causa extorquendi aliquid inde'.

[42] '. . . et si luna transtulerit inter eos lumen erit initium pacis per manus legatorum'.

transfer light between them, see if another planet transfers light between them, because if it is so, some people who will make them agree will involve themselves <in the suit> even if the parties have already begun to sue.[43]

Commentary - Here Bonatti adds another planet besides the Moon which may transfer light between the significators. The phrase 'transfer of light' (or, in most English astrology texts, 'translation of light') is the way in which two significators that would not normally be connected by aspect can be connected by a third planet or the Moon. It occurs when a fast moving planet [A] makes an aspect to a slower planet [B] which is not currently in aspect to another slower-moving planet [C]. A carries B's nature to C by first being joined to B and then to C. This most commonly happens with the Moon but other planets can perform this function as well, so long as the planet A is swifter than either B or C.

7. Sahl - After this look at the place of both planets, namely the lord of the Ascendant and the lord of the matter, that is, of the seventh house, and the fortitude of these planets.[44]

   Bonatti - look at the lord of the Ascendant which signifies for the querent and the lord of the seventh which signifies for the adversary, and see which of them is stronger, because that one whose significator is stronger ought to prevail, . . .[45]

Commentary - No difference here.

8. Sahl - This is how you will know the strength of those sides which are engaged in struggle, for that one will be the stronger of the two whose significator is in an angle and which is received. He will have the most allies.[46]

---

[43] 'Deinde aspice lunam et vide si ipsa transfert lumen inter dominum ascendentis et dominum septime: et si luna non transtulerit lumen inter eos vide si alius planeta transfert inter eos lumen: quoniam si sic fuerit intromittent se aliqui qui concordabunt eos etiam si iam incepissent litigare'.

[44] '. . . post hec aspice locum vtrorum planetarum domini ascendentis, scilicet, ac domini rei, id est, domini septimi et fortitudine eorum:'

[45] 'Post hoc aspice dominum ascendentis qui habet significare querentem et dominum septime qui habet significare adversarium: et vide quis eorum fuerit fortior: quia ille cuius significator fuerit fortior debebit obtinere fortior . . .'

[46] 'per hoc intelliges fortitudinem eorum qui contendunt: fortior enim est ille cuius significator fuerit in angulo: et qui fuerit receptus ex eis habebit plures auxiliatores:'

Bonatti – . . . for the stronger one will be that one which is in an angle and *especially if it is in one of its own dignities; and however much the dignity is greater and however more fortitudes one of them should have, so much more it will be the stronger,* and especially if it should be received in the place in which it is located because <the one signified> will be stronger in and of himself and he will have helpers who will assist him.[47]

Commentary – Bonatti adds the significator's own dignity here to the possibility of its being received and in an angle as a factor indicating its strength. This may not be a very important addition since it follows logically from the doctrine of dignities as reported by any number of other sources.

9. Sahl – Know that the beginning of peace will be according to that planet which pushes, that is, from the one that seeks the joining together, which is the swifter planet, and from <any> planet which is cadent if it is the swifter.[48]

Bonatti – If it should be that the two sides ought to come together as I have described, the beginning of the settlement will come from the side <represented> by the swifter planet which also commits disposition to the other: . . . Also a planet which is cadent from the angles is said to be weaker *unless another planet which is in a strong place supports and receives it.*[49]

Commentary – Bonatti's main contribution here is a circumstance which can mitigate the debilitating effect of a planet's location in a cadent house. Once again it is reception by a strongly placed planet.

10. Sahl – Know that when the lord of the seventh is in the Ascendant, it

---

[47] 'enim erit ille qui fuerit in angulo: et maxime si fuerit in aliqua suarum dignitatum: et quantumcunque dignitas fuerit maior: et quantumcunque plures fortitudines habuerit aliquis eorum tanto magis erit fortior: et maxime si fuerit receptus in loco in quo erit: quoniam erit fortis per se et habebit auxiliatores qui iuvabunt eum'.

[48] '. . . et scito quod initium pacis erit a planeta pulsanti, id est, ab eo qui petit coniunctionem qui est leuior et a planeta cadenti si fuerit leuior:'

[49] 'Et si debuerint componere sicut dixi veniet inicium compositionis ex parte planet levioris et qui committit dispositionem alteri: nam si dominus ascendentis fuerit levior et dominus septime ponderosior veniet ex parte interrogantis. Si vero dominus ascendentis fuerit ponderosior et dominus septime fuerit levior veniet inicium concordie ab adversario: et planeta qui fuerit cadens ab angulo dicitur esse debilior nisi alius planeta sublevet eum qui sit in loco forti et recipiat eum'.

signifies the strength of the querent, and the lord of the Ascendant in the seventh signifies the strength of him about whom the question is asked <, the opponent,> because he is like one <already> defeated.[50]

Bonatti – Likewise, it is necessary that one look out and see whether the lord of the seventh is in the Ascendant because it is a complete indication that the . . . querent will win and the adversary will give way. And if the lord of the Ascendant is in the seventh, it signifies that the adversary will prevail and the querent will give way . . . *Also, this not only will happen in lawsuits or in monetary cases, indeed, it will even happen in battles and wars.* <This is> always <so> because the significator of whichever side is found in the house of the other is said to be already overcome and is like one conquered.[51]

Commentary – The Latin of the Sahl passage, at least in the edition consulted, is ambiguous. But from the context and from a knowledge of the principles involved it is clear that the words I have added in < > restore the intention of the original Sahl passage. The Latin of the Bonatti has the very same words in the corresponding section. In the Bonatti passage he states for the first time that the logic of questions about lawsuits can be applied without alteration to questions about who will win at battle. This point is made again at the end of this chapter.

11. Sahl – . . . if one significator is retrograde, it signifies weakness and rout, and also underhanded dealing and falsehood for that one whose significator it is, that is, if the lord of the Ascendant is retrograde, it will be the weakness of the querent, but if it is the lord of the seventh which is retrograde, it will be

[50] 'et scito quod dominus .7. cum fuerit in ascendente significat fortitudinem interrogantis:

et dominus ascendentis in .7. significat fortitudinem eius de quo interrogatur: quia similis victo . . .'

[51] 'Item oportet prospicere et videre utrum dominus septime sit in ascendente: quia tunc significat ex toto quod dominus ascendentis scilicet interrogator vincet et adversarius succumbet.

Et si dominus ascendentis fuerit in septima significat quod adversarius obtinebit et interrogator succumbet: quicumque enim significatorum invenitur in domo alterius significatur victus.

Et non solum accidet hoc in litibus seu causis pecunariis: verum etiam accidet in preliis atque guerris: quia semper cuiuscunque significator invenitur in domo alterius dicitur esse iam victus et est victo similis'.

the weakness of the opponent.[52]

Bonatti - Then it is necessary for you to see whether the lord of the Ascendant or the lord of the seventh is retrograde because if the lord of the ascendant is retrograde it signifies the querent's weakness and that he will not be firm in standing up to the lawsuit *and he will deny the truth to the adversary, nor will he confess it, and he will not believe that he has the right <on his side>*. But if the lord of the seventh is retrograde, it signifies weakness on the part of the adversary, and that he will flee the suit insofar as he is able; *he will also deny the truth and he will not believe that he has a good case.*[53]

Commentary – What Bonatti has added is clear enough.

12. Sahl - Moreover, if the lord of the Midheaven aspects them and it is retrograde, this signifies the unjustness of the judges and that the quarrel will be prolonged.[54]

Bonatti - Look also at the significator of the judge, whether it is a king, podesta, or <an actual> judge who must pronounce sentence between them. It will be the lord of the tenth house. <*See*> *whether or not he aspects the significators of the lawsuit. If he aspects them and is direct, he will proceed according to the order of the law in that case and he will strive to shorten the case and finish it quickly*. However, if the significator of the judge is retrograde, it signifies that the judge or king or person in authority will not proceed in that case according to the order of the law, he will not end it, indeed, it will be prolonged longer than it should be according to law.[55]

---

52 '. . . et si vnus significator fuerit retrogradus significat debilitatem et fugam negociationem quoque atque mendacium illi cuius fuerit significator, id est, si fuerit dominus ascendentis retrogradus erit debilitas interrogantis: si vero fuerit dominus septime retrogradus: erit debilitas contentoris'.

53 'Postea opportet te videre utrum dominus ascendentis vel dominus septime sit retrogradus quoniam si dominus ascendentis fuerit retrogradus significat debiltatem querentis et quod ipse non erit bene firmus in stando ad litem: et quod ipse negabit veritatem adversario et non confitebitur illam nec credet se habere ius. Si vero dominus septime fuerit retrogradus significat debilitatem ex parte adversarii: et quod ipse fugiet litem prout poterit: et negabit vertitatem; nec credet se habere bonam causam'.

54 'Si autem dominus medii celi aspexerit eos and fuerit retrogradus significat iniustitiam iudicum et contentio prolongabitur.'

55 'Aspice etiam significator iudicis sive fuerit rex sive potestas sive iudex qui debuerit sentenciare inter eos qui erit dominus decime domus utrum aspiciat significatores litis an

Commentary - What Bonatti adds seems clearly based on his experiences with judges and mediators in actual legal conflicts. He adds considerable detail as to the nature of the 'unjustness of the judges' and describes the judges' behaviours, both good and bad, in considerably more detail.

13. Sahl - <It is> likewise if one of the significators is being separated from the other. I call the lord of the ascendant and the lord of the matter the significators.[56]

    Bonatti - One must say the same thing about prolonging of the case if the lord of the Ascendant is separated from the lord of the seventh, or if the lord of the seventh is separated from the lord of the Ascendant.[57]

Commentary - Not much difference here.

14. Sahl - Also know this about the Luminaries, that is, the Sun and the Moon; if one of them is being joined to one of the significators, or a significator is in the domicile of one of Luminaries, it will be stronger and more dignified.[58]

    Bonatti - Next see if the lord of the Ascendant has been joined with the Sun or Moon or either of them has been joined with the lord of the Ascendant *so that no other planet impedes their joining together (as long as the joining <in question> is not a bodily conjunction with the Sun because that would signify impeding of the lord of the ascendant (unless the planet is in the cazimi of the Sun since then it would become strong)* or the lord of the Ascendant is in the domicile of a luminary, or the Sun or Moon are in the Ascendant; because, if it is so, it signifies the strength of the querent. But if the lord of the seventh house is disposed as I have said with respect to the lord of the Ascendant, it

---

non qui si aspexerit eos et fuerit directus incedet secundum ordinem iuris in causa illa et quod ipse nitetur abreuiare ipsam et diffinire cito.
Si autem fuerit retrogradus significat quod iudex sive rex sive potestas non incedet in causa illa secundum ordinem iuris nec curabit eam diffinire immo prolongabitur plusquam debeat prolongari de iure'.

56 'Similiter si vnus significatorum fuerit separatus ab alio: signficatores dico dominum ascendentis et dominum rei:'

57 'Idem dicendum est de prolongatione cause si dominus ascendentis fuerit separatus a domino septime: vel si dominus septime fuerit separatus a domino ascendentis'.

58 'et scito quod luminaria, id est, sol et luna si vnus eorum iuncti fuerit vni significatorum: aut fuerit in domo eius erit fortior et dignior'.

signifies the strength of the adversary.[59]

Commentary – The Bonatti passage adds considerable astrological detail that might be derived more from theory than from practice. Sahl implies that any joining by or to the Sun or Moon is good. However, it is standard astrological doctrine in the period that a bodily conjunction (both planets in the same position) of a planet with the Sun does not strengthen the planet, but weakens it. This is called 'combustion' and is derived from the fact that a planet too close to the Sun cannot be seen at any time during the day or night. The Sun is said to have burnt the planet up (combustion) and the planet becomes powerless. However, when a planet is within 0° 17' of the Sun on either side the effect reverses and the planet becomes very strong again. This is called *cazimi, zamini*, or *zamin.*

15. Sahl – . . . if the lord of the Ascendant is being joined to the lord of the Midheaven, the lord of the question <, the querent,> will seek assistance from the king. But if the lord of the Midheaven is being joined to the lord of the Ascendant, the king will give him aid without his asking. If the lord of the seventh is being joined to the lord of the Midheaven, the adversary will ask for assistance from the king, but if the lord of the Midheaven is being joined to the lord of the seventh, the king will give aid to the adversary.[60]

Bonatti – Also, see if the lord of the ascendant is joined with the lord of the tenth house. <If so,> the querent will ask for aid from the judge or from that person who must decide concerning the case. *And perhaps, <it may be> that he will strive to corrupt the judge so that the judge will bring a decision for him. And if the lord of the tenth receives the lord of the second from the Ascendant the judge will require some of the querent's money. And if the lord of the tenth house house receives*

---

[59] 'Preterea vide si dominus ascendentis fuerit iunctus cum sole vel cum luna vel aliquis eorum iunctus fuerit ei ita quod alius non impediat eorum coniunctionem dummodo non sit coniunctio solis corporalis: quia illa significaret eius impedimentum nisi esset planeta in zamini solis quia tunc fieret fortis vel fuerit dominus ascendentis in domo luminaris alicuius: vel fuerit sol vel luna in ascendente: quia si sic fuerit significat fortitudinem querenti. Si vero dominus septime fuerit ita dispositus ut dixi de domino ascendentis signficat fortitudinem adversarii'.

[60] 'et si dominus ascendentis iunctus fuerit domino medii celi queret dominus interrogationis auxilium a rege. Si vero dominus medii celi coniunctus fuerit domino ascendentis auxilabitur ei rex absque rogatu suo: si dominus .7. iunctus fuerit domino medii celi postulabit auxilium contentor a rege. Si vero dominus medii celi iunctus fuerit domino septimi auxiliabitur rex contentori'.

the lord of the Ascendant, the judge will acquiesce to the entreaties of the querent; but if it is otherwise, it will not happen. And, likewise, see if the lord of the tenth house is swifter than the lord of the Ascendant, and is joined to it; <if so> the judge or podesta will do the querent's business even if the querent does not make an entreaty. But if the lord of the seventh is joined with the lord of the tenth house, the adversary will seek aid from the judge or podesta. *But if the lord of the tenth receives the lord of the seventh, the judge will acquiesce to the entreaties of the adversary and will allow himself to be corrupted and will offer up his own cloak; otherwise, he will not. But if the lord of the tenth receives the lord of the eighth, the judge will accept the adversary's money.* But if the significator of the judge, namely, the lord of the tenth house is swifter than the lord of the seventh and is joined to him, then the judge or podesta in authority will strive to do the adversary's good business, even if the adversary makes no entreaty.[61]

Commentary - Here we see a great deal of added detail in Bonatti all having to do with the behaviour of judges and litigants. There is also a good deal of added astrological detail.

16. Sahl - When you know the strength of each of the sides with respect to the other and you know that the two sides will not be pacified, look at the king or judge who will judge between them according to the lord of the midheaven. Then see which of the significators he aspects, that is, whether the aforementioned lord of the midheaven (which is the significator of the king or judge) aspects the lord of the ascendant or the lord of the seventh. Know that the king or judge is with the side which he aspects.[62]

---

[61] 'Et aspice si dominus ascendentis fuerit iunctus domino decime domus interrogator postulabit auxilium a iudice seu ab illo qui debuerit cognoscere de causa: et forte quod nitetur eum corrumpere ut ferat sentenciam pro ipso. Et si dominus decime domus receperit dominum secunde ab ascendente petet iudex de pecunia querentis. Et si dominus decime secundi ceperet dominum ascendentis acquiescat iudex precibus interrogantis: sin autem non. Et similiter prospice si dominus decime domus fuerit levior quam dominus ascendentis et iunctus fuerit ei iudex sive potestas faciet rem querentis etiam ipso non petente. Si autem dominus septime fuerit iunctus domino decime domus adversarius queret auxilium a iudice seu potestate. Quod si dominus decime receperit dominum septime acquiescet iudex precibus adversarii et dimmittet se corrumpi et prestabit suum aminiculum aliter non. Sed si receperit dominum octave accipiet pecuniam adversarii. Sed signficator iudicis scilicet dominus decime domus si fuerit levior quam dominus septime et fuerit iunctus ei tunc iudex sive potestas nitetur facere rem adversarii bonam etiam eo non petente'.

[62] 'Cumque noueris fortitudinem vniuscuisusque eorum ex altero: et noueris quod non

Bonatti – After this should you look at the disposition and state of both significators, . . . and see that they do not wish to settle, . . . see then if the lord of the tenth is being joined to one of the significators, . . . or that one of them is being joined to it *such that neither planet is impeded in their joining together* because then the judge or one who will pronounce the decision will be favorable to that one with whose significator the lord of the tenth is being joined . . . *If none of these is being joined with any other of these, the judge will be favorable but he will proceed only according to the way of the law. But if it may be joined to both with reception, as sometimes it happens, the judge will make a settlement between them and he will make them reach agreement together, whether they want to or not.*[63]

Commentary – Again the Bonatti adds much detail about describing the behavior of the principals in a lawsuit, the litigants and the judges. Note once again the role played by reception in determining the outcome.

17. Sahl – If there is a peregrine planet in the Midheaven which does not aspect the significators, and the lord of the Midheaven does not aspect them, the two sides will decide among themselves who will judge justly between them.[64]

---

pacificabuntur aspice regem vel iudicem qui iudicat inter eos a domino medii celi: deinde aspice quem eorum significatorum aspiciat, id est, vtrum dominum ascendentis vel dominum septimi aspiciat predictus dominus medii celi qui est significator regis vel iudicis: et scito quod rex vel iudex sit cum eo quem aspicit'.

[63] 'Postquam vero videris dispositionem et esse amborum signifactorum domini scilicet ascendentis et domini septime et videris quod nolunt componere nec videbitur tibi quod component sed potius videbuntur velle litegare: vide tunc si dominus decime domus iungitur alicui significatorum domino scilicet ascendentis vel domino septime: vel quis eorum iungatur illi ita quod alius planeta non impediat eorum coniunctionem quoniam iudex seu sententiator erit favorabilis illi cum cuius significatore* ipse coniungitur: hoc est si iungitur cum significatore prime erit fauorabilis querenti: si iungitur cum significatore septime erit fauorabilis adversario: si cum nullo eorum iungitur nulli eorum erit favorabilis sed solum per tramitem iuris incedet. Si vero iungatur cum ambobus cum receptione sicut aliquando fit componet iudex inter eos et concordabit eos simul velint nolint'.

*I read *significatore* for the text's *significatori* following the rendition in Codex Vindobonensis Palatinus 2359. This is the emendation of the Ratdolt text I have made in this paper.

[64] 'et si fuerit in medio celi planeta peregrinus non aspiciens eos: et dominus medii celi non aspexerit eos: ipsi inter se constituunt qui iuste iudicet inter eos'.

Bonatti - *Then look at the tenth house which is the house of the one who announces the decision, and see if there is a planet in it; if it is the lord of the tenth, the judge will judge that case as carefully and as quickly as he can according to his own honor, unless that planet is Saturn. But if the planet is the lord of the bound, triplicity, or face, he will judge the case but he will not be so careful in the announcing of the decision.* But if there is a planet in the tenth which has no dignity there, nor is it received by the lord of the tenth, it signifies that the parties will not stand contented with that judge (or any other one who annouces the decision) because they both fear him and will agree on another judge and they will stand by his judgment.[65]

Commentary - Here again Bonatti adds considerable detail to the broad pattern described by Sahl.

18. Sahl - If Saturn is in the Midheaven, and he is himself the lord of the Midheaven, the judge will not judge justly, nor truly. If Mars impedes Saturn <under these conditions>, this judge will be reviled because of this judgment, and he will be defamed because of it.[66]

Bonatti - Also, see whether Saturn is the significator of the judge and whether he is in the tenth; that judge will not judge according to the law nor according to what he ought. *If at that time either Jupiter, the Sun, Mercury, Venus, or the Moon is being joined to Saturn by any aspect whatever except <the aspect> by opposition, or it is void in course, evil will be spoken of concerning the judge but that speech will be quickly suppressed and that judge will not be defamed. But if one of these planets is being joined to Saturn by opposition, evil will be said of the judge because of his unjust judgment and it will endure for a long time.* But if Mars aspects Saturn at the time by the opposition or square aspect, whatever is Mars' condition at that time, the judge or podesta will be defamed from

---

65 'Deinde aspice decimam domum que est sententiatoris: et vide si aliquis planeta sit in ea si fuerit dominus eius iudicabit ille iudex causam illam quam cautius et quam citius poterit cum honore suo nisi sit ipse saturnus. Si vero fuerit dominus termini vel triplicitatis vel faciei iudicabit eam sed non erit ita sollicitus in sententiando. Si autem fuerit in decima planeta qui non habeat ibi dignitatem nec fuerit receptus a domino decime domus significat quod partes non stabunt contente illo iudice seu sententiatore: quoniam ambe timebunt eum et convenient in alium iudicem et stabunt iudicio illius'.

66 'et si fuerit in medio celi planeta peregrinus non aspiciens eos: et dominus medii celi non aspexerit eos: ipsi inter se constituunt qui iuste iudicet inter eos. Si fuerit saturnus in medio celi: et fuerit ipse dominus medii celi: iudex non iudicabit iuste nec vere. et si mars impedierit saturnus: vituperabitur propter hoc iudex et erit inde diffamatus'.

this. *However, if Mars has an evil condition, he will be defamed with allegations worthy of blame unless Saturn is then in Capricorn, because then Mars restrains some of its malice, especially if it has a good essential dignity.*[67]

Commentary - Bonatti adds the effects of the other planets besides Mars and Saturn on the behavior of the judge. He also notes a number of factors which alter and mitigate the judgment.

19. Sahl - If Mars is in the Midheaven, the judge will be swift, and the judgment of great swiftness, intelligent and fast. If Jupiter is in the Midheaven, the judge will be just. And if it is Venus, the judge will be easy-going, of good heart, and readily sustained. If it is Mercury, the judge will be sharp in vision. *If the Midheaven is in a common sign, the first judge will not finish the judgment of the two sides, until they go to another judge.*[68]

Bonatti - *But if you find that the parties do not stand content with the previous judge but would settle upon another judge as has been said, see if there is some planet in the tenth because through that planet you will be able to know the state of of the judge upon whom the parties will settle between themselves because* if Jupiter is present in that place, the judge whom they settle upon will be a good one, benevolent, just, and benign, and will in no manner permit himself to be corrupted neither with a gift nor by entreaties, but will proceed only by the way of truth. But if it is Mars, the judge will *be false, wrathful, unfaithful, not one who loves justice,* and one who is quickly moved and changed *from proposition to proposition such that there will be yet a new error worse than the previous and they will repent that they have chosen such a judge. But if the Sun is*

---

67 'Et vide etiam si saturnus fuerit significator iudicis et fuerit in decima iudex ille non iudicabit secundum ius neque secundum quod debuerit. Si tunc iungitur ei iupiter vel sol vel mercurius vel venus vel luna a quocunque aspectu nisi ab oppositione vel fuerit vacuus cursu dicetur malum de iudice sed cito opprimetur illud dicere et non diffamabitur ob hoc iudex. Si vero fuerit iunctus ei aliquis istorum ab oppositione dicetur malum de iudice causa iniusti iudicii et durabit diu. Si vero mars aspexerit tunc saturnus ab oppositione vel quarto aspectu cuiuscunque esse tunc fuerit mars diffamabitur inde iudex sive potestas. Si autem fuerit mars mali esse diffamabitur diffamatione vituperabili nisi tunc saturnus in capricorno quia tunc refrenat mars aliquid de malicia sua maxime si fuerit boni esse'.

68 'et si fuerit mars in medio celi: erit iudex leuis et multe celeritatis acutus et velox. si vero iuppiter fuerit: erit iudex iustus. et si fuerit venus: erit leuis et boni animi: et leuiter suscipitur. et si fuerit mercurius: erit visu acutus. et signum medii celi commune fuerit: primus iudex non finet eorum iudicium donec eant ad alium iudicem'.

> *there, the judge will have a good character, yet he will let himself by dragged along by the entreaties of friends, and run himself around to them, and will give them ear and the hope of doing what they wish; yet in the end he will judge rightly.* And if Venus is in that place, the judge will be just and have good opinions *but he will not be very profound in law,* yet he will judge in good faith. And if it is Mercury in the tenth, he will be a judge having a good and acute intellect, and one who quickly sees the matter of the case, *but he will judge accordingly as Mercury is applied to by the <other> planets; if it is by fortunes, <he will judge> justly, if by malefics, unjustly; if it is applied to by no planet, the judge will judge accordingly as he himself finds the evidence.*[69]

Commentary - Here is yet more detail on the subject of the behaviour of judges in Bonatti.

Material at the End of the Chapter Found in Bonatti but not in Sahl.

> And in all of the aforesaid accidents the lord of the Ascendant and the lord of the seventh and the significators mentioned previously are considered without the participation of the Moon; even though she is herself a sharer naturally in every matter, yet something is to be derived from her <state>. For if the Moon is in the tenth house the judge will be light and unstable and one who will judge just as it seems to him. Not considering much what the law may be nor caring what he may judge, nor what will be said concerning his judgment whether good or bad.
>
> You will also consider a certain secret which I do not remember having ever found in the sayings of the ancients; yet I have tried this and found it

[69] 'Si quidem inveneris quod partes non stent contente priori iudice sed constituant fidialium sicut dictum est: aspice si fuerit aliquis planeta in decima: quoniam per illum poteris scire esse iudicis quem constituent inter se partes: quoniam si fuerit ibi iupiter erit iudex quem constituent bonus et benivolus iustus atque benignus: et per nullum modum permittere se corrumpi neque precio neque precibus sed solum via veritatis incedet. Si vero fuerit mars erit iudex falsus iracundus infidelis non amans iusticiam et qui cito movetur et mutatur de proposito ad propositum ita quod erit novissimus error peior priore et penitebit eos elegisse talem iudicem. Si fuerit sol erit iudex boni animi tamen dimittet se trahi precibus amicorum et flectit se ad illa et dabit illis aures et spem faciendi quod volunt ultimo tamen iudicabit recte. Et si fuerit ibi venus erit iudex iustus et bone opinionis sed non erit multum profundus in iure tamen iudicabit bona fide. Et si fuerit mercurius in decima erit iudex boni ingenii et acuti et cito videns rem cause: sed iudicabit secundum quod ipse applicabitur planetis: si fortunis iuste: si malis iniuste si nulli applicabitur iudicabit secundum quod ipse invenerit probationes'.

genuine, namely, that you consider the place of the lord of the Ascendant and the place of the lord of the second, and you should take the lesser from the greater and that which remains is the residual of the lord of the first and the lord of the second. Then consider the place of the lord of the seventh and the place of the lord of the eighth and subtract the lesser from the greater and that which remains will be the residual of the lord of the seventh and the lord of the eighth. And take the two residuals and subtract that which is the less from the greater and save that third residual. Then take the place of the lord of the ninth and the place of the lord of the twelfth and subtract the lesser from the greater and that will be the residual of the lord of the ninth and the lord of the twelfth, and take that and the third residual, subtract the lesser from the greater and that which remains will be the Part Signifying Aid and Strength of the Querent or Quesited. Add this onto the degree of the sign of the Ascendant and project from the Ascendant just as you do in the <computation of the> Part of Fortune if <the chart> is in the daytime; If it is at night, project from the Nadir,[70] and see in whose domicile, exaltation, bound, or triplicity that number has ended because the planet which is the lord of that place and is stronger and more powerful in it will be what has been sought for, namely, the one that is helper of that one whose significator it more <powerfully> or better aspects to the minute, or which is nearer to that place (provided that it has in that place some dignity which renders it stronger). And this will be the more so if <the preceding> is with reception. But if both the residuals are equal, it will be signified by the Ascendant in the daytime but the Nadir in the night. And when you do this work, always prefer the lord <of the sign>. If it is impeded, work by means of the lord of the exaltation. And if that is impeded, work with the lord of the bound. If that is impeded, work at last with the lord of the triplicity because the planet into the rulership of which of any of the places which have been mentioned the Part should fall, or which it aspects the more, or which is the nearest having dignity in that place will be the one which signifies the case wherefore and in what manner things happen and from whence they happen.

But if the lord of the first and the lord of the second are the same place, it will be as if that place is the residual of the lord of the first and the lord of the second. And if the lord of the seventh and the lord of the eighth are the same,

[70] The term nadir, as used here, is a little unusual. In modern astronomical terminology it means the point directly opposite the zenith. However, the Arabic meaning of the word according to Charles Burnett is 'opposite'. Therefore, here it most likely refers to the descendant, the point opposite the ascendant, not the usual nadir.

it will be as if its place is the residual of the lord of the seventh and the lord of the eighth. Subtract then the lesser from the greater and do as has been described previously concerning the residual of the lord of the first and second, and concerning the residual of the lord of the seventh and eighth. Understand the same in battles and wars and in all controversies as it has been described concerning lawsuits.[71]

---

[71] 'Et in omnibus supradictis accidentibus considerantur dominus ascendentis et dominus septime et alii predicti significationes sine participatione lune licet ipsa sit particeps omnis rei naturaliter: tamen derogatur ei aliquid. Si autem fuerit luna in decima erit iudex levis et instabilis et qui iudicabit prout sibi videbitur non considerans multum quid sit ius nec curans quid iudicet nec quid dicatur de suo iudicio bonum seu malum.

Considerabis etiam quoddam secretum quod nunquam memini me in dictis antiquorum invenisse: fui tamen expertus et illud inveni veridicum videlicet ut consideres locum domini ascendentis et locum domini secunde et minuas minorem de maiori: et illud quod remanserit erit residuum domini prime et domini secunde. Deinde considera locum domini septime et locum domine octave et minue minorem de maiori: et illud quod remanserit erit residuum domini septime et domini octave. Et accipe illa duo residua et minue quod minus fuerit de maiorie et serva illud residuum tercium. Deinde accipe locum domini none et locum domini dudecime et minue minus de maiori et illud erit residuum domini .9. et domini .12. et accipe illud et residuum tercium et minue minus de maiori et illud quod remanserit erit pars significans auxilium atque fortitudinem querentis seu quesiti: adde desuper gradum signi ascendentis et proice ab ascendente sicut facis in parte fortune si fuerit in die: si autem in nocte proice a nadir: et vide in cuius domum vel exaltationem vel terminum vel triplicitatem finitus fuerit numerus ille: quoniam planeta qui fuerit dominus illius loci ac in eo fortior et potentior erit quesitus scilicet adiutor illius cuius significatorem magis ac melius aspexerit minuto per minutum: vel qui proprior fuerit illi loco dummodo habeat in eo aliquam dignitatem et qui fortiorem eum reddit: et eo magis si hoc fuerit cum receptione. Quod si ambo illa residua equalia fuerint erit significatum in die in ascendente: in nocte vero in nadir. Et cum operatus fueris prepone semper dominum: qui si fuerit impeditus operare per dominum exaltationis. At si fuerit impeditus operare per dominum termini. Qui si fuerit impeditus operare ultimo per dominum triplicitatis quoniam planeta in cuius <dominio> aliquorum dictorum locorum pars illa ceciderit: vel qui magis cum aspexerit vel qui ei propior fuerit habens ibi dignitatem erit significans causam quare et quomodo dicta fiant et unde accidant. At si dominus prime et dominus secunde sint idem locus eius erit tamquam residuum domini prime et domini secunde: Si quidem dominus septime et dominus octave sint idem erit locus eius tamquam residuum domini septime et domini octave: munie tunc minorm de maiorem et fac sicut dictume est de residuo domini prime et secunde et de residuo domini septime et domini octave. Quod dictum est in litibus illud idem intelligas in preliis et guerris ac in omnibus controversiis'.

Commentary – None of this material is to be found in Sahl. Also, beginning in the second paragraph we have an excellent example of how Bonatti often concludes a section with material derived from his own experience. He explicitly does this here with something he did 'not remember having ever found in the sayings of the ancients'. In this case what he adds is quite complex and not, to my knowledge, to be found in any other source, but then Bonatti's additions to the lore that he received were not always simple.

Concluding Comments

To sum up, the purpose of all of the foregoing comparison of Bonatti and Sahl is not to prove that Bonatti was a better or more learned astrologer than Sahl or that he had done anything like modern scientific research in coming to his conclusions. The additional material that one finds in Bonatti is simply an indication that Bonatti had encountered the material presented in Sahl and come to his own conclusions. This would not have happened unless Bonatti used the material in his own practice. As I will demonstrate in a lengthier analysis in my subsequent work, there are parts of Bonatti where he does not add anything to his sources, where he faithfully duplicates his sources, if not *verbatim*, certainly in equivalent words. There are even instances where he perpetuates errors of doctrine originating from his own sources. By 'errors of doctrine' I mean teachings that were not in accord with the majority of other sources which for some reason Bonatti did not have access to or chose not to consult. So Bonatti does not always add to the lore or even always transmit it accurately.

Again, my point is not to prove that Bonatti was employed for purposes of military planning. The point is to show that in an area of astrological application which some moderns might think unlikely and improbable, military strategy and intelligence, where we know that he was employed, we see exactly the kind of evolution of material that one would expect from a practitioner. This is useful to the historian because it is another way of finding what astrology was actually used for in a particular time and place. This technique of textual analysis can be used alongside of external evidence, references to astrology in philosophical and theological writings, literary allusions (Dante, Chaucer), references to the use of astrology in chronicles, records of academic curricula, and legal documents, to mention several. This method also helps us with texts themselves to sort out what a particular author may or may not have used of the material he presented in his text, material that was simply handing on the tradition or material that he himself confronted.

PAUL OF MIDDELBURG'S PROGNOSTICUM *FOR THE YEARS 1484 TO 1504*

Stephan Heilen

Paul of Middelburg (1445–1533) first published his *Prognosticum* in August 1484. Its objects were two upcoming, rare astronomical events, the conjunction of Saturn and Jupiter in Scorpio in November 1484 and a total solar eclipse in Aries in March 1485. Unlike the countless annual predictions that were published by Renaissance astronomers (including Paul himself), this prediction covers twenty years, the approximate interval between Saturn–Jupiter conjunctions. This value had been standardised in the Perso-Arabic theory of the effects of the so-called 'Great Conjunctions' on the sublunar world.[1] Paul's prediction became the most influential Renaissance text on the conjunction of 1484. The present contribution originates from the preparation of a critical edition with commentary of Paul's *Prognosticum*. As a precursor to that forthcoming edition, it aims at providing a detailed summary of the text and discussing its major characteristics.[2]

Biographical Introduction

Our author was born at Middelburg, a prosperous merchant city, capital of the Dutch province of Zeeland.[3] After a first period of schooling at Bruges, he went

---

1 The most important source text is Abū Maʿšar, *On Historical Astrology: The Book of Religions and Dynasties (On the Great Conjunctions)*, trans. and ed. Keiji Yamamoto and Charles Burnett, 2 vols., Islamic Philosophy, Theology and Science: Texts and Studies, vols. 33–34 (Leiden: Brill, 2000). See vol. I, pp. 573–613, for an overview of its sources and doctrines.

2 Up to now, there has been only one summary of this *Prognosticum*: Karl Sudhoff, *Aus der Frühgeschichte der Syphilis. Handschriften- und Inkunabelstudien, epidemiologische Untersuchung und kritische Gänge*, Studien zur Geschichte der Medizin, vol. 9 (Leipzig: J.A. Barth 1912), pp. 161–68, which consists mostly of long Latin quotations and is of no analytical value with respect to the astrological content.

3 On Paul's life, see the dictionary entries of C.G. van Leijenhorst, 'Paul of Middelburg', in *Contemporaries of Erasmus: A Biographical Register of the Renaissance and Reformation*, ed. Peter G. Bietenholz and Thomas B. Deutscher, vol. 3 (Toronto: University of Toronto Press, 1987), pp. 57–58, and Menso Folkerts, 'Paul von Middelburg' in *Lexikon des Mittelalters*, vol. VI, pt. 9 (Munich: Artemis, 1999), p. 1827. (Some details in this and the following paragraph are literal borrowings from van Leijenhorst). See further J.D. Struik, 'Paulus van Middelburg (1445–1533)', *Mededeelingen van het Nederlandsch Historisch*

to Louvain to study philosophy, theology, medicine, mathematics, and astronomy. The young doctor was ordained as a priest in his native town of Middelburg. In 1479 he became professor of astronomy in the University of Padua, an honourable appointment because he was the successor of Regiomontanus, arguably the leading mathematician and astronomer of the fifteenth century. Two years later (1481) Paul resigned from this position to enter the service of Federico da Montefeltro, duke of Urbino.[4] At that time Jacob of Speyer was the official court astrologer to the dukes of Montefeltro. Since this German had held that office for a very long time, Paul's initial employment at Urbino was that of personal physician to the duke; only later the office of court astrologer (at Jacob's side) was added.[5] We do not have evidence of horoscopes cast by Paul for Federico da Montefeltro.[6]

After Federico's death (1482) Paul remained in the service of his successors, travelling, however, for at least one extended period to the Netherlands, where he advocated a reform of the Julian calendar and engaged in a dispute over its theological implications. In 1494 Paul was appointed to the see of Fossombrone, near Urbino, and was thus in a position to participate in the fifth Lateran council (1512–1517) which was also concerned with the reform of the calendar. He was appointed head of the committee for the reform of the calendar by Pope Leo X.[7] During the council, Paul's most important work went to press: the *Paulina de recta Paschae celebratione et de die passionis Domini nostri Iesu Christi*.[8] He was

---

Instituut te Rome 5 (1925): pp. 79–118 and J.D. Struik, 'Paolo di Middelburg e il suo posto nella storia delle scienze esatte', *Periodico di Matematiche* ser. 4, 5 (1925): pp. 337–47 (with special emphasis on Paul's mathematical pursuits) and Patrizia Castelli, 'Gli astri e i Montefeltro' *Res publica litterarum* 6 (1983): pp. 78–86.

4 On this famous individual see Gino Benzoni, *'Federico da Montefeltro'*, in *Dizionario Biografico degli Italiani*, vol. 45 (Roma: Istituto della Enciclopedia italiana, 1995): pp. 722–43. For the entire lineage of the Montefeltro see Gino Franceschini, *I Montefeltro* (Milano: Dall'Oglio, 1970).

5 Castelli, 'Gli astri', p. 80. Jacob of Speyer is first attested as court astrologer in Urbino in a letter written by Regiomontanus on 15 February 1465, and last attested in a letter written by Ottaviano Ubaldini on 15 October 1494 (Castelli, 'Gli astri', pp. 79, 86). He was highly esteemed by Regiomontanus, and it was this Jacob who introduced Paul of Middelburg to Federico da Montefeltro on the occasion of a visit made by Paul who was traveling back north from Aquila (ibid. p. 79).

6 Castelli, 'Gli astri', p. 83.

7 On Paul's role in the calendar project, see John David North, *The Universal Frame: Historical Essays in Astronomy, Natural Philosophy and Scientific Method* (London: Hambeldon Press, 1989), pp. 58–64 and 70.

8 This *opus magnum* in thirty-three books contains the history of chronology and

disappointed with the council's meagre results. In 1533 Pope Paul III called the aged Dutch scholar to Rome with the intention of making him a cardinal but upon his arrival in Rome Paul of Middelburg died, half a century before the overdue reform was eventually enacted under Pope Gregory XIII (1582).[9] Numerous outstanding humanists thought highly of Paul of Middelburg; suffice it to mention Erasmus, Pico, Ficino, and Scaliger. Apart from six annual prognostications for the years 1479–83 and 1486, two astrological writings are devoted to conjunctions of Saturn and Jupiter, those of 1484 and of 1524. While the latter, written on 1 December 1523, aimed to dispel the widespread fear of a new deluge that others had predicted for the impending conjunction of all the planets in Pisces, the former was written forty years earlier, in the summer of 1484. It is the longest extant astrological treatise written by Paul of Middelburg.

Introduction to the Text

The text of the *editio princeps* was composed, or given the finishing touch, in Louvain in the days and weeks preceding its publication on 31 August 1484.[10] Paul was about to return to Italy in order to resume his work as court physician to the Duke of Urbino. Compared to other texts of the same genre, Paul's *Prognosticum* is rather long. The *editio princeps* comprises forty-three pages with thirty lines per page. Since its first leaf is blank and unsigned, there is no official title. The absence of a title indicating the technical content of this work may be due to the fact that the treatise takes the form of a letter to Maximilian of Habsburg (1459–1519). What comes closest to a title is Paul's characterisation of the text in the following words of his preface: 'equum mihi persuasi coniunctio-

---

discussions of the various scholarly opinions on how the calendar ought to be reformed. The title translates as *Work by Paul (of M.) on the right manner of celebrating Easter and on the day of the passion of our Lord Jesus Christ* (Fossombrone, 1513).

9 Struik, 'Paulus van Middelburg', p. 87, and Lynn Thorndike, *A History of Magic and Experimental Science*, 8 vols. (New York: Columbia University Press, 1923–1958), vol. 4: p. 561.

10 'Gesamtkatalog der Wiegendrucke' (GW) N° M 3021210; 'Incunabula Short Title Catalogue' (ISTC) N° ip00187550. I used the copy from the university library of Cologne which is available online at http://inkunabeln.ub.uni-koeln.de/vdib-info/kleioc/ip00187550. One more copy of the *editio princeps* is extant in the university library at Cambridge. It presents marginal corrections by the same hand that annotated the Cologne copy. Two of these corrections concern astronomical data (see the section 'Astronomy and astrology in the *Prognosticum*'). Another handwritten correction in the Cologne copy is printed in the Cambridge copy which must, therefore, be a subsequent printing. I am grateful to Dr Emily Dourish (Cambridge) for providing me with this information.

nis magne atque horrende eclipsis solis future prognosticum nomini tuo dicare'.[11] Paul's addressee, the later Holy Roman Emperor, was a keen supporter of the arts and sciences. He was, at that time, twenty-five years old and Count of Zeeland, Paul's home province. Therefore Paul addresses Maximilian as his sovereign.[12]

The Preface

Paul's long preface (fol. a2^{r}–<a5>^{r}) begins with a typical early modern praise of the virtues of the addressee, Maximilian, who is even called divine (*divus*).[13] This praise is resumed at the end of the preface, thus making it a ring composition. We learn from these extremely flattering pages that Paul did not know Maximilian personally. Nevertheless, Paul writes that he came to love and revere Maximilian with all his heart because of the latter's widely known, excellent virtues. As a second reason for his reverence, Paul adduces Maximilian's role as a patron of scholars which leads him, generally speaking, to consider himself fortunate for being one of Maximilian's subjects and, more specifically, to greet the learned patron and send him the latest product of Paul's scholarship before leaving Zeeland on his way to Italy. The implicit quest for patronage is resumed at the end of the text.

Federico da Montefeltro, in whose service Paul had been since 1479, had died in 1482. The duke had been one of the most important patrons of the arts in Italy. When that powerful, impressive man was succeeded by his twelve-year-old son Guidobaldo (1472–1508), the court of Urbino was likely to have lost much of its attraction for Paul. The Dutch scholar could not foresee, in 1484, that Guidobaldo's marriage with Elisabetta Gonzaga (1471–1526) two years later (1486) would lay the foundation for re-establishing the splendour of Federico's court and that another child at the time, Baldassare Castiglione (1478–1529), would start writing his famous *Book of the Courtier* at the court of Urbino in 1508.

---

[11] Fol. a2^{v}; trans.: 'I thought it proper to dedicate to you a prediction on the great conjunction and the dreadful future solar eclipse'. This and all subsequent references are to the foliation of the *editio princeps* unless explicitly stated otherwise. A slightly modified version of this implicit title became the official title in a revised edition that Paul prepared in 1486 for the court of Urbino which will be quoted in n. 22. The classification of the conjunction of 1484 as 'great' is inappropriate. More on this in the analysis of Chapter I.

[12] Fol. a2^{r}: 'domine mi obseruandissime'. As to the Latin spelling *u/v*, quotations in this contribution will follow the sources without an attempt at standardising the orthography.

[13] Fol. a2^{r}: 'Illustrissimo ac maximo principi diuo Maximiliano Austrie duci Burgondie Brabantie etc. domino suo colendissimo Paulus de Middelburgo Zelandie illustrissimi ducis Vrbini phisicus Salutem plurimam dicit'.

Paul may have been looking for a new patron after Federico's death. Although he pretends that the opportunity of writing to Maximilian came entirely unexpectedly,[14] the *Prognosticum* was certainly not written in a hurry while Paul was preparing his departure from Zeeland. As an astronomer and astrologer, he must have known for years that this conjunction would occur in 1484. In addition, the unprecedented length and elaboration of the *Prognosticum*, including hundreds of unacknowledged borrowings from all eight books of Firmicus Maternus' *Mathesis* that are interspersed in the text, indicates a longer process of composition.[15] The official reason given by Paul is, therefore, most likely a pretext, a well-chosen one because the alleged *insperata occasio* emphasises the chronological relevance of the *Prognosticum* to an imminent danger and provides Paul with a good reason for flattering Maximilian by choosing a place of publication in this sovereign's province. There is one detail that seems to confirm Paul's claim of having written the *Prognosticum* in Louvain not long before its publication, namely the reference to the death of Pope Sixtus IV on 12 August 1484.[16] It is, however, likely that Paul brought a more or less complete draft of the *Prognosticum* with him from Italy to Louvain and added the detail concerning the pope's death when the news reached him there.

There are further arguments for this assumption. Apart from the aforementioned time-consuming, rhetorical elaboration based on Firmicus Maternus, there is a series of anonymous references by Paul to a personal enemy in Italy which makes little sense in the cultural and scholarly environment north of the Alps. In addition, while no relevance of that enemy of Paul's to Maximilian is discernible, there is one to Guidobaldo da Montefeltro; the 'protonotary apostolic', as our author calls his opponent, is Giovanni Barbo, a Venetian with good connections to the Roman Curia. Giovanni's uncle, Pietro Barbo, had been Pope Paul II (1464–71) who appointed his nephew as one of the apostolic protonotaries. Giovanni had been a student of Paul's at Padua, but they fell out with each other because Paul predicted that Giovanni would not enjoy further support by way of nepotism after his uncle's death.[17] As a consequence of this alienation,

---

14 Fol. a2r: 'nescio profecto, quonam pacto insperata occasio ad te scribendi sese obtulerit'.

15 One may even doubt the availability of a copy of the *Mathesis* in Louvain, while there certainly was one in the duke's famous library in Urbino (now Vat. Urb. lat. 263). On all this, see my forthcoming article 'Paul of Middelburg's use of the *Mathesis* of Firmicus Maternus', from the proceedings of the conference *Astrologers and their Clients in Medieval and Early Modern Europe* (Erlangen, 29-30 Sept. 2011), ed. David Juste and Wiebke Deimann (forthcoming).

16 More on this will be presented in the analysis of Chapter V.

17 See Franco Gaeta, 'Barbo Giovanni', in *Dizionario Biografico degli Italiani*, vol. 6 (Roma:

Barbo criticised his former teacher's annual prediction for 1483 in print, calling himself (in the title) 'Giovanni Barbo, apostolic protonotary' and his former teacher (in the first sentence) 'astutissimus et maliciosissimus'.[18] By doing so, he not only roused Paul's wrath but also discredited him with Guidobaldo da Montefeltro to whom Paul had, for the first time after Federico's recent death on 10 September 1482, dedicated his annual prediction for 1483. We do not know if the young duke and his tutor Ottaviano Ubaldini, an extraordinary man with a strong interest in magic and astrology,[19] somehow obtained a copy of Giovanni Barbo's pamphlet. But it is very likely that they came to learn about the confrontation between the court physician and his former student because Paul, who was obviously furious, published no less than three increasingly longer retorts written between March 1483 and February 1484.[20]

The same year (1484) saw, only a few months later, the first edition of the *Prognosticum* that is under scrutiny here. Interestingly, Paul dedicated a revised version to Guidobaldo da Montefeltro and his tutor Ottaviano Ubaldini in late 1486.[21] In this revised version some details regarding Maximilian are omitted, especially allusions to his military prowess which would not make sense in the case of fourteen-year-old Guidobaldo, while some others regarding the new addressees and various Italian cities are added.[22] However, the substance and

---

Istituto della Enciclopedia italiana, 1964): pp. 243–44.

18 *Antipauli* [sic]. *Johannis Barbi Prothonotarii Apostolici Veneti Patricii iudicium De Anno 1483*. At the end, the text is dated Padua, 11 March 1483. The date of printing is unknown but must have been in the following days.

19 See Castelli, 'Gli astri', p. 85.

20 Paulus de Middelburgo, *Antiprothonotarii categoria* ('Accusation directed against the protonotary'). *Ineptiarum per dominum iohannem barbum apostolicum prothonotarium patriciumque uenetum calumniatorem meum contra me propositarum confutatio* (12 pages long), not dated, printed in Venice, probably very soon after Barbo's pamphlet had been published; an expanded version followed immediately afterwards: *Venatio apri siue piscatio barbi et antiprothonotarii categoria*, dated Venice, 27 March 1483 (18 pages long); a still more elaborate attack, *Prothonotariomastix* ('Protonotary-whip'), was dated Urbino, 28 February 1484 (28 pages, printed at Louvain sometime later the same year).

21 Paul dated the text 31 December 1486. It was printed soon afterwards (i.e., 1487) in Venice by Thomas de Blavis. Only one copy is extant (Sevilla, Biblioteca Colombina). Immediately after the three-line salutation of the two addressees, and before the rewritten preface begins, the following title is inserted: *Magne coniunctionis ac tetre Solis eclypsis pronosticum xx annorum* (fol. a<1>^{r}).

22 This 'zooming' into the geographical and political details of the Italian peninsula is limited to the final part of Chapter IV. Note that not all changes can be explained with respect to the change of addressee. Some changes are modifications of astronomical,

the length of the text remained basically the same. In view of the public controversy described above it is reasonable to assume that the anonymous allusions to the 'apostolic protonotary', which remained unchanged from the first to the revised edition, would be intelligible to Guidobaldo and his tutor. Their polemic inclusion in the *Prognosticum* of 1486 would be a reasonable strategy of the Dutch scholar to continue defending his reputation at the court of Urbino. At the same time the omission of the odious name of the protonotary in question could have been a strategy of *damnatio memoriae*.[23]

Taken together, the evidence suggests that the *Prognosticum* was originally conceived for use at the court of Urbino and only temporarily adapted to an additional use abroad. Paul seems to have had, from the very beginning, the intention of dedicating his text to his own patron, Guidobaldo da Montefeltro, and to Ottaviano Ubaldini who had, as mentioned above, a strong interest in astrology. If that was so, Paul's visit to the Netherlands in 1484 would have provided him with the *insperata occasio* of using the unpublished draft of his *Prognosticum* twice by dedicating the text to different addressees.

We shall now, after this historical excursus, return to the preface of the *editio princeps*. It continues by specifying that the object of the prediction will be two upcoming astronomical events, a 'great conjunction and a dreadful solar eclipse'.[24] The *Prognosticum* will be useful both for the *docti* of Maximilian's court and for the *vulgus indoctum*. This leads to a praise of divination and three polemics, one individually directed against the aforementioned anonymous opponent of Paul's own divination (Giovanni Barbo), which will be iterated several times in the course of the text, and two others more generally directed against the opponents of astrology. The praise of divination contains numerous examples from the ancient world when diviners of all sorts—Paul mentions *astrologi, augures, auspicia, haruspices, magi, mathematici*, and the *Sibilla*—allegedly were more highly esteemed than in Paul's own time. The examples are mostly drawn from Quintus's arguments in the first book of Cicero's *De divinatione* (partly also from Livy) and suitable to the new context because they are about various ancient kings; Maximilian will have understood the relevance of this art

astrological, or theological details and quotations.

23 One wonders what motivated Paul to include the polemical allusions to Barbo in his first edition at all, because Maximilian would probably not have understood them. Maybe Paul did so with respect to another group of readers, namely his colleagues in Louvain and other northern universities who were somewhat more likely than Maximilian to have taken notice of Barbo's invective against his former teacher.

24 Fol. a2v: 'coniunctionis magne atque horrende eclipsis solis future prognosticum nomini tuo dicare'.

to his own present and future power. Passing from Antiquity to his own time, Paul claims to have, himself, predicted correctly the events that troubled Italy in the preceding years.[25]

Paul briefly sums up that all peoples of all times hold divination in high esteem and moves on from this *argumentum a consensu gentium*[26] to attack the opponents of astrology. Their alleged folly is first qualified as a gross lack of education, even as blasphemy, because they refuse to acknowledge that the movements of the stars are God's instrument for governing the world. Paul gives his polemic rhetorical emphasis by directly and coarsely attacking one hypothetical, individual denier of the astrologically meaningful structure of the cosmos.[27] The punishment that allegedly awaits such people is then exemplified with a reference to the ancient philosopher Plotinus who, as Paul has it, inconsiderately thought himself exempt from stellar influences and was punished with terrible illness and painful death. This extensive polemic (it occupies more than half a page in the *editio princeps*)[28] is an abridged version of the same polemic in the first book of the *Mathesis* of Firmicus Maternus.[29] This substantial borrowing, unlike the previous ones from Cicero and Livy,[30] lacks acknowledgement. It is difficult to judge whether Paul intended to dissimulate his largely literal borrowing or whether he thought the source was so well known as to need no explicit reference. The latter, however, seems unlikely: in the absence of printed copies of the *Mathesis* (the *editio princeps* was published in 1497) the low number of available manuscripts in 1484 seems to exclude the possibility that there existed a widespread knowledge of Firmicus Maternus' polemic against Plotinus.[31]

---

[25] He must be referring to his earlier annual predictions for the years 1479–83.

[26] Vgl. 'ea, que omnium gentium firmata sunt consensu' (fol. a3^r).

[27] Fol. a3^r: 'heus tu . . .'

[28] Fol. a3^v.

[29] Firmicus Maternus, *Mathesis* 1.7.14–22. On this passage, see Paul Henry, *Plotin et l'Occident: Firmicus Maternus, Marius Victorinus, Saint Augustin et Macrobe*, Spicilegium sacrum Lovaniense, Études et documents, vol. 15 (Louvain: Peeters, 1934), pp. 25–43, who gives an analysis of Firmicus' source (Porphyry's *Vita Plotini*), references to earlier secondary literature, and the retrospective diagnosis of Plotinus' disease as leprosy.

[30] They are summarily acknowledged with the words 'Cicerone teste … Cicerone teste … Liuio teste' (fol. a2^v).

[31] According to Michele Rinaldi, *'SIC ITUR AD ASTRA': Giovanni Pontano e la sua opera astrologica nel quadro della tradizione manoscritta della Mathesis di Giulio Firmico Materno*, Studi Latini, vol. 45 (Naples: Loffredo, 2002), pp. 27, 51, 235–51, a total of thirty-four manuscripts from the eleventh to fifteenth centuries is extant and not mutilated in the section regarding Plotinus (1.7.14–22).

Paul then returns to addressing Maximilian and humbly implores his sovereign's benevolence, associating him with Jupiter and Mercury.[32] He anticipates the possible objection that Maximilian, having plenty of astrological advisers in Louvain, does not need Paul's *Prognosticum*, but justifies his initiative by saying that he hopes to be recognised and favoured as a devoted servant.[33] Paul declares himself ready to serve Maximilian if the sovereign wishes to make use of his service. On this thought the prefatory letter ends. It is dated Louvain, 31 August 1484.[34]

Now the astrological treatise begins. In its introduction, Paul emphasises the immense difficulty of his task. He mentions the imperfect kinematic models of stellar movements of his day, the complexity of parameters (especially the overwhelming number of previous conjunctions) to be taken into account, and the imponderable effects of both divine providence and human free will. As a consequence, he proclaims that his goal will be accomplished if his predictions match the future events not exactly, but roughly.[35] In view of the *immensa difficultas* (fol. a4^v^) of his task he digresses into a long, rhetorically elaborate prayer for divine assistance in which various chunks of text from Firmicus Maternus (especially from his prayer in the preface to the fifth book of the *Mathesis*) and from Virgil are interwoven.[36] Eventually, he announces that his treatise will fall into seven chapters in accordance with the number of the seven planets, and what the content of each chapter will be. This peculiar structure is again, like the previous polemic against Plotinus and the prayer for divine assistance, inspired by Firmicus Maternus who says explicitly, in the last chapter of his work (8.33.1), that the *Mathesis* falls into eight books, one for the introduction plus

---

32 Fol. a3^{v}: 'iouiali humanitate ac mercuriali benignitate . . . iouiali fronte'.

33 Fol. a3^{v}–a4^{r}: 'Et quamquam apud me dubium minime sit excellentiam tuam [. . .] complures peritissimos et insignes mathematicos Louanii residentes habere, non tamen importunum mihi uisum est mearum quidem litterarum ad te aliquid dare [. . .]'. Paul does not pretend to have anything to add to or improve on the work of Maximilian's astrologers at Louvain.

34 Fol. a4^{r}: 'Vale et lege feliciter. Louanii pridie kalendas Septembris anno domini Mccccclxxxiiii'.

35 He metaphorically speaks of seeing but shadows and trying to predict bodies not too different from those blurred outlines, or—negatively put—to deny the coming of bodies that are substantially different from those blurred outlines: 'satis fructus ex hoc uaticinio nostro percepisse nobis persuadeamus, si ex qualitate umbrarum sese offerentium in celestibus causis possimus non ualde dissimilium corporum formas promittere uel ualde dissimilium negare' (fol. a4^{v}).

36 Firmicus Maternus, *Mathesis* 1.5.7; *Mathesis* 5 praefatio 3–6; *Mathesis* 7.1.2; Virgil, *Aeneid* 1.663.

seven in accordance with the number of the planets. Paul's unacknowledged exploitation of Firmicus Maternus continues throughout the *Prognosticum* and leads to some oddities when Paul starts discussing astrological details.[37]

Chapter I

The first chapter provides the astronomical data on which the prediction will be based. Paul informs the reader that the conjunction of Saturn and Jupiter will occur on 25 November 1484, at 6:04 PM, at 23° 43′ ♏, with 13° ♋ ascending.[38] He does not specify the longitudes of the luminaries and the remaining three planets nor the geographical coordinates to which his data apply.[39] As is to be expected, Paul's data imply that he means the true conjunction which, according to the Alfonsine tables, occurred on the day and afternoon mentioned by Paul, not the mean conjunction which, according to the same tables, occurred several months earlier.[40] Paul's astronomical data of all three alignments that are central to his arguments will be illustrated and discussed comprehensively after our review of the text.[41]

The effects of this conjunction will, according to Paul, be terrible, due to a combination of negative features: the conjunction will take place in the sign of Scorpio, which is both an evil sign in itself and a house of malevolent Mars; in addition, Mars will be in Aries, his own house, in the midheaven; and, most importantly, Saturn will be 'elevated' over Jupiter.[42] In addition, Mars will be the lord of the conjunction (*dominus coniunctionis*). Thus both malefic planets will prevail over Jupiter and render the effects of the conjunction dire.

Paul continues arguing that numerous other celestial events need to be taken

---

37 Cases of astrologically inappropriate recycling of formulations contained in the *Mathesis* will be discussed in my forthcoming article cited in n. 16.

38 The *editio princeps* contains two typographical mistakes that are corrected in the subsequent editions: instead of 25 November, it has 29 (*xxix*, fol. <a5>v), and instead of 23° 43′ ♏, it has 23° 23′ ♏ (error of perseveration). The true date of the conjunction was 18 November (more on this in the second paragraph below Figure 2 from the section 'Astronomy and astrology in the *Prognosticum*'.

39 Some planetary data are interspersed in later chapters where Paul, wishing to explain specific details of his prediction, refers to this or that planet being in a certain house (to be discussed in the section 'Astronomy and astrology in the *Prognosticum*').

40 Computed with *Deviations 11*, developed by Raymond Mercier, Cambridge, UK.

41 See the section entitled 'Astronomy and astrology in the *Prognosticum*'.

42 'Elevation' is a polyvalent criterion that Paul uses in the sense that Saturn will be at a more northerly celestial latitude than Jupiter. This is true, as computation based on the Alfonsine tables reveals.

into consideration because they, too, contribute in various measure and quality to the effects of the conjunction of 1484. This is in keeping with the Arabic doctrine of the 'Great Conjunctions' and, more generally, with the tendency of astrologers of all times towards complex sets of parameters that allow—from their own point of view—for adequate interpretations of a complex world or—from the point of view of their critics—for flexible excuses if predictions happen to fail. Paul argues that the strongest and most detrimental contribution will be made by a total solar eclipse four months later, on 16 March 1485.[43] He further mentions two conjunctions that had already occurred in 1483, one between Jupiter and Mars and one between Saturn and Mars. They can be dated to 2 and 30 November, respectively.[44]

The remainder of the first chapter is devoted to the profections and directions of important earlier conjunctions in world history, namely those that preceded the Deluge, the birth of Jesus Christ and the appearance of Muhammad (571 CE) as well as those of four other years: 848 CE (a great conjunction with the beginning of a new cycle), 1365 CE (a middle conjunction with change of triplicity), 1425 CE (a triple conjunction), 1464 CE (the one in whose final phase of influence Paul is writing). He further computes the vernal equinox of the year of the upcoming conjunction, saying that it occurred during the night of 10/11 March 1484, with ♏ ascending, and the preceding conjunction of the luminaries (New Moon) on 26 February 1484, at 1:15 PM, with 1° ♌ ascending.[45] Altogether the quality of Paul's astronomical data is, within the limits of early modern astronomy, good. In the last sentence of this chapter he apologises for sometimes calling the conjunction of 1484 a great one (although it ought to be classified as a small one because it does not imply a shift of triplicity). He does so with the odd justification that it is bigger than other small conjunctions.[46] Apparently Paul wishes to enhance the importance of his topic.

---

43 On this date there was, indeed, a total solar eclipse whose umbra went through central Europe (see the third paragraph from the end of the section 'Astronomy and astrology in the *Prognosticum*'. In Chapter V we learn that the longitude of the eclipse was 6° ♈.

44 The *editio princeps* erroneously gives the longitude of the conjunction of Jupiter and Mars as 18° ♏ (*re vera* 25° 30′ ♎) which was actually the longitude of the Sun (18° 38′ ♏). The revised edition of 1486 no longer contains the reference to this conjunction, probably because Paul had realised that it did not take place in the house of Mars (♏).

45 For all this, see fol. <a6>r–<a7>r. The New Moon actually occurred some twenty minutes earlier than calculated by Paul, when the last degrees of Cancer were rising.

46 Fol. <a7>r: 'si coniunctionem hanc aliquando magnam appellauerimus, id ad minores eam referendo intelligi uelimus'. One example of such terminology is quoted above in n. 25.

In the following three chapters Paul examines the effects of the conjunction of November 1484. Chapter II is devoted to its general—or, in modern terms, global—effects,[47] Chapter III to its specific effects on various individuals, and Chapter IV to some single predictions.

Chapter II

The second chapter begins with a protestation of Paul's Christian orthodoxy: the conjunction of 1484 will neither limit the omnipotence of God nor the free will of man. Its effects are, therefore, subject to change (*mutabilia*). This, combined with the difficulty of taking those many other astronomical parameters into account which had been mentioned in the previous chapter and which all allegedly contribute somehow to the effects of our conjunction, makes the adequate interpretation of the conjunction of 1484 a very complex task.

After this clarification Paul gives a thoroughly negative overall characterisation of the upcoming conjunction which will bring all sorts of want and calamity.[48] Its most obvious general consequence, which is described at considerable length in highly rhetorical style, will be misery for the virtuous and prosperity for the wicked.[49] This will be brought about by the already-mentioned elevation of evil Saturn over benign Jupiter. All sorts of severe illnesses will be another effect.[50] Apart from the conjunction itself, the impending calamities will also be announced by meteorological and seismological phenomena, especially by comets and earthquakes.

Next, the conjunction will cause misfortune for kings, especially those who live in mountains. For this detail Paul explicitly quotes the Latin version of Abū Maʿshar's *Book of Religions and Dynasties*,[51] possibly with the intention of alluding to Maximilian or (since Maximilian was not king in 1484) to his father Frederick III, the holy Roman emperor, whose residence in Austria (Vienna) might, by one who is writing in the Netherlands (Louvain), be thought of as being *in montibus*.

The fact that the conjunction will occur in the fifth house, which symbolises

47 Fol. <a7>^{r}: 'per omnem terrarum tractum'.

48 Fol. <a7>$^{r-v}$: 'maligna hec constellatio uidetur et plurimum minax ac maliciosa potestate composita [. . .], ut recte angustiarum significatio et calamitatum denunciatio appellari possit'.

49 Fol. <a7>^{v}–<a8>^{r}.

50 Fol. <a8>$^{r-v}$: repeated in briefer wording towards the end of Chapter II (fol. b2^{v}).

51 Album. *De magn. coni.* 6.8.1–3 (Abū Maʿšar, *On Historical Astrology*, ed. Yamamoto and Burnett, vol. II, p. 244).

children,[52] combined with the additional circumstance that Saturn is the infamous child devourer of ancient myth,[53] will cause great suffering to embryos and newborn children, as well as to women who are pregnant or about to give birth. Paul takes this opportunity to speak profusely of abortions, terrific birth pains and premature deaths of both mothers and newborn children.

But he is not yet finished: our expert reminds his reader that the fifth house signifies pleasure (*voluptates*), too. This will make people impudent, gluttonous, and—more than anything else—sexually licentious. The conjunction will (again in view of the prominent role of shabby Saturn in it)[54] produce all kinds of perversion, prostitution, incest and adultery, not only among men but among women as well, because Venus will, at the time of conjunction, join Saturn and Jupiter in the fifth house. Even nuns and priests will indulge in despicable vanity and outrageous carnal pleasures. In his description of all this Paul keeps drawing extensively on Firmicus Maternus who was similarly indefatigable in describing sexual matters (fol. b1^{r-v}).

The remainder of Paul's long second chapter on general effects examines both the chart of the conjunction itself and that of the preceding vernal equinox. There will be extreme climatic conditions, precipitations of immoderate quantity (too large when not needed, insufficient in other seasons) and of harmful astrological quality, crop failure, devastation of crop by armies, sickness-provoking winds, and so on. At the conclusion of Chapter II, Paul asserts that the effects of the conjunction will last twenty years, with the most detrimental period to be expected from the eighth to the sixteenth year, i.e., between November 1491 and November 1499 (to be further explored in the analysis of Chapter V).

Chapter III

After these general effects discussed in the second chapter, the third contains more specific predictions for individuals in whose natal charts 'the principal places or the primary cardines or the hyleg or almuten' will be contaminated by the conjunction.[55] Such persons will suffer countless misfortunes that will, in

52 Fol. b1^{r}: 'in quinta ab horoscopo hoc est in filiorum et nouiter natorum domo'. Since Paul regularly calls the sections of the dodecatropos 'houses' (*domus*), this term will be used in discussing his text, even if the ancient term 'places' (*loci*), which Firmicus Maternus employs, is in principle preferable because it avoids confusion with the zodiacal houses of the planets.

53 Fol. b1^{r}: 'quem puerorum comestorem fingunt'.

54 Paul does not say this, but his description contains numerous adjectives such as *impurus, sordidus, fetidus*, etc., that are typical of Saturn.

55 Fol. b2^{v}: 'quorum principalia natiuitatis loca uel primos geniture infecerit cardines, aut

each individual case, depend on the nativity's ascendant and dominating planet. After some random examples of the misfortunes to be expected Paul concludes that it is difficult to imagine that any individual could escape the vast variety of harmful effects of the conjunction unless he or she has bright fixed stars in the ascendant or is suitably protected by one of the benevolent planets (Jupiter and Venus).[56] He then embarks upon a systematic theoretical discussion of various possible cases based on the twelve astrological houses.[57] Depending on which house of an individual's natal chart happens to be affected by the impending conjunction of Saturn and Jupiter, either bodily or by aspect, the effects on the individual in question will be different. In the first house, they will be health problems (including psychological distress and mental disorders such as epilepsy); in the second, poverty; in the third, impiety, blasphemy, fraternal strife; in the fourth, parricide and dissipation of patrimony; in the fifth, sterility, impotence, difficult pregnancy and miscarriage; in the sixth, dangers from servants and maids; in the seventh, all sorts of marriage problems and undesired brides (ugly, old, poor, adulterous, crippled, sterile, socially unacceptable, quarrelsome);[58] in the tenth, loss of political power or physical fall from an elevated position. With regard to the eighth, ninth, eleventh and twelfth houses, Paul asserts summarily that their effects will be in accordance with these houses' natural properties and powers.

Chapter IV

The fourth chapter in this *Prognosticum* had by far the strongest impact on contemporary ideas, expectations for the future and retrospective interpretations of history. In it, Paul examines the significance of the impending conjunction for the history of religion and announces the birth of a 'minor prophet'. This technical term is prominently placed at the beginning of the chapter's first sentence:

---

quorum inimica aliqua radiatione hyleg aut almutas percusserit aut aliqua ex parte damnauerit'. Paul uses the indeclinable form *almutas* for the lord of the geniture, thus transliterating the Arabic *al-mubtazz* ('mighty'). See As'as Masri, 'Arabisches Lehnwortgut im Englischen' (Dissertation, FU Berlin, 1982), p. 38. In the Latin translation of Abū Maʻshar the term is transliterated as *almubtez*.

[56] Fol. b3r: 'ut uix aliquis humanam fragilitatem indutus huius seuissime coniunctionis discrimina poterit subterfugere, nisi claras aliquas stellas in horoscopo habuerit aut beniuole alicuius stelle presidio protectus fuerit'. On bright fixed stars see Firmicus Maternus, *Mathesis*, 6.2 'De claris signorum stellis'.

[57] A similar discussion of various cases is found in the last paragraph of the analysis of Chapter VI.

[58] Paul does not envisage undesired bridegrooms.

'Surely this prodigious alignment portends that a minor prophet will be born who will dazzle through [his] astonishing interpretation of the gospels and give responses with almost divine authority, one who will subject the souls of mortals that descended [from heaven] to earth to his power'.[59]

Although Paul expects to meet the consensus of all other astrological experts, he finds it appropriate to justify the core of his prediction before giving detailed information about the 'minor prophet'. With this in mind, he first contextualises the upcoming conjunction in the series so far by informing the reader of the signs (partly also the degrees) and triplicities of the conjunctions since 1325 CE:

1325	♊, air
1345	♒, air
1365	8° ♏, water, a 'great conjunction with change of triplicity'[60]
1385	♊, air
1405	♒, air
1425	13° ♏, water
(1444)[61]	water
(1464)	water
1484	water

He further asserts that the next change of triplicity will occur in 1563 and that the next following conjunction (1583) will switch back to the watery triplicity (♓). All this is astronomically correct except for the presumed future change of triplicity in 1563 which actually occurred forty years later, in 1603 (a detail irrelevant to Paul's purpose).[62] Based on these data, Paul explains that the small

59 Fol. b4^{r-v}: 'Prophetam quippe minorem mira quadam scripturarum interpretatione fulgentem ac quadam diuinitatis auctoritate responsa proferentem, qui mortalium animas ad terram delapsas sue subiiciet ditioni, prodigiosa hec constellatio nasciturum portendit'.

60 Fol. b4^{v}: 'coniunctionem magnam mutate triplicitatis'.

61 Paul does not actually mention the years 1444 and 1464 in this chapter. He only says that the conjunctions had not left the watery triplicity since 1425. He explicitly mentions the year of the conjunction of 1464 in an earlier passage on fol. <a6>^{v}.

62 This is a pardonable mistake on Paul's side if one takes into consideration that almost a century later Tycho Brahe (1546–1601) still thought that he had, in 1563, witnessed a change from the watery to the fiery triplicity. Cf. Tycho Brahe, *De disciplinis mathematicis oratio* (1574), in *Tychonis Brahe Dani Scripta Astronomica*, ed. John Louis Emil Dreyer

conjunction of 1484 will 'expand and bring to light whatever had been signified and decreed by the great conjunction with its change of triplicity in 1365'.[63] The time of this delayed effect will be that of the sixth immediately following conjunction, i.e., the year 1484. For this detail, which is of central importance to his argument, Paul refers to Abū Ma'shar whose relevant lines he quotes thus:

> 'The time of the appearance of the event will, in the watery triplicity, be two conjunctions after the return to the sign of the triplicity'. And explaining this he says: 'this means after six immediately following conjunctions'. And indeed it is established that this one will be the sixth from the first of this triplicity and the second of a (or: characterised by a) return to the sign of Scorpio.[64]

In view of both the importance and the difficulty of these lines we shall examine first what Abū Ma'shar actually means, second how Paul departs from the teaching of his authority and last, why he does so. Abū Ma'shar says, in the English translation by Yamamoto and Burnett:

> As for the time of the appearance of the indication, the fiery triplicity indicates three conjunctions after the return of the conjunction to the sign of the triplicity to which the conjunction shifts; in <the case of> the airy and earthy triplicities, four conjunctions, and in the watery triplicity, two conjunctions. It is possible that the times of the indications are different: according to this scheme, the indications of the shift to the fiery triplicity occur after nine conjunctions from the time of the shift, in <the case of> the airy and earthy <triplicities> after eight conjunctions, and in the watery triplicity after six conjunctions.[65]

(Hauniae: Libraria Gylendaliana, 1913, repr. Amsterdam: Swets & Zeitlinger, 1972), p. 156, 20–21: 'Sic anno M.D.LXIII, cum magna contigißet Saturni et Jouis combinatio, in initio Leonis partiliter, . . .'

[63] Fol. 4bv: 'his sic premissis dicimus coniunctionem hanc minorem expansuram et in lucem producturam, quecunque significata sunt et decreta per coniunctionem magnam mutate triplicitatis in octauo scorpionis factam anno christi Mccclxv teste Albuma [fol. <b5>r] sare tractatu primo coniunctionum magnarum differentia ii dicente 'tempus apparitionis etc' (this quotation will be continued above in the main text).

[64] Fol. <b5>r: ' "tempus apparitionis euentus in triplicitate aquea ad duas erit coniunctiones post reuersionem ad triplicitatis signum", quod exponens dicit "hoc est post sex coniunctiones immediate sequentes". hanc autem sextam a prima huius triplicitatis fore constat atque secundam reuersionis ad scorpionis signum.' I hesitatingly take *reuersionis* as a *genetivus definitivus.* The fact that it is repeated without change in the revised edition of 1486 speaks against emendation to *reuersionem*.

[65] Album. *De magn. coni.* 1.2.4 (Abū Ma'šar, *On Historical Astrology*, ed. Yamamoto and Burnett, vol. I, p. 31). The editors add the following note: 'In the second scheme one would expect 9, 12, and 6 conjunctions after the shift, in symmetry with the 3, 4, and 2

The Latin translation is preserved in two different versions, **V** and **C**.[66] We shall present the Latin text as edited by Yamamoto and Burnett (vol. II, p. 19) together with the variants of both versions of the textual transmission as given by the editors in their *apparatus*:

> De tempore autem apparitionis significationis triplicitatis ignee, erit ad tres coniunctiones post reversionem scilicet coniunctionis ad ipsum; in triplicitate vero aerea et terrea, ad .4. coniunctiones; in triplicitate aquatica, ad duas coniunctiones. Acciditque ut sit corruptio ex parte universitatis significationum mutationis ad triplicitatem igneam secundum hunc ordinem post novem coniunctiones ab hora mutationis; in aereis quoque et terreis, post .8. coniunctiones; et in triplicitate aquatica, post .6. coniunctiones.
>
> **2** *scilicet* om. **C** **3** *ad ipsum*] *ad signum triplicitatis ad quod mutata est coniunctio* **C** **3-4** *et terrea* om. **V** **4** *in*] *et in* **C** **5** *acciditque*] *accidit ergo* **C** | *corruptio*] *mutatio* **C**

It is obvious from the first two entries of the apparatus that Paul is following version C of the textual tradition.[67] It is further clear that the first sentence of version C is—except for the perfect tense of *mutata est*—the literal equivalent of the corresponding words of the Arabic original. Somewhat less obvious is what Abū Ma'shar means with 'after the return of the conjunction to the sign of the triplicity to which the conjunction shifts' (= 'post reversionem coniunctionis ad signum triplicitatis ad quod mutata est coniunctio', version C).[68] The *return*

conjunctions of the first scheme'.

[66] See Abū Ma'šar, *On Historical Astrology*, ed. Yamamoto and Burnett, vol. II, pp. xv–xvi. The majority of the MSS belong to version C.

[67] It is unclear how and where Paul had access to manuscripts of version C. The library of Federico da Montefeltro seems not to have included a manuscript copy of *De magnis coniunctionibus* (there is no such codex Vaticanus Urbinas extant), nor is any relevant codex Lovaniensis extant today. Paul may have had access to cod. Vat. lat. 5713 (1388 CE) or to cod. Flor. Ashburnham 127 (201/133) (saec. XV, 'provides a very poor text' according to Yamamoto and Burnett [eds.], Abū Ma'šar, *On Historical Astrology*, vol. II, p. xxviii). Needless to say, Paul did not have a printed copy available either for his *editio princeps* or for his revised edition of 1486 because the *editio princeps* of *De magnis coniunctionibus* was published only in 1489.

[68] The following analysis gained greatly from a discussion with Dorian G. Greenbaum who contributed important observations on some other details as well.

(*reversio*) seems to be that which occurs sixty years after a shift of triplicity when the conjunction of Saturn and Jupiter occurs again in the same zodiacal sign in which the shift had previously taken place. This meaning of *return* (*reversio*) is attested to beyond doubt in at least two other passages (ibid. 1.3.10; 2.8.32). The alternative interpretation of our passage is to take *return* (*reversio*) to mean the shift of triplicity to where the conjunctions had taken place 960 years earlier. This meaning is equally attested in *De magnis coniunctionibus*, and its first occurrence (1.1.16) is the only instance of the noun *reversio* or the verb *reverti* that precedes our passage in question (1.2.4). Therefore this alternative interpretation might, *prima facie*, seem easier and preferable. On the other hand, Abū Ma'shar would be speaking in a very clumsy and complicated manner (why not just say '*after the shift*'?), and would be blurring the terminological distinction between 'return' (*reversio*) and 'shift' (*mutatio*) within one and the same sentence. In conclusion, it seems safe to assume that in 1.2.4 Abū Ma'shar meant the small sort of return, that which occurs after sixty years.

If we also take into account his subsequent discussion of various cases and apply the rule to our specific case, the result is that after the shift of the cycle from the airy to the watery triplicity (in the year 1365) the effects of the conjunction of the shift will be delayed until the second conjunction following the return to the shift (1425), i.e., to the year 1464. There is, however, an alternative scheme that Abū Ma'shar describes in the second part of the above quotation: if that applies, the delay of the effects after a switch of the cycle (from the airy to the watery triplicity) is delayed until the sixth conjunction following the shift: in our case, from that of 1365 to that of 1484.

One sees that Paul has incorrectly reported the original teaching of Abū Ma'shar. His mistake consists in the establishment of a false logical relationship between the two numerical schemes by introducing the words *exponens* and *hoc est* which are absent from the manuscript tradition of the Latin translation of Abū Ma'shar. They suggest identity of meaning instead of alternative applicability. Paul tries to harmonise the second scheme with the first: more specifically, to show that the conjunction of 1484 is, depending on the method of counting, the sixth as well as the second after that of 1365. The sixth conjunction immediately following that of 1365 equals the second return of the cycle to the sign of the 1365 conjunction with its shift of triplicity (Scorpio). Even if this explanation is mathematically impeccable, is it not supported by Abū Ma'shar's original teaching. Nevertheless, Paul's erroneous explanation is pardonable in view of one decisive word hidden in the *apparatus criticus*: At the beginning of the second part of paragraph 1.2.4, where Yamamoto and Burnett print *acciditque*, version C has *accidit ergo*. Whoever made *ergo* part of version C distorted the sense of the Arabic original by giving the transition from the description of the first to the second scheme the appearance of logical coherence instead of what is actually intended: a contrast. A reader of version C such as Paul of Middelburg would in all likelihood find the text of paragraph 1.2.4 with its two incompatible numerical schemes connected by *ergo* confusing and fail in his attempt at correctly understanding Abū Maʿshar's intention.

Let us now take the problematic claim for granted that the effects of the conjunction of 1365 will be delayed: not until 1464, as Abū Maʿshar's main scheme would have it (a year of no use to Paul of Middelburg), but until 1484, as Abū Maʿshar's alternative scheme would have it. The quality of the effects of the conjunction of 1484 will then be determined by the astrological house in which the conjunction of 1365 took place. Paul asserts that this was, in most parts of Europe, the third and that this signified the coming of a prophet: 'illa mutate triplicitatis coniunctio aduentum prophete significabat, cum in pluribus Europe regionibus in tercia ab horoscopo facta extit<er>it'.[69] This crucial sentence implicitly refers to the following passage:

> And let us say that, when the conjunctions shift from triplicity to triplicity and (if) any one of the three superior planets is in the ninth or third (house) from the ascendant of the same conjunction that signifies their appearance, and especially Saturn, this will signify the births of prophets.[70]

Paul does not mention the discrepancy between his confidence expressed in the present passage that the remote conjunction of 1365 can be dated to the day and hour (the hour is needed to determine the house of the conjunction chart) and his earlier, much more cautious remark about the difficulty of determining the precise day of a conjunction of Saturn and Jupiter: 'cum uix coniunctionis diem certum et constitutum ob motuum tarditatem habere possimus'.[71] In fact, he misdated the conjunction in November 1484 by an entire week. Even if Paul could not know the impressive magnitude of his astronomical mistake, his own words show that he must have been aware of the extreme uncertainty of the result of his (or any contemporary's) calculation of the conjunction house in 1365

---

69 Fol. <b5>^{r}.

70 'Dicamusque quia, quando mutantur coniunctiones a triplicitate in triplicitatem et fuerit aliquis planetarum trium superiorum in nono vel in tertio [scil. loco] ab ascendente eiusdem coniunctionis significantis apparitionem eorum, et maxime Saturnus, significabit hoc nativitates prophetarum'. Album. *De magn. coni.* 1.3.3 (Abū Maʿšar, *On Historical Astrology*, ed. Yamamoto and Burnett, vol. II, p. 23).

71 Fol. <a8>^{v}–b1^{r}.

and, consequently, of the prominence of the religious dimension in his prediction. He never breaks his silence about these things. Instead, he adds, in the passage that is here under scrutiny, that he could adduce much corroborating evidence from the writings of 'the very wise Abū Ma'shar and the divine Māshā'allāh', such as the aspect of Mars from the third house of the horoscope of the vernal equinox of the year 1484 to Saturn (being located in the ascendant: see Fig. 1, below), from Saturn being lord of the ninth house of the conjunction (because its cusp happens to fall into Aquarius: see Fig. 2, below), and so on, but that he will, for the sake of brevity, refrain from providing a complete list of arguments.[72]

Next, Paul addresses the place, time, portents, and circumstances of the appearance of the prophet as well as his character. He will be born in a country subject to Scorpio in the fifth *clima*,[73] but emigrate later and engage in his miraculous activity in a country subject to Aquarius or Leo, the signs in square aspect to Scorpio. Since Scorpio is a solid sign (a so-called *signum fixum* or *stabile* or *immobile*),[74] Paul predicts that the prophet will be born no earlier than after a complete cycle of profections,[75] i.e., no earlier than twelve years after the conjunction: in other words, not before late 1496. He will be preaching over a time-span equal to 'the minor years of the Sun', i.e., 19 years,[76] and establish a

---

[72] Fol. <b5>r: 'possent et alia multa sapientissimi Albumasaris et diuini messehale testimonia adduci ex marte coniunctionis dispositore a tercia reuolutionis saturnum respiciente, tum ex saturno domino none coniunctionis et reliqua, que breuitatis gratia missa faciemus'. Instead of really stopping his argumentation at that point, he continues to refer to the characteristics of the conjunction of 1425 and to the horoscope of the vernal equinox of that year.

[73] On this technical term see Ernst Honigmann, *Die sieben Klimata und die πόλεις ἐπίσημοι: eine Untersuchung zur Geschichte der Geographie und Astrologie im Altertum und Mittelalter* (Heidelberg: C. Winter), 1929.

[74] This Latin terminology was translated from Arabic; see Wolfgang Hübner, *Die Eigenschaften der Tierkreiszeichen in der Antike: ihre Darstellung und Verwendung unter besonderer Berücksichtigung des Manilius*, Sudhoffs Archiv. Beiheft 22 (Wiesbaden: F. Steiner, 1982), pp. 74–76 (n° 1.311.1–2).

[75] Fol. <b5>v: 'non nisi post complementum reuolutionis unius profectionum'. On the technical term 'profectio', meaning the movement of one sign a year, see Abū Ma'šar, *On Historical Astrology*, ed. Yamamoto and Burnett, vol. I, p. 578.

[76] See, for example, Hugo of Santalla, *Liber Aristotilis* 3.1.8 (*De annis stellarum*), in: *The* Liber Aristotilis *of Hugo of Santalla*, ed. Charles Burnett and David Pingree (London: The Warburg Institute, 1997), p. 40; for Antiquity, Auguste Bouché-Leclercq, *L'astrologie grecque* (Paris: E. Leroux, 1899), p. 410.

new religion.[77] The colour of his clothes will either be reddish (Mars) or white (Jupiter, Moon). He will be recognised easily because his body will be stained with black marks and will be disgraced by dark spots on the right side of his abdomen, groin or thigh because of the position of the Lot of Fortune.[78] These marks will be concentrated on the back of his body because of the 'effeminate nature' of the ascending signs of both charts (the vernal equinox and the conjunction itself), i.e., Scorpio and Cancer (see figs. 1 and 2 below). He will have another mark (*signum*) on the chest because 'the lot of the mark' (*signi pars*) will be in 6° Leo.[79]

The prophet will be an extremely strong personality that Paul describes in terms borrowed (this time with acknowledgement)[80] from Firmicus Maternus'

---

77 Fol. <b6>^{r}: 'nouam religionem instituet'.

78 Fol. <b6>^{r}: 'Nam notis quibusdam nigris immaculatum corpus et fuscis uarietatibus aut maculis in dextro ipocondrio, inguine uel femore dedecoratum corpus habebit ex parte fortune in dextro celi atque in decima ab horoscopo collocata'. Cf. Album. *De magn. coni.* 1.3.5 (Abū Ma'šar, *On Historical Astrology*, ed. Yamamoto and Burnett, vol. I, p. 37, with n. 4). Instead of calculating the Lot of Fortune of the horoscope of the vernal equinox of 1365 as prescribed by Abū Ma'shar, Paul seems to have calculated the Lot of Fortune of the conjunction horoscope of 25 November 1484. I plan to show this with a detailed argument in the commentary to my forthcoming edition.

79 Fol. <b6>^{r}. Paul is here referring to Album. *De magn. coni.* 1.3.7 where the computation of a lot for discovering the position of birthmarks is described (cf. Abū Ma'šar, *On Historical Astrology*, ed. Yamamoto and Burnett, vol. II, p. 24 and comm. vol. I, p. 594). The details of Paul's computation will be commented on *in extenso* in the forthcoming edition of this text. Abū Ma'shar wants the interpretation of the lot to be based on zodiacal melothesia which traditionally associates the chest with Cancer, the heart and the two sides with Leo. For the early modern period, see the numerous manuscript illustrations of the so-called 'zodiac man' (ex. gr. Karl Sudhoff, *Graphische und typographische Erstlinge der Syphilisliteratur aus den Jahren 1495 und 1496* (München: Carl Kuhn, 1912), plates III–IV). They usually place Cancer on the chest and Leo a little lower. See, for example, the most famous and most beautiful one in the *Très Riches Heures du Duc de Berry* (http://upload.wikimedia.org/wikipedia/commons/7/76/Anatomical_Man.jpg). A monographic study of these 'zodiac men' by Wolfgang Hübner is *Körper und Kosmos. Untersuchungen zur Ikonographie der zodiakalen Melothesie*, Gratia, vol. 49 (Wiesbaden: Harrassowitz, 2013). Note also that according to Firm. math. 6.2.2 the bright fixed star Regulus is at 5° Leo on the chest of the celestial Lion.

80 It is the only explicit reference to Firmicus Maternus in Paul's *Prognosticum*. In his revised version of the text (1486), Paul slightly rephrased this passage and substituted the reference to Firmicus Maternus with one to Henricus de Malinis (Henry Bate of Malines). The literal quotation from Firmicus Maternus, however, remained mostly intact.

description of an exorcist: He will be 'frightening to gods and demons', work miracles, and free people that are possessed by evil spirits without a word, simply through his appearance.[81] In Firmicus Maternus' *Mathesis*, this prediction is the apodosis of a conditional clause referring to people born with Mars located in one of his zodiacal houses and in the ninth house of the *dodecatropos*. While the first condition is fulfilled in the chart of the conjunction of 1484 (Mars in Aries), the second is not, because Mars was—according to Paul—in the tenth house.[82]

With reference to the Lot of Rulership in the eleventh house of the conjunction horoscope and the interpretation of this datum by Antonio da Montolmo, Paul characterises the future prophet as highly intelligent and learned but also a hypocrite, an unscrupulous liar, one who will have a 'branded conscience' (because of Mars, lord of Scorpio) and who will, like a scorpion, splash his martial poison by agitating wars and causing much bloodshed.[83] Since he is signified by Mars, Paul presumes (with reference to Māshā'allāh) that the prophet's intention will be to reconfirm the 'Chaldean' faith, i.e., Mazdaism.[84] Despite his

81 Fol. <b6>r: 'Erit nanque Firmico teste diis et demonibus terribilis. signa multa et prodigia faciet, eius quoque aduentum praui demonum spiritus fugient, talique morbo laborantes homines non ui uerborum sed sola sui ostensione liberabit'. Cf. Firmicus Maternus, *Mathesis*, 3.4.27. Paul's use of the *Mathesis* will be analyzed in detail in the forthcoming article cited in n. 16.

82 Fol. <b5>v: 'ex marte in decima' (scil. *domo*).

83 Fol. <b6>r. The calculation of the Lot of Rulership (*pars regni*) is described by Album. *De magn. coni.* 1.4.6 (Abū Ma'šar, *On Historical Astrology*, ed. Yamamoto and Burnett, vol. II, p. 29). If its position is in the eleventh or twelfth place (Paul would say 'house'), it indicates a discrepancy between these individuals' words and deeds ('Que si fuerit in .11.° vel .12.° [sc. loco], quod dicunt hoc et non faciunt', ibid.; cf. the English translation of the apodosis from the Arabic original, ibid., vol. I, p. 47: 'it indicates that they say that but they do not do it'). An alternative method for calculating the Lot of Rulership is described in Album. *De magn. coni.* 1.4.8. For Antonio da Montolmo see Vittorio de Donato, 'Antonio da Montolmo', in *Dizionario Biografico degli Italiani*, vol. 3 (Roma: Istituto della Enciclopedia italiana, 1961), pp. 559–60. I have not been able up to now to identify the text and passage to which Paul is referring here.

84 Fol. <b6>r. Paul's unspecific reference to the name of Māshā'allāh is difficult to interpret. As the editors of this volume point out to me, Paul may have been using an intermediary source such as Al-Qabīṣī. On the association of planets with religions however, see, Album. *De magn. coni.* 1.4.4 (Abū Ma'šar, *On Historical Astrology*, ed. Yamamoto and Burnett, vol. II, p. 28) who interprets specific conjunctions of Jupiter with each one of the six remaining planets as signifying one of six world religions. About Jupiter in conjunction with Mars he says: 'Et si complexus fuerit ei Mars, significat culturam ignium et fidem paganam' (ibid.). The Arabic original means 'If the mixer with

ability to work miracles, good Christians must not follow him; on the contrary, he will be one of those to whom the warning of the gospel applies (Matth. 24, 23–26).

The fourth chapter finishes with a remark that the whole explanation could be further substantiated with reference to 'the wise men of Egypt and Babylon' as well as to Ptolemy, Hali Abenragel, Albumasar, Al-Kindī, and even Archimedes.[85]

Chapter V

The fifth chapter is about the total solar eclipse of 16 March 1485. Solar eclipses always signify major events, as Paul asserts with a quotation from chapter 7 of Māshā'allāh's letter on eclipses and planetary conjunctions,[86] all the more when and where they happen to be total. The eclipse in question will enhance the dire effects of the preceding conjunction of Saturn and Jupiter, and it will do so with more or less intensity based on the expected path of its umbra. Paul declares that the north-western part of Europe will be most affected by the conjunction because the eclipse will be total there; in other parts of Europe it will be partial; in distant regions such as Scythia, India and Taprobane (Sri Lanka) it will not be visible at all. Italy, Germany, France, Spain, and England will all be affected more or less strongly. It goes without saying that this geographical area, especially the north-western part of Europe where the eclipse will be total, includes the territories that are subject to Paul's addressee, Maximilian.

Mars will govern the eclipse because it will occur in his sign (Aries). He will do so with some weak participation of Venus and Mercury: of Venus because she will be the almuten (i.e., the ruling planet) of the eclipsed cardine (i.e., of the

---

it [i.e., Jupiter] is Mars, it indicates the worship of fire and the faith of Mazdaism' (ibid., vol. I, p. 45). Paul's term *Chaldaei* for Mazdaism in this context is found in other Latin authors, too. See, for example, Roger Bacon, *Opus maius*, pars IV, ed. John Henry Bridges (Oxford: Clarendon Press, 1897), 1: p. 256.

85 Paul had recently translated a treatise of Archimedes on spherical geometry from Greek into Latin.

86 Fol. <b7>r. Māshā'allāh's *Epistola in rebus eclipsis lune et in coniunctionibus planetarum ac reuolutionibus annorum* reads thus (cap. 7, fol. 148va [wrongly numbered '143'] of the *editio Veneta* 1493): 'Capitulum 7 in eclipsi solis et eius significatione. dixit messahallah: Scito quod in eclipsi solis non potest fieri quin significetur aliquod magnum accidens secundum quantitatem eclipsis ipsius, hoc est ut sit ex quarta corporis solis et supra'. The *editio Veneta* of 1493 is *Liber Quadripartiti Ptholemei cum commento Haly Heben Rodan*, available online at http://nbn-resolving.de/urn:nbn:de:bvb:12-bsb00060372-7. In this print version, the text of Ptolemy and his commentator is followed by several works of Māshā'allāh and other astrological authors.

descendant = Pisces); of Mercury because he will be lord of the ascendant (Virgo).[87] The effects of this solar eclipse will be far worse than any preceding eclipse in the people's collective memory, including the terrifying solar eclipse that occurred on 12 February 1431, which was total in central Italy and preceded the death of Pope Martin V on 20 February.[88]

Since the eclipse of 1485 will take place in the royal sign of Aries,[89] its effects will be worst on kings. They ought to expect a wide variety of misfortunes including the loss of their lives and kingdoms, especially if their enthronement takes place in that very year. Similar effects will apply to smaller rulers and governors of cities. The effects will come about more quickly for those who hold the highest positions in their respective hierarchies. The two individuals that are at greatest risk will be the Holy Roman Emperor Frederick III (Maximilian's father) and the newly elected Pope, unless one considers these two most powerful individuals on earth are directly subordinate to the will of God and therefore exempt from stellar influences. Sixtus IV had died on 12 August 1484. He was succeeded by Innocent VIII on 29 August, two days before the date of publication that is specified in the colophon of Paul's *editio princeps*. These latest events were apparently not yet known to Paul because he continues with a prayer that the new pope may be elected on a favourable day and enthroned at a favourable hour. In any case the Church will be exposed to various dangers that can, according to Paul, be understood from the great conjunction that preceded the birth of Christ.[90] He then returns to the matters of kings and describes all sorts of misfortunes that they ought to expect. Paul makes anonymous predictions for a few rulers, one individual who has Aries ascending (in his horoscope) and another one who is called a *scorpionista*, i.e., one who has Scorpio ascending. The reader will remember that Aries and Scorpio are the respective signs of the eclipse (1485) and the conjunction (1484).

In a second step, the consequences for private individuals are envisaged. Particularly endangered are those who have 6° Aries or 13° Gemini ascending. It is to be understood (but never explicitly stated by the author) that these are the

---

87 Fol. <b7>v: 'Mars namque loci eclipsati dominus summo de celo deficientem solem ac lunam exagono respiciens eclipsis gubernationem sibi uendicat cum debili ueneris eclipsati anguli almutas ac mercurii ascendentis domini participatione'. See the diagram in Figure 3.

88 See the discussion of contemporary reports on this eclipse by Francis Richard Stephenson, *Historical Eclipses and Earth's Rotation* (Cambridge: Cambridge University Press, 1997), pp. 407–08.

89 Fol. <b7>v: 'in signo regali et in capite fiet zodiaci'.

90 He does not explain how.

zodiacal longitudes of the eclipse and of Mars, lord of the zodiacal sign of the eclipse. The former individuals will lose their eyesight, presumably because it will be at 6° Aries that the luminaries, symbolising the right (Sun) and left (Moon) eye, will be eclipsed; the latter will be burned alive, presumably because of the fiery character of Mars. More generally speaking, all those will suffer from the eclipse in whose horoscopes the first cardines and principal places are contaminated and troubled by the eclipse. Those whose 'giver of life' (*hyleg*) occupies 6° Aries will die. Brute animals such as rams and kids will also suffer, and there will be famine and drought because Aries belongs to the fiery triplicity.

According to Paul the eclipse will occur in the seventh house.[91] This is surprising for reasons that will be explained below. Nevertheless, there is not the slightest doubt about the correct transmission of this datum. The ordinal *septima* is confirmed by its astrological interpretation, which is all about women and marital affairs (see below), and matches a piece of 'hidden' astronomical information given soon afterwards in the same chapter, namely that Virgo was ascending at the time of the eclipse.[92] On the other hand, Paul locates Mars in the tenth house.[93] Soon after the entry of the luminaries into the seventh house, Mars will cross the midheaven and move from the tenth house into the ninth. All this leads to the conclusion that Paul imagined the house division of the eclipse chart as very similar to the one that is given as Figure 3 below,[94] when Mars is still in the tenth house but the luminaries are already in the seventh and the ascendant in Virgo, thus satisfying all the given data.

Paul interprets his datum that the eclipse will take place in the seventh house thus: it signifies manifold dangers to women, especially because Venus, the planet with the highest dignity (*almuten*) in the sign of the seventh house, is 'infected' by Saturn.[95] The results will be marital dissensions, hatred, forbidden

---

91 Fol. <b8>^{v}: 'obscuratio [. . .] in septima ab horoscopo facta'.

92 Fol. c1^{v}: 'Grecia quoque que ascendenti eclipsis subiicitur'. In astrological geography, Greece belongs to Virgo.

93 Fol. <b7>^{v}: 'summo de celo' (see above n. 86).

94 With the obvious difference that he would have drawn up a square diagram, not a circular one.

95 Fol. c1^{r}: 'Saturnus . . . uenerem septime domus almuten inficiens'. Paul does not explain his reasoning. He seems to be taking Venus as the *almuten* of the seventh house (Pisces) because her astrological exaltation is there and/or because Venus rules the watery triplicity, to which Pisces belongs, in daytime charts. As to her being 'infected' by Saturn, he was probably thinking of a quartile aspect between Saturn and Venus. According to the Alfonsine tables (computed with *Deviations 11*) the longitude of Saturn was 29° 55′ ♏, that of Venus 27° 47′ ♒. The true longitudes were 0° 12′ ♐ (Saturn) and 27° 4′ ♒ (Venus)

desires, prostitution, and so on. Mars (in Gemini) in opposition to the lord of the seventh house (Jupiter, lord of Pisces, located in Sagittarius across the zodiac from Gemini) will add wantonness, petulance, a burning desire to satisfy their passions, and many other misfortunes, including various kinds of death connected to the natives' amorous pursuits.

Towards the end of this chapter Paul returns to geographical questions. The eclipse will affect primarily countries that belong to the sixth and seventh climates, that are western rather than eastern, and that are, according to astrological geography, governed by Aries, such as Tuscany, France, and Britain, but also all those countries that are governed by signs of the same fiery triplicity as Aries, namely Leo and Sagittarius.

Last, Paul analyses the time when the effects of the total solar eclipse will come about. He mentions two different methods of computation, both based on the distance of the eclipse from the ascendant. One method—anonymously championed by *alii*—consists in counting one month for each hour or sign of that distance. This would, according to Paul, result in a peak of the bad effects of the eclipse in the course of the second year after its occurrence (i.e., between March 1486 and February 1487; it is not quite clear how Paul arrived at this result). The other method—explicitly attributed to Ptolemy and his commentator ʿAlī ibn Riḍwān (*Halirodoan*)—counts one year for each hour of that distance. This would, again according to Paul, result in a peak of the bad effects of the eclipse in the tenth and eleventh years after its occurrence (i.e., between March 1494 and February 1496). In view of the totality of the future obscuration of the Sun's disk, Paul assents to this latter doctrine.[96]

This reasoning is somewhat obscure due to the brevity of Paul's explanation. It will be useful to clarify at least some details and show that Paul is not really following Ptolemy. Paul explicitly refers to the second book of Ptolemy's

---

(computed with *Galiastro* 4.3, developed by Paessler Software, Erlangen [Germany] based on modern planetary theory and SwissEphem).

96 Fol. c1v: 'Verum de tempore quo hec euenient uarias auctorum inueni sentencias. nam et si omnes per distantiam eclipsis ab ascendente hoc inuestigare conentur, alii tamen per horas distantie alii per signa id inquirunt qui tamen adhuc inter se diuersitatem non modicam recipiunt. Alii namque pro qualibet hora aut signo mensem accipiendum iubent, alii uero non minoris auctoritatis ut Ptholomeus et Halirodoan pro qualibet hora distantie ab ascendente annum unum accipiendum censent. primos itaque imitando maiora erunt hec mala anno secundo post eclipsim currente, Ptholomei tamen secundo quadripartiti sentencia maxima erunt hec mala et fortiori calamitate preualida anno decimo atque undecimo post eclipsis diem, cui etiam propter obscurationis magnitudinem satis assentimus'.

Quadripartitum (i.e., the *Tetrabiblos* or, more correctly, *Apotelesmatika*). The relevant chapter is the seventh in Hübner's authoritative count. It equals chapter 6 in the count of Robbins ('Of the Time of the Predicted Events'). We will have to pay special attention to the Ptolemaic concepts of 'duration' and 'delay'. Ptolemy associates the equinoctial hours of the duration of an eclipse in a specific locality with the duration of its effects counted either in years (in the case of solar eclipses) or months (in the case of lunar eclipses).[97] Applied to our case, that rule would lead to, roughly speaking, two years for the duration of the effects because it takes roughly two hours from the beginning of a solar eclipse to its end.[98] Immediately afterwards Ptolemy speaks of the delay between the time of the eclipse and the beginning of its effects.[99] This delay is to be deducted from the position of the place of the eclipse relative to the cardines and to be counted in months. Ptolemy does not mention years in the context of computing the delay, nor does he distinguish between the luminaries. The maximum delay envisaged by Ptolemy is twelve months, regardless of which luminary happens to be eclipsed. Applied to our case, the delay would amount to a figure close to the maximum of twelve months because the eclipse will, as quoted above, take place in the seventh house, almost opposite the ascendant. Ptolemy further says that the effects of an eclipse near the ascendant are worst in the first third of the time span of the effects, of an eclipse near midheaven in the second third of that time span, and of an eclipse near the descendant during the last third of that time span.[100] Applied to our case, then, they would be worst during the last third of the approximate two-year time span following the approximate one-year delay, i.e., by many years earlier than Paul's prediction has it.

Paul does not mention the Ptolemaic distinction between the delay of the beginning of the effects and their ensuing duration. He inaccurately combines the chronological unit 'year'—which Ptolemy uses only in the computation of the duration of the effects (and only of solar eclipses)—with Ptolemy's criterion

---

97 Ptolemy, *Apotelesmatika*, 2.7.2 lines 560–62 Hübner [= ch. 2.6 pp. 166–67 Robbins]).

98 The reason is simple: Since the Sun's and the Moon's diameters are both ca. 0° 30′ (with obvious variations depending on the Moon's distance from earth and the earth's distance from the Sun), the Moon will have to move ca. 1° from the first to the last contact with the Sun; the Moon moves at an average speed of ca. 13°/day = ca. 1°/2h; therefore a solar eclipse will take ca. two hours. The eclipse in question actually lasted 2h 2m 30s along its path of totality. This figure was computed with *Astrowin* by Dr Wolfgang Strickling (http://www.strickling.net/software.htm).

99 Ibid. l. 563–565 Hübner.

100 Claudius Ptolemy, *Apotelesmatika* 2.7.3 lines 565–572 Hübner (= ch. 2.6 pp. 166–7 Robbins).

for the delay, namely the distance of the eclipse from the cardines. However, it becomes somewhat easier to follow Paul's rationale when we take a look at his second authority, 'Alī ibn Riḍwān. The Arabic commentator recommends a slightly different method from that which Ptolemy prescribes.[101] He omits the separation between the respective calculations of delay and duration. Instead, he determines the three moments in time when the effects of the eclipse will begin, reach their middle and end, from the respective elongations of the eclipse (i.e., of the longitude of the luminaries) from three different ascendants: that of the beginning of the eclipse, that of its middle (in our case, totality) and that of its end.[102] These elongations are supposed to be counted clockwise, in seasonal hours, from the ascendant.[103] The results must be converted into larger time units—the commentator does not say which ones, but the inner logic of his argument requires years for solar eclipses and months for lunar eclipses. The reason is this: both Ptolemy and 'Alī ibn Riḍwān obtain the duration of the effects of a solar eclipse by converting the hours of the duration of the eclipse into years. While this procedure is arithmetical in the relevant chapter of the *Quadripartitum*, it becomes geometrical in the commentary where the duration of the eclipse corresponds to the final section of an arc extending clockwise from the ascendant to the zodiacal position of the luminaries at the time when the eclipse will end. If this final section of arc must be converted into years, it would be absurd to convert the remaining section in a different time unit. Applied to our case, that means the following: as has been shown above, Paul envisages the eclipse as taking place right after the entry of the luminaries into the seventh house. This entry occurs roughly ten hours after sunrise.[104] By 'taking place' (*facta*)[105] Paul must mean the few minutes of totality of the solar eclipse.[106] The

---

[101] The relevant section is fol. 39rb in the *editio Veneta* of 1493, cited in n. 85.

[102] 'Alī ibn Riḍwān (ed. Veneta 1493, fol. 39rb) speaks of the 'elongatio eclypsis ab ascendente principij eclypsis' as indicating the time 'quando incipiet accidens [i.e., the effect] eclypsis. Similiter quando sciueris horas elongationis eclypsis ab ascendente medij [scil. eclypsis], scies quando erit medium accidentis, et quando horas sciueris elongationis ab ascendente finis [scil. eclypsis], scies quando complebitur accidens eclypsis'.

[103] The maximum elongation possible is 180° (= 12 hours) if the eclipse takes place on the descendant. Eclipses in the lower, invisible hemisphere are irrelevant. Cf. ex. gr. Anon. comm. on Ptolemy, *Apotelesmatika* 2.6 (Hieronymus Wolf, ed., [Basel: Petri, 1559], p. 64): 'Nam subterranei defectus, cum nobis non appareant, nihil ad nos attinent'.

[104] It is more or less irrelevant whether we compute this time-span in seasonal or equinoctial hours because the equinoctial points (0° ♈ and 0° ♎) were near the horizon and moving towards it.

[105] See the quotation in n. 90.

[106] This is because of Mars moving from the tenth into the ninth house soon afterwards;

first contact between the luminaries occurs roughly one hour earlier, the last contact one hour later. The eclipse would then comprise the tenth and eleventh hours of that day. That would nicely match Paul's expectation of the effects of the eclipse during the tenth and eleventh year after the astronomical event.

This is no more than an attempt at understanding Paul's method. One could object that Paul speaks of the period of the worst (!) effects in the tenth and eleventh years and that the entire duration of the effects must therefore be longer, actually three times as long in view of Ptolemy's rule quoted above.[107] But this objection is not valid because it would require that the eclipse have a duration of six hours from the first to the last contact of the luminaries, which is impossible. If Paul really had that Ptolemaic rule of the tripartition of the years of the effects of the eclipse in mind, the worst period would last less than one year; in this case Paul's speaking of two years, the tenth and the eleventh, would make sense only if the tenth hour is assigned to the western part of Europe and the eleventh to the eastern part where the local time of the eclipse would be one hour later for 15 degrees of longitudinal distance. However, Paul does not mention longitudinal differences with regard to the time of the effects; if he did, one would rather expect him to speak of the tenth *or* (not 'and!') the eleventh year because each of these two periods would refer to only one of two separate geographical regions, not both of them together. Be this as it may, the easiest explanation is that Paul, wishing that his *Prognosticum* be read all over Europe, did not make geographical differentiations, that he did not bother to observe Ptolemy's tripartition of the duration of the effects, and that he exaggerated a bit by speaking, with regard to the tenth and eleventh year, not just of the period of the effects but of the period of the worst effects.

As mentioned earlier, the tenth and eleventh year means the period from March 1494 to February 1496. This period coincides chronologically with the middle of the period of the worst effects of the conjunction which, as the attentive reader will remember, will extend from November 1491 to November 1499.[108] And the most disastrous single effect, the birth of a false prophet, will not take place before late 1496. The years 1494 to 1496 will then be thoroughly dire.

Chapter VI

The title of the sixth chapter announces a treatment of the fortunes of various

---

see the fifth paragraph of the analysis of Chapter V, above.

107 Ptolemy, *Apotelesmatika* 2.7.3.

108 See above in the analyses of Chapters II (last paragraph) and IV (fourth paragraph from the end).

nations and of the clergy. Christian ecclesiastical environments will all suffer from the two impending astronomical events. Paul exploits the late antique metaphor of the *Navicula Petri* to envisage storms, hurricanes, agitated waves, tossing about and ultimately the shipwreck of the Church—if God does not protect it in his mercy. There will be grave dissensions among the prelates, hatred and ambition; they will devote themselves more than they usually do (*plus solito*) to delights and banquets and they will be involved in lewd passions that will cause deadly diseases.[109] Only some will manage to escape: not because of moral qualities and self-control but because of bright fixed stars in favourable positions in their natal charts.

The situation of the monastic life will not be any better, especially with regard to quarrels, contentions and dissensions of all sorts, first of all because Mars, the *dispositor* of the conjunction of 1484, will be located in the third house—signifying religious affairs[110]—of the horoscope of the vernal equinox

---

[109] Paul could not know in 1484 that the outbreak of syphilis, which caused a significant mortality rate among the clergy, would retrospectively be dated to the year 1495 and counted among the effects of the conjunction of 1484. See Dieter Wuttke, 'Sebastian Brants Syphilis-Flugblatt des Jahres 1496'. In Girolamo Fracastoro. *Lehrgedicht über die Syphilis. Herausgegeben und übersetzt von Georg Wöhrle*, zweite, erweiterte Auflage, Gratia, vol. 18 (Wiesbaden: Harrassowitz, 1993 [1988]), pp. 128–29, 133, 138–39, and Stephan Heilen, 'Fracastoros Götterversammlung im Krebs (Syph. 1,219–246)', in *In Pursuit of Wissenschaft: Festschrift für William M. Calder III zum 75. Geburtstag*, ed. Stephan Heilen, et al., Spudasmata, vol. 119 (Hildesheim: Georg Olms Verlag, 2008), pp. 143–76, here: pp. 144–47. The belief that syphilis had been caused by the conjunction of 1484 is central to the broadsheet of Dietrich Ulsen (Nürnberg 1496) where it is illustrated by a well known woodcut attributed to the young Albrecht Dürer (1471–1528). Analyses and/or reproductions of this broadsheet are in Conrad Fuchs, ed., *Theodorici Ulsenii Phrisii Vaticinium in epidemicam scabiem, quae passim toto orbe grassatur, nebst einigen anderen Nachträgen zur Sammlung der ältesten Schriftsteller über die Lustseuche in Deutschland* (Göttingen: Dieterich, 1850), and in Johann Ueltzen, 'Das Flugblatt des Arztes Theodoricus Ulsenius vom Jahre 1496 über den deutschen Ursprung der Syphilis und seine Illustration', *Virchows Archiv für pathologische Anatomie und Physiologie und für klinische Medizin* 162 (1900): pp. 371–73, as well as in Sudhoff, *Erstlinge der Syphilisliteratur* and Philipp Portwich, 'Das Flugblatt des Nürnberger Arztes Theodoricus Ulsenius von 1496', *Berichte zur Wissenschaftsgeschichte* 21 (1998): pp. 175–83. The woodcut alone is most easily accessible at http://upload.wikimedia.org/wikipedia/commons/d/d7/D%C3%BCrerSyphilis1496.jpg. A few years after the publication of the broadsheet we find Ulsen (together with Joseph Grünpeck) as Maximilian's court physician (Ueltzen, 'Flugblatt', p. 372).

[110] The third house is in that passage (fol. c2^r) characterised as that of 'claustralium religiosorum castitas iusticia pietas charitas fides et parsimonia spes sobrietas ac omnis sanctimonia'. Cf., for example, Haly Abenragel, *De iudiciis astrorum*, ch. 29 (ed. Norimb.

(*revolutio anni*) of 1484. They will also indulge in all sorts of unlawful lust, monks as well as nuns. To avoid misunderstandings, Paul profusely describes their future sins. Again, an exception must be made for a small number of unwavering nuns, those who have Virgo or Pisces (i.e., presumably, symbols of chastity and of Christianity) ascending in their horoscopes and who happen to be protected by the benevolent radiation of Jupiter.

Entirely different will be the consequences for the Jews. Since Saturn, the planet of Judaism,[111] will be elevated over Jupiter during the conjunction of 1484, the Jews will concentrate their expectation of a future Messiah on the arrival of the prophet whom this conjunction foretells. Nevertheless, they will also be mistreated by the Christians and suffer expulsions.

Paul then repeats some of the general predictions regarding kings that he already made in the previous chapter, adding the new point that he has individual predictions for some of them in store, based on their respective birth horoscopes. This announcement is likely to create a state of curiosity and expectation on the part of a reader who will, however, immediately afterwards be disappointed by the news that Paul deems it wiser not to divulge such delicate details to the broad public, but to keep them secret for later confidential revelation to select 'illustrious men'.[112] In other words, Maximilian, the addressee, or any other powerful man who happens to read the *Prognosticum*, is invited to enrol Paul of Middelburg in his service and learn the important details about his allies and opponents on the thrones of Europe. The only detail that Paul drops is that the Venetian government will experience grave adversity because the eclipse will occur in the sign of their city's foundation horoscope. Interestingly, this detail is missing in the revised edition of 1486 which has, instead, an addendum about the sufferings of various Italian cities at the end of Chapter IV; but Venice is missing among those place names, too. Maybe Paul wanted to avoid giving offense in Venice where the revised edition was published.

When those dire years are over, a new period of happiness will begin. Paul's description of it remains vague yet runs to almost a page, which is surprising in view of his declared pursuit of brevity. Maybe he wanted to convey to his noble

---

1539): 'De lege, religione & uisionibus nati: Aspice in re fidei & somniorum ad istas duas domos, Tertiam uidelicet & nonam, quia ex illis scitur de lege & uisionibus'.

111 See Album. *De magn. coni.* 1.4.4 (Abū Maʿšar, *On Historical Astrology*, ed. Yamamoto and Burnett, vol. II, p. 28): 'iudaismus [. . .] congruit substantie Saturni'; Roger Bacon, *Opus maius*, pars IV, vol. I, p. 256 Bridges: *significat de sectis Judaicam* [scil. *Saturnus*]. Cf. above, n. 83.

112 Fol. c3^{r}: '[. . .] que a nobis precognita sunt, in pectore nostro reseruabimus et illustribus uiris tantum reseranda custodiemus, ne ad ignobilis vulgi aures perueniant'.

addressee the idea that it was worth seeking expert advice for the frightening yet transient period of dangers to come. This section is missing from the revised edition of 1486.

Last, after the clergy and the nobility, come the ordinary people. They will experience a similarly broad spectrum of dangerous or even deadly misfortunes, including some that had not been mentioned to that point and that originate from the ordinary people's being subject to jurisdiction. They ought to expect accusations, imprisonment, and so on. Their fates will, however, be diverse depending on their individual horoscopes. Therefore Paul embarks on a second theoretical discussion of various cases.[113] He goes systematically through all the signs of the zodiac, starting with those who had Aries ascending (or otherwise in a strong position) at birth and ending with Pisces. The underlying silent assumption is that these individuals are all males. Only once is an addendum made in which the possibility is envisaged that the native be female. This occurs in the context of the *infelicissimum Scorpionis signum* in which the conjunction will take place and which therefore receives the fullest discussion. In some cases Paul makes use of a special, lexicographically interesting terminology to denote the natives (*Taurini, Geministe, Cancrini, Leonini, Virginiste*). Being created from the respective signs' names, this terminology resembles that which was used for the children of the planets (*viri Mercuriales, viri Ioviales,* etc.). In this twelvefold systematic discussion of cases the textual borrowings from Firmicus Maternus are particularly numerous and dense.

Chapter VII

Lastly comes chapter seven, which contains advice on remedies by which the evil effects of the impending alignments can be avoided or partly mitigated.[114] Being a physician, Paul explains his intention with reference to medicine: while therapeutic medication is good, prophylactic medication is better. Accordingly, it is important to take individual precautions against the astrological effects of the conjunction and the eclipse, effects that he explicitly claims to be avoidable.[115]

Paul distinguishes two sorts of medications, corporal and spiritual. He first treats the former. In principle everyone will have to consult his or her own physician who will be able to take the individual complexion and the regional,

---

113 See the last paragraph of the analysis of Chapter II, above.

114 Fol. c4v: '[. . .] remedia, quibus prauarum constellationum improbitas euitari aut aliqua ex parte mitigari possit'.

115 Fol. c4v: 'danda est igitur opera (postquam euitandi facultas non abest), ne accidens superueniat'.

temporal and habitual specifics into account.[116] Nevertheless Paul wishes to give at least some appropriate advice from humoural pathology. In many individuals, the elevation of Saturn over Jupiter during the conjunction will cause disturbances of the four humours. That will require treatment with continued administration of a certain kind of pills prepared by a pharmacist following a physician's prescription. Paul specifies numerous ingredients and their respective doses, the pharmaceutical preparation of the pills and the modalities of their administration, adding a few optional modifications for delicate patients such as the substitution of aloe with scammony and the administration of the medication in a lekvar prepared with honey. In any case, the recipe as given (before the additional information on optional modifications) is preferable, and the pills thus prepared cannot harm.[117] Paul then adds brief remarks on other kinds of pills that will also be convenient. These other pills are of more simple composition and partly recommendable to special groups of patients who are either rich enough to afford the ingredients or robust enough to tolerate them. In the latter case, the administration of a compound preparation at least four times per year will be sufficient. Paul ends his pharmaceutical excursus by emphasising again that for more information each person should consult his or her own physician. He then inserts an interesting polemical remark that sheds light on his view of the relationship between medicine and astrology. He claims that the substance of the human body, being composed of the four elements, contains occult properties whose understanding goes beyond medicine; it falls in the domain of the 'most excellent, divine' science of astrology which is indispensable for physicians yet studied far too little by them due to the scarcity of reward, 'because in our days it is preferable or at least much more useful to become a mendacious empiric than to profess the true art of medicine'.[118] Since the ancient

---

116 Fol. <c5>r: 'quibus autem aut qualibus sit utendum medicinis, cum hec complexionum qualitatem ac regionum temporum et consuetudinum uarietatem insequantur, a proprio quisque medico requiret'.

117 Fol. <c5>r: 'sunt enim incolumes'.

118 Fol. <c5>v: 'Verum quia corporis formam atque substantiam ex quatuor elementorum commixtione prouidi numinis artificio constat esse formatam, in qua plures quidem indiuiduales et materie latent proprietates, quas medicorum scole appropriato satis uocabulo occultas uocant, cum eorum noticia medicinam transcendens altiorem quidem scientiam, ymo omnium artium preclarissimam diuinam quippe astrologiam attingat, que et si non parum utilis ymo necessaria foret medicis, ob premii tamen hac tempestate tenuitatem uix partem modicam studii his artibus tribuendam putant, cum eligibilius aut saltem multo utilius sit hoc seculo nostro mendacem fieri empericum (sic) quam ueram phisicam profiteri'.

medical school of the empirics considered the enquiry into hidden causes of diseases fruitless, its tenets are irreconcilable with Paul's interest in the occult properties of human bodies and in the potential for healing them by way of iatromathematical medicine.

This brings Paul to the spiritual medications. To select something suitable, the occult properties of an individual bodily complexion and the details of that individual's horoscope must be taken into account. Since that requires an astrological specialist, Paul can give only some general advice. First of all, the reader should purify his soul from the marks of sin. Then he should cast his birth horoscope, examine all parameters carefully (including directions, profections and revolutions), and eventually create, at the right time, the appropriate astrological talismans.[119] This section ends with a renewal of Paul's earlier statement that all this requires the assistance of an expert; therefore everyone should turn to his personal astrologer.

Three aspects of this chapter are worth being emphasised. First, Paul's pharmaceutical recipes are part of a long iatromathematical tradition that harks back to Ptolemaic Egypt. Already the legendary King Nechepsos of Hellenistic astrology is reported to have given a recipe for the preparation of a 'sun pill' of allegedly marvelous healing powers.[120] Note, however, that Paul's recipes serve to prepare not remedies but protective medication, a kind of early modern 'flu

119 On such talismans see Nicolas Weill-Parot, *Les "images astrologiques" au Moyen Âge et à la Renaissance. Spéculations intellectuelles et pratiques magiques (XIIe–XVe siècle)*, Sciences, techniques et civilisations du Moyen Âge à l'aube des lumières, vol. 6 (Paris: Champion, 2002).

120 Our source for that is a report by Thessalus of Tralles (Thess. virt. herb. 1 prooem. 6–7 [cod. T], p. 47,5–11 Friedrich = Nech. et Pet. frg. 35,1–8). When making the rounds of the libraries in Alexandria, Thessalus 'came upon a book by the wise Egyptian king Nechepso, containing twenty-four remedies based on the use of stones and plants for every part of the body and every disease arranged according to the signs of the zodiac. The book promised amazing results, but when Thessalos tried to put the remedies of Nechepso into practice, he failed completely'. (Ian S. Moyer, *Egypt and the Limits of Hellenism* (Cambridge: Cambridge University Press, 2011), p. 209; see also Ian S. Moyer, 'Thessalos of Tralles and Cultural Exchange', in *Prayer, Magic, and the Stars in the Ancient and Late Antique World*, ed. Scott Noegel, Joel Walker and Brannon Wheeler (University Park: Pennsylvania State University Press, 2003), p. 42). The latest state of research on Nechepsos is summarised in Stephan Heilen, 'Some metrical fragments from Nechepsos and Petosiris', in *La poésie astrologique dans l'Antiquité: Actes du colloque organisé les 7 et 8 décembre 2007*, ed. Isabelle Boehm and Wolfgang Hübner, Collection du Centre d'études et de recherches sur l'Occident romain CEROR, vol. 38 (Paris: Diffusion De Boccard, 2011), pp. 23–93, here: pp. 23–29.

injection'.[121] It will require further study to contextualise and classify Paul's recipes in the history of early modern pharmacy and iatromathematics.[122] Paul's interest in astrological medicine obviously stems from his own medical training and practice. As mentioned earlier he was, in 1484, personal physician to the duke of Urbino and in his dedication of the *Prognosticum* he refers to this office alone, not to his being also a court astrologer.[123]

Second, the medical content of this chapter recalls the polemic against Plotinus in the preface, thereby creating a ring composition and providing unity to the *Prognosticum* as a whole.

Third, this chapter conveys a clear message to Maximilian. He is in danger and will need personalised protective medication of both kinds: corporeal (pills) and spiritual (talismans), prepared by an expert—ideally speaking, by Paul himself.

Chapter VII and the whole *Prognosticum* ends with a long apostrophe to Maximilian. Paul says that the young sovereign's military prowess is such as to obliterate the memory of Alexander the Great, Hannibal, and Scipio Africanus.[124] Human tongues are not sufficient to praise Maximilian's unsurpassed virtues. In his enthusiasm, Paul goes so far as to include even a praise of Maximilian's six-year-old son (Philip I of Castile, 1478–1506), whose qualities he considers such as to require angelic rather than human speech to be praised adequately. Amidst these flatteries Paul does not forget to emphasise that his addressee ought to pay attention to the advice of astrologers. They are the only ones who can preserve Maximilian and his state unharmed because it is

---

121 A pill is, of course, not an injection, but the comparison is not entirely inappropriate in view of the immunising potential of Paul's pills and of the lexical origin of 'flu' from Italian *influenza*, i.e., an epidemic illness caused by astral influences. According to the Oxford English Dictionary (2nd ed. 1989), vol. VII, p. 941 s.v. *influenza*, the Italian term is attested in this sense as early as 1504. I actually found it in Italian predictions for the conjunction of Saturn and Jupiter of 1504 and assume that it will turn up even earlier in one or several of the five printings of Lichtenberger's adaptation of Paul's *Prognosticum* that were, according to the ISTC, published in Italian between 1492 and 1500 (More on this below in 'Reception and editions of the *Prognosticum*'.)

122 As to the ingredients mentioned by Paul, see Willem F. Daems, *Nomina simplicium medicinarum ex synonymariis medii aevi collecta / Semantische Untersuchungen zum Fachwortschatz hoch- und spätmittelalterlicher Drogenkunde*, vol. 6 of *Studies in Ancient Medicine* (Leiden: E.J. Brill, 1993).

123 See the quotation above, in n. 14. The official court astrologer with a longer history of service at the court of Urbino was Jacob of Speyer (see n. 6 above).

124 This is a reference to Maximilian's bravery and victory in the battle of Guinegate (1479).

exclusively to them among mortals that God reveals his plans through the motions of the celestial bodies.[125] The astrologer's self-advertisement ends with a request for a gracious reception of the *Prognosticum* and for benevolent patronage in the future.[126]

Astronomy and Astrology in the Prognosticum

As to be expected from a professional mathematician and astronomer, Paul's *Prognosticum* is based on solid knowledge of astronomical computation and astrological sources. However, at no point in the text does he provide a full list of the astronomical data of any of the alignments that he discusses and analyses, nor does he provide horoscopic diagrams to illustrate them. The data of the three alignments that are, from the point of view of the Arabic theory, most important for his purpose—those of the vernal equinox of 1484, of the conjunction of 1484, and of the eclipse of 1485—are all scattered incompletely and unsystematically throughout the text. It will be useful to comprehensively collect, illustrate and discuss these data.[127] The astronomical parameters that Paul specifies are the following:

a) vernal equinox (*revolutio anni*) of 1484:

- date: 10 March 1484
- time: night
- ascendant: ♏

The position of the Sun is implicitly clear (0° ♈). That of Mars is alluded to by reference to the house of the equinoctial chart in which his position happens to fall (the 3rd).[128] The positions of the Moon, Saturn, Jupiter, Venus, and Mercury,

---

125 Fol. <c6>v–<c7>r: 'astrologos obserua: soli enim sunt inter mortales, qui te statumque tuum incolumem preseruare possunt. voluit namque benignissimus et idem optimus ac sapientissimus deus bonitatis et sapientie sue dispositionem in rebus per secundarum causarum motus atque influxus ita ostendere, ut solis ipsis astrologis deoque dilectis innotesceret'.

126 Fol. <c7>r: 'a te, principe munificentissimo diis et hominibus gratissimo, munus hoc peto suauissimum, ut me quanquam in Italia residentem in tuorum numero fidelissimorum seruitorum collocare digneris [. . .]'.

127 The following footnotes will contain occasional references to additional information given by Paul in his revised editions of 1486 and 1492, which will be described in the next to last paragraph of this article.

128 In the editions of 1486 and 1492 Paul provides the explicit information that Mars was in Capricorn.

are not mentioned.

b) conjunction of 1484:

- date: 25 November 1484 [ed. pr.: 29 November][129]
- time: 6:04 PM
- longitude (Saturn, Jupiter): 23° 43′ ♏ [ed. pr.: 23° 23′ ♏]
- ascendant: 13° ♋
- 'elevation': Saturn over Jupiter[130]

The positions of Mars, Venus, and the Lot of Fortune are alluded to by reference to the houses of the conjunction horoscope in which they happen to fall (Mars and Lot of Fortune: 10th, Venus: 5th).[131] The ascending node is mentioned, but not localised. The positions of Sun, Moon, and Mercury are not mentioned at all.[132]

c) solar eclipse of 1485:

- date: 16 March 1485
- longitude (Sun and Moon): 6° ♈

The positions of Mars, Jupiter and the ascendant as well as the time of day are given only implicitly (Mars: 13° ♊, Jupiter: ♐; ascendant: ♍, time: late afternoon). To be understood, they require the combination of various chunks of information scattered over the text and basic astronomical knowledge to draw the appropriate conclusions. The positions of Saturn, Venus, and Mercury are

---

129 The erroneous numerals for the day and for the minutes of arc of the ecliptical longitude that made their way into the *editio princeps* were detected and corrected very early, as shown by the handwritten corrections in the two extant copies of the *editio princeps* (described in n. 11). The corrections are included in the text of all later editions and also in Lichtenberger's plagiarism of 1488 on which see the section 'Reception and editions of the *Prognosticum*'.

130 On this datum see the paragraph just above Figure 3, below.

131 In the editions of 1486 and 1492 Mars is explicitly said to be located in Aries. Regarding Paul's reference to the Lot of Fortune in Chapter IV, it is not certain but very likely that he means the conjunction whose data are here summarised (see above n. 77).

132 Some contemporary authors take a different approach. Take, for example, John of Lubecca who provides a systematic exposition of all planetary longitudes of the conjunction of 1504 in his *Pronosticum super Antechristi adventu Iudeorumque Messiae* (Padua, 1474), fol. <3>v.

not mentioned at all.

The incompleteness of the astronomical data, the lack of diagrams, and the brevity with which certain points are asserted without explanation, fit the general picture; this is not a didactic text with the intention of providing exact demonstrations of each astronomical or astrological detail but rather an attempt to exercise psychological effects on the reader—such as fear of the future and desire for Paul's services. To arouse this interest, it is sufficient to appear learned (without proving one's learning in detail) by using technical terminology, quoting renowned authorities, and embellishing the whole with rhetorical ornament. The technicalities must, of course, be correct (to avoid criticism and derision by other experts) but not always intelligible to the addressee and the broad public.

It will be useful to illustrate the alignments (a) to (c) with diagrams. All three were computed with *Galiastro* 4.3.[133] The respective times were chosen so as to emulate Paul's view of the alignments as closely as possible (as far as can be discerned from the data that he provides), not to match the results of modern recomputation of the astronomical events in question. In the absence of explicit information regarding the system of house division practised by Paul of Middelburg,[134] that of Regiomontanus—Paul's predecessor on the chair of astronomy at Padua—was chosen because it quickly became the most popular.[135]

After each diagram the collected and illustrated data will be discussed briefly in historical perspective, especially with regard to the astronomical data that would be obtained with the Alfonsine tables. That Paul used these tables is suggested by a passing remark in the first chapter which refers, strictly speaking, only to Paul's calculation of the New Moon preceding the vernal equinox of 1484.[136] A universally applicable remark is found in the revised edition of 1486 which repeats all the astronomical data of the *editio princeps* (with the exception of two obvious misprints) and informs the reader in its last, newly written section that Paul based his calculations on the Alfonsine tables, whose default meridian is that of Toledo (4° West), and their Oxford variant: 'Calculum etiam et supputationes nostras ex approbatissimis Alfonsi tabulis toletanis et Oxoniensibus exarauimus' (fol. <a10>^{r}).[137] The Alfonsine data that will be given on the fol-

---

133 Mentioned in n. 98, above.

134 At least I did not find such information to the present.

135 See John David North, *Horoscopes and History*. Warburg Institute Surveys and Texts, vol. 13 (London: The Warburg Institute, University of London, 1986), p. 158.

136 Fol. <a6>^{v}: 'secundum vulgatum Alphonsi calculum'.

137 See John David North, *Cosmos: an Illustrated History of Astronomy and Cosmology* (Chicago: University of Chicago Press, 2008), pp. 264–65 ('Oxford and the Alfonsine tables').

lowing pages were computed with Raymond Mercier's software *Deviations 11*.

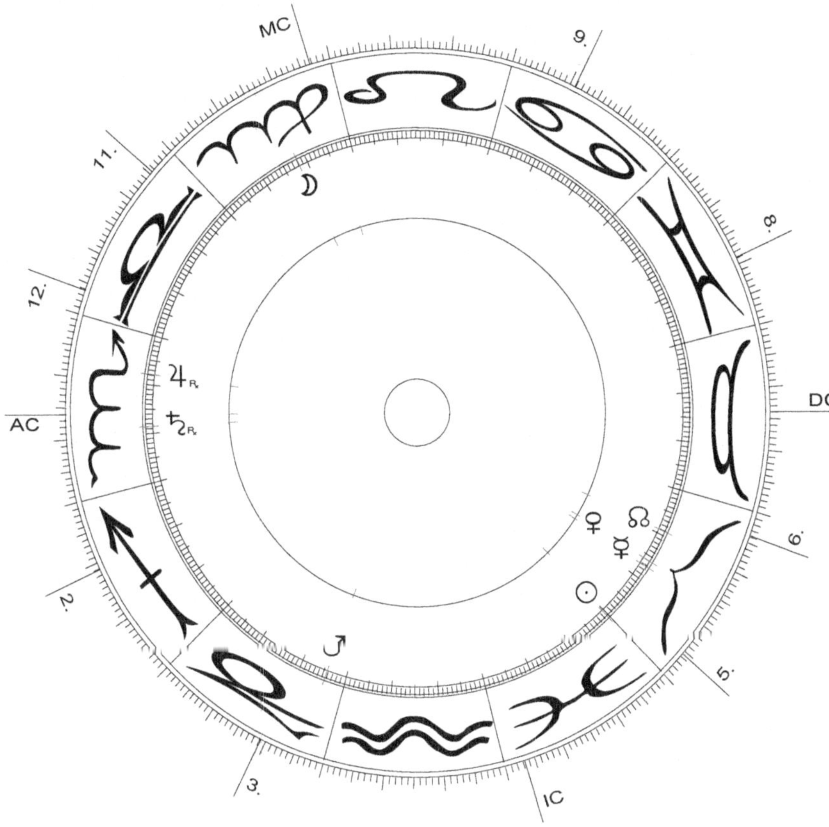

Fig. 1: The vernal equinox (revolutio anni) *of 1484.*

This diagram has been computed for 10 March 10:30 PM (local mean time at Louvain) to match Paul's datum that Scorpio was ascending. The Alfonsine tables lead, for the same day and the longitude of Louvain (4° 42′ East) to 8:40 PM as the time of the Sun's entry into Aries, for Urbino (12° 38′ East) to 9:11 PM, for Vienna (16° 22′ East) to 9:26 PM. At these respective local times Scorpio was ascending in Urbino and Vienna but not in Louvain where Scorpio began to rise some twenty minutes after 8:40 PM. It would, however, be rash to conclude from these data that Paul computed the vernal equinox for a locality further east than

Louvain. He may simply have overestimated the eastern longitude of that city by 5° (= 20 min of clock time) or more.[138]

According to modern recomputation, the exact time of the equinox was several hours later, on 11 March 6:30 AM (LMT Louvain), when Aries was ascending.

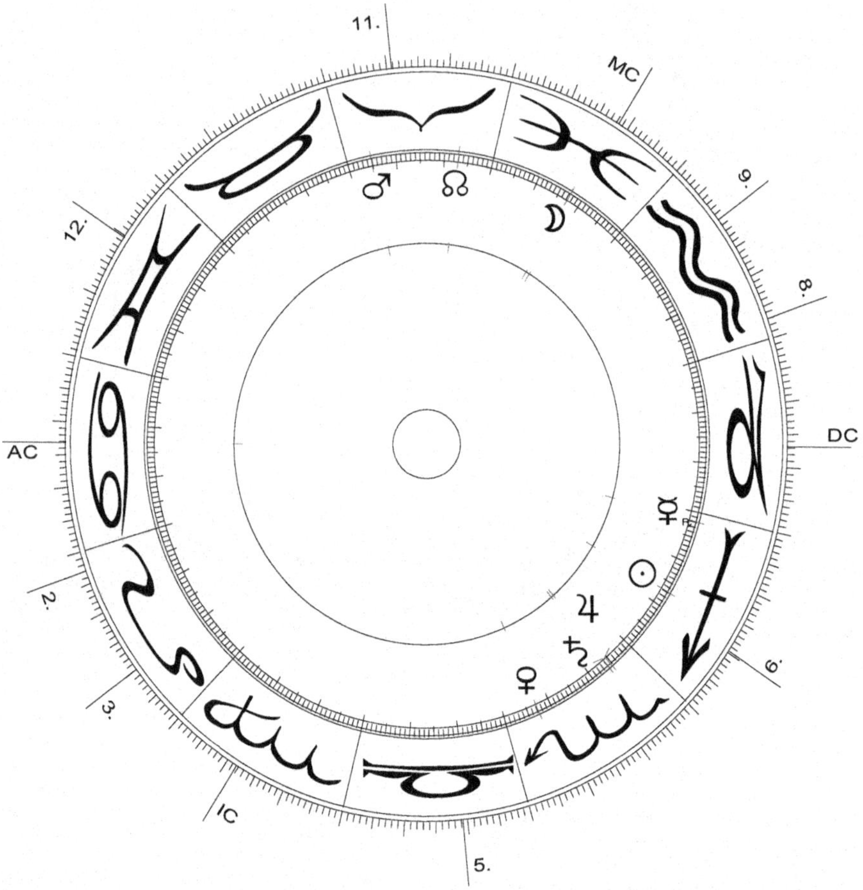

Fig. 2: The conjunction of Saturn and Jupiter in 1484.

[138] For more information on this problem see the first paragraph below Figure 3 (eclipse chart).

This diagram has been computed for 25 November 1484, at 5:57 PM (LMT Louvain) to match Paul's datum of the ascendant (13° ♋). The time of day given by Paul is only seven minutes later. This good match is nevertheless surprising because the Alfonsine tables lead, for their default meridian (4° West, = Toledo), to 25 November, 7:23 PM,[139] for Louvain (4° 42′ East) to 7:58 PM, for Urbino (12° 38′ East) to 8:30 PM, for Vienna (16° 22′ East) to 8:44 PM. It remains to be investigated how Paul arrived at his conjunction time 6:04 PM, and what city or longitude he had in mind.

Modern recomputation reveals that the conjunction actually took place on 18 November, 5:45 PM (LMT Louvain), at 23° 10′ ♏. For the gross mistake in computing the date of the conjunction (one week off the true date) see Paul's apology that has been quoted above.[140] Note that he did not correct the tables' mistake when he revised the text in 1486. In the meantime there had been the opportunity of verifying or at least improving the date of the conjunction by way of direct observation. It is hard to believe that Paul was not interested in this or that he and other astronomers with whom he entertained correspondences were all precluded from direct observation by protracted unfavourable weather conditions.

In this context another shortcoming deserves to be mentioned. Not only the date of the conjunction but also its other astronomical parameters are repeated without any change in the revised version of 1486. While Paul declares to have written the *editio princeps* at Louvain—which probably implies that the coordinates of Louvain were used—the revised edition was prepared at Urbino and for the court of Urbino.[141] Consequently, Paul should have recomputed the ascendant, which is more than six degrees lower at the geographical coordinates of Urbino. The ascendant is, by definition, a specific locality's ascendant and cannot be used for all of Europe indiscriminately. Paul's mistake can only partly be excused by imperfect knowledge of longitudinal distances.[142] It seems that he did not expect the ascendant data of his two versions of the text after their publications in far distant cities (Louvain and Venice) to be compared by experts.

The 'elevation' of Saturn over Jupiter is a criterion of crucial astrological importance. Already the Arabic authorities on conjunctionism admitted various definitions of this technical term (*al-mamarr* in Arabic) which were continued and variously applied by their Western successors. Paul concentrates on

---

139 This is to be understood as the true conjunction. For the mean conjunction, the Alfonsine tables lead to 29 July 1484, at 15° 09′ ♏.

140 See the fifth paragraph from the end of the analysis of Chapter IV.

141 This information is given in the respective colophons of the two editions.

142 More information on this point will be given below with respect to the eclipse chart.

'elevation' defined as a higher northern celestial latitude of one planet compared to another. He says (fol. <a5>^{v}): 'rigidus ille saturnus maliuolus ecentrici sui eleuatione ac circuli sui latitudinis in septentrionem altitudine et sublimitate Iouem benignum opprimet'. The Alfonsine tables lead, for the calendrical date given by Paul, to the result that the ecliptic latitude of Saturn was 1° 50′ 46″, that of Jupiter 0° 54′ 43″.[143] Hence Saturn was indeed 'elevated' over Jupiter.

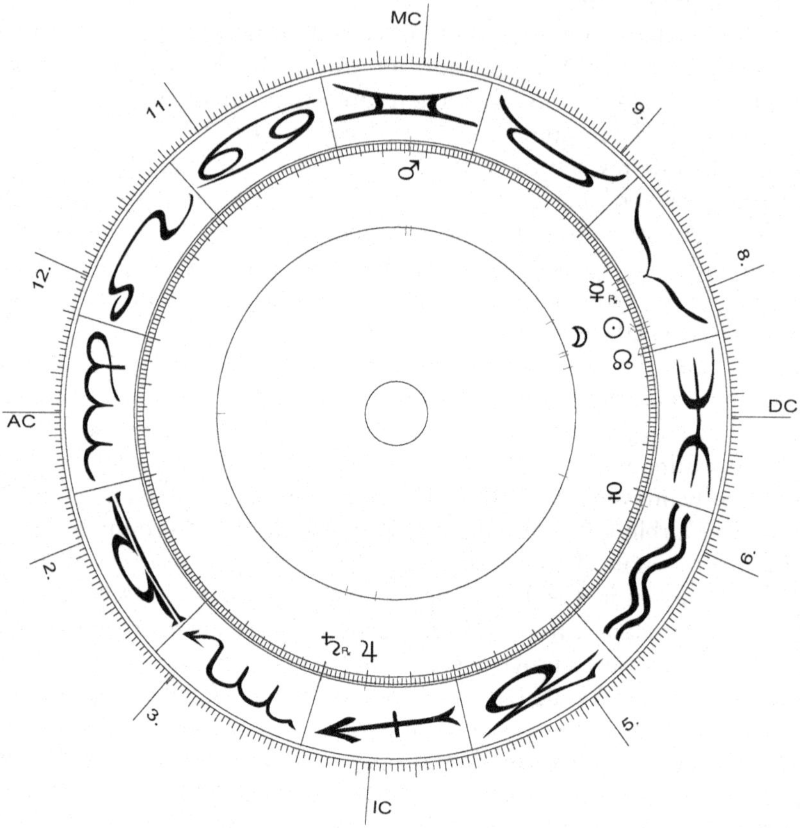

Fig. 3: The solar eclipse of 16 March 1485.

[143] Computed with *Deviations 11*. I am grateful to Raymond Mercier for giving me advice on the use of the Alfonsine tables and his software, and particularly for helping me better understand the present passage on 'elevation'. Saturn's higher northern latitude on the date in question is confirmed by modern recomputation.

This diagram has been computed for 16 March 1485, at 4:30 PM (LMT Louvain) to match Paul's data regarding the positions of the luminaries in the seventh house, of Mars in the tenth, and of the ascendant in Virgo. The Alfonsine tables lead, for Toledo (4° West), to 1:48 PM as the time of the conjunction of the luminaries (i.e., the totality of the eclipse), for Louvain (4° 42′ East) to 2:23 PM, for Urbino (12° 38′ East) to 2:56 PM, for Vienna (16° 22′ East) to 3:12 PM, for Jerusalem (34° 12′ East) to 4:21 PM. Only in the eastern Mediterranean would the house division of Regiomontanus, at the eclipse time given by the Alfonsine tables, result in a satisfactory chart, i.e., one with the properties of Figure 3 above. At Louvain the house division at 2:23 PM is such that the ascendant is still in Leo and the luminaries in the eighth house near the cusp of the ninth; in other words, incompatible with Paul's three data that must be matched.[144] At Vienna at 3:12 PM the house division is such that the eclipse would still be in the middle of the eighth house, now with the first degrees of Virgo ascending: better than Louvain, but still unsatisfactory. How can this be explained? The answer to this question is complicated by two uncertainties that pertain to house division and longitudinal distances. Maybe our hypothesis (see the second paragraph above Figure 1)—that Paul used Regiomontanus' system of domification—is wrong. However, I do not know of an alternative historical system that would lead to satisfactory results. It seems that the conjunction of the luminaries would in any case take place in the eighth house, more or less close to the cusp of the ninth. The other problem is that fifteenth-century astronomers had very inaccurate knowledge of the longitudinal distances between various geographical locations which are notoriously more difficult to determine than latitudinal distances.[145] In all likelihood Paul overestimated the longitudinal distance of whatever city he had in mind from Toledo. Suffice it to mention that in the version of the Alfonsine tables that was printed by Erhard Ratdolt in Venice in 1483[146] the final three pages contain a list of latitudes and longitudes of various cities measured 'from the most western point of the inhabited world' (*Tabula latitudinis et longitudinis ciuitatum ab occidente habitato*) which is thought to be 11° West of Toledo, i.e., the Canary islands.[147] In this list—which is arranged by longitudes so as to guarantee the typographical accuracy—astronomical mistakes of seven

---

144 The same situation is found at 2:43 PM (LMT Louvain) which is the true time of the eclipse as obtained with modern planetary theory (*Galiastro* 4.3). The rising time of 0° Virgo was 2:58 PM.

145 On this problem see Wolfgang Kokott, 'Astronomische Längenbestimmung in der Frühen Neuzeit' *Sudhoffs Archiv* 79 (1995): pp. 165–72.

146 The title is *Tabulę astronomicę illustrissimi Alfontij regis castellę* (source: www.gallica.fr).

147 I.e. 15° West of the modern prime meridian (Greenwich).

or even more degrees are frequent.[148] Interestingly, there is a somewhat later volume of tables adapted to our city in question, Louvain;[149] these show the same rearrangement as Ratdolt's, i.e., they equally suppose their prime meridian at 11° West of Toledo. Since Louvain is located at 28° 45′ East in these tables, the difference is 17° 45′, far more than the true longitudinal difference between Toledo and Louvain which amounts to 8° 44′.[150] In view of such historical documents Paul's data appear somewhat less surprising. It remains to be further investigated if, and to what extent, our uncertainties regarding his house division and his grasp of longitudinal distances are relevant to the explanation of his view of the eclipse chart. A third potential factor that seems less likely, but cannot *a priori* be ruled out, is astrological considerations.[151]

It remains to be mentioned that the eclipse in question was total along a west-east path through southern Germany (for example, at Konstanz and Augsburg) but only partial in Louvain and in Urbino.[152]

As far as astrology is concerned, Paul mentions ten authorities by name, some of them with literal quotations: Abdalla (al-Khwārizmī), Albumasar (Abū

---

148 Toledo (*Toletum*) is at 11° 0′ East, Mecheln (*Machlinia*), which is very near Louvain, at 24° 20′ East, Utrecht (*Traiectum*) at 27° 20′ East, Augsburg (*Augusta Vindelicorum*) at 32° 50′ East, Siena and Perugia (*Sena* and *Perusium*) both at 34° 20′ East, Vienna (*Vienna pannonie*), which is much further East than Siena and Perugia, at 34° 5′, Danzig (*Dantiscum*) at 44° 20′ and Jerusalem (*Hierusalem*) at 56° 0′ (to quote just a few). Since Toledo, in our modern system, is at 4° 2′ West, all these figures must be lowered by 15° before they can be compared to the modern longitudes of the cities in question. It then becomes clear that Paul's contemporaries thought of the cities in question as being much further East than they actually are. The mistake for Perugia (modern: 12° 23′ East), for example, is ca. 7° (= 34° 20′ - 15° - 12° 23′); for Danzig (modern: 18° 39′ East) ca. 11°; for Jerusalem (modern: 34° 12′ East) ca. 7°.

149 Henri Baers, *Tabule perpetue longitudinum ac latitudinum planetarum noviter copulate ad meridiem alme Universitatis Lovaniensis ac plerumque aliorum necessariorum in nativitatibus requisitorum* (Lovanii: Gilb. Maes 1528), fol. K4ʳ (repr. with introd. trans. and comm. Emmanuel Poulle and Antoine De Smet [Bruxelles: Études Culture et civilization, 1976]).

150 I thank Raymond Mercier for directing my attention to the problem as such and to the specific data in the Louvain Tables of 1528. Any inaccuracies in interpreting the material are my fault.

151 Did Paul maybe postpone the time of the eclipse a bit in order to make it shift from the eighth house (*mors*) into the seventh (*uxor*) and thus obtain astrological effects of a more scandalous nature?

152 A simple diagram of the eclipse path of 16 March 1485 together with the essential astronomical data is available at http://eclipse.gsfc.nasa.gov/5MCSE/5MCSE-Maps-09.pdf, plate 414. Details can be visualised with *Astrowin* (http://www.strickling.net/software.htm).

Ma'shar), Anthonius de Monte Ulmo (Antonio da Montolmo),[153] Firmicus Maternus, Hali or Halirodoan ('Alī ibn Riḍwān), Haliabenragel ('Alī ibn abī-l-Rijāl), Hermes (*pseudepigraphon*), Messehala (Māshā'allāh), and Ptolemy. In later editions (1486 and 1492, see below) he also refers to Henricus de Malinis (Henry Bate of Malines).[154]

Although the name of Firmicus Maternus is mentioned only once, hundreds of chunks of the text of the *Mathesis* are interspersed in Paul's text.[155] His application of the Arabic doctrine of the Great Conjunctions is primarily, but not exclusively, based on Abū Ma'shar. More than once he offers two different predictions depending on which authority one wishes to follow, for example, with regard to the climate where the prophet will be born (fol. <b5>$^{r-v}$) or to the colour of his clothes (fol. <b5>^{v}– <b6>^{r}). In several such cases Paul does not pronounce himself in favour of one theory and against another, even when he admits that the opinions contradict each other.[156]

Reception and Editions of the Prognosticum

The primary goal that Paul aimed at with the *editio princeps*, i.e., to attract the attention of Maximilian of Habsburg, was achieved, even if not immediately and not to the full extent that Paul may have been hoping. Maximilian did not offer Paul an employment as court physician or court astrologer, but he is reported to have recommended the Dutch scholar and priest to Pope Alexander VI (elected in 1492) for the bishopric of Fossombrone, the see to which Paul was actually appointed in 1494.[157] In the meantime, the *editio princeps* saw several reprints north of the Alps: at Antwerp (28 September 1484), at Cologne (7 December 1484), at Augsburg (about 1484), and at Leipzig (about 1492).[158]

However, there was also a less welcome form of reception in northern Europe—one that preceded Maximilian's request to Alexander VI. Only four

---

153 See De Donato, 'Antonio da Montolmo'.

154 See L. Hödel and John David North, 'Heinrich Bate von Mecheln', in *Lexikon des Mittelalters*, vol. 4 (Munich: Artemis, 1999), pp. 2088–89.

155 Apart from astrological authorities, Paul also quotes Cicero, Livy, and the New Testament explicitly. Further quotations without source references are from Sallust, Virgil, Juvenal, and Silius Italicus.

156 Regarding the question of the climate, we have 'tam discrepantes auctorum sentencie, ut recte sibi inuicem contrarie videantur esse' (fol. <b5>^{v}).

157 See Joseph Schmidlin, *Geschichte der deutschen Nationalkirche in Rom: S. Maria dell'Anima* (Freiburg im Breisgau: Herderische Verlagshandlung, 1906), p. 350.

158 In addition, the text was reprinted in Italy.

years after the text was first published, Johannes Lichtenberger (1440–1503), who may have been court astrologer to Maximilian's father, Emperor Frederick III,[159] wrote an extremely successful *Pronosticatio* (ed. pr. Heidelberg 1488). Despite the promise given in the title of being thoroughly new and original,[160] this text is, over many pages, a blatant yet unacknowledged plagiarism of Paul's *Prognosticum*. Lichtenberger's important innovation was to create a hybrid text by mingling Paul's astrological prediction with prophetic material based on the revelations of Joachim, Saint Bridget, Reinhard the Lollard, the sibyls, and Francis. What gained Lichtenberger's plagiarised text enormous popularity were, apart from the inclusion of prophetism, three features: a series of woodcut illustrations, the publication in both Latin and the vernacular languages German and Italian,[161] and the fact that he described the false prophet as a monk. This latter detail almost inevitably led to his later association with Martin Luther. However, this implies a substantial departure from some central features of the prediction made by Paul, especially those (documented in the analysis of Chapter IV) regarding the prophet's year of birth (1496), his home country (in the fifth climate, i.e., south of the Alps), and especially his religious agenda (revival of Mazdaism).[162]

---

[159] Although it is often taken for granted that Lichtenberger held that office, actual proof cannot be adduced (Gerd Mentgen, *Astrologie und Öffentlichkeit im Mittelalter*, Monographien zur Geschichte des Mittelalters, vol. 53 (Stuttgart: Hiersemann, 2005), pp. 229–30, and Daniel Carlo Pangerl, 'Sterndeutung als naturwissenschaftliche Methode der Politikberatung: Astronomie und Astrologie am Hof Kaiser Friedrichs III. (1440–1493)' *Archiv für Kulturgeschichte* 92 (2010): pp. 315–16).

[160] The title is *Pronosticatio in Latino. Rara & prius non audita* (!) *que exponit & declarat nonnullos celi influxus & inclinationem certarum constellacionum magne videlicet coniunctionis et eclipsis que fuerant istis annis* [. . .]. This text, which is available online at http://diglib.hab.de/inkunabeln/1-quod-3/start.htm, has been analyzed by Dietrich Kurze in *Johannes Lichtenberger († 1503). Eine Studie zur Geschichte der Prophetie und Astrologie*, Historische Studien, vol. 379 (Lübeck: Matthiesen, 1960) and 'Popular Astrology and Prophecy in the fifteenth and sixteenth Centuries: Johannes Lichtenberger', in *'Astrologi hallucinati': Stars and the End of the World in Luther's Time*, ed. Paola Zambelli (Berlin: Walter de Gruyter, 1986), pp. 177–93.

[161] Cf. Steven Vanden Broecke, *The Limits of Influence. Pico, Louvain, and the Crisis of Renaissance Astrology*. Medieval and Early Modern Science, vol. 4 (Leiden – Boston: Brill, 2003), p. 62: 'Whereas Paul of Middelburg published exclusively in Latin for an audience of courtly patrons, urban *literati*, and academic physicians, at least half of the pre-1500 Lichtenberger editions were vernacular versions'.

[162] Paul also contributed with his *Prognosticum* to the difficulties that the self-proclaimed prophet Girolamo Savonarola experienced; cf. Vanden Broecke, *Limits of Influence*, p. 79.

Lichtenberger's *Pronosticatio* saw more than fifty editions and became so extremely popular that Martin Luther personally prefaced one of these editions in order to protest against the widespread identification of himself with the monk prophesied by Lichtenberger. Nevertheless, some of the reformers around Luther, such as Melanchthon, tried to modify the astronomical data slightly so as to retain the prediction of a prophet or religious reformer while removing the odious and aggressive characteristics described by Paul and Lichtenberger.

My edition of Paul of Middelburg's *Prognosticum* will be the first critical edition of this text. It will be based on the *editio princeps* and take the ten extant subsequent editions into account.[163] Most of these are corrected reprints. However, there is the important revised version of 31 December 1486 that Paul dedicated to Guidobaldo da Montefeltro and his tutor Ottaviano Ubaldini. The modifications in this revised version are mostly due to the choice of new addressees, but Paul changed and added some other details, too. Several years later Paul prepared yet another edition that is part of an invective against Lichtenberger (*In superstitiosum vatem lucubratio*). In the highly polemical preface, which Paul completed in Urbino on the first of January 1492, he unmasks the plagiarist and accuses him both of technical shortcomings and disciplinary transgressions.[164] It is obvious that Paul considers himself a serious scientist but Lichtenberger a brazen fraud who not only stole Paul's intellectual property but diluted its scholarly substance in a hotchpotch of prophetic *deliramenta, picturae inanes* and a new message—that the Antichrist was about to come—which was not at all supported by conjunctionist theory and therefore *profecto ridiculum non minus quam absurdum*.[165] After this preface, Paul moves on to reprint the revised

---

163 It is well underway thanks to a research grant from the Ministry of Education of the State of Lower Saxony for research on the predictions regarding the conjunctions of both 1484 and 1504.

164 This text was printed soon afterwards by Johannes and Gregorius de Gregoriis at Venice. Paul's date of the completion of the preface is on fol. a2^r. Again, only one copy of this printing is extant (Sevilla, Biblioteca Colombina). There is, however, a reprint from Antwerp (without date) of which several copies are extant (see urn:nbn:de:bvb:12-bsb00017536-8).

165 To quote just a few expressions from the first page of Paul's preface. Cf. Vanden Broecke's discussion of Paul of Middelburg's position in the contemporary intellectual environment on the Italian peninsula and of his invective against Lichtenberger (*Limits of Influence*, pp. 61–65). As to Lichtenberger's merger of two different traditions, see also Kurze, 'Popular Astrology and Prophecy', pp. 179 and 184, and Michael H. Shank, 'Academic Consulting in Fifteenth-Century Vienna: The Case of Astrology', in *Texts and Contexts in Ancient and Medieval Science: Studies on the Occasion of John E. Murdoch's Seventieth Birthday*, ed. Edith Sylla and Michael McVaugh, Brill's Studies in Intellectual

text of 1486, so that every reader can make a comparison between the original and Lichtenberger's plagiarism. The extensive correspondences between these revised versions (1486 and 1492) and the first edition of 1484 will be documented in the forthcoming critical edition. The edition will be accompanied by an extensive commentary to clarify the manifold philological, biographical, historical, astronomical and astrological aspects of the text.

Is this ongoing effort worthwhile? Yes, it is, because already at the present, incomplete stage of research one new insight into the characteristics of Renaissance astrology has emerged. The potential of combining two different astrological prose traditions, that of the Arabic theory of the 'Great Conjunctions', appreciated for its content, and that of Firmicus Maternus' *Mathesis*, appreciated for its rhetorical style, in one elaborate prognostication, has been exploited only once. The product is not only unique in its kind but also proved to be very influential, both directly by way of reprints and indirectly by way of Lichtenberger's plagiarism. Curiously, it originated from a man of the clergy and had consequences for another man of the clergy, both of them prolific Christian authors and important reformers in the history of the Church: the former as head of the committee for the reform of the calendar under Pope Leo X, the latter as seminal figure of the Protestant Reformation. In short, this *Prognosticum* is a text with an unusually broad spectrum of dimensions: astronomical, astrological, rhetorical, sociological, and religious.

History, vol. 78 (Leiden: Brill, 1997), pp. 245–70, here: p. 266.

AL-BĪRŪNĪ ON THE COMPUTATION OF PRIMARY PROGRESSION (TASYĪR)

Jan P. Hogendijk

Introduction

The *Masudic Canon* (al-Qānūn al-Mas'ūdī) of al-Bīrūnī in eleven 'Books' (or large chapters) is one of the most important works of Islamic astronomy. The work is comparable in size and structure to the *Almagest* of Ptolemy (ca. 150 CE). Al-Bīrūnī completed this work between 1030 and 1040 for sultan Mas'ūd of Ghazna, now Ghazni in Afghanistan. An overview of the contents of the *Masudic Canon* can be found in Kennedy's *Studies in the Exact Islamic Sciences*.[1] Unlike Ptolemy in the *Almagest*, al-Bīrūnī added a Book (11) on mathematical astrology, of which Chapter 5 deals with the doctrine of primary progressions. The Arabic text of the *Masudic Canon* was published in an uncritical edition in India[2] which was reprinted in Beirut.[3] The work was also translated into Russian under communist rule; one of the translators, Boris Rozenfeld, once remarked to me that it was the first book on astrology that was printed in Russia after the revolution of 1917.[4] An English translation of the *Masudic Canon* would be important for our knowledge of Islamic astronomy but would require many years of highly specialized work. Al-Bīrūnī wrote in Arabic in a peculiar literary style which is more difficult to understand than the rather straightforward language used by most Islamic mathematicians and astronomers. The appendix to this paper contains a literal translation of Sections 1–4 of Chapter 5 of Book 11,

---

1 Edward Stuart Kennedy, 'Al-Bīrūnī's Masudic Canon', *Al-Abḥāth* 24 (1971), pp. 59–81, repr. in E.S. Kennedy, Colleagues and Former Students, *Studies in the Islamic Exact Sciences* (Beirut: American University of Beirut, 1983), pp. 573–95.

2 Al-Bīrūnī, *al-Qānūn al-Mas'ūdī*, 3 vols (Hyderabad: Osmaniya Oriental Publications Bureau, 1954–56).

3 Al-Bīrūnī, *al-Qānūn al-Mas'ūdī, qaddama lahu wa-ḍabaṭahu wa-ṣaḥḥahu 'Abd al-Karīm Sāmī al-Jundī*, 3 vols (Beirut: Dār al-Kutub al'ilmiyya, 1422 H./2002).

4 Abu Raikhan Beruni (973–1048), Izbrannye Proizvedeniya V, part 2, *Kanon Mas'uda, knigi VI–XI*, trans. Boris Abramovich Rozenfeld and Ashraf Akhmedovich Akhmedov (Tashkent: Fan, 1976).

which are related to astrological doctrines of ultimately Greek origin, although some of the mathematical methodology was developed in the Islamic middle ages. I have omitted the final Section 5 of Chapter 5 of Book 11 because it concerns Indian astrology and does not involve advanced mathematics.

I begin the appendix with a translation of al-Bīrūnī's cynical introduction to astrology in his preface to Book 11 of the *Masudic Canon*. Al-Bīrūnī also shows a sceptical attitude towards astrology in his more elementary *Introduction to the Art of Astrology* (*kitāb al-tafhīm li-awā'il ṣinā'at al-tanjīm*), which he wrote in the form of approximately 500 questions and answers for the daughter of a high dignitary, Rayḥāna bint Ḥasan. In that work, al-Bīrūnī begins the final section on astrology as follows:

> We now mention the subjects in the art of the judgement of the stars [i.e., astrology], because its aim is the solution of the question of a person who asks [something about his future], and because it [astrology] is for the majority of people the fruit of the mathematical sciences, although our opinion about this fruit and this art is similar to the opinion of the minority (translation mine).[5]

Commentary on Sections 1–4 of Chapter 5 of Book 11 of the Masudic Canon

The following commentary is introductory; mathematical details will be discussed in a subsequent section of this paper on worked examples. In this and the following section I will assume some familiarity with the concept of the celestial sphere, the coordinate systems on the sphere (ecliptical, equatorial, azimuthal), and the basics of spherical trigonometry, as explained, e.g., in Chapter 1 of Smart's *Textbook on Spherical Astronomy* or Chapter 1 of volume 1 of Chauvenet's *A Manual of Practical and Spherical Astronomy*, (freely accessible on the internet).[6]

Al-Bīrūnī begins section 1 with a brief description of the doctrine of *tasyīr* in general. This doctrine was introduced in Book 3, Chapter 10 of the *Tetrabiblos* of

---

[5] Al-Bīrūnī, *The Book of Instruction in the Elements of the Art of Astrology* reproduced from Brit. Mus. Ms. Or. 8439, tr. Robert Ramsay Wright (London: Luzac, 1934; repr. in *Islamic Mathematics and Astronomy*, ed. Fuat Sezgin, vol. 29 [Frankfurt: Institute for History of Arabic-Islamic Sciences, 1998]), p. 210.

[6] W.M. Smart, *Textbook on Spherical Astronomy* (Cambridge: Cambridge University Press, 1977); William Chauvenet, *A Manual of Spherical and Practical Astronomy*, 2 vols (London: Trübner and Philadelphia: J. B. Lippincott and Co., 1868), *Vol. 1: Spherical Astronomy*, http://books.google.nl/books?id=KlhRAAAAYAAJ

Ptolemy (ca. 150 CE);[7] it is also known under its Greek name *aphesis* and in the West as the theory of *primary progression(s)* or *direction(s)*.[8]

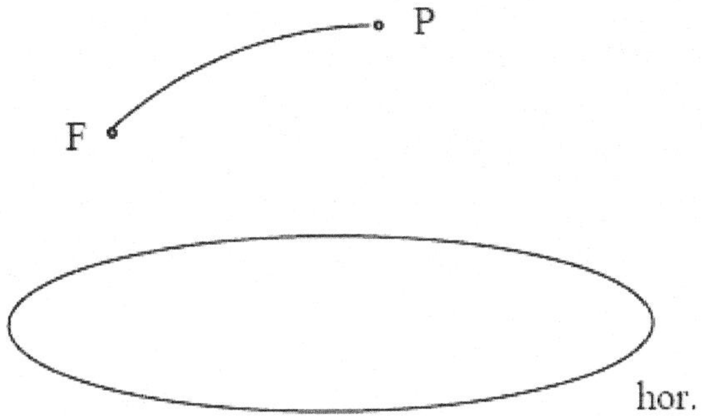

Fig. 1: F and P on same parallel circle.

In the celestial constellation at the moment of birth of a person, two planets or other relevant places are selected using astrological arguments which do not concern us here.[9] For the sake of explanation, I will assume that both places are planets above the horizon. In this case, al-Bīrūnī calls the planet which is more to the West the 'preceding' planet *P*, and the planet which is more to the East the 'following' planet *F*. For the computation of the duration of the life of the person, point *P* was called in Greek the 'aphetic' body, in Arabic the *haylāj*, from Persian *haylij*, 'lord of a building' and in Latin the *hyleg* or *significator*.[10] Point *F* was called the *anairetic* body in Greek, *qāṭi'* ('cutting-off') in Arabic, and *promissor* in Latin.[11]

We now consider the apparent motion of the sky, which was called in ancient

---

[7] Ptolemy, *Tetrabiblos*, trans. Frank Egleston Robbins, Loeb Classical Library 435 (Cambridge, MA: Harvard University Press, 1940; repr. 1980), pp. 270–307.

[8] Oskar Schirmer, 'Tasyīr', in *Encyclopaedia of Islam*, first ed. (Leiden: Brill, 1934), vol. 4: pp. 751–55.

[9] Auguste Bouché-Leclercq, *L'Astrologie grecque* (Paris: Leroux, 1899), pp. 411–22.

[10] C.L. Nallino, *Al-Battānī sive Albatenii Opus Astronomicum*, editum, Latine versum, adnotationibus instructum, 3 vols (Milano: Pubblicazioni del reale osservatorio di Brera, 1903, 1907, 1899; repr. ed., Frankfurt: Minerva, 1969), 2, p. 355.

[11] Schirmer, 'Tasyīr'.

and medieval terms the daily rotation of the universe (and which is, as we now know, caused by the rotation of the Earth). By means of this daily rotation, the planet *F* will appear to move in a western direction, on a path along the celestial sphere parallel to the celestial equator. After a few hours it may end up at the same position in the sky where *P* was at the beginning (Fig. 1). The astrologer then computed the length of the *tasyīr* arc *FP* in degrees, and converted each degree into one solar year. For example, a *tasyīr* arc of 57 degrees and 11 minutes would be converted to $57\frac{11}{60}$ solar years. Then *F* and *P* could be astrologically connected to an event which would occur this amount of time after the birth of the individual, although the period could be modified on the basis of other astrological arguments.

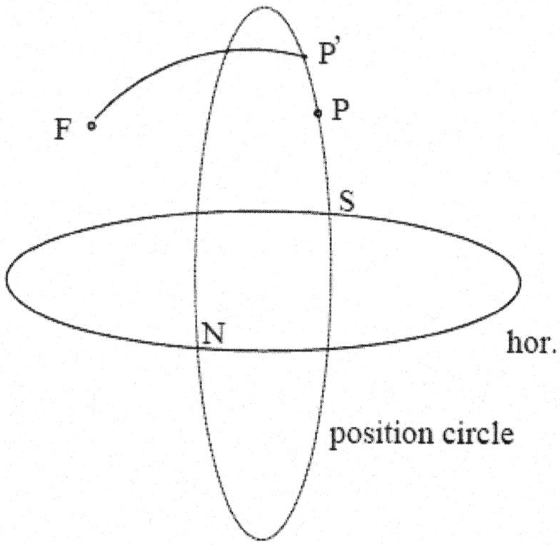

Fig. 2: F and P on different parallel circles.

Usually, the planet *F* will not pass through the initial position of *P* in the sky but will appear to move lower or higher, as in Figure 2. Then the astrologers considered what I will call the *position circle* of *P* – that is, the great circle of the celestial sphere through *P* and the north point *N* and south point *S* of the horizon. I will also use the term *position semicircle* of *P* for the arc *NPS* of the position circle with endpoints *N* and *S*. Now the *tasyīr* arc is arc *FP′* where *P′* is the intersection of the position semicircle of *P* and the path of *F*. I note that the whole process is only concerned with the (apparent) daily rotation of the universe caused by the rotation of the earth, and not with real motions of P and F with respect to the fixed stars.

If P is on the meridian, arc FP' is the difference between the (modern) right ascensions of P and F. If P is on the Eastern horizon, FP' is the difference between the 'oblique ascensions' of F and P, which also depend on the geographical latitude of the observer. Oblique ascensions are no longer used in modern astronomy but they were standard in Ptolemaic and medieval astronomy; for didactical explanations see Evans and Pederson.[12] For P on the Western horizon, arc FP' is the difference between the oblique descensions, which are directly opposite the oblique ascensions of F and P. In these cases the computation caused no problem for Ptolemy, who had computed tables of right and oblique ascensions in *Almagest* II:8.[13] These tables are widely available and will be used in the worked examples in the subsequent section of this paper. For P not in the meridian or horizon plane, Ptolemy presents an approximate computation[14] which al-Bīrūnī discusses in Section 1 and which was often used in the Islamic world. The method only requires tables of right ascension and of oblique ascension for one's locality. Before al-Bīrūnī the same method had also been presented by al-Battānī (ca. 900 CE),[15] and by Kūshyār ibn Labbān (tenth century).[16] Below I will discuss the numerical examples given by Ptolemy, using al-Bīrūnī's methodology. Ptolemy only discusses the case where P and F are on the ecliptic but, at the end of Section 1, al-Bīrūnī slightly adapts the procedure so it can also be used for planets with non-zero latitude.

Al-Bīrūnī makes the following remark on terminology. Although F is carried

---

12 James Evans, *History and Practice of Ancient Astronomy* (New York: Oxford University Press, 1998), pp. 109–21; Olaf Pedersen, *A Survey of the Almagest* (Odense: Odense University Press, 1974; repr. ed. New York: Springer, 2010), pp. 98–101, 110–15.

13 Gerald J. Toomer, *Ptolemy's Almagest* (London: Duckworth, 1984; repr. ed. Princeton: Princeton University Press, 1998), pp. 18, 100–01.

14 Ptolemy, *Tetrabiblos*, pp. 292–95.

15 Carlo Alfonso Nallino, *Al-Battānī sive Albatenii Opus Astronomicum*, editum, Latine versum, adnotationibus instructum (Milano: Pubblicazioni del reale osservatorio di Brera, 1903, 1907, 1899; repr. ed., Frankfurt: Minerva, 1969), 1: pp. 131–34, 3: pp. 200–02.

16 Michio Yano and Merce Viladrich, 'Tasyīr computation of Kūshyār ibn Labbān', *Historia Scientiarum* 41 (1991): pp. 4–7; Kūshyār Ibn Labbān, *Introduction to Astrology*, ed. and trans. Michio Yano (Tokyo: Institute for the Study of Languages and Cultures of Asia and Africa, 1997), pp. 160–67.

to P by the daily rotation of the universe, the astrologers say that P 'progresses' to F, and al-Bīrūnī also uses this standard terminology. This 'progression' is visualized in Figure 3. For point P on the ecliptic, we can define a series of points $F_1, F_2, \dots F_n$ on the ecliptic such that the distance of F_n (along its circle parallel to the equator) to the position semicircle NPS is exactly n degrees in the direction of the daily rotation of the universe.

Then we can say that in the *tasyīr* doctrine, P after one year progresses to F_1, after two years to F_2, and so on. I note that this 'progression' is in the usual order of the signs of the ecliptic, and that the ecliptical longitude increases if P 'progresses' to F_1, then to F_2, etc.

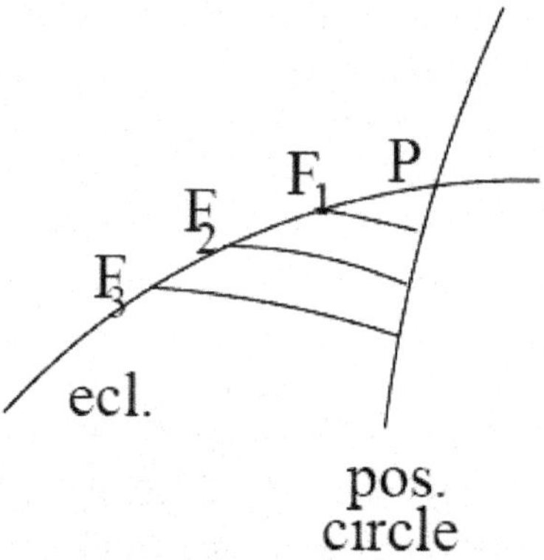

Fig. 3: Progression of P towards F.

Al-Bīrūnī's Section 2 has the somewhat mysterious title 'on mixing degrees with ascensions'. The word 'degree' (*daraja*) in the title must refer to ecliptical degrees; time-degrees on the equator are called *azmān*, 'times'. Section 2 begins with a general introduction to variable quantities and the process of interpolation. Al-Bīrūnī goes on to discuss another computation preliminary to the determination of *tasyīr* for planets with non-zero latitude, as an alternative to his own computation at the end of Section 1. By 'mixing degrees with ascensions' the astrologers wanted to compute for such a planet P, which is outside the ecliptic, the intersection T of its position semicircle with the ecliptic. The ecliptical longitude λ_T of this point of intersection may differ by a few degrees from the planet's ecliptical longitude λ_P obtained from astronomical handbooks (unless the position circle of the planet passes through the pole of the ecliptic and is perpendicular to the ecliptic). The computation of λ_T from λ_P is complicated and al-Bīrūnī only sketches an approximate method which resembles the computation in Section 1. The astrologers apparently continued the *tasyīr* computation with λ_T instead of λ_P.

Remarkably, λ_T emerged again in the twentieth century in the Dutch astrological school headed by Theo J.J. Ram (1884–1961) as the 'true zodiacal longitude' of a planet. The concept was introduced by the Dutch astrologer Leo Knegt (1882–1957).[17]

Al-Bīrūnī was aware of the fact that the computations in Section 1 and 2 are based on a geometrically approximate method. In Section 3 he describes a geometrically exact method of computation. He says that this method requires tables of oblique ascensions, not only for one's own geographical latitude but also for sufficiently many latitudes between one's own latitude and zero. Al-Bīrūnī says that the method can be used if one's mathematical competence is limited, but this is rather optimistic; the crux is a complicated trigonometrical computation of a quantity that he calls the 'latitude' of the position circle through the planet *P*. Al-Bīrūnī considers this position circle as a horizon for a new locality and then proceeds to compute the 'latitude' of that locality, which latitude is the length of the great circle arc from the celestial pole perpendicular to the new 'horizon'. Once this has been done, al-Bīrūnī prescribes that the computation of *tasyīr* should be based on oblique ascensions for the latitude of this new horizon. His point of view is abstract because if *P* is in the Western hemisphere, he considers the necessary oblique 'descensions' as oblique ascensions for localities of southern latitude. If a celestial object sets on the Western horizon at a locality on the Northern hemisphere of the Earth, it rises on the diametrically opposite locality on earth, in the Southern hemisphere. Thus al- Bīrūnī considers oblique ascensions of localities that were believed to be uninhabited in his time.

The worked examples below illustrate the computation of the 'latitude' of the position circle, and also the resulting exact determination of the *tasyīr* arc. Our worked examples for al-Bīrūnī's sections 1 and 3 are the same and will illustrate

---

[17] See Leo Knegt, *Astrologie, Wetenschappelijke Techniek, een studiewerk voor meergevorderden* (Amsterdam: J.F. Duwaer en zonen, 1928), pp. 76–79 for an introduction, computations, and a list of λ_T and λ_P for the horoscope of the Dutch Queen Wilhelmina (1880–1962). See also the website, www.wva-astrologie.nl.

the difference between the approximate and exact computation. In these examples, the differences correspond to 9 months and 2.5 years for the astrological prediction. We may conclude that, for a serious astrological prediction, the standard approximation method in Section 1 is pretty useless. This is probably the reason why computations on the basis of Section 3 are often met with in later Islamic astrology – for example in the *Zīj* of Ulugh Beg (ca. 1420).[18]

In Section 4, al-Bīrūnī describes the solution of an inverse problem: if the position of P on the ecliptic and the *tasyīr* arc is given, find the position of F on the ecliptic. In Figure 3, we have to find the ecliptical longitude of point F to which P 'progresses' in a given amount of time. Al-Bīrūnī presents an approximate solution which seems to agree well with the approximation in his Section 1 and therefore must have been rather useless for the exact solution of the problem, at least if the given number of years is sufficiently large.

In order to facilitate the *tasyīr* computation for a fractional number of solar years, al-Bīrūnī then presents a table in which any number of days of a solar year can be converted to minutes and seconds of arc (assuming that a complete solar year is equivalent to one degree of *tasyīr* arc). The manuscripts and printed edition contain this table in alphanumerical (*abjad*) notation. The table has been transcribed in the Appendix and some obvious scribal errors have been corrected in the process.

Worked examples, and some additional commentary

The following numerical examples were treated by Ptolemy.[19] I use the same latitude that was used by Ptolemy and also his tables of right and oblique ascensions in *Almagest* I:15, II:8.[20] Al-Bīrūnī computed slightly different tables of oblique ascensions which are not easily available to the reader who does not know Arabic.

Example 1: The locality is such that the longest day is 14 hours (Lower Egypt, latitude $\phi = 30°22'$); P and F are on the ecliptic at 0° Aries (P) and at 0° Gemini = 30° Taurus (F). One is required to compute the *tasyīr* in the following four cases:

---

[18] Louis Pierre Eugene Amelie Sédillot, *Prolégomènes des Tables astronomiques d'Oloug-Beg* (Paris: Typographie de Firmin Didot Frères, 1853), pp. 208–09, 211–12.
[19] Ptolemy, *Tetrabiblos*, III:10, pp. 294–305.
[20] Toomer, *Ptolemy's Almagest*, pp. 100–03.

(a) P is on the meridian, above the horizon (at midheaven) or below the horizon (imum coeli). Solution: the *tasyīr* arc is the right ascension of the signs Aries plus Taurus, that is 57°44′.

(b) P is at the Eastern horizon. Solution: the *tasyīr* arc is the oblique ascension of the signs Aries plus Taurus, taken from the oblique ascension table for Lower Egypt ($\phi = 30°22'$), namely 45°5′.

(c) P is on the Western horizon. Solution: the *tasyīr* arc is the oblique descension of the signs Aries and Taurus, which is equal to the oblique ascension of the two diametrically opposite signs of Libra and Scorpio, taken from the table for Lower Egypt: $250°23' - 180°0' = 70°23'$.

(d) P is in the Western quadrant above the horizon, with distance 45° to the meridian plane (measured on the celestial equator). In modern terms, the hour angle of P is 3^h. Solution: Since P is on the celestial equator, its half-day arc is 90°, and Ptolemy's seasonal ('ordinary') hours coincide with his equinoctial hours which are still used today. In this case, al-Bīrūnī's first arc is the right ascension arc 57°44′ determined in (a), and his second arc is the oblique descension arc 70°23′ determined in (c). His and Ptolemy's approximate computation boils down to the following.

If the distance of P to the meridian plane is $a°$, and the half-day arc of P is D, the *tasyīr* arc is the weighted average $57°44' + \frac{a}{D}(70°23' - 57°44')$. In Ptolemy's case, $D = 90°$ and $a = 45°$ so the *tasyīr* arc is 64°4′. In the *Tetrabiblos* III:10 Ptolemy rounds all *tasyīr* arcs to integer degrees.

I finish by one more working example for the same locality, but with $D \neq 90°$:

(e) Take P and F on the ecliptic such that $P = 0°$ Taurus, $F = 0°$ Cancer, and assume that P is in the Eastern quadrant above the horizon, at a distance of $a = 20°$ from the meridian plane measured along a parallel circle. (In modern terms, the hour angle of P is 22^h40^m.) Solution: The day arc $2D$ of P is the part of this parallel circle above the horizon, and its length can be computed as the oblique ascension of $P + 180°$ minus the oblique ascension of P; so $2D = 214°47' - 20°53' = 193°54'$, whence $D = 96°57'$.

Al-Bīrūnī's first and second arcs are the right and oblique ascensions ($\phi = 30°22'$) of arc PF, that is $90°0' - 27°50' = 62°10'$ and $75°0' - 20°53' = 54°7'$.

Thus the *tasyīr* arc is $62°10' - \frac{20}{96°57'}(62°10' - 54°7') = 60°30'$.

In the more refined method for planets P of non-zero latitude, the ecliptical coordinates longitude and (non-zero) latitude of the planet are first transformed into the equatorial coordinates declination δ, and right ascension α. Using the geographical latitude ϕ, one can then compute the point on the equator which rises or sets together with *P* as $\alpha \pm \arcsin(\tan\delta \tan\phi)$, without reference to ecliptical coordinates. Using tables of right and oblique ascensions, one can then compute al-Bīrūnī's 'degree of the rising point', the point on the ecliptic that rises at the same moment as *P*, and the 'degree of transit', which is the point on the ecliptic which passes through the meridian plane at the same time as *P*.

Section 1 of Chapter 5 of Book 5 of the *Masudic Canon* agrees with al-Bīrūnī's non-technical explanation of *tasyīr* in the *Introduction to Astrology*:

> . . . the meaning of *tasyīr* here, concerning births, is not by equal (ecliptical) degrees, but by degrees of ascension. As for the degree of the ascendent and the stars which are in it, its *tasyīr* is by oblique ascension of the locality, for every degree one year. And as for the degree of the descendent and the planets which are in it, it is by the descensions of the locality, and they are the ascensions of the degree opposite the [setting, that is the] rising (degree) and the signs which follow it, because the descensions of every sign in the locality are equal to the ascensions of the (sign) opposite it. For the degrees of the midheaven and the imum coeli, and the planets which are in it, will have *tasyīr* in all localities in right ascension. If a planet which is 'progressing' is not in these four degrees, but if it is between two degrees in the cardinal planes, its *tasyīr* is by ascensions which are mixed between the ascensions of the two cardinal degrees, by a long procedure and a difficult computation.[21]

The computation by Ptolemy and by al-Bīrūnī in his Section 1 is based on the idea that position circles are approximately the same as hour lines for seasonal hours. We can see this in the following way. If the sun is in *P* in the Western or Eastern quadrant above the horizon such that $\frac{a}{D} = \frac{n}{6}$ for constant $n = 1,...5$, the time of day is the beginning of a constant seasonal hour, namely $(7-n)$ if *P* is in the Eastern quadrant and $(7+n)$ if *P* is in the Western quadrant.

In Section 3 (see Figure 4 below), al-Bīrūnī assumes that the preceding planet is *K* and that its altitude *KZ* and azimuth *ZE* (reckoned from the East or West point of the local horizon) have been computed from the declination and the hour angle. His idea is to first find arcs *KH* and *HZ* from arcs *KZ* and *ZE*; mathematically speaking he performs a transformation of coordinates of *K* to a

---

[21] Al-Bīrūnī, *The Book of Instruction*, pp. 326–27.

new system, in which the basic circle of reference is the prime vertical. The computation can be described in more modern notation as follows. Make $R = 60$ equal to the radius of the sphere and write Sin and Cos for the sine and cosine functions used by al-Bīrūnī; so Sin $x = R\sin x$ and Cos $x = R\cos x$, where sin and cos are the modern sine and cosine.

Step 1: We have Sin HK = Sin $EZ\cdot$ Cos KZ / R = Sin $EZ\cdot$ Sin KS / Sin ZS and hence we find arc HK.

Step 2: We have Sin EH = Sin KZ / [Cos HK / R] and hence we find arc EH.

Step 3: We have Sin TM = Cos EH Sin ϕ / R where $\phi = TD$ is the geographical latitude. Then TM is the 'latitude' of the 'horizon' $HKMD$. Thus, from the intersection of the ecliptic with the position circle $HKMD$ can find the intersection with the celestial equator using the table of oblique ascensions for 'latitude' TM. Al-Bīrūnī's figure (Figure 4 below) is not realistically drawn; because K is a planet, it will not be too far away from the celestial equator.

For worked example (e) in Section 1, this computation is as follows. For $P = K$ standard computations produce a zenith distance $z = 26°20'$, and azimuth $a = 42°18'$ reckoned from the East point of the horizon, or $47°42'$ reckoned from the South point. In modern terms $\sin(HK) = \sin z \sin a$, so arc $HK = 17°22'$ (where K should be left of the prime vertical); $\sin EH = \cos z/\cos HK$ so $EH = 69°54'$ (note that E is also left of the prime vertical); $\sin TM = \sin EH \sin\phi$ so $TM = 10°0'$. For this latitude, the oblique ascension for the arc FP is the oblique ascension of 30 Gemini (85°32′) minus that of 30 Aries (25°45′), so the correct *tasyīr* arc is 59°47′. The standard approximation method in Section 1 produced 60°30′. For the astrological interpretation, the difference between correct and approximate computation corresponds to a difference of nine months in the life of the person.

In worked example (d) we find in the same or easier ways, $HE = 40°47'$ and $TM = 22°30'$. Because $P = K$ is in the Western quadrant above the horizon, we need to compute for this latitude the oblique descension of Taurus and Gemini, which is equal to the oblique ascension for Libra and Scorpio. This can be found, either by linear interpolation between Ptolemy's two tables of oblique ascensions for $\phi = 16°27'$ and $\phi = 23°51'$ or by direct trigonometrical computation, as 66°39′. This accurate *tasyīr* arc differs from the approximation 64°6′ of Section 1 by 2°33′, corresponding to a difference of more than 2.5 years in the astrological predictions for the person who was born at the time when the celestial configuration was as in example (d).

I illustrate the computation in Section 4 by a worked example similar to (e).

Assume that the locality is again the same ($\phi = 30°22'$), that P is again the point 0° Taurus on the ecliptic, and that the *tasyīr* arc is 60°30′, and that P is in the Eastern quadrant above the horizon with a distance 20° to the meridian (measured along a circle parallel to the equator).

We find al-Bīrūnī's first arc as follows. Since the right ascension of 0° Taurus is 27°50′, we look for an ecliptical degree whose right ascension is 27°50′ + 60°30′ = 88°20′ and we find (by linear interpolation in Ptolemy's table for right ascensions) 28°28′ Gemini, which is the endpoint of the first arc; hence the first arc is 58°28′.

We then find al-Bīrūnī's second arc. Since the oblique ascension of 0° Taurus is 20°53′, we look for an ecliptical degree whose oblique ascension is 20°53′ + 60°30′ = 81°23′. We find the endpoint of the second arc as 5°42′ Cancer, so the second arc is 65°42′. As above we have $a = 20$, $D = 96°57'$, so the correction is $\frac{20}{96°57'}(65°42' - 58°28') = 1°30'$. Thus arc $PF = 58°28' + 1°30' = 59°28'$, so F is in 29°58′ Gemini, very close to 30° Gemini in worked example (e) in Section 1. If al-Bīrūnī had believed in the value of astrology, he probably would have given a more correct solution such as the one in Section 3.

Appendix: Translations from the eleventh Book of the Masudic Canon

The following abbreviations will be used:
H: the Arabic edition in vol. 3 of Al-Bīrūnī, *al-Qānūn al-Mas'ūdī*, 3 vols (Hyderabad: Osmaniya Oriental Publications Bureau, 1954–56),
J: the Arabic edition in vol. 3 of Al-Bīrūnī, *al-Qānūn al-Mas'ūdī, qaddama lahu wa-ḍabaṭahu wa-ṣaḥḥahu 'Abd al-Karīm Sāmī al-Jundī*, 3 vols (Beirut: Dār al-Kutub al'ilmiyya, 1422 H./2002), which seems to be largely a reprint of H,
R: the Russian translation in Abu Raikhan Beruni (973–1048), Izbrannye Proizvedeniya V, part 2, *Kanon Mas'uda, knigi VI–XI*, trans. Boris Abramovich Rozenfeld and Ashraf Akhmedovich Akhmedov (Tashkent: Fan, 1976).
All explanatory additions by me appear in square brackets.

The Eleventh Book of the Masudic Canon

[H 1354, J 317, R 449]

This art [of astronomy] to which this book is devoted, is sufficient in itself, because of its great intrinsic value. Thus it is not very attractive to the hearts [of students], who cannot imagine any delight except in preparations for sensual pleasures, and who cannot see any use except in worldly matters. Since they found nothing desirable in it, they disliked and loathed it, so they turned their back on it and on its people. For this reason, the ancients versified the events of this world in terms of the rulings [of the stars], and they found somewhat satisfactory methods for obtaining knowledge of them [the events] by means of the influences of it [astronomy]. They founded the art of the judgements [of the stars, i.e., astrology] on these [methods], all the time presenting it to them [i.e., the 'hearts' of the students] as absolutely the fruit of that [i.e., astronomy], so they would pursue [it]. They [the ancients] knew that the greed of the general public for knowledge on how to increase the good and how to avoid harm would take severe blame and harsh disasters away from them [the students of astronomy and astrology].[22]

Some of the principles of the art of the judgements of the stars are related to computation. The astrologers find it sufficient to slavishly follow the relevant rules without critical investigation. But since that [i.e., such rules] cannot be reduced to [logical] necessity, it is possible to have differences [i.e., different opinions] in it, so the methods in it have become manifold. This [eleventh] book describes most of them, so it is distinguished from the earlier [works on the subject].[23]

The fifth chapter on the procedures of *tasyīr*, in five sections [H 1393, J 343, R 474]

The first section, on the well-known method in this

The astrologers assume some planet or place in the ecliptic in order to make predictions. They make (1) the [number of] time-degrees between it and another planet or its ray or something similar, correspond to (2) [real] amounts of time, in such a way that the first resembles the second or exemplifies the second. They call the procedure for obtaining these time-degrees *tasyīr* [i.e., 'progression']. By this term they indicate that we make [in our imagination] some planet progress to some [other planet or place], and then it will reach [that planet or place] in a certain amount of time: years, months or days. For easy expression, let us call the first of the two [planets] the 'preceding', since it precedes in the primary [i.e., daily] motion, and the other [planet], at which [the *tasyīr*] ends, the 'following'. The terminology and the procedure of them [the astrologers] may give the impression that the *tasyīr* is directed from the preceding [planet] and ends at the following [planet], but this is not the case. Its [real] meaning is contradictory to that impression: it is the arrival of the following[24] [planet], by

---

[22] Al-Bīrūnī probably means that because the general public believes that astrology can be useful, a skilled astronomer and astrologer can have a good reputation and make a living.

[23] Al-Bīrūnī means that Book 11 of the Qānūn is the first collection of different, mutually inconsistent astrological computations.

[24] Following R, p. 475 n. 69, p. 607, I read instead of *al-awwal* in H 1393:14 and J 343:12 *al-tālī* to make mathematical sense.

the primary motion [i.e., the daily motion of the sky], at the place of the preceding [planet]. They [the astrologers] agree that if the circle of the preceding [planet] is the meridian above or below [the horizon], the time-degrees of the *tasyīr* are degrees of right ascension of the [arc] between it and the following [planet]; and that if the circle of the preceding [planet] is the horizon, these time-degrees are degrees of oblique ascension of the [arc] between the two [planets] if the [preceding planet] is on the Eastern horizon, and degrees of oblique descension if the [preceding planet] is on the Western horizon. Thus, if [the preceding planet] is between these fundamental [half-]planes, it is necessary that the procedure for them is by means of the ascensions [defined] by the [semi]circle [H 1394] passing through the preceding [planet] and through the two poles of the prime vertical, or by their descensions, in analogy with what has been explained above[25] for the procedure for [computing] the projection of rays by means of ascensions that are mixed between the ascensions for the fundamental semicircles. For that procedure [for the rays] is adapted from the procedure for the *tasyīr*. So in this [procedure for the *tasyīr*] also: the ratio of the difference between the right ascension and the ascension of the circle through the preceding [planet] to the difference between the right ascension and the ascension or descension of the locality is [supposed to be] equal to the ratio of the distance [arc] between the preceding [planet] and the meridian to half its day arc [if it, sc. the preceding planet, is] above the earth or half its night arc [if it is] below the earth.

Its computation: we derive the distance [arc] of the preceding [planet] from the meridian circle above the horizon:[26] if it [the preceding planet] is above the earth, we subtract the right ascension of the tenth [house] from its [i.e., the planet's] right ascension, if it is in the Eastern quadrant; and we do the opposite of that [i.e., we subtract the planet's right ascension from

---

[25] See Section 1 of Chapter 4 of Book 11 of the *Masudic Canon* [H].

[26] In Chapter 3 of Book 11 of the *Masudic Canon,* Al-Bīrūnī explains that the 'distance' is computed along a circle parallel to the celestial equator.

the right ascension of the tenth house], [if it is] in the Western [quadrant]; or [we derive] its distance from the meridian circle below the horizon, if it [the preceding planet] is below the earth: we subtract the right ascension of the fourth [house] from its right ascension if it is in the Eastern quadrant and we do the opposite [if it is] in the Western [quadrant]. Then we subtract the right ascension of the preceding [planet] from the right ascension of the following [planet], and the remainder is the first [arc of] time-degrees. We do the same [subtraction] with the two oblique ascensions [of the preceding and following planet] for the locality, if the preceding [planet] is in the rising half [of the celestial sphere], and with the two oblique descensions if it is in the setting half. I mean by the oblique descensions the two oblique ascensions of the degrees diametrically opposite to the two degrees of them for the same [locality]. The remainder is the second [arc of] time-degrees. Then we multiply the difference between these two [arcs of] time-degrees by the distance of the preceding [planet to the meridian] and we divide the result by half its day arc if it is above the earth and by half its night arc if it is under the earth. Then the result is [called] the correction. We add it to the first [arc of] time-degrees if they are less than the second, and we subtract it from them [the first time-degrees] if they are more than the second. The result after the addition or subtraction is the desired time-degrees of the *tasyīr*. [J 344] [H 1395]

A more refined method: if we desire a more refined method, just as we desired in the projection of rays for the case where the planet is at a distance of a [non-zero] latitude from the ecliptic, then it is necessary to consider the preceding celestial body by itself, regardless of its ecliptical degree. If it is in the orb of the meridian itself, above or below the horizon,[27] then we use the right ascensions, and[28] we take them between the two [ecliptical] degrees of transit of the preceding and the following [planet]. Then

[27] For *nqshmā* in H 1395:7 I read *nafsihimā*. J 344:14 incorrectly changes the word to *naqsimuhumā*, as in the footnote on H 1395.

[28] I have emended *aw* in H 1395:8 and J 344:15 to *wa-*.

the result is the time-degrees of the *tasyīr*. And if the preceding [planet] is on the Eastern horizon, the time-degrees of the *tasyīr* are the difference between the oblique ascensions for the locality of the two [ecliptical] degrees of their rising points; and if on the Western horizon, then [the *tasyīr* arc is] the difference between the oblique ascensions of the degrees diametrically opposite to the [ecliptical] degrees of their setting points. According to this analogy, the ascensions of [bodies] between these fundamental planes are mixed between these [right and oblique] ascensions. Their procedure is that we compute the distance in right ascension between the [ecliptical] degree of transit of the preceding [planet] and the midheaven or the *imum coeli*, and the first [arc of] time-degrees in them [right ascensions] also, between the [ecliptical] degrees of transit of the preceding and the following [planets], and the second [arc of] time-degrees between the oblique ascensions for the locality of the two [ecliptical] degrees of their rising points, if the preceding [planet] is in the rising hemisphere, or between the oblique ascensions of the two [ecliptical] degrees diametrically opposite to the degrees of their setting points, if the preceding [planet] is in the setting hemisphere. For the correction, and the condition about adding or subtracting [it], we follow what has been explained above. Thus the time degrees of the *tasyīr* are obtained by means of half the day arc of the preceding [planet] itself or half its night arc, but not by means of half the day arc or night arc of its [ecliptical] degree.

[H 1396]

The second section. On mixing the degrees [of a planet] by means of the ascensions and the use of them

Magnitudes which change in the neighbourhood of two consecutive cardinal planes [horizon, meridian] share in that change according to the distance from them, if they happen to be between the two circles which define them [the cardinal planes]. Ascensions belong to them [i.e., to such magnitudes], as has been explained above in sufficient [detail]. So there is a rule for their similarity which is in two types. One type is for a magnitude which is bounded between its [maximal] value and its absence [i.e., being zero], either at the beginning or at the end, such as the altitude [of a celestial body]. For this begins with its absence [zero] at the horizon and reaches its [maximal] value in the meridian. Another example is the distance in azimuth, taken from the meridian line. It begins at its maximum, at the rising [of the planet] at the horizon, it ends with its absence [being zero] in the meridian circle. The case of the 'equation of day' is similar. [J 345]

The second type is the [magnitude] which oscillates between the two cardinal planes, between two [maximal and minimal] values: it is greater than the minimum and less than the maximum according to its position with respect to the cardinal plane[s]. Such is the day arc. Just like the distance between rising point and East point, the day arc is different in magnitude for horizons [of localities] with [non-zero] latitude, and fixed at its average magnitude in the meridian.[29] Another example is the ortive amplitude for them [i.e., for these horizons], for the ortive amplitude reduces to the declination [of the planet] when it is at midheaven, and if it is [computed for a position circle] between them [meridian and local horizon] it is less than the ortive amplitude [on the local horizon] and greater than the declination. For it is always [equal to an arc] on the [position] circle which is the horizon of a latitude less than the latitude of the locality.

And to this specialism belongs what they do,[30] because they

---

[29] The day arc of a planet is the arc of its apparent daily orbit above the horizon. This arc is always 180° for an observer on the terrestrial equator and it varies between a minimum and a maximum value with average 180° for observers in the tropical and temperate latitudes. In the context of *tasyīr*, the 'horizon' through the planet is the circle through the planet and the North and South point of the local horizon, so if a planet is at the meridian, its 'horizon' is the meridian itself and the celestial pole is located on it. So mathematically speaking, the 'horizon' of the planet is then the horizon for an observer on the terrestrial equator.

[30] Al-Bīrūnī is a bit sarcastic.

urgently need it, where they use both the degrees of rising and transit. If they use [only] one of these degrees [i.e., one of the two values] for the whole distance between the cardinal planes, the transition to the other [value] is [with a jump] at the [moment of] reaching the other cardinal plane without any orderly approach [H 1397] towards it [the new value]. This is unsatisfactory from a theoretical point of view.

The computation of the degree which is a mixture between the two above-mentioned degrees follows the analogy which has been mentioned for the projection of rays and the *tasyīr*. We obtain half the day arc of the body of the planet, not [necessarily] for the planet itself, but for its ecliptical degree. Then we multiply (1) the difference between the degree of transit and the rising degree in the ascending hemisphere, or the difference between the degree of transit and the degree of setting in the descending hemisphere by (2) the distance of the degree of transit from[31] the tenth house [if it is] above the earth, and we divide the product by (3) half the day arc of the planet; or [we multiply (1)] by (2) the distance of the degree of transit from the fourth house [if it is] below the earth, and we divide the product by (3) half the night arc of the planet. Thus we find the correction of the degree. Then we see: if the degree of transit is before the degree of rising or setting, whichever of the two is used, then we add the correction of the degree to the degree of transit. And if it [the degree of transit] is after [the degree of rising or setting] we subtract it [the correction] from it [the degree of transit]. The result is the degree which belongs to the planet in accordance with its position between the two cardinal planes. According to this analogy, the *tasyīr* will be made for the [astrological] powers of the planets, if they are between[32] the two cardinal planes.

---

[31] I have corrected *fī l-ʿāshir* in H 1397:6 J 345:19 to *ʿani l-ʿāshir*, in analogy with H 1397:7, J 345:21 *ʿani l-rābiʿ*.

[32] Instead of *fī*, 'in' in H 1396:12 and J 345:25 I read *bayna*, 'between' to make mathematical sense.

The third section. On the method which I preferred in tasyīr computation

For someone who can obtain [tables of] ascensions for the [i.e., all] latitudes less than the latitude of his locality, the above-mentioned procedure can be reduced from complexity to simplicity, and one can get rid of the carelessness and approximation which are involved in it, even if one's [mathematical] power is but little. [J 346]

For this, let *ABGD* be the circle of the meridian with pole *E*, and *BED* the horizon with
pole *S*, and *AEG* the equator with pole *T*, [H 1398]

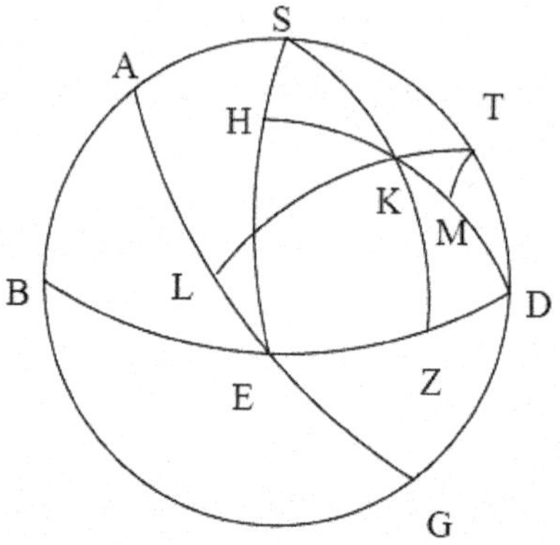

Fig. 4: Al-Bīrūnī's own computation.

and *K* the position of the preceding planet, between two fundamental [half-planes], and *TKL* the [declination] circle of its distance from the equator, and by this circle its position is known at the [given] time. We let pass through it *SKZ*, its altitude circle, to find its azimuth, and we draw *SHE*, the prime vertical. Then it is known that, if the azimuth is known, the ratio of the Sine of *EZ* to the Sine of *ZS*, the quadrant, is equal to the ratio of the Sine of *HK* to the Sine of *KS*, the complement of the altitude of the preceding [planet], so *KH* is known. But the ratio of the Sine of *DK*,[33] the complement of *KH*, to the Sine of *KZ*, is equal to the ratio of the Sine of *DH*, the quadrant, to the Sine of *EH*. So *EH* is known, but it

[33] I have corrected the scribal error *ZK* in H 1398:9 and J 346:7.

is the magnitude of the angle *EDH*, so the angle *SDH* is known, because it is the complement of it. But the ratio of the Sine of it to the Sine of the right angle *M* is equal to the ratio of the Sine of *TM*, which is perpendicular to *DH*, to the Sine of *DT*, the latitude of the locality. But *TM* is the latitude of the locality whose horizon is circle *DKH*. If it [the planet] is in the ascending hemisphere, it [the latitude *TM*] is in the [same] direction of the latitude of the locality [of the observer, i.e., Northern latitude], and therefore ascensions are used for it. But if it [the planet] is in the descending hemisphere, then *TM* is the latitude of that position [i.e., of the position circle through the planet], but in the direction different from the latitude of the locality [of the observer], and therefore the descensions of that locality are used in it, since they are equal to the ascensions there [for a locality of Southern latitude].

So either we compute the ascensions or descensions between the preceding [planet] and the following [planet], by [computing ourselves] the equation of day of the preceding [planet] on the [H 1399] horizon *DKH*, or we use the [tables of] ascensions which have been issued for the above-mentioned [i.e., all] latitudes; then [the result] is the [arc of] *tasyīr* which we wanted, in time-degrees.

The computation of this is as follows: we compute the altitude of the preceding [planet] and its azimuth from the given moment of time. Then we multiply the Sine of the azimuth by the Cosine of the altitude, and we divide by sixty. The result is a Sine, of which we take the arc. We divide the Sine of the altitude by the Cosine of it [i.e., of the arc] divided by sixty, and we take the arc corresponding to the result [considered as Sine]. We multiply the Cosine of it by the Sine of the latitude of the locality divided by sixty. The quotient is the Sine of the latitude of the circle of the *tasyīr* [i.e., the position circle of the preceding planet], and that is the horizon such that its ascensions or descensions are used for the *tasyīr* of the preceding [planet].

The fourth section, on the determination of the amounts of the tasyīr

If a known [amount of] time is assumed for us, and one wants to know where the preceding [planet] arrives in this [amount of

time] as a result of
tasyīr, we take for each complete solar year of the designated period one time-degree; and [we take] for the remainder in months, days, and smaller intervals, the share[34] of one time-degree which is allotted to it, [one time degree being] sixty minutes – by converting the remaining days of the year in our amount [of time], expressed in their smallest units, into minutes of days and higher sexagesimal fractions [of days], and by multiplying them by the sixty minutes which are in one time-degree, and by dividing the result by the magnitude of the year, and the result is the desired [number of] minutes of the time-degree. They are added to them [the integer number of time-degrees]. [J 437]

It is easier to compute for the remainder which does not complete a solar year, the argument of the sun and its apogee. We multiply the sum of these two [arcs] by ten minutes [= 1/6], and in this way we also extract the minutes of the time-degrees, which are added to the integer [time-degrees].[35] So if our time-degrees have been obtained, we add them to the right ascensions of

---

[34] I have emended *wa-ḥiṣṣatuhā* in H1399:13 and J 347:2 to *ḥiṣṣatuhā* for mathematical sense.

[35] Since the mean sun moves with constant speed and makes one complete revolution in one solar year, al-Bīrūnī can use the arc of the mean sun from the beginning of Aries in the first column of his table. In Book 6 of the *Masudic Canon,* he adds a table in which he lists for the n-th day ($n = 1...60$) two columns in six sexagesimals, namely the increase of the argument of the mean sun, reckoned from the apogee, from the beginning of the first day to the beginning of the n-th day, and the motion of the apogee in the same period, see [1, vol. 2, pp. 697–700]. The first column in the present table is adapted from the table in Book 6 by adding the two columns and truncating the sum. The second column in the present table is obtained from the first by means of division by 360, because 360 degrees of solar motion, one solar year, correspond to a *tasyīr* arc of one degree. The division by 360 is accomplished by multiplication by 1/6 ('ten minutes') and shifting the result by one sexagesimal place. Al-Bīrūnī indicates the sexagesimal shift by his statement that the quotient is in 'minutes of the time degree' rather than 'time-degrees' itself.

the degree of transit of the preceding [planet], and we convert the result into an [ecliptical] arc, and the result is the first arc. [H 1400]

Then we also add to the [oblique] ascensions for the locality of its rising degree, if it is in the rising half, the same [amount] which we have added to the ascensions of its degree of transit, and we convert the result to an [ecliptical] arc by means of the [oblique] ascensions for the locality, and the result is the second arc. And if it is in the setting half, we add this amount to the [oblique] ascensions of the degree diametrically opposite to its setting degree for the locality, and we convert the sum to an arc by means of these [oblique ascensions], and we add to the result one hundred and eighty degrees, and the result is the second arc.

Then we multiply the difference between it and the first [arc] by the distance between the preceding [planet] and the tenth [house] and we divide the product by half the day arc if it is[36] above the earth and by half the night arc if it is under it, then the result is the correction. We add it to the first arc if it is less than the second and we subtract it from it is if it is more. The result after the addition or the subtraction is the place to which the preceding [planet] is transported by the tasyīr, that is to say, the place in the ecliptic to whose [position] circle it is transported by the prime motion. Further, it is clear that the first arc is the desired [arc] if the preceding [planet] is on the meridian, above or under the earth, and then we do not need the second [arc]; and that the desired [arc] is the second arc if it [the preceding planet] is on the horizon, and then we do not need the first [arc].

I have placed in this table opposite the elapsed days the mean [motion] of the sun and its share of one time-degree. From this is also found, by the property of four numbers in proportion, the days and their fractions which correspond to [given] fractions of degrees in the *tasyīr*. [H 1401, J 438]

36 I have changed *fawqa* in H 1400:8 and J 347:16 to *in kāna fawqa* for mathematical sense.

day	solar year			time deg.			day	solar year			time deg.		
	°	′	″	°	′	″		°	′	″	°	′	″
1	0	59	8	0	0	10	31	30	33	18	0	5	5
2	1	58	16	0	0	20	32	31	32	27	0	5	15
3	2	57	23	0	0	30	33	32	31	35	0	5	25
4	3	56	33	0	0	40	34	33	30	43	0	5	35
5	4	55	41	0	0	49	35	34	29	51	0	5	45
6	5	54	50	0	0	59	36	35	29	0	0	5	55
7	6	53	58	0	1	9	37	36	28	8	0	6	5
8	7	53	6	0	1	19	38	37	27	15	0	6	14
9	8	52	15	0	1	29	39	38	26	24	0	6	24
10	9	51	23	0	1	39	40	39	25	33	0	6	34
11	10	50	31	0	1	48	41	40	24	41	0	6	44
12	11	49	40	0	1	58	42	41	23	50	0	6	54
13	12	48	48	0	2	8	43	42	22	58	0	7	4
14	13	47	56	0	2	18	44	43	22	6	0	7	14
15	14	47	5	0	2	28	45	44	21	15	0	7	24
16	15	46	13	0	2	37	46	45	20	23	0	7	33
17	16	45	21	0	2	47	47	46	19	31	0	7	43
18	17	44	30	0	2	57	48	47	18	40	0	7	53
19	18	43	38	0	3	7	49	48	17	48	0	8	3
20	19	42	47	0	3	17	50	49	16	56	0	8	13
21	20	41	55	0	3	27	51	50	16	5	0	8	23
22	21	41	3	0	3	37	52	51	15	13	0	8	32
23	22	40	11	0	3	46	53	52	14	21	0	8	42
24	23	39	20	0	3	56	54	53	13	30	0	8	52
25	24	38	28	0	4	6	55	54	12	38	0	9	2
26	25	37	36	0	4	16	56	55	11	47	0	9	12
27	26	36	45	0	4	26	57	56	10	55	0	9	22
28	27	35	53	0	4	36	58	57	10	3	0	9	32
29	28	35	2	0	4	46	59	58	9	12	0	9	41
30	29	34	10	0	4	56	60	59	8	20	0	9	51

day	solar year			time deg.			day	solar year			time deg.		
	°	′	″	°	′	″		°	′	″	°	′	″
61	60	7	29	0	10	1	91	89	41	39	0	14	57
62	61	6	37	0	10	11	92	90	40	47	0	15	7
63	62	5	45	0	10	21	93	91	39	56	0	15	17
64	63	4	54	0	10	31	94	92	39	4	0	15	26
65	64	4	2	0	10	41	95	93	38	12	0	15	36
66	65	3	10	0	10	50	96	94	37	21	0	15	46
67	66	2	19	0	11	0	97	95	36	29	0	15	56
68	67	1	27	0	11	10	98	96	35	38	0	16	6
69	68	0	35	0	11	20	99	97	34	46	0	16	16
70	68	59	44	0	11	30	100	98	33	54	0	16	26
71	69	58	52	0	11	40	101	99	33	3	0	16	35
72	70	58	0	0	11	50	102	100	32	11	0	16	45
73	71	57	9	0	11	59	103	101	31	19	0	16	55
74	72	56	17	0	12	9	104	102	30	28	0	17	5
75	73	55	25	0	12	19	105	103	29	36	0	17	15
76	74	54	34	0	12	29	106	104	28	44	0	17	24
77	75	53	42	0	12	39	107	105	27	53	0	17	34
78	76	52	50	0	12	49	108	106	27	1	0	17	44
79	77	51	59	0	12	59	109	107	26	9	0	17	54
80	78	51	7	0	13	9	110	108	25	18	0	18	4
81	79	50	15	0	13	18	111	109	24	27	0	18	14
82	80	49	24	0	13	28	112	110	23	34	0	18	24
83	81	48	32	0	13	38	113	111	22	43	0	18	34
84	82	47	40	0	13	48	114	112	21	51	0	18	43
85	83	46	49	0	13	58	115	113	21	0	0	18	53
86	84	45	57	0	14	8	116	114	20	8	0	19	3
87	85	45	6	0	14	18	117	115	19	17	0	19	13
88	86	44	14	0	14	27	118	116	18	25	0	19	23
89	87	43	22	0	14	37	119	117	17	33	0	19	33
90	88	42	31	0	14	47	120	118	16	41	0	19	43

day	solar year			time deg.			day	solar year			time deg.		
	°	′	″	°	′	″		°	′	″	°	′	″
121	119	15	50	0	19	52	151	148	50	0	0	24	48
122	120	14	58	0	20	2	152	149	49	8	0	24	58
123	121	14	6	0	20	12	153	150	48	16	0	25	8
124	122	13	15	0	20	22	154	151	47	25	0	25	18
125	123	12	23	0	20	32	155	152	46	33	0	25	28
126	124	11	31	0	20	42	156	153	45	41	0	25	38
127	125	10	40	0	20	52	157	154	44	50	0	25	47
128	126	9	48	0	21	1	158	155	43	58	0	25	57
129	127	8	56	0	21	11	159	156	43	6	0	26	7
130	128	8	5	0	21	21	160	157	42	15	0	26	17
131	129	7	13	0	21	31	161	158	41	23	0	26	27
132	130	6	21	0	21	41	162	159	40	31	0	26	37
133	131	5	30	0	21	51	163	160	39	40	0	26	46
134	132	4	38	0	22	1	164	161	38	48	0	26	56
135	133	3	46	0	22	11	165	162	37	56	0	27	6
136	134	2	55	0	22	20	166	163	37	5	0	27	16
137	135	2	3	0	22	30	167	164	36	13	0	27	26
138	136	1	11	0	22	40	168	165	35	21	0	27	36
139	137	0	20	0	22	50	169	166	34	30	0	27	46
140	137	59	28	0	23	0	170	167	33	38	0	27	56
141	138	58	36	0	23	9	171	168	32	46	0	28	5
142	139	57	45	0	23	19	172	169	31	55	0	28	15
143	140	56	53	0	23	29	173	170	31	3	0	28	25
144	141	56	2	0	23	39	174	171	30	12	0	28	35
145	142	55	10	0	23	49	175	172	29	20	0	28	45
146	143	54	18	0	23	59	176	173	28	29	0	28	55
147	144	53	26	0	24	9	177	174	27	37	0	29	4
148	145	52	35	0	24	18	178	175	26	45	0	29	14
149	146	51	43	0	24	28	179	176	25	54	0	29	24
150	147	50	51	0	24	38	180	177	25	2	0	29	34

day	solar year			time deg.			day	solar year			time deg.		
	°	′	″	°	′	″		°	′	″	°	′	″
181	178	24	10	0	29	44	211	207	58	21	0	34	39
182	179	23	19	0	29	54	212	208	57	29	0	34	49
183	180	22	27	0	30	3	213	209	56	38	0	34	59
184	181	21	35	0	30	13	214	210	55	46	0	35	9
185	182	20	45	0	30	23	215	211	54	54	0	35	19
186	183	19	52	0	30	33	216	212	54	3	0	35	29
187	184	19	0	0	30	43	217	213	53	11	0	35	39
188	185	18	9	0	30	53	218	214	52	19	0	35	48
189	186	17	17	0	31	3	219	215	51	28	0	35	58
190	187	16	25	0	31	13	220	216	50	37	0	36	8
191	188	15	33	0	31	22	221	217	49	44	0	36	18
192	189	14	42	0	31	32	222	218	48	53	0	36	28
193	190	13	50	0	31	42	223	219	48	1	0	36	38
194	191	12	59	0	31	52	224	220	47	9	0	36	48
195	192	12	7	0	32	2	225	221	46	18	0	36	58
196	193	11	15	0	32	12	226	222	45	26	0	37	7
197	194	10	24	0	32	22	227	223	44	34	0	37	17
198	195	9	32	0	32	31	228	224	43	43	0	37	27
199	196	8	40	0	32	41	229	225	42	51	0	37	37
200	197	7	49	0	32	51	230	226	42	0	0	37	47
201	198	6	57	0	33	1	231	227	41	8	0	37	57
202	199	6	6	0	33	11	232	228	40	16	0	38	7
203	200	5	14	0	33	21	233	229	39	25	0	38	16
204	201	4	22	0	33	31	234	230	38	33	0	38	26
205	202	3	31	0	33	41	235	231	37	41	0	38	36
206	203	2	39	0	33	50	236	232	36	50	0	38	46
207	204	1	47	0	34	0	237	233	35	58	0	38	56
208	205	0	56	0	34	10	238	234	35	6	0	39	6
209	206	0	4	0	34	20	239	235	34	15	0	39	16
210	206	59	12	0	34	30	240	236	33	22	0	39	26

day	solar year			time deg.			day	solar year			time deg.		
	°	′	″	°	′	″		°	′	″	°	′	″
241	237	32	31	0	39	35	272	268	5	50	0	44	41
242	238	31	40	0	39	45	273	269	4	58	0	44	51
243	239	30	48	0	39	55	274	270	4	6	0	45	1
244	240	29	56	0	40	5	275	271	3	15	0	45	11
245	241	29	5	0	40	15	276	272	2	23	0	45	20
246	242	28	13	0	40	24	277	273	1	31	0	45	30
247	243	27	21	0	40	34	278	274	0	40	0	45	40
248	244	26	30	0	40	44	279	274	59	48	0	45	50
249	245	25	38	0	40	54	280	275	58	56	0	46	0
250	246	24	46	0	41	4	281	276	58	5	0	46	9
251	247	23	55	0	41	14	282	277	57	13	0	46	19
252	248	23	3	0	41	24	283	278	56	21	0	46	29
253	249	22	11	0	41	33	284	279	55	30	0	46	39
254	250	21	20	0	41	43	285	280	54	38	0	46	49
255	251	20	28	0	41	53	286	281	53	46	0	46	59
256	252	19	36	0	42	3	287	282	52	55	0	47	8
257	253	18	45	0	42	13	288	283	52	3	0	47	18
258	254	17	53	0	42	23	289	284	51	12	0	47	28
259	255	17	2	0	42	33	290	285	50	20	0	47	38
260	256	16	10	0	42	43	291	286	49	29	0	47	48
261	257	15	18	0	42	52	292	287	48	37	0	47	58
262	258	14	26	0	43	2	293	288	47	45	0	48	7
263	259	13	35	0	43	12	294	289	46	54	0	48	17
264	260	12	43	0	43	22	295	290	46	2	0	48	27
265	261	11	51	0	43	32	296	291	45	10	0	48	37
266	262	11	0	0	43	42	297	292	44	19	0	48	47
267	263	10	5?	0	43	52	298	293	43	27	0	48	57
268	264	9	16	0	44	1	299	294	42	35	0	49	7
269	265	8	25	0	44	11	300	295	41	43	0	49	17
270	266	7	33	0	44	21	301	296	40	51	0	49	26
271	267	6	41	0	44	31	302	297	40	0	0	49	36

day	solar year			time deg.			day	solar year			time deg.		
	°	′	″	°	′	″		°	′	″	°	′	″
303	298	39	8	0	49	46	334	329	12	27	0	54	52
304	299	38	16	0	49	56	335	330	11	35	0	55	2
305	300	37	25	0	50	6	336	331	10	44	0	55	12
306	301	36	33	0	50	16	337	332	9	52	0	55	22
307	302	35	41	0	50	26	338	333	9	0	0	55	31
308	303	34	50	0	50	35	339	334	8	9	0	55	41
309	304	33	58	0	50	45	340	335	7	17	0	55	51
310	305	33	6	0	50	55	341	336	6	25	0	56	1
311	306	32	15	0	51	5	342	337	5	34	0	56	11
312	307	31	23	0	51	15	343	338	4	42	0	56	21
313	308	30	31	0	51	25	344	339	3	50	0	56	30
314	309	29	40	0	51	35	345	340	2	59	0	56	40
315	310	28	48	0	51	45	346	341	2	7	0	56	50
316	311	27	56	0	51	54	347	342	1	15	0	57	0
317	312	27	5	0	52	4	348	343	0	24	0	57	10
318	313	26	13	0	52	14	349	343	59	32	0	57	20
319	314	25	21	0	52	24	350	344	58	40	0	57	30
320	315	24	30	0	52	34	351	345	57	49	0	57	39
321	316	23	38	0	52	44	352	346	56	57	0	57	49
322	317	22	46	0	52	54	353	347	56	6	0	57	59
323	318	21	55	0	53	3	354	348	55	14	0	58	9
324	319	21	3	0	53	13	355	349	54	22	0	58	19
325	320	20	12	0	53	23	356	350	53	31	0	58	28
326	321	19	20	0	53	33	357	351	52	39	0	58	38
327	322	18	29	0	53	43	358	352	51	47	0	58	48
328	323	17	37	0	53	53	359	353	50	56	0	58	58
329	324	16	45	0	54	3	360	354	50	4	0	59	8
330	325	15	53	0	54	13	361	355	49	12	0	59	18
331	326	15	2	0	54	23	362	356	48	21	0	59	28
332	327	14	10	0	54	33	363	357	47	29	0	59	37
333	328	13	19	0	54	42	364	358	46	38	0	59	47
							365	359	45	46	0	59	57

COSMOLOGICAL TRADITIONS IN JUDEO-BYZANTINE SOUTH ITALY: A PRELIMINARY ANALYSIS

Piergabriele Mancuso

The vision of the starred sky, the observation of the cosmos and the perception of the unalterable movements of the stars, planets and constellations is one of the intellectually most impressive experiences that for centuries—and to some extent also today—was considered one of the most tangible proofs of the existence of an immutable order governing the universe and human destinies. Virtually all human civilisations—from the ancient Greeks to the Romans, through the Indians to the Jews and the Babylonians—have interpreted the events of the celestial world through the language of myth, the account of an imaginary story aiming to explain—or at least make intuitively understandable by means of a metaphorical language—the causes of natural phenomena such as earthquakes, the eclipses of the luminaries or the (only apparent) irregular motion of some celestial bodies.

One of the most vexing questions in ancient geocentric cosmology concerned the seemingly irregular movements that some planets seem to perform while moving around the earth, stopping and then moving backward. Greek and Hellenistic astronomers, taking for granted the geocentric system, had found a plausible explanation for this phenomenon, assuming that the planets, while moving around the earth, were rotating also around their own axes. The superimposition of the circular movements—the epicycles—would eventually result in the visual phenomenon of the retrograde motion of the planets to the eyes of a terrestrial observer. The practical application of this theory—the aim of which was to justify the geocentric system, rather than explain the physiognomy of the heliocentric cosmos—involved a series of extremely difficult and intricate mathematical-geometrical demonstrations that not all astrologers were able to perform. As pointed out by Sharf in his research on medieval Byzantium,[1] the

[1] Andrew Sharf, *The Universe of Shabbetai Donnolo* (New York: Ktav Publishing House, 1976), p. 37: 'The explanation of the planetary motion by epicycles was not accepted unanimously in Byzantium with the rest of the Ptolemaic system. Symeon Seth, for

theory of epicycles remained largely unpractised by Byzantine astrologers who, while accepting the fundamental tenets of classic cosmology (the geocentric idea of the universe as an agglomerate of sealed spheres, each one allotted to a planet or a luminary moving through it), preferred to it other less mathematically grounded and more mythically oriented hypotheses about the motion of the planets and the governance of the universe. As appears from the extant literary witnesses in the Jewish astrological milieus, particularly those of the southern Italian *themes* (districts) of the Byzantine empire, such a cognitive vacuum was filled with new cognitive hypotheses and new narrative strategies. Some probably stemmed from ancient Hebrew sources and, more specifically, from the cosmological lore of Babylonian Judaism, as attested in the so-called *Babli* (Babylonian Talmud, ca. sixth century CE) and by other contemporary exegetical sources (*midrashim*, rabbinical commentaries). Such a switch entailed in some cases, especially among southern Italian Jewish astrologers, radical rethinking of the fundamental tenets of classic cosmology, depicting the cosmological scheme according to new and unique cosmological coordinates.

In this paper I will focus primarily on a set of Jewish astrological texts written or circulating in Italy between the ninth and tenth centuries, corresponding to the peak of the phenomenon of cultural Renaissance that, between the eighth and eleventh centuries, led to a profound revitalisation of Jewish learning and culture among southern Italian Jews, eventually taking Hebrew—a language that the Jewish intellectual had until then neglected in favour of other, more sophisticated languages such as Arabic—back to its primeval role of the 'language of the Jews', particularly as a tool of written communication.[2]

---

example, could not, it seems, stomach the complex celestial machinery required . . .'. Sharf was the author of a number of studies on Byzantine Jewry and their cosmological ideas. See, for example, his '*Tli* and *Jawzahr* in the Macrocosm of Shabbetai Donnolo', in *Jews and Other Minorities in Byzantium* (Ramat-Gan: Bar-Ilan University Press, 1995), pp. 178–89. For more information about the study of astrology in late antique and medieval Byzantium, see Anne Tihon, 'L'Astronomie byzantine (du Ve au XVe siècle)', *Byzantion* 51 (1981): pp. 603–24 and Joseph Mogenet, 'L'Influence de l'astronomie arabe à Byzance du XIe au XIV siècle', in *Colloques d'Histoire des Sciences* (Louvain: Presses universitaires de Louvain, 1976), pp. 44–55.

[2] It is still not entirely clear what led the Jews of the Diaspora to return to Hebrew. The earliest evidence of this process can be found in the tombstones of the Hebrew catacombs of Venosa (Basilicata, near Naples) which attest to a gradual switch from Latin and Greek

Particular attention will be paid to the *Baraita of Samuel*, a pseudepigraphic work attributed to the Talmudic sages Samuel bar Abba or Shemu'el ha-Katan (Samuel the Young), produced probably in Palestine around the eighth century but well known in ninth-century southern Italy.[3] But our focus will be mostly on the astrological writings by Shabbatai Donnolo (912–913–after 982), a tenth-century polymath born in Oria (not far from Brindisi, in south Apulia), the author of some of the oldest written Hebrew texts in medieval Europe such as *Sefer ha-mazzalot* (*Book on the Constellations*),[4] and, above all, *Sefer Hakhmoni* (*The*

(the languages of Italian Jews since the early centuries of the common era) to Hebrew—a process which began around the eighth century, first at an onomastic level and then in more specific literary contexts. This suggests that the linguistic process was not a mere intellectual phenomenon but a part of a much more complex process concerning the socio-political character of the Mediterranean Jewish Diaspora which, at that time, was facing Muslim domination and socio-political restriction in Christian Europe. On this see Cesare Colafemmina, 'Hebrew Inscriptions of the Early Medieval Period in Southern Italy', in *The Jews of Italy – Memory and Identity*, eds. Bernard Dov Cooperman and Barbara Garvin (Potomac: University Press of Maryland, 2000), pp. 65–81; Nicholas de Lange, 'Hebrew Scholarship in Byzantium', in *Hebrew Scholarship and the Medieval World*, ed. Nicholas de Lange (Cambridge: Cambridge University Press, 2001), pp. 23–37 and Piergabriele Mancuso, *Shabbatai Donnolo's Sefer Hakhmoni – Introduction, Critical Text, and Annotated English Translation* (Leiden-Boston: Brill, 2010), pp. 3–11.

[3] The text of Samuel's *Baraita* was transmitted by a single manuscript whose text was edited for the first time by Nathan Amram, *Baraita di-Shemu'el* (Thessaloniki, 1861). The text was then republished with an introduction and notes by Judah David Eisenstein in *Otzar midrashim* (New York: 1915), II: pp. 542–47. The attribution of this *Baraita* (which is a text not included in the Talmudic canon) to the Talmudic sage Samuel the Young is merely hypothetical.

[4] *Sefer ha-mazzalot* is an astrological commentary on the *Baraita of Samuel*. The work is extant only in a long fragment preserved in the form of citation in the commentary on Job by the French exegete Joseph ben Shim'on Qara (born ca. 1060–1070). On Qara and the work by Donnolo, see Moshé Max Ahrend, *Le commentaire sur Job de Rabbi Joseph Qara* (Hildesheim: Gerstenberg, 1978), pp. 45–47 and Mancuso, *Shabbatai Donnolo's Sefer Hakhmoni*, pp. 23–24. The text of the citation was published as an independent text by Samuel David Luzzatto ('Mikhtav gimel', *Kerem Hemed* 7 [1843]: pp. 60–67) and a few years later with notes and commentary by Zachariah Frankel ('Der Commentar des R. Joseph Kara zu Job', *Monatsschrift für Geschichte und Wissenschaft des Judentums* 5 [1856]: pp. 223–29; 6 [1857]: pp. 270–74; 7 [1858]: pp. 255–63, 345–58). Parts of the same citation attested in Qara's text are attested in *Sefer Peli'ah, Sefer Razi'el* and *Sefer Hassidim*. For

Wise Book or *Book of the Wise*),[5] one of the major literary creations of medieval south Italian Jewry, and on the *Sefer Yetzirah* (*Book of Formation*, hereafter *SY*). This is an anonymous text pseudepigraphically attributed to the Patriarch Abraham but probably produced, as we will see immediately below, in Palestine between the third and the sixth centuries.[6]

Celestial Hierarchies, Astrological Myths: the Sphere, the Dragon, and the Wain

SY is one of the oldest, shortest and, from several points of view, most enigmatic texts of the Hebrew literature. Nothing can said with certainty either about its place and time of origin or its authorship except that, since the early tenth

---

more information on this, see Mancuso, *Shabbatai Donnolo's Sefer Hakhmoni*, p. 24, nn. 88–89.

[5] The Hebrew text of Donnolo's *Hakhmoni* was published for the first time by David Castelli, a nineteenth-century Italian scholar, on the basis of some manuscripts that he had collected in Paris, Florence and other Italian libraries. See David Castelli, ed., *Il commento di Sabbatai Donnolo sul Libro della Creazione* (Florence: Le Monnier, 1880). As pointed out by Ithamar Gruenwald ('Some Critical Notes on the First Part of Sefer Yezirah', *Revue des études juives* 132, [1973]: pp. 475–512, particularly p. 483), Castelli's edition is not reliable, being dotted by mistakes and several omissions. A new critical edition based on a comprehensive analysis of all the extant manuscripts was recently published by the author of the present paper in both Italian and English translation: see Piergabriele Mancuso, *Shabbatai Donnolo – Sefer Hakhmoni – Introduzione, testo critico e traduzione italiana annotate e commentata a cura di Piergabriele Mancuso* (Florence: La Giuntina, 2009) and Mancuso, *Shabbatai Donnolo's Sefer Hakhmoni*.

[6] I have not included in this study the analysis of *Baraita de-mazzalot (The External Collection on the Constellations)*, an anonymous astrological text written probably around the tenth century. The hypothesis that the work was by Donnolo was formulated by Gad B. Sarfatti according to the result of a comparative analysis that he conducted of the quotations attributed to Donnolo in later Hebrew works. On this see Gad Ben-Ami Sarfatti, 'An Introduction to *Barayta de-Mazzalot*', *Bar-Ilan University Annual* 3 (1965): pp. 56–82 [in Hebrew]; Sarfatti, 'The Astrological Books of Shabbetai Donnolo', *Korot* 8 (1981): pp. 27–29 [English section] and 31–35 [Hebrew section]; Sarfatti, 'I trattati di astrologia di Sabbetay Donnolo', in *Sabbetay Donnolo – Scienza e cultura ebraica nell'Italia del X secolo*, ed. Giancarlo Lacerenza (Naples: Università degli studi di Napoli L'Orientale, 2004), pp. 141–47. This *Baraita* consists mainly of a commentary on the *Baraita of Samuel*—as does Donnolo's *Sefer ha-mazzalot*—and even though it shows remarkable linguistic similarities with Donnolo's *Sefer Hakhmoni* and *Sefer ha-mazzalot* itself, its authorship as well as the place and time of composition are uncertain.

century, as far as we can infer from the literary testimonies, *SY* became an important text among the Jews of the Mediterranean basin: from the ninth- to tenth-century Neoplatonist Isaac Israeli to Sa'adiah Gaon, and Shabbatai Donnolo (the only one out of the four early commentators who explicitly defined *SY* as a divinely inspired text comprising part of the Sinai revelation, the Pentateuch canon) to Dunash ben Tamim (one of Israeli's pupils), who all commented on it, stemming from Neoplatonic gnoseological and philosophical premises. As underscored by Joseph Dan, although in the Talmudic writings there are some references to the theory of creation by letters and, more specifically, to a series of *hilkot ha-yetzirah* (rules of formation, a name closely resembling *Sefer Yetzirah*), there is no evidence that those 'rules' were the same as the text we have known since the tenth century today.[7]

SY probably originated from the confluence and eventual conflation of two main cosmogonic/cosmological traditions: one centred on the letters of the Hebrew alphabet (the *otiyyot*) as an active factor and element of the creation, another one based on the action of the so-called *sefirot*, a term of very uncertain meaning, commonly understood as emanations or ontological influences. *SY* contains some passages of astrological interest, most of which are very simple in nature and concern fundamental elements of cosmological knowledge such as the order of the planets in the universe—particularly their positions with respect to the earth and their physical characteristics—their mutual associations and the relationships they have with the elements of the sublunar world (such as the organs of the human body) and sublunar time (such as the hours of the day, the weekdays and the months of the year). These associations, however, do not seem to be linked to any other astrological tradition; the very core of *SY*'s cosmology seems to be based on a sort of celestial triad which *SY* places in relation with the three principal *otiyyot*, the three main and most important letters of the Hebrew alphabet:

ואלו הם שלש אמות אמ"ש ויצאו מהם שלשה אבות... ותולדותיהם ושבעה כוכבים וצבאותיהם ושנים עשר גבולי אלכסון. ראיה לדבר עדים נאמנים בעולם שנה נפש ושנים עשר חק ושבעה

---

7 See Joseph Dan, 'The Three Phases of the History of *Sefer Yezirah*', in *Jewish Mysticism – Late Antiquity* (Northvale: Jason Aronson, 1998), pp. 155–87. On *SY* there is a plethora of studies; for a list of the most comprehensive and authoritative I refer to *La mistica ebraica – Testi della tradizione segreta del giudaismo, dal III al XVIII secolo*, eds. Giulio Busi and Elena Loewenthal (Turin: Einaudi, 1995), pp. xxiv–xxxv and 658–59. On Donnolo and *SY*, see also Mancuso, *Shabbatai Donnolo's Sefer Hakhmoni*, pp. 41–46.

ושלשה פקדן בתלי וגלגל ולב...

> ... These are the Three Mothers, *alef-mem-shin,* and from them emanated the Three Fathers . . . and their descendents, and seven stars and their hosts, and twelve diagonal boundaries. A proof of this true witness in the Universe, in the year and in the body [lit. 'spirit'] and the rule of twelve, and seven and three: He set them in the *Tly,* in the Cycle and in the heart.[8]

Some of the astronomical terms employed in this passage are intuitively clear and simple. The *seven stars* presumably refer to the five planets (Saturn, Jupiter, Mars, Venus, Mercury) and the two luminaries (the Sun and the Moon); the *twelve diagonal boundaries* are probably related to the twelve parts into which the zodiacal belt is divided (in other words, the signs of the zodiac), while the quite explicit aim is to define a correspondence between the elements of the micro- and macrocosm, the fundamental theme of *SY*'s cosmological and philosophical discourse. Far from clear, however, is the meaning of two terms, *tly* and the *galgal* ('Cycle'), two celestial entities apparently playing a dominant role in the cosmological context.

An explanation of this passage comes from the first chapter of the *Baraita of Samuel* which describes the structure and hierarchical principles governing the universe, at the head of which is said to be a celestial trilogy dominated by the *tly*, the *galgal* and—instead of the *lev* (heart) of *SY*—the *'agalah*, a noun that rabbinical tradition had identified with a northern constellation, probably the Wain, which is also called the Great Bear. Just as in *SY*, here the *tly* is said to be like a 'king', that is, a supreme entity. This entity is not, however, actively involved in any practical activity; the charge of this is given to its subjects, namely the constellations (comparable to the generals of a king's army) and,

[8] Hebrew text from A. Peter Hayman, *Sefer Yesira – Edition, Translation and Text Critical Commentary* (Tubingen: Mohr Siebeck, 2004), p. 168. *SY*, as already mentioned, has been the subject of several studies and several hypotheses were formulated about its genesis. Very little, however, has been done about its astrological contents and, more specifically, the peculiar characteristics of its cosmological theories and micro-macrocosmic correspondences. From this standpoint, the 'heterodoxy' of *SY*'s cosmological scheme is so explicit but also internally consistent that we can exclude it as the product of mere misunderstanding or mishaps in the transmission of the text. My hypothesis is that the author (or authors) of *SY* were somehow trying to outline a new cosmological scheme, Jewish insofar as 'peculiarly' different from any other one.

above all, the Wain: the real mover of the entire celestial stage. In Samuel's view the movement is generated mechanically from the Wain, to be subsequently transmitted to the Pleiades (which are connected to the twelve sections of the zodiacal belt by means of *chains* (*ma'danot*) and *reins* (*moshekot*), which Samuel derives from the exegesis of a verse from the book of Job), to the *sphere* to which all the other celestial bodies are attached:

> ...מצפון לדרום עש עולה כסיל הגלגל כימה ומזלות מן המזרח למערב. התקשר מעדנות כימה (ומושכות) [או מושכות] כסיל תפתח (איוב לח לא). שבעה מעדנות כימה וחמשה מושכות כסיל. שבעה וחמשה י"ב. סובב הגלגל ז' מקושרים מבית וה' מפותחים מבחוץ... זריחת ז' מצפון לימין וה' משמאל... תאומים סוף ז' ועקרב סוף החמשה. מן תאומים לקשת כמן עקרב לסרטן. בין עקרב לסרטן כבין עגלה לעקרב, עגלה בצפון ועקרב בדרום. זורח עיגול כלפי דרום ושוקע עיגול כלפי צפון ובצפון עגלה חוזרת ומשרתת את התלי. והתלי למזלות והמזלות לגלגל והגלגל חוזר כגלגל דלי מים. המזלות כסדינים. התלי כמלך ועגלה המנהיג ברוח שנאמר (איוב כו יג) ברוחו שמים שפרה חוללה ידו נחש בריח. נחש בריח זה התלי

> [. . . from north to south the *'ash* [Bear] rises, the *galgal* [sphere], the *kimah* [Pleiades] and the constellations, from east to west. *Canst thou bind the chains* (*ma'danot*) *of the Pleiades, or loose the reins* (*moshekot*) *of Orion* [*kesil*]? (Job 38:31). The seven chains are the Pleiades, the five reins are Orion. Seven and five makes twelve...The sphere [*galgal*] turns the seven bound from inside and the five opened from outside... The rising of the seven [constellations] from the north in the right and of the five from the left... Gemini marks the end of the [group of the first] seven [constellations], and Scorpio [marks] the end of the [other] five constellations. [The distance] from Gemini to Sagittarius is like [the distance] from Scorpio to Cancer and [the distance] from Scorpio to Cancer is like [the distance] from the Wain [*'agalah*] to Scorpio, the Wain staying in the north and Scorpio in the south. The circle [*'igul*] rises in the south and sets in the north, and in the north the Wain turns and serves the *tly*. The *tly* [dominates?] the constellations and the constellations [move?] the sphere which turns around like a water bucket. The constellations are like generals and the *tly* is like a king. The Wain [*'agalah*] drives [all] by means of the spirit, as is said: *By His spirit the heavens are serene; His hand hath pierced the slant serpent* [*nachas bariach*] (Job 26:13). The *slant serpent*, this is the *tly* . . .]

Why, however, does Samuel focus so much on the constellations set in the north part of the vault, ignoring the rest of the firmament? This was due to the fact that to a terrestrial observer living in a parallel above the northern tropic (in Palestine or in southern Italy, for example), the constellations of the northern hemisphere appear to turn much more rapidly than the other constellations, in some cases never disappearing from his view, being visible for longer and thus, in astrological terms, being 'dominant' in comparison to the other asterisms. This is what led ancient civilisations—the Egyptians, for example, as well as Samuel and some other later astrologers such as Shabbatai Donnolo—to bestow on the northern side of the vault a dominant role in their cosmology.

Donnolo, one of the earliest and most systematic commentators on the *Baraita of Samuel* and *Sefer Yetzirah*, which he considered the most authoritative Hebrew texts on astrology, moves from the same cosmological assumptions of Samuel. However, he gives the *tly* a series of cosmological prerogatives and conceives it not as a static—although theoretically dominant—factor, but as an active element of the celestial hierarchy, acting directly in the universe and over all its elements. In Donnolo's view, in sum, the *tly* is the main cosmological factor; it is the source of all phenomena, everything depending on it and being performed without mediation. The aim of Donnolo's interpretation of the *Baraita*'s text is to weaken the mechanical character of Samuel's north universe, to deconstruct and then redefine a new celestial hierarchy dominated directly and actively by the *tly*. To do so, Donnolo needs to break up the components which comprise the celestial hierarchy outlined by Samuel, to deconstruct its constituent parts and, by singling them out, to insert each of them into an independent and self-sufficient mythological narrative frame. Donnolo took this frame from the Babylonian Talmud, without any doubt the most authoritative rabbinical work at that time and the only 'legitimate' source of cosmological knowledge. The following text is taken from *Sefer ha-mazzalot*:[9]

...וראיתי בספר ר'[בי] שבתי ז[כר]צ[דיק]"ל[ברכה] שמפרש בו ברייתא דשמואל וחשבון י"ב מזלות נמצא מכימה וכסיל כדברי שמואל החכם שאמר בברייתא שלו כי **ז'** הם **מעדנות כימה וה' מושכות כסיל**... יש חכמים שאומרים הוא כסיל והוא עגלה ועש שהולך אחר הכימה. ויש שאומרים שהעגלה הוא עש וכסיל זה שהולך אחר הכימה שהעגלה הוא כסיל ומביאין[10] ראייה מן חמשה מושכות כסיל. כלומר כי יש לעגלה כוכבים השנים נקראים כסיל והחמשה נקראים מושכות כסיל, כי השנים

---

[9] The following citation follows the Samuel David Luzzatto edition of *Sefer ha-mazzalot*. The footnotes to the Hebrew letter ר indicate the reading variants of the text of *Sefer Razi'el*. Round brackets indicate omissions while the square brackets refer to words of longer sentences not attested in the main text. For the sake of clarity, the passages from the *Baraita of Samuel* on which Donnolo is commenting are written in bold characters in both in the Hebrew text and in the English translations.

[10] ר (ומביאין...נקראים כסיל)

נחשבים אופני[11] העגלה וחמשה מושכותיהם ומגלגלותם. ולכימה יש ז' כוכבים והם מעדנות כימה. ועש הוא שהולך אחר הכימה ואומרים שכשהביא הקב"ה להעביר מימי[12] המבול מעל הארץ לקח שני כוכבים[13] מן העש וסתם את המקומות של ב'[14] כוכבים שלוקחו מן הכימה ועל זה הולך העש אחר הכימה ומבקש[15] ממנה שני כוכבים ואומר לה הבי לי בניי הבי בניי...

[I have seen in the book by Shabbatai of blessed memory where he comments on the *Baraita of Samuel*, the calculation of the twelve constellations which terminates with the Pleiades and Orion according to the word of Samuel the Wise who said in his *Baraita* that **seven are the chains** [*ma'danot*] **of the Pleiades and five the reins** [*moshekot*] **of Orion**... There are some sages who affirm that Orion [*kesil*] is the Wain [*'agalah*] and that the Bear [*'ash*] moves behind the Pleiades. There are some other [sages] who say that the Wain is the Bear and that Orion moves behind the Pleiades, the Wain being the same as Orion. In support of it they refer to the five *reins of Orion* (Job 38:31), that is to say, that the Wain has two stars called Orion and five [stars] called the *reins of Orion*, the [first] two being considered like the wheels of the Wain, and the [other] five like the reins that make them move. The Pleiades have seven stars, which are the *chains of the Pleiades* (ibid.). The Bear moves behind the Pleiades, and [the sages] say that when the Holy One - blessed be He - was going to let the waters of the Flood on the earth, He took two stars from the Bear and with them closed the two holes [lit. "places"] corresponding to the two stars which he had previously taken from the Pleiades. For this the Bear moves behind the Pleiades asking for the two stars, saying: 'Give me my

11 ר אל פני

12 ר (להעביר מימי)

13 ר [מכימה והיה המבול וכשמבקש להעביר לקח שני כוכבים]

14 ר (של ב'...מן הכימה)

15 ר לבקש (ממנה...שאמר) בניה עי"ש שהוא עש וזה

daughters, give me my daughters!’].[16]

By referring to the cosmological legend attested in the Babylonian Talmud—but with some important variations[17]—Donnolo has in some way been able to

---

[16] Donnolo’s reference to the ‘chains’ and the interpretation he offers of their role closely reminds us of the notion of ‘sky-cords’, not uncommon in several sixth- and seventh-century Asian cosmological traditions. On this see the very interesting article by Kevin Van Bladel, ‘Heavenly Cords and Prophetic Authority in the Qur’an and its Late Antique Context’, *Bulletin of the School of Oriental and African Studies* 70 (2007): pp. 223–46. Here, there is a graphical representation of the cosmological ‘drama’ taking place in the universe.

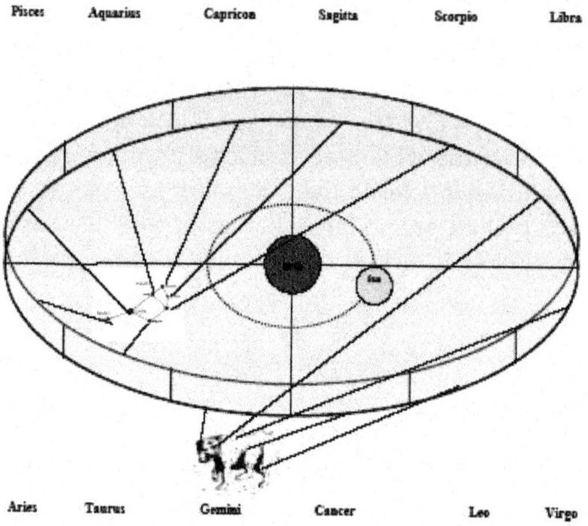

The earth occupies the centre of the universe and is surrounded by the planets which move around it (in the figure above we have indicated only the Sun) and the zodiacal belt whose movement originates, as Donnolo explains, from the conflict between the Bear and the Pleiades.

[17] See for instance *Berakhot* 58b–59a: ‘. . . What is meant by *Kimah* [Pleiades]? Samuel said: About a hundred [*ke’me-ah*] stars. Some say they are close together; others say that they are scattered. What is meant by *Ash* [the Bear]? Rab Judah said: Jutha. What is Jutha? Some say it is the tail of the Ram; others say it is the hand of the Calf. The one who says it is the tail of the Ram is more probably right, since it says: *Ayish* will be comforted for her children. This shows that it lacks something . . .’, but see also *bRosh ha-shanah* 11b where is said: ‘. . . R. Joshua said: That day was the seventeenth day of Iyar, when the constellation of Pleiades sets at daybreak and the fountains begin to dry up, and because they

decontextualise the role of the two constellations (Pleiades and Orion) and dismantle them as the mechanisms of Samuel's scheme, leaving a vacuum in the celestial hierarchy that only a cosmologically empowered *tly* will be able to fill. Unlike Sa'adiah, Dunash and many other later commentators on *SY* who understood the *tly* in the mere 'inert' astronomical terms of the *axis mundi*, Donnolo depicts it in a completely different vein as a celestial creature acting directly on the universe, over the sub- and super-lunar spheres. The *tly*, says Donnolo, governs the entire universe, moves the celestial bodies back and forward or makes them stop. In Donnolo's cosmology, in sum, the *tly* is the source of all phenomena, everything depending on and being attributed to it. Donnolo refers extensively to the *tly* in his *Sefer ha-mazzalot*, the commentary on the *Baraita of Samuel*, but the more systematic and comprehensive analysis of this subject appears in his *Sefer Hakhmoni* where Donnolo comments on a passage of *SY* (§ 55)[18] where it is said that

וזה ה ו ז ח ט י ל נ ס ע צ ק וכולן אדוקין בתלי וגלגל ולב

> [This is *he, waw, zayin, het, tet, yod, lamed, nun, samekh, 'ayin, sade, qof*, they all adhere to the *tly*, the Sphere and the heart]:[19]

This is Donnolo's commentary on the above.

> This is ***he, waw, zayin, het, tet, yod, lamed, nun, samekh, 'ayin, tzade, qof***... [This is] the order of the twenty-two letters, their foundation, combination and rotation, their measure, the words [they generate] and their formation, their secret, their permutations and their actions, all adhering to the Dragon (*tly*), the [celestial]

[mankind] perverted their ways, the Holy One, blessed be He, changed for them the work of creation and made the constellation of Pleiades rise at daybreak and took two stars from the Pleiades and brought a flood on the world. R. Eliezer said: That day was the seventeenth of Marheshvan, a day on which the constellation of Pleiades rises at daybreak, and [the season] when the fountains begin to fill, and because they perverted their ways, the Holy One, blessed be He, changed for them the work of creation, and caused the constellation of Pleiades to rise at daybreak and took away two stars [from it] and brought a flood on the world . . .'.

[18] See Hayman, *Sefer Yesira*, p. 168.

[19] For the sake of clarity the text of *SY* in this passage is written in bold characters. The Hebrew text and English translation are in Mancuso, *Shabbatai Donnolo's Sefer Hakhmoni*, p. 201–02, 343.

> sphere and the heart. Who is the Dragon? When God created this firmament, which is above us and which is divided into seven firmaments, He created the Dragon out of water and fire, in the likeness of a large sea monster, like a large writhing serpent (Cf. Is. 27:1). He made for it a head and a tail and set [literally, 'stretched'] it in the fourth firmament, which is the middle one and the abode of the sun. He stretched it from end to end as an axis, like a writhing serpent, twisted half way along its length and stretched out in the shape of a circular ring. All the planets, the luminaries and the constellations are attached to it, as the threads of the warp and woof are attached to the weaver's loom. Likewise are attached to it all the planets in the seven firmaments, from the lowest to the uppermost one, as well as the two luminaries and the twelve constellations. It [the Dragon] was appointed king over them all, to guide them, either benignly or malignly. It darkens the light of the two luminaries and the five planets, it moves the luminaries forward and backward and the planets and the constellations from east to west and from west to east; it draws the planets back and holds them in one place, preventing them from straying either forwards or backwards. It conducts them in a straight path, and it comes from fire and water; its quality is like [the quality of] water, and it cannot be seen with the naked eye, but rather it is by the study of the ancient texts transmitted to us that we gain knowledge of the Dragon and its quality, its dominion, its kingship, its creation, its beneficence and its malignity, the features of those who are born under it, the time it takes to move from constellation to constellation, when it reverses its course, how its head follows its tail, its ascent and descent and how the twelve constellations are attached to it, six to the south, six to the north.

According to Donnolo, the Dragon (*tly*) has complete control over the sphere and everything: from the ordinary movements of the planets around the earth to the less frequent phenomena of lunar and solar eclipses and the apparent stopping and retrograde motions of the planets. In this respect, as pointed out by Sharf,[20] *tly* reminds us quite closely of the concept of the 'celestial dragon' of Gnostic cosmology, vestiges of which probably survived and also circulated to some extent in Judeo-Byzantine southern Italian milieux.[21] Donnolo sets the *tly*

---

[20] See Sharf, *The Universe of Shabbetai Donnolo*, p. 33–51. For a short but exhaustive explanation of the idea of the celestial dragon/serpent in Gnostic thought, see Bernard Simon, *The Essence of the Gnostics* (London: Arcturus Publishing, 2004), pp. 137–56.

[21] In support of this hypothesis, however, Sharf does not bring any really convincing evidence. In light of the extant documentation, the only possible and plausible *trait d'union* between forms of Gnostic thought and the Jewish milieux of southern Italy are

in the fourth sky, the abode of the Sun and the middle one between the sphere of the Moon—the lowest and nearest to the earth—and the path of Saturn, the most distant from the earth and nearest to the eighth sphere of the fixed stars, the constellations. The spatial centrality allotted to the *tly* in the universe justifies *SY*'s dictum that the *tly* is 'like a king' (i.e., a king seated in the middle of a celestial court), a ruler who acts, however, directly upon his subjects, without mediation. In order to fulfil all its celestial duties, the *tly* needs to be conceived not as a mere astronomical concept, but as a dynamic being able to move throughout the universe from its abode (the fourth sky) through the site of the fixed stars to the abode of the Moon. The inclusion of such a dynamic entity within the universal framework mitigates the rigid structures of the classic cosmological scheme, weakening the boundaries which divide planets, each one moving along its own path, from the constellations. It is within this conceptual framework of 'cosmological malleability' and spatial mobility of the elements making up the cosmos that Donnolo outlines a new map of the universe where the constellations—in classic cosmology thought to be outside the planetary spheres—are said to lie together with the Moon in the first sky:

> . . . the Moon is set in the lowest firmament, which is above us, and it absorbs the cold from earth and the lower waters. Being far above the earth and the lower waters, it is not as cold as Saturn. *The moon possesses a little heat, which it absorbs from the constellations and from the planets [making up] their hosts and their armies, which are set in the lowest firmament, together with the moon* [italics mine]. For this reason, the quality of the Moon is a mixture of cold and heat.[22]

As was already pointed out, one cannot rule out that here Donnolo is elaborating on, or was to some extent influenced by, older sources where similar

---

admittedly only *SY* and the *Baraita of Samuel*, two works that, in light of extant evidence and according to the most plausible hypotheses, may well have been composed roughly around the same time (sixth–eighth centuries CE) and in the same or close geographical milieux (Byzantium and Palestine), so as to have incorporated and elaborated concepts and ideas from a common, older Gnostic source, independent of each other.

22 ...ולבנה סדורה ברקיע התחתון אשר מעלינו ומקבלת את הקור מן הארץ ומן המים התחתונים ועל אשר היא ברום מאד למעלה מן הארץ ומן המים התחתונים איננה קרה כשבתאי ויש ללבנה חום מעט כי מקבלת חום מעט מן המזלות ומן כוכבי צבאותיהם וחיילותיהם הנתונים ברקיע התחתוני עם הלבנה.
Hebrew text and English translation in Mancuso, *Shabbatai Donnolo's Sefer Hakhmoni*, pp. 188 and 321. For the sake of clarity the critical notes are omitted here.

(but not identical) 'non-conforming' pictures of the universe are attested.[23] However it is clear that at the basis of Donnolo's unorthodox cosmological view, what conceptually justifies such a peculiar representation of the universe is the *tly*, the creature that moves the constellations to the first sky together with the Moon. Whether Donnolo shared such a view with other Judeo-Byzantine astrologers or astronomers or not is not an easy question to answer. Donnolo's writings played a not-insignificant role in the development of cosmological studies among the Jews, contributing mostly to the development of a specific astrological terminology. But his peculiar views about the form of the universe and the very notion of *tly*—an idea removed from any mathematical reasoning and with a quasi-magical flavor—were given no place in the field of astrological studies. They disappeared, for example, from the writings of Abraham Ibn Ezra who, as we have recently argued, probably knew and studied the astrological works by Donnolo. No traces of the *tly*, by the same token, appear in the writings of the Haside Ashkenaz group—probably the most faithful and most legitimate heirs of the southern Italian intellectual legacy—not even in the commentary on *SY* by El'azar of Worms's (ca. 1176–1238, Haside Ashkenaz's last major leader), most of which consists of a systematic paraphrase of Donnolo's *Sefer Hakhmoni*. Probably for the same reasons as its disappearance in these contexts, Donnolo's *tly* survived to some extent at the cost of a substantial redefinition in more mystically-oriented literary contexts. A telling example is offered by *Sefer ha-Peliah*, a pseudepigraphic text probably composed in the fifteenth century in a Byzantine milieu, which states that the celestial vault is made up of ten spheres encompassed by two sea-monsters (two *tanninim*). The author of *Sefer ha-Peliah* certainly knew Donnolo's works (particularly the *Sefer*

[23] I have not been able to identify any Hebrew or non-Hebrew source from which Donnolo may have derived his notion of universe. As observed by Castelli in his Italian introduction to the first edition of the Hebrew text of *Sefer Hakhmoni* (see Castelli, ed., *Il commento*, pp. 59–60) some similarities to Donnolo's cosmology can be found in a passage of the first book of the *Bibliotheca Historica* by the first-century CE Diodorus Siculus, even though it cannot be proved that Donnolo knew this text or that the two authors were referring to a common older source. Some other similarities can be found also in *Liber Gaphar de mutatione temporis*, a Latin translation of an astrological work by the eighth-century Ja'far al-Hindi. For more information on this, see Mancuso, *Shabbatai Donnolo's Sefer Hakhmoni*, p. 321, n. 104.

ha-mazzalot, which he often quotes *verbatim*) and it seems plausible that his theory was derived directly from a passage of *Sefer Hakhmoni*, here compared:

Sefer ha-Peliah:[24]

> וסביב העגולה של גלגלים מצויירים שם התנינים הגדולים שברא השם יתברך בששת ימי הבראשית
> זנב עם ראש בצד אחד: זנב עם ראש בצד אחד

> ['And all around the circumference of the spheres are the two big sea-monsters which God – blessed be He – created during the six days of the Creation. The tail and the head (of one) is to one side, the tail and the head (of the other) is on the other side'] (my translation).[25]

Sefer Hakhmoni:[26]

---

[24] *Sefer ha-qanah we-hu sefer ha-peli'a* (Koretz, 1784), f. 30a.

[25] In the *editio princeps* and in several later editions of the text a graphical representation of this passage is offered:

Although it is plausible that the author of *Sefer ha-Peliah* knew Donnolo's work from which he probably took the notion of the two celestial dragons, his understanding of the universe and its structures differs from it substantially. According to the author of *Sefer ha-Peliah*, as pointed out above, the cosmos consists of ten spheres, presumably corresponding to ten celestial bodies moving around the earth and, more precisely, its physical and spiritual centre, the Temple of Jerusalem.

[26] Mancuso, *Sefer Hakhmoni*, p. 226.

ויש ספרים שאומרים כי שנים תליים הם כשני תנינים גדולים וכשני נחשים עקלתונים והעוקל.
שלהם כשני טבעות זה כנגד זה אחד נטוי בצד דרום ואחד נטוי בצד צפון ראשו של זה דבוק בזנבו
של זה וראשו של זה דבוק בזנבו של זה ומתוך הלוכם מתחלפים להיותם הדרומי צפוני והצפוני
דרומי והם ברקיע הרביעי במעונה של חמה וששה מזלות אדוקין בתלי אחד וששה

[According to some books, there are two *t^e^layyim*, which are like two big sea-monsters (*tanninim*), or like two writhing serpents (*nehashim 'aqaltonim*) twisted in the shape of two (half) rings facing each other, one to the south, the other to the north, with the head of the one attached to the tail of the other and vice versa. As they progress along their course, they change over: the one to the south turns north, and the one to the north turns south. They are in the fourth firmament, the abode of the sun. Six constellations are attached to the first *tly*, and six other to the second *tly*…]

Conclusions

What we have seen so far is just a detail of the very complex relationship which occurred within the cosmological debate between myth and astrology, between what I would like to call two dimensions or aspects of pre-scientific intellectual plausibility. The lack of knowledge that afflicted early medieval Byzantium broke the fragile balance that in astrological practice existed between the coherence of the mathematical calculus (not a prerogative of astronomy!) and the formulation of plausible cosmological suppositions, giving free range to a plethora of hypotheses from which further ideas and cosmological thoughts sprouted. Donnolo's *tly*, as has been mentioned, was probably an answer to such a misbalance, a response to a quest for clarity and cosmological plausibility.

In spite of the interest that, since the times of the *Wissenschaft des Judentums*, Jewish scholarship has expressed for the intellectual legacy of southern Italian Jewry in the early Middle Ages and the works that originated from there, several details of that cultural debate—especially those concerning the study of astrology and the overall problem of Hebrew cosmology—are unknown or at least have not yet completely come into focus. Only a deeper and more comprehensive examination of the rich corpus of cosmological and astrological texts produced in the early Middle Ages by southern Italian and Byzantine Jews, I think, will enable us to enter a field that for the time being remains largely unexplored.

QUANTITATIVE CONCEPTS IN HELLENISTIC AND MEDIEVAL ASTROLOGY[1]

Josefina Rodríguez-Arribas

'Be careful and do not give any judgement unless according to two valid witnesses (*'edim kešerim*)'.
Abraham ibn Ezra[2]

The status of Medieval astrology was certainly hybrid; its validity was supported by the generally acknowledged influence of heavenly bodies upon terrestrial beings (natural astrology) that was part of Medieval science, and by the apparently arbitrary and frequently contradictory judgements that astrologers could formulate about a horoscope, relying on their experience and the tradition (judicial astrology). The theory of *testimonies/witnesses* and *powers* tried to build a bridge over the gap that separated astrology from science by imposing a quantitative system. I have already analysed in a previous article the concept *witness/testimony* in Hellenistic and Medieval sources.[3] There, I

---

[1] I would like to express my appreciation to the Warburg Institute and the Sophia Trust for the Sophia Fellowship that made this research possible. It was also supported by a scholarship of the Spanish Ministerio de Asuntos Exteriores y Cooperación intended for the mobility of researchers. I wish to thank Charles Burnett and Dorian Gieseler Greenbaum for having read and improved this article with their comments. Needless to say, only the author is responsible for the contents. Since the acceptance of my article for publication in the proceedings of the conference *From Masha'allah to Kepler: The Theory and Practice of Astrology in the Middle Ages and the Renaissance* some of the Hebrew manuscripts that I used in the preparation of this article have been edited and published. I thank Charles Burnett for having updated most of these references with Shlomo Sela's editions. We have included the reference of these editions, but have kept the reference to the manuscripts that I originally used in my research. Unless otherwise noted, all the translations in this article are by the author.

[2] Abraham Ibn Ezra, *Sefer ha-moladot* (*The Book of Nativities*), MS BNF 1056 f. 48a (now Shlomo Sela, *Abraham Ibn Ezra on Nativities and Continuous Horoscopy* [Leiden: Brill, 2013], pp. 102–03).

[3] Josefina Rodríguez-Arribas, 'Testimonies in Medieval Astrology: Finding Degrees of

considered the evolution of this term from a general to a more specific meaning in Arabic and Hebrew sources, and its application by certain kinds of astrologers who were also scientists or were especially concerned with the certainty of astrological judgements (Ibn Labbān and Ibn Ezra). In these sources this concept is crucial for understanding that trend in Medieval astrology to endow astrology with a more scientific and ascertainable basis.[4] In this article, I will consider the concept of *power/strength* and three other minor quantitative concepts—*claims, victory,* and *sign*—in Hellenistic and Medieval sources. Like the term *testimony/witness,* all these terms are evidence of a specific trait of Medieval astrology concerned with the reliability of astrological judgements.

The Astrological Concept of Testimony/Witness*: An Outline*

As the concept of *testimony/witness* is closely related to the concept of *power* in astrological sources, I present here a short introduction to the former in order to make clearer the main subject of the present article.[5] In Greek astrology the concept of *testimony* (root 'martyr-') is very close to the concept of astrological aspect, with which it frequently overlaps. The first writer to employ this term in astrological contexts is Manetho (Egypt, second–first century BCE) in his *Apotelesmatika*.[6] Manetho's uses of this term seem to imply that the *testimony* of a planet strengthens the aspect and influence of others. In Latin literature, the

---

Certitude in Astrological Judgments', in *Doxa, Études sur les formes et la construction de la croyance,* ed. Pascale Hummel (Paris: Philologicum, 2010), pp. 115–33.

[4] For an overview on the accuracy and certainty of astrological judgements and their scope, see Dimitri Gutas, 'Certainty, Doubt, Error: Comments on the Epistemological Foundations of Medieval Arabic Science', *Early Science and Medicine* 7 (2002): pp. 276–89; Charles Burnett, 'The Certitude of Astrology: The Scientific Methodology of al-Qabīṣī and Abū Ma'shar', *Early Science and Medicine* 7 (2002): pp. 198–213; and Peter Adamson, 'Abu Ma'shar, al-Kindi and the Philosophical Defense of Astrology', *Recherches de théologie et philosophie médiévales* 69 (2002): pp. 245–70. None of these articles refer to the existence of a quantitative system to express degrees of certainty in the field of astrological judgements.

[5] For a detailed analysis of the term witness/testimony, see Rodríguez-Arribas, 'Testimonies in Medieval Astrology'.

[6] Robert Lopilato (Greek ed. and English tr.), *The Apotelesmatika of Manetho,* PhD dissertation, Brown University, 1998, p. 61 [3. 63–64] and 224 (tr.), also in p. 53 [2. 400–401], p. 28 [1.124], p. 124 [6.324], and forms with prefix in p. 72 [3.355] and 235, p. 80 [4.176] and 245, etc.

equivalent term is *testimonium* which is present in Firmicus Maternus' *Mathesis* (fourth century CE).[7] In the Arabic version of Dorotheus Sidonius' *Carmen astrologicum* (c. 75 CE), the Arabic root that translates the Greek concept is *š-h-d*.[8] The meaning of this root in the *Carmen* also suggests an aspect or relationship among planets that strengthens (testifies/bears witness to) the judgement coming from another aspect or relationship among the planets.[9] In Medieval Arabic literature, Māshā'allāh (fl. ca. 762–815) includes in his astrological works a concept (*šahāda*) equivalent to the testimony already existing in Greek and Latin literature.[10] Pingree's and Kennedy's translation of *šahāda* as *aspect* (instead of *testimony*) is a proof of the overlapping of the two concepts in old sources. In this text the two notions, *testimony/witness* and *power/strength*, appear several times together.[11] From Māshā'allāh's use of testimony it becomes clear that the concept 'testimony' has to do with the strength/power of the planets, i.e., the stronger the planet, the stronger the testimony or the larger its degree. The fact that testimony also emerges in the plural is an indication that this is a countable term.[12] However, I have not found in Māshā'allāh's text an account of witnesses as we will find in later sources.

The unidentified Latin translator (working in or before the twelfth century) of Māshā'allāh's work on the solar annual revolutions (historical astrology) employs the same term as Firmicus (*testimonium*).[13] However, something new emerges: we see together, for the first time (as far as I know), the word *testimonium* in a nominal group in which it is in the genitive (the first noun) and

---

[7] Pierre Monat (Latin ed. and French tr.), Firmicus Maternus, *Mathesis*, v. 2 (Paris: Les Belles Lettres, 1994), p. 15–16 [3.1.2], p. 199 [4.21.7], and p. 66 [6.29.4].

[8] David Pingree (Arabic, Greek and Latin ed. and English tr.), *Dorotheus Sidonius, Carmen astrologicum* (Leipzig: Teubner, 1976), for instance, 1.26.19, 23, 35, and 2.12.

[9] Dorotheus, *Carmen*, p. 191 [1.26.19].

[10] Edward Stewart Kennedy and David Pingree (Arabic facsimile and English tr.), *The Astrological History of Māshā'allāh: On Conjunctions, Religions, and Peoples*, (Cambridge MA: Harvard University Press, 1971), p. 45 [229v, 1–2].

[11] Kennedy and Pingree, *The Astrological History*, p. 49 [230v, 17–19], and also p. 64 [222v, 1–2].

[12] Kennedy and Pingree, *The Astrological History*, p. 51 [232r, 1].

[13] Concerning the translations of Māsha'allāh's treatises into Latin, see the references by David Juste and Charles Burnett on the webpage of the Warburg Institute, *Bibliotheca astrologica latina numerica*, <http://warburg.sas.ac.uk/pdf/fah765mesahw.pdf>.

the second noun makes reference to quantity/amount (*testimonii illius quantitas*).[14] The definitive text regarding the word *testimonium* as a quantitative technical term is the chapter of Māshā'allāh's *De revolutionibus annorum mundi* that starts with the revealing title of *de partibus ac testimoniis planetarum* ('the shares and testimonies of the planets').[15] In this section, *testimonium* and *fortitudo* overlap, for the word *testimonium* in the title disappears in the text where the word *fortitudo* takes its place. Thus, the concept *fortitudo* seems to be, for Māshā'allāh (or for his translator), the expression of the degrees of the testimonies of the planets, as the expression *ex fortitudine testimonii* in the *Liber Messahalae de receptione* also proves (Latin version by John of Seville in the twelfth century).[16] I will come back later in this article to the apparent overlap of *testimonium* and *fortitudo* in the Latin sources (Robert Grosseteste, thirteenth century). The meaning of *testimonium* as a quantitative term is missing in the Arabic work of Abū Ma'shar (787–886), where only the general meaning of this term (*witness*) emerges.[17]

The Persian Al-Bīrūnī (973–1048) mentions the word testimony in several places within his *Book of Instruction in the Elements of the Art of Astrology*, written in Arabic. Al-Bīrūnī's text is highly significant, for we find in it for the first time a clear distinction between the two meanings of testimony: quantitative and general. The first meaning concerns the so-called *essential dignities* of the planets and, in this sense, *testimony* (quantitative) and *dignity* are synonymous.[18] The most restricted (quantitative/countable) meaning of testimony has only one

---

14 Māshā'allāh, *De revolutionibus annorum mundi*, caput XII, *Quando dominus anni fuerit cadens*, sig. B viii v, caput XIIII, *De adversario regis*, sig. C i r, and also caput XXIX, *De inimicis regis*, D iii r. This text is available on the webpage of the Warburg Institute, *Bibliotheca astrologica latina numerica*, <http://warburg.sas.ac.uk/pdf/fah765mesahw.pdf>.

15 Māshā'allāh, *De revolutionibus annorum mundi*, caput VI, *De partibus testimoniis planetarum, ex quibus agnoscitur dominus anni*, B iii r.

16 John of Seville, *Liber Messahalae de receptione*, caput II, *De re, quae speratur utrum fiat an non*, sig. M i r. This text is also available on the webpage of the Warburg Institute, *Bibliotheca astrologica latina numerica.*

17 Keiji Yamamoto and Charles Burnett, *Abū Ma'šar, On Historical Astrology, The Book of Religions and Dynasties (On the Great Conjunctions)*, 2 vols (Leiden: Brill, 2000), v. 1 (Arabic ed. and English tr.), for instance, pp. 32–33 [2.8].

18 See R. Ramsay Wright (Arabic facsimile and English tr.), Al-Bīrūnī, *Book of Instruction in the Elements of the Art of Astrology* (London: Luzac, 1934), pp. 306–07 [493].

precedent, the *Introduction to Astrology* of Kūshyār ibn Labbān (eleventh century). According to Ibn Labbān, the planet with more dignities in a certain house (by domicile, exaltation, triplicity, and term) is considered the lord according to a calibrated scale: the lord of the household holds four testimonies, the lord of the exaltation three, the first lord of the triplicity two and the second lord of the triplicity and the lord of the term hold one testimony each (*shahāda*).[19] In his text, Ibn Labbān goes further than Al-Bīrūnī in the quantitative aspect of the term *testimony* and allots a different number of testimonies to every planet according to its position in some of its dignities in the zodiac (domicile, exaltation, triplicity, term, and decan—the decan was not mentioned in Al-Bīrūnī's text).[20] As we have mentioned, the association of testimonies with dignities is already attested to in Al-Bīrūnī's text, save that Al-Bīrūnī does not introduce any measurement associated with the term testimony but only with the dignities of the planets.[21]

Moving to Hebrew literature, Abraham bar Hiyya (d. after 1136) uses the biblical Hebrew word *'edut* (testimony) to translate the Arabic root *š-h-d*. The sense of the term *testimony* in Bar Hiyya's *'Iggeret* (*Letter*) to Yehudah ben Barzillai and in his *Sefer Megillat ha-megalleh* (*The Book that Reveals*) is the influence of stars in general, although it also entails the idea that an aspect strengthens another aspect or the influence of another planet, as we have already seen in previous sources. Abraham ibn Ezra (1089/92–1164/67) employs in Hebrew, for the first time, the very same technical (quantitative) meaning of witness/testimony (*'ed*/*'edut*) with the same intention as Ibn Labbān. Ibn Ezra aims to prove the certainty of an astrological judgement, which stems from a certain astrological aspect and certain position of the planets and is relevant to any of the astrological branches (natal, historical, electional, interrogational, and medical astrology). Ibn Ezra also states, as Ibn Labbān did, that at least two valid testimonies (i.e., two conclusive relationships of elements in the horoscope indicating the very same judgement on the same issue) are required to validate a prognostication.[22] For this purpose, Ibn Ezra introduces (as far as I know, for the

[19] For a complete explanation of this theory, see Michio Yano (Arabic ed. and English tr.), *Kūshyār ibn Labbān's Introduction to Astrology* (Tokyo: ILCAA, 1997), pp. 66–69 [1.22.1–4] and pp. 66–67 [1.22.1–2].

[20] See Ibn Labbān, *Introduction*, pp. 66–67 [1.22.1–2].

[21] Al-Bīrūnī, *Book of Instruction*, pp. 329–30 [525].

[22] See, for instance, the second version of Ibn Ezra's *Sefer ha-še'elot*, MS Paris BNF 1058 f.

first time with respect to previous sources in the languages analysed in this article) the notion of a valid/apt witness (*'ed kašer*) in astrological contexts, which is any testimony guaranteeing and backing up the certainty of a judgement deduced from the positions and relations in a horoscope. An identical meaning is conveyed by the other term of the same root, *'edut*, which I translate as *testimony*. Both *'ed* and *'edut* are quantitative terms and it is possible to refer to a half, one, two, three, or more witnesses/testimonies at the moment of weighing up the certainty of a prognostication.[23] The concept of *testimony* seems to overlap with the Hebrew term *koaḥ* (power, strength) in Ibn Ezra's texts (as in Ibn Labbān's texts and in previous sources), and it is not infrequent that the two appear together in the same sentence. The following section explores this other astrological term.

Hellenistic and Medieval Sources on the Concept of Power/Strength

The word *dynamis* is already used by Homer (c. eighth century BCE) and denotes power, might, and especially bodily strength—also influence.[24] It appears in the *Septuaginta* (third century BCE), in the form *hai dynameis*, with or without the genitive form *tōn ouranōn*, meaning the heavenly bodies (literally, 'the powers of the heavens').[25] Manetho (Egypt, second–first century BCE) does

---

1b (now Shlomo Sela, *Abraham Ibn Ezra on Elections, Interrogations and Medical Astrology* [Leiden: Brill, 2011], pp. 352–53).

[23] For instance, the first version of Ibn Ezra's *Sefer ha-še'elot*, MS BNF 1056 fols 64a and 64b. See also Ibn Ezra's *Sefer ha-moladot*, MS Paris BNF 1056 fols 48a and 48b, and *Sefer ha-me'orot* (*Book of the luminaries*), Y.L. Fleischer (Hebrew ed.), *Sinai* 5 (1933): p. 45, and in the second version of the *Sefer ha-še'elot*, MS Paris BNF 1058 fol. 3b (now Sela, *Abraham Ibn Ezra on Elections, Interrogations and Medical Astrology*; see pp. 256–67 and 468–69, and Sela, *Abraham Ibn Ezra on Nativities and Continuous Horoscopy*, pp. 102–05).

[24] Henry G. Liddell and Robert Scott, *A Greek-English Lexicon* (Oxford: Clarendon Press, 1925–1940).

[25] Evangelinus Apostolides Sophocles, *Greek Lexicon of the Roman and Byzantine Periods (From BC 146 to AD 100)* (New York: Chas Scribner's Sons, 1887). For the meaning of the Greek terms I have used Liddell and Scott, *A Greek-English Lexicon* with the *Supplements* of 1968 and 1996; and Henri Etienne, *Thesaurus Linguae Graecae*, 8 vols (Paris, 1842–46). See also Geoffrey William Hugo Lampe, *A Patristic Greek Lexicon* (Oxford: Clarendon Press, 1961), pp. 389–91: power, might, also of spiritual beings, as in *kyrios tōn dynameōs* (literally, 'lord of the powers') where the meanings of 'heavenly powers', 'angelic hosts', and 'forces' are combined.

not employ this root, but uses the noun 'power' (*kratos*) in his *Apotelesmatika* to denote a similar meaning, in the context of the direction of a degree in order to determine the years of life of a person: '. . . begin with that star which rules the geniture, since it has great power (*mega te kratos iskhei*)'.[26] Ptolemy (second century CE) uses *dynamis* several times in his *Tetrabiblos* denoting the powers of the planets, the specific power of every planet, the powers of the signs, and the power of the ruling planet.[27] However, Ptolemy also employs, although less frequently, other words, like energy (*energeia*) to express the same concept, and the interesting expression 'the characteristic active powers (*poiētikē idiotropia*) of the planets'.[28] Vettius Valens (second century CE) also employs *dynamis* several times in his *Anthologiae* for denoting the power of a planet or other element in the horoscope. For instance, he refers to the power of directing a planet or a degree with the expression *dynamin ekhein* (to have power), whose meaning in this context is clearly 'to have influence'.[29] In Paulus of Alexandria's (fl. c. 378 CE) *Eisagōgika* (*Introduction*) there is also mention of the term *dynamis* (power) with the verbs *ekhein* and *epekhein* (to have power); in the *Scholia* (*Commentaries*) to his work, we find *dynamis* with the same meaning. All the contexts refer to the power/influence of the planets:[30]

> For just as the Sun when in the <face> of Ares by reason of <its being> in the first decan of Aries clearly has another power (*dynamin ekhein*) . . . , so again the same Sun, when in the second decan, takes another strength (*iskhyn*) which it clearly has in itself and by itself.[31]

---

[26] Lopilato, *Apotelesmatika of Manetho*, p. 74 [3.413] (Greek text) and p. 237 [3.410] (English tr.).

[27] Frank Egleston Robbins (Greek ed. and English tr.), *Ptolemy, Tetrabiblos* (Cambridge, MA, and London: William Heinemann Ltd. and Harvard University Press, 1980), pp. 34–35 [1.3], pp. 36–37 [1.4], pp. 44–45 [1.8], pp. 64–65 [1.11], and pp. 238–239 [3.3], respectively.

[28] Ptolemy, *Tetrabiblos*, pp. 178–79 [2.8].

[29] David Pingree (Greek ed.), *Vettii Valentis Antiocheni Anthologiarum Libri Novem* (Leipzig: Teubner, 1986), p. 165 [4.11.17]. See also, for instance, p. 235 [6.2.29] (*the powers of the stars*).

[30] Emilie Boer (Greek ed.), *Paulus Alexandrinus, Eisagōgika* (Leipzig: Teubner, 1958), p. 27, line 2, p. 27, line 10, and p. 106, line 9, respectively.

[31] Dorian Gieseler Greenbaum (English tr.), *Late Classical Astrology: Paulus Alexandrinus and Olympiodorus with the Scholia from Later Commentators*, Reston VA: Arhat, 2001, p. 11.

The Latin word *vis-vires* (power) emerges in Manilius' (fl. beginning first century BCE) *Astronomica* with the general meaning of influence/power, very frequently referring to the zodiacal signs: '. . . and the influences (*vires*) it <the celestial vault> radiates from afar are faint when they reach the earth'; or 'the individual signs vary on account of the distribution of their divisions and modulate their respective powers (*vires*) in the dodecatemories'.[32] The term *vis* is sometimes clearly equivalent to *effectus* (effect/influence) referring to a planet or any other element in the horoscope: 'each cardinal, however, enjoys a different influence (*vis*)', 'Saturn exercises the powers (*vires*) that are his own', and 'the influence (*vires*) of heaven'.[33] However, Firmicus Maternus (fourth century), in his *Mathesis*, prefers the word *potestas* (power/strength) to denote this meaning, referring to the planets and houses. The planet (in this case, Saturn) increases its power as the result of its position in certain parts of the horoscope where it is especially strong (domicile, decan, term, etc.):

> But the malice of Saturn grows more strongly, when, provoked by the quality of the place, terms, decan or sign or from the sect, receives the power to harm . . .[34]

The Arabic version of Dorotheus Sidonius' *Carmen astrologicum* (c. 75) also contains some evidence of this concept (Arabic *quwwa*) in different contexts, also referring to the power of the planets. This quotation is taken from a context of the calculation of lots:

For the Greek text, see *Eisagōgika*, p. 96, line 4.

32 G.P. Goold (Latin ed. and English tr.), *Manilius, Astronomica*, Cambridge MA: Harvard University Press, 1977, pp. 112–13 [2.378] and pp. 138–39 [2.712], similar meaning in pp. 278–79 [4.700], pp. 288–89 [4.840], and pp. 302–03 [5.30]. Regarding the meanings of the Latin words, I have used the *Oxford Latin Dictionary*, (Oxford: Clarendon Press, 1968) for Classical Latin and, for Medieval Latin, Albert Blaise, *Lexicon Latinitatis Medii Aevi*, (Turnholt: Brepols, 1975), and Charles du Fresne du Cange, *Glossarium mediae et infimae latinitatis*, new ed. by Léopold Favre, 10 vols, (Niort-London, 1884–1887).

33 Manilius, *Astronomica*, pp. 146–47 [2.808], pp. 156–57 [2.931–932] and pp. 150–51 [2.859].

34 'sed et malitia Saturni fortius crescit, cum ex loci qualitate uel ex finium uel ex decani uel ex signi uel ex conditione prouocata ad nocendum acceperit potestatem': Firmicus Maternus, *Mathesis*, v. 1, p. 108 [2.13.5]. See also, for instance, v. 3, p. 129 [6.33.2] (*potestas loci*).

> . . . similarly if Venus is in a cardine or what follows a cardine, except that its strength (*quwwa*) is not the equal of Jupiter's strength (*quwwa*) save in the matter of women, . . .[35]

In the same context, we find *quwwa* as the complement of a verb: 'to be a planet in strength (*quwwa*)'; in a context of interrogations, Dorotheus employs the expression 'to increase its (the planet's) power (*quwwa*)'.[36] We also find the group *quwwat al-kawākib* (the power of the planets), when Dorotheus explains that the benefics are strong in their dignities and the malefics less harmful. The planets are also strong when they are eastern with respect to the Sun, are not under the solar rays and when they are direct in their motions.[37] Here, we find an echo of one of the meanings of *testimony* in Ibn Ezra's writings (countable testimonies according to the positions of the planets with respect to the Sun).[38]

Māshā'allāh's treatise on historical astrology (fl. ca. 762–815), which survived partially quoted and modified in the work of a Christian astrologer, Ibn Hibintā (ninth century), also contains several references to *quwwa*. For instance, in the context of the calculation of the lord of the year in which the conjunction of planets indicating the deluge took place, Ibn Hibintā's text says: '. . . it <the Sun> confers its power (*quwwa*) upon it <Jupiter>, and it <Jupiter> receives power (*quwwa*) from Venus'.[39] These relations are two of the 'conditions' of the planets.[40] In a similar context—the change of the conjunction to the triplicity of fire, in which the conjunction indicating the birth of Christ took place—we read: 'And because Saturn, which receives the strength (*quwwa*) of the two luminaries from the ascendant . . .'.[41] John of Seville's translation of Māshā'allāh's treatise on the solar revolutions (twelfth century) employs the word *fortitudo*, another possible Latin translation for the Arabic *quwwa*: '. . . sicut alias aspicis

---

[35] Dorotheus, *Carmen*, p. 195 [1.27.36].

[36] Dorotheus, *Carmen*, p. 195 [1.27.37] and p. 285 [5.25.30].

[37] Dorotheus, *Carmen*, pp. 164–65 [1.6].

[38] See Tables 3 and 4 in Rodríguez-Arribas, 'Testimonies in Medieval Astrology'.

[39] Kennedy and Pingree, *The Astrological History*, p. 40 [215v, 2–3].

[40] Concerning these 'conditions', see, for instance, Charles Burnett, Keiji Yamamoto and Michio Yano (Arabic and Latin ed. and English tr.), *The Abbreviation of the Introduction to Astrology of Abū Ma'šar* (Leiden: Brill, 1994), pp. 40–51 [3.1–54].

[41] Kennedy and Pingree, *The Astrological History*, p. 45 [228r, 4].

testimonium planetarum et fortitudinem ipsorum in locis suis'.[42] The classical term *vis* seems to have disappeared in Medieval astrological texts to denote the power of the planets.

Abū Ma'shar (787–886), in his *Abbreviation of the Introduction to Astrology*, uses *quwwa* in two senses, one general and not quantitative (the only one found in the previous sources), the other with a quantitative nuance:

> Each one of them <the planets> in its body has power (*quwwa*) over a certain number of degrees before and after it. The power of the body of the Sun is 15 degrees in front of it, and the same number behind it. The power (*quwwa*) of the body of Saturn and Jupiter, both of them, is nine degrees in front and behind them both. The power (*quwwa*) of the body of Mars is eight degrees in front and behind it. The power (*quwwa*) of the body of Venus and Mercury, both of them, is seven degrees in front and behind them both.[43]

The meaning of power in this passage is general and describes how far the influence of the planet reaches. However, it proves to have a quantitative connotation because it acknowledges degrees of power expressed by the number of the degrees in front of and behind the body of any planet. However, the power is not itself countable (one half, one, two, three, etc.) as in later texts. The plain general meaning is clear in the following fragment, where Abū Ma'shar explains positions of the planets in which they have a special power:

> Their power (*quwwa*) is if they are rising in the north or are northern, or are rising in the orb of their apogee or in their second station, or leaving the rays of the Sun, or in a cardine or succedent <houses>. Or the three superior ones are east of the Sun—and if they aspect it from sextile, it is more powerful for them—or they are in the two masculine quadrants. If the Sun is in these two quadrants or in the signs of males (i.e. masculine signs), then it is powerful also, except if it is in Libra. With regard to the power (*quwwa*) of the three inferior planets, it is if they are western or in the two feminine quadrants.[44]

Again, there is mention, among other things, of the power of the planets according to their positions with respect to the Sun, which Ibn Ezra names

---

[42] Māshā'allāh, *De revolutionibus annorum mundi*, caput XXI, *De bello*, sig. C iv r.
[43] Abū Ma'šar, *The Abbreviation*, pp. 34–35 [2.11–12].
[44] Abū Ma'šar, *The Abbreviation*, pp. 52–53 [4.4–7].

testimony instead of *power*.[45] In his book on historical astrology Abū Ma'shar refers, in this particular context, to the power (*quwwa*) of an astrological aspect ('according to the position of the aspect and its *power*'), the power of a planet ('if Mars has *strength* in one of the cardines'), the power of a sign ('according to the *strength* of the sign'), and the power of a conjunction ('even if its <Mars'> conjunction with Saturn does not have such *power*').[46] In all these cases the meaning entailed is the general one, not the quantitative. Abū Ma'shar also uses the particular expressions 'to be equal in power of position' (*al-quwwa al-muwaḍa'iyya*), 'to push power' (*daf' quwwa*), and 'to be a planet in its power' (*fī quwwihi*).[47] The Latin version of this book by John of Seville (twelfth century) shows the equivalent Latin term *fortitudo* in all the previous passages.[48] The Latin version by Adelard of Bath (c. 1116–1142) of Abū Ma'shar's *Abbreviation of the Introduction to Astrology* employs the Latin word *potentia* to denote power: 'Illud autem pretereundum non est quia singule stelle sue potentie ante et retro gradus habent determinatos' [2.11] and 'potentia vero stellarum est ut shemeli [sic] oriantur vel site sint' [4.4].[49]

Al-Bīrūnī only mentions the term *power* when he quotes Abū Ma'shar and his explanation of the relations between signs *by course* and *by power* (*quwwa*), i.e., what are called signs/degrees equidistant from the equinoxes and from the solstices, respectively (also called contra-antiscia and antiscia). The relation of power between signs is already in Ptolemy (*isodynamountes*), referred to by a word containing the same root as *dynamis*.[50] The prolific translator John of

[45] See Ibn Ezra's second version of the *Sefer ha-še'elot*, Ms. Paris BNF 1058 fol. 3b, and *Sefer ha-me'orot*, Fleischer [Hebrew ed.], p. 45 (now Sela, *Abraham Ibn Ezra on Elections, Interrogations and Medical Astrology*, pp. 468–69).

[46] Abū Ma'šar, *On Historical Astrology*, v. 1, pp. 54–55 [2.1.4], pp. 62–63 [2.3.8], pp. 64–65 [2.4.3], and pp. 122–23 [2.8.2], respectively.

[47] Abū Ma'šar, *On Historical Astrology*, v. 1, pp. 84–85 [2.5.4], pp. 136–37 [2.8.22], and pp. 486–87 [8.1.19], respectively.

[48] Abū Ma'šar, *On Historical Astrology*, v. 2, pp. 36 [2.1.4] (*fortitudinem eius*), 43 [2.3.8] (*fortitudo*), 45 [2.4.3] (*fortitudinis signi*), 57 [2.5.4] (*equantur in fortitudine*), 80 [2.8.2] (*fortitudinem*), 89 [2.8.22] (*porrexerit fortitudinem suam*), and 302 [8.1.19] (*apud fortitudinem suam*).

[49] Abū Ma'šar, *The Abbreviation*, pp. 106 and 120, respectively.

[50] See Al-Bīrūnī, *The Book of Instruction*, pp. 228–29 [377]. Cf. al-Qabīṣī's *Introduction to Astrology*, Keiji Yamamoto, Michio Yano and Charles Burnett (Arabic ed. and Latin and English tr.) (London: Warburg Institute, 2004), pp. 46–47 [1.54]: 'Every two degrees which

Seville employs the Latin terms *virtus* and *fortitudo* to denote strength in Abū Ma'shar's *Great Introduction to Astrology*:

> . . . who think that the motions of the planets do not have either power or significance over everything that happens in this world[51]

> . . . by the power of the motion of the planets[52]

In the two texts the meaning of power overlaps with the meaning of influence/effect.

The Quantitative Term koaḥ *in Hebrew Sources*

The Hebrew term *koaḥ* means, in a general way, the *strength/power* of a planet, a luminary, a zodiacal sign, a house, an aspect or any other part of a horoscope; or the influence of the elements altogether in a horoscope or the horoscope as a whole.[53] For instance, we find this general meaning in the following passage of

---

are the same distance from the beginning of any of the tropical signs are called powerful and sharing in power (*quwwa*)'. For the same general meaning of power, see also pp. 66–67 [2.10] and 98–99 [3.20] (the power of a planet). Regarding Ptolemy, see *Tetrabiblos*, pp. 76–77 [1.15].

[51] '... qui putant quod nulla *virtus* sit motibus planetarum, et quod nulla significatio sit eis super res que fiunt in hoc mundo (ex *virtute* motus planetarum)', see Richard Lemay (Arabic and Latin ed.), *Abū Ma'šar, Kitāb al-Madḫal, Liber introductorii maioris ad scientiam judiciorum astrorum* (Naples: Istituto Universitario Orientale, 1995–96), v. 5: p. 2 [1.prologus.22–25], but also in p. 5 [1.1.126–127]. However, this meaning overlaps with the more usual meaning of *virtus* as *quality*, see p. 15 [1.2.479] ('ex virtutibus universalibus'), p. 23 [1.3.782] ('et virtus que pervenit ad hec corpora terrestria est ex parte corporum celestium'), and p. 23 [1.3.784–86] ('et ex motu corporum superiorum erga corpora terrestria fiunt corpora terrestria mutabilia et convertibilia ad invicem, quia virtute Sunt in invicem').

[52] '... ex fortitudine motus planetarum': Abū Ma'šar, *Kitāb al-Madḫal, Liber introductorii*, v. 5, p. 15 [1.2.499–500].

[53] This meaning is shown, for instance, in the first version of Ibn Ezra's *Sefer ha-mivḥarim*, Y.L. Fleisher, pp. 9 and 13; the first version of the *Sefer keli ha-neḥošet* (M. ben Yitzhaq Baqal, Jerusalem, 1971), p. 118, which is a copy of the edition of this treatise by H. Edelman (Könisberg, 1845); the *Sefer ha-meo'rot* (Fleischer, p. 42); the *Sefer Māšā'allāh be-qadrut* (Bernard R. Goldstein, 'The Book on Eclipses of Masha'allah', *Physis* 6, (1964): 205–13 (p. 208); the first version of the *Sefer ha-'olam* (MS BNF 1056 fol. 81b); the second

Ibn Ezra:

> Know that Venus removes the damage of Mars in conjunction or in any aspect until Mars' damage is not visible except in thoughts or in words, but Venus does not have power (*koaḥ*) to remove the damage of Saturn from a horoscope (*be-nolad*). Only Jupiter, either in conjunction or in any aspect, removes the damage of Saturn.[54]

The meaning *influence* also emerges in the term *koaḥ*/power, especially in Bar Hiyya's texts (d. after 1136), where we also find the word *koaḥ* to denote it:

> For all Israel is unanimous and believes that the influence (*ha-koaḥ*) conferred on stars has been given to them on condition (*'al tena'i*). They do not have power (*koaḥ*) to benefit or to harm of their own free will and with their knowledge, but everything is by decree and command (*be-ma'amar u-be-ṣiwui*).[55]

However, it is also possible to find a very different use of the term *koaḥ*, meaning

---

version of the *Sefer ha-mivḥarim* (MS BNF 1058 fol. 12b); the first version of the *Sefer ha-še'elot* (MS BNF 1056 fol. 62a); the second version of the *Sefer ha-še'elot* (MS BNF 1058 fol. 2a); the *Sefer ha-moladot* (MS BNF 1056 fol. 46a); the second version of the *Sefer ha-'olam* (MS Vatican 477 fol. 87a); the second version of the *Sefer ha-te'amim* (Shlomo Sela [Hebrew ed. and English tr. of the two versions], *The Book of Reasons* [Leiden: Brill, 2007], pp. 246–47 [7.2.10–11]); and the *Sefer mišpeṭei ha-mazzalot* (ed. Meir Ben Yitzhaq Baqal, *Seder 12 ha-mazzalot*, v. 2, Jerusalem, 1994, p. 159). It appears also in the *Iggeret še-šalḵu ḥaḵemei Monpišler le-rabbi Moses ben Maimon 'al gezirat ha-koḵavim*, see S. Sela, 'Queries on Astrology Sent from Southern France to Maimonides: Critical Edition of the Hebrew Text, Translation, and Commentary', *Aleph* 4 (2004): pp. 89–190 (p. 110 [14]). It is likewise employed in the anonymous prognostication for the year 1166; see Bernard R. Goldstein, 'A Prognostication Based on the Conjunction of Saturn and Jupiter in 1166 [561 AH]', ed. C. Burnett et al, *Studies in the History of the Exact Sciences in Honour of David Pingree* (Leiden: Brill, 2004), pp. 735–57 (p. 754 [2]). See also the word indexes s.v. 'power' and 'koah' in Sela, *Abraham Ibn Ezra on Elections, Interrogations and Medical Astrology*, and Shlomo Sela, *Abraham Ibn Ezra: The Book of the World* (Leiden: Brill, 2010).

54 First version of Ibn Ezra's *Sefer ha-'olam* (*Book of the World*), MS BNF 1056 fol. 82a (Sela, *Abraham Ibn Ezra: The Book of the World*, pp. 70–71). Unless otherwise noted, all translations from Hebrew are mine.

55 Z. Schwartz, ''Iggeret R. Abraham bar Hiyya ha-Nasi še-katav le-Rabbi Yehudah bar Barzilai *'al še'ilah ba-kalda'im*', *Festschrift Adolf Schwartz*, ed. Samuel Krauss (Berlin–Vienna: R. Löwit, 1917), p. 25.

a quantitative concept, like *'ed/'edut*; as far as I know, this appeared for the first time in Ibn Ezra's writings. In the following passage, it means the degree of influence of the ruler, any of the angles in a horoscope, or any other part of it, which can be reckoned:

> Also consider <which planet> has government in its position and give to it one power (*koaḥ 'eḥad*). If it is one of the superior planets (*ha-kokavim ha-'elionim*) and it is eastern, in its great power (*koḥo ha-rav*), give to it five in the number of power<s> (*koaḥ*). . . . You also have to consider the house where any of the lords (*ba'alim*) is. If it is in the tenth house, give to it six powers (*koḥot*), in the first house, five, in the eleventh, four, . . .[56]

We also find it in the context of the dignities of the planets, the typical context of this term in Arabic astrology and a familiar one in this paper in the context of *testimonies* in Medieval Arabic and Latin sources:

> The lord of the house (*ba'al ha-bayit*) receives a power of five (*ha-koaḥ ḥamišša*); the planet in its exaltation (*ba'al ha-kavod*), four; the lord of the term (*ba'al ha-gevul*), three; the lord of the triplicity (*ba'al ha-šelišut*), two; and the lord of the decan (*ba'al ha-panim*), one. The <planet> in the first house has, for the Sun, a power (*koaḥ*) of twelve, <in> the tenth house a power (*koaḥ*) of eleven, in the eleventh house <a power> of ten . . . Saturn, Jupiter, and Mars, when they are rising from below the light of the Sun (*taḥat 'or ha-šemeš*) and they are eastern, have a power of twelve, and up to thirty degrees from the position of the Sun, <a power of> eleven, and up to sixty <a power of ten>, up to seventy-nine <a power of nine>, and up to the first station (*ha-ma'amad ha-ri'šon*) <a power of eight>.[57] In the second station, seven, up to being ninety degrees away from the position of the Sun, six, and if sixty, five, in the second station, four, and in the aspect of opposition with the Sun, three. When <the planet> is thirty degrees away from the Sun and it is western, <it has a power

---

[56] First version of Ibn Ezra's *Sefer ha-še'elot* (*Book of questions*), MS Paris BNF 1056 fol. 66a (now Sela, *Abraham Ibn Ezra on Elections, Interrogations and Medical Astrology*, pp. 270–73). This meaning is also involved in the following passages: the second version of the *Sefer ha-še'elot* (MS BNF 1058 fol. 1a, now Sela, *Abraham Ibn Ezra on Elections, Interrogations and Medical Astrology*, pp. 348–51); the *Sefer ha-moladot* (MS BNF 1056 f. 48a, now Sela, *Abraham Ibn Ezra on Nativities and Continuous Horoscopy*, pp. 102–05); the second version of the *Sefer ha-'olam* (MS Vatican 477 f. 88b, now Sela, *Abraham Ibn Ezra: The Book of the World*, pp. 166–69); and the *Sefer mišpeṭei ha-mazzalot* (p. 161).

[57] In other words, when the planet changes from direct to retrograde motion.

> of> two, and if it is fifteen degrees <away>, one. When it is below the Sun (*taḥat ha-šemeš*), it has no power; only Jupiter and Saturn <have power> after their western rising thirty degrees away from the orb of combustion (*gevul ha-serefah*).[58]

As we can see in this passage by Ibn Ezra, the resemblance to the concept of testimony is very close. We can also find *koaḥ* in nominal groups: the power of the solar light (*koaḥ 'or ha-šemeš*), the power of the ray of a planet (*koaḥ niṣoṣ ha-mešaret*), the power of an astrological direction or prorogation (*koaḥ ha-nihug*), the power of a *dodecatemorion* (*koaḥ šenayim ha-'eser*), i.e., a twelfth of the sign, and the power of the *ninth* (*koaḥ ha-tiš'ah* or *ha-tiš'i*), i.e., a ninth of the sign.[59] In all these expressions it is simply the general meaning of power that emerges. There are also fractions of power given by the Hebrew expression *ḥelqei ha-koaḥ*. These are divisions in degrees of influence of the rulers according to their positions in the horoscope, which also seems very close to the concept of testimony. For instance:

> If there are not ten degrees between the Sun and Mars, it does not have powers (*koḥot*). If it is eastern, then it has. Venus and Mercury have the same number of fractions of power (*ḥelqei ha-koaḥ*) as the superior planets>; the only difference between them is that if the former are western, they have much more power (*koaḥ*).[60]

---

[58] Second version of Ibn Ezra's *Sefer ha-'olam,* MS Vatican 477 fol. 88b (now Sela, *Abraham Ibn Ezra: The Book of the World,* pp. 166–69).

[59] See Ibn Ezra, *Sefer ha-moladot,* MS BNF 1056 fol. 52b (power of the solar light) and fol. 61b (the power of the *dodecatemorion*); the *Sefer mišpeṭei ha-mazzalot,* p. 185 (power of the ray of a planet and power of a direction); the first version of the *Sefer ha-'olam,* MS BNF 1056 fol. 82b and the second version of this treatise, MS Vatican 477 fol. 89b, and the first version of the *Sefer ha-te'amim,* pp. 50–51 [2.11.1] (power of the *dodecatemorion*); and the second version of the *Sefer ha-še'elot,* MS BNF 1058 fol. 2a and the second version of the *Sefer ha-te'amim,* pp. 202–03 [3.9.9] (power of the ninth). See the word indexes s.v. 'power' and 'koah' in Sela, *Abraham Ibn Ezra on Elections, Interrogations and Medical Astrology*; *The Book of Reasons* and *The Book of the World.*

[60] Second version of Ibn Ezra's *Sefer ha-'olam,* MS Vatican 477 fol. 89a (now Sela, *Abraham Ibn Ezra: The Book of the World,* pp. 168–69). In any case, the number of powers with respect to the Sun cannot be the same in all the cases for the superior and the inferior planets, for the maximum elongation of Venus from the Sun is 48 degrees and that of Mercury is 28 degrees, see the first version of Ibn Ezra's *Sefer ha-te'amim* (pp. 32–33 [1.3.11]).

Finally, as in the testimonies, we find the word *koaḥ* as the complement of a verb, for instance, *natan koaḥ*[61] and *qibbel koaḥ*.[62] The two expressions have nothing to do with the general or the specific technical meaning that I am discussing here. They are respectively the regular translation into Hebrew (the same in Bar Hiyya's and in Ibn Ezra's texts) of the Arabic expressions *daf' al-quwwa* (pushing of power) and *qabūl* (reception of power) employed, for example, by Abū Ma'shar.[63] 'Giving power' is the relation that takes place when a planet is in its domicile, exaltation, triplicity, term or decan and forms a conjunction or any aspect with another planet. Then the former transfers its own power to the latter. The concept of 'receiving power' is the same relationship considered from the opposite point of view.[64] Concerning these two relationships among planets, Ibn Ezra employs a different and more general meaning for the two expressions. In the second version of his *Sefer ha-te'amim*, he considers the reception of power to be the reception of the power of a fast planet by another slower in motion when there is an astrological aspect between the two:

> The power (*koaḥ*) of the inferior planet is always given to the superior, either in conjunction or in any aspect.[65]

---

[61] See the first version of the Sefer *ha-mivḥarim*, p. 10; the first version of the *Sefer ha-'olam*, MS BNF 1056 fol. 83b; the second version of the *Sefer ha-mivḥarim*, MS BNF 1058 fol. 9a; the first version of the *Sefer ha-še'elot*, MS BNF 1056 fol. 62a; the second version of the *Sefer ha-še'elot*, MS BNF 1058 fol. 2a; the *Sefer ha-moladot*, MS BNF 1056 fol. 48b; the second version of the *Sefer ha-'olam*, MS Vatican 477 fol. 90a; and the second version of the *Sefer ha-te'amim*, pp. 212–13 [4.9.1]. See the word indexes s.v. 'power' and 'koah' in Sela, *Abraham Ibn Ezra on Elections, Interrogations and Medical Astrology* and *The Book of the World*.

[62] See the second version of Ibn Ezra's *Sefer ha-te'amim*, pp. 212–13 [4.9.1].

[63] See Abū Ma'šar, *The Abbreviation*, pp. 46–47 [3.31] and pp. 50–51 [3.52].

[64] For a definition of reception (*qibbul*) in Hebrew astrology, see the seventh chapter of Ibn Ezra's *Sefer re'šit ḥokmah*, Raphael Levy and Francisco Cantera (Hebrew ed. and faulty English tr.), *The Beginning of Wisdom, an Astrological Treatise by Abraham ibn Ezra* (Baltimore: The John Hopkins Press, 1939), pp. LXI (Hebrew text). Cf. the Arabic concept *qabūl*, for instance, in Al-Bīrūnī, *The Book of Instruction*, p. 312 [#507] and in Ibn Labbān, *Introduction*, p. 53 [1.18.6].

[65] See the only extant version of Ibn Ezra's *Sefer mišpeṭei ha-mazzalot* (*Book of the judgements*

> . . . for the Moon is like a body and it receives the power<s> (*koaḥ*) of the superior <planets> and gives them to the sublunary beings (*taḥtiyyim*).[66]

As a precedent of the powers as they appear in Ibn Ezra's texts, we find in Ibn Labbān's *Madkhal* (11th c.) the following text:

> The essential power (*quwa dhātiyya*) is if a planet is in one of its shares (i.e. dignities). The most powerful of the shares is the house, then the exaltation, then the triplicity, then the term, and then the decan. ... Also among the essential powers is <the planet's> ascent in the orb of its apogee . . . The accidental power (*quwa 'araḍiyya*) is if the planets are in one of the cardines or its succedents. The most powerful of them is the ascendant, then the tenth place, then the seventh, then the fourth, then the eleventh, then the fifth, then the ninth, then the third, then the second, and then the eighth. The sixth and the twelfth are not considered <to be powerful>. Again this is speaking generally, . . .[67]

Ibn Labbān's distinction between an essential power (*quwa dhātiyya*) and an accidental power (*quwa 'araḍiyya*) distantly corresponds to Ibn Ezra's distinction of five groups of factors that help to determine the degree of power of any planet; however, as we can see in the text quoted below, in this case Ibn Ezra does not refer to the number of powers, as he does in other texts. This paragraph from Ibn Ezra emerges in a context of historical astrology and refers to the power of a planet in a horoscope according to five possible ways of considering

---

of the zodiacal signs), p. 180.

[66] See the first version of Ibn Ezra's *Sefer ha-še'elot*, MS Paris BNF 1056 fol. 62a (now Sela, *Abraham Ibn Ezra on Elections, Interrogations and Medical Astrology*).

[67] Ibn Labbān, *Introduction*, pp. 54–55 [1.19.2, 1.19.3, and 1.19.4]. A similar distinction of *powers* and a quantitative application of the term *power*, in addition to the concept of accidental and essential *shares* (*ḥuṣṣūṣ*), emerge in al-Qabīṣī's *Introduction to Astrology*, pp. 60–61 [1.415, 77] prior to Ibn Labbān's text: 'For example, if your question is concerning property, and you want to know the ruler over property, <and> it is in the fifth degree of Aries, then the place [i.e., house] belongs to Mars (so it has five powers in that place), the exaltation is the Sun's (so it has four powers in it), the triplicity belongs to the Sun (so it has three powers in it) – that gives the Sun a total of seven powers in the place, the term belongs to Jupiter (so it has two powers), and the decan belongs to Mars (so it has one power). Six powers, therefore, come to Mars, and seven to the Sun; so the Sun is the ruler over the place of property'.

it: superior planet *versus* inferior, combination, angle, dignity, and the position of a planet in its epicycle.

> You will know the power (*koaḥ*) of any of the planets through five aspects (*ḥamiššah panim*) in the following way.[68] First, if it is one of the superior planets (*ha-'elionim*), it should rise in the east before the Sun. If it is one of the inferior <planets> (*ha-šefalim*), it should set after the Sun and be about to get out from under the light of the Sun (*taḥat 'or ha-šemeš*). Second, through combination (*mimsak*). If it is in combination with a benefic or malefic planet, in conjunction or in aspect, it will change its nature. Third, when it is in one of the angles (*yetedot*) with respect to the rising-sign. Fourth, when it is in its domicile, its exaltation, <its> term, its triplicity or in the sign of the culmination (*beit romah*) of its nature:[69] if hot in a hot sign, if cold in a cold sign, if male in a male sign, and if female in a female sign. Fifth, when it has northern latitude and is increasing (*nosef be-ḥešbon*), i.e., it goes faster than its mean motion. Many say that if the planet is in its apogee, then it is benefic.[70]

A curious case of the reception (or more precisely, return) into Medieval Latin of the two traditions, *testimonium/testis* (testimony/witness) and *fortitudo/potestas* (power), is Robert Grosseteste's (1170–1253) treatise *De impressionibus aeris* in which the two distinct, although close, notions (*testimonium* and *fortitudo*) finally merge into the one term *testimonium*.[71] It seems that Grosseteste wrote this treatise before 1209 as a handbook to use in the classroom, which could explain the oral style and the practical examples proposed at the end.[72] The term (*testimonium/testimonia/testis*)[73] emerges in a treatise devoted to the

---

[68] As is clear from the context, in our translation 'aspects' do not have the technical meaning usual in astrology, which corresponds to the Hebrew term *mabbaṭ*.

[69] The concept of nature (Hebrew *toledet*) in relation to the planets has a broad meaning, which concerns the general character of its influence, and a restricted meaning, which refers exclusively to the primordial qualities of the type hot/cold, dry/humid, and male-female.

[70] *Sefer ha-'olam* (second version), MS Vat 477 fol. 94a–94b (now Sela, *Abraham Ibn Ezra: The Book of the World*, pp. 190–1).

[71] I am indebted to Jose Luis Pascual, who generously drew my attention to Grosseteste's treatise.

[72] See Richard C. Dales, 'Grosseteste's Views on Astrology', *Medieval Studies* 29 (1967): pp. 357–63.

[73] The form *testis*: 'Item Saturnus frigidus et siccus est in 10 gradu Scorpionis, et sic in

prognostication of weather according to the horoscope of a particular moment. Grosseteste distinguishes between *testimonia essentialia* and *testimonia accidentalia*. The former stems from the positions of the planets in the signs, the latter from the planets in themselves; we have already found this classification in Ibn Labbān's text.[74] Despite the fact that Grosseteste explains neither the two categories (essential and accidental) nor the elements that comprise them, the reading of his treatise allows us to conclude that what Grosseteste calls *essential testimonies* are, in traditional terminology, the *dignities* of the planets (domicile, exaltation, triplicity, term, and decan). He allotted to them the values five, four, three, two and one testimonies, respectively, as did Ibn Labbān.[75] *Accidental testimonies* are those derived from the aspects between planets and the different positions of each planet in its epicycle and in its deferent. Whereas the *testimonia essentialia* are also alluded to by the Latin words *fortitudines, potestates,* and *dignitates* (p. 42), Grosseteste qualifies as *accidentalia* the *fortitudines* and *debilitates* of the planet (p. 44).[76] They work in the following way in the example that he

---

opposito aspectu cum Venere carens testimoniis est retrogradus, et sic testes Veneris non permittit fructificare. Sed quia exaltatur in suo deferente et est prope augem, et sic quasi favorem iudicii adquirens testes Veneris reddit suspectos, et sic debilitatur Venus in sua significatione' (ibid. p. 50). 'The cold and dry Saturn is in the tenth degree of Scorpio, therefore it is in the aspect of opposition with Venus lacking testimonies and retrograde. Hence Venus' witnesses do not allow it to become fruitful. However, as it is raised in its deferent and close to its apogee, wins the favour of the judgements and makes Venus' witnesses suspect, and so Venus becomes weak in its signification' (my translation from the Latin text).

[74] See note 67 and the quotation to which corresponds in the text of the article.

[75] See the text referred to in note 19.

[76] Cf. the use of accidental dignities (*ḥuṣṣūṣ*), for instance, in al-Qabīṣī's *Introduction to Astrology*, pp. 54–55 [1.70] and 60–61 [1.78]. This edition translates *ḥuṣṣ* as *share* in most cases: (p. 55) 'Each of the seven planets has a share (*ḥuṣṣ*) in one of these places [i.e. houses]; these are the shares (*ḥuṣṣūṣ*) which are accidental, and they are called the joys (*farāḥ*). Mercury has its joy in the ascendant; the Moon in the third; Venus in the fifth; Mars in the sixth; the Sun in the ninth; Jupiter in the eleventh; Saturn in the twelfth'; (p. 61) 'One of the accidental shares of the planets is the *ḥalb*. This is if a diurnal planet is by day above the earth and by night under the earth, and a nocturnal planet is by night above the earth and by day under the earth. If, in addition to this, a masculine planet is in a masculine sign, and a feminine planet in a feminine sign, it is said that it is in its domain (*hayyiz*); its power (*quwwa*) is like the power of a man in the place of his benefits,

proposes to his disciples:

> Proceed as follows: the Sun is by nature very temperate or mildly warm and dry at 22 degrees of Aries, i.e., in its exaltation, where it has four testimonies; it has three testimonies in its triplicity; in total, seven. . . . Likewise, Venus is warm and humid at 17 degrees of Taurus, which is its domicile, where it has five testimonies. However, Mercury is by nature cold and dry at 14 degrees of Taurus, where it has two testimonies.[77] Therefore, it takes from Venus two testimonies, so that Venus has then but three testimonies.[78]

The adjective *essentialia* alerts us that Grosseteste is really dealing with the 'powers' of the planets (Arabic *quwa*, Hebrew *koḥot*) by means of the term *testimonium*, and not with the 'testimonies' in the meaning that they received in Ibn Labbān's and in Ibn Ezra's writings. In any case, it seems that the two concepts, already close in Arabic and Hebrew sources, merge: the Latin word *testimonium* takes on the quantitative meaning of *fortitudo*, but loses the specific quantitative meaning of the Arabic root *š-h-d* in Ibn Labbān's work and the Hebrew *'ed/'edut* of Ibn Ezra's texts. With Grosseteste, the Latin word *testimonium* which, as far as I know, appeared for the first time in Firmicus Maternus (general meaning), re-enters Medieval Latin through the translations from Arabic (or from Hebrew), this time carrying along with it the specific

---

his gain, and his good fortune'. Regarding essential dignities (*ḥuṣṣūṣ*), see ibid. pp. 32–33 [1.22]: 'Since we have completed the shares (*ḥuṣṣūṣ*), of the planets in the signs, which are the house, the exaltation, the triplicity, the term and the decan, we will mention their powers (*quwwa*) in them. The lord of the house has five powers (*quwwa*), the lord of the exaltation has four, the lord of the triplicity has three, the lord of the term has two, and the lord of the decan has one. Some of them put the term in front of the triplicity'.

[77] The reason is, likely, that degree 14 of Taurus belongs to the term of Mercury.

[78] For the Latin text of Grosseteste, see Ludwig Baur (Latin ed.), *Die philosophischen Werke des Robert Grosseteste, Bischofs von Lincoln* (Münster i. W.: Aschendorff, 1912), pp. 42–51: 'Procede ergo sic: Sol in natura summe temperatus vel temperate calidus et siccus est in 22 gradu Arietis, videlicet in exaltatione sua, ubi habet quattuor testimonia, et in triplicitate sua, ubi habet tria testimonia; et sic in universo habet 7. ... Item Venus calida et humida est in 17 gradu Tauri, qui est domus sua, ubi habet 5 testimonia. Sed Mercurius in sua natura frigidus et siccus est in 14 gradu tauri, ubi duo habet testimonia Aufert ergo a Venere duo testimonia, et sic non remanent Veneri nisi tria testimonia.' (p. 49, my translation from the Latin text).

meaning (quantitative) of the Arabic and Hebrew *powers*.[79]

Other Quantitative Terms in Hellenistic and Medieval Astrological Sources

Among the few quantitative concepts existing in astrology I have found, in Hellenistic texts, the term (*psēphos*) (frequently associated with the verb *ekhein*, 'to have'). This term means literally 'a small stone' used to count (equivalent to the Latin term *calculus*) and to elect candidates in Greek democracy ('a vote').[80] In Ptolemy's *Tetrabiblos*, this term denotes the number of the (essential) dignities that any of the planets holds. The context of the word in Ptolemy's text is the determination of the planet ruling a certain element of the horoscope related to a certain matter (an action, the father, etc.):

> . . . if one planet is lord in all these ways <domicile, exaltation, triplicity, term, and decan>, we must assign to him the rulership of that prediction; if two or three, we must assign it to those which have (*ekhousi*) the more claims (*psēphous*).[81]

The following passage of Ptolemy relates the concept of *stones/reckonings* with the concept of *power* (*dynamis*). The context is the same as in the previous passage: to determine the rulership over the positions indicating the parents in the horoscope of a person. The more 'stones/reckonings' the planet has, the more its power and the more the information provided by it determines the astrological judgement. From the passage it is clear that 'stones/reckonings' (in

[79] Cf. John of Seville's Latin version of al-Qabīṣī's *Introduction to Astrology*, pp. 264–67 [1.77], where there is also a mention of *testimonia* and *de virtutibus seu de fortitudinibus* of the planets in the context of the calculation of the planet ruling a question: '. . . ex fortitudinibus [i.e., *powers*] quas prediximus, id est ex numero quem prediximus dum de fortitudine potestatum [i.e., *dignities*] planetarum tractaremus, et qui fortior omnibus fuerit in loco rei, ipse erit dominator eius. . . . v gradus signi Arietis, quia domus est Martis, habet in loco Mars quinque fortitudines; . . . Similiter aspicies in loco partis substantie et Partis Fortune et participem illorum facies Iovem, qui est significator substantie naturaliter, et miscebis significationes partium et planetarum *testimonia*'. John of Seville, like Ibn Ezra and Ibn Labbān, and contrary to Grosseteste, clearly distinguishes powers from testimonies.

[80] See Pierre Chantraine, *Dictionnaire étymologique de la langue grecque, Histoire des mots*, (Paris: Klincksieck, 1999), p. 1289: petit caillou, jeton de vote, vote, suffrage, opinion, décret, jugement; and Lampe, *A Patristic Greek Lexicon*, p. 1542: number, cypher, decree, sentence, calculation, reckoning.

[81] Ptolemy, *Tetrabiblos*, pp. 238–39 [3.3].

every instance always in the plural) are a means to determine levels of power among the planets in order to make astrological judgements more accurate. This is a logical procedure if we take into consideration that, from the beginning of astrology, the influence of any planet is determined by the degree of power that it holds in the horoscope with respect to the other planets. Astrological judgements are usually difficult to ascertain because of the different, and even contradictory, information that several planets frequently provide for the very same issue. Because of this to determine the prevailing or more influential planet in an astrological judgement is decisive for any prognostication.

> However, both here and everywhere it is well to recall the mode of mixture of the planets, and, if it happens that the planets which rule the places under inquiry are not of one kind but different, or bring about opposite effects, we should aim to discover which ones have (*ekhontes*) most claims (*psēphous*), from the ways in which they happen to exceed in power (*dynamin*) in a particular case, to the rulership of the predicted event.[82]

Paulus Alexandrinus (fl. c. 378) in his *Eisagōgika* also refers to this term with the same meaning (the essential dignities of the planets) and also with the verb *ekhein* (to have *small stones*, i.e., counts/reckonings), as Ptolemy did:

> Of the aforesaid ways, when one star has (*ekhēi*) more counts (*psēphous*) than the others and is found at morning rising on a cardine and in its own throne, this one <then> has the rulership, especially if it oversees the luminary of the sect.[83]

The context of this passage is the calculation of the ruling planet in a natal horoscope (diurnal or nocturnal). Paulus explains that the rulership of any planet depends on several factors, the first among which is the number of *stones/reckonings* that the planet has, followed by its position in a cardinal house at the moment of rising or in a house where it has a certain dignity ('throne').[84] However, the text does not explain how and according to which rules these

---

[82] Ptolemy, *Tetrabiblos*, pp. 248–49 [3.4].

[83] Greenbaum, *Late Classical Astrology*, p. 75 (I have slightly modified Greenbaum's translation). For the Greek text, see Boer, p. 96, line 4.

[84] The term 'throne' refers to the position of a planet in that part of the zodiac where it has more than one dignity, see Giuseppe Bezza, *Glossario dei termini tecnici*, (<http://www.cieloeterra.it/glossario4.html#Trono>).

stones/reckonings were allotted to the planets in a horoscope. Let us look for the occurrence of this term in Medieval sources for, as far as I know, it is missing in Hellenistic texts in Latin.

In Arabic sources the 'reckonings' of a planet in relation to its dignities are denoted mainly by the words *ḥuṣṣ* (Abū Ma'shar, Ibn Labbān and al-Qabīṣī), *šahāda* (Ibn Labbān and Al-Bīrūnī), and *quwwa* (al-Qabīṣī).[85] In Hebrew, the equivalent concept is conveyed by *koaḥ* (Ibn Ezra),[86] in Medieval Latin sources by *testimonium* (Māshā'allāh and Grosseteste) and *fortitudo/potestas/dignitas* (Grosseteste).[87] In Medieval Latin sources, we also find the equivalent term *pars/dignitas* to express the number of the dignities of any of the planets. For instance, the Latin version of Abū Ma'shar's book on historical astrology by John of Seville (twelfth century) employs the Latin word *partes* (parts/shares) to translate the Arabic word *ḥuṣṣūṣ* (dignities/shares).[88] The context is the calculation of the disasters that the king of the dynasty will meet with and the day on which they will happen:

> If Saturn is received in a strong position, and Mars is in a weak position without any of its shares (Arabic *ḥuṣṣūṣ*/Latin *partibus*, i.e. dignities), it indicates that <men> desire his killing.[89]

---

[85] See, for instance, Abū Ma'shar, *On Historical Astrology*, v. 1 (Arabic text and English tr.), pp. 106–07, pp. 118–19, and pp. 126–27 (*ḥuṣṣ*); Ibn Labbān, *Introduction*, pp. 66–69 [1.22.1–4] (*ḥuṣṣ* and *šahāda*); Al-Bīrūnī, *Book of Instruction*, pp. 306–08 [493–94] (*šahāda*). For al-Qabīṣī's terms (*ḥuṣṣ* and *quwwa*), see the texts quoted in the note 76 of this article.

[86] See, for instance, the second version of Ibn Ezra's *Sefer ha-'olam*, MS Vatican 477 f. 88b (now Sela, *Abraham Ibn Ezra: The Book of the World*, pp. 168–69) and the texts referred to in note 56 of this article.

[87] Concerning *testimonium*, see, for instance, the Latin version of Māshā'allāh's *De revolutionibus annorum mundi*, p. 9r (caput VI, *De partibus ac testimoniis planetarum, ex quibus agnoscitur dominus anni*). See also Grosseteste's *De impressionibus aeris*, p. 49 (*testimonium*) and p. 42 (*fortitudo, potestas,* and *dignitas*).

[88] See also Dorotheus, *Carmen*, p. 237 [3.1.26] (*ḥuṣṣūṣ*, which Pingree translates as *portions*). For more details on partes and *ḥuṣṣūṣ* see Giuseppe Bezza, 'The Development of an Astrological Term—from Greek *hairesis* to Arabic *ḥayyiz*', in 'The Winding Courses of the Stars: Essays in Ancient Astrology', eds. Charles Burnett and Dorian Greenbaum, *Culture and Cosmos* 11 (2007), pp. 229–60.

[89] Abū Ma'šar, *On Historical Astrology*, v. 2 (Latin text), p. 70 [2.7.3], cf. v. 1 (Arabic text and English tr.), pp. 106–07. For the same use of this word to denote the dignities of the

John of Seville translates the Arabic *quwwa* of the *Introduction to Astrology* of al-Qabīṣī with the Latin word *potestas* (equivalent to *dignitas* in the quoted passage): 'Et quia, annuente Deo, iam tractavimus de potestatibus planetarum in signis, que sunt domus, exaltatio, triplicitas, termini et facies . . .'.[90] It seems that the counting of the (essential) dignities of the planets (*psēphos, ḥuṣṣ, pars/dignitas/potestas*) is a method consistently employed by Hellenistic and Medieval astrologers to determine the strongest of two or more planets in order to ascertain any astrological judgement in which they are involved. The scope of this technique is more limited than the scope of the quantitative term 'testimony' for it only concerns the dignities of the planets, while the method of 'testimonies' is concerned not only with dignities but with other elements in the horoscope. However, it is very close to the quantitative concept 'power', as the texts quoted in this article show. In any case, the overlap of terms in the different authors and languages makes it difficult to keep separate these terms ('reckonings', 'testimonies', and 'powers') and their respective meanings. Finally, the quantitative concept 'reckoning'/'share'/'count' is not so conspicuous in astrological literature as 'testimony' or 'power'.

Another intriguing quantitative term is *victory*, which I have detected only in Medieval sources. In the few sources where it emerges this term reveals a meaning very close to the general meaning of 'power'. In this way, the 'victory' of a planet depends directly on its strength/power in a horoscope. The Latin translation by John of Seville of Māshā'allāh's treatise on the solar revolutions gives the Latin word *victoria* as the likely rendering of a likely Arabic *ghalaba* in the unknown Arabic text: 'aspice adeptionem et victoriam ex fortiori planetarum, quia ipsa significat multitudinem militum, et eorum fortitudinem'.[91] Abū Ma'shar (787–886) also refers to the term 'victory' (Arabic *ghalaba*) in the

---

planets, see also ibid. v. 2, p. 78 [2.7.11] (Arabic text, v. 1, pp. 118–19). Cf. the Latin *dignitas* for the same Arabic word, ibid. v. 2, p. 83 [2.8.5] (Arabic text, v. 1, pp. 126–27).

[90] al-Qabīṣī, *Introduction to Astrology*, pp. 238–39 [1.22]. See also, al-Qabīṣī's *Introduction to Astrology*, pp. 32–33 [1.22]: 'the shares (*ḥuṣṣūṣ*) of the planets in the signs' and 'their powers (*quwwa*)'; and pp. 58–59 [1.77]: 'the powers of their shares [i.e., dignities] (*quwwa al-ḥuṣṣūṣ*)'.

[91] *De revolutionibus annorum mundi*, caput XXI, *De bello*, sig. C iv r: 'Consider the achievement and the victory of the strongest among the planets, for it signifies the number of the soldiers and their strength' (my translation of the Latin text).

Arabic version of his *Great Introduction to Astrology*, whose Latin translation by John of Seville keeps the Latin *victoria*. However, in this context 'victory' makes reference to the four elements (fire, air, water, and earth), which are ascribed to the signs:

> Therefore, the signs inform about the four elements and there are three <signs per element>, for the signs are the houses of the planets. These signs do not <receive> the corruption <in> themselves, but indicate ... the effect and the corruption <in the elements> ... However, the elements do not receive the corruption from themselves, but by means of the temporal changes <taking place> above them and because of their mutual combination and victory.[92]

The meaning of 'victory' in these texts is far from the technical and the quantitative meaning that we find, as far as I know for the first time, in Ibn Ezra's terminology (one, two, three victories of a planet with respect to another). In Ibn Ezra's texts *niṣṣuaḥ* (victory) emerges denoting the dominance of a planet in a certain position over another planet in another certain position according to an order of priorities of the planets and their positions in a horoscope. It is clearly a quantitative noun and in this sense it is new in astrological literature.[93] Some of the relevant positions are mentioned in the text of Ibn Ezra that is quoted below: direct motion over retrograde motion, any aspect with the sun (except combustion or being under the solar rays) over the aspects with the remaining planets, and superior planets over inferiors. All these positions are clearly positions of power/weakness for the planets or positions of strong (superior) planets *versus* weak (inferior) planets, which determine the victory of some of them over the others. The concept emerges in the form of a transitive verb in *pi'el* (*niṣṣaḥ*, i.e., to triumph over) and also in the form of a quantitative

---

92 *Kitāb al-Madkhal, Liber introductorii,* v. 2, p. 42 (*ghalaba*) and v. 5, p. 72 [2.3.201–211] (*victoria*), respectively: 'Et ideo facta sunt signa significantia super IIII. elementa et esse eorum tria quia signa sunt loca planetarum. Et hec signa non <recipiunt> corruptionem <in> semetipsis, sed significant . . . effectum et corruptionem <in elementis> . . . Elementa vero non recipiunt corruptionem ex semetipsis, sed recipiunt corruptionem per diversitatem temporum super ea, et per complexionem eorum ad invicem, ac victoriam eorum in invicem' (my translation of the Latin version).

93 The technical term 'victory' is closed to the Arabic concept (*al-mubtazz*, i.e., 'the strong one') transliterated into Latin with the word *almuten*. However I have not found this term with a quantitative use in astrological texts and it is not considered in this study.

noun (*niṣṣuaḥ*, i.e., victory):

> The planet direct in its motion triumphs over (*yenaṣṣeaḥ*) the retrograde planet and the planet that is in aspect with the Sun triumphs over (*yenaṣṣeaḥ*) the <planet that is> burnt or the one that is under the light of the Sun. . . . If one of the planets were superior and the other inferior, the superior would always triumph over (*yenaṣṣeaḥ*) the inferior. There is no need to mention if the two are superior or inferior, for this cannot be. . . Look, you have to consider the number of all the victories (*niṣṣuḥim*) that I have mentioned and the <planet> with the largest number will triumph over (*yenaṣṣeaḥ*) the other.[94]

The perusal of Ibn Ezra's writings and language reveals another original term that Ibn Ezra employs with a slight quantitative nuance: *siman* (sign, signal, mark, indication). We find *siman* in the context of the prognostication of prices at the moment of the annual revolution of the Sun (first text) and in a context of medical astrology (second text):

> One has always to consider that Jupiter makes prices go down and Saturn <makes them> go high. If the two are placed in signs of fire, it is an indication (*siman*) of high (prices). If they are in signs of air, <the prices are> less high.[95]

> When the Moon is in the aspect of square with its position at the beginning of the illness, or in the aspect of opposition, or in the sign of its exaltation <Taurus>, this is half of a good indication (*ḥeṣi siman ṭov*).[96]

This term is always employed in relation to a planet and its position in the horoscope or in relation to an aspect. A distinctive trait of this term, which separates it from the others analysed so far in this article, is that its presence in favour of a judgement does not seem to make the judgement conclusive. In other words, it seems that an 'indication/sign' is not sufficient proof to make an astrological judgement certain. Whatever the employment of these two concepts (sign and victory) in Ibn Ezra's writings, they are not used as systematically and

---

[94] The first version of Ibn Ezra's *Sefer ha moladot* (*Book of nativities*), MS BNF 1056 fol. 56a (now Sela, *Abraham Ibn Ezra on Nativities and Continuous Horoscopy*, pp. 162–63).

[95] The second version of Ibn Ezra's *Sefer ha-'olam*, MS Vatican 477 fol. 90a (now Sela, *Abraham Ibn Ezra: The Book of the World*, pp. 174–75).

[96] Ibn Ezra, *Sefer ha-me'orot*, pp. 44–45 (now Sela, *Abraham Ibn Ezra on Elections, Interrogations and Medical Astrology*, pp. 462–63).

frequently as the concepts of testimonies and powers. Neither of them is present in Bar Hiyya's writings or in the previous astrological literature in Hebrew; they are unusual (victory) or non-existent (sign/indication) in Arabic sources prior to Ibn Ezra. For this reason, I should conclude that they were introduced into astrology in Hebrew by Ibn Ezra.

Conclusions

My research in this article regarding the concept of 'power/strength' and three other minor quantitative/countable terms in Hellenistic and Medieval astrology confirms the conclusions of my previous article on the concept of 'testimony' ('Testimonies in Medieval Astrology'). In the ensemble of Medieval manuscripts on the science of the stars, writers frequently considered the relationship between astronomy and astrology and the different status that each one held in the Medieval classification of sciences. All Medieval scientists considered astronomy a science, which means that it was considered evident and relied on clear proofs whereas astrology, even for its practitioners, seemed to rely more upon experience and tradition; its conclusions were approximate and frequently fallible. For this reason astrologers devised different systems in order to establish degrees of certainty in the judgements that they could formulate about the positions or configurations of the elements in a horoscope. These systems left an imprint in the astrological terminology of Hellenistic and especially Medieval texts, which I have analysed in my two articles. The Medieval Arabic concepts *šahāda* (testimony or witness) and *quwwa* (power or strength), like their equivalents in Hebrew *'ed/'edut* and *koaḥ*, are quantitative nouns. The former allows degrees of measurement (half testimony, two, three testimonies, etc.) that represent degrees of proximity to a complete certainty in the judgement. At the same time, this concept allows the expression of nuances of quality (a clear/sure/right/valid/not valid/complete testimony), but only in Ibn Ezra's texts. The meaning of *quwwa/koaḥ* is close to testimony for its quantitative aspect; but while 'testimony' denotes degrees in judgement, 'power' denotes degrees of influence or strength of the planets. As far as I know, only Ibn Labbān in Arabic and Ibn Ezra in Hebrew employed the two expressions as countable terms in their texts for similar contexts. Ibn Ezra and Ibn Labbān seem to have been very concerned, both with the uncertainty of astrological judgements and with the validity of the practice of astrology. The concepts 'power' and 'testimony' (and also the minor concepts 'reckoning', 'victory', and 'sign') allowed astrologers to approach and explain astrology as a science: still relying on experience and tradition, but endowed with a group of reasoned rules that established the probability of truth to be expected from a judgement, and the degree of the influence of any planet on the horoscope at the moment of establishing that judgement.

The quantitative concept *psēphos*, i.e., reckoning stone (Arabic *ḥuṣṣ*, Latin *dignitas/pars/potestas*) expresses the number of the dignities of the planets and therefore the degree of influence of the planets in any judgement in which they are involved. The quantitative term 'victory' (Arabic *ghalaba*, Hebrew *niṣṣuaḥ*, Latin *victoria*) determines, according to a set of rules based on the strength/weakness of the planets and of certain positions, which is the prevailing planet in a position, house or aspect and, therefore, in an astrological judgement according to the number of its victories. The Hebrew word *siman* (sign/indication) is poorly documented in astrological texts and, as far as I know, non-existent in sources prior to Ibn Ezra. Its use has to do with the influence of a planet or aspect in the determination of an issue, but it is not conclusive about it. The perusal of all five terms in astrological lore in different languages from the second century BCE until the thirteenth century CE proves that astrological terminology, even if referring to the same concepts, fluctuates throughout its texts, authors and languages. In this way, not infrequently, close meanings and usages interchange their terms in Arabic and Medieval Latin, either because of confusion in transmission or because of specific linguistic choices made by writers and translators. In any case, the tradition of making astrological judgements as precise as possible seems to be consistent throughout the history of astrology, as the technical terminology of the analysed texts proves.

TEACHING ASTROLOGY IN THE 16TH CENTURY: GIULIANO RISTORI AND FILIPPO FANTONI ON PSEUDO-PROPHETS AND OTHER EFFECTS OF GREAT CONJUNCTIONS[1]

H. Darrel Rutkin

PART I: CONTEXT

Introduction: Astrology and Mathematics

How was astrology configured within the structures of European premodern medieval, Renaissance and early modern natural knowledge? In important articles from the 1970s, Charles B. Schmitt discussed mathematics teaching at the University of Pisa before Galileo studied and taught there, from roughly 1581 to 1592.[2] Although Schmitt added a great deal to our knowledge, he also reaffirmed a fundamental and widespread confusion concerning astrology's relationship to mathematics, disparaging astrology as 'occult mathematics', stating strongly—and wrongly—that at least Galileo himself would have had nothing to do with such endeavours.[3] Far from astrology being an 'occult science', however (whatever this overworked locution might mean), I have

[1] My grateful thanks to Villa I Tatti, the Harvard University Center for Italian Renaissance Studies, for supporting the manuscript research for this article, the Huntington Library for supporting its writing, and the organizers of this conference for inviting me to present it as a paper and to publish it here. I would also like to thank my I Tatti coaevus Stefano Dall'Aglio for many useful suggestions concerning Savonarola and his legacy.

[2] Charles B. Schmitt, 'The Faculty of Arts at Pisa at the Time of Galileo', in *Studies in Renaissance Philosophy and Science*, ed. Charles B. Schmitt (London: Variorum, 1981 [1972]), pp. 243–72 and Schmitt, 'Filippo Fantoni: Galileo Galilei's Predecessor as Mathematics Lecturer at Pisa', in *Studies* [1978], pp. 53–62.

[3] I discuss the extensive evidence for Galileo's astrological practice in my article, 'Galileo Astrologer: Astrology and Mathematical Practice in the Late-Sixteenth and Early-Seventeenth Centuries', *GALILAEANA: Journal of Galilean Studies* 2 (2005): pp. 107–43, from which most of these paragraphs are taken.

found that astrology was a normal and legitimate part of premodern Aristotelian-Ptolemaic-Galenic natural knowledge. Indeed, astrology was taught within three distinct scientific disciplines—mathematics, natural philosophy and medicine—in the finest premodern universities in Italy and elsewhere, from the thirteenth through seventeenth centuries.[4]

According to the University of Bologna's 1405 statutes, which provided a model for the basic structures of arts education in the premodern Italian universities, astrology was primarily taught in the four-year mathematics course; it was also taught in different respects in the natural philosophy and medical courses, in relation to core texts by Aristotle and Galen respectively.[5] After prerequisites in arithmetic, geometry and elementary mathematical astronomy, the students began their study of astrology proper in the third year with al-Qabīṣī's *Liber introductorius*.[6] In the fourth year, they advanced to the higher levels of scientific astronomy and astrology by reading two of Ptolemy's fundamental texts, the *Almagest* and *Quadripartitum* (*Tetrabiblos*).[7]

---

[4] I argue for this concisely in my chapter, 'Astrology', in *The Cambridge History of Science, Vol. 3: Early Modern Science,* eds. Lorraine Daston and Katharine Park (Cambridge: Cambridge University Press, 2006), pp. 541–61, and at length in chapter 3 of my dissertation, 'Astrology, Natural Philosophy and the History of Science, c. 1250–1700: Studies Toward an Interpretation of Giovanni Pico della Mirandola's *Disputationes adversus astrologiam divinatricem*' (PhD Thesis, Indiana University, 2002), as well as in my forthcoming monograph, *Reframing the Scientific Revolution: Astrology, Magic and Natural Knowledge, ca. 1250–1800,* Volume 1, part 4 (*Medieval Structures, 1250–1500: Conceptual, Istitutional, Socio-Political, Religious and Cultural*) and Volume 3 (*Early Modern Structures, 1500-1800: Continuities and Transformations*) (Dordrecht: Springer) in which I discuss this and many other relevant issues.

[5] These include but are not limited to Aristotle's *De generatione et corruptione* and Galen's *De criticis diebus.*

[6] 'Abd al-Azīz Ibn 'Uthmān al-Qabīṣī (Alcabitius), *The Introduction to Astrology: editions of the Arabic and Latin texts and an English translation,* eds. Charles Burnett, Keiji Yamamoto and Michio Yano (London: Warburg Institute, 2004).

[7] For the evidence and further bibliography: in addition to my works mentioned in n. 4 ['Astrology', et al.], see Graziella Federici Vescovini, 'I programmi degli insegnamenti del collegio di medicina, filosofia e astrologia dello statuto dell'universitaria di Bologna del 1405', in *Roma, magistra mundi: Itineraria culturae medievalis. Melanges offerts au père L.E. Boyle* (Louvain: La Neuve, 1998), I: pp. 193–223, and Paul Grendler's annotated translation, *The Universities of the Italian Renaissance* (Baltimore: Johns Hopkins University

When Cosimo I de' Medici (1519–74) refounded the University of Pisa in 1543, statutes were composed for the mathematics course that are clear and straightforward. I quote them in full: 'The mathematics teacher in the first year will teach (literally 'read') the author of the *Sphere*; in the second, Euclid; in the third, certain works of Ptolemy (*quaedam Ptolemaei*)'.[8] Since the Ptolemy requirement was left open with respect to the specific work to be studied, we find that some professors taught from the *Almagest*, some from the *Geography*, and others from the *Quadripartitum*. It is worthwhile to quote *in extenso* Schmitt's discussion of the *Quadripartitum* at Pisa:

> In fact, this brief work of Ptolemy's, one of the mainstays of the astrological [...] side of medieval and Renaissance thought, played quite a central role in mathematics and astronomy teaching at Pisa. [...] Lectures on the *Tetrabiblos* were given quite often at Pisa and there are a number of manuscript commentaries, especially by Ristori and Fantoni, which remain to be studied. The teaching of this material was apparently considered to be useful particularly for medical students, for when Filippo Fantoni lectured on the First Book of the work in 1585 it was spelled out that he was to deal with the *quaestiones ad facultatem medicam pertinent*.[9] Ristori in particular was strongly oriented toward the occult sciences and produced, in addition to his lectures and commentary on the *Tetrabiblos*, a *Prognostico sopra la genitura* [. . . *di*] *Cosimo I*, works on chiromancy and physiognomy, and perhaps also a series of horoscopes.[10] Fantoni was perhaps not

Press, 2002), pp. 410–11 (and more generally, pp. 408–29). I will now briefly define 'astrology' in relation to 'astronomy'. Both were indifferently called either '*astronomia*' or '*astrologia*' in the premodern period, but *each* term (both of which may be translated neutrally as 'the science of the stars') refers to *both* of two clearly distinguished practices: [1] what we call 'astronomy', which studies and predicts the *motions* of the planets over time, and [2], what we call 'astrology', which studies the *influences* of the planets on the earth, its atmosphere and inhabitants.

8 Schmitt, 'Faculty of Arts', p. 257: 'Astronomi primo anno legant Auctorem Spherae, secundo Euclidem interpretent, tertio quaedam Ptolomaei'. This is my translation, as are translations in this paper, unless otherwise indicated.

9 Schmitt, 'Filippo Fantoni', p. 57: 'Primum Euclidis, primum librum Quadripartiti Ptolomei, quaestiones ad facultatem medicinae pertinent[es], et secundum planetarum delineationes et non aliud'.

10 All of which are extant. Schmitt provides references in 'Faculty of Arts', p. 259 (nn. 84–86). Raffaella Castagnola has published Cosimo's horoscope, which I discuss briefly below: 'Un oroscopo per Cosimo I', *Rinascimento* 29 (1989): pp. 125–89.

> so completely oriented toward the occult side of astronomical and mathematical science, but he did expand upon and embellish Ristori's extensive *In quadripartitum Ptolomaei Regis expositio praeclara*. All of this indicates quite clearly that there was a strong [astrological] element in the teaching of mathematics and astronomy at Pisa from the reopening of the studio in 1543 until the time of Galileo.[11]

In fact, however, far from the 'occult sciences' being taught at Pisa, Schmitt's description places the teaching of astrology, before and during Galileo's time there, squarely into the normal premodern configuration of the mathematical disciplines at Italian (and other) universities.[12]

Schmitt develops some of this material in a fuller treatment of Filippo Fantoni, Galileo's immediate predecessor as professor of mathematics at Pisa.[13] Focusing on the record of what Fantoni taught (including while Galileo was a student there),[14] Schmitt treats the books Fantoni left in manuscript, including an exposition of all four books of the *Quadripartitum*, which he taught in 1585–86.[15] Schmitt notes: 'from this we can get a good indication of what was being taught in the Pisan classroom at the time Galileo was himself a student and in the immediately succeeding years'.[16] Schmitt considers Ristori and Fantoni to be the two most important mathematics teachers at Pisa before Galileo.[17]

In this essay, I will open a window on what it was like to study scientific astrology at a fine Renaissance university, and one where Galileo studied and taught before heading off to teach at the University of Padua from 1592 to 1610. From this wider focus, we will zoom down by steps into two Pisan classrooms of the 1540s and 1580s to explore how astrology was actually taught on the ground. Let us first meet the professors.

---

[11] Schmitt, 'Faculty of Arts', pp. 258–59. I substitute 'astrological' for Schmitt's term 'occult' in the last sentence. I also removed 'and pseudo scientific' following 'astrological' from the first sentence. Although there is some justification for using these terms, they are much more misleading than useful as terms of analysis.

[12] I discuss this further in my 'Galileo Astrologer'.

[13] Schmitt, 'Filippo Fantoni'.

[14] There is, however, no direct evidence that Galileo heard his lectures; Schmitt, 'Filippo Fantoni', p. 58 (n. 14).

[15] Schmitt reconstructs Fantoni's teaching at 'Filippo Fantoni', p. 57.

[16] Schmitt, 'Filippo Fantoni', p. 57.

[17] Schmitt, 'Faculty of Arts', p. 256.

Giuliano Ristori and Filippo Fantoni

Who was Giuliano Ristori?[18] A Carmelite monk, Ristori was a leading member of his mother church, the famous Santa Maria del Carmine in Florence, home to the Brancacci chapel and its important paintings by Masaccio.[19] In the colophon to the 1537 horoscope he composed for Cosimo I,[20] Ristori describes himself as 'Messer Giuliano Ristori from Prato, a Carmelite theologian and professor of theology'.[21] Installed by Cosimo at its refounding, Ristori taught astrology and mathematics at Pisa from 1543 to 1550, in which capacity he was sometimes called '*mathematico*' and sometimes '*astrologo*', which were interchangable in contemporary usage.[22] During this time, Francesco Giuntini (1523–90), another Carmelite theologian and Ristori's most famous pupil, studied the *Quadripartitum* with Ristori in 1548,[23] before taking his doctorate in theology there in 1554.[24] Ristori also taught at the universities of Florence and Siena. His

---

[18] In addition to Schmitt ('Faculty of Arts' and 'Filippo Fantoni'), and Castagnola ('Oroscopo'), see Claudia Rousseau's richly informative 'Cosimo I de' Medici and Astrology: The Symbolism of Prophecy' (PhD thesis, Columbia University, 1983), 17ff., and Janet Cox-Rearick, *Dynasty and Destiny in Medici Art: Pontormo, Leo X, and the Two Cosimos* (Princeton: Princeton University Press, 1984).

[19] For the religious and cultural life of the Carmine in the Quattrocento, see Megan Holmes, *Fra Filippo Lippi. The Carmelite Painter* (New Haven: Yale University Press, 1999)

[20] Castagnola's introduction is very informative: 'Oroscopo', pp. 125–29. For a splendid evocation of the broader political context at this pivotal moment in Florentine history, see Eric Cochrane, *Florence in the Forgotten Centuries, 1527–1800* (Chicago: University of Chicago Press, 1973), pp. 13–21.

[21] At the beginning (Castagnola, 'Oroscopo', p. 133): 'Messer Giuliano Ristori pratese e teologo carmelitano'; at the end (189): 'Iuliano Ristoro carmelitano da Prato, theologia professo (28 June 1537)'.

[22] Schmitt, 'Faculty of Arts', pp. 255–56 (and n. 65).

[23] 'Frater Iulianus Ristorus Pratensis, Carmelita, Theologus, et Mathematicus excellentissimus cum exponeret anno domini 1548. in Gymnasio Pisano publice Ptolemaei quadripartitum, quem ego audivi [. . .]'. Giuntini, *Speculum astrologiae*, 2 vols. (Lyon: P. Tinghi, 1583), I: p. 126.

[24] Vanni Bramanti, 'Sulle istorie della città di Fiorenza di Jacopo Nardi: Tra autore e copista (Francesco Giuntini)', *Rinascimento* 37 (1997): pp. 321–40, 334. For more on Giuntini (in addition to Bramanti, 'Sulle istorie', 330 ff.) see Germana Ernst, s.v., *Dizionario biografico degli Italiani* (*DBI*), ed. Alberto Ghisalberti (Rome: Istituto della Enciclopedia Italiana, 1960– (2001)), 57: pp. 104–08, and her 'Dalla bolla "Coeli et terrae" all' "Inscrutabilis": l'astrologia tra natura, religione e politica nell'età controriforma',

other teachings and writings included a textbook on Sacrobosco's *Sphere* and astronomical matters, as well as theological writings and a work on physiognomy.[25]

When he died in 1556, the Carmelites of the Carmine set up a still visible marble relief of Ristori reading a book with the following inscription:

> Mourning Giuliano Ristori da Prato, a Carmelite theologian and their provincial of the greatest merit, the Carmelites have placed [this memorial]. Not only those at Siena, Pisa and Florence, where he taught publicly for at least 22 years, but also the entire world acknowledges how greatly he was esteemed in philosophy and all the mathematical disciplines, but especially in *astrologia*. He lived for 64 years, 5 months, 11 days. He died 7 December 1556.[26]

Given the statement of Ristori's name here by the monks of the Carmine and that at the end of Cosimo's horoscope, Castagnola reasonably suggests that the two horoscopes signed 'Giuliano Rustico carmelitano theologo atque mathematico', attached to a letter by Francesco Guicciardini dated 21 July 1534, are also by Ristori.[27]

We know something about Ristori's astrological activities before he constructed and interpreted Cosimo's horoscope in 1537. For example, Ristori made annual prognostications (or 'revolutions') for 1528 and 1529, one of which

---

chap. 11 of her *Religione, ragione e natura: Ricerche su Tommaso Campanella e il tardo Rinascimento* (Milan: F. Angeli, 1991), pp. 255–77, 261ff. My thanks to Stefano Dall'Aglio for bringing the Bramanti article to my attention.

[25] Castagnola, 'Oroscopo', p. 131 (nn. 8–10).

[26] Quoted in Castagnola, 'Oroscopo', pp. 130–31, taken from *Biblioteca Carmelitana,* p. 209: 'Juliano Ristori Pratensi carmelitano theologo / suo provinciali optime merito lugentes / Carmelitae posuerunt / qui quanto in philosophia ac mathenticis (sic) disciplinis omnibus praecipue autem in astrologia / valuerit non Senae Pisae ac Florentiae tantum / ubi annis non minus XXII / publice est professus verum totus terrarum / orbis agnovit. Vixit annis LXIIII / mensibus V diebus XI. Obiit VII / decembris MDLVI'.

[27] Castagnola, 'Oroscopo', p. 131 (n. 7). For Francesco Guicciardini and his brother Luigi's interest in astrology, see Raffaella Castagnola, *I Guicciardini e le scienze occulte: L'oroscopo di Francesco Guicciardini: Lettere di alchimia, astrologia e cabala a Luigi Guicciardini* (Florence: Olschki, 1990). Stefano Dall'Aglio also kindly informs me that there is a reference to a nativity by Ristori in a letter of 1549 by Donato Giannotti; see Donato Giannotti, *Lettere italiane (1526–1571),* ed. Furio Diaz (Milan: Marzorati, 1974), pp. 154–55.

was printed.[28] In 1534, Ristori was officially involved in determining the astrological timing (or 'election') for placing the cornerstone of the massive Fortezza da Basso at this turning point in Florentine political history.[29] We know that several astrologers in an official capacity had suggested different precise moments with positive astrological connotations for setting the stone. To break the deadlock, Francesco Guicciardini went to Bologna to consult the astrologers there, in particular, Ludovico Vitali (1475/78?–1554), a professor at the university and himself a prolific author of annual prognostications.[30] Ristori's timing was ultimately chosen as the best.[31]

Finally, soon before interpreting Cosimo's horoscope, Ristori's fame had spiked due to his accurately predicting the first duke of Florence, Alessandro de' Medici's (1510–37), violent death.[32] In 1537, then, the first troubled year of

---

[28] *Comento. Sopra le occurrente constellationi generali & particulari del anno salutifero MDXXIX di maestro Giuliano Ristoro theologo carmelita da Prato* [. . .]; printed probably in Siena; Castagnola, 'Oroscopo', p. 132 (n. 12). Giuntini mentions Ristori's prognostication and its impact in the rich introduction to his *Speculum astrologiae*, I: pp. 1–15, 2: 'Ut taceam observationes doctissimi Mathematici Magistri Iuliani Ristori Pratensis mei praeceptoris, qui anno 1528 obstupefecit non solum Senarum civitatem, sed et Romam, et universam quasi Italiam, et utrunque et Gallorum et Hispanorum exercitum. Unde translata fuit eius prognosticatio dicti anni sub nomine Ioannis Stoflerini Astrologi Germani'. The prognostication for 1529 may be a copy of that for the previous year. For the rich range of uses of the term *'observatio'* which has a broader semantic field than its cognate English term, see Katharine Park, 'Observation in the Margins, 500–1500', in *Histories of Observation* , eds. Lorraine Daston and Elizabeth Lunbeck (Chicago: University of Chicago Press, 2011). We will have occasion to observe another peculiar usage below.

[29] John R. Hale discusses this episode within its political context in, 'The End of Florentine Liberty: The Fortezza da Basso', in *Renaissance War Studies* (London: Hambledon Press, 1983), pp. 31–62, 48–50. Hale also discusses other examples of such practices, as does Mary Quinlan-McGrath, 'The Foundation Horoscope(s) for St. Peter's Basilica, Rome, 1506: Choosing a Time, Changing a *Storia*', *Isis* 92 (2001): pp. 716–41.

[30] For Vitali, see Fabrizio Bonolì and Daniela Pilarvu, *I lettori di astronomia presso lo studio di Bologna dal XII al XX secolo* (Bologna: CLUEB, 2001), pp. 129–30.

[31] Hale, 'End', p. 49.

[32] Castagnola, 'Oroscopo', p. 127; she does not cite the evidence, which Stefano Dall'Aglio kindly supplied me from Benedetto Varchi, *Storia fiorentina*, ed. Lelio Arbib, vol. III (Rome: Edizioni di Storia e Letterature, 2003 (reprint)), pp. 262–63: 'Né voglio lasciar di dire che gli fu predetto e pronosticato più volte, e per via di sogni, come da un paggio da Perugia, il quale era infermo, e per arte d'astrologia, come da maestro Giuliano del

Cosimo's rule, Ristori composed an extensive 53-folio-page interpretation of Cosimo's geniture or nativity—his birth horoscope—that explored the astrologically informed nature of his body and mind, and predicted a range of experiences—the accidents of fortune—that he would encounter during the course of his life.[33] Thus we see Ristori engaged in three of the four canonical

---

Carmine, il quale fece la sua natività (benché costui, secondo l'usanza di cotali astrologi, andava indovinando più quello ch'egli pensava che dovesse piacere al principe, che quello che fosse la verità) non solo ch'egli sarebbe ammazzato, ma scannato; e scannato, chi diceva il proprio nome, da Lorenzo de' Medici, e chi lo descriveva [. . .] si conosceva espressamente che intendevano di lui'.

[33] In addition to astrological analysis, Ristori also provided a running treatment of Cosimo's physiognomy that follows the structure of the horoscope. Ristori's interpretation of Cosimo's horoscope is a spectactularly interesting document for studying astrology's importance in the political sphere, especially with the striking Machiavellian overtones of Ristori's introductory section. In the meantime, one should consult Anthony J. Parel's provocative but problematic *The Machiavellian Cosmos* (New Haven: Yale University Press, 1992). A synthetic study of astrology's centrality in European politics from the twelfth to the eighteenth centuries would be of tremendous interest. Among others, see for Italy, Anthony Grafton, *Cardano's Cosmos: The Worlds and Works of a Renaissance Astrologer* (Cambridge, MA: Harvard University Press, 1999) and Monica Azzolini's 'Reading Health in the Stars: Politics and Medical Astrology in Renaissance Milan', in *Horoscopes and Public Spheres: Essays on the History of Astrology*, eds. Günther Oestmann, H. Darrel Rutkin and Kocku von Stuckrad (Berlin: Walter de Gruyter, 2005), pp. 183–205; as well as her *The Duke and the Stars: Astrology and Politics in Renaissance Milan* (Cambridge, MA: Harvard University Press, 2013); for Germany, see Gerd Mentgen, *Astrologie und Öffentlichkeit im Mittelalter* (Stuttgart: Hiersemann, 2005) and Claudia Brosseder, *Im Bann der Sterne: Caspar Peucer, Philipp Melanchthon und andere Wittenberger Astrologen* (Berlin: Akademie Verlag, 2004); for France, Jean-Patrice Boudet, *Recueil des Plus Celebres Astrologues de Simon de Phares*, ed. Jean-Patrice Boudet, 2 vols. (Paris: Champion, 1997–99) and Herve Drevillon, *Lire et Ecrire l'Avenir: L'Astrologie dans la France du Grand Siecle, 1610–1715* (Seyssel: Champ Vallon, 1996); for England, Hilary M. Carey, *Courting Disaster: Astrology at the English Court and University in the Later Middle Ages* (New York: St. Martin's, 1991) and Patrick Curry, *Prophecy and Power: Astrology in Early Modern England* (Princeton: Princeton University Press, 1989). Further, Ristori was by no means Cosimo I's only astrologer. Towards the end of Cosimo's rule (and life), Egnazio Danti (1536–86) served this function, as we can see in Danti's treatise on the astrolable, *Trattato dell'uso e della fabbrica dell'astrolabio,* second enlarged edition (Florence, 1569; also Florence, 1578). For more on Danti, see Bonolì and Piliarvu, *I Lettori*, pp. 137–41. This is a rich and understudied topic.

types of astrological practice: revolutions, elections and nativities. I know of no evidence for the fourth, namely, interrogations.[34]

*

A Camaldolese monk, Filippo Fantoni, lived from roughly 1530 to 1591. He taught mathematics at the University of Pisa from 1560 to 1567, and then again from 1582 to 1589, when he was replaced by Galileo.[35] We do not know very much about Fantoni's life, beyond that he was a monk at Santa Maria degli Angeli in Florence, and that he rose to be the abbot of SS. Giusto e Clemente in Volterra (1569–70) and, ultimately, to be general of his order (1586). He refers to himself as a Florentine, and as a doctor in theology.[36]

With respect to his writings Fantoni only published one book, an extensive work on the reform of the calendar: *De ratione reducendi anni ad legitimam formam et numerum* (1560).[37] In the same year, Fantoni began teaching mathematics at Pisa as an extraordinary lecturer, junior colleague of Francesco Ottonaio, who had himself succeeded Ristori after his death in 1556.[38] Fantoni wrote another work on the calendar in 1578, entitled *Compendiarium totius anni reductionem,* which he dedicated to Francesco de' Medici, Cosimo's successor.[39]

---

[34] The best discussion I know of the four types of practical astrology is in Keith Thomas's magisterial chapters on astrology in his *Religion and the Decline of Magic* (New York: Scribners, 1971), chapters 10–12, especially pp. 286–87. They are clearly articulated for the most part in the *Speculum astronomiae* often attributed, but probably wrongly, to Albertus Magnus. It was most likely composed in the 1260s and certainly by 1270. Zambelli argues for the 1260s in *The* Speculum Astronomiae *and its Enigma: Astrology, Theology and Science in Albertus Magnus and his Contemporaries* (Dordrecht: Kluwer, 1992). Weill-Parot demonstrates the *terminus ante quem* of 1270 in Nicolas Weill-Parot, *Les "images astrologiques" au Moyen Age et à la Renaissance: Spéculations intellectuelles et pratiques magiques (XIIe–XVe siècle)* (Paris: Champion, 2002), pp. 39–40.

[35] My knowledge of Fantoni comes from Schmitt's articles, and A. Pagano, 'Filippo Fantoni', *DBI* (1994), 44: pp. 672–74, which, for the material we are interested in here, is mainly derived from Schmitt.

[36] This biographical material comes from Schmitt, 'Filippo Fantoni', pp. 55–58.

[37] Schmitt, 'Filippo Fantoni', p. 55 and n. 9.

[38] Schmitt discusses the other sixteenth-century professors of mathematics at Pisa in 'Filippo Fantoni', p. 54, and more fully in 'Faculty of Arts', pp. 255–63.

[39] At 'Filippo Fantoni', p. 59, Schmitt mistakenly states that it was dedicated to Cosimo I, but in n. 17 he attributes it correctly to Francesco. Fantoni dedicated the 1560 edition to

Although Fantoni's teaching in his first period at Pisa (1560–67) is mostly shrouded in obscurity, much more is known about the second period (1582–89), including his teaching of the *Quadripartitum*. Schmitt reconstructs Fantoni's teaching as follows from the rotoli:[40]

1582–3 The fifth book of Euclid and *Theorica of the Planets*.
1583–4 The *Sphere* of Ptolemy and the first book of Euclid.
1584–5 The fifth book of Euclid and *Theorica of the Planets*.
1585–6 The first [book] of Euclid, the first book of Ptolemy's *Tetrabiblos*, questions pertaining to the medical faculty, and according to the delineations of the planets and nothing else.
1586–7 The Sphere of Orontio [Fine] and the first book of Euclid.
[1587–8][41] [Pifferi is also listed] Euclid [no indication of book] and *Theorica of the Planets*.
1588–9 The first [book] of Euclid, the *Sphere* of Orontio together with the *Sphere* of Ptolemy.

Teaching manuscripts from several of these courses exist, including ones on Ptolemaic geography and cosmology which discuss (*inter alia*) some of the recent maritime discoveries, and a cycle of lectures on Peurbach's *Theoricae novae planetarum*.[42] Fantoni dedicated these lectures to Francesco de' Medici when he was grand duke of Tuscany, which allows us to date them to between 1576 and

---

the general of his order, a certain Antonio (55).

[40] Schmitt, 'Filippo Fantoni', p. 57:
1582–3 Quintum librum Euclidis et theoricas planetarum
1583–4 Sphaeram Tholomei et primum librum Euclidis
1584–5 Quintum librum Euclidis et planetarum theoricas
1585–6 Primum Euclidis, primum librum Quadripartiti Ptolomei, quaestiones ad facultatem medicinae pertinent[es], et secundum planetarum delineationes et non aliud
1586–7 Sphaeram Horontii et primum librum Euclidis
[1587–8] [Pifferi is also listed] Euclides [no indication of book] et theoricas planetarum
1588–9 Primum Euclidis et spheram Orontii simul cum sphaera Ptolomei
Schmitt discusses Pifferi, another professor of mathematics at Pisa, briefly in 'Faculty of Arts', p. 257.

[41] Schmitt prints 1586–7 twice; this appears to be a typo.

[42] Schmitt discusses his writings at 'Filippo Fantoni', pp. 58–62.

1587.[43] The work on cosmology was supposed to be published in 1590, but those plans fell through when Fantoni died in 1591.[44] We also possess small works on the motion of heavy and light things and on the certainty of mathematics. Commentaries on Sacrobosco's *Sphere* and Peter Lombard's *Sentences* (his only known work on theology) are no longer extant.[45] We will now explore Ristori's and Fantoni's teaching commentaries on Ptolemy's *Quadripartitum*.

The Ptolemy Lectures: Textual Introduction

According to Schmitt, Ristori taught mathematics-slash-astrology at the University of Pisa from 1543 to 1550. Of his teaching, several manuscripts exist for Ristori's course on the *Quadripartitum*,[46] two of which I will discuss here.[47] MS Riccardiana 157 consists of 61 lectures on the first two books of the *Quadripartitum*, and runs to 257 double-sided octavo pages.[48] The colophon states that the lectures were recorded *viva voce* by Amerigo Droncioni (*De roncionibus*), about whom I have been unable to find any further information.[49] The text of the manuscript is clean and legible, and does not have many corrections. The other manuscript I have studied offers the same basic lectures by Ristori, but as modified and presented by Filippo Fantoni at Pisa in the academic year 1585–86, including lectures on Books III and IV. Fantoni's manuscript (Conventi Soppressi B.VII.479, 2 volumes)[50] at the Biblioteca

---

[43] Schmitt, 'Filippo Fantoni', p. 60 and n. 36.

[44] His nephew, Antonio Savino, prepared an Italian translation, two manuscripts of which exist. Schmitt tells this story in 'Filippo Fantoni', pp. 59–60 and nn. 31–32.

[45] Schmitt, 'Filippo Fantoni', p. 62.

[46] Castagnola notes these in 'Oroscopo', p. 131 (n.11).

[47] See also Giuseppe Bezza's contribution in this volume.

[48] Germana Ernst signals this manuscript in *Firenze e la Toscana dei Medici nell'Europa del Cinquecento: La corte il mare i mercanti, La rinascita della scienza editoria e società, Astrologia, magia e alchimia* (Scala: Electa, 1980), p. 372 (3.3.11), as does Schmitt, 'Faculty of Arts', p. 259 (n. 62).

[49] 'Lectura super Ptolomei Quadripartitum reverendi ac eximii magistri Iuliani ristorii Pratensis, per me Amerigum de roncionibus dum publice legeretur; almo Pisarum gimnasio currenti calamo collecta:. (1r; my transcription, as are the rest unless otherwise noted)'.

[50] Schmitt signalled but only briefly discussed this manuscript in two articles ('Faculty of Arts' and 'Filippo Fantoni'), the fruit of research undertaken while he was a Fellow at Villa I Tatti. Schmitt also discusses another manuscript at the BNCF, which he identifies

Nazionale Centrale in Florence contains a complete course on Ptolemy's *Quadripartitum* in 118 lectures, written out in Latin in a less clear hand than the Riccardiana manuscript; there are many additions, corrections and deletions in another hand, perhaps Fantoni's. The manuscript is very long, consisting of 673 double-sided folio pages in two volumes.[51]

*

For his Ptolemy course, which was delivered in Latin, Ristori used Joachim Camerarius's Latin translation of the *Tetrabiblos* (1535).[52] One of Philipp Melanchthon's closest associates and a highly skilled textual scholar, Camerarius established the Greek text, publishing its *editio princeps* in 1535 at Nuremberg with Johannes Petreius, who later published Copernicus's *De revolutionibus orbium coelestium* (1543) and some of Cardano's writings.[53]

---

as F.9.478 in the text ('Filippo Fantoni', p. 59) and as Conv. Soppr. B.7.478 in the corresponding footnote (n. 29). The former is correct. Schmitt identifies the manuscript as having 441 folios; I found 430, with 113 *lectiones*. This manuscript remains to be studied. Pagano ('Filipo Fantoni', p. 673) follows Schmitt's second and erroneous citation. Furthermore, Schmitt's description of what he numbers B.7.479 does not correspond to the manuscript I study here: 'FBN [=BNCF], conv. soppr. B.7.479, in two parts of 50+24 fols'. Although B.7.479 has two parts, they are rather longer and contain lectures on all four books. More work needs to be done to identify which manuscripts Schmitt examined and how all the manuscripts relate. I hope this essay contributes usefully to this endeavor. I would also like to take this opportunity to correct a misprint for this manuscript in my 'Use and Abuse of Ptolemy's *Tetrabiblos*' (cited just below), which I erroneously called B.7.749. My thanks, once again, to Stefano Dall'Aglio for helping me straighten this out.

51 This is my description of the manuscript, which I examined *in situ* while a Fellow at I Tatti. The text here derives from my transcription; the text offered is a working text. The three photographs are from this manuscript.

52 I draw the next two paragraphs from my 'The Use and Abuse of Ptolemy's *Tetrabiblos* in Renaissance and Early Modern Europe: Two Case Studies (Giovanni Pico della Mirandola and Filippo Fantoni)', in *Ptolemy in Perspective: Use and Criticism of his Work from Antiquity to the Present* ed. Alexander Jones (Dordrecht: Springer, 2010), pp. 135–49.

53 [. . .] *Claudii Ptolemaei Pelusiensis libri quatuor compositi* [. . .] *Traductio in linguam Latinam librorum Ptolemaei duum priorum* [. . .] *Ioachimi Camerarii Pabergensis* (Nuremberg: J. Petreius, 1535). For more on Camerarius, see Frank Baron, 'Camerarius and the Historical Doctor Faustus', in *Joachim Camerarius (1500–74): Essays on the History of Humanism during the Reformation*, ed. Frank Baron (Munich: William Fink, 1978), pp. 200–22. For Petreius, a printer worthy of greater attention, see (e.g.) Noel M. Swerdlow, 'Annals of Scientific Publishing: Johannes Petreius's Letter to Rheticus', *Isis* 83 (1992): pp. 270–74, and

Camerarius's Greek text was reprinted several times; it was only replaced when the first two modern editions of *Tetrabiblos* were published independently in 1940.[54]

In addition to providing the 1535 Greek text, Camerarius also translated the first two books of Ptolemy's treatise into Latin, providing brief summaries of books III and IV. In 1548 Antonio Gogova, an associate of Gerard Mercator and Gemma Frisius at the University of Louvain,[55] published a complete Latin translation of the *Tetrabiblos*, in which Gogova took over, whole cloth, Camerarius's translation of books I and II and himself rendered books III and IV into Latin.[56] Gogova's translation became standard in the Catholic world, whereas Philipp Melanchthon translated anew all four books in 1553, based on the revised edition of Camerarius's Greek text; this was the standard edition in Protestant lands.[57] Cardano used the Camerarius-Gogova translation in his published 1554 commentary on the *Quadripartitum*,[58] as did Fantoni for his course at the University of Pisa in 1585–86.

Brosseder, *Im Bann der Sterne*, pp. 147–49. For Melanchthon and the astrological context, see Sachiko Kusukawa, *The Transformation of Natural Philosophy: The Case of Philip Melanchthon* (Cambridge: Cambridge University Press, 1995) and Brosseder, *Im Bann der Sterne.*

54 Ptolemy, *Tetrabiblos*, trans. and ed. F.E. Robbins, Loeb Classical Library (Cambridge, MA. Harvard University Press, 1940), and *Claudii Ptolemaei Opera quae extant omnia*, Vol. III, chap. 1, *Apotelesmatika*, eds. Franz Boll and EmilieBoer (Leipzig: Teubner). Wolfgang Hübner's recent Teubner text is the first to take both modern editions into account: *Claudii Ptolemaei Opera quae extant omnia*, Vol. III, 1, *Apotelesmatika*, ed. Wolfgang Hübner (Stuttgart: Teubner, 1998). I do not know of a satisfactory account of Ptolemy's textual history, especially of the Latin translations and commentaries. A proper critical edition of Ptolemaeus Latinus is a desideratum for both the *Tetrabiblos* and the *Centiloquium*, as is a study in the *Corpus translationum et commentariorum: Medieval and Renaissance Latin Translations and Commentaries*, ed. Virginia Brown (Washington, DC: Catholic University of America Press, 1960–). The new long-term Ptolemaeus Arabus et Latinus project at the Bavarian Academy of Sciences intends to fulfill these desiderata.

55 For more on Gogova and this milieu, see Steven Vanden Broecke, *The Limits of Influence: Pico, Louvain, and the Crisis of Renaissance Astrology* (Leiden: Brill, 2003).

56 *Operis quadripartiti, in latinum sermonem traductio. Adiectis libris posterioribus, Antonio Gogova Graviens. Interprete* (Louvain: P. Phalesius and M. Rotarius, 1548).

57 *Claudii Ptolemaei de praedictionibus astronomicis, cui titulum fecerunt Quadripartitum Grece & Latine, libri IIII. P. Melanthone interprete,* [. . .] 2 vols. (Basel: J. Oporinus, 1553).

58 *Hieronymi Cardani* [. . .] *In Cl. Ptolemaei Pelusiensis. IIII de astrorum iudiciis, aut, ut vulgo vocant, quadripartitae constructionis, libros commentaria* [. . .] (Basel: Petri, 1554).

Contextual Introduction: Savonarola and Great Conjunctions (Historical Astrology)
In his lectures of the 1540s on Ptolemy's *Tetrabiblos*, Giuliano Ristori identified Girolamo Savonarola (1452–98) as the pseudo-prophet predicted by a great(er) conjunction in Scorpio in 1425; others had identified Martin Luther as the prophet (or pseudo-prophet) predicted by the great conjunction of 1484, also in Scorpio.[59] Although Ristori's successor at Pisa, Filippo Fantoni, used these lectures as the basis of his own Ptolemy course there, Fantoni made no such identification. Rather, manuscript evidence reveals that Fantoni scratched out Savonarola's name quite emphatically in the text of Ristori's lectures. Although many interesting topics are discussed in their commentaries, I will focus here on transcribing and exploring the text of Ristori's identification from MS Riccardiana 157 (**R** in what follows) and of Fantoni's modifications from MS Conventi Soppressi B.VII.479 (vol. 1) of the Biblioteca Nazionale Centrale in Florence (**F** in what follows). My interpretation may best be read as an exploratory sounding in mostly uncharted waters.

An influential and incendiary figure in late Quattrocento Florence was Girolamo Savonarola.[60] He appears three times in the first 18 *lectiones* of Ristori's commentary (F: fols 1r–81v).[61] The first two times occur in the text examined in

---

59 Aby Warburg, 'Pagan-Antique Prophecy in Words and Images in the Age of Luther' (originally published 1920), in his *The Renewal of Pagan Antiquity: Contributions to the Cultural History of the European Renaissance*, trans. David Britt (Los Angeles: Getty Research Institute, 1999), pp. 597–697, 760–75, esp. 603–13. Warburg brilliantly brings out the complexities of this story on both Catholic and Protestant sides, especially the attempt to redate Martin Luther's birth date and year from 1483 to 1484, the year of the great conjunction. For Scorpio being a sign deleterious to religion, see Laura A. Smoller, *History, Prophecy and the Stars: The Christian Astrology of Pierre d'Ailly* (Princeton: Princeton University Press, 1994), p. 76. Perhaps this is why pseudo-prophets are supposed to arise when a great conjunction takes place in Scorpio and Mars, its ruling planet, is in the ninth house of religion (or its complement, the third), as we will see below.

60 Savonarola is too well known to require extensive discussion here. First of all, one should consult Donald Weinstein's masterly *Savonarola and Florence: Prophecy and Patriotism in the Renaissance* (Princeton: Princeton University Press, 1970). For important recent studies on Savonarola and his influence, see Lorenzo Polizzotto, *The Elect Nation: The Savonarolan Movement in Florence, 1494–1545* (Oxford: Clarendon Press, 1994) and the more recent researches of Stefano Dall'Aglio and Tamar Herzig. For this article, I have learned a great deal from a pre-publication copy of Dall'Aglio's richly informative *Savonarola and Savonarolism*, trans. John Gagné (Toronto: Centre for Reformation and Renaissance Studies, 2010), for which I am deeply grateful.

61 These are the folios I have transcribed and studied so far.

Part II below, once in the company of Giovanni Pico della Mirandola (1463–94), the precocious humanist who famously rejected astrology at the end of his short but intense life.[62] The other time occurs in *Lectio* 6 in an extensive and interesting text where Ristori argues that '*astrologia*' is a true science. Here too Fantoni crossed out Savonarola's name, but this time substitutes for it the anonymous 'quidam vir' (F: 34r [see image in *Appendix* 5]).[63] In the overall conclusion, I will address possible reasons why Fantoni softened Ristori's attack on Savonarola.

In the text transcribed, translated and examined here (see *Appendix* 3), Ristori identified Savonarola as a pseudo-prophet in a discussion of historical astrology, in particular, according to the theory of great conjunctions, which provided an influential astrological framework for understanding and interpreting the patterns of history ever since it was developed in Sasanian Persia (226–642) CE.[64]

---

[62] For a splendid orientation to Pico and his work on astrology, see Anthony Grafton, 'Giovanni Pico della Mirandola: Trials and Triumphs of an Omnivore', in *Commerce with the Classics: Ancient Books and Their Renaissance Readers* (Ann Arbor: University of Michigan Press, 1997), pp. 93–134; see also my thesis, especially chaps. 4–6. For the text of Pico's extensive attack on astrology, originally published posthumously in 1496, see Giovanni Pico della Mirandola, *Disputationes adversus astrologiam divinatricem*, ed. Eugenio Garin, 2 vols. (Florence: Vallecchi, 1946–52). I am currently preparing the first English translation for the I Tatti Renaissance Library (Harvard University Press). Pico dedicated Book V to a critique of historical astrology, including the theory of great conjunctions. John D. North discusses this briefly, including the significant lag time between the great conjunction in 571 that predicted the arrival of a prophet, and Mohammed's actual arrival in 620, a horoscope we shall encounter later: 'Astrology and the Fortunes of Churches', in his *Stars, Minds and Fate: Essays in Ancient and Medieval Cosmology* (London: Hambledon Press, 1989 [1980]), pp. 59–89, 81–83.

[63] 'Arguit ~~Savonarola~~ <quidam vir>'. This *lectio* is also worthy of further study, and I hope to treat it more fully elsewhere. I discuss Savonarola's ambivalent and changing attitude toward astrology in its cultural context in chapter 6 of my thesis. For the editorial conventions I use, see the introduction to the textual appendices below.

[64] For its origins, see David Pingree, *From Astral Omens to Astrology: From Babylon to Bīkāner* (Rome: Istituto Italiano per l'Africa et l'Oriente, 1997), especially chap. 4, 'The Recovery of Sasanian Astrology', pp. 39–50, but also scattered throughout the following chapters. For its ideological location in the Arabic world and the close relation to its Persian roots, see Dmitri Gutas, *Greek Thought, Arabic Culture: The Graeco-Arabic Translation Movement in Baghdad and early 'Abbasid Society (2nd–4th/8th–10th Centuries)* (London: Routledge, 1998). See also Edward S. Kennedy, 'The World Year Concept in Islamic Astrology', in *Astronomy and Astrology in the Medieval Islamic World* (Aldershot: Ashgate, 1998 [1962]), pp. 23–43, 30–37 on great conjunctions. Kennedy accepts Pingree's arguments for its Sasanian origins (p. 41), primarily because there is no mention of any

Pico fundamentally despised historical astrology—which he treated in detail in *Disputations,* Book V—because he thought it subordinated religion to astrology, although this would have been justified within the context of God's providential creation and ordering of the world, while also protecting God's absolute power to modify things as He wished.[65] Nevertheless, even though Ristori's and Fantoni's discussion of great conjunctions was inspired by a lemma in the *Quadripartitum,* Ptolemy himself did not mention them, as we will see; nor could he have done so, since the theory had not yet been developed.

*

Great conjunctions played a significant role in the European understanding of history from at least the thirteenth century with Roger Bacon[66] (and in the fourteenth with, e.g., Matteo Villani) until well into the seventeenth with Johannes Kepler (favourably) and Giovanni Battista Riccioli (critically).[67] Such analyses were also often mixed with prophetic speculation and the interpretation of apocalyptic texts, as with Roger Bacon on the *Book of Revelations* in *Opus maius* IV.[68] This was also the case at the end of the fifteenth century with

---

such doctrine in any earlier Hindu or Hellenistic texts. Yet in this volume Giuseppe Bezza will argue for precursors of the Sasanian great conjunctions in certain Hellenistic natal astrological practices.

65 Astrology and providence is a fundamentally significant but understudied topic.

66 John Henry Bridges, ed., *The 'Opus maius' of Roger Bacon*, 3 vols. (Oxford: Clarendon, 1897–1900), I: p. 263. See the full quotation and translation in Giuseppe Bezza's contribution to this volume.

67 For the earlier period, see (e.g.) Smoller, *History, Prophecy*, 78ff., and for the later period, Germana Ernst, 'From the Watery Trigon to the Fiery Trigon: Celestial Signs, Prophecies and History', in "Astrologi Hallucinati": *Stars and the End of the World in Luther's Time*, ed. Paola Zambelli (Berlin: De Gruyter, 1986), pp. 265–80. For a penetrating earlier treatment, see Friedrich von Bezold, 'Geschichtskonstruction aus Mittelalter', reprinted in his *Aus Mittelalter und Renaissance: Kulturgeschichtliche Studien* (Munich: R. Oldenbourg, 1918). Abū Maʿshar's *De magnis coniunctionibus*, the central text in this tradition, was translated twice into Latin in the second quarter of the 12th century; one of the translations was then published twice (1489 and 1515). See Keiji Yamamoto and Charles Burnett, *Abū Maʿšar on Historical Astrology: The Book of Religions and Dynasties (On the Great Conunctions)*, 2 vols. (Leiden: Brill, 2000), II: pp. xi–xxix.

68 Bridges, *'Opus maius'*, I: p. 266. North, 'Fortunes', discusses this as well, and with much reference to Marjorie Reeves, *Influence of Prophecy in the Middle Ages: A Study in Joachimism* (Oxford: Clarendon, 1969).

Johannes Lichtenberger's extremely popular, prophetically augmented revision of Paul of Middelburg's extremely influential, but strictly astrological, prognostication of 1484,[69] and at Florence in particular.[70]

Historical astrology had numerous influential proponents. Among others, Roger Bacon used great conjunction theory, which he describes at length, to provide evidence for astrology's utility *qua* religion in *Opus maius* IV (pp. 238–69). I will refer to his analysis where helpful in what follows.[71] In the early fifteenth century, Pierre d'Ailly (1350–1420?), whom Bacon deeply influenced, used historical astrology–including great conjunction theory with other techniques–to clarify the timing of the Antichrist's advent. Armed with this knowledge, Cardinal d'Ailly almost singlehandedly resolved the Church's Great Schism at the Council of Constance (1414).[72]

Not surprisingly, these views elicited strong reactions. Henry of Hesse (ca. 1325–97) criticised historical astrology in the mid-to-late-fourteenth century.[73] But the major attack came in Book V of the *Disputations against Divinatory Astrology*, where Giovanni Pico della Mirandola was concerned primarily to defend religion from its perceived subordination to astrology. Among others, Pico ferociously attacked Bacon and d'Ailly, as well as Abū Ma'shar, the central figure in this tradition. Amid fervid apocalyptic speculation, Pico wrote his *Disputations* and Savonarola rose to power in the same late Quattrocento power vacuum in Florence following Lorenzo de' Medici's death on 9 April 1492.[74]

---

69 Warburg also discusses this, especially in relation to Johannes Lichtenberger, who lifted the astrological part of his prophecy-prognostication from Paul of Middelburg. On Lichtenberger himself, see Dietrich Kurze, *Johannes Lichtenberger: Eine Studie zur Geschichte der Prophetie und Astrologie* (Lübeck: Matthiesen, 1960) and his 'Popular Astrology and Prophecy in the Fifteenth and Sixteenth Centuries: Johannes Lichtenberger', in "Astrologi hallucinati": *Stars and the End of the World in Luther's Time*, ed. Paola Zambelli (Berlin: De Gruyter, 1986), pp. 177–93. On Paul of Middelburg, see Stefan Heilen's contribution to this volume. Paul's deeply influential prognostication for 1484 and the following 20 years seem to have inspired many to attempt to identify the predicted pseudo-prophet.

70 See Weinstein, *Savonarola and Florence*.

71 I treat Roger's astrology in detail in Volume I of my forthcoming monograph.

72 For the development of d'Ailly's thought and Roger Bacon's influence thereon—as well as his work at the Council and how his astrologico-historical views influenced that—see Smoller, *History, Prophecy*.

73 This is discussed briefly in North, 'Fortunes'. For more on Henry, see Hubert Pruckner, *Studien zu den astrologischen Schriften des Heinrich von Langenstein* (Leipzig: Teubner, 1933).

74 In *Savonarola and Florence*, Weinstein brilliantly reconstructs this context. For related

Ristori and Fantoni offered their sixteenth-century courses on Ptolemy's *Quadripartitum* in the long shadows cast by these events, including intense and broadly spread speculation on the effects of the great conjunctions of 1484 (in Scorpio) and of 1524 (in Pisces), both in the water triplicity. The latter inspired widespread fears of an impending deluge of biblical proportions.[75]

*

Very briefly, there are three types of great conjunctions, that is, conjunctions of the two outermost planets known at the time, Jupiter and Saturn: great, greater and greatest.[76] By the nature of our solar system, Jupiter (with its twelve year cycle) and Saturn (with its 29.5 year cycle) conjoin once every twenty years at roughly 242.5 degrees distant from the previous conjunction,[77] and thus normally within the same elemental triplicity, whether fire, earth, air or water

---

issues, see Michael J.B. Allen on Golden Age speculation in his *Synoptic Art: Marsilio Ficino on the History of Platonic Interpretation* (Florence: Olschki, 1998), and Claudia Rousseau on the great conjunction and what came after: 'Cosimo I de Medici and Astrology'.

75 Much has been written on the great conjunction of 1524, including "Astrologi Hallucinati": *Stars and the End of the World in Luther's Time*, ed. Paola Zambelli (Berlin: de Gruyter, 1986); Heike Talkenberger, *Sintflut: Prophetie und Zeitgeschehen in Texten und Holzschnitten Astrologischer Flugschriften* (Tübingen: Niemeyer, 1990) and Ottavio Niccoli, *Prophecy and People in Renaissance Italy,* trans. Lydia Cochrane (Princeton: Princeton University Press, 1990), pp. 140–67. Such practices and their critiques continued well into the seventeenth century (and beyond?). A worthwhile topic for future research is to determine when historical astrology ceased to be a factor in European history writing. Albeit somewhat modified, the subject has seen a recent resurgence in certain 'New Age' writings, in particular, those of Richard Tarnas, *Cosmos and Psyche: Intimations of a New World View* (New York: Viking, 2006) and his earlier, *Prometheus the Awakener: An Essay on the Archetypal Meaning of Uranus* (Woodstock, CT: Spring Publications, 1995). The new great conjunctions refer, of course, to conjunctions of the new outer planets: Uranus, Neptune and Pluto.

76 For descriptions of this theory, see for example North, 'Fortunes', p. 64ff; Kennedy, 'World Year', p. 30ff.; Smoller, *History, Prophecy,* p. 20ff; Yamamoto and Burnett, *On Historical Astrology,* I: pp. 573–613. Abū Ma'shar himself describes it in detail in Book 1, Ch. 1. There are some minor differences in terminology in the lengths of cycles, but the basic structures are very clear.

77 In Book I, chapter 1, par. 16, Abū Ma'shar gives the precise number for the mean conjunction as: 242°, 25', 17", 10"', 6""; Yamamoto and Burnett, *On Historical Astrology,* I: p. 13. Kennedy, 'World Year', gives a table of the slightly different figures in different authors (31).

(in order).[78] Conjunctions within the same triplicity are called 'great' *simpliciter*. After twelve (or thirteen) such triangular cycles, however, the conjunctions shift into the next triplicity in order, for example, from air to water signs. This happens every 240 or so years, and the conjunction that inaugurates the shift is called a 'greater' conjunction, with its characteristic indication of great changes in politics and religion. After four such cycles (960 years or so), the conjunctions return to the first sign of the zodiac, namely, to Aries, thus marking a 'greatest' conjunction.[79]

Al-Kindī's most influential student, Abū Ma'shar (Abū Ma'shar Ja'far ibn Muḥammad ibn 'Umar al-Balkhī, 787–886) provided the core text in this tradition for the identification of prophets.[80] In *Differentia* 3 of the first *Tractatus* of his classic *De magnis coniunctionibus*,[81] Abū Ma'shar informs us about the changes (*mutationes*) of conjunctions that signify the birth of prophets:[82]

---

78 For elementary details about astrology, see J.C. Eade, *The Forgotten Sky: A Guide to Astrology in English Literature* (Oxford: Clarendon, 1984), and any basic astrological textbook, past and present; for example, Derek and Julia Parker, *Parker's Astrology*, in numerous editions. Abū Ma'shar describes these three permutations in detail plus the 30 year patterns of Saturn and Mars conjunctions in Book I, Chapter 1.

79 The numbers 20-240-960 are not precise because the planets do not maintain constant speeds in their cycles, and they regularly go retrograde. We will see this with the main conjunctions under discussion here (1365 [W], 1385 [A], 1405 [A], 1425 [W]), where that for 1365 moved from air to water, whereas the next two were back in air signs. It was only in 1425 that the conjunctions returned to water signs where they remained for the rest of that cycle; North, 'Fortunes', p. 73. As we will see, Ristori used 1425 as a greater conjunction because, although it was not the first water conjunction to have marked a change of triplicity, it did so after two retrograde passes in air signs. Smoller discusses the great conjunction of 1365 at 8° Scorpio, in *History, Prophecy*, p. 76.

80 Yamamoto and Burnett, *On Historical Astrology*, discuss al-Kindi's influence on Abū Ma'shar in I: pp. 606–09.

81 For the text, I use the Huntington Library's copy of the 1489 *editio princeps* published by Erhard Ratdolt, Regiomontanus's protégé. Yamamoto and Burnett publish a somewhat different text that is closer to the Arabic original. For our purposes, however, the differences are trivial. For the nature of Yamamoto and Burnett's Latin text, see *On Historical Astrology*, II: pp. xxx–xxxiii. The Latin text for this passage is in Book I, Chap. 3, par. 3 (II: p. 23).

82 'Nunc narremus in hac differentia mutationes coniunctionum significantium nativitates prophetarum qui elevantur ad hoc ut sint reges violentum et reliquum esse eorum' (a7r). The Sasanian Persians mainly used historical astrology for political purposes. When their views were translated and transposed into an Islamic context under 'Abbasid rule, however, the religious dimension also came to the fore; Yamamoto and Burnett, *On*

> Let us say that when [1] the conjunctions are changed from [one] triplicity into [another] triplicity, and [2] one of the three superior planets is in the ninth or third [place, i.e. terrestrial house][83] from the ascendant of the same conjunction, [this] signifies their [sc. the prophets] appearance. And especially Saturn signifies the nativities of prophets in this [way].[84]

For Abū Ma'shar, then, there are two primary astrological factors necessary for predicting the advent of prophets: [1] a greater conjunction, and [2] the appearance of Mars, Jupiter and/or Saturn in either the ninth house of religion or its complement, the third. According to Abū Ma'shar, these horoscopes were not constructed for the time of the greater conjunction itself, but rather for the time of the sun's ingress into Aries that marked the beginning of the year in which the conjunction occurred; this is the horoscope of an annual revolution (*Revolutio anni*).[85]

In our text Ristori also emphasized a conjunction that shifted from one triplicity to the next, which must therefore be either a greater or greatest conjunction. Since the relevant conjunction occured in Scorpio, namely, a water sign (and thus triplicity) and not in a fire sign of any sort (let alone Aries), it must be a greater conjunction. Following Abū Ma'shar, then, whom Ristori cites explicitly, the location of a planet in the ninth (or third) house from the ascendant is also significant because the ninth house rules the religious domain, and the third house is its complement. Roger Bacon discusses this doctrine in a

---

Historical Astrology, I: p. 599.

83 'Nono' or 'tertio' implies 'locus' (m.) – as opposed to 'domus' (f.), the other likely candidate—which can refer either to houses or signs, namely terrestrial or celestial houses. The ambiguity in modern terminology derives from the ambiguous premodern terminology. Roger Bacon clarifies this admirably in his *Opus maius*, Book IV. As we will see, the language here is very similar to that in Ristori's discussion (*fuit aliquis planetarum* [. . .]) as is their location in the houses in relation to the ascendant. This allows the identification as houses and not signs, which would not be tied to the ascendant.

84 'Dicamusque quando mutantur coniunctiones a triplicitate in triplicitatem et fuit aliquis planetarum trium superiorum in nono vel in tercio ab ascendente eiusdem coniunctionis significantis apparitionem eorum et maxime saturnus significabit hoc nativitates prophetarum' (a7r).

85 Yamamoto and Burnett, *On Historical Astrology*, Book I, Chap. 1, par. 12ff. (I: p. 11). They also call this *Revolutio anni mundi*, which amounts to the same thing, and is opposed to *Revolutio anni nati*, the revolution horoscope for an individual's nativity.

richly detailed and interesting passage of *Opus maius* IV, where an analysis of Christ's nativity is used to illustrate astrology's utility for religion.[86]

Abū Ma'shar's treatment differs from Ristori's. As we saw, Abū Ma'shar informs us that a superior planet, especially Saturn, should be located in the ninth (or third) house. As we will see, Ristori discusses Mars. As far as I can tell, however, Abū Ma'shar only mentions the signifying of prophets, not *pseudo*-prophets. Further, it is obvious that whether someone is understood to be an authentic or spurious prophet is deeply culturally conditioned. For example, whereas Mohammed would be accounted a legitimate prophet by Muslims (indeed, he is referred to precisely as '*The* Prophet'), for Christians he would have, and continues to have, a much more problematic identity. Likewise, in the case of Martin Luther. It is no surprise that as controversial a figure as Savonarola would receive the same double-edged treatment.

PART II: TEXTS

Ptolemy's Lemma: Quadripartitum *I.2*

With this background, let us now zoom in closer and enter a sixteenth-century Pisan classroom. We will begin by turning to the passage in Ptolemy that Ristori used as a stepping-off point for our text identifying Savonarola as a pseudo-prophet. Book I, chapters 1–3 of the *Quadripartitum* are introductory to the entire treatise. I.1 introduces the subject matter, distinguishing astronomy from astrology. Both are modes of foreknowledge through the science of the stars. As mentioned above, what we call 'astronomy' studies and predicts the *motions* of the planets over time, and what we call 'astrology' studies and predicts the *influences* of the planets on the earth, its atmosphere and inhabitants. *Quadripartitum* I.2–3 argues for astrology's validity as an art or science: for the attainability of its knowledge (2), and for its utility (3).[87]

After establishing astrology's complexity and validity in general, the text

86 For an insightful analysis, see Ornella Pompeo Faracovi, *Gli oroscopi di Cristo* (Venice: Marsilio, 1999); the discussion in Bacon occurs in Bridges, *'Opus maius'* 1: p. 258ff. I am not certain where the interpretation of pseudo-prophets arises, perhaps with Paul of Middelburg's 1484 prognostication.

87 These are very interesting chapters with much broader philosophical and cultural interest, including Ptolemy's comparisons of astrology with medicine; both are types of conjectural (not certain) knowledge.

under discussion from *Quadripartitum* I.2 arises in response to criticisms about astrology's status as a science, and particularly addresses why astrologers err.[88] The first source of errors Ptolemy discusses are due to the inexperience of some astrological practitioners, which reflects more on *their* deficiencies than on those of the science itself. Another source of error, broadly speaking—and one reason for astrology's bad reputation—arises because sometimes non-astrological arts are called types of astrology by disreputable practitioners. Although Ptolemy himself does not mention any, Cardano in his commentary gives the example of geomancers.[89] These unscrupulous practitioners then make prognostications about matters that cannot properly be known by means of astrology, which casts the natural and legitimate subjects of astrological prediction in a bad light.

Ptolemy then acknowledges two main structural difficulties and discusses each in turn. We will focus on the second. After discussing the first, namely, matter's recalcitrance, Ptolemy raises another deep structural issue that also militates against astrology ever being a certain science, that is, one capable of predictive certainty: that the ancient configurations of the planets are similar to but different from modern ones. Since the celestial bodies, whether stars, planets or luminaries, are understood to be efficient causes in the economy of nature, if these efficient causes differ, even slightly, then their effects must differ as well.[90] Thus predictions sometimes fail because the historical examples on which they are based differ structurally (positionally) from those in the current situation. At this point in his argument, Ptolemy uses this celestial efficient factor to explain why both revolutions and nativities are more difficult to prognosticate about

---

88 For the Greek text, I use Ptolemy, *Tetrabiblos*, ed. Robbins, pp. 12–17, and for the Latin of texts XIII–XV, I use Camerarius's translation printed in Cardano's commentary, *Opera omnia*, ed. Charles Spon, 10 vols. (Lyon, 1663; repr. Stuttgart, 1966), V: pp. 103–5. All of my references to Cardano's *Tetrabiblos* commentary are to this edition.

89 Cardano, *Opera omnia*, p. 104. For more on geomancy, see Thérèse Charmasson, *Recherches sur une technique divinatoire: La géomancie dans l'Occident médiéval* (Geneva: Droz, 1980). Ristori treats these illegitimate divinatory practices in *Lectio* 2 (R: fol. 8v), mentioning, among others, hydromancy, pyromancy and aeromancy.

90 In his commentary, Cardano notes that the two reasons Ptolemy gives for astrology's essential uncertainty as a science are the material and efficient causes: 'Cum in omni actione naturali duae causae sint omnibus quidem manifestae atque principales, scilicet materia et efficiens (105)[.]' I also discuss this dimension of astrological causality in much greater detail in ch. 2 of my thesis. For Ristori's and Fantoni's use of the efficient cause, see my 'Uses and Abuses'.

than, for example, the weather. This is because individual temperaments are involved, and thus a more complex and highly structured material dimension.[91]

Ristori took a different approach. To explain Ptolemy's text in Camerarius's Latin translation Ristori takes this opportunity to discuss a very different sort of example, namely, that of great conjunctions, leading ultimately to the identification of pseudo-prophets.[92] In addition to planetary locations, Ristori also discusses the fixed stars and their slow movement over great expanses of time due to the precession of the equinoxes. We will also see that this discussion is relevant for understanding astrology's epistemological foundations: in particular, what can be known and how. I will first discuss Ptolemy's lemma, turning then to Ristori's two-fold exposition thereof. In this way, we can catch a glimpse of how an early modern professor of mathematics taught astrology as a discipline of natural knowledge at a fine, premodern university.

*

Ptolemy's passage (*Textus* XV) begins as follows:

> But it is obvious that even the most diligent [practitioners] and those skilled in mathematics at the highest levels err much in this part [sc. making predictions]. This does not happen due to any of those things that we mentioned, but by the nature of the thing (*rei natura*), and by the weakness of those professing such a weighty subject. For we believe that, due to[93] matter and its general consideration, [astrology] is not a certain science, but conjectural (*nec certa scientia, sed coniectura*), especially when concerned with what is made from many diverse things.[94]

---

[91] As noted above, in the medieval and early modern periods, there were four canonical types of astrological practices: revolutions, nativities, elections and interrogations. Great conjunctions which also came later were configured with revolutions.

[92] A question for further research is to see if this is a normal locus for discussing great conjunctions in earlier *Tetrabiblos* commentaries that Ristori simply follows. Cardano, too, discusses great conjunctions here, but not the identification of authentic or pseudo-prophets.

[93] 'praeter' is printed here, but 'propter' seems clearly to be what was meant.

[94] 'At est manifestum, multum falli in hac parte etiam diligentissimos et summo studio in Mathematicis versatos. Non fit hoc propter quicquam eorum quae diximus, sed rei natura, et infirmitate profitentium in tanto onere professionis. Nam [praeter] <propter> id quod materiam quomodo se habeat generaliter consideramus, nec certa scientia, sed coniectura, praesertim quae ex multis diversisque rebus concreta sit (104–05)[.]' I use the

Here Ptolemy explicitly states that, by its very nature astrology is a conjectural, not a certain science—in implicit contrast to astronomy[95]—and that even the finest mathematically sophisticated practitioners err due to the complex natures of material things.

Ristori uses the next passage as a lemma:

> This also happens in relation to the *configurationes* which the ancients passed down (*ut configurationes quas veteres tradiderunt*)[96] and to which we are accustomed to fit judgements (*iudicia accomodare*), making pronouncements about those which we now observe as they did formerly. And it happens that these configurations were not even once found to be similar (*similes*) to and congruent with ours.[97]

What does Ptolemy mean by the phrase 'τοῖς παλαιοῖς τῶν πλανωμένων συσχηματισμοῖς', which Camerarius translates simply as '*configurationes*'? For Ptolemy himself, the fuller phrase—which Robbins accurately translates as 'the ancient configurations of the planets'—clearly indicates that he means planetary configurations, whereas Camerarius's decision to compress Ptolemy's phrase into the one word '*configurationes*' easily admits a significant ambiguity between [1] 'configurations *of the planets*' per se (as in Ptolemy), and [2] configurations of any and all types of celestial entities, including the fixed stars, which would thereby admit issues related to precession. As we will see, Ristori uses the term '*constellationes*' with precisely the same ambiguity that Camerarius invited with his term '*configurationes*'. Needless to say, Ptolemy discussed this issue for his own time, the mid-second century CE, and he explicitly drew the connection of this structural problem with the making of astrological prognostications or

---

text of Camerarius's Latin translation of Ptolemy as printed in the Lyon edition of Girolamo Cardano's commentary (Textus XV), pp. 104–06 (text, 104–05). This is my translation from Camerarius's Latin, but I refer to Robbins's Loeb translation for assistance where necessary, always comparing the Greek original with the Latin translation.

[95] Here it is implicit. In I.1, it is explicit.

[96] As we will see, this is the text of the lemma underlined by Ristori in MS. Ricc. 157 (R).

[97] '[H]oc quoque accidit, ut configurationes quas veteres tradiderunt, et quibus nos iudicia accomodare consuevimus, pronunciantes de iis, quas nunc observamus, ut illi olim: eas configurationes ne semel quidem cum nostris similes, et congruentes reperire contigerit' (105).

judgements.

Ptolemy continues:

> For indeed, they [sc. the configurations of the planets] can take the same positions (*concordare*)[98] more or less [sc. with ours], and that indeed in the immense pathways of time. Moreover, they do not meet wholly in any way, since the renewal (*instauratio* ['συναποκατάστασις'])[99] of all things, celestial and likewise terrestrial (except for one who rejoices in displaying, with a certain ostentatious vapidity [*inanitate quadam gloriosa*], the knowledge [*scientia*] and perception of those things of which there can be none ['περὶ τὴν τῶν ἀκαταλήπτων κατάληψιν καὶ γνῶσιν']),[100] is either not to be fully hoped for, or not, at any rate, within a time grasped by the human mind.[101]

Precise knowledge is impossible, and the difficulties are patent, except to fools and blowhards; only people with glorified senses of their own abilities lay claim to such impossible knowledge. In such circumstances, then, erring should come as no surprise: 'When, therefore, if an error is committed in predicting, it comes from this experience, that the subject examples were dissimilar among themselves (*dissimilia inter se*)'.[102] Thus Ptolemy concludes the relevant passage

---

[98] There is a proper astronomical definition in the *Oxford Latin Dictionary*: '2 (of things) [. . .] c (of stars): to take up the same or proper relative positions, move according to a pattern'. They quote a passage from Paulus Diaconus, *Epitoma Festi* (p. 147M) of the 8th century CE, who gives a great year (*magnus annus*) as an example: 'magnum annum dicunt mathematici, quo septem sidera errantia, expletis propriis cursibus sibimet concordare'. They also note Seneca, *Historia naturalis* 1, pr. 12 without offering a quotation.

[99] Robbins adduces an illuminating quotation from Nemesius, *De natura hominis*, at n. 3 (Loeb, pp. 15–17).

[100] Robbins notes that 'καὶ γνῶσιν' is missing in Camerarius's Greek, but Camerarius has obviously translated it in the Latin ('scientiam'). (But he has reversed 'perception' and 'knowledge' from what they are in the Greek.)

[101] 'Nam magis quidem, aut minus concordare possunt, atque id quidem immensis temporum ambagibus, prorsus autem convenire nullo modo, cum omnium rerum, coelestium simul ac terrestrium instauratio (nisi cui lubeat inanitate quadam gloriosa ostentare scientiam et perceptionem earum rerum quarum nulla esse potest) aut non sit prorsus expectanda, aut non intra saltem tempus, quod humano intellectu comprehendatur' (105).

[102] 'Si quando igitur in praedicendo erratum fuerit commissum, ex eo usu venit, quod

by acknowledging a deep structural problem that profoundly affects the accuracy of astrological predictions.

Ristori's Exposition of Ptolemy's Lemma (see *Appendix 1*)

In discussing this lemma from *Tetrabiblos* I.2 in his third lecture, Ristori first expounds the text (*exponemus textum*; R: 9v–11v), then he discusses various problems. In discussing the lemma, Ristori raises the issue of great conjunctions—which Ptolemy did not do—and also the distinction between the real and imaginary zodiac—also not in Ptolemy; both features also recur in Ristori's later discussion identifying Savonarola as a recent pseudo-prophet.

Ristori begins expounding the text by first reiterating Ptolemy's point that even experienced astrologers err:[103]

> Moreover, it happens to be the case that even an experienced astrologer errs from the difficulty of the art due to the magnitude of the things to be known, he [sc. Ptolemy] declares by speaking first in general [and then] in particular. First, he says that it is not untoward (*inconveniens*) for an experienced astrologer (*peritus astrologus*) to err, if he compares (*conferat*) his [sc. contemporary] celestial configurations (*constellationes*) to the observations of the ancients.

As for Ptolemy, comparing modern to older celestial configurations is the core of the problem. We can see here and below that Ristori prefers the term '*constellatio*' for what Camerarius translated as '*configuratio*' and that he too, like Camerarius, does not qualify the term with the phrase 'of the planets'.

To explain why this dislocation is a problem, Ristori offers a causal analysis:

> The reason is that the effect ought to be referred (*reduci*)[104] to its similar causes (*in suas causas similes*), but contingent effects at the time of more recent [astrologers] and at present times come forth from causes that are not similar to the causes of the ancients (*proficiscuntur ex causis non similibus causis antiquorum*). Therefore, in prognosticating with their (*illorum* [sc. the ancients']) observation and not by means of these configurations (*has constellationes* [i.e. contemporary ones]), it

---

subiecta exempla dissimilia inter se fuerint'.

[103] This is my translation of Ristori (MS Ricc. 157 = R). My interpolations for clarity are in brackets []. The texts are transcribed in the appendices. This text is in *Appendix 1*.

[104] Thomas Aquinas uses this exact term in a similar causal context in his *De occultis operibus naturae*.

happens that they err.

Effects are referred to their causes. In prognosticating, then, errors will occur if dissimilar causes provide the basis of astrological judgments.

Ristori continues, this time adducing an example:

> Therefore, the upshot of the argument (*summa rationis*) is that, since these [present] celestial configurations (*h[a]e constellationes*) are not altogether similar to those (*illis*), therefore the effects are not altogether similar to those. For example, I would say that before the flood of Deucalion, a configuration (*constellatio*) occured, namely, a conjunction (*coniunctio*) of Saturn and Jupiter at 14 degrees of Cancer, and this configuration (*constellatio*) was the efficient cause of that flood (*efficit illud diluvium*).

The first part of Ristori's example establishes that the great flood of Deucalion—the Greek Noah[105]—was caused by a great conjunction of Jupiter and Saturn at 14° Cancer, a water sign. We can see here that Ristori continues to use '*constellatio*' for Camerarius's '*configuratio*'. This time, however, Ristori's example of a '*constellatio*' (celestial configuration) is the conjunction of two planets, so here he actually refers to the same sort of example that Ptolemy did: a configuration of the planets, namely, a great conjunction (*coniunctio*) of Saturn and Jupiter.

On this basis, Ristori turns to the problem of predicting future floods:[106]

> Therefore, [if] I wanted to prognosticate a flood again by means of that configuration (*illa constellatio*), namely, by a conjunction of Saturn and Jupiter, but

---

105 I get my information on Deucalion from the eponymous article in the *Oxford Classical Dictionary*, 3rd ed., eds. Simon Hornblower and Antony Spawforth (Oxford: Oxford University Press, 1996), p. 460; and the more extensive article in Pauly-Wissowa, *Realencyclopädie der classischen Altertumswissenschaft*, series 1, vol. 5 (Stuttgart: Metzler, 1905), column 261ff.

106 It would not be surprising if traces of anxiety were still apparent in the 1540s due to the tremendous publicity drummed up for what turned out to be a great astrological non-event: the widely predicted but never occurring flood of 1524, supposedly indicated by a great conjunction in Pisces; see *"Astrologi Hallucinati"*; Niccoli, *Prophecy and People*; Talkenberger, *Sintflut*, and Grafton, *Cardano's Cosmos*. The anxiety had been building—with an accelerating velocity—ever since it was first predicted in 1499 by Johannes Stöffler, professor of mathematics and astrology at the University of Tübingen.

> [if] the triplicity were changed,[107] I would easily fall into error, since I will be observing a present conjunction of Saturn and Jupiter. And [if] the change of triplicity was made into [another] triplicity, I could predict a flood, but if I wished to predict a similar flood, I can be deceived because this configuration (*h[a]ec constellatio*) will not be altogether similar to that one (*illi*), since if it happens to be in Cancer, it will not be at the 14th degree.

Here Ristori instantiates his causal analysis. Although he could in theory predict another flood, nevertheless, if the great conjunction—and thus the efficient celestial cause—were not at 14° Cancer, it would not be the same kind of flood.[108] There are, thus, two crucial elements for analyzing the effects of a great conjunction as an efficient cause: [1] the conjunction itself of two particular planets—here Jupiter and Saturn—and [2] their precise location—in a particular zodiacal sign at a particular degree—which is required to condition the nature of the planetary effects. Implied here (and discussed in *Lectio* 4 and elsewhere) is a geometrical optical model of planetary action, where celestial influences are understood to act as rays of light with different angular relationships and thus intensities.[109]

Ristori continues, but now shifts his analysis from the simple case of different planetary positions to probe some of the deeper cosmologico-astronomical problems that arise from the vast differences of time involved. Here we can see a shift from the constrained focus of Ptolemy's original text to the greater range of issues permitted by Camerarius's less specific translation:

> Again, if that (*illa*, sc. *constellatio* [the older configuration]) were under the eighth sphere (*orbis*)[110] [and] this one (*h[a]ec*) under the ninth, or more correctly in the

---

[107] That is, if the conjunction took place in a different triplicity, in this case, *not* in a water sign.

[108] In his commentary on the pseudo-Aristotelian *De causis proprietatibus elementorum*, Albertus Magnus discusses the causal relationship of great conjunctions to floods. I discuss these texts in Volume I, Part I of my monograph.

[109] I discuss this more fully in relation to Fantoni in my 'Use and Abuse', and I reconstruct it in detail for the 13th century in Volume I, Part I of my monograph. I will take it ultimately through the 18th century in Volume II. We will see more traces of this model below.

[110] In his *Lexicon Mathematicum Astronomicum Geometricum* (1668), Gerolamo Vitali distinguishes '*orbis*', properly so-called, from '*sphaera*', which orbs are commonly called,

> imaginary zodiac (*in inmaginario zodiaco*), as moreover you have heard that in that elapsed year at the time of Deucalion and Pyrrha it was under the real zodiac (lit. 'sign-bearer', *sub signifero reali*), therefore I would not be able to prognosticate a future flood.

What do we have here? That earlier (*illa*) configuration (a conjunction) was in the eighth sphere.[111] *Haec*, on the other hand, refers to the modern configuration (conjunction) as taking place in the ninth sphere, which Ristori immediately says is more correctly called the 'imaginary' zodiac. The eighth sphere is the sphere of the fixed stars and actual constellations, and is also known as the firmament. The ninth sphere contains the 360° circle of the zodiac and its twelve 30° signs. It is fixed and unmoving, anchored to the *primum mobile*, and superimposed on the slowly moving eighth sphere, whose motion is measured in relation to the fixed ninth sphere. I will explore below what Ristori means by this curious terminology of the two zodiacs, imaginary and real, and its clearly stated implications for prognosticatory practice.[112]

Ristori's next example explicitly alludes to precession:

> Again, that was the case with the image (*imago* = constellation) of the ship (*navis*), which is one of the 48 constellations (*una ex 48 figuris*).[113] Moreover, this [is] not [what it used to be before] because the stars had gone beyond and above (*ulterius*

---

s.v. *orbis* (341). Vitali's *Lexicon* is very useful for terminology; Gerolamo Vitali, *Lexicon Mathematicum Astronomicum Geometricum* (anastatic reprint of the 1668 Paris edition), ed. Giuseppe Bezza (La Spezia: Agora Edizioni, 2003).

[111] *illa* in the paragraph above also related to the older configuration, refering to 14° Cancer, which Ristori identified as the site of the flood conjunction with Deucalion and Pyrrha.

[112] The distinction between the eighth and ninth orb or sphere and the corresponding real vs. imaginary zodiac is essentially the same distinction as that between sidereal and tropical zodiacs/years. In *The Heavenly Writing: Divination, Horoscopy, and Astronomy in Mesopotamian Culture* (Cambridge: Cambridge University Press, 2004), pp. 123–33, Francesca Rochberg discusses what we currently know about the origins of the zodiac. For the Babylonians, who created the grid of the zodiac with twelve signs of 30 degrees each, apparently around 500 BCE, the zodiac, including the equinoxes and solstices, were tied directly to the fixed stars. Thus, their zodiac was sidereally based and there is no evidence that they knew of precession. With the *Almagest* of circa 150 CE, however, the two zodiacs have split, and Ptolemy offers a theory of precession.

[113] For Ristori, then, *imago* and *figura* both refer here to actual constellations.

> *et superius processerunt*) [where they were before]. With respect to this, therefore, in order for a good astrologer (*bonus astrologus*) to prognosticate well, he ought to attend to these things.

According to Ristori, then, awareness of precession is important to an astrologer for prognosticating successfully. He does not, however, spell out *how* the astrologer ought to incorporate such an understanding in practice.

Completing his exposition of Ptolemy's lemma with another example, Ristori draws out some of the implications for astrological practice:

> Moreover, that configurations (*constellationes*) cannot be altogether similar (*non possint omnino similes*), he [Ptolemy] derives (*deducit*) from the length of time (*ex longitudine temporis*). For to the extent that there is such a great interval (*intercapedo*) of time, to that extent there is [also] a great restoration (*restitutio*) of the stars to their proper place (*in proprio loco*),[114] for understanding which, a person's lifetime (*vita hominis*) does not suffice. For if I wished to find that conjunction which would return Saturn and Jupiter to the 14th degree of Cancer in the *zodiacus mobilis*,[115] one person's lifetime does not suffice for knowing and having this. And also the Greek (*Grecus*)[116] says likewise that [the lives] of many men [does not suffice].

Ristori concludes by restating Ptolemy's conclusion that such complete knowledge is fundamentally beyond our grasp—given the short duration of our lives in the face of the heavens' long-term courses—and that good astrologers need to take this fundamental factor into account. In addition to explicitly alluding to precession, Ristori also adds the *zodiacus mobilis* to his earlier talk of real and imaginary zodiacs.

---

114 This seems to refer to the Stoic great year with its return to the beginning. 'Συναποκατάστασις' is Ptolemy's stoicizing term. It is also known as the world year or the Platonic great year (originally from *Timaeus* 39D), as we find in Macrobius's *Commentary on the Dream of Scipio* (William H. Stahl, ed. and trans., ch. XI, 219–222) and in Cardano's *Tetrabiblos* commentary (106). For the world year in Islamic astronomy, see Kennedy, 'World Year'.

115 That is, in the eighth sphere, as we will see, since it is the only zodiac that can move.

116 In his commentary, Ristori often uses the anonymous Greek commentator on Ptolemy, who was first published by Hieronymus Wolf, *In Claudii Ptolemaei Quadripartitum enarrator ignoti nominis* (Basel: Petri, 1559).

Ristori on the Identification of Pseudo-Prophets (see *Appendix* 3)

With Ristori's basic exposition of Ptolemy's passage in hand, we may now examine our key text, in which Ristori identifies Savonarola as the pseudo-prophet predicted by a recent great conjunction. Ristori begins by posing three difficulties inspired by Ptolemy's text:

> But it happens that there are doubts concerning the text (*circa textum dubitare*). First, whether it is possible to obtain the times of the return (*restitutio*) of the stars to their proper places. Secondly, that, if we cannot compare (*conferre*) our celestial configurations (*constellationes nostras*) [sc. with those of the ancients], how can we have a *scientia astrologiae*, from which every science and art comes to be by experiences (*ex quo omnis scientia et ars experimentis fit*)? Third, since it has been declared that celestial bodies act on things below (*corpora c[a]elestia agere in inferiora*): [a] Is it true, and [b] how do they [sc. the celestial bodies] act: by light only, or in another manner.[117]

Ristori makes the stakes clear and explicit. We will focus here on the second difficulty. Ristori begins by restating the problem more precisely:[118]

> With respect to the second difficulty, when it is said: How can a *scientia astrologiae* be made if the celestial configurations (*constellationes*) of the more recent [astronomer astrologers] (*iuniorum*) cannot be compared (*non possunt conferri*) to the observations of the ancients (*ad observationes antiquorum*)? To which we say that, although [1] the present configurations (*constellationes*) are not entirely similar (*non sint omnino similes*) and [2] they do not have every likeness (*omnis similitudo*) whatsoever for comparing, nevertheless, they [sc. the ancient and modern constellations] can be compared in something general and universal (*in aliquo comuni et universali*).

Although precise comparisons are out of the question, Ristori begins confronting the difficulty by offering another approach. He develops his position by clarifying the fundamental distinction between universal and particular predictions:

---

[117] The text of the statement of the three difficulties and Ristori's analysis of the first is in *Appendix 2*, in a composite Ristori base text with Fantoni's modifications. I discuss the third difficulty partially in my 'Use and Abuse', Part II.

[118] This text is in *Appendix 3*.

> Therefore, the art of astrology can be considered in two ways (*dupliciter*): [1] in one way, as a practitioner (*artifex*) predicts future events in their proper form (*praedicat futuros eventus in propria forma*) **[*]**, or [2] that he predicts such events in general [and] not distinctly (*in universali non distincte*). With respect to the first, it is not fitting for a human being to predict events in their proper form. Moreover, if we want universal and general understanding (*cognitio universalis et comunis*), I say that from these configurations compared with those (*ex his constellationibus collatis ad illas*) we can have this knowledge **[*]**.[119]

Ristori here distinguishes two styles of astrological prognosticatory practices. The first 'predicts future events in their proper form'. This practice is illegitimate, as we are informed by Thomas Aquinas in his *Summa Theologiae* IIª, IIªᵉ, 95, which was still authoritative on these matters in the sixteenth century.[120] The second practice predicts future events in general and not distinctly, that is, not in precise and particular detail. Ristori says that we can gain this second type of universal and general knowledge by comparing ancient and modern celestial configurations, the very crux of Ptolemy's lemma.

To begin instantiating his approach, Ristori introduces the major authority in the field of historical astrology, namely, Abū Ma'shar, and immediately begins discussing great conjunctions to exemplify what he means by 'constellationes', namely, celestial configurations:

> Albumasar says in his book *On Great Conjunctions* (*De magnis coniunctionibus*) that [1] [when there is] a conjunction of the two superior [sc. planets: Jupiter and Saturn], having changed from [one] triplicity to another, and [2] there were some one of the inferior [sc. planets] in the third [place = house][121] from the ascendant or in the ninth, this signifies a pseudo-prophet (*significat Pseudoprofetam*).

For Abū Ma'shar as for Ristori's adaptation here, the astrological structures are fundamentally the same: both require great conjunctions with a planet in the

[119] [*] indicates a marginal note added by Fantoni into Ristori's lecture. I discuss them in the following section.

[120] I discuss this text in Volume I, Part 2 of my forthcoming monograph.

[121] As we saw above, both place and house can be ambiguous, but here it must refer to the terrestrial houses, since it is defined in relation to the ascendant, which is not the case with celestial houses = the signs of the zodiac.

third (or ninth) house. The primary difference between them, however, is that for Abū Ma'shar the relevant planet in the ninth (or third) house is Saturn, whereas for Ristori it is Mars, which Ristori considers an inferior planet, as we will see. Another significant difference is that Abū Ma'shar only mentions prophets, whereas Ristori explicitly states that this configuration indicates *pseudo*-prophets. Perhaps the different planets in the ninth house—Saturn and Mars—account for the different outcomes.

Ristori then provides a significant historical example to instantiate Abū Ma'shar's slightly modified formula which, at the same time, illustrates the differences of 'constellationes' (celestial configurations) present and past, and their relevance for the two modes of prediction (we will recall that Ptolemy himself was also concerned with the implications for prediction):

> Let us accept that after the year of the savior in the year 571 there was a conjunction (*coniunctio*) of Jupiter and Saturn [that marked the shift] from [one] triplicity to [another] triplicity at the fifth degree of Scorpio, and Mars was in the ninth house from the ascendant. Therefore it signified a prophet (*significabat ergo profetam*). Afterwards, Mohammed (*Maumeth*) rose up (*surrexit*) against the law of Christ, promising gifts and the goods of fortune, and it predicted [that it would take place] in the year 620 from the incarnation of Christ.

Here we have a case where Saturn and Jupiter conjoined at 5° Scorpio (from a previous conjunction in the air triplicity, with Mars in the ninth house (in Gemini). The great conjunction indicates the advent of a prophet, who appeared as such in 620. We possess several historical examples of horoscopes for both: [1] the annual revolution for 571 that indicated the birth of a prophet, which took place the year before Mohammed's birth, and [2] the nativity of the religion (the year of the Hijra).[122]

Ristori then turns to a more recent example:

> Also in the year 1425 I observed (*observavi*) a conjunction of Jupiter and Saturn at the 25th degree of Scorpio, and Mars was in the ninth [house] from the ascendant. Therefore, it signified a pseudo-prophet, as Mohammed was not. But it well signified a pseudo-prophet, although both (*ambae* [sc. conjunctions]) were in a

---

122 Kennedy and Pingree discuss these famous horoscopes in Edward S. Kennedy and David Pingree, *The Astrological History of Masha'allah* (Cambridge, MA: Harvard University Press, 1971) as do Yamamoto and Burnett in *On Historical Astrology*.

> water triplicity. Therefore, a good astrologer (*bonus astrologus*) will say that a pseudo-prophet will arise (*orietur pseudopropheta*). Afterwards, in the year 1492 the pseudo-prophet Fra Girolamo Savonarola (*pseudoprofeta frater Hieronimus Savonarola*) appeared in Italy.

Ristori's second example took place in the relatively recent past, fully 854 years after the earlier one, although both great conjunctions occurred in Scorpio. The great conjunction of 1425 was at 25° Scorpio, and also has Mars in the ninth house. These are indeed strikingly similar configurations, and for Ristori, following but modifying Abū Ma'shar, the first indicates a prophet and the second a pseudo-prophet.[123] We should also note that Ristori uses the seemingly strange locution 'I observed' (*observavi*) for something that happened well before his birth in 1492. He seems to mean 'observation' in the sense of looking something up in a table or ephemeris.[124]

Ristori now compares the two situations:

> Let us see [1] how they [sc. Mohammed and Savonarola] agree among themselves, and [2] [how] each (*utraque* [sc. conjunction]) signified a pseudo-prophet [*], as they appeared to be. This cannot be denied. [ad 1] But let us see how these men agreed. They agreed in that each affirmed that Christ was a prophet, and they [sc. each] prophesied (*profetarunt*) a prophet. [And] they agreed in something else, that just as Mohammed contradicted the Church, likewise did he (*ille* [sc. Savonarola]), because he contradicted the apostolic see.[125] Again, how Mohammed promised and affirmed joys and wealth of the body (*divitias corporis*), as is clear in the *Koran* (*in Alcorano*), and as Avicenna says in the ninth [book] of his *Metaphysics*, and likewise misery. Likewise, he [Savonarola] promised great joys and miseries to his fellow citizens,[126] just as Mohammed did, and that that city will be most flourishing (*florentissima*) and increasing day by day.

---

123 Ristori here seems not to characterize Mohammed as a pseudo-prophet, even though he rose to attack Christianity. In the next section this sanguine characterization changes.

124 See Park, 'Observation'.

125 See Weinstein, *Savonarola and Florence*, for Savonarola's problematic relations with Rome in the context of Florence's also difficult relationship with Rome at this time. I must also reiterate that Savonarola's rise to power only took place within the context of the power vacuum created at the time of Lorenzo de' Medici's death and in relation to the anxiety surrounding the French king, Charles VIII's profoundly disruptive invasion of Italy.

126 Including the famous *Flagellum Dei* as found on coins, etc.

For Ristori, then, Savonarola compares closely with Mohammed in their activities as prophets and/or pseudo-prophets, both of whom were predicted by structurally similar but inexact great(er) conjunctions in Scorpio, with Mars (its ruling planet) in the ninth house.

Now Ristori addresses the crucial structural issue identified in Ptolemy's lemma: can there be a science of astrology if ancient celestial configurations cannot be compared with modern ones?

> [ad 2] But because the configurations (*constellationes*) were not altogether similar (*non fuerunt omnino similes*), since that (*illa* [sc. *coniunctio*]) was at 5 degrees of actual Scorpio (*scorpio realis*) but that (*illa*) was at 25 degrees of *scorpio imaginarius*. But it refers basically to the same thing[127] (*sed quasi ad idem revertitur*), since by taking away the 2nd immovable degree (*auferendo secundo gradus inmobilis*), which the sun crossed (*sol pertransivit*) when it went to the first degree of the mobile [movable, sc. zodiac], it remains that the sun finished at the 5th movable degree [= of the *zodiacus realis*]. But the configurations (*constellationes*) were not altogether similar, because those stars inhering (*haerentes*) in the heavens were different from those at that birth (*in ista nativitate*), for which reason they also said different things, since this[128] affirms that Christ is the son of God, but not Mohammed.[129]

Here Ristori returns to the distinction between the two zodiacs, one real (sidereal) and one imaginary (tropical), from his exposition of Ptolemy's lemma.

The conjunction of 571 took place at 5° of Scorpio *realis*, that is, on the eighth sphere or moving zodiac with actual stars; that of 1425 took place at 25° Scorpio in the imaginary zodiac, which is fixed and unmoving, anchored to an original location of 0° Aries on the *primum mobile*. The major question, then, is how far did the eighth sphere move during those 854 years between the two great conjunctions, and how does this modify (or diminish) the 20° differential between the two locations? The rate of precession according to Vitali is 1° in 53.5 years, so the point of the conjunction seems to have precessed almost exactly 16° since 571.[130] This would precess the location where the 571 conjunction took

---

[127] Sc. to the same point or place.

[128] [*hic* (he?); I am not sure what the referent is.]

[129] I wonder if the technical details of the analysis got confused in the recording.

[130] I have not encountered an explicit discussion by Ristori or Fantoni of the rate of precession, so for now I use Vitali's as found in the article 'Aries' in his *Lexicon*.

place on the moving eighth sphere (*zodiacus realis*) to 21° Scorpio on the imaginary (tropical) zodiac, and thus much closer to the later conjunction, but still not exact. Nevertheless, instead of discussing this, which is implicit, Ristori seems to offer a different type of adjustment relating to the motion of the sun and involving the difference between the mobile and fixed zodiacs.[131]

Now Ristori returns to the earlier distinction between universal and particular predictions of future events as he offers his resolution of the difficulty:

> From which, what should be said concerning that difficulty appears, [namely,] that [1] either the astrologer predicts 'in particular' and in its proper form (*in particulari et propria forma*) or [2] 'in general' (*in universali*). The first is [the prerogative] of God alone, not of men, because it is necessary that [He] foreknow all causes (*praecognoscere omnes causas*). Human beings and astrologers can understand future events with a certain indistinct understanding (*cognitione quadam non distincta*), but with some knowledge making for generality (*aliqua notitia faciente ad universalitatem*), as we will discuss in another *lectio*,[132] and the second [sc. doubt] is resolved.

With such questions about God's foreknowledge in relation to man's, astrology enters the theologian's purview. As Ristori had stated before, astrology can legitimately supply general knowledge; this is in no way problematic, at least according to Thomas Aquinas, whom Ristori cites with approval, as we will see. It is unclear to me what Ristori's conclusion here has to do with his example beyond that precise knowledge (and thus predictions) are impossible and that general conjectural knowledge (and predictions) are both possible and legitimate.

Ristori then goes on to introduce his response to the third difficulty, which will lead into *Lectio* four. It also concerns the efficient cause, but this time how it acts, thereby providing insight and instruction into astrology's natural philosophical foundations:

> But in the third [difficulty is to be sought] whether celestial bodies act on these things below, in which question not only do we wish to explain (*exponere*) that

---

[131] I do not fully understand what Ristori is doing here. Nor is his reference to *ista nativitas* and its implications for Christ's status as a Prophet and Son of God vis-à-vis Mohammed's clear to me.

[132] As we will see, Fantoni crosses out this cross-reference, which seems to be to *Lectio* 6.

celestial bodies act, but we intend to declare how they act: either by motion alone, or by light, or by a *virtus spiritualis*, namely, '*influentia*', or in all these modes. Again, whether they act on everything which is under the moon, [and] whether they distinguish particular effects, since they say that it is only a universal cause (*causa universalis*), against Pico and Girolamo Savonarola. Therefore, let us hold with D[ivine] Thomas. And we will respond to Pico.

This is the subject of *Lectio* 4, whose contents I discuss elsewhere.[133] Thus Ristori completes *Lectio* 3 by mentioning Savonarola for the second time, but this time in the company of Giovanni Pico della Mirandola, whom Fantoni does not cross out.

As we can see, Ristori continues to develop his analysis of universal vs. particular knowledge by discussing how the celestial bodies act and, in particular, whether their action can distinguish particular effects, thus addressing the ontological side of the epistemological dimension addressed in *Lectio* 3. As Ristori correctly notes, universal vs. particular action was a central distinction used by Pico in the analysis and attempted refutation of astrology's natural philosophical foundations in *Disputations* Book III.[134]

Fantoni's Modifications of Ristori's Lectures (see *Appendix* 4)

Let us now explore Ristori's analysis more deeply as we address Fantoni's more prominent modifications of Ristori's lectures, including his expurgations of Savonarola's name. I will also indicate how both Ristori and Fantoni used Thomas Aquinas's analysis and authority to interpret Ptolemy. Fantoni modified Ristori's lectures in two primary domains: [A] The universal vs. particular distinction in relation to texts by Thomas Aquinas, and [B] the direct discussion of sensitive religious matters. In the first and less sensitive domain, Fantoni's changes are more fine-tuning than revisionist. In the second, however, his revisions are more dramatic. I will treat each theme in turn.[135]

The first texts to be compared are those treating the universal-particular

---

133 Rutkin, 'Use and Abuse', Part II.

134 For more on this, see chapter 6 of my thesis.

135 The texts and translations here are represented as they appear in *Appendix 4*, namely, with Ristori's base text as modified by Fantoni, whose deletions are indicated with lines struck through, and additions with < >.

distinction in relation to texts by Thomas Aquinas.[136] The first text is rather long and includes two extensive marginal notes by Fantoni in addition to minor revisions. The longer notes have a mark in the text and the associated note in the margin:[137]

> Therefore, the art of astrology can be considered in two ways: in one way as a practitioner (*artifex*) predicts future events ~~in their proper form~~ (~~*in propria forma*~~) [*] <in their causes (*in suis causis*), but not in themselves (*in seipsis*), as we say>, or [2] that he predicts such events in general and not distinctly. With respect to the first, it is not fitting for a human being to predict events in their proper form. Moreover, if we want universal and general understanding, I say that from these configurations compared with those we can have this knowledge [*] <by the inclination of the celestial bodies, and naturally, not in another manner, since God alone knows future things in themselves (*in seipsis*)>[.][138]

In this rich passage we can see that Fantoni first changes Ristori's initial formulation from *in propria forma* to *in suis causis*, which he then contrasts to *in seipsis*. This slight modification in terminology brings Fantoni's lectures into closer connection with Thomas's language in *Summa Theologiae* II^{a}, II^{ae}, 95. Secondly, in a parallel passage, Fantoni tells us that we get this universal and

---

136 D. P. Walker describes Thomas's stature as a pro-astrological authority in the 16th century, especially in the richly astrological commentaries of Cardinal Caietanus (Tommaso de Vio), which were embraced as the official version authorized by the Council of Trent in *Spiritual and Demonic Magic from Ficino to Campanella* (London: Warburg Institute, 1958; repr. 1975, University of Notre Dame Press), p. 215. On Thomas's authority in the Renaissance in general, see Paul Oskar Kristeller, 'Thomism and the Italian Thought of the Renaissance', in *Medieval Aspects of Renaissance Learning: Three Essays by Paul Oskar Kristeller*, trans. and ed. Edward P. Mahoney (Durham, NC: Duke University Press, 1974), pp. 29–91.

137 < > represent additions by Fantoni. If they follow [*], they are marginal additions put in their proper place in the text.

138 [F: 15v–16r] 'itaque ars astrologi(a)e dupliciter considerari potest[,] uno modo ut artifex predicat eventus futuros ~~in propria forma~~ [*] <in suis causis[,] non autem in seipsis sicut dicimus> vel quod predicat tales eventus in universali non distincte; quo ad primam non convenit homini predicere eventus in propria forma[.] si autem velimus cognitionem universalem et comunem[,] dico quod ex his constellationibus collatis ad illas possumus habere hanc cognitionem [*] <per inclinationem corporum celestium, et naturaliter non altero modo[,] quia solus deus cognoscit futura in seipsis>[.]'

general knowledge from the inclination of the celestial bodies, which are thus the causes. To this he contrasts, once again, knowledge of future things in themselves, which is not the proper way for human beings to gain knowledge.[139]

Ristori's second mention of Savonarola, which we just examined, occurs in a similar context of the discussion of universal vs. particular causation, as Ristori and Fantoni end *Lectio* 3:

> [F: 17r (see image in *Appendix* 5)] rursus an agant omnia qu(a)e sub luna sunt an distinguant effectus particulares quia dicunt quod est tantum causa universalis contra Picum ~~et Hieronimum Savonarolam~~[140] tenemus igitur cum D. Thoma[141] et respondebimus Pico:.

We can now see that both Ristori and Fantoni allude to Thomas's authoritative analysis to defend astrology against Pico's and Savonarola's attacks. Fantoni, however, responded only tacitly to Savonarola, for reasons about which we can only speculate (as I will in the conclusion).[142]

*

The second set of modified texts relate to the direct discussion of sensitive religious matters. Here there are many more deletions. In our first text, Ristori identified Savonarola as the predicted pseudo-prophet:

> Afterwards, in the year 1492 appeared ~~in Italy the pseudo-prophet brother Girolamo Savonarola~~.[143] Let us see how they [sc. Mohammed and Savonarola]

---

139 Fantoni also reiterates some of these points elsewhere, but they need not detain us here: [1] [F: 16v–17r] 'quia aut Astrologus predicit in particulari <et in se ipsis> ~~et propria forma~~ vel in universali[.]' [2] [F: 17r] 'homines et astrologi possunt cognoscere <et> futuros eventus cognitione quadam non distincta[,] sed aliqua notitia faciente ad universitalitatem ~~ut dicemus in alia lectione~~ <et denique per inclinationem corporum celestium>'.

140 With the '*Hieronimus*' double lined and the Savonarola blotched, but with the S and L clear. This reading thus confirms the other one just below.

141 Sc. *Aquinas*.

142 We can more fully understand Ristori's and Fantoni's analyses by exploring Thomas Aquinas's discussion of astrology in relation to the divinatory part of supersition in *Summa Theologiae* II^{a} II^{ae} 95, which I do in Volume I, Part 2 of my monograph.

143 As we can see in the photograph (*Appendix 5*, F: 16r), this line is blotted out pretty

> agree among themselves, and that each (*utraque* [sc. conjunction]) signified ~~a pseudo-prophet~~ [*] <an inclination of a certain false person>, as they appeared. ~~This cannot be denied~~. But let us see how these [sc. prophets] agreed. They agreed that each affirmed ~~that Christ was a prophet and they prophesied a prophet. [And] they agreed in something else, that just as Mohammed contradicted the Church, likewise does he (*ille* [sc. Savonarola]) because he contradicted the apostolic see. Again, how Mohammed promised and affirmed joys and wealth of the body, as is clear in the *Koran*, and [as] Avicenna says in the ninth [book] of his *Metaphysics*, and likewise misery~~, <since> he [Savonarola] likewise promised great joys and miseries to his fellow citizens, just as Mohammed did, and that that city will be most flourishing (*florentissima*) and increasing day by day.[144]

In this passage, Fantoni anonymizes Ristori's pointed and particular identification (however controversial), and thus ironically instantiates Ristori's own proviso that astrology cannot make particular but only general predictions. As we can see, Fantoni crossed out the entire discussion, including all mention of pseudo-prophets, and the fact that they both agree that Christ was a prophet.

In another passage, we see Fantoni do something similar:

> Since there were some stars inhering in the heavens and different stars in that nativity, wherefore they also said that they are different ~~since this [he?] affirmed that Christ was the son of God, but not Mohammed~~[.][145]

---

thickly, especially the name, but it also seems clear that it says Savonarola: the '*mus*' from the first name, and the S and L from the last are pretty clear.

144 [F: 16r–17v] 'apparuit postea anno 1492 ~~in italia pseudoprofeta frater Hieronimus Savonarola~~, videamus quomodo conveniant inter se utraque significavit ~~pseudoprofetam~~ <inclinationem cuiusdam falsi hominis> sicut et apparuerunt, ~~hoc non potest negari~~, sed videamus quomodo convenerunt isti[.] convenerunt quod uterque affirmavit ~~christum fuisse profetam et profetarunt profetam convenerunt in alio quia sicut Maumeth contradixit eccles(a)e similiter. et ille quia contradixit sedi apostolic(a)e, rursus quemadmodum Maumeth. promittebat ac pollicebatur felicitates et divitias corporis ut patet in Alcorano et refert Avicenna 9.o su(a)e Methaph(ysi)ces. et similiter miseriam~~ <quoniam> similiter ille promisit magnas felicitates et miserias suis civibus sicut Maumeth et civitatem illam florentissimam futuram esse ac in dies crescendam[.]'

145 [F:17v] 'quia ali(a)e fuerunt ill(a)e stell(a)e c(a)elo h(a)erentes et ali(a)e in ista nativitate, quapropter diversa quoque dicebant ~~quia hic affirmabat christum filium Dei, sed non Maumeth~~[.]'

Fantoni thus continues to remove all the material relating astrology and religion, especially where astrology might seem to confirm (and thus subordinate) religion. Perhaps Fantoni follows Pico here, at least in this respect.

We can also see this in Fantoni's modifications to the first difficulty (*Appendix* 2), in which Ristori discusses the eternity of the world and the eternity of time implied by perpetual tables. Fantoni removes both references, as we can see:

> With respect to the first [difficulty], they say that it is easy to discover the return of the stars to their proper places because, given ~~the eternity of the world and of men~~ [*] <the multitude of years of the world up to the day of judgment> and the continuous generation of men [*] <up to that time>, we can have continuous observations and observe the celestial configurations (*constellationes*). Secondly, there are ~~perpetual~~ tables (*tabulae* ~~*aeternae*~~) <made, computed and calculated up to the end of the world>. Therefore, ~~for all time~~ (~~*eterno tempore*~~) <for a virtually infinite time (*tempore fere infinito*)> we can compute and calculate, and discover these returns.[146]

Ristori here made two strong claims, but not in his own name and without identifying who made them, concerning the likelihood that knowledge of the 'world-year' can be attained. As stated by Ristori, this position implies the eternity of the world.

In his modifications to Ristori's lecture, Fantoni primarily addresses theologically sensitive issues. In particular, Fantoni here transforms the eternity of the world and its concommitant eternal tables from a truly infinite eternity into vast but finite expanses of time. Aristotelian views of the world's eternity were in pointed tension with Judeo-Christian views of the world's creation in time by an all-powerful deity. Although Ristori ultimately rejects this position, he does present it. Fantoni, on the other hand, softens its theologically sensitive contours, even in a hypothetical formulation.

---

[146] [F: 14v–15r] 'Ad primum dicunt quod facile est invenire restitutionem stellarum ad propria loca quia data ~~eternitate mundi et hominum~~ <mundi multitudine annorum usque ad diem iudicii> et continua hominum generatione <usque ad illud tempus>[,] poterimus continuas observationes habere et constellationes observare. Secundo tabul(a)e sunt <usque ad mundi finem facte supputate et calculate> ~~(a)etern(a)e~~[,] ergo ~~eterno tempore~~ <tempore fere infinito> possumus supputare et calculare et invenire illas restitutiones[.]'

Conclusion

Why then did Fantoni soften Ristori's attack on Savonarola? Perhaps the answer lies at least partially in the fact that Fantoni's lectures were offered at a particular moment in the context of Savonarola's changing fortunes in sixteenth-century Florence.[147] As we know, Ristori offered his lectures at the University of Pisa in the 1540s, that is, at the troubled beginnings of Cosimo's reign before he had securely established his own power.[148] By lending prophetic support, Savonarola's legacy in Florence had heretofore played an important religio-political role in promoting a pro-Republican and thus anti-Medici (as well as anti-papal) political agenda that had flared up several times already, especially from 1494 to 1512 and from 1527 to 1530. Also in early 1537 Lorenzino de' Medici murdered his cousin Alessandro de' Medici, the first duke of Florence, which Republicans hoped would stir up significant anti-Medici sentiment.

As it turned out, the last major flare-up of anti-Savonarolan polemics in Florentine politics occurred from 1545 to 1550, precisely while Ristori was teaching at Pisa. Extremely sensitive to the Savonarolan threat, Duke Cosimo took controlling pro-Savonarolan discourse and activism very seriously indeed, especially at San Marco, where he squashed it effectively with the repressive arm of an increasingly absolutist state. In this context it is not surprising that Ristori, the duke's personal astrologer, would take the opportunity in his lecture course to further blacken Savonarola's name.

By the 1580s, however, the political dimension of Savonarola's legacy had almost completely dissipated, having transformed now almost entirely into a devotional mode. In fact, Savonarola had, by now, became such a symbol of Counter-Reformation sanctity that Fantoni could simply erase Savonarola's name from even mildly controversial contexts; at the same time he removed the entire discussion of pseudo-prophets altogether.[149]

---

147 Dall'Aglio's accessable and authoritative *Savonarola and Savonarolism* deeply informs this conclusion. Investigating Ristori's and Fantoni's personal motives for attacking or defending Savonarola would also be extremely valuable.

148 For an accessable discussion, see Cochrane, *Florence in the Forgotten Centuries*.

149 Dall'Aglio brings attention to another text, the Servite Cosimo Favilla's *Flagellum Pseudoprophetarum* (1524–25), which attacked Savonarola heatedly. In it, Savonarola's name was subsequently erased in manuscript by a censor, but, unusually, to *defend* Savonarola's good name. In the event, the censor was so effective that the pseudo-prophet in question was not identified as Savonarola until Dall'Aglio himself recently did

Furthermore, in 1581, soon before Fantoni's course at Pisa (1585–86), Tommaso Buoninsegni, a Dominican professor of theology at the University of Florence, whose mother house was San Marco—Pico's and Savonarola's church—translated Savonarola's attack on divinatory astrology into Latin from its originally published Italian.[150] Buoninsegni's translation began with a long apologetic introduction concerning Pico's and Savonarola's anti-astrological writings. Here is D.P. Walker's account:

> This *apologia* is more like a plea for leniency than a defense. Opponents of their works, we are told, claim that they have proved nothing against sober and prudent astrologers, who are strictly orthodox, do not pretend to foretell particular events, and are careful to subject all their predictions to the inscrutable will of God. Moreover, these defenders of good astrology have the authority of Thomas Aquinas on their side, who 'in innumerable places' teaches that even man's mind and will are indirectly influenced by the stars, through their effect on his body. Buoninsegni, then, instead of answering these critics, says: 'Indeed, to speak freely my opinion in so grave a matter, I have never been able to convince myself, nor be led to believe that Pico, Savonarola and other excellent men wished to condemn true and legitimate astrology'.
>
> Good astrologers, like Ptolemy himself, take care to safeguard free-will and [God's] providence. It was against the bad astrologers, who subject man's will entirely to the heavens and who derive religions from planetary conjunctions, that Pico and Savonarola were writing. If sometimes, carried away by their just anger against this bad, superstitious astrology, they went too far and also attacked good astrology, Buoninsegni begs the reader to forgive them[.] [...]
>
> Not content with this curious *apologia* for Pico and Savonarola, Buoninsegni does his best to transform the latter's treatise into a work in favour of astrology by means of copious annotation. The authorities he uses in this are mainly Thomas Aquinas and his pro-astrological commentator, Cardinal Caietano (57–8)[.]

---

so: 'Il *Flagellum pseudoprophetarum* di Cosimo Favilla: Nota su un'opera antisavonaroliana del primo cinquecento', *Memorie Domenicane* 29 n.s. (1998), pp. 442–51. A similarly defensive erasure seems also to be the case in Fantoni's lectures.

[150] I get my information for this paragraph from Walker (*Spiritual and Demonic Magic*, pp. 57–58), and U. Tucci's *DBI* article (s.v., [1972] 15: pp. 260–64), who mentions but does not discuss Buoninsegni's relevant translation. See also Claudio Gigante, 'Un interprete cinquecentesco della polemica antiastrologica di Savonarola: Tommaso Buoninsegni' in *Nella luce degli astri. L'astrologia nella cultura del Rinascimento*, ed. Ornella Pompeo Faracovi, (Sarzana: Agorà Edizioni, 2004), pp. 101–17.

Ironically, resuscitating Savonarola's standing in the 1580s also seems to have promoted a pro-astrological refashioning of his original, strongly anti-astrological stance.[151] Finally, it seems worth noting that, in a context discussing pseudo-prophets in mid- and late-sixteenth-century Catholic Italy, neither Ristori nor Fantoni mention Martin Luther, as Cardano and Luca Gaurico had done.[152] Even with this limited sounding, I hope I have shown that there is much of interest in exploring the teaching of astrology in sixteenth-century commentaries on Ptolemy's *Tetrabiblos*.[153] There is much more work to be done on these rich, but understudied texts. This is also true for commentaries on the pseudonymous *Centiloquium*, and for the Arabic and Latin traditions of both.

---

[151] For some of the complexities of the reading and response to Savonarola's and Pico's attacks on astrology, primarily in the 16th century and with much rich bibliography, see Stefano Dall'Aglio, 'Da Girolamo Savonarola a Tommaso Erasto: Itinerari di una polemica astrologica tra Firenze e Heidelberg', in *Scritti in ricordo di Armando Saitta* (Milan: Franco Angeli, 2002), pp. 42–71.

[152] See Warburg, 'Pagan-Antique Prophecy'.

[153] Comparing Ristori and Fantoni's treatments with Cardano's would also be worthwhile.

Appendices 1–4 (Primary Texts)

[R: MS Riccardiana 157] Ristori Version: I put [*] in the text where Fantoni adds something, whether a few words in the text, or a significant note in the margin; I distinguish them with normal type for the former and bold for the latter. The paragraphing, punctuating and capitalising is from Ristori's text, with my added punctuation in brackets []. '(a)e' indicates an e with a cedilla. The symbols of planets and zodiac signs in the text have been left as written.

Appendix 1: Ristori's 'exponere textum'; From R: Lectio Tertia (9r–10v)

[R: 9r] Hoc quoque accidit ut configurationes quas veteres tradiderunt. Exponemus textum[.] [...]

[R: 9v][154] Quod autem contingat errare etiam apud peritum Astrologum ex difficultate artis ob magnitudinem rerum sciendarum[,] declarat prius in universum dicendo in particulari[.] primum dicitur non esse inconveniens peritum Astrologum errare si conferat suas constellationes ad observationes antiquorum[.] ratio est quia effectus reduci debeat in suas causas similes, sed effectus contingentes tempore iuniorum et pr(a)esentis temporibus proficiscuntur ex causis non similibus causis antiquorum[.] Igitur prognosticando cum observatione illorum non per has constellationes contingit errare[.]

est igitur summa rationis quia h(a)e constellationes non sunt omnino similes illis[,] ideo effectus [R: 10r] non omnino similes illis[.] ut si gratia exempli, ego dicam ante diluvium Deucalionis contingit constellatio scilicet coniunctio ♄i et ♃ in 14.o gradu ♋i et h(a)ec constellatio efficit illud diluvium[.] ergo per illam constellationem voluero rursus prognosticari diluvium[,] scilicet per coniunctionem ♄i et ♃[,] sed mutata sit triplicitas[,] facile capiam errorem[,] quoniam ego observabo ad praesens coniunctionem ♄ et ♃[,] et facta sit mutatio triplicitatis in triplicitatem[,] possem prognosticari diluvium, sed si simile diluvium prognosticari voluero[,] possum decipi quia h(a)ec constellatio non erit omnino similis illi, quia si continget esse in ♋ non erit in 14 gradu[.]

154 There is no paragraphing in the text, so I have added what seems reasonable here.

rursus si fuit illa sub 8.o orbe[,] h(a)ec sub 9.o vel rectius in maginario (*sic* [*imaginario*]) zodiaco, ut autem audistis anno elapso illo tempore Deucalionis et Pirrh(a)e fuit sub signifero reali[,] ideo non potero prognosticari futurum diluvium[.] rursus fuit illa cum imagine navis qu(a)e est una ex 48 figuris, h(a)ec autem non[,] quia stell(a)e ulterius et superius processerunt[.]

Ad hoc ergo ut bonus Astrologus debeat bene prognosticari, h(a)ec debet advertere, quod autem constellationes non possint esse omnino similes, deducit ex longitudine temporis[,] nam est adeo magna intercapedo temporis et adeo magna restitutio stellarum in proprio loco [*][,] quod non sufficit vita hominis ad id cognoscendum[,] nam si illam coniunctionem voluero reperire quod redeat ♄s et ♃ ad 14 gradum ♋ in zodiaco mobili[,] non est sufficiens [R: 10v] ad cognoscendum et habendum hoc vita unius hominis et etiam Grecus dicit nec plurium hominum:—

Appendix 2: [A] Ristori's text of the three difficulties, and [B] the text of Ristori's treatment of the first difficulty with Fantoni's modifications

[A][R: 11v–12v] Sed contingit circa textum dubitare et primo, an possibile sit nancisci tempora restitutionum stellarum ad propria loca; 2.o quia si non possemus conferre constellationes nostras[,] quomodo possemus habere scientiam Astrologi(a)e ex quo omnis scientia et ars experimentis fit; 3.o quia declaratum est corpora c(a)elestia agere in inferiora, an verum sit et quomodo agunt an lumine tantum vel alio modo:—

[B][155] Ad primum dicunt quod facile est invenire restitutionem stellarum [F: 15r] ad propria loca quia data ~~eternitate mundi et hominum~~ <mundi multitudine annorum usque ad diem iudicii> et continua hominum generatione <usque ad illud tempus> poterimus continuas observationes habere et constellationes observare.

---

155 I offer Ristori's base text here with Fantoni's changes because Fantoni's modifications relate to theologically sensitive subjects, as they do in the second difficulty, as we can see in *Appendix 4*, which also gives Fantoni's modifications; see the editorial conventions discussed there.

Secundo tabul(a)e sunt <usque ad mundi finem facte supputate et calculate> ~~(a)etern(a)e~~[,] ergo ~~eterno tempore~~ <tempore fere infinito> possumus supputare et calculare et invenire illas restitutiones[.] tamen habemus in oppositum experientiam[,] fuerunt enim aliqui qui crediderunt restitutionem fieri in 10000 annis[,] Macrobius in (*sic*) de somnio scipionis dixit in 15000[,] tertius ut Iosephus dixit id fieri in 40000 annis[,] alii in 36000[,] iuniores dicunt in 49000[.] si igitur haberemus restitutiones stellarum ad propria loca[,] haberemus tempus mensurans has restitutiones[,] quia cum sint numeri compositi[,] igitur ex 2.a 7.i elementorum [Euclid?] habebimus eodem communem mensuram metientem[,] sed non est id tempus[,] ergo vultis videre quia cursus 8.i orbis secundum omnes transit 30000 annos[,] sed dato quod fiat in 36000 annis[,] utrum sit numerus metiens hos numeros? <quo videtur> ~~non~~ quia [Saturn]i motus sit in 30 annis[,] [Jupiter]is in 12 et similiter de reliquis secundum proprios motus, ~~ut scitis~~[.] ergo non dantur ~~ist(a)e~~ restitutiones[,] nec per successionem id fieri [F: 15v] potest[,] quia dicunt tempus esse infinitum; patet quoniam propter <magnas> ~~grandes~~ mutationes sicut habetur in fine primi Metheo(rum) deficiunt artes et primo methaf(ysicae), et scienti(a)e continuo innovantur [R: 12v] quia adveniunt bella magna, pestes universales et homines moriuntur et scienti(a)e deperduntur:—

Quod autem dicunt de tabul~~is externis~~ <arum calcula(ret?) supputatione> falluntur quia tabul(a)e que fuerunt fact(a)e ante Hipparcum delet(a)e sunt[.] postea Pto(lemaeu)s fecit tabulas, quae delet(a)e sunt[,] similiter tabul(a)e Pisarum et Alfonsi delet(a)e sunt[.] sed necesse est saltem singulis 200is annis restaurare tabulas:—

Appendix 3: The second difficulty, with Ristori's identification of Savonarola as a false prophet

[R: 12v–14r] Ad secundam difficultatem quando dicitur si non possunt conferri constellationes iuniorum ad observationes antiquorum quomodo scientia Astrologi(a)e facta? ad quam dicimus quod licet constellationes presentes non sint omnino similes et omnem similitudinem omnino non habeant conferendi[,] tamen in aliquo comuni et universali possunt conferri[.] itaque ars astrologi(a)e dupliciter considerari potest[,] uno modo ut artifex predicat eventus futuros in propria forma [*] vel quod predicat tales eventus in universali non distincte; quo ad primam non convenit homini predicere eventus in propria forma[.] si autem velimus cognitionem universalem et comunem[,] dico quod ex his constellationibus collatis ad illas possumus habere hanc cognitionem [*][.] dicit Albumasar in libro de magnis coniunctionibus quod coniunctio duorum superiorum mutata de triplicitate ad aliam et fuerit aliquis[156] inferiorum in 3.o[157] ab ascendente vel in 9.o significat Pseudoprofetam. accipiamus quod post annum Salvatoris anno [R: 13r] 571 facta est coniunctio ♃ et ♄ de triplicitate in triplicitatem in 5 gradu ♏ et ♂ fuit in 9.a[158] ab ascendente[;] significabat ergo profetam[.] surrexit postea Maumeth contra legem christi qui promisit dona et bona fortun(a)e, et predicavit anno 620 a christi incarnatione.

Observavi quoque anno 1425 coniunctionem ♃ et ♄ i. in 25.o gradu ♏ et ♂ erat in 9.a ab ascendente[,] igitur significavit Pseudoprofetam ut fuit Maumeth non, sed bene significavit pseudoprophetam[,] licet amb(a)e fuerint in triplicitate aquea, igitur bonus astrologus dicet quod orietur pseudopropheta[.][159] apparuit postea anno 1492 in italia pseudoprofeta frater Hieronimus Savonarola[.] videamus quomodo conveniant inter se utraque significavit pseudoprofetam [*] sicut et apparuerunt[.] hoc non potest negari, sed videamus quomodo convenerunt isti[.] convenerunt quod uterque affirmavit christum fuisse profetam et profetarunt profetam[.] convenerunt in alio quia sicut Maumeth contradixit eccles(a)e[,] similiter et ille quia contradixit sedi apostolic(a)e[.] rursus quemadmodum Maumeth promittebat ac pollicebatur felicitates et divitias corporis ut patet in Alcorano[,] et refert Avicenna 9.o su(a)e Methaphysices et similiter miseriam[.] similiter ille promisit magnas felicitates et miserias suis civibus sicut Maumeth et civitatem illam florentissimam futuram esse ac in dies crescendam[,] sed quia constellationes non [R: 13v] fuerunt omnino similes, quia illa fuit in 5.o gradu ♏ realis, illa vero in 25.o gradu ♏ imaginarii[,] sed quasi ad

---

156 Fantoni inserts '*planeta*' here.
157 Sc. '*loco*'; '3.*a domo*' in F.
158 Sc. '*domo*'.
159 R: *pseudoprofeta*; F: *falsus propheta* (in base text of F).

idem revertitur[,] quia auferendo 2.o gradus inmobilis quos [sun] pertransivit cum ad primum gradum mobiles ivit[,] remanet [sun] finisse 5 gradus mobilis[.] sed constellationes non fuerunt omnino similes[,] quia ali(a)e fuerunt ill(a)e stell(a)e c(a)elo h(a)erentes et ali(a)e in ista nativitate, quapropter diversa quoque dicebant[,] quia hic affirmabat christum filium Dei, sed non Maumeth[.] ex quibus apparet quod ad hanc difficultatem dicendum est, quia aut Astrologus predicit in particulari [*] et propria forma vel in universali[.] primum est Solius Dei, non hominum quia necesse est precognoscere omnes causas, homines et astrologi possunt cognoscere futuros eventus cognitione quadam non distincta[,] sed aliqua notitia faciente ad universitalitatem[,] ut dicemus in alia lectione [*] et soluta est secunda.[160]

Tertia vero [*] an corpora c(a)elestia agant in h(a)ec inferiora, in qua questione non tantum volumus exponere corpora c(a)elestia agere, sed intendimus declarare quomodo agunt vel motu tantum vel lumine vel virtute spirutuali scilicet influentia vel omnibus his modis[,] rursus an agant omnia qu(a)e sub luna sunt an distinguant effectus particulares quia dicunt quod est tantum causa universalis contra Picum et Hieronimum Savonarolam[.] tenemus igitur cum D. Thoma[161] et respondebimus Pico.

Appendix 4: Fantoni's Version with modifications

[BNCF MS Conv. Soppr. B.VII.479 (vol. 1) [F] with Ristori's text from MS Ricc. 157 as the base text, and with the very few significant variant readings from Fantoni's MS. Brackets < > indicate Fantoni's additions in the text, and those in brackets with a mark (bold asterisk **[*]**) indicate a marginal addition with an explicit mark in the text. Images of selected folia from this text are in *Appendix 5*.

From Lectio 3: [F: 14v–17r]
[F: 14v] 2.o quia si non posse<u>mus conferre constellationes nostras quomodo posse[u]mus habere scientiam astrologi(a)e ex quo omnis scientia et ars experimentis fit[.]. 3.io quia declaratum est corpora

160 Sc. *'dubitatio'*.
161 Sc. *Aquinas*.

c(a)elestia agere in inferiora, an verum sit et quomodo agunt an lumine tantum vel alio modo:.

[ad 2 (F: 15v)] Ad secundam difficultatem quando dicitur si non possunt conferri constellationes iuniorum ad observationes antiquorum quomodo <fieri potest> scientia Astrologi(a)e ~~facta~~? ad quam dicimus quod licet constellationes presentes non sint omnino similes et omnem similitudinem omnino non habeant ~~conferendi~~ tamen in aliquo comuni et universali possunt conferri[,] itaque ars astrologi(a)e dupliciter considerari potest[,] uno modo ut artifex predicat eventus futuros in ~~propria forma~~ **[*]** <in suis causis non autem in seipsis sicut dicimus> vel quod predicat tales eventus in universali non distincte; quo ad primam non convenit homini predicere eventus in propria forma si autem velimus cognitionem universalem et comunem[,] dico quod ex his constellationibus collatis ad illas possumus habere hanc cognitionem **[*]** <per inclinationem corporum celestium, et naturaliter non altero modo quia solus deus cognoscit futura in seipsis> dicit [F:16r (image in *Appendix 5*)] Albumasar in libro de magnis coniunctionibus quod coniunctio duorum superiorum mutata de <una> triplicitate ad aliam et fuerit aliquis <planeta> inferiorum in 3.o[162] ab ascendente vel in 9.o significat Pseudoprofetam. accipiamus quod post annum Salvatoris anno 571 facta est coniunctio ♃ et ♄. de triplicitate in triplicitatem in 5. gradu ♏ et ♂ fuit in 9.a[163] ab ascendente[,] significabat ergo profetam, surrexit postea Maumeth contra legem christi qui promisit dona et bona fortun(a)e, et predicavit anno 620.[164] a christi incarnatione:.
~~Observavi~~ quoque anno 1425 coniunctio~~nem~~ ♃ et ♄i. in 25.o gradu ♏ et ♂ erat in 9.a ab ascendente[,] igitur significavit Pseudoprofetam ut fuit Maumeth non, sed bene significavit pseudoprophetam[,] licet amb(a)e fuerint in triplicitate aquea, igitur bonus astrologus dicet quod orietur pseudoropheta,[165] apparuit postea anno 1492 ~~in italia pseudoprofeta frater Hieronimus Savonarola~~,[166] videamus quomodo

[162] Sc. '*loco*'; '3.*a domo*' in F.
[163] Sc. '*domo*'.
[164] 620. in margin also.
[165] R: *pseudoprofeta*; F: *falsus propheta*.
[166] This is blotted out quite thickly, especially the name, but it is also pretty clear that it is

conveniant inter se utraque significavit ~~pseudoprofetam~~ <inclinationem cuiusdam falsi hominis> sicut et apparuerunt, ~~hoc non potest negari,~~ sed videamus quomodo convenerunt isti, [F:16v] convenerunt quod uterque affirmavit ~~christum fuisse profetam~~[167] ~~et profetarunt profetam convenerunt in alio quia sicut Maumeth contradixit eccles(a)e similiter. et ille quia contradixit sedi apostolic(a)e, rursus quemadmodum Maumeth. promittebat ac pollicebatur felicitates et divitias corporis ut patet in Alcorano et refert Avicenna 9.o su(a)e Methaph(ysi)ces. et similiter miseriam~~ <quoniam> similiter ille promisit magnas felicitates et miserias suis civibus sicut Maumeth et civitatem illam florentissimam futuram esse ac in dies crescendam[,] sed quia constellationes non fuerunt omnino similes, quia illa fuit in 5.o gradu realis, illa vero in 25. gradu imaginarii sed quasi ad idem revertitur quia auferendo 2.o gradus inmobilis quos [sun] pertransivit cum ad primum gradum mobiles ivit[,] remanet [sun] finisse .5. gradus mobilis sed constellationes non fuerunt omnino similes quia ali(a)e fuerunt ill(a)e stell(a)e c(a)elo h(a)erentes et ali(a)e in ista nativitate, quapropter diversa quoque dicebant ~~quia hic affirmabat christum filium Dei, sed non Maumeth~~[.] ex quibus apparet quod ad hanc difficultatem dicendum est, quia aut Astrologus [F: 17r (image in *Appendix* 5)] predicit in particulari <et in se ipsis> ~~et propria forma~~ vel in universali[.] primum est Solius Dei, non hominum quia necesse est precognoscere omnes causas, homines et astrologi possunt cognoscere <et> futuros eventus cognitione quadam non distincta sed aliqua notitia faciente ad universitalitatem ~~ut dicemus in alia lectione~~ <et denique per inclinationem corporum celestium> et soluta est secunda.[168] Tertia vero <querendum est> an corpora c(a)elestia agant in h(a)ec inferiora, in qua questione non tantum volumus exponere corpora c(a)elestia agere, sed intendimus declarare quomodo agunt vel motu tantum vel lumine vel virtute spirutuali scilicet influentia vel omnibus his modis[,] rursus an agant omnia qu(a)e sub luna sunt an distinguant effectus particulares quia dicunt quod est tantum causa universalis contra Picum ~~et~~

Savonarola: the '*mus*' from the first name, and the 'S' and 'L' from the last are reasonably clear.

[167] Double lines indicate words thickly blotted out.

[168] Sc. 'dubitatio'.

~~Hieronimum Savonarolam~~[169] tenemus igitur cum D. Thoma[170] et respondebimus Pico.

Appendix 5: Images of Selected Folia

Reproduced with permission of the Biblioteca Nazionale Centrale, Florence

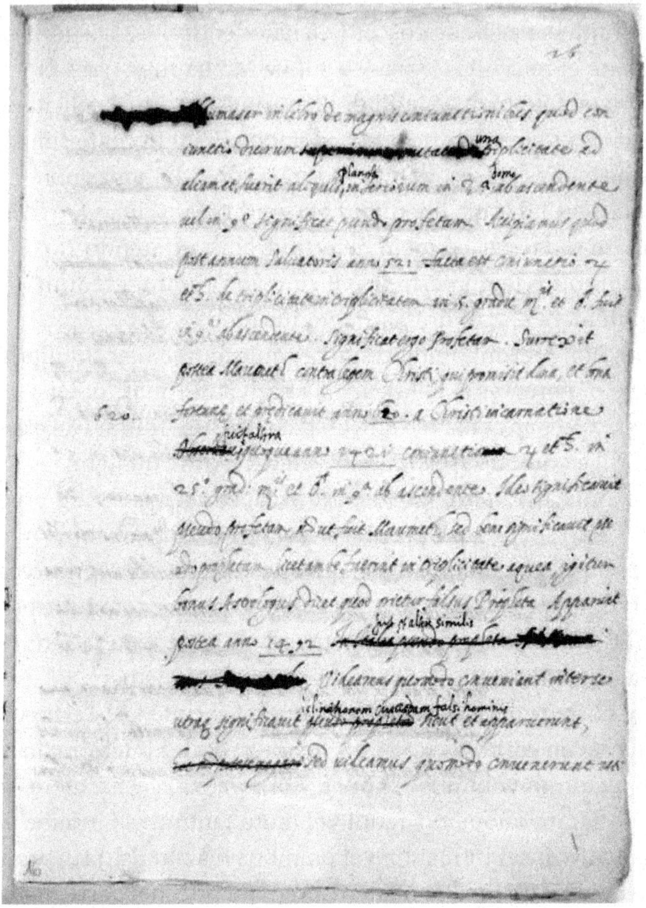

Fig. 1: BNCF MS Conv. Soppr. B.VII.479 (vol. 1) [F: 16r].

---

169 The Hieronimus is double lined and the Savonarola blotched, but with the S and L clear again, thus confirming the reading in n. 166 above!

170 Sc. *Aquinas*.

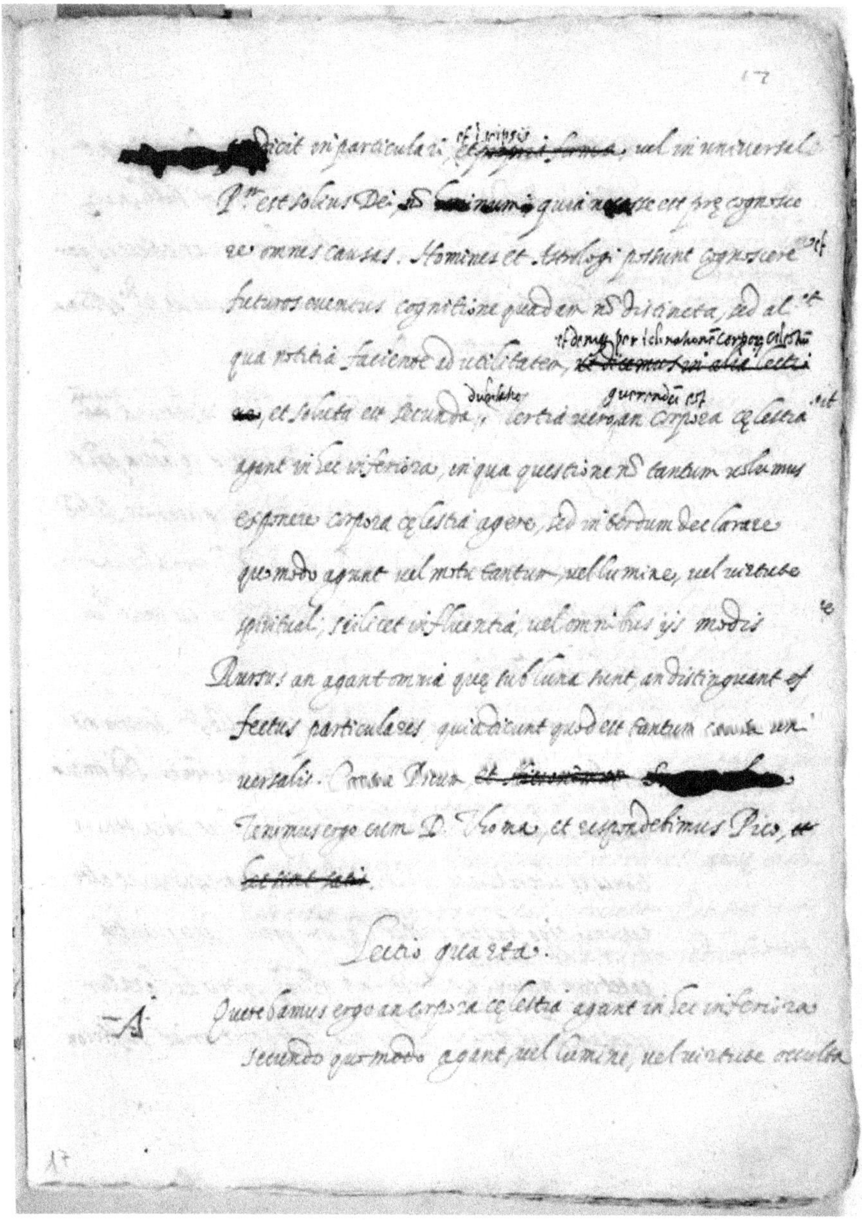

[redacted] dicit in particulari, vel in universali.
P.us est solus Dei, [redacted] quia necesse est pre cognoscere omnes causas. Homines et Astrologi possunt cognoscere futuros eventus cognitione quadam non distincta, sed alia qua petitia faciente ad utilitatem, et soluta est secunda, tertia vero an corpora celestia agant in hec inferiora, in qua questione non tantum volumus exponere corpora celestia agere, sed in ordinem declarare quomodo agant vel motu tantum, vel lumine, vel virtute spirituali, scilicet influentia, vel omnibus iis modis. Rursus an agant omnia que sub luna fiunt, an distinguant effectus particulares quidam dicunt quod est tantum causa universalis. Contra Picum [redacted]
Tenemus ergo cum D. Thoma, et respondebimus Pico.

Lectio quarta.

Querebamus ergo an corpora celestia agant in hec inferiora secundo quomodo agant, vel lumine, vel virtute occulta

Fig. 2: BNCF MS Conv. Soppr. B.VII.479 (vol. 1) [F: 17r].

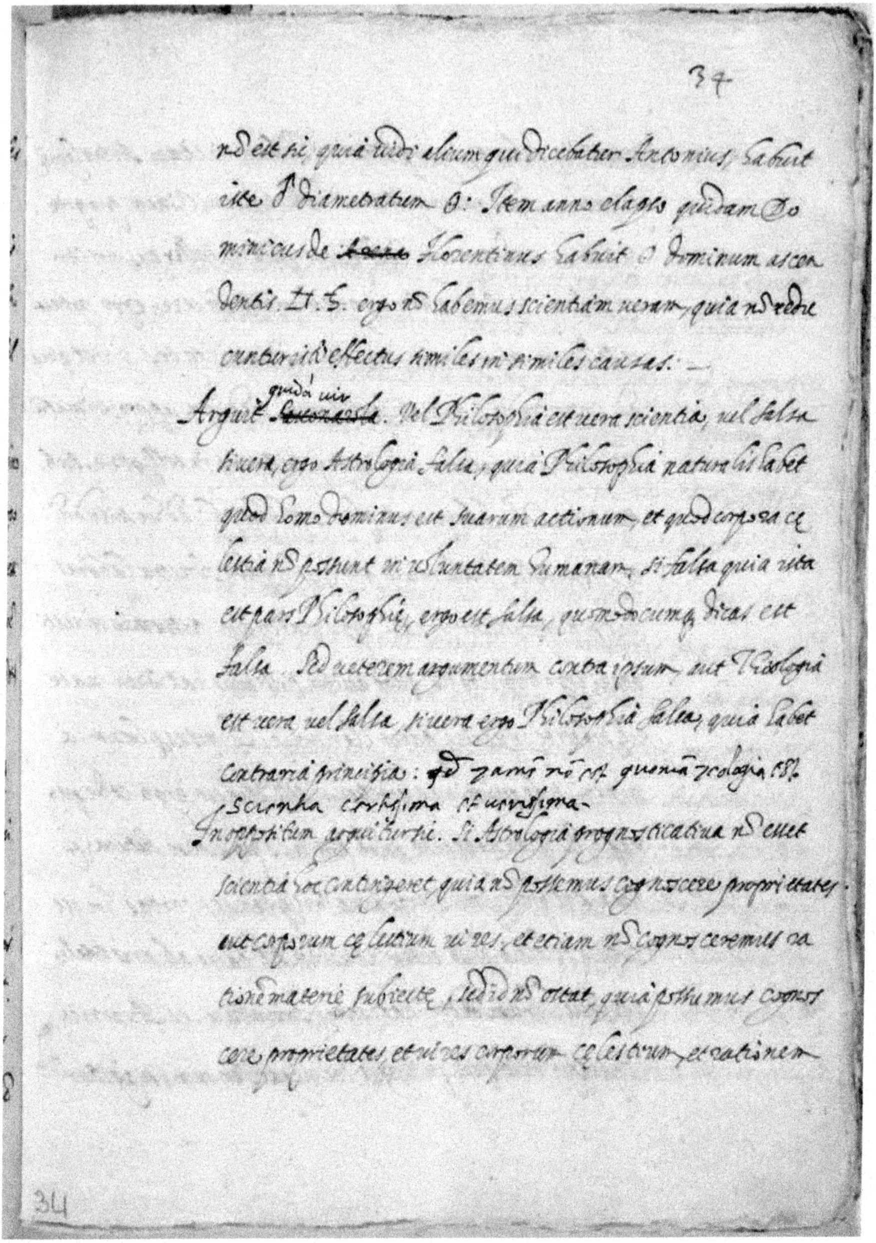

Fig. 3: BNCF MS Conv. Soppr. B.VII.479 (vol. 1) [F: 34r].

ASTROLOGY IN MOROCCO TOWARDS THE END OF THE FOURTEENTH CENTURY AND BEGINNING OF THE FIFTEENTH CENTURY

Julio Samsó

Introduction

Towards the middle of the fourteenth century the scholar Ibn Marzūq (1310–1379) wrote an hagiographic portrait of the tenth Marīnid sultan of Morocco Abū l- Ḥasan b. ʿAlī (r. 731/1331–752/1351), one chapter of which is dedicated specifically to Abū l-Ḥasan's rejection of astrology as a consequence of his extreme orthodoxy.[1] One of the most important events during his reign was his defeat at the battle of El Salado or Faḥṣ Ṭarīf (1340) in which the Muslim army formed by Marīnid and Naṣrid troops was overcome by the Castilian army of King Alfonso XI. Curiously enough, an astrologer, Ibn ʿAzzūz al-Qusanṭīnī (d. Constantina 755/1354), who lived in Fez, cast several horoscopes related to the issue of the battle; the result of his first failed attempt to predict its outcome led him to compile a new set of astronomical tables (*al-Zīj al-Muwāfiq*) using an experimental method in which the data were obtained using both astronomical and astrological criteria.[2]

Abū l-Ḥasan's orthodoxy did not put an end to the practice of astrology in

[1] See Muḥammad ibn Marzūq al-Tilimsānī, *al-Musnad al-ṣaḥīḥ al-ḥasan fī ma'āthir wa-maḥasin mawlā-nā Abī l-Ḥasan*, ed. María Jesús Viguera (Algiers: al-Sharikah al-Waṭanīyah lil-Nashr wa-al-Tawzīʿ, 1981), pp. 438–44; Muḥammad ibn Marzūq al-Tilimsānī, *El Musnad: hechos memorables de Abū l-Ḥasan, sultán de los Benimerines*, Spanish trans. and comment. María Jesús Viguera (Madrid: Instituto Hispano-Arabe de Cultura, 1977), pp. 361–66.

[2] Julio Samsó, 'Horoscopes and history: Ibn ʿAzzūz and his retrospective horoscopes related to the battle of El Salado (1340)', in *Between Demonstration and Imagination. Essays in the History of Science and Philosophy Presented to John D. North*, eds. Lodi Nauta and Arjo Vanderjagt (Leiden: Brill, 1999), pp. 101–24; Julio Samsó, 'Andalusian Astronomy in 14th century Fez: *al-Zīj al-Muwāfiq* of Ibn ʿAzzūz al-Qusanṭīnī', *Zeitschrift für Geschichte der Arabisch-Islamischen Wissenschaften*, 11 (1997): pp. 73–110. Both papers repr. in Julio Samsó, *Astronomy and Astrology in al-Andalus and the Maghrib* (Aldershot: Ashgate, Variorum, 2007), nos. IX and X.

Morocco during the second half of the fourteenth century. As a matter of fact, I am not sure of the origin of Ibn ʿAzzūz' horoscopes of the battle; was he asked to prepare them by the circles of power surrounding Abū l-Ḥasan? Besides, we know of important persons from this period who were interested in astrology, such as the sultan Abū Sālim Ibrāhīm ibn Abī l-Ḥasan (760/1359–762/1361), one of the sons of the aforementioned Abū l-Ḥasan, who owned two astrolabes made in gold and silver,[3] and the vizier Ghāzī ibn al-Kās to whom Ibn Qunfudh al-Qusanṭīnī (1339–1407) dedicated the commentary (*sharḥ*) on the *Urjūza fī l-aḥkām al-nujūmiyya* (an astrological poem written in *rajaz* meter) by the famous astrologer of the eleventh century, Ibn Abī l-Rijāl.[4]

The latter work must have been quite popular, as it is extant in many manuscripts. This small book is dedicated to Abū Yaḥyā Abū Bakr, son of the dead vizier Abū Mujāhid Ghāzī, identified by Manūnī[5] as Abū Bakr b. Abī Mujāhid Ghāzī ibn al-Kās, vizier of the Marīnī sultans Abū Fāris (767/1366–774/1372) and his son Abū Zayyān (774/1372–776/1374). As Ibn Qunfudh's writing contains a series of historical horoscopes—the last (chronologically speaking) corresponding to the *bayʿa* (oath of fidelity) of Abū Fāris and including a very precise estimation of the length of his reign—we must conclude that the work was written after 1372. On the other hand, since Ibn Khaldūn says that minister Ibn Ghāzī was exiled to Majorca towards the end of 776/1375,[6] I suggest that the *sharḥ* was written during the short reign of Abū Zayyān (1372–1374), although Ibn Qunfudh states that 'our time' is 'the beginning of the third third of the eighth century of the Hijra', which implies a date around 766H (1 Muḥarram 766 corresponds to 27 September 1364), some ten years before the aforementioned

---

[3] See Muḥammad Manūnī, *Waraqāt ʿan ḥaḍārat al-Marīniyyīn* (Rabat: Jāmiʿah Muḥammad al-Khāmis, 2000), p. 366.

[4] The text has been edited by Marc Oliveras in *La* Urŷūza astrológica *de ʿAlī b. Abī l-Riŷāl junto al comentario de Ibn Qunfuḏ al-Qusanṭīnī* (Barcelona: Grup Millàs Vallicrosa d'Història de la Ciència Árab, 2012). A previous study of this work appears in Julio Samsó, 'Cuatro horóscopos sobre muertes violentas en al-Andalus y el Magrib', in *De muerte violenta. Política, religión y violencia en al-Andalus, EOBA*, ed. Maribel Fierro (Madrid: CSIC, 2004), 14: pp. 479–519. Repr. in Julio Samsó, *Astrometeorología y Astrología Medievales* (Barcelona: Universidad de Barcelona, 2008), nº XIII; Julio Samsó, 'La *Urŷūza* de Ibn Abī l-Riŷāl y su comentario por Ibn Qunfuḏ: Astrología e Historia en el Magrib en los siglos XI y XIV', *Al-Qanṭara* 30 (2009): pp. 7–39, 321–60.

[5] Manūnī, *Waraqāt*, p. 366.

[6] Ibn Khaldūn, *Histoire des berbères et des dynasties musulmanes de l'Afrique septentrionale*, New Edition, trans. W.M. Baron De Slane, 4 vols. (Paris: P. Casanova, 1978), IV: p. 416.

date. In fact two manuscripts of the *Sharḥ* (Rabat Hassaniya 4805 and British Library ADD 9599) give a precise date according to which Ibn Qunfudh's commentary was finished towards the end of *shawwal* 774/ mid-April 1373.[7]

Ibn Qunfudh's commentary is one of the two sources I would like to consider here, although very briefly because practically all the information I can offer has already been published. The second source is slightly later: the *Kitāb al-amṭār wa l-as'ār* (Book on rains and prices) by Abū 'Abd Allāh al-Baqqār about whom we only know that he was the author of two interesting books: the *Amṭār* and the *Kitāb al-adwār fī tasyīr al-anwār* (Book on cycles for the prorogation of the luminaries). The first of these books has been preserved in only one manuscript: Escorial 916 (fols 187v–236r); it was edited by Chedli Guesmi, presented as a Ph.D. dissertation at the University of Barcelona in 2005.[8] The *Anwār,* on the other hand, is extant in at least three manuscripts (Escorial 916 and Rabat, Hassaniyya 826 and 5372) and it is clearly divided into two parts. The first is mainly astronomical and has been edited and studied by Montse Díaz Fajardo,[9] who has also prepared an edition of the astrological part for her Ph.D. dissertation, presented at the University of Barcelona in 2008. This second work has the obvious interest of showing that al-Baqqār was a competent astronomer and that he lived in a period in which Maghribī astronomers were beginning to abandon the Andalusī astronomical tradition, represented by the *zījes* of the school of Ibn Isḥāq, and to adopt the new Eastern *zījes* which were appearing in the Maghrib.[10] The *Adwār,* on the other hand, is the only source which allows us to date the activities of its author, for it states that it was written in 821/1418, the year in which al-Baqqār

[7] See Oliveras, La Urŷūza astrológica, p. 36.

[8] Chedli Guesmi, 'El *Kitāb al-amṭār wa l-as'ār* de Abū 'Abd Allāh al-Baqqār' (unpublished PhD dissertation, Universidad de Barcelona, 2005).

[9] Montse Díaz Fajardo, 'La teoría de la trepidación en un astrónomo marroquí del siglo XV. Estudio y edición crítica del *Kitāb al-adwār fī tasyīr al-anwār* (parte primera) de Abū 'Abd Allāh al-Baqqār' see *Anuari de Filologia* XXIII [2001] B4), pp. 6-109.

[10] Julio Samsó, 'An Outline of the History of Maghribī Zijes from the End of the Thirteenth Century', *Journal for the History of Astronomy* 29 (1998): pp. 93–102; Julio Samsó, 'Astronomical Observations in the Maghrib in the Fourteenth and Fifteenth Centuries', *Science in Context* 14 (2001): pp. 165–78. Both papers repr. in Samsó, *Astronomy and Astrology in al-Andalus and the Maghrib*. Mercè Comes, 'Some new Maghribī sources dealing with trepidation', in *Science and Technology in the Islamic World,* ed. S.M. Razhuallah Ansari (Turnhout: Brepols, 2002), pp. 121–41. Repr. in Mercè Comes, *Coordenadas del Cielo y de la Tierra* (Barcelona: Universidad de Barcelona, 2013), pp. 299-322.

made, in Fez, an observation of the solar altitude after he had very carefully determined the latitude of the city. Apart from this, we only know that he was probably the copyist of the collection of five astrological texts extant in MS Escorial 939, copied in 813/1411 by a Muḥammad b. ʿAlī al-Baqqār.[11]

The *Kitāb al-amṭār* has attracted the attention of scholars because it is one of the two known sources[12] that contain an Arabic text explaining the astrological predictions based on the 'system of the crosses' (*aḥkām al-ṣulub*) used by the ancient Romans (*rūm*) of al-Andalus, Ifrīqiyā and the Maghrib.[13] This system is also known through a Castilian version extant in the Alfonsine *Libro de las Cruzes*, based on a later revision of a primitive Arabic original prepared in the eleventh century (after the Saturn–Jupiter conjunction of year 459/1066–67, quoted in the text) by a certain ʿAbd Allāh b. Aḥmad al-Ṭulayṭulī.[14]

---

[11] Julio Samsó and Hamid Berrani, 'The Epistle on *Tasyīr* and the projection of rays by Abū Marwān al-Istijī', *Suhayl* 5 (2005): pp. 163–242 (see a description of the manuscript and of its contents on pp. 171–76). Repr. in Samsó, *Astrometeorología y astrología medievales*, nº XIV. One of the aforementioned texts copied by al-Baqqār has been edited and translated into Spanish by María José Parra, 'El "Sirr al-asrār" de ʿUṭārid b. Muḥammad al-Ḥāsib y sus aforismos', *Anaquel de Estudios Árabes* 20 (2009): pp. 165–86.

[12] The other one is MS Escorial 918. See Rafael Muñoz, 'Textos árabes del *Libro de las Cruces* de Alfonso X', *Textos y Estudios sobre Astronomía Española en el siglo XIII*, ed. Juan Vernet (Barcelona: Universidad autónoma de Barcelona, 1981), pp. 175–204. Incidentally, MS Escorial 939 contains one page (fol. 34v) with two short chapters (on the division of al-Andalus between the zodiacal signs and the planets) related to the 'system of the crosses'.

[13] See Juan Vernet, 'Tradición e innovación en la ciencia medieval', in *Oriente e Occidente nel Medioevo; Filosofia e Scienze* (Roma: Accademia nazionale dei Lincei, 1971), pp. 741–57. Repr. in Juan Vernet, *Estudios sobre Historia de la Ciencia Medieval* (Barcelona-Bellaterra: Universidad autónoma de Barcelona, 1979), pp. 173–89; Julio Samsó, 'The Early Development of Astrology in al-Andalus', *Journal for the History of Arabic Science* 3 (1979): pp. 228–43. Repr. in Julio Samsó, *Islamic Astronomy and Medieval Spain* (Aldershot: Ashgate, Variorium, 1994), nº IV; Samsó, 'Astrology, pre-Islamic Spain and the conquest of al-Andalus', *Revista del Instituto Egipcio de Estudios Islámicos en Madrid* 23 (1985–86): pp. 79–94. Repr in Samsó, *Islamic Astronomy* nº II.

[14] Margarita Castells, 'Un nuevo dato sobre el *Libro de las Cruces* en el *al-Zīŷ al-Muṣṭalaḥ* (obra astronómica egipcia del siglo XIII)', *al-Qanṭara* 13 (1992): pp. 367–76. Quite recently Charles Burnett ('Al-Qabīṣī's *Introduction to Astrology*: From Courtly Entertainment to University Textbook', in *Studies in the History of Culture and Science: A Tribute to Gad Freudenthal*, ed. R. Fontaine, et al. [Leiden-Boston: Brill, 2011], pp. 43-69) has identified a new manuscript of the Alfonsine work (Vienna, Österreichische Nationalbibliothek,

We have, therefore, two astrological treatises written in Morocco between 1372–1374 (Ibn Qunfudh) and, probably, after 1418. They can give us an idea about the practice of astrology in Morocco during a period of some fifty years corresponding to the last quarter of the fourteenth century and the first quarter of the fifteenth century.

Astrology and Islam

A recent study by Robert Morrison[15] has highlighted the peculiar case of a religious scholar, Niʿām al-Dīn al-Aʿraj al-Nīsābūrī (ca. 1270–ca. 1330), an Eastern scholar earlier than our Maghribī authors, who defends the legitimacy of astrology, which is permitted (*mubāḥ*) if one considers that the heavens act as an intermediary in God's control over the world. In a chapter in his *Kashf-i ḥaqā'iq-i Zīj-i Īlkhānī*, al-Nīsābūrī argues that the stars act as secondary causes and that their influence is not the result of their own nature. Astrology provides men with *conjectural* knowledge of how God controls the world through celestial motions; and thus intelligent people may draw conclusions about future events by way of intuition (*ḥads*) and experience (*tajriba*).

A similar attitude is adopted by our two authors, one of whom (Ibn Qunfudh) was clearly interested in Sufism and, therefore, considered to be a man of religion.[16] Both seem to worry about the compatibility between the practice of astrology and their own Islamic orthodoxy. Ibn Qunfudh classifies sciences into religious (*dīnī*) and rational (*ʿaqlī*) sciences. Religious sciences are contained in the *sharīʿa* while the rational sciences can be applied or practical (*ṣināʿī*) or not (*ghayr ṣināʿī*). Within the first subgroup we find Logic, Geometry, Arithmetic (*ḥisāb*), Medicine, Astrology and Astronomy (*ʿilm al-nujūm*), secretarial disciplines (*kitāba*) and others. The *ghayr ṣināʿī* sciences include the Fundaments of Religion (*Uṣūl al-Dīn*) and of Law (*Uṣūl al-Fiqh*), as well as the Arabic language (because the *sharīʿa* is written in Arabic). Ibn Qunfudh says that indications (*dalāla*) given by celestial bodies are just this—not causes—and that God may alter the motions of planets and change such indications. Astronomy is a useful science because of its

Hebr. 199, second part, fols 1v-47r), written in Castilian but in Hebrew script.

[15] Robert G. Morrison, *Islam and Science: The Intellectual Career of Niʿām al-Dīn al-Nīsābūrī*, Culture and Civilisation in the Middle East (London and New York: Routledge, 2007).

[16] The same could be said about the mathematician and astronomer Ibn al-Bannā' (1256–1321), whose interest in Sufism is well known. See A. Jabbār (= Djebbar) and M. Aballāgh, *Ḥayāt wa-muʾallafāt Ibn al-Bannā al-Murrākushī maʿa nuṣūṣ ghayr manshūra* (Rabat: Kullīyat al-Ādāb wa-al-ʿUlūm al-Insānīyah, 2001). On pp. 160–78 Djebbar and Aballāgh edit several short astrological texts by Ibn al-Bannā'.

applications to *mīqāt*. The study of planetary sizes and distances as well the irregularity of their motions reflects divine wisdom. He quotes religious authorities such as ʿAlī ibn Abī Ṭālib, who had an adequate knowledge of Astronomy, as well as authors of the *anwāʾ* literature, a kind of folk-astronomy which was considered acceptable in orthodox circles.

Al-Baqqār expands on this topic at much greater length: in the introduction of his *Kitāb al-amṭār* he explains that scholars adopt three different attitudes towards astrology, then continues with some remarks on its usefulness. One of these attitudes is that of the polemicists (*ahl al-jadal*) who reject astrology, and the opposite one corresponds to those who practise talismanic magic and consider that celestial bodies have effects (*afʿāl*) and exert influences (*taʾthīrāt*) on the sublunary world. Both attitudes are rejected by al-Baqqār who, like Ibn Qunfudh, considers that practising astrologers believe that the celestial bodies offer indications (*dalālāt*) which allow them to make predictions due to their knowledge based on experience (*tajārib*) and analogical reasoning (*qiyāsāt*), the results of which they recorded in their books. Celestial influences offer suggestions but they are not causes of future events (*wa huwa mushāhid ghayr mudāfiʿ*). In this respect, he quotes *Qurʾān* 32, 34 on the five things only God knows about, among which we find rainfall, the main topic of his book. He also quotes *Qurʾān* 37, 88–89 on Abraham's capacity to use astrology to predict that he was going to fall ill. Rain cannot be caused by the celestial bodies, but men are able to analyse the indications that allow them to foresee the possibility of rain. In this respect he gives several historical examples: Caliph ʿUmar did not allow the prayer of the *istisqāʾ* (i.e., *ad petendam pluviam*) until the moment of the *nawʾ* of the Pleiades, traditionally considered a period of rain in the solar year.[17] Similarly, al-Ghazālī did not want to say the prayer of the *istisqāʾ* until Venus was combust in the sign of Pisces. This has two different interpretations. On the one side Pisces is a watery sign and Venus which, together with the Moon, has a clear influence on rainfall, has its exaltation in its twenty-seventh degree; on the other, from a more rational point of view, if Venus is combust in Pisces the Sun should also be in the same sign, very near the vernal equinox, a period of the year in which, at least in the Mediterranean area, rainfall is quite common. Astrology, being compatible with the Islamic religion, is obviously useful, for it makes it possible to predict the future and to adopt the adequate preventive measures (among which he mentions praying to God in order to avoid a catastrophic future event). This kind of knowledge is particularly important for kings and political leaders like Heraclius,

---

[17] See Henri Paul Joseph Rénaud, *Le Calendrier d'Ibn al-Bannāʾ de Marrakech (1256–1321)* (Paris: Larose, 1948), pp. 54–55.

king of Byzantium, who was able to foresee that he would be ejected from Syria due to the advent of Prophet Muḥammad. Heraclius observed the stars, as did the Banū ʿUbayd when they built the city of Mahdiyya; the site for the new city was chosen by ʿUbayd Allāh al-Mahdī in 300/912–13 and the official inauguration took place on 8 Shawwāl 308/ 19 February 921 with Leo in the ascendant, because of its being a fixed sign and the domicile of the Sun, which is an indicator of kings.[18] In another passage al-Baqqār tells us that a Roman king foresaw, through a horoscope, the transfer of the capital of the Roman Empire from Rome to Byzantium and this allowed him to adopt preventive measures.

Ibn Qunfudh's standard astrology

Both Ibn Abī l-Rijāl's *Urjūza* and its commentary by Ibn Qunfudh correspond to what we might call 'standard' astrology. The first of these authors is a well-known Tunisian astrologer of the eleventh century who wrote the *Kitāb al-Bāriʿ fī aḥkām al-nujūm,* one of the most popular astrological handbooks in Europe during the Middle Ages, which was translated in a great many versions, including the only one that has been well edited: the Alfonsine Castilian translation entitled *Libro conplido en los iudizios de las estrellas.*[19]

His *urjūza* contains 467 verses and it does not seem to be a summary of the *Kitāb al-Bāriʿ*, as has often been thought; it seems clear to me that the contents of *al-Bāriʿ* are more general. The *urjūza* deals with: 1. Introduction (vv. 1–22); 2. Interrogations (*masāʾil*) (vv. 23–343) on topics related to aspects of private and public life. Seventy-five verses of this group (almost a quarter of the whole) deal with questions which refer to the supreme political power (the sultan or king); 3. Elections (*ikhtiyārāt*): establishing the propitious moment for beginning a particular activity, most of which correspond to different aspects of common life. Only in a few cases does the election correspond to something directly concerned with political power, such as choosing the propitious moment for the *bayʿa* (oath

---

[18] See Ibn al-Khaṭīb's *Aʿmāl al-aʿlām* in *Tārīkh al-Magrib al-ʿarabī fī l-ʿaṣr al-wasīṭ. Al-qism al-thālith min kitāb Aʿmāl al-aʿlām li l-wazīr al-gharnāṭī Lisān al-Dīn ibn al-Khaṭīb,* eds. Aḥmad Mukhtār al-ʿAbbādī and Muḥammad Ibrāhīm al-Kattānī (Dār al-Kitāb, al-Dār al-Bayḍāʾ, 1964), p. 47.

[19] The first five books were edited by the Real Academia Española, Madrid, 1954. Books 6–8 have recently appeared in the Castilian version (book 6, pp. 3–77; book 8 pp. 191–327) or in the Judaeo-Portuguese translation (book 6, pp. 78–86; book 7, pp. 87–190) published by the Instituto de Estudios Islámicos y del Oriente Próximo, with the collaboration of the Instituto Millás-Vallicrosa de Historia de la Ciencia Árabe of the University of Barcelona, in Zaragoza, 2005.

of fidelity) of a monarch; 4. World anniversaries (*taḥwīl sinī al-ʿālam*) (vv. 425–468) are concerned with problems of world astrology and based on the use of prorogations (*tasyīr*) and the theory of Saturn-Jupiter conjunctions. It is quite surprising that topics such as nativities and their anniversaries (*taḥāwīl sinī al-mawālīd*) have been totally omitted.[20] If we add this fact to the depth with which problems related to the political power are addressed, my conclusion is that the *urjūza* was dedicated to an important figure in the Zīrī court of Tunis.

Ibn Qunfudh's *sharḥ* is a collection of glosses explaining the contents of Ibn Abī l-Rijāl's *urjūza*, often excessively concise, to which it adds extra information in the form of passages called *fā'ida, faṣl, tafṣīl, tanbīh, qāʿida, ilḥāq, muʿāraḍa, ishāra* or *mushāhada*. These additions sometimes contain extra information that is not to be found in the *urjūza* or even in the *Bāriʿ*. The most interesting item in Ibn Qunfudh's commentary is the fact that he gives, as examples of astrological predictions, a series of twelve commented horoscopes which I have numbered according to the order in which they appear in the text. Horoscope 10 corresponds to the spring equinox of year 571 CE, the year of a Saturn-Jupiter conjunction which coincided, approximately, with the presumed date of the birth of Prophet Muḥammad and which announced the arrival of Islam (*al-qirān al-dāll ʿalā l-Milla*).[21] The other eleven horoscopes are quite unusual in the Maghribī astrological tradition, as they form a kind of astrological history of the dynastic crisis which took place after the murder of sultan Abū ʿInān (1348–1358). This history deals with the period between 1348 and 1372 and the horoscopes included are related to the following topics:

- *Bayʿa* of Abū ʿInān (1348–1358) (HOROSCOPE 7)
- Siege of Constantina (1354) (HOROSCOPE 11)
- *Bayʿa* of Abū Yaḥyā al-Saʿīd (1358–59) (HOROSCOPE 9)
- *Bayʿa* of Abū Sālim Ibrāhīm b. Abī l-Ḥasan (1359–61) (HOROSCOPE 6)
- Nativity horoscope (unidentified subject) dated in 1361 (HOROSCOPE 1)
- *Bayʿa* of Tāshufīn (1361) (HOROSCOPE 4)
- Siege of Fās Jadīd in 1361 (HOROSCOPE 12)
- The horoscope corresponding to the *bayʿa* of Abū Zayyān (1361–66) is missing

---

[20] These topics are dealt with in books IV–VI of the *Libro conplido*.

[21] See another horoscope of the same kind, cast by al-Battānī (before 858–929), in Edward S. Kennedy's last work which has recently been published: Edward S. Kennedy, Colleagues and Former Students, 'Al-Battānī's Astrological History of the Prophet and the Early Caliphate', *Suhayl* 9 (2009–10): pp. 13–148 (see pp. 34–41, 88–92).

- Release of an anonymous captive in 1362 (HOROSCOPE 3),
- Nativity horoscope (unidentified subject) dated in 1363 (HOROSCOPE 2),
- An anonymous ʿ*āmil* (governor of a district) holds office in 1363 (HOROSCOPE 8).
- *Bayʿa* of Abū Fāris (1366–1372) (HOROSCOPE 5)

The subjects of these horoscopes are not identified in the text but, knowing that Ibn Qunfudh is using a set of tables in the tradition of Ibn Isḥāq,[22] it is easy to establish a date for each horoscope (when the text does not give it) and the subject of the horoscope has been identified in seven cases which correspond to the royal *bayʿa*s or to well-known historical facts such as the siege of Constantina

[22] Ibn Isḥāq (fol. 1193–1222) prepared a set of astronomical tables (*zīj*) which he could not finish. Three different Maghribī astronomers of the 13th century prepared 'editions' of Ibn Isḥāq's *zīj*, which have been studied during the last twenty years. They are 1) the anonymous editor of the Hyderabad recension (fl. 1266–1281), 2) Ibn al-Bannā' al-Marrākushī (1256–1321), and 3) Ibn al-Raqqām al-Mursī (d. 1315), who compiled three *zīj*es following Ibn Isḥāq's tradition. Any of the aforementioned five *zīj*es could be used for the computation of Ibn Qunfudh's horoscopes for they all employ the same parameters. See Ángel Mestres, 'Maghribī Astronomy in the 13th Century: a Description of Manuscript Hyderabad Andra Pradesh State Library 298' in *From Baghdad to Barcelona*, eds. Josep Casulleras and Julio Samsó (Barcelona: Instituto 'Millás Valicrosa' de Historia de la Ciencia árabe, 1996), pp. 383–443; Julio Samsó and Eduardo Millás 'The computation of planetary longitudes in the *zīj* of Ibn al-Bannā'', *Arabic Sciences and Philosophy* 8 (1998): pp. 259–86. Repr in Samsó, *Astronomy and Astrology in al-Andalus and the Maghrib*, nº VIII; Edward S. Kennedy, 'The astronomical tables of Ibn al-Raqqām, a scientist of Granada', *Zeitschrift für Geschichte der Arabisch-Islamischen Wissenschaften* 11 (1997): pp. 35–72; Muḥammad ʿAbd al-Raḥmān, 'Ḥisāb aṭwāl al-kawākib fī l-Zīj al-Ḥāmil fī tahdhīb al-Kāmil li-Ibn al-Raqqām', (unpublished PhD dissertation, University of Barcelona, 1996); Montse Díaz Fajardo, '*Al-Zīŷ al-Mustawfà* de Ibn al-Raqqām y los apogeos planetarios en la tradición andaluso-magrebí', *Al-Qanṭara* 26 (2005): pp. 19–30; Julio Samsó, 'The computation of the degree of mediation of a star or planet in the Andalusian and Maghribī Tradition', in *Mathematics Celestial and Terrestrial: Festschrift für Menso Folkerts zum 65. Geburtstag*, ed. Joseph Warren Dauben, et al., Acta Historica Leopoldina 54 (Halle: Deutsche Akademie der Naturforscher Leopoldina; Stuttgart: Wissenschaftliche Verlagsgesellschaft, 2008), pp. 395–404; J. Samsó, 'Ibn al-Raqqām's *al-Zīj al-Mustawfī* in MS Rabat National Library 2461', in *From Alexandria, Through Baghdad. Surveys and Studies in the Ancient Greek and Medieval Islamic Mathematical Sciences in Honor of J.L. Berggren*, eds. Nathan Sidoli and Glen Van Brummelen (Springer, Berlin-Heidelberg, 2014), pp. 297-328.

(1354) by the troops of Abū ʿInān or that of Fās Jadīd (1361) during the reign of Tāshufīn.[23] There are, however, four cases in which all my attempts at identification have failed: the nativity horoscopes of 1361 (HOR. 1) and 1363 (HOR. 2), the release of a captive in 1362 (HOR. 3), or the governor who held office in 1363 (HOR. 8).

On the whole my impression is that the horoscopes, clearly retrospective, were cast by a direct witness of the events and included in a work dedicated to another witness, the vizier Abū Bakr Ghāzī ibn al-Kās, with whom the author was playing a kind of guessing game, asking him whether he could establish the identity of the subject of each horoscope with the limited data he was providing.

Al-Baqqār's Kitāb al-amṭār: *simple techniques for astrological predictions*

Al-Baqqār's 'Book on Rains and Prices' corresponds to an entirely different kind of astrology; al-Baqqār is mainly concerned with predictions based on a small number of variables, which can easily be listed using combinatorial techniques. With this method the astrologer will have to establish the variables that concern a particular case and read the corresponding prediction already given to him in one of the lists, without having to bother about the computation of planetary longitudes, the division of houses or other technicalities of standard astrology. This makes me think of a kind of popular astrology used by cheap astrologers working in the *sūq* of a city. This resembles what we find in two other astrological works produced in the Iberian Peninsula: the *Alchandreana* collection[24] (although it lacks the astronomical contents we find in al-Baqqār) and Raimundus Lullius' *Tractatus de nova astronomia*.[25] All this is entirely different from the more sophisticated kind of astrology, based on Classical and Islamic developments, that is to be found in Ibn Qunfudh's commentary.

The 'system of the crosses' in the Kitāb al-amṭār

The first part of the *Kitāb al-amṭār* is related to the astrological techniques of the 'system of the crosses'. Its contents correspond quite closely to chapters 1, 4, 5, 6,

---

[23] The historical sources used for this analysis are Ibn al-Aḥmar, *Rawḍat al-nisrīn fī dawlat Banī Marīn*, introduction and annotated Spanish translation by Miguel Angel Manzano (Madrid: CSIC, 1989); Ibn Khaldūn, *Histoire des berbères*.

[24] David Juste, *Les* Alchandreana *primitifs. Étude sur les plus anciens traités astrologiques latins d'origine arabe (Xe siècle)*, Brill's Studies in Intellectual History, Vol. 152 (Leiden-Boston: Brill, 2007).

[25] Julio Samsó, 'Notas sobre la astronomía y la astrología de Llull', *Estudios Lulianos* 25 (1981–83), pp. 199–220. Repr. in Samsó, *Astrometeorología y astrología medievales* nº XI.

57, 60, 61, 62, 63, 64 and 65 of the Alfonsine *Libro de las Cruzes*. The equivalence shows that al-Baqqār was using a source related to the revision made in the eleventh century by ʿAbd Allāh al-Ṭulayṭulī, the *Oveidalla* of the Alfonsine translation. The text also quotes thirty-nine verses of the *urjūza* of ʿAbd al-Wāḥid ibn Isḥāq al-Ḍabbī (fl. Algeciras and Cordova ca. 788–ca. 852),[26] which is the oldest known Andalusī astrological text and a versification of chapter 57 of the *Libro de las Cruzes*. Its antiquity, the fact that it was composed in a period of history in which Eastern astronomical texts had not yet reached al-Andalus, the references made both by the Castilian translation and al-Baqqār's book explaining that the system was the one used by the ancient Romans of al-Andalus, Ifrīqiya and the Maghrib and the primitive techniques used for astrological predictions led both my master, Juan Vernet, and myself to assume a late Latin origin for this system.

This part of the book deals mainly with weather prediction,[27] periods of drought and rains and their influence on the evolution of prices of agricultural products using mainly the positions of the superior planets. The system of the crosses uses well-known aspects such as quartile, together with others such as the *iḥtirāq* ('quemazón/combustion')—when the planets are together in the same sign or scattered in either even or odd houses—[28] or the *ighlāq* ('lock'), in which the planets are *mughlaqa* (locked) when they retrograde. The planets can also be *mutasattara* (on line) when they are found in four consecutive signs. When no sign (of these four) is empty, the disposition is called *mughlaqa* (locked); if there is an empty sign, it receives the name of *mughlaqa maftūḥa* (locked and open). The text also speaks about aspects, called *ittiṣāl* (application), although the Alfonsine translation uses the term 'catamientos' which seems to be a translation of *naẓar*. These aspects are used when the author tries to establish which of the two

---

[26] Julio Samsó, 'La primitiva versión árabe del Libro de las Cruces' in *Nuevos Estudios sobre Astronomía Española en el siglo de Alfonso X*, ed. Juan Vernet (Barcelona: CSIC, 1983), pp. 149–61. Repr. in Samsó, *Islamic Astronomy* no. III; on the biography of al-Ḍabbī see Samsó, 'Sobre el astrólogo ʿAbd al-Wāḥid b. Isḥaq al-Ḍabbī (fl. c. 788– c. 852)', *Anaquel de Estudios Árabes* 12 (2001), pp. 657–69. Repr. in Samsó, *Astrometeorología y astrología medievales* nº X.

[27] On weather prediction see Gerrit Bos and Charles Burnett, *Scientific Weather Forecasting in the Middle Ages: The Writings of al-Kindī*, (London: Routledge, 2000), although its contents bear no relation to those of the *Kitāb al-amṭār*. See also Charles Burnett, 'Weather Forecasting in the Arab World', in *Magic and Divination in Early Islam*, ed. Emilie Savage-Smith (Aldershot: Ashgate, 2003), pp. 201–10.

[28] Mª Dolores Poch, 'El concepto de quemazón en el Libro de las Cruces', *Awrāq* 3 (1980): pp. 68–74.

superior planets (Saturn and Jupiter) dominates when they are in trine or quartile. A new aspect is also introduced—besides quartile, trine, conjunction and opposition—because the text speaks about a 'septile' (*tasabbu*ʿ).

There is sometimes evidence of the practice of a more developed astrology, such as passages which mention dignities (*ḥuẓūẓ*), falls (*suqūṭ*), aspects between propitious and malefic planets, opposition and conjunction.[29] This may imply that such passages could correspond to additions made by ʿAbd Allāh al-Ṭulayṭulī, who quotes other sources that are independent of the system of the crosses. Thus, in chapter 63 of the *Libro de las Cruzes* (in a passage also preserved by al-Baqqār), the text quotes an Eastern source (*baʿḍ al-mashriqiyyīn*) or (in al-Baqqār's book only) a quotation from the *Kitāb al-ʿarḍ fī l-asʿār* of Hermes al-Ḥakīm. This kind of more sophisticated astrology appears in what seems to be the remnant of a possible horoscope, indicating heavy rainfall:[30]

Saturn in the House of Illness (VI) which is Scorpio (210°–240°)
Sun in the House of Brethren (III) which is Leo (120°–150°)
Jupiter in the House of Happiness (XI) which is Aries (0°–30°)
Ascending node in the House of Life (I) which is Gemini (60°–90°)

Bearing in mind the possible time period in which ʿAbd Allāh al-Ṭulayṭulī lived, these data may correspond to 1 August 1015 when the planetary positions, according to al-Khwārizmī's *Zīj*, were:

	True long.	*Mean long.*
Saturn	234;28	238;36
Jupiter	33;30	19;53
Sun	125;58	127;39
Asc. node	77;14	

Saturn's passage through the triplicities and zodiacal signs: the Lāmiyya *of Ibn al-Khayyāṭ*

In the second part of the *Kitāb al-amṭār,* al-Baqqār deals with the passage of Saturn through the four triplicities and the twelve zodiacal signs. This part seems to be independent of the 'Book of Crosses', although the simplicity of the astrological techniques used is the same. Al-Baqqār quotes Andalusian sources, mainly the

[29] Cf. *Cruzes* cap. 5, pp. 11 a & b, 12 a.

[30] Analogous information, although less complete, can be found in the *Libro de las Cruzes* chap. 65, p. 167a, paragraph 2.

Lāmiyya (poem rhyming in *lām* = *l*) of Abū Bakr Yaḥyā b. Aḥmad, known as Ibn al-Khayyāṭ. This astrologer lived from ca. 367/977 until 447/1055–56, when he died in Toledo. He served professionally several monarchs of the period including the caliph Sulaymān b. al-Ḥakam al-Nāṣir li-Dīn Allāh (r. in 400/1010 and from 403/1013 until 407/1016), during the period of the *fitna* (anarchy after the fall of the Cordovan Caliphate) and the king of Toledo al-Ma'mūn (435/1043–467/1074–75).[31] The last king of Granada, ʿAbd Allāh b. Buluqqīn adds, in his memoirs (*Ṭibyān*)[32] that Ibn al-Khayyāṭ predicted the conquest of Denia by al-Muqtadir b. Hūd, king of Zaragoza and father of the famous king-mathematician al-Mu'taman b. Hūd, in 468/1076, followed by the death of al-Muqtadir himself in 475/1082–83. According to al-Baqqār, Ibn al-Khayyāṭ dedicated to al-Ma'mūn a *Risāla fī l-qirānāt al-nujūmiyya* (Epistle on planetary conjunctions) dealing, among other things, with the events of al-Andalus, how long the Muslims will stay in this country and signs indicating that they will soon have to leave.

Al-Baqqār is, apparently, the only source that has preserved Ibn al-Khayyāṭ's *Lāmiyya*. The *Kitāb al-amṭār* reproduces 90 verses of the poem, scattered through this second part of the work, dealing with the passage of Saturn through the four triplicities (15 verses). The three final verses of this group allow us to conjecture a possible date for the poem (around 1050):

> Listen to what I am going to describe and do not ignore what I am going to say today
> I began at the moment in which I found it stationary (*muqīm*) according to its position calculated with tables
> And I found it at the end of Capricorn, leaving the sign and moving towards Aquarius in which earthquakes are frequent.

Using the tables of al-Khwārizmī, we can easily calculate that towards 8 Jumādā I 442 (28 September 1050) Saturn reached a station, after retrograding, at 25° Capricorn. It entered 0° Aquarius on 3 Shaʿbān 442 (21 December 1050). Saturn had also entered Aquarius about thirty years earlier (22 Shawwāl 411/7 February

---

[31] Ṣāʿid, *Ṭabaqāt al-Umam*, ed. Ḥayāt Bū ʿAlwān (Beirut, 1985), p. 199. French trans. by Régis Blachère (Paris: Larose, 1935), p. 153.

[32] Ibn Buluggīn, *Tibyān*, ed. Évariste Lévi-Provençal (Cairo, 1955), p. 78 (= *Al-Andalus* 3 (1935), p. 323 and 4 (1936), p. 43); Spanish trans. by Évariste Levi-Provençal and Emilio García Gómez, *El Siglo XI en 1ª persona* (Madrid: Alianza, 1982), p. 164. English trans. by Amin T. Tibi, *The Tibyān. Memoirs of ʿAbd Allāh b. Buluggīn Last Zīrid Amīr of Granada* (Leiden: Brill, 1986), p. 94.

1021) but, in this case, there was no retrogradation before or after this date and, therefore, Ibn al-Khayyāṭ could not have found it stationary.

- Saturn in Aries (8 vv): the penultimate verse of the series is concerned with a war with the Berbers.
- Saturn in Taurus (3 vv), Gemini (4 vv) and Cancer (8 vv): The last verses (Cancer) refer to an earthquake in Cordova and a solar eclipse at midday which allowed people to see the lunar mansions during the day. This may refer to the solar eclipse which took place on 29 June 1033, with the line of totality crossing the northern part of the Iberian Peninsula. At the moment of the eclipse, Saturn was in Cancer. On the other hand, the first verse of the Cancer series mentions the presence, in the sign of Cancer, of *al-qahhārān* or *al-qāhirān* (the two powerful ones); this is probably a reference to Saturn and Mars which, again according to the tables of al-Khwārizmī, had a conjunction in Cancer (110°) on 15 September 1033.
- Saturn in Leo (6 vv), Virgo (8 vv) and Libra (6 vv): the passage of Saturn through 21° Libra, which is the degree of its exaltation, produces all kinds of disasters.
- Saturn in Scorpio (5 vv) and Sagittarius (8 vv): the sixth verse of the Sagittarius series seems to allude to an occultation of Saturn by the full Moon which was advancing towards the ascending node together with the planet.
- Saturn in Capricorn (5 vv), Aquarius (10 vv) and Pisces (2 vv):

Al-Baqqār ends with two other verses, dealing with different topics, and the whole gives the impression that he has not quoted Ibn al-Khayyāṭ's *Lāmiyya* in full.

More elaborate techniques of astrometeorological prediction in the Kitāb al-amṭār

The book continues with the analysis of the passage of Saturn through the zodiacal signs using other sources and techniques. Thus al-Baqqār refers to *tasyīr* when he uses terms such as *ṭāli*ʿ (ascendant), *qaṭ*ʿ (cut) or *haylāj* (indicator). Among his sources he quotes 'Some Roman/ or Greek wise men' (*baʿḍ ḥukamāʾ al-Rūm*), which contain references to al-Andalus. This makes me think of the possibility of a relation of this source to the aforementioned 'system of the crosses'. Other authorities are Hermes and ʿUmar ibn al-Farrukhān al-Ṭabarī (second half of the eighth century–beginning of the ninth century) whom he seems to have known through an Andalusian recension of a book of his, written by somebody called ʿAbd al-ʿAzīz ibn al-Bayṭār, possibly the author of a set of tables of planetary latitudes (perhaps derived from those of Ibn al-Kammād) mentioned by the anonymous author of the Tunisian recension of the *Zīj* of Ibn Isḥāq extant in the

Hyderabad manuscript.[33] Al-Baqqār also mentions another anonymous source considered reliable by him: a conjunction of Saturn and Mars in the sign of Pisces in 626/1228–29, which brought prosperity to al-Andalus and poverty to the Eastern part of the Maghrib, Egypt and Syria. Using modern tables, it is easy to check that such a conjunction took place at 324° (near Pisces) on 21 November 1228.[34] It would have been possible to obtain similar results with the medieval tables used at that time.

This is followed by another passage in which al-Baqqār, after considering the transit of Saturn through triplicities, tropical, fixed and bicorporeal signs, adds other variables such as conjunctions of Saturn–Mars and Jupiter–Venus, as well as the already mentioned conjunction of Saturn and Jupiter. He insists on the importance of Venus and the Moon, whose relation to rainfall is a well-known astrological commonplace; he makes predictions based on the lunar mansions in which Venus rises and on the direct or retrograde motion of the superior planets.[35] He applies medical ideas (such as the moments of crisis of an illness) to the study of astrometeorology; the position of the Moon allows him to predict moments of crisis which imply a change of weather in a particular month. He also introduces refinements such as the projection of rays, the idea of the *ḥayyiz* (domain) of every planet, decans, *ḥudūd* (terms), as well as the *ziyāda/nuqṣān* (increase/decrease) in *ḥisāb* (calculation) or *masīr* (velocity).

The last part of the book is divided into three chapters which deal with 1) meteorology and rains, 2) prices and 3) solar and lunar eclipses. In the first chapter a new source appears: Ibn Abī l-Rijāl's *Kitāb al-Bāriʿ fī aḥkām al-nujūm* which offers new techniques for weather prediction. Such predictions can be made for yearly periods with the standard method of casting the horoscope of the conjunction or opposition of the Sun and the Moon before the vernal equinox, although there are other significant moments. There are also predictions for seasons (horoscope of the conjunction or opposition before equinoxes and solstices), for half months (application of the Moon to a planet when the former leaves the place of the conjunction or opposition), for each week (horoscopes of syzygies and

33 Mestres, 'Maghribī Astronomy in the 13th Century', p. 428.

34 William D. Stahlman and Owen Gingerich, *Solar and Planetary Longitudes for Years –2500 to +2000* (Madison: University of Wisconsin Press, 1963), p. 456; Bryant Tuckerman, *Planetary, Lunar and Solar Positions A.D. 2 to A.D. 1649* (Philadelphia: American Philosophical Society, 1964), p. 632.

35 On predictions based on the Moon see Charles Burnett, 'Lunar Astrology: The Varieties of Texts Using Lunar Mansions, with Emphasis on *Jafar Indus*', *Micrologus XII: Il sole e la luna* (Florence: SISMEL, 2004), pp. 43–133 + 7 plates.

quadratures), and for periods of two-and-a-half days (passage of the Moon through the twelve zodiacal signs). For predictions of this kind al-Baqqār introduces cycles of world-astrology (*qisma* and *ifrādiyya*) and defines new theoretical instruments:

a) Three lots (*sihām*) which are the *sahm al-maṭar, sahm al-riyāḥ* and *sahm al-ayyām* which correspond, respectively, to the lots of rain, winds and 'days'. Only the *sahm al-riyāḥ* is calculated with the same method as in Eastern sources; this is not the case of the *sahm al-maṭar*. Al-Baqqār ascribes the *sahm al-ayyām* to Abū Maʿshar, as does Ibn Abī l-Rijāl, although I have not been able to find this *sahm* in the *Madkhal Kabīr*.

b) *Ta'sīsāt* which seem equivalent to the *fashīshāt* mentioned by al-Bīrūnī:[36] they are a series (12 according to al-Bīrūnī, 24 according to al-Baqqār) of elongations of the Moon from the Sun, at unequal intervals, which are considered sensitive points in the monthly displacement of the Moon.

c) 'Opening of the doors' (*abwāb al-futūḥ, abwāb al-futuḥāt*), a concept which appears, with minor differences, in many Eastern sources such as ʿUmar ibn al-Farrukhān, al-Kindī,[37] al-Qabīṣī,[38] Kūshyār ibn Labbān[39] and al-Bīrūnī[40]. Al-Baqqār's definition is not the same as that of his Eastern predecessors; there is 'opening of the doors' when the Moon separates from one planet of two which have their domiciles in opposite signs[41] and enters into application with the other one.

d) Increase and decrease in number (*ʿadad*), equation (*taʿdīl*) and light (*nūr*) as well as *sāʿid/hābiṭ fī falaki-hi* (ascending/descending in its sphere) and *baṭī'/sarīʿ al-sayr* (slow/fast of motion).

[36] al-Bīrūnī, *Kitāb al-Tafhīm li-awā'il ṣināʿat al-tanjīm*, facsimile ed. and English trans. by R. Ramsay Wright (London: Luzac, 1934), p. 153.

[37] Bos & Burnett, *Scientific Weather Forecasting*, pp. 19, 385–94, 447–48.

[38] Charles Burnett, Keiji Yamamoto and Michio Yano, *Al-Qabīṣī (Alcabitius): The Introduction to Astrology*, eds. of the Arabic and Latin texts and an English trans. (London and Turin: Warburg Institute, 2004), pp. 136–37.

[39] Kushyār Ibn Labbān, *Introduction to Astrology*, ed. and trans., Michio Yano (Tokyo: Institute for the Study of Languages and Cultures of Asia and Africa, 1997), pp. 86–89, 90, 95.

[40] al-Bīrūnī, *Tafhīm*, pp. 314–15.

[41] Venus (Libra and Taurus) and Mars (Scorpio and Aries); Mercury (Virgo and Gemini) and Jupiter (Sagittarius and Pisces).

The second chapter of this last part deals with the oscillation of prices of agricultural products which, according to al-Baqqār, depends on periods of rainfall or drought. His ideas on this topic are interesting because he states that an increase of the offer of products in the market does not necessarily imply a reduction in their price. In his opinion, the Moon is the cause of an opposition between merchandise and *ʿayn*; he never explains the meaning of *al-ʿayn* although it is clear that he is referring to gold and silver coins.[42] His attitude to high and low prices is not always clear although, in most cases, he associates good (*khayr*) with increases in prices and evil (*al-sharr wa-l-fasād*) with falls. Thus when propitious indicators (*suʿūd*) are in a favourable situation, prices rise, and when their position is unfavourable, prices fall, but similar things are also said about the malefics (*nuḥūs*), which is a clear contradiction. In most of the cases, however, the second attitude corresponds to quotations of other authors such as ʿAlī ibn Riḍwān's commentary on the *Tetrabiblos* or an unidentified Ibrāhīm al-Yahūdī. Al-Baqqār's attitude, however, seems to change in his analysis of the oscillation of prices using concepts derived from world astrology: when the malefic Saturn is in the sign of the last conjunction with Jupiter, or in the *Burj al-Milla* (sign of the Religion) or in the *Burj al-qirān al-dāll ʿalā l-Milla* (sign of the conjunction which indicated the rise of Islam)—which should be considered privileged positions—the price of food will go up and there will be widespread famine. It is clear that the *al-qirān al-dāll ʿalā l-Milla* is the conjunction of Saturn and Jupiter, with a change of triplicity, which took place in 571 (coinciding approximately with the birth of the Prophet) in the sign of Scorpio.[43] As for the *Burj al-Milla* the interpretation is doubtful, although I believe that al-Baqqār is referring to the sign of Cancer, which was the sign of Saturn at the moment of the spring equinox of the year of the beginning of the Hijra (19 March 622). Two days later (21 March 622) there was a conjunction of Saturn and Mars, also in Cancer, according to Abū Maʿshar.[44] Cancer corresponded, again, to the mean longitude of Saturn on the day of the beginning of the Hijra (14 July 622), while its true longitude was in the beginning of Leo. If we realise that the sign of the last mean conjunction of Saturn and Jupiter before

---

[42] Reinhart Dozy, *Supplement aux dictionnaires arabes* II (repr. Leiden-Paris: Brill, 1967) p. 197.

[43] On this topic see, recently, Kennedy et al., 'al-Battānī's astrological history', pp. 34–41, 88–92; Samsó, 'La *Urŷūza* de Ibn Abī l-Riŷāl', in *al-Qanṭara* 30 (2009): pp. 322–26.

[44] Keiji Yamamoto and Charles Burnett, eds., *Abū Maʿshar on Historical Astrology: The Book of Religions and Dynasties (On the Great Conjunctions)*, 2 vols (Leiden-Boston-Köln: Brill, 2000), I: pp. 124–25 and David Pingree, *The Thousands of Abū Maʿshar* (London: Warburg Institute, 1968), p. 80.

the beginning of the era (25 September 610) was Pisces, we have three signs (Cancer, Scorpio and Pisces) which, curiously enough, form the triplicity of water.

The predictions on the oscillation of prices use the same methodology as those related to meteorology; the same periods of time are used (years, seasons, months, half months and weeks) and the Moon, whose importance for the prediction of rainfall has already been mentioned—followed by the Sun, Venus and Mercury—is the most important indicator.

The chapter gives frequent lists of the products subject to price oscillations. The products are the ones we would expect in the economy of the Maghrib at the beginning of the fifteenth century: agricultural products used for human nourishment or weaving, as well as dyeing, all kinds of cattle but not a single reference to fishing. Allusions to metals and mining are scarce and only one luxury product is mentioned: perfumes. The aforementioned products have astrological associations which may be the triplicities or specific planets.

It is interesting that al-Baqqār makes three different attempts to quantify rises and falls in prices. The clearest one establishes that the difference in degrees of longitude between the planet which indicates the change in the price and the planet with which it enters into application will correspond to the number of dinars or dirhams of the increase or decrease.

The third chapter deals with the indications of solar and lunar eclipses and it is the only part of the whole book unrelated to rains or prices. Interestingly, however, it contains quotations from Ibn Hibintā and passages where the *al-Kitāb al-Mughnī* has clearly been used although its author is not mentioned. Thus, using information gathered in the *Tetrabiblos*, in the *Karpós* and in Ibn Hibintā's *Mughnī*, the author studies the period of time during which the influence of an eclipse will last as well as the moment in which this influence will be most powerful. He also deals with the people that will be affected by the eclipse according, among other things, to the zodiacal sign or the lunar mansion in which the eclipse will take place.

*LUNAR ELECTIONS IN IBN RAḤĪQ'S FOLK-ASTRONOMICAL TREATISE**

Petra G. Schmidl

Ibn Raḥīq, most probably a legal scholar from eleventh-century Hijaz in the northwestern part of the Arabian Peninsula, integrates in his folk-astronomical treatise with an incomplete title— . . . *ʿalā madhāhib al-ʿArab* ('. . . according to the methods of the Arabs')—a lengthy chapter on the lunar mansions which also includes astrological information on elections. This is a common topic here dealt with in an unexpected place.

Elections

Choosing the appropriate time to start an activity has been a standard procedure of astrology at least since Greek antiquity and was commonly used in the Middle Ages.[1] The terms used for this procedure either reflect the first aspect, 'choices': in Latin *electiones*, in Arabic *ikhtiyārāt*, in Hebrew *mivrahīm*, or the second, 'beginnings': in Greek *katarchai*, in Arabic *ibtidāʾāt*. These elections are often either given in lists arranged by month, day or hour, or described by the position of the moon with respect to the signs of the zodiac and in relation to the

---

* Many people were involved in preparing this paper by listening, correcting, commenting, annotating, and providing additional data. I wish to express my special gratitude to Sabine Arndt, Charles Burnett, Benno von Dalen, Moritz Epple, Sharon S. Horowitz, Teije de Jong, David A. King, Paul Kunitzsch, Tzvi Langermann, Thebe Medupe, Jay Rovner, Christine Wern, Joshua V. Schmidl and Martin Schmidl. All remaining mistakes are the author's responsibility.

Without the support of the library of the Institute for the History of Arabic-Islamic Science, Frankfurt, and the library of the former Institute for the History of Science, Frankfurt, the work on this topic would have been much more cumbersome. Parts of the research done for this project were generously founded by the Cusanuswerk, Bonn and the Fritz Thyssen Stiftung, Düsseldorf.

1 See, e.g., Nicholas Campion, *A History of Western Astrology*, 2 vols. (London, New York: Continuum, 2008), 1: p. 205, n. 15 (with a different explanation of the derivation of the Greek word), and 2: p. 22.

other planets. They are qualified either as auspicious, inauspicious, or ambiguous for specific activities.[2] Additionally, there are elections defining these times by means of the position of the moon with respect to the lunar mansions. They are designated in this article as 'lunar elections'.[3]

---

[2] E.g., Dorotheus of Sidon, *Carmen Astrologicum*, trans. David Pingree, Book V (Leipzig: Teubner, 1976); see also Toufic Fahd, *Nudjūm, Aḥkām al-, II. Hemerology and menology, The Encyclopaedia of Islam, New Edition*, 12 volumes and indices (Leiden: Brill, 1960–2009; henceforth *EI*²), VIII: pp. 107b–108b with a list of Arabic treatises dealing with elections; David Juste, *Les Alchandreana primitifs: Étude sur les plus anciens traités astrologiques latins d'origine arabe (Xe siècle)* (Leiden, Boston: Brill, 2007), pp. 167–74; R.Y. Ebied and M.L.J. Young, 'A Treatise on Hemerology Ascribed to Ǧa'far al-Ṣadīq', *Arabica* 23 (1976): pp. 296–307; Toufic Fahd, *La divination arabe* (Leiden: E.J. Brill,1966), pp. 483–84; Wilhelm Gundel, *Sternglaube, Sternreligion und Sternorakel. Aus der Geschichte der Astrologie*, 2nd Aufl. Neu bearb. von Hans Georg Gundel (Heidelberg: Quelle und Meyer, 1959), pp. 66–67 and 77–78; Viktor Stegemann, *Beiträge zu Geschichte der Astrologie I: Der griechische Astrologe Dorotheos von Sidon und der arabische Astrologe Abu 'l-Ḥasan 'Ali ibn abi 'r-Riǧāl, genannt Albohazen*, Quellen und Studien zur Geschichte und Kultur des Altertums und des Mittelalters, Reihe D: Untersuchungen und Mitteilungen 2 (Heidelberg: F. Bilabel, 1935), p. 6; Auguste Bouché-Leclercq, *L'astrologie grecque* (Paris, 1899), pp. 461–66.

[3] E.g., Carlo Alfonso Nallino, 'Astrology', in *The Encyclopaedia of Islam, First Edition* (Leiden, London: Brill, 1913–1936; Photomechanical Reprint in 9 volumes, [Leiden: Brill, 1987]; henceforth *EI*¹), p. 496a: '2. The system of 'electiones' (*ikhtiyārāt*, καταρχαί), *i.e.*, the choice of the auspicious moment for accomplishing such and such an act; this moment is determined by observing in which of the twelve celestial houses the moon is. Astrologers who preferred the Indian methods employed the 28 lunary stations (*manāzil*) in place of the twelve houses.' and Charles Burnett, 'Astrology' in *The Encyclopaedia of Islam, Three* (Leiden: Brill, 2007, henceforth *EI*³), pp. 164–75 (see p. 173a), Brill Online, 2015, http://referenceworks.brillonline.com/entries/encyclopaedia-of-islam-3/astrology-COM_0162, section 3.4: 'Arabic texts of this genre were called *ikhtiyārāt* ('choices'), often with the addition *al-sā'āt* ('of hours'). [. . .] Some works of this genre use the lunar mansions for choosing the times to act or avoid action, and some of these in turn include references to making talismans. Among the latter are various versions of a work attributed to Hermes, [. . .].'

The Lunar Mansions

The lunar mansions comprise twenty-eight stars and groups of stars arranged in a belt extending some degrees north and south of the ecliptic, the apparent path of the sun around the earth (see Table 1).[4]

	Name	Modern Designation
(1)	*al-sharaṭān, al-ashrāṭ*, or *al-naṭḥ*	βγ Ari or βα Ari
(2)	*al-buṭayn*	εδρ Ari
(3)	*al-thurayyā*	the Pleiades (M 45 and η Tau)
(4)	*al-dabarān*	α Tau
(5)	*al-haqʿa*	$\lambda\varphi^{1,2}$ Ori
(6)	*al-hanʿa*	γξ Gem
(7)	*al-dhirāʿ*	αβ Gem
(8)	*al-nathra*	ε Cnc or εγδ Cnc
(9)	*al-ṭarf*	δ or χ Cnc und λ Leo
(10)	*al-jabha*	ζγηα Leo
(11)	*al-zubra*, or *al-kharātān*	δθ Leo
(12)	*al-ṣarfa*	β Leo
(13)	*al-ʿawwāʾ*	βηγε Vir, sometimes in addition δ Vir

4 For a general introduction see Paul Kunitzsch, 'al-Manāzil' in *EI*^{2}, s.v. The list of the lunar mansions in this work is primarily found on pp. 374a–b, with additional information extracted from Varisco, 'Islamic Folk Astronomy', in *Astronomy across Cultures: The History of Non-Western Astronomy*, Helaine Selin and Xiaochun Sun, eds. (Dordrecht: Kluwer Academic Publishers, 2000), p. 621. See also the description in chapter 56 of al-Bīrūnī in C. Edward Sachau, *Alberuni's India: An Account of the Religion, Philosophy, Literature, Geography, Chronology, Astronomy, Customs, Laws and Astrology of India about A.D. 1030 edited in the Arabic Original* (London, 1887), pp. 242–46 (Arabic text) and al-Bīrūnī, Sachau, *Alberuni's India: An Account of the Religion, Philosophy, Literature, Geography, Chronology, Astronomy, Customs, Laws and Astrology of India aboul A.D. 1030. An English Edition with Notes and Indices*, 2 vols. 2nd ed. (London, 1910) 2: pp. 81–89 (English translation).

	Name	Modern Designation
(14)	*al-simāk*	α Vir
(15)	*al-ghafr*	ικλ Vir or ικ Vir
(16)	*al-zubānā*	αβ Lib
(17)	*al-iklīl*	βδπ Sco
(18)	*al-qalb*	α Sco
(19)	*al-shawla*, *al-ibra*, or *ibrat al-ʿaqrab*	λν Sco
(20)	*al-naʿāʾim*	γδεη Sgr and σφτζ Sgr
(21)	*al-balda*	a void region without stars
(22)	*saʿd al-dhābiḥ*	$\alpha^{1,2}$ νβ Cap
(23)	*saʿd bulaʿ*	με Aqr, sometimes in addition Fl. 7 Aqr or ω Aqr
(24)	*saʿd al-suʿūd*	βξ Aqr and c^1 Cap
(25)	*saʿd al-akhbiya*	γπζη Aqr
(26)	*al-fargh al-muqaddam*, or *al-fargh al-awwal* [5]	αβ Peg
(27)	*al-fargh al-muʾakhkhar*, or *al-fargh al-thānī* [6]	γ Peg and α and/or γδ Peg
(28)	*baṭn al-ḥūt*, or *al-rishāʾ*	β and ???

Table 1: The lunar mansions.

While the zodiacal signs subdivide this belt into twelve equal parts of 30 degrees each, the lunar mansions subdivide it into twenty-eight equal parts of 12 6/7 degrees each and thus represent a lunar zodiac. The twelve zodiacal signs can be regarded as the twelve *monthly* mansions of the sun. Approximately once each month the sun changes its mansion, until it returns to the same sign after one year. On the other hand the lunar mansions can be regarded as the twenty-eight

[5] Ikhwān al-Ṣafāʾ, *Rasāʾil*, 4 vols. (Beirut: Dār Ṣādir, 1957), 4: p. 441: *muqaddam al-dalw*.
[6] Ikhwān al-Ṣafāʾ, *Rasāʾil*, vol. 4, p. 442: *muʾakhkhar al-dalw*.

daily mansions of the moon. Approximately every day of a lunar month the moon changes its mansion, until it returns to the same mansion after a month.[7] In their function as a lunar zodiac the lunar mansions can also be used similarly to the zodiacal signs, the Egyptian decans, or the Babylonian *ziqpu*-stars, for timekeeping by night and calendrical purposes.[8]

Folk Astronomical Sources

The lunar mansions play a prominent part in folk astronomical sources, although they are also mentioned in scientific treatises, e.g., in astronomical handbooks with tables (singular *zīj*, plural *zījāt*).[9] Current research on pre-

---

[7] See e.g., David Pingree, 'Ḳamar 1: Astronomy' in *EI*², s.v., p. 517a: 'The risings of the 28 *manāzil*, which are individual stars or groups of stars that the moon conjoins with roughly at the rate of one each night of a sidereal month, [. . .]'; and Manfred Ullmann, *Die Natur- und Geheimwissenschaften im Islam*, Handbuch der Orientalistik 1. Abt., VI:2 (Leiden: Brill, 1972), p. 351: 'Die zwölf Zodiakalbilder sind gewissermaßen die monatlichen Stationen der Sonne in ihrem Jahreslauf. Entsprechend wurden die Sterngruppen, in denen der Mond jede Nacht bei seinem Umlauf von 27 oder 28 Tagen erscheint oder 'Station macht', als Mondstationen (*manzil al-qamar*, plur. *al-manāzil*) bezeichnet'.

[8] For Egypt and the decans see Otto Neugebauer, 'The Egyptian "Decans"', *Vistas in Astronomy* 1 (1960): pp. 47–51; Otto Neugebauer and Richard A. Parker, *Egyptian Astronomical Texts: The Early Decans*, vol. 1 (Providence, London: Lund Humphries,1960), pp. 95–121; and, more briefly for Mesopotamia and the *ziqpu*-stars Hermann Hunger and David Pingree, *Astral Sciences in Mesopotamia*, Handbuch der Orientalistik Abt. 1, Bd. 44 (Leiden, Boston, Köln: Brill, 1999), pp. 84–90; Hermann Hunger and David Pingree, *MUL.APIN: An Astronomical Compendium in Cuneiform*, Archiv für Orientforschung Beiheft 24 (Horn / Austria: Berger, 1989), esp. pp. 137–45.

[9] The preliminary version of September 2007 of Benno van Dalen's, *A New Survey of Islamic Astronomical Tables*, kindly provided by the author, lists approximately 200 known *zīj*es, and describes more than half of these in detail with a full table of contents. According to the information given, the lunar mansions were mentioned in *ca.* 20 *zīj*es. The earliest of these appears to be Kūshyār b. Labbān''s *al-Zīj al-Jāmi'* (Gurgān [?], 1025, see Edward S. Kennedy, *A Survey of Islamic Astronomical Tables*, Transactions of the American Philosophical Society. New Series 46:2 [Philadelphia: American Philosophical Society, 1956, repr. 1989], 9; Mohammed Bagheri, *al-Zīj al-Jāmi', an Arabic astronomical handbook by Kūshyār b. Labbān. Books I and IV*, Islamic Mathematics and Astronomy 114 [Frankfurt am Main: Institut für Geschichte der arabisch-islamischen Wissenschaften, 2009], chap. I.8.10), on which the anonymous *Dustūr al-munajjimīn* (Raqqa or Alamut, *ca.* 1110 [?]) and the anonymous *al-Zīj al-Muṣṭalaḥ* (ibid., 47; Egypt, *ca.* 1250 [?]) rely. Ibn al-

modern astronomy in Islamicate societies uses the concepts of folk or popular astronomy on the one hand and scientific or mathematical astronomy on the other to distinguish different ways of practising astronomy.[10] Usually the genre of the texts, the authors who wrote them and the methods they describe are the criteria used to distinguish these two astronomical traditions. But the distinction is problematic. Texts like the *Kitāb al-Tabṣira fī ʿilm al-nujūm* by al-Ashraf ʿUmar (Yemen, d. 1296) contain methods of both traditions for the same problem and authors like al-Fārisī (Yemen, d. 1278/79) wrote treatises in both traditions.[11] Additionally, the designations coined for these astronomical traditions may be misleading. The terms 'folk' or 'popular' astronomy suggest that they describe how common people practised astronomy. But all that is preserved are the records of scholars about this practice. Although the concept of folk astronomy thus has its problems, it is nevertheless useful in understanding pre-modern astronomy in Islamicate societies.

The Lunar Elections in Ibn Raḥīq's Folk Astronomical Treatise

Ibn Raḥīq: His Life and Work

The unexpected discovery of a description of lunar elections in a folk astronomical treatise initiated this investigation.[12] Its author, Ibn Raḥīq, is unknown except through some meagre hints given in his treatise. According to this information he lived in the Hijaz, a region in the northwestern part of the

---

Shāṭir's highly influential *al-Zīj al-Jadīd* (ibid., 11; Damascus, *ca.* 1365) also deals with the lunar mansions, and so do a range of *zījāt* depending on it, including Kawm al-Rīshī's *al-Lumʿa* (Cairo, *ca.* 1415), Shihāb al-Dīn al-Ḥalabī's *Nuzhat al-nāẓir* (Damascus, *ca.* 1435), his *al-ʿIqd al-yamānī* (Damascus, *ca.* 1440), and his *al-Durr al-fākhir* (Damascus, *ca.* 1450).

[10] Petra Schmidl, *Volkstümliche Astronomie im islamischen Mittelalter. Zur Bestimmung der Gebetszeiten und der Qibla bei al-al-Aṣbaḥī, Ibn Raḥīq und al-Fārisī* (Leiden: Brill, 2007), pp. 78–92. Concerning astrology there is a similar distinction in use between 'scientific / mathematical astrology' and 'folk astrology' (Burnett, 'Astrology', pp. 165b–166a).

[11] On al-Ashraf ʿUmar see n. 25, and on al-Fārisī n. 24.

[12] Lunar elections in astrological and magical sources are not the subject of this paper, but some examples are mentioned in a later section (see below). In most cases the general character of the treatises mentioned in Daniel M. Varisco, 'The Magical Significance of the Lunar Stations in the 13th Century Yemeni *Kitab al-Tabsira fi ilm al-nujum* of al-Malik al-Ashraf', *Quaderni di Studi Arabi* 13 (1995): p. 25, n. 30, is difficult to determine (see also n. 32).

Arabian Peninsula which includes the cities of Mecca and Medina, most probably at the beginning or the middle of the eleventh century. His treatise demonstrates that Ibn Raḥīq was trained in Quranic studies and Islamic jurisprudence. Familiar with astronomy and timekeeping, he also knew about the folk-astronomical traditions of the Yemen and of Egypt.[13]

Ibn Raḥīq's Folk Astronomical Treatise

Ibn Raḥīq's treatise is preserved in only one manuscript, most probably copied in the thirteenth or fourteenth century and now in Berlin (Staatsbibliothek Preußischer Kulturbesitz, Lbg. 108 [=Ahlwardt 5664]).[14] The manuscript consists of seventy-one folios and is in poor condition. Some sheets are missing and the remaining folios are mixed up. The edge is damaged and parts of the text are pasted over. On the first page only the second part of the title is visible: ...*ʿalā madhāhib al-ʿArab* ('. . . according to the methods of the Arabs'); the first part is pasted over.[15]

The treatise consists of forty-five chapters of varying length. Apart from the sections concerning the prayer times and the *qibla*, it includes chapters dealing with lexicographical lists, timekeeping, Islamic worship and calendrical matters (see Table 2).[16]

fols.	Title	Contents
1a	(title page)	—
1b	(introduction)	—
2a–3b	(on several traditions)	—
3b–4a	The names of the hours	*anwāʾ, azmina*
4a	The names of the hours of the night	*anwāʾ, azmina*
4b	The names of the days	*anwāʾ, azmina*
4b	The names of the days in pre-Islamic times	*anwāʾ, azmina*

13 Schmidl, *Volksastronomie*, p. 14; David A. King, *Mathematical Astronomy in Medieval Yemen: A Biobibliographical Survey*, American Research Centre for Egypt (Malibu: Udena Publications, 1983; henceforth *MAY*), pp. 20–21; Carl Brockelmann, *Geschichte der arabischen Litteratur*, vol. 1 (Leiden: Brill, 1937–1942; henceforth *GAL*), pp. 224, 257.

14 See https://ismi.mpiwg-berlin.mpg.de/om4-ismi/public/publicCodex.jsp?eid=101488.

15 Schmidl, *Volksastronomie*, pp. 15–16.

16 Schmidl, *Volksastronomie*, pp. 17–18; see also King, *MAY*, p. 21.

fols.	Title	Contents
4b–5a	The names of the months in Arabic	*anwāʾ, azmina*
5a–6a	The names of the lunar nights	*anwāʾ, azmina*
6a	The length of the Arabic months	*azmina,* chronology
6a	The names of the months in Syrian	*azmina,* chronology
6a–6b	The names of the months in Byzantine	*azmina,* chronology
6b	The names of the months in Coptic	*azmina,* chronology
6b	The names of the months in the language of the Himyarites	*azmina,* chronology
7a	The names of the months in Persian	*azmina,* chronology
7b–8a	The names of the lunar mansions	descriptive astronomy
8a–8b	On the prayer times	sacred astronomy, timekeeping
8b–10a	On the determination of the break of dawn	sacred astronomy, timekeeping
10b–11a	On the determination of sun set, the breaking of the fasting and the duty of the evening prayer	sacred astronomy, timekeeping
11a–11b	On the changing of dawn during the seasons	sacred astronomy, timekeeping
11b–12a	On the determination of the time of midday	sacred astronomy, timekeeping
12a–12b	On shadow measurements in Mecca	sacred astronomy, timekeeping
12b–13a	On the longest shadow length at several places	sacred astronomy, timekeeping
13a–14a	Chapter on the knowledge of the lunar motion (*masīr al-qamar*)	descriptive astronomy
14a	Abū Jaʿfar al-Rāsibī on the moon	descriptive astronomy
14a–15a	On observations of the moon	descriptive astronomy
15a	Chapter on the oddities of this discipline	descriptive astronomy
15b	On the determination of (the position) of the moon in the zodiacal signs	descriptive astronomy
15b–17b	On the characteristics of the waning and waxing of the moon	descriptive astronomy
18a	On the appearing of the new moon at the beginning of the year	descriptive astronomy, chronology
18a–19b	On the determination of the *qibla* by means	sacred geography

fols.	Title	Contents
	of the sun, the moon, the stars, and the winds	
19b	On the determination of the *qibla* by means of the winds	sacred geography
19b–22b	On the determination of the *qibla* in the Qur'an and the *sunna*	sacred geography
22b–23a	On the determination of the *qibla* in the *ḥadith*s	sacred geography
23a–25b	On the determination of the *qibla* according to Ibn Surāqa	sacred geography
25b–27a	On the division of the seasons	*azmina*, calendars
27a–28a	On different divisions of the year	*azmina*, calendars
28a–29a	On the determination of what has passed of the day	Timekeeping
29a–30b	On different opinions about the increasing and decreasing of the day and the night	Timekeeping
30b–31a	The descendents (*al-raqā'ib*) of the zodiacal signs	descriptive astronomy
31a–32a	The descendents (*al-raqā'ib*) of the lunar mansions and the (northern) pole (*al-quṭb*)	descriptive astronomy
32a–32b	On the spherical pole	descriptive astronomy
32b–33b	On mentioning the milky way	descriptive astronomy
33b–34b	The seven spheres of the scientist of the stars (*ahl al-nujūm*)	Cosmology
34b–39a	On the lunar mansion in which the moon rises	Chronology
39b–71b	On the lunar mansions	chronology, timekeeping, astrology

Table 2: Table of contents of Ibn Raḥīq's folk-astronomical treatise … 'alā madhāhib al-ʿArab ('… according to the methods of the Arabs').

The Chapter on the Lunar Mansions

The final chapter in Ibn Raḥīq's treatise deals with the lunar mansions. It covers almost half the manuscript, although the information on almost half the lunar mansions is missing: that related to lunar mansions 1 to 11 (i.e., *al-sharaṭān* to *al-kharaṭān*) and to lunar mansion 25 (*sa'd al-akhbiya*). It is written very systematically and starts with a general introduction describing a simple and approximate method for timekeeping by means of the lunar mansions that is very common in folk astronomical sources. The main part of the chapter lists similar data for each section describing a lunar mansion.[17]

Each section for a lunar mansion starts with the date for its heliacal rising in the Coptic, Syrian, Julian and Persian calendars. Condensed information follows, within which is hidden the simple and approximate way of timekeeping by night by means of the lunar mansions; this is explained briefly by Ibn Raḥīq in the general introduction of the chapter. Using this method, three of the five daily prayers of Islam related to twilight can be determined, namely the evening (*al-maghrib*), the night (*al-'ishā'*) and the morning prayer (*al-fajr* or *al-ṣubḥ*).[18] Afterwards, Ibn Raḥīq explains the number and the arrangement of the stars in the lunar mansion, gives a derivation of its name, and adds more general information concerning it. Then he mentions the length of the midday shadow in Mecca, which suffices for determining the two remaining of the five daily prayers of Islam: the midday (*al-ẓuhr*) and the afternoon prayer (*al-'aṣr*). Always starting with 'The Indians say', Ibn Raḥīq then introduces the lunar elections. He states which actions are auspicious and which inauspicious when the moon in its monthly course finds itself in that particular lunar mansion. The elections end with 'God knows best' or an equivalent saying. The final part of the description presents meteorological and agricultural data.[19]

---

[17] The chapter of Ibn Raḥīq's treatise dealing with the lunar mansions, and including the lunar elections, is edited, translated and annotated in Schmidl, *Volksastronomie*, pp. 280–305. (B, 39b–71b); the elections themselves are not discussed in the commentary on pp. 602–14, mainly because the project was focused on the determination of the prayer times and of the *qibla*, the sacred direction towards Mecca.

[18] Schmidl, *Volksastronomie*, pp. 602–08; Schmidl, 'On Timekeeping by the Lunar Mansions in Medieval Egypt', in *Time and Astronomy in Past Cultures: Proceedings of the Conference, Toruń, 30 March – 1 April, 2005*, Arkadiusz Soltysiak, ed., pp. 75–87 (Warszawa: Institute of Archaeology, Warsaw University, 2006), pp. 77–78; Forcada, 'Mīqāt en los calendarios andalusíes', *al-Qantara* 11:1 (1990): pp. 63–67; see also Julio Samsó, 'Lunar Mansions and Timekeeping in Western Islam', *Suhayl* 8 (2008): pp. 122–36.

[19] These parts are omitted in Schmidl, *Volksastronomie*, pp. 280–305.

Ibn Raḥīq makes use of the lunar mansions in two different ways, a monthly and a daily use (see above). By means of their heliacal risings the lunar mansions subdivide the year into sections of thirteen days. To get the 365 days of a regular solar year an additional day is necessary, which is usually added to *al-jabha*.[20] The information in this chapter on timekeeping, as well as the meteorological and agricultural data, belongs to this monthly use of the lunar mansions. But the elections are given for each day and change with the waxing and waning of the moon. At first sight it seems somewhat awkward to deal with the monthly and daily use of the lunar mansions at the same time.

The Lunar Elections

The activities recommended or disapproved by Ibn Raḥīq on a given day, based on the location of the moon in a particular lunar mansion, concern economic, social and political matters. Most of them focus on buying and selling and the appropriate time to call on kings and noblemen. Elections concerning social life concentrate on the appropriate time for marriage. Recommendations concerning health, agriculture, and warfare are scattered and do not appear very often. The most detailed section is that on lunar mansion 22 (*sa'd al-dhābiḥ*), which may be a hint that originally there was more information related to the other lunar mansions as well, lost in the transmission and/or copying process (see Appendix).

RELATED TEXTS

There are at least three folk astronomical texts related to Ibn Raḥīq's folk astronomical treatise, primarily because of their similarities in content, but also because of their time and place of compilation. However, none of these treatises deals with lunar elections.

---

[20] Abū Muḥammad 'Abd Allāh Ibn Qutayba, *Kitāb al-Anwā': On Meteorology of the Arabs*, M. Hamidullah and Charles Pellat, eds. (Hyderabad: Maṭba'at Majlis al-Ma'ārif, 1375H/1956), p. 7; al-Bīrūnī, *Chronology*, in C. Edward Sachau, *The Chronology of Ancient Nations. An English Version of the Athâr-ul-Bâkiya of Albîrûnî, or "Vestiges in the Past"* (London: Oriental translation fund of Great Britain & Ireland, 1879, repr. Frankfurt: Institut für Geschichte der Arabisch-Islamischen Wissenschaften, Frankfurt am Main, 1998), p. 339; al-Fārisī in Schmidl, *Volksastronomie*, p. 634; different al-Aṣbaḥī in Schmidl, *Volksastronomie*, p. 535.

Tenth-Century al-Andalus: Aḥmad b. Fāris

Although written in tenth-century al-Andalus, the part of the Iberian Peninsula under Muslim rule in the Middle Ages, the *Mukhtaṣar fī al-Anwāʾ* ('Concise Treatise on *anwāʾ*') by Aḥmad b. Fāris contains certain parts that are related to Ibn Raḥīq's treatise or, more precisely, which appear to be based on a common source. In particular, the list with the hour-names in the Andalusi treatise is quite similar to that in the Hijazi text. The title of Aḥmad b. Fāris's treatise makes it clear that its main topic is *anwāʾ* and folk astronomy, although about a quarter of its content deals with astrology.[21] But, unlike Ibn Raḥīq, he does not mention lunar elections.[22]

---

[21] Forcada, 'Astrology and Folk Astronomy: the *Mukhtaṣar min al-Anwāʾ* of Aḥmad b. Fāris', *Suhayl* 1 (2000): p. 117: 'The lists <with the names of the twelve hours of day and of night> most similar to these two are the ones attributed to Ibn Raḥīq, a Meccan scholar who flourished in the 5th/11th century, so we must assume the existence of common sources prior to Ibn Fāris'. Apart from these lists there is also a conspicuous coincidence. The full title of Aḥmad b. Fāris' treatise reads *Kitāb fihi Mukhtaṣar min al-anwāʾ ʿalā madhhab al-ʿArab* ('Concise treatise on *Anwāʾ* according to the *method* of the Arabs'). Its final part is similar to the only legible part of the title of Ibn Raḥīq's book . . . *ʿalā madhāhib al-'Arab* ('according to the *methods* of the Arabs'). Forcada, 'Astrology and Folk Astronomy', pp. 111–13, and Miquel Forcada, 'A New Andalusian Historical Source from the Fourth / Tenth Century: the *Mukhtaṣar min al-anwāʾ* of Aḥmad Ibn Fāris', in *From Baghdad to Barcelona. Studies in the Islamic Exact Sciences in Honour of Prof. Juan Vernet*, Josep Casulleras and Julio Samsó, eds. (Instituto "Millás Vallicrosa": Barcelona, 1996), pp. 769–80 (pp. 775–77), identifies Aḥmad b. Fāris with Aḥmad b. Fāris al-Baṣrī (or al-Miṣrī), the chief astrologer at the court of al-Ḥakam II, while Ekmeleddin Ihsanoğlu and Boris A. Rosenfeld, *Mathematicians, Astronomers and other Scholars of Islamic Civilisation and Their Works (7th–19th c.)*, Series of Studies and Sources on History of Science 11 (Istanbul: Research Centre for Islamic History, Art and Culture, 2003), pp. 105–06; Fuat Sezgin, *Geschichte des arabischen Schrifttums*, vol. 7 (Leiden: Brill, 1967–1984: henceforth *GAS*), pp. 360–61, and Brockelmann, *GAL* I, pp. 130–31, 135–36 identify him with the philologist Abū al-Ḥusayn Aḥmad b. Fāris b. Zakariyāʾ (Qazwīn, 10th c.).

[22] Forcada, 'Astrology and Folk Astronomy', pp. 143–49; see also Forcada, 'New Source', pp. 771–74; Paul Kunitzsch, *Über eine Anwāʾ-Tradition mit bisher unbekannten Sternnamen*, Sitzungsberichte der Bayrischen Akademie der Wissenschaften, Philosophisch-historische Klasse 5, Beiträge zur Lexikographie des Klassischen Arabischen 4 (München: Verlag der Bayrischen Akademie der Wissenschaften, 1983), pp. 13–16; Sezgin, *GAS* VII, pp. 360–61.

Thirteenth-Century Yemen: al-Aṣbaḥī and al-Fārisī

Two other folk astronomical books from thirteenth-century Yemen, one by al-Aṣbaḥī (al-Janad (?), d. *ca.* 1265) and another by al-Fārisī (Aden, d. 1278/79) are, in some parts, very similar to Ibn Raḥīq's treatise. While al-Aṣbaḥī's *Kitāb al-Yawāqīt fī ʿilm / maʿrifat al-mawāqīt* ('Treasures of Timekeeping') mainly deals with the determination of the prayer times and their legal and traditional background, al-Fārisī's *Tuḥfat al-rāghib wa-turfat al-ṭālib fī tasyir al-nayyirayn wa-ḥarakāt al-kawākib* ('Present for Desiring and Seeking the Revolutions of the Two Luminaries and the Motions of the Planets') concentrates on more general information concerning calendars, timekeeping, and methods useful for an 'astronomy in the service of Islam'.[23] But neither al-Aṣbaḥī's nor al-Fārisī's treatises contain any astrology, let alone a treatment of lunar elections.[24]

LUNAR ELECTIONS IN OTHER FOLK ASTRONOMICAL SOURCES?

al-Ashraf ʿUmar's Tabṣira

Another treatise from thirteenth-century Yemen, the *Kitāb al-Tabṣira fī ʿilm al-nujūm* ('The Enlightenment on the Science of the Stars'), most probably written by the third Rasulid sultan al-Ashraf ʿUmar (Taiz, d. 1296), lists lunar elections in chapter XXV.[25] Although both the *Tabṣira* and Ibn Raḥīq's treatise describe the

---

[23] *Cf.* the title of David King's studies in 1993: *Astronomy in the Service of Islam* (London: Variorum Publications, 1993).

[24] Extracts of both treatises are introduced, edited, translated, and annotated in Schmidl, *Volksastronomie*. On al-Aṣbaḥī see also King, *MAY*, pp. 22–23. On al-Fārisī see also Petra Schmidl, 'al-Fārisī' in *Biographical Encyclopedia of Astronomers*, ed. Thomas Hockey et al. (New York: Springer, 2007, henceforth *BEA*), 1, 357b–59a; Ihsanoğlu and Rosenfeld, *Mathematicians*, p. 219; King, *MAY*, pp. 23–26; Brockelmann, *GAL* I, pp. 474, 625, and Supplementband I, pp. 866–67; Heinrich Suter, 'Die Mathematiker und Astronomen der Araber und ihre Werke', in *Abhandlungen zur Geschichte der Mathematischen Wissenschaften mit Einschluß ihrer Anwendungen* 10 (1900): p. 139, no. 349 and p. 218, n. 72; Heinrich Suter, 'Nachträge und Berichtigungen zu „Die Mathematiker und Astronomen der Araber und ihre Werke"', *Abhandlungen zur Geschichte der Mathematischen Wissenschaften mit Einschluß ihrer Anwendungen* 14 (1902): p. 175, no. 349.

[25] Translation and commentary in Varisco, 'Magical Significance'. On al-Ashraf ʿUmar see also Schmidl, 'al-Ashraf ʿUmar', in *BEA*, 1, 66a–67b; Daniel M. Varisco, *Medieval Agriculture and Islamic Science: The Almanac of a Yemeni Sultan*. Seattle: University of Washington Press, 1994), pp. 12–16; King, *MAY*, pp. 27–29; Suter, 'Mathematiker und

appropriate time to start or avoid an activity depending on the position of the moon with respect to the lunar mansions, and their elections deal mainly with similar topics, there are several differences. While the main part of al-Ashraf ʿUmar's section on elections focuses on magical activities like making charms, Ibn Raḥīq's elections concentrate on economics. In the *Tabṣira* there are, mainly in the margins, notes on the type of child born when the moon is in a certain lunar mansion, another topic not found in Ibn Raḥīq's text.[26] Furthermore, al-Ashraf ʿUmar does not attribute this sort of election to the Indians. Ibn Raḥīq does not mention the ecliptical longitude for defining the position of a lunar mansion. Apart from these differences in content there is another significant distinction. The *Tabṣira* of al-Ashraf ʿUmar contains elements of both astronomical traditions mentioned above: it is not a folk astronomical treatise proper. The contents presented in the *Tabṣira* are different from that of Ibn Raḥīq's treatise; e.g., more than half of the chapters in al-Ashraf ʿUmar's treatise deal with descriptive astrology: astrological methods distinguished from mathematical astrology that is mainly concerned with the computation of horoscopes.[27] The religious background that has a prominent place in Ibn Raḥīq's text is missing completely in the *Tabṣira*.

A Judaeo-Arabic tiklāl *Book*

Another treatise of interest is preserved in a late Judaeo-Arabic manuscript of Yemeni provenance, most probably compiled in 1720 (Jewish Theological Seminary of America, MS. 10236 fols. 112a–113a, or 106a–107a in Hebrew foliation). This anonymous *tiklāl* text, a prayer book, contains a part with entries for all twenty-eight lunar mansions, and which includes lunar elections. The beginning of the relevant paragraph refers to the *Rasāʾil* ('Letters') of the Ikhwān al-Ṣafāʾ (Brethren of Purity; Basra [?], 2nd half of tenth century).[28] It reads

---

Astronomen', pp. 160–61, no. 394; Suter, 'Nachträge', p. 177, no. 394.

[26] Omitted in Varisco, 'Magical Significance', pp. 28–33.

[27] Schmidl, 'Magic and Medicine in a 13th c. Treatise on the Science of the Stars. The *Kitāb al-Tabṣira fī ʿilm al-nujūm* of the Rasulid Sultan al-Ashraf ʿUmar', in *Herbal Medicine in Yemen: Traditional Knowledge and Practice, and Their Value for Today's World*, ed. Ingrid Hehmeyer, Hanne Schönig, Islamic History and Civilization 96 (Leiden: E. J. Brill 2012), pp. 43–68, 43–49.

[28] Text discussed in Paul Kunitzsch and Y. Tzvi Langermann, 'A Star Table from Medieval Yemen', *Centaurus* 45 (2003): pp. 165–66. Additional information was kindly

(respectively, text in the manuscript kindly provided by Jay Rovner, corresponding Arabic, and English translation by the author):

בשמל (?) רחמן . קיל אן הד'א אלכתאב מנתזע מן רסאיל א כ'ואן אלצפה פיה וצ'ע מנאזל אלקמר ומא יתצל מנה מן אלרוחאנייאת ... ולתחויל אלכתאב מן מכאן אלא מכאן, אוול ד'אלך ...

بسمل (؟) رحمن (= باسم الله الرحمان الرحيم) . قيل أنّ هذا الكتاب منتزع من رسائل إخوان الصفاء فيه وضع منازل القمر وما يتّصل منه من الروحانيات ... وتحويل الكتاب من مكان علي مكان , أوّل ذلك ...

'In the name of God, Almighty. It is said that this note is taken from the *Letters* of the Ikhwān al-Ṣafā', in it the lunar mansions are laid down, and what is connected of them of the *pneumata* . . . and adjusting (the information) (?) in the book to different places (?). The first of them is: [. . .].'

A preliminary investigation of this text shows some differences from Ibn Raḥīq's and al-Ashraf 'Umar's sections on the lunar elections, but also some topics in common.[29] The *tiklāl* book provides general characteristics of the lunar mansions, a topic missing from the two other texts, e.g., the seventh lunar mansion, *al-dhirā'*, is described as windy, soft, beneficent, stable, and of good spirits. As in al-Ashraf 'Umar's *Tabṣira* the elections focus on magic, but also include recommendations concerning worship, another topic missing from the two other examples. But most important is the kind of text where these elections are described. As in Ibn Raḥīq's treatise, this *tiklāl* book appears to be a text with a sound religious background.

---

provided in January 2010 by Jay Rovner, Manuscript Bibliographer of the Library of the Jewish Theological Seminary of America, New York. See also Ikhwān al-Ṣafā', *Rasā'īl* IV, pp. 428–43. On the Ikhwān al-Ṣafā' see also Yves Marquet, *Ikhwān al-Ṣafā'* in *EI²*; Ihsanoğlu and Rosenfeld, *Mathematicians*, pp. 90–91; Brockelmann, *GAL* I, pp. 213–14, 236–38, and Supplementband I, pp. 379–81.

[29] Kunitzsch and Langermann, 'Star Table', p. 166 only provide the data for the 7th lunar mansion. Correspondence with both authors in October 2009 revealed that the entries belonging to the other lunar mansions appear to be arranged in a similar way.

Bilāl b. Malik

Apart from these examples taken from Yemeni sources,[30] there is another one known to the author, preserved in a text of Sub-Saharan provenance: two astrological sections either written or copied by Bilāl b. Malik b. Alfā Bilāl Muḥammad, most probably a local scholar from the region around Timbuktu.[31] The first section bears the title *Bāb maʿrifat al-manāzil al-qamar* [*sic*] ('On the knowledge of the lunar mansions') and covers two thirds of the manuscript. The character of the elections in Bilāl b. Malik's astrological section is closer to Ibn Raḥīq than to the later Yemeni examples, al-Ashraf ʿUmar's *Tabṣira* and the anonymous *tiklāl* text. As in Ibn Raḥīq's text the Sub-Saharan treatise does not deal with magical topics, but concentrates on economic activities. Both end with an invocation, namely 'God knows what is concealed!' They do not mention precise ecliptical longitudes. In contrast to Ibn Raḥīq, Bilāl b. Malik additionally describes the general character of a lunar mansion as auspicious, inauspicious or ambiguous, and informs the reader about the expected type of boy or girl born when the moon is in a certain lunar mansion. Most probably these two

---

30 Another Yemeni text of the early fourteenth century, an anonymous ephemeris compiled for the year 727H (1326–1327) now preserved in Cairo (*Dār al-kutub, mīqāt,* 817(2)), comprises tables with *ikhtiyārāt* in the title, apparently elections by the moon, but not those of the 'astrologers who preferred the Indian methods' (Carlo Nallino, 'Astrology' in *EI*[1], p. 496, see also n. 3). On the ephemeris itself see David A. King, *A Survey of the Scientific Manuscripts in the Egyptian National Library*. American Research Center in Egypt, Catalogues, vol. 5 (Winona Lake, IN: Eisenbrauns, 1987), p. 132, no. E11; King, *A Catalogue of the Scientific Manuscripts in the Egyptian National Library* (in Arabic), 2 vols (Cairo: General Egyptian Book Organization, 1981/1986), 2: p. 148, no. 2/3/2; King, *MAY,* p. 33, and plate 2 and 3; see also the photos in David A. King, 'Astronomie im mittelalterlichen Jemen', in *Jemen,* ed. Werner Daum (Frankfurt am Main: Pinguin-Verlag, Frankfurt and Umschau-Verlag, Innsbruck, 1987), pp. 299, 300.

31 Thebe Medupe and Petra Schmidl, *The Astronomical Manuscripts in the* Institut des Hautes Études et de Recherches Islamiques – Aḥmad Bābā (IHERI-AB, formerly *Centre de Documentation et de Recherches Aḥmad Bābā* [CEDRAB]) *in Timbuktu, Mali: A Preliminary Handlist,* forthcoming, no. 4169; Julian Johansen and Sidi Amar Ould Ely, eds., *Handlist of Manuscripts in the Centre de Documentation et de Recherches Historiques Ahmad Baba Timbuktu,* 5 vols., al-Furqān Heritage Foundation Catalogue of Islamic Manuscripts Series V (London: Al-Furqān Islamic Heritage Foundation, 1995–1998), p. 498, no. 4169. Copies of the manuscript kindly provided by the *Timbuktu Science Project* of Cape Town University supported by the National Research Foundation of South Africa.

astrological sections by Bilāl b. Malik are fragments surviving from a larger treatise that has not yet been identified. Therefore the astronomical tradition to which the text belongs cannot yet be determined.

Further Folk Astronomical Texts

Even if a treatise is complete, it is often difficult to decide whether a text belongs to the folk astronomical tradition or not without examining its manuscript context. The titles mentioned in the modern literature are frequently misleading and do not help in identifying folk astronomical texts that may contain lunar elections.[32] An extensive reading by the author of published folk astronomical texts, *anwāʾ*- and *azmina*-books, calendars and almanacs, revealed no lunar elections. But some similarities deserve closer investigation. Ibn Qutayba (Baghdad, ninth century) reports in his *Kitāb al-Anwāʾ* economic activities carried out at the same time every year determined by the heliacal rising of a lunar mansion. However, he does not link the economic activities and the lunar mansions to astrology, but uses them for timekeeping.[33] Ibn Māsawayh (Baghdad, *ca*. 786–857) arranges his *Kitāb al-Azmina* ('Book of Azmina'—despite the title it is an almanac) according to the Syrian months. The first part of each entry lists for specific days of a month the customs, events and activities that repeat themselves every year, as well as meteorological, astronomical, biological, navigational, agricultural, economic and liturgical data. Astrological predictions are missing. The second part of Ibn Māsawayh's *Kitāb al-Azmina* offers general advice valid for the whole month, mainly concerning diet,

---

[32] Varisco, 'Magical Significance', p. 25, n. 30 lists about a dozen of published and unpublished texts preserved in Cairo and Milan that provide data similar to that of al-Ashraf ʿUmar's *Tabṣira,* and therefore of Ibn Raḥīq's treatise, too. They deserve further research to establish their main characteristics, and their relation to specific astronomical and astrological traditions.

[33] *Cf*. Varisco, 'Folk Astronomy', p. 624 referring to Ibn Qutayba (p. 21): 'When *al-buṭayn* rose, debts were paid, finery appeared, the perfumer and the smith were pursued. In this time pastures begin to dry up and the nomads are forced to return to permanent water sources and larger camps. As the smaller herding units come together, the Bedouins pay their debts'. On Ibn Qutayba see also Gérard Lecomte, 'Ibn Ḳutayba' in *EI*[2] s.v.; Brockelmann, *GAL* I, pp. 120–24, 124–27, and Supplementband I, pp. 184–87; Ihsanoğlu and Rosenfeld, *Mathematicians*, p. 94; Sezgin, *GAS* VII, pp. 350–51.

hygiene and health.[34] Some of these recommendations can be interpreted as a basic form of election by means of the solar months and may also have been inspired by seasonal supplies and requirements.[35] The *Long Calendar* of Ibn Mammātī (Egypt, d. 1209) provides data of the same kind and arranges it in a similar way. The first part lists for specific days of a Coptic month the customs, events and activities repeating themselves every year; the second part gives general recommendations but diet, hygiene, and health play a less prominent rôle than in Ibn Māsawayh's *Kitāb al-Azmina*.[36]

Although the activities described in these sources show similarities to those incorporated in the lunar elections, they do not have an explicit astrological background. The difference between describing the appropriate time for an activity in respect to seasonal changes and electing the moments auspicious or inauspicious for that activity by astrological means would seem to be small, and is most apparent in the general advice related to each month.

Other Relevant Aspects

Some Examples of Lunar Elections in Astrological and Magical Texts

At the moment Ibn Raḥīq's treatise is the only known, purely folk astronomical treatise listing lunar elections. They occur more commonly in astrological and magical texts; e.g., both, the *Ghāyat al-ḥakīm* ('The aim of the sage') and the *Kitāb al-Bāriʿ fī aḥkām al-nujūm* ('Book of the Skillful on Astrology') by ʿAlī b. Abī Rijāl (Tunis, d. after 1041), contain chapters on lunar elections. The *Ghāyat al-ḥakīm*, known in the European Middle Ages as the *Picatrix*, was written by Pseudo-Maslama al-Majrīṭī in tenth-century al-Andalus. It mentions lunar elections

---

[34] Gérard Troupeau, 'Le Livre des temps de Jean Ibn Māsawayh' (translation), *Arabica* 15 (1968): pp. 117–35; Paul Sbath, 'Le livre des temps d'Ibn Massawaïh, médecin chrétien célèbre décédé en 857', *Bulletin de l'Institut d'Egypte* 15 (1933): pp. 241–56 (edition). On Ibn Māsawayh see also Jean-Claude Vadet, 'Ibn Māsawayh', *EI*[2] s.v.; Ihsanoğlu and Rosenfeld, *Mathematicians*, p. 32; Sezgin, *GAS* VII, p. 326; Brockelmann, *GAL* I, pp. 232, 266, and Supplementband I, p. 416.

[35] Moreover the characterizing of the months by combinations of hot or cold with moist or dry, and their association with one of the four humours of Greek Antiquity, have influence on the diet recommended (Schmidl, 'Magic and medicine', pp. 61–63).

[36] Charles Pellat, *Cinq calendriers égyptiens*, Textes Arabes et Études Islamiques 26 (Cairo: Institut Français d'Archéologie Orientale du Caire, 1986), pp. 2–93.

twice, in chapters I:4 and IV:9 (missing in the Arabic version), both times focusing on magical purposes, the making of amulets and talismans.[37] In his *Kitāb al-Bāriʿ*, ʿAlī b. Abī Rijāl lists the lunar elections in chapter VII:101; the advice given concerns hygiene, medicine, and agriculture, as well as social and economic topics.[38]

---

[37] Pseudo-Majrīṭī, *Das Ziel des Weisen I: Arabischer Text*, ed. Hellmut Ritter, Studien der Bibliothek Warburg. Herausgegeben von Fritz Saxl 12 (Leipzig, Berlin: Teubner, 1933), pp. 14–26; Martin Plessner and Hellmut Ritter, *Picatrix: Das Ziel der Weisen von Pseudo-Mağrīṭī: Translated into German from the Arabic*. Studies of the Warburg Institute 27 (London: The Warburg Institute, 1962), pp. 14–24; David Pingree, *Picatrix: The Latin Version of the Ghāyat al-Ḥakīm: Text, Appendices, Indices*, Studies of the Warburg Institute 39 (London: The Warburg Institute, 1986), pp. 8–15, 228–34. On the possible authorship of Maslama b. Qāsim al-Qurṭubī (al-Andalus, d. 964) see Maribel Fierro, 'Bāṭinism in Al-Andalus: Maslama b. Qāsim al-Qurṭubī (d. 353/964), Author of the *Rutbat al-Ḥākim* and the *Ghāyat al-Ḥākim*', *Studia Islamica* 84 (1996): pp. 87–112.

[38] Charles Burnett, 'Lunar Astrology: The Varieties of Texts Using Lunar Mansions, with Emphasis on *Jafar Indus*', *Micrologus* 12 (2004): pp. 43–133 (pp. 49–50); Ullmann, *Natur- und Geheimwissenschaften*, pp. 336, 353. On ʿAlī b. Abī al-Rijāl see also David Pingree, 'Ibn Abi 'l-Ridjal' in EI^2 s.v.; Ihsanoğlu and Rosenfeld, *Mathematicians*, p. 157; Sezgin, *GAS* VII, pp. 186–88; Brockelmann, *GAL* I, pp. 224, 256, and Supplementband I, p. 401; Suter, 'Mathematiker und Astronomen', p. 100, no. 219; Suter, 'Nachträge', pp. 172–73, no. 219, and Henri-Paul-Joseph Renaud, 'Additions et corrections à Suter "Die Mathematiker und Astronomen der Araber"', *Isis* 18 (1932): p. 172, no. 219. For further examples of lunar elections see Charles Burnett, 'Nīranj: A Category of Magic (Almost) Forgotten in the Latin West', in *Natura, scienze e società medievali. Studi in onore di Agostino Paravicini Bagliani*, ed. Claudio Leonardo and Francesco Santi, Micrologus Library 28 (Florence: SISMEL, 2008), pp. 37–66 (pp. 39–44); Burnett, 'Lunar Astrology', pp. 48–51; Charles Burnett, 'Arabic, Greek, and Latin Works on Astrological Magic Attributed to Aristotle', in *Pseudo-Aristotle in the Middle Ages*, ed. Jill Kraye, W.F. Ryan, and Charles B. Schmitt, Warburg Institute Surveys and Texts 11 (London: Warburg Institute, 1987), pp. 84–96; Ullmann, *Natur- und Geheimwissenschaften*, p. 358; *cf.* also David Pingree, 'Astronomy and Astrology in India and Iran', *Isis* 54 (1963): pp. 229–46 (p. 230). Ibn al-Ḥātim's treatise on the talismans of the lunar mansions is for the most part stripped of the lunar elections (Kristin Lippincott and David Pingree, 'Ibn al-Ḥātim on the Talismans of the Lunar Mansions', *Journal of the Warburg and Courtauld Institutes* 50 (1987): pp. 57–81).

The lunar elections even made their way into Europe, e.g., in the *Picatrix*, the Latin version of the *Ghāyat al-ḥākim* or in *De Luna* attributed to Aristotle.[39] But there they never became as popular as they were in the Islamicate realm.[40]

Possible Origins of the Lunar Elections

Ibn Raḥīq introduces his elections always with 'the Indians said'. Lunar elections were known in India; e.g., they are listed in the *Yavanajātaka* of Sphujidhvaja (India, third century, CE). The advice given there concerns warfare and politics.[41] In addition Ibn Raḥīq's reference supports the widely accepted way of transmission of the lunar mansions from India to Islamicate societies, where they were mingled with the already-existing *anwāʾ*-system.[42] From there the lunar mansions and their names found their way into Europe.[43]

---

[39] On the *Picatrix* see n. 37, and also n. 51; on *De Luna* see Burnett, 'Nīranj', pp. 56–64; Burnett, 'Astrological Magic', pp. 90–93; see also Dilwyn Knox and Charles B. Schmitt, *Pseudo-Aristoteles Latinus: a guide to Latin works falsely attributed to Aristotle before 1500*, Warburg Institute Surveys and Texts 12 (London: Warburg Institute, 1985), p. 76, no. 84.

[40] For further examples in European treatises see also Ute Müller, 'Deutsche Mondwahrsagetexte aus dem Spätmittelalter' (Inaugural-Dissertation zur Erlangung eines Doktors der Philosophie des Fachbereichs Germanistik der Freien Universität Berlin, 1971), esp. pp. 21–23; Bodo Weidemann, 'Kunst der Gedächtnüss' und 'De Mansionibus', zwei frühe Traktate des Johann Hartlieb (Inaugural-Dissertation zur Erlangung eines Doktors der Philosophie der Philosophischen Fakultät der Freien Universität Berlin, 1964); Emanuel Svenberg, *Lunaria et Zodiologia Latina: Edidit et Commentario Instruxit*, Studia Graeca et Latina Gothoburgensia 15 (Göteborg: Acta Universitatis Gothoburgensis, 1963); Robert Vian, *Ein Mondwahrsagebuch: Zwei altdeutsche Handschriften des XIV und XV Jahrhunderts* (Halle: Niemeyer, 1910).

[41] David Pingree, *The Yavanajātaka of Sphujidhvaja*, 2 vols., Harvard Oriental Series 48 (Cambridge, MA, London: Harvard University Press, 1978), pp. 175, 393; see also Pingree, 'India and Iran', p. 230, n. 9. On Sphujidhvaja see also eds., 'Sphujidhvaja' in *BEA*, s.v.

[42] Kunitzsch, 'Manāzil' *EI*[2] s.v.; Miquel Forcada, 'Books of *Anwāʾ* in al-Andalus', in *The Formation of al-Andalus, Part 2: Language, Religion, Culture and the Sciences*, ed. Maribel Fierro and Julio Samsó (Aldershot: Ashgate, 1998), pp. 305–28 (pp. 308–10); see also Emilie Savage-Smith and Marion B. Smith, 'Islamic Geomancy and a Thirteenth-Century Divinatory Device: Another Look', in *Magic and Divination in Early Islam*, ed. Emilie Savage-Smith, The Formation of the Classical Islamic World 42 (Aldershot: Ashgate, 2004), pp. 211–76 (pp. 245–46); Daniel M. Varisco, 'The Origin of the Anwāʾ in Arab Tradition', *Studia Islamica* 74 (1991): pp. 5–28 (pp. 6–9); Daniel M. Varisco, 'The Anwāʾ Stars according to Abū Isḥāq al-Zajjāj', *Zeitschrift für Geschichte der arabisch-islamischen*

From the other folk astronomical texts discussed above only the Judaeo-Arabic *tiklāl*-book attributes the paragraph on the lunar elections to a source, the Ikhwān al-Ṣafāʾ.[44] Their *Rasāʾil* give evidence for a different, purportedly Greek origin, for the lunar elections. In the chapter dealing with the lunar mansions the first part lists the lunar mansions and gives a reference to the 'Book of al-ʾ-r-s-ṭ-mākh-s'.[45] The second part discusses several topics related to lunar elections and mentions Idrīs, Hermes, Aristotle and the *Kitāb al-makhzūn* attributed to him, as well as the 'companion of al-ʾṣ-ṭīṭās'.[46] In addition another Greek element shines through, namely the four elements attributed to the lunar mansions.[47] Most probably the 'Book of al-ʾ-r-s-ṭ-mākh-s' refers to the *Kitāb al-Isṭamākhīs* and the 'companion of al-ʾṣ-ṭīṭās' to the *Kitāb al-Ustuwwaṭās*. Both Hermetic treatises are attributed or related to Aristotle.[48] The great amount of pseudepigrapha connected with Aristotle reflects his high standing in pre-modern educated

---

Wissenschaften (1989): pp. 145–66 (pp. 150–51); Daniel M. Varisco, 'The Rain Periods in Pre-Islamic Arabia', *Arabica* 34 (1987): pp. 251–66 (p. 253); David Pingree, 'The Indian and Pseudo-Indian Passages in Greek and Latin Astronomical and Astrological Texts', *Viator* 7 (1976): pp. 141–95 (pp. 174–76); Pingree, 'India and Iran', pp. 229–46; see also the description in ch. 56 of al-Bīrūnī in *India,* ed. Sachau, pp. 242–44 (Arabic text), and al-Bīrūnī *India* II, trans. Sachau, pp. 81–85.

[43] Juste, *Alchandreana*, p. 123; Silke Ackermann, 'The Path of the Moon Engraved. Lunar Mansions on European and Islamic Scientific Instruments', *Micrologus* 12 (2004): pp. 147–78; Burnett, 'Lunar Astrology', pp. 44, 60; Paul Kunitzsch, *Arabische Sternnamen in Europa* (Wiesbaden: Harrassowitz, 1959), pp. 54–57; Burnett, 'Nīranj', pp. 39–40.

[44] See n. 28.

[45] Ikhwān al-Ṣafāʾ, *Rasāʾil*, vol. 4, p. 429: كتاب ارسطماخس .

[46] See Ikhwān al-Ṣafāʾ, *Rasāʾil*, vol. 4, pp. 443–46, esp. 445: صاحب الاسطيطاس .

[47] Ikhwān al-Ṣafāʾ, *Rasāʾil*, vol. 4, pp. 429–43. The *nakṣatra*s however were qualified by six categories, fixed, sharp, fierce, swift, soft, common, and unstable (Pingree, 'Indian Passages', p. 175).

[48] Burnett, 'Astrological Magic', pp. 95–96; see also Ullmann, *Natur- und Geheimwissenschaften,* pp. 374–75; Sezgin, *GAS* VII, p. 57; Pseudo-Mağrīṭī, *Picatrix,* ed. Plessner and Ritter, p. 15, n. 3. On Aristotle see also Cristina D'Ancona, 'Aristotle and Aristotelianism' in *EI*³; Richard Walzer, 'Arisṭūṭālīs' in *EI*² s.v.; Stephen Hetherington, 'Aristotle' in *BEA*, s.v.; Ullmann, *Natur- und Geheimwissenschaften,* pp. 287–88; Sezgin, *GAS* VII, pp. 60–63. On Hermes see also Kevin van Bladel, 'Hermes and Hermetica' in *EI*³; Martin Plessner, 'Hirmis' in *EI*² s.v.; Ullmann, *Natur- und Geheimwissenschaften,* pp. 289–93, and pp. 368–74; Sezgin, *GAS* VII, pp. 50–58. On Idrīs see Georges Vajda, 'Idrīs' in *EI*² s.v.

circles in Islamicate societies as *the* philosopher and the teacher of Alexander the Great, as well as his assumed familiarity with many different topics. They include, most famously, the *Sirr al-asrār* (*Secretum secretorum*, 'Secret of Secrets'), also dealing with magical topics,[49] and even a treatise concerning lunar elections.[50]

From the astrological and magical texts mentioned above the *Ghāyat al-ḥakīm* attributes the lunar elections to the Indians in chapter I:4, while in chapter IV:9 (missing in the Arabic version) a purportedly Greek source is mentioned: 'he autem sunt viginti octo mansiones Lune secundum *Plinionem*,' probably referring to Pseudo-Apollonius (of Tyana).[51] In his *Kitāb al-Bāriʿ* ʿAlī b. Abī Rijāl relates the lunar elections to the Indians. He seems to add to some of the lunar mansions' *katarchai* attributed to Dorotheus of Sidon (Greece, first century CE),

---

[49] W.F. Ryan and Charles B. Schmitt, eds., *Pseudo-Aristotle: The Secret of Secrets, Sources and Influences*, Warburg Institute Surveys 9 (London: The Warburg Institute, 1982), esp. pp. 1–2; Mahmoud Manzalaoui, 'The Pseudo-Aristotelian *Sirr al-asrār*: Facts and Problems, *Oriens* 23 (1974): pp. 147–257; Sezgin, *GAS* VII, pp. 62–63, 147–48; ʿAbdalraḥmān Badawī, *al-Uṣūl al-yūnāniyya, lil-naẓariyyāt al-siyāsiyya fī al-Islām*, Juzʾ I, Dirāsāt Islāmiyya 15 (Cairo: s.n., 1954); Robert Steele, *Opera hactenus inedita Rogeri Baconi*, Fasc. V, *Secretum secretorum* (Oxford: Clarendon Press, 1920).

[50] Sezgin, *GAS* VII, p. 62. There is another copy in Cairo bearing the title *Kitāb fī tadbīr fī* (!) *manāzil al-qamar* ('Book on the planning [?] by means of [?] the lunar mansions') (King, *Cairo Survey*, p. 23, no. A3; King, *Cairo Catalogue II*, pp. 651–52, no. 5/1/2). But it seems doubtful if the *Kitāb fī manāzil al-qamar*, attributed to Hermes and reworked by Aristotle, contains different content (Sezgin, *GAS* VII, pp. 54–55). See also Burnett, 'Astrological Magic', p. 89, n. 6.

[51] See n. 37, and esp. Pingree, *Latin Version of the Picatrix*, p. 228; David Pingree, 'Between Ghāya and Picatrix I: The Spanish Version', *Journal of the Warburg and Courtauld Institutes* 44 (1981): pp. 27–56 (pp. 29–30); David Pingree, 'Some of the Sources of the Ghāyat al-Ḥakīm', *Journal of the Warburg and Courtauld Institutes* 43 (1980): pp. 1–15 (p. 8); see also Burnett, Lunar 'Astrology', p. 53, equating Plinio(n) with Bālīnūs, *i.e.* Pseudo-Apollonius (of Tyana). On Apollonius of Tyana see Martin Plessner, 'Balīnūs' in *EI*[2] s.v.; Ullmann, *Natur- und Geheimwissenschaften*, pp. 378–81; Sezgin, *GAS* VII, pp. 64–66. For another example relating Bālīnūs to lunar election *cf.* Ullmann, *Natur- und Geheimwissenschaften*, p. 380: 'In der Vorrede des *Muṣḥaf al-qamar* des Balīnās (n. 3: Dublin, Chester Beatty 4890, I [fol. 1–8]) wird behauptet, daß Balīnās das Buch von Hermes bekommen habe, und daß es später ins Arabische übersetzt worden sei. Sein Inhalt sind Talismane, die unter bestimmten Bedingungen angefertigt werden sollen. Vor allem sollen sie auf die 28 Mondstationen (daher der Name der Schrift) ausgerichtet sein'.

apparently depending on the position of the moon in the zodiacal signs.[52] A Greek text that must derive from the same source as that of ʿAlī b. Abī Rijāl, also refers to the opinions of the Persians.[53] The *Safīnat al-aḥkām* ('Ship of Astrology') of Naṣīr al-Dīn al-Ṭūsī (Tus, 1201–Baghdad, 1274) provides us with further information. In this book al-Ṭūsī apparently classifies one of his sources, an anonymous treatise with the title *Ikhtiyārāt ʿalā al-manāzil* ('Elections by means of the lunar mansions'), as being of Indian origin. He also seems to mention that ʿUmar b. al-Farrukhān (Baghdad, eighth century) translated or commented on the predictions according to the lunar mansions by Dorotheus.[54]

In fact, Greek astronomy did not know the concept of a lunar zodiac. Two reasons may have prompted the attribution to Dorotheus of Sidon.[55] On the one hand, Dorotheus mentions in his astrological poem catarchic astrology by the

---

[52] See n. 38, and also Viktor Stegemann, 'Dorotheos von Sidon: Ein Bericht über die Rekonstruktionsmöglichkeiten seines astrologischen Werkes', *Rheinisches Museum für Philologie: Neue Folge* 91 (1942): pp. 326–49 (p. 345).

[53] Burnett, 'Lunar Astrology', p. 49.

[54] Sezgin, *GAS* VII, pp. 22–24, 34–35; Ullmann, *Natur- und Geheimwissenschaften,* pp. 338–39 assuming another author of the *Safīnat al-aḥkām,* al-Nuṣairī. *Cf.* also Ibn al-Qifṭī, *Ta'rīkh al-ḥukamā',* Auf Grund der Vorarbeiten August Müller's herausgegeben von Julius Lippert (Leipzig: Dieterich'sche Verlagbuchhandlung, 1903), p. 184. See also the table of contents of the Berlin manuscript in W. Ahlwardt, *Handschriften-Verzeichnisse der Königlichen Bibliothek zu Berlin, 17. Band: Verzeichniss der arabischen Handschriften.* Band 5 (Berlin, 1893), pp. 293–97, no. 5895. On Naṣīr al-Dīn al-Ṭūsī see also Hans Daiber and F. Jamil Ragep, 'al-Ṭūsī' in *EI*² s.v.; Ragep, 'al-Ṭūsī' in *BEA,* s.v.; Ihsanoğlu and Rosenfeld, *Mathematicians,* pp. 211–19; Brockelmann, *GAL* I, pp. 508–12, 670–76, and Supplementband I, pp. 924–33; Suter, 'Mathematiker und Astronomen', pp. 146–53, no. 368; Suter, 'Nachträge', pp. 307–08, no. 368; Renaud, 'Additions', p. 172, no. 368 (all without mentioning the *Safīnat al-aḥkām*). On ʿUmar b. Farrukhān see also Ihsanoğlu and Rosenfeld, *Mathematicians,* pp. 18–19; Ullmann, *Natur- und Geheimwissenschaften,* pp. 18–19, 280; Sezgin, *GAS* VII, pp. 111, 36; Brockelmann, *GAL* I, p. 221, 249, and Supplementband I, p. 364; Suter, 'Mathematiker und Astronomen', pp. 7–8, no. 13; Suter, 'Nachträge', p. 158, no. 13; Renaud, 'Additions', p. 170, no. 13.

[55] *Cf.* Ibn ʿĀṣim, *Kitāb al-Anwāʾ wa-l-azmina - al-qawl fī l-šuhūr - (Tratado sorbre los anwāʾ y los tiempos – capítulo sobre los meses –),* Estudio, traducción y edición crítica por Miquel Forcada Nogués, Fuentes arabico-hispanas 15 (Barcelona: Consejo Superior de Investigaciones Científicas, 1993), p. 21, or Pingree, 'Sources of the Ghāyat', p. 8; see also Ullmann, *Natur- und Geheimwissenschaften,* p. 351; Bouché-Leclercq, *L'astrologie grecque,* p. 463.

moon. The position of the moon with respect to the zodiac and in relation to the other planets allows the election of the most appropriate time for an activity.[56] Although this method differs from that of lunar elections it is relatively close to the subject, closer than Ptolemy's *Tetrabiblos* ever comes to it.[57] On the other hand, it seems that Dorotheus' text reached Islamicate societies through Indian and Persian mediators.[58] Thus the lunar elections could have been added to Dorotheus' text in the process of its transmission.[59]

These examples show two possible lines of transmission for the lunar elections. One points towards Indian sources, sometimes enriched with Persian traditions and (Pseudo-) Dorotheana.[60] The other refers to some Hermetic traditions, and to (Pseudo-) Aristoteliana. A connection between these two lines is not completely improbable, if one assumes a 'Hermetic route for this "Indian" material'.[61]

---

[56] Dorotheus, *Carmen Astrologicum,* Book V, esp. V.6–25; see also Stegemann, *Beiträge I,* pp. 14–25. On Dorotheus of Sidon see also Ullmann, *Natur- und Geheimwissenschaften,* p. 280–81; Sezgin, *GAS* VII, pp. 32–38.

[57] *Cf.* Sezgin, *GAS* VII, p. 43.

[58] Pingree, 'India and Iran', pp. 230, n. 10, and 241; see also Ullmann, *Natur- und Geheimwissenschaften,* p. 280; Sezgin, *GAS* VII, p. 34.

[59] An example for such a supplement in the course of transmission is found in the *Yavanajātaka* of Sphudjidhvaja, where the Greek associations of the planets with various sublunar substances were enriched with Indian data (Pingree, 'Sources of the Ghāyat', p. 6).

[60] *Cf.* Pingree, 'Indian Passages', pp. 174–75: 'At some point a text (in Pahlavī or in Arabic) concerning activities to be undertaken or avoided when the moon is in each of the *nakṣatras* (*manāzil al-qamar* in Arabic) was put together from three sources: an Indian text, the fifth book of Dorotheus, and a Persian tradition. The Arabic version of this text was copied by ʿAlī ibn abī Rijāl, through whom it reaches the Latin West; and it was translated into Byzantine Greek; it was also used in part by the author of the *Picatrix,* through which again it appears in Latin'.
A possible transmission from India to the Islamicate societies by Abū Maʿshar has not yet been verified, but *De electionibus lunae* preserved in Paris (Bibliothèque Nationale, no. 7435) is attributed to Abū Maʿshar (Nallino, *Raccolta* V, p. 12; Steinschneider, *Übersetzungen aus dem Arabischen,* p. 36).

[61] Burnett, 'Weather Forecasting in the Arabic World' in Savage-Smith, Emilie (ed.): *Magic and Divination in Early Islam,* The Formation of the Classical Islamic World 42 (Aldershot: Ashgate Variorum, 2004), pp. 201–10, p. 208, n. 25: 'A Hermetic route for this 'Indian' material is not implausible, since the 28 lunar mansions are also characteristic of

Conclusion

Possible reasons for Ibn Raḥīq to include the lunar elections in his treatise, or at least not to omit them, are a practical component concerning their use, and a theoretical, or philosophical, one concerning the relationship of religion and astronomy. Calculating a horoscope is a demanding task. Apparently it is less difficult to use the information on the *katarchai* given in Dorotheos' fifth book. But it is probably still too complicated for a non-professional astrologer or astronomer.[62] Lists with the lunar elections like those given by Ibn Raḥīq appear to be easier to use for an amateur. Their occurrence in religious texts may be due to the use of the lunar or luni-solar calendar. For someone trained in observing the moon for religious purposes it seems only natural to make use of the moon for elections, as well.

At the moment Ibn Raḥīq's treatise is the only known purely folk astronomical treatise listing lunar elections, while other astrological concepts are not entirely unknown to pre-modern folk astronomical traditions in Islamicate societies.[63] But Ibn Raḥīq's elections are not a singular phenomenon. Lunar elections are found in treatises of unknown or uncertain background, as well as in astrological and magical works. Although less commonly known than other astrological concepts, they nevertheless seem to be widespread. In contrast to other sources dealing with lunar elections Ibn Raḥīq only mentions them as an astrological method without any further magical connotation, possibly due to the genre of his text. Most probably the absence of this topic in folk astronomical treatises is more due to the small number of sources investigated, than to their non-existence.[64] It is safer to say, at the moment, that Ibn Raḥīq's treatise presents a common topic in an unexpected place.

Hermetic works on using talismans'.

[62] Bouché-Leclercq, *L'astrologie grecque*, p. 464: 'Elle (la méthode des καταρχαί) était aussi plus facile à appliquer que la généthlialogie'.

[63] See Forcada, 'Astrology and Folk Astronomy', pp. 107–16.

[64] Schmidl, *Volksastronomie*, pp. 85–91; Varisco, 'Islamic Folk Astronomy', pp. 615–17; Forcada, 'Books of *Anwā'*', pp. 305–08.

Appendix
Ibn Raḥīq on Lunar Elections

The following translation is an extract from Ibn Raḥīq's . . . *ʿalā madhāhib al-ʿArab* (B, 39b–71b), taking into consideration only the sentences on the lunar elections.[65] The paragraphs on the lunar mansions from no. 1 (*al-sharaṭān*) to no. 11 (*al-zubra*), and no. 25 (*saʿd al-akhbiya*) are missing in the manuscript (see also above).

no. 12: *al-ṣarfa* (B,45a-9–11)

The Indians say: When the moon stations in (*al-ṣarfa*), then do not do any work, because it is reprehensible – and only God knows what is concealed.[66]

no. 13: *al-ʿawwāʾ* (B,47a,2–5)

The Indians say: When the moon stations in (*al-ʿawwāʾ*), then enter before kings, sultans, and nobles, begin any work, travel, buy farms (?) and slaves, and marry – and only God knows what is concealed.[66]

no. 14: *al-simāk* (B,49a,6–9)

The Indians say: When the moon stations in (*al-simāk*), then do not begin any work, do not buy slaves, do not wield the plough, do not enter before anybody, do not associate with them, and do not marry – and only God knows what is concealed.[66]

no. 15: *al-ghafr* (B,50a,11–50b,2)

The Indians say: When the moon stations in (*al-ghafr*), associate with kings, brothers, and everybody you want, marry, buy slaves, and wear clothes that are suitable (?) – and only God knows what is concealed.[66]

no. 16: *al-zubānā* (B,52a,12–52b,3)

The Indians say: When the moon stations in (*al-zubānā*), then enter before kings, nobles, and every person you want, travel, marry, plant,[67] do any work apart

---

[65] Arabic text and German translation in Schmidl, *Volksastronomie*, pp. 282–305.

[66] See *sura* 53,36/35.

[67] Misread in Schmidl, *Volksastronomie*, p. 290.

from (forging) iron, and do not wear (new clothes) – and only God knows what is concealed.[66]

no. 17: *al-iklīl* (B,54a,10–11)

The Indians say: When the moon stations in (*al-iklīl*), then do not enter before kings, do not join anybody, do not marry, and do not do any work – and God knows best.

no. 18: *al-qalb* (B,56a,11–56b,2)

The Indians say: When the moon stations in *al-qalb*, associate with kings and nobles, begin any work, buy slaves and farms (?), do (any work) you want to do, and do not travel during (this time), (because) it is reprehensible by them – and God knows best.

no. 19: *al-shawla* (B,58a,10–58b,1)

The Indians say: When the moon stations in (*al-shawla*), then enter before kings, nobles and others, marry, wear new (clothes), buy slaves, do not plant, do not bind together (the harvest) (?), do not travel, and do not imbibe medicine – and God knows best what He concealed.[66]

no. 20: *al-na'ā'im* (B,60a,8–11)

The Indians say: When the moon stations in (*al-na'ā'im*), then buy slaves and farms (?), wage war, associate with enemies, travel, and do (any work) you want to do, (because) it is recommended – and only God knows what is concealed.[66]

no. 21: *al-balda* (B,62a,12–13)

The Indians say: When the moon stations in (*al-balda*), then do not do any work and do not dispose (freely) over any affair.

no. 22: *sa'd al-dhābiḥ* (B,63b,13–64a,7)

The Indians say: When the moon stations in (*sa'd al-dhābiḥ*), then do not do any work. It is recommended for poetry during (this time) apart from the last third of the day. For the people (making) jewelry it is in the middle (between what is recommended to do, and what is disapproved). They maintain that a marriage contracted (during this time) will bring inevitably for both a separation. If both (nevertheless) agree (on the marriage), one has to be afraid of the death of one partner before the end of the year or in any case an inauspicious separation. Give up the military slave who ran away, and because of that they disapprove of buying them. During (this time) seafaring is auspicious, and a partnership appropriate. There is hope during (this time) for the release of those that are captured – and only God knows what is concealed.[66]

no. 23: *saʿd bulaʿ* (B,65b,12–66a,2)

The Indians say: When the moon stations in (*saʿd bulaʿ*), then do not do any work, (because) it is reprehensible. Some say, treat (the sick) during (this time), (meet) (?) beautiful women, and (make) jewelry. Travel at the beginning of the day and marriage are recommended. Buying slaves in the middle (of the day) is reprehensible and at its end recommended – and only God knows what is concealed.[66]

no. 24: *saʿd al-suʿūd* (B,67b,3–4)

The Indians say: When the moon stations in (*saʿd al-suʿūd*), then do not avoid any work and do any work you want (to do), (because) it is recommended – and only God knows best what He concealed.[66]

no. 26: *al-fargh al-muqaddam* (B,70a,12–70b,3)

The Indians say: When the moon stations in (*al-fargh al-muqaddam*), then associate with kings and nobles, enter before them, plant,[68] harvest, bind together (the harvest) (?), wield the plough, do not (forge) iron, and (do not make) jewelry – and only God knows what is concealed.[66]

no. 27: *al-fargh al-muʾakhkhar* (B,40b,2–6)

The Indians say: When the moon stations in (*al-fargh al-muʾakhkhar*), then it is appropriate to enter before kings and nobles, (to begin) a war, a travel, and a partnership. During this time seafaring, entrusting (goods), buying slaves and marrying are disapproved – and only God knows what is concealed.[66]

no. 28: *baṭn al-ḥūt* (B,42b,6–13)

The Indians say: When the moon stations in (*baṭn*) *al-ḥūt*, then it is recommended to trade and to travel apart from the final half of the day. Marriage during (this time) is appropriate. Association with kings and brothers, selling, buying, and

---

[68] Misread in Schmidl, *Volksastronomie*, p. 302.

any work during (this time) is appropriate. Some of them disapprove during (this time) of buying military slaves and seafaring (because) it is inauspicious for captives – and only God knows what is concealed.[66]

Survey of the Manuscripts Consulted

B = Berlin, Staatsbibliothek Preußischer Kulturbesitz, Ahlwardt 5664 (= Lbg. 108)
Ibn Raḥīq: … *ʿalā madhāhib al-ʿArab*

H = Oxford, Bodleian Library, Huntington 233
al-Ashraf ʿUmar: *Kitāb al-Tabṣira fī ʿilm al-nujūm*

C = Cambridge, Cambridge University Library, Arberry Supp. 110 (a) (= Or. 1236 (11))
al-Aṣbaḥī: *Kitāb al-Yawāqīt fī ʿilm al-mawāqīt*

D = Dublin, Chester Beatty Library, 3640,1
Naṣīr al-Dīn al-Ṭūsī: *Safīnat al-aḥkām*

G = Berlin, Staatsbibliothek Preußischer Kulturbesitz, Ahlwardt 5731 (= Glas. 163)
(al-Fārisī: *Tuḥfat al-rāghib wa-turfat al-ṭālib fī taysīr al-nayyirayn wa-ḥarakāt al-kawākib*)

K = Cairo, Dār al-Kutub, Mīqāt 948
al-Aṣbaḥī: *Kitāb al-Yawāqīt fī ʿilm al-mawāqīt*

M = Milan, Biblioteca Ambrosiana, X 73 sup. (Griffini 37)
al-Fārisī: *Tuḥfat al-rāghib wa-turfat al-ṭālib fī taysīr al-nayyirayn wa-ḥarakāt al-kawākib*

O = Oxford, Bodleian Library, Marsh 134
al-Aṣbaḥī: *Kitāb al-Yawāqīt fī l-mawāqīt*

T = Timbuktu, Institut des Hautes Études et de Recherches Islamiques – Aḥmad Bābā (IHERI-AB), formerly Centre de Documentation et de Recherches Aḥmad Bābā (CEDRAB), no. 4169
Bilāl b. Malik: *Bāb maʿrifat al-manāzil* (!) *al-qamar*

ABRAHAM IBN EZRA'S INTERPRETATION OF ASTROLOGY ACCORDING TO THE TWO VERSIONS OF THE BOOK OF REASONS

Shlomo Sela

Abraham Ibn Ezra (1089–1167) is mainly known as a prolific writer on a great variety of subjects, almost exclusively in Hebrew, although some original Latin works are also ascribed to him or appear to have been written with his active collaboration. He rose to fame principally because of his outstanding biblical exegesis; but he also wrote religious and secular poetry, a series of religious-theological monographs, grammatical treatises and a scientific corpus comprising roughly thirty treatises dealing with the main scientific branches pursued in his time: mathematics, astronomy, scientific instruments and tools, calendrics and, especially, astrology. We currently know of nineteen Hebrew treatises on the main systems of Arabic astrology; these include four recently discovered works.[1] As part of his astrological endeavors, Ibn Ezra composed two treatises that bear the same title: *Sefer ha-Ṭeʿamim* or the *Book of Reasons*.[2]

---

1 For an updated list, see *Abraham Ibn Ezra on Nativities and Continuous Horoscopy*, A Parallel Hebrew English Critical Edition of the Book of Nativities and the Book of Revolution, Edited, Translated and Annotated, by Shlomo Sela (Leiden: Brill, 2013), pp. 1-4. For a chronological listing, see Shlomo Sela and Gad Freudenthal, 'Abraham Ibn Ezra's Scholarly Writings: A Chronological Listing', *Aleph* 6 (2006): pp. 13–55. The new discoveries are: (a) the complete text of *Sefer ha-Tequfah* (Book of the Revolution), a treatise on continuous astrology (see Shlomo Sela, '*Sefer ha-Tequfah*: An Unknown Treatise on Anniversary Horoscopy by Abraham Ibn Ezra', *Aleph* 9 (2009): pp. 241–54; (b) the third version of *Sefer ha-Mivḥarim* (Book of Elections) and the third version of *Sefer ha-She'elot* (Book of Interrogations) (see Shlomo Sela and Renate Smithuis, 'Two Hebrew Fragments from Unknown Redactions of Abraham Ibn Ezra's *Sefer ha-Mivḥarim* and *Sefer ha-Šeʾelot*', *Aleph* 9 [2009]: pp. 225–40); (c) a fragment of the second version of *Reshit Ḥokhmah* (see Shlomo Sela, 'A Fragment From an Unknown Redaction of *Reʾšit Ḥokmah* by Abraham Ibn Ezra', *Aleph* 10 [2010]: pp. 43–66).

2 For a recent critical edition, see *The Book of Reasons, A Parallel Hebrew-English Critical Edition of the Two Versions of the Text*, edited, translated, and annotated by Shlomo Sela (Leiden: Brill, 2007). This edition is used for all quotations from or references to the Hebrew text of the first and the second redactions of *Sefer ha-Ṭeʿamim*, in the format: (a)

These twin treatises (the first version will be referred to here as *Ṭeʿamim* I and the second version as *Ṭeʿamim* II) were written to accomplish a similar, although not identical, purpose: to offer the *Ṭeʿamim*—'reasons', 'explanations' or 'meanings'—of the raw astrological concepts formulated in two different introductions to astrology also composed by him: the two versions of *Reshit Ḥokhmah*, or the *Beginning of Wisdom*. One of them is a well-known work which survives in more than 50 manuscripts, has enjoyed several editions and translations, and is considered to be the pinnacle of Ibn Ezra's astrological corpus.[3] The existence of the second version of *Reshit Ḥokhmah* was suggested by a comparison of the two redactions of the *Book of Reasons;* the hypothesis was confirmed very recently by the discovery of a fragment of it.[4]

In fact, the two versions of the *Book of Reasons,* although they share the same name and were composed to accomplish the same ostensible purpose, are quite different. To begin with, whereas the first version is full of quotations from the extant complete version of *Reshit Ḥokhmah,*[5] the second version incorporates quotations from a completely different work.[6] Secondly, major topics covered in

---

Ṭ(I), §3.2:1, pp. 70–71 = first version of *Sefer ha-Ṭeʿamim*, ed. Sela, chapter 3, section 2, passage 1 on pp. 70–71; (b) *Ṭ*(II), §3.2:1, pp. 223–24 = second version of *Sefer ha-Ṭeʿamim*, ed. Sela, chapter 3, section 2, passage 1, on pp. 223–24.

3 Raphael Levy and Francisco Cantera, *The Beginning of Wisdom* (Baltimore: The Johns Hopkins Press, 1939).

4 *Ṭeʿamim* I is full of quotations from the extant version of *Reshit Ḥokhmah* (henceforth *RḤ* I). By contrast, even though *Ṭeʿamim* II includes obvious quotations from an underlying text and many parts of *Ṭeʿamim* II do not make sense unless one assumes that they are commenting on quoted passages, it is virtually impossible to find explicit and obvious quotations from *RḤ* I in *Ṭeʿamim* II. The theory that *Mishpeṭei ha-Mazzalot* (an additional introduction to astrology by Ibn Ezra) was the text on which *Ṭeʿamim* II expands is rendered untenable by the fact that *Mishpeṭei ha-Mazzalot* does not contain the vast majority of the quotations and does not employ the same terminology as in *Ṭeʿamim* II. Given that at the very start of *Ṭeʿamim* II Ibn Ezra wrote that 'I wish to lay the foundation of the *Book of Reshit Ḥokhmah*', we are forced to conclude that *Ṭeʿamim* II is commenting on a second version of *Reshit Ḥokhmah*. For an expansion of these arguments, see *The Book of Reasons*, ed. Sela, pp. 6–8 and 359–64; Renate Smithuis, 'Abraham ibn Ezra the Astrologer and the Transmission of Arabic Science to the Christian West' (PhD dissertation, University of Manchester, 2004), pp. 156–63. For the recently found fragment of the second version of *Reshit Ḥokhmah,* which confirms this theory, see Sela, 'A Fragment From an Unknown Redaction of *Reʾšit Ḥokmah* by Abraham Ibn Ezra'.

5 For an example, see *The Book of Reasons*, ed. Sela, pp. 341–44.

6 For examples, see ibid., pp. 347–51.

the second version are omitted from the first, and *vice versa*; those topics that are addressed in both versions are treated in a different order and sometimes in a different fashion.[7] Thirdly, in at least seven Hebrew and one Latin manuscript collections of Ibn Ezra's astrological treatises the two versions were copied side by side (or one after the other), as if they were two dissimilar treatises that should be read sequentially.[8] In other words, in the Middle Ages and early modern period the two versions of the *Book of Reasons* circulated as distinct treatises rather than as variants of a single text.

My main purpose here is to address Ibn Ezra's interpretive strategy and highlight the main characteristics of the interpretation of astrology that emerges from these twin treatises. At the outset we should note that the two versions of the *Book of Reasons* constitute a special case in Ibn Ezra's astrological corpus. As a rule, his astrological treatises are textbooks or reference works, aimed chiefly at providing conventional astrological knowledge. As such, they have a clear didactic character and make no pretence of innovation. The bulk of the astrological material is offered, explicitly or implicitly, as paraphrases of or quotations from earlier sources. However, providing the 'reasons' behind the astrological doctrines presented in another text presupposes a more resourceful reorganization of the available data, a more innovative explanatory strategy and, in particular, a more creative approach to astrology. Let us see now whether *Ṭeʿamim* I and *Ṭeʿamim* II bear out these assumptions.

Interpretive Organization

It is not surprising that Ibn Ezra felt a need to compose two books designed to offer the 'reasons' behind the astrological doctrines presented in another text. For one thing, such an approach is to be expected from a writer whose main

7 For example, two chapters of *Ṭeʿamim* II, §6 and §8, address a variety of concepts related to nativities, which are totally absent from the extant text of *Reshit Ḥokhmah* and consequently are not expanded on in *Ṭeʿamim* I.

8 MS Munich, Bayerische Staatsbibliothek, Cod. Hebr. 202, fols 35a–67a; MS New York, Columbia University Library, X 893 Ib 53, fols 1–35; MS Paris, Bibliothèque nationale de France, héb. 1044, fols 192b–239b ; MS Vatican, Biblioteca Apostolica Vaticana 47, fols 25a–34b, 44b–53b; MS Berlin, Staatsbibliothek 220, fols 1b–32a, 51b–54a; MS Cambridge, University Library, Add. 1186, fols 36b–51b, 87a–100a; MS Jerusalem, Benyahu ע133, fols 1a–35a; MS Leipzig University 1466, fols 49^{b}2–60^{b}2.28 and 60^{b}2.35–73^{b}1 (Henry Bate's Latin translations of *Ṭeʿamim* II and I).

literary form was the biblical commentary. It should be recalled that his biblical exegesis, which attained extraordinary recognition in the Middle Ages, may be divided broadly into two periods, Italian and French; during the French period he wrote second versions of some of the commentaries he had already produced in Italy.[9] In fact, in both versions of the *Book of Reasons* we observe the same interpretive strategy adopted by Ibn Ezra in his biblical commentaries: on the one hand, brief notes glossing an underlying text; on the other hand, long digressions or exegetical asides in which Ibn Ezra takes the liberty of deviating from the ordinary rigorous reference to the words of the underlying text and adds new perspectives to the problem under discussion, applying knowledge drawn from all the scientific disciplines of his age.[10] As in his biblical commentaries, not only are these digressions the most interesting and fascinating portions of both versions of the *Book of Reasons*, they are also the sections in which he articulated his most creative ideas.

---

[9] In Rome, in 1140–1142, Ibn Ezra wrote commentaries on Ecclesiastes, Esther, Job, Lamentations, Daniel, Song of Songs and Psalms: see Sela and Freudenthal, 'Abraham Ibn Ezra's Scholarly Writings', nn. 1, 2, 5, 6, 7, 8, 9; J.L. Fleischer, 'R. Abraham Ibn Ezra and his Literary Work in Rome' (Heb.) *Oṣar ha-ḥayyim* 8 (5692 [1932]), pp. 98, 100, 129–31; *Oṣar ha-ḥayyim* 9 (5693 [1933]), pp. 134–36; M. Friedlander, *Essays on the Writings of Abraham Ibn Ezra* (London: Society of Hebrew Literature, 1877), p. 195; D. Rosin, 'Die Religionsphilosophie Abraham Ibn Esra's', *Monatsschrift für Geschichte und Wissenschaft des Judentums* 42 (1898): p. 25. In Lucca, in 1142–1145, he wrote commentaries on the twelve Minor Prophets, a complete commentary on the Pentateuch, and commentaries on Ruth and Isaiah: see Sela and Freudenthal, 'Abraham Ibn Ezra's Scholarly Writings', nn. 10, 11, 12, 13; J.L. Fleischer, *R. Abraham Ibn Ezra: A Collection of Articles on his Life and Works* (Tel Aviv, 5730 [1970]), pp. 116–124; Friedlander, *Essays*, pp. 142–95, esp. p. 195. Subsequently, in Rouen, in 1154–1157, he composed a second commentary on Esther, Daniel, Genesis, Exodus, Psalms, Song of Songs, and on the Minor Prophets: see Sela and Freudenthal, 'Abraham Ibn Ezra's Scholarly Writings', nn. 50, 51, 52, 53, 54, 55, 56; Norman Golb, *The History and Culture of the Jews of Rouen in the Middle Ages* (Heb.) (Tel Aviv, 5736 [1976]), pp. 264–67; J.L. Fleischer, 'R. Abraham Ibn Ezra in France' (Heb.), *Mizraḥ u-maʿarav* 4 (5690 [1930]), pp. 219–20; Friedlander, *Essays*, pp. 142–95.

[10] I am referring here to the exegetical excursus, in which Ibn Ezra illuminates some burning and controversial exegetical issue by providing supplemental information related to astronomy, astrology, mathematics, cosmology, Hebrew grammar, and logic. For some examples, see Shlomo Sela, *Abraham Ibn Ezra and the Rise of Medieval Hebrew Science* (Leiden: Brill, 2003), pp. 273–76 and 288–323.

Linguistic Strategy

Although Ibn Ezra was not the first Jewish writer to compose astrological works in Hebrew,[11] he was the first to address all branches of Arabic astrology and thereby coin a comprehensive astrological vocabulary in Hebrew. This is evident in both versions of the *Book of Reasons*, which include the terminology of all branches of Arabic astrology.[12] The formidable task of creating a comprehensive astrological vocabulary should not be dismissed as a mere technical undertaking, but as an interpretation of astrology at its most basic and essential level. This is made clear by the significant fact that Ibn Ezra's approach to it is unique among Jewish translators. He preferred, in some remarkable cases, biblical words to Arabic calques, loanwords, or other more usual expressions because, in his opinion, the available biblical vocabulary included a few original and authentic scientific terms that represented central concepts of nature and reality. Ibn Ezra considered these scientific words to be vestiges of the original Hebrew language, 'the most comprehensive and the first among the languages

---

[11] The Hebrew astrological terminology in two works from the early Middle Ages—the *Baraita de-Shemu'el* and the *Baraita de-Mazzalot*—reveals Greek and Arabic origins: see G. B. Sarfati, 'Introduction to the Baraita de-Mazzalot' (Heb.), *Bar Ilan* 3 (1965): pp. 56–82. There is also significant astrological content in *Sefer Ḥakhmoni* and *Sefer ha-Mazzalot*, two Hebrew works by Shabbetai Donnolo (913–ca. 982), as well as in the *Commentary on Sefer Yeṣirah* (Book of Creation) by Judah ben Barzillai ha-Bargelloni, the leading rabbinic authority of Barcelona in the first half of the twelfth century: see *Shabbatai Donnolo's Sefer Ḥakhmoni*, Introduction, Critical Text, and Annotated English Translation by Piergabriele Mancuso (Leiden: Brill, 2010), pp. 138–39, 156, 186–95 (Hebrew part); 230–34, 283, 317–34 (English part); *Sefer ha-Mazzalot* by Shabbetai Donnolo in S.D. Luzzato, *Kerem Ḥemed* 7 (1843): pp. 60–67; Shlomo Sela, 'Dos textos astrológicos conservados en el comentario al *Sefer Yeṣiráh* de Yehudáh ben Barzilay al Bargeloni', *Sefarad* 68 (2008): pp. 261–90. The contribution to the creation of a Hebrew astrological vocabulary made by Abraham Bar Ḥiyya (ca. 1065–ca. 1140) is of great importance but limited mainly to general astrology and continuous horoscopy. For Bar Ḥiyya's astrological work and thought, see Shlomo Sela, 'Abraham Bar Ḥiyya's Astrological Work and Thought', *Jewish Studies Quarterly* 13 (2006): pp. 127–58; idem, 'A Newly Identified Essay on Anniversary Horoscopy Embedded in Abraham Bar Ḥiyya's Astronomical Tables: Hebrew Edition, Translation and Commentary', *Aleph* 13(1) (2013): pp. 27–76. For a comparison between the astrological lexicons of Bar Ḥiyya and Ibn Ezra, see idem, *Abraham Ibn Ezra and the Rise of Medieval Hebrew Science*, pp. 103–04; Josefina Rodríguez-Arribas, 'Terminology for Historical Astrology According to Bar Hiyya and Ibn Ezra', *Aleph* 11 (2011): pp. 11–54.

[12] See *The Book of Reasons*, ed. Sela, pp. 377–90.

of all the nations'.[13] Reviving the use of those forgotten words stood at the heart of his terminological strategy.[14]

For example, in both versions of the *Book of Reasons* we find the Hebrew word *muṣaq* (taken from the Book of Job)—literally 'solid'—is used to denote the concept of centre;[15] the Hebrew word *gevul* (Ps. 74:17), literally 'border', to mean 'climate' (in the sense of a region);[16] *mishpaṭim* (Ps. 19:10) to mean 'astrological judgments';[17] *ḥeshev ha-ʾafuddah* (based on Exodus 28:8), which speaks of the girdle in the ceremonial vestments of the High Priest, to denote the ecliptic.[18] Perhaps the most outstanding example is the neologism *mesharetim,* literally 'servants', but frequently employed by Ibn Ezra to mean the planets. Ibn Ezra found the word in Psalm 103:21, where he glossed it in his commentary as a reference to the seven planets. Endowed with this meaning, the biblical word conveyed the message that the seven planets are not self-sufficient astrological agents but work as *servants* of God to *do his pleasure.*[19]

Another ubiquitous Hebrew term is *nissayon,* 'experience', which appears in the *Book of Reasons* in various collocations to denote the main tool of the astrologers. Through this very frequent term, Ibn Ezra conveys the idea that the method employed by the astrologers is not based on deduction from theoretical principles but on induction and analogies, mathematical calculations, astronomical observation and, especially, on knowledge accumulated by astrologers in their writings over the generations.[20]

---

[13] *Keli ha-Neḥoshet* (Book of the Astrolabe), third version, MS Paris, BNF, héb. 1054, f. 4b.

[14] On Ibn Ezra's strategy for the creation of a new scientific Hebrew vocabulary, see Sela, *Abraham Ibn Ezra and the Rise of Medieval Hebrew Science*, pp. 93–143.

[15] See *Ṭ*(I), §5.2:3, pp. 82–83 and p. 164n. For other cases, see *The Book of Reasons*, ed. Sela, p. 378.

[16] See *Ṭ*(I), §2.1:1, pp. 36–37 and p. 122n. For other cases, see *The Book of Reasons*, ed. Sela, p. 379.

[17] See *Ṭ*(II), §1.3:2, pp. 184–85 and p. 266n. For other cases, see *The Book of Reasons*, ed. Sela, p. 383.

[18] See *Ṭ*(I), §1.2:1, pp. 182–83 and p. 262n. For other cases, see *The Book of Reasons*, ed. Sela, p. 388.

[19] See *Ṭ*(II), §1.2:1, pp. 28–29 and p. 122n. For other cases, see *The Book of Reasons*, ed. Sela, p. 380.

[20] See *Ṭ*(I), §1.4:1, pp. 32–33 and p. 118n. For other cases, see *The Book of Reasons*, ed. Sela, p. 381.

Ibn Ezra's Approach to his Astrological Sources

Both versions of the *Book of Reasons* offer extensive information about Ibn Ezra's astrological sources; his references to them are an excellent means for learning about the astrological texts available in al-Andalus in the twelfth century and earlier. He names a relatively long list of celebrated astrologers, referring to the work, occupation and speciality of his sources, along with generic references that highlight their geographical and national affiliations and their time periods.[21]

In most cases Ibn Ezra invokes the name and opinion of some prominent authority in order to buttress the case for some astrological reason (i.e., 'Yaʿqub al-Kindī said …'; 'Enoch said …'; 'Māshā'allāh said …'; 'Abū Maʿshar said …'; 'Doronius [Dorotheus] said …'). However, it is Claudius Ptolemy who emerges as the chief astrological source; in the two versions of the *Book of Reasons* Ibn Ezra refers to Ptolemy more than to any other astrologer.[22] But the persona with whom Ibn Ezra was acquainted was surrounded by a cluster of myths. Thus, in the first version of the *Book of Reasons* Ibn Ezra refers to *Baṭlmiyūs*, Ptolemy, in Arabic transliteration;[23] in the second version he refers to Ptolemy not only as *Talmai*, the post-biblical or Talmudic Hebrew equivalent of Ptolemy, but also as '*Talmai* the King'.[24] In fact, Ibn Ezra inherited the mythical King Ptolemy from Abū Maʿshar, in all likelihood from his *Great Introduction*;[25] but in turn Ibn Ezra

---

21 See *The Book of Reasons*, ed. Sela, pp. 353–56.

22 See *The Book of Reasons*, ed. Sela, p. 355, s.v. Ptolemy.

23 See *Ṭ*(I), §1.2:3, pp. 30–31, et passim.

24 See *Ṭ*(II), §5.5:6, pp. 230–231, et passim.

25 Abū Maʿshar al-Balkhī (Albumasar), *Kitāb al-mudkhal al-kabīr ilā ʿilm ʾaḥkām an-nujūm*, eds. Charles Burnett and Keiji Yamamoto, forthcoming, IV:1: 'إنّ عدّة من ملوك اليونانيين كانوا على اثر ذي القرنين ٱلإسكندر بن فلفس يقال لكلّ واحد منهم بطلميوس وهم عشرة اناس تسعة رخال وامراة وكانوا ينزلون مصر وكان سنو ملكهم مائتين وخمسة وسبعين سنه وكان عامّتهم حكماء ومنهم بطلميوس الحكيم الذي ألّف كتاب المجسطي على علل حركة الفلك وما فيها من الكواكب وبعضهم الف كتابا في أحكام النجوم ونسبه الى بطلميوس صاحب كتاب المجسطي وقد يقال إنّ علّامة الذي الف كتاب الآحكام هو الذي ألف كتاب المجسطي' = 'There were a number of Greek kings immediately after the Two-Horned, Alexander, son of Philip, each of whom was called Ptolemy, namely ten, nine men and a woman. They lived in Egypt and their rule lasted 275 years (i.e., BCE 305–30). The majority of them were wise, and one of them was Ptolemy, who composed the book of the *Almagest* on the causes of the motion of the sphere and all the planets within it. Another of them

created a new ('Jewish') mythical King Ptolemy—not only the flesh-and-blood astrologer of antiquity but also the 'King Ptolemy' who commissioned the Septuagint, the Greek translation of the Bible, in an attempt to steal the astrological secrets concealed in the Torah.[26]

Ibn Ezra frequently expresses approval of Ptolemy,[27] but does not abstain from highlighting what he considers to be Ptolemy's errors and even unleashes harsh attacks on him with regard to some fundamental astrological issues. A notable instance is found in the first version of the *Book of Reasons,* where we read: 'I now give you a general rule: anything that Ptolemy says about the orbs is correct and no one surpasses him; but his astrological decrees and judgments do not befit his wisdom. You should rely only on what Doronius the king and Māshāʾallāh, who was from India, said about astrological decrees'.[28]

Most of Ibn Ezra's Ptolemaic references can be readily located in the *Tetrabiblos* or the *Centiloquium*. In some cases, however, they enable us to identify unknown or lost works by Ptolemy. A notable example is found in a parallel passage in the two versions of the *Book of Reasons*. According to *Ṭeʿamim* II: 'Ptolemy, the King, said that the number of the Sun is 18, and of the Moon 12, and the number of Mercury and of Venus is 16, and the number of Mars is 21⅓, and the number of Jupiter is 24, and the number of Saturn is 32. He said that this number was obtained from the ratio of the planets' orbs to the Earth's orb. For this reason Saturn and Mars are malefic, because they do not have a good ratio

---

composed a book on astrology and attributed it to Ptolemy, the author of the book of the *Almagest*. It is sometimes said that the very learned man who wrote the book of astrology also wrote the book of the *Almagest*'. See also Ṣāʿid al-Andalusī, *Kitāb Tabaqāt al-umam* in *Science in the Medieval World, 'Book of the Categories of Nations' by Said al-Andalusi*, trans. and ed. Sema'an I. Salem and Alok Kumar (Austin: University of Texas Press, 1991), p. 27: 'There is also Batlymus al-Qaluzi (Claudius Ptolemy) the author of the book *al-Majisti* (*Almagest*), the book *al-Manazir* (*Optics*) and the book *al-Maqalat al-Arbaʿ* (*Tetrabiblos*) on the study of astronomy. ... Many people who claim knowledge of the history of nations include Claudius Ptolemy with the Greek Ptolemies who reigned after Alexander'.

26 This point is fleshed out in Sela, *Abraham Ibn Ezra and the Rise of Medieval Hebrew Science*, pp. 296–313.

27 See *Ṭ*(I), §2.5:12, pp. 46–47; *Ṭ*(I), §2.16:9, pp. 56–57; *Ṭ*(I), §3.5:7, pp. 64–65; *Ṭ*(I), §7.1:1, pp. 88–89; *Ṭ*(I), §8.1:6, pp. 90–91; *Ṭ*(II), §4.8:2, pp. 212–13; *Ṭ*(II), §5.1:15, pp. 218–19 et passim.

28 *Ṭ*(I), §2.18:2, pp. 58–59: see also *Ṭ*(I), §1.5:1–5, pp. 32–35: 'The explanation of the natures of the planets is complicated and may be found in the *Tetrabiblos* by Ptolemy. ... But I, Abraham, the author, say that this book was not written by Ptolemy, because there are many things in it that have in them nothing of rational thought or experience'.

to the luminaries, but the maleficence of Saturn is removed because Saturn and Mars have a good ratio; and the same applies to Venus and Mercury with Mars'.[29]

We shall look in vain for this information in Ptolemy's *Tetrabiblos, Almagest,* or *Planetary Hypotheses*. But it turns out that a virtually identical list, which incorporates the planets, their corresponding numbers and, also, the name of a corresponding musical note, is part and parcel of the *Canobic Inscription,* an early work by Ptolemy, predating the *Almagest.*[30] In fact, the list in the *Canobic Inscription,* as well as the lists in the two versions of the *Book of Reasons,* pertains to the Pythagorean tradition of the 'music of the spheres', which regards the proportions in the movement of the celestial bodies as a form of music.[31] But where did Ibn Ezra obtain these lists and the information that the numbers somehow correspond to ratios between the orbs of the planets and the orb of the Earth? Perhaps he had access to some now-lost work of Ptolemy, such as a lost chapter of *Harmonics,* where Ptolemy is supposed to have included information about the musical tones of the planets.[32] It is more plausible, however, that he derived the information from some Arabic work, closer to his time and cultural climate, such as the *Epistle on Music* that is part of the Encyclopedia of the Brethren of Purity.[33] In fact, in the *Epistle* we find not only a similar account of

---

29 *Ṭ*(II), §5.5:6–7, pp. 230–31; *Ṭ*(I), §4.1:1–4, pp. 68–71.

30 N.M. Swerdlow, 'Ptolemy's *Harmonics* and the "Tones of the Universe" in the *Canobic Inscription*', in *Studies in the History of the Exact Sciences in Honour of David Pingree* (Leiden and Boston: Brill, 2004), pp. 166–67. I am grateful to Lenn Schramm for alerting me to this fact.

31 The Pythagoreans, according to Aristotle's *De caelo* 2.9, 'starting from the observation that the stars' speeds, as measured by their distances, are in the same ratios as musical concordances, assert that the sound given forth by the circular movement of the stars is a harmony'.

32 Chapter 3.14 of Ptolemy's *Harmonics* is entitled 'By which least numbers the fixed tones (notes) of the perfect system may be compared to the primary spheres in the universe'; this is presumably where Ptolemy explained the relation between the musical tones and certain astronomical properties of the planets. But the contents of this chapter are unfortunately lost.

33 *Epistle on Music of the Ikhwân al-Ṣafâ'*, trans. Amnon Shiloah (Tel Aviv: Tel-Aviv University, Faculty of Fine Arts, 1978), pp. 45–46.

the musical tones of the planets, but also a very similar explanation of the maleficence and beneficence of the planets.[34]

Explanations of Astrological Doctrines

From a technical perspective, the most interesting parts of the two versions of the *Book of Reasons* are Ibn Ezra's explanations of astrological doctrines. In most cases he defends a particular view, though it is not clear whether it is an innovative position or a paraphrase from an earlier source. This applies to the reasons for the physical properties of the zodiacal signs, which Ibn Ezra attributes to their visual shapes,[35] or the cardinal points of the quadrants of the horoscope, where he overtly endorses the opinion of the astrolabists.[36] Sometimes he tries to reconcile opposing opinions about an astrological issue by offering a middle-ground solution. This is noticeable regarding whether Venus and Mercury are above or below the Sun, where Ibn Ezra surprisingly endorses a partially heliocentric theory;[37] whether the intensity of the planets' astrological

---

[34] Ibid., pp. 34–35.

[35] *Ṭ*(II), §2.1:11, pp. 186–87: 'In my opinion, they made <the sign of> Aries hot because the shape <formed by the stars resembles> a ram, and similarly <Taurus has> the shape resembling a> bull, and Gemini <they made> hot and moist because it has the shape of a man, and Cancer <they made> cold and moist because that is its nature, and <they made> Leo hot and it is like that'. This corresponds to *Ṭ*(I), §1.4:4, pp. 32–33.

[36] *Ṭ*(I), §3.4:8–9, pp. 62–63: 'Abraham said: there is a disagreement among the scholars of this art. Some say that <the quadrant> between the degree of the ascendant and the line of lower midheaven is eastern, and <the quadrant> from the line of midheaven to the degree of the ascendant is southern, and <that> from the line of lower midheaven to the degree of the descendant is northern, and <that> from the degree of the descendant to the line of midheaven is western. This is the way in which it was divided by the experts in the astrolabe, and I tend to agree with them'.

[37] *Ṭ*(II), §2.5:1–2, pp. 194–95: 'There is a great dispute among scholars about whether Venus and Mercury are above or below the Sun; this uncertainty arose because nobody can see them when they are in conjunction with the Sun, and also because they both have the same eccentric circle. But in my opinion all of them are right, for sometimes they [i.e. Venus and Mercury] are below and sometimes they are above <the Sun>, and this requires a long explanation'. This corresponds to *Ṭ*(I), §1.3:8–9, pp. 30–31. A partially heliocentric theory, according to which Mercury and Venus circle the Sun, was advocated in antiquity by Theon of Smyrna and had a vigorous Latin tradition. It is mentioned by three late (fourth and fifth centuries CE) Latin writers—Calcidius, Macrobius, and Martianus Capella—and also by twelfth-century philosophers—William of Conches and Hermann of Carinthia: see James Evans, *The History and Practice of Ancient Astronomy*

influence depends on their distance from Earth; and whether the Head and Tail of the Dragon should be considered to be astrologically beneficent or maleficent.[38] To demonstrate the truth or falsity of an astrological tenet he sometimes incorporates an account of empirical work he himself has carried out.[39]

In a few places Ibn Ezra takes personal credit for a new approach to an astrological doctrine; a notable instance is his explanation of the distribution of the pains of the planets among the zodiacal signs. In contrast to introductions to

---

(New York and Oxford: Oxford University Press, 1998), pp. 349, 413–14; John L.E. Dreyer, *A History of Astronomy from Thales to Kepler* (New York: Dover, 1953), p. 128. Since it is not found in Arabic sources, it is possible that Ibn Ezra was acquainted with this theory via Latin sources. I am grateful to Prof. Charles Burnett for this information.

38 Ṭ(II), §5.9:1–5, pp. 234–35: 'The Tail. When the Moon is in the south side it loses power; hence it [the Dragon's Tail] indicates then a lack of good fortune and a lack of honor, which is disgrace and shame ... They said that if a benefic planet is in the Head it increases good fortune; if a malefic, it diminishes <good fortune>, and they said that the Tail diminishes the good fortune of a benefic planet and diminishes the misfortune of a malefic <planet>. Hence they said that the Head is a benefic with the benefics and a malefic with the malefics, and the Tail is a malefic with the benefics and a benefic with the malefics. They said <all that> about the Head of the Dragon of the Moon's orb and its Tail. In my opinion their statements are true, but every planet has its own Head of the Dragon and its Tail'. This corresponds to Ṭ(I), §5.3:1–5, 84–85. See also Abū Maʿshar, *The Abbreviation of the Introduction to Astrology*, together with the Medieval Latin translation of Adelard of Bath, ed. and trans. Charles Burnett, Keiji Yamamoto, and Michio Yano (Leiden: Brill, 1994), p. 57; al-Qabīṣī, *Introduction to Astrology*, II:48, p. 89.

39 Ṭ(I), §2.2:17, pp. 40–41: 'As for the reason for the days and hours, I saw it in Abū Maʿshar's book and I verified it by experience'. Ṭ(I), §2.18:1, pp. 58–59: 'Ptolemy disagrees <with them> regarding the houses of the triplicities. We have tested his statements empirically but were unable <to confirm them>'. Ṭ(I), §5.2:7, pp. 84–85: 'But if a planet that is at perigee is in charge of the soul, it indicates that the native will be a fool and ignoramus; and if it is in charge of the body it indicates that he will have a large and powerful body. I have verified this by experience many times.' Ṭ(II), §6.1:4–5, pp. 234–35: 'Ptolemy said that the number <of degrees> of one of the cardines is equal to the number of degrees of the planet that rules the place of the conjunction or the opposition <of the luminaries>. Now I have tested <this> many times, taking the degrees and minutes of the Sun's apogee at the time of birth, and for most years I corrected the places of the planets in the Indian <scientists'> tables and Ptolemy's tables and the Persian <scientists'> tables and the tables that seem to be correct, but I did not find any of the cardines <to be equal to> the number <of degrees> of any of the planets'. Ṭ(I), §6.8:3, pp. 242–43: 'I have found out by empirical experience that the lords of the aspects are more complete than the lords of the terms'.

astrology—such as Ibn Ezra's first version of *Reshit Ḥokhmah* or al-Qabīṣī's *Introduction to Astrology,* which merely list the pains of the planets in the signs[40]—in both versions of *Ṭeʿamim* Ibn Ezra undertakes to elucidate the mechanism behind the distribution of the pains of the planets among the signs. He attributes the doctrine to the Egyptian astrologers and considers it to be derived from the doctrine of melothesia, which distributes the parts of the body among the zodiacal signs, beginning with Aries (the head), Taurus (the neck), and so on.[41] Ibn Ezra's explanation of the mechanism of distribution is based on the assumption that one of the planetary houses of the planet in question is taken as equivalent to Aries, such that the planet in this sign is assigned the head, in the following sign it is assigned the neck, and so on. Therefore the pain of Mars in Aries is the head, because Aries is one of the planetary houses of Mars, the pain of Mars in Taurus is the neck, and so on.[42] In *Mishpeṭei ha-Mazzalot* ('Judgments of the Zodiacal Signs'), another introduction to astrology by Ibn Ezra, he refers to this explanation as a secret, concealed by the Ancients, which he is now disclosing.[43]

---

[40] Levy and Cantera, *The Beginning of Wisdom,* chapter II (Hebrew part), p. x, lines 11-16 et passim; al-Qabīṣī (Alcabitius), *The Introduction to Astrology,* editions of the Arabic and Latin texts and an English translation, Charles Burnett, Keiji Yamamoto, and Michio Yano (London and Turin: Warburg Institute, 2004), I:37–48, pp. 37–41.

[41] *Ṭ*(I), §2.3:2–3, pp. 40–41: 'They assigned the head to this sign [i.e., Aries] because it is the first [lit. 'head'] of all the signs and indicates the head. Taurus <indicates> the neck ... and Pisces the feet. The Egyptian scientists said that the chest is the pain of Saturn in it [i.e., in Aries], and the heart <is the pain> of Jupiter <in Aries>'. Corresponds to *Ṭ*(II), §2.4:20–21, pp. 194–95.

[42] *Ṭ*(I), §2.3:4–7, pp. 40–41: 'This is the reason for it: they put the first house of the planet facing Aries as if it were equivalent to Aries, and therefore say that the pain of Jupiter in Sagittarius, which is the first of its houses, is in the head, just like Aries, which indicates the head. Therefore the pain of Mars in Aries is in the head. The feet were assigned to Pisces' portion with respect to the sign of Aries [i.e., the feet are the pain of Mars in Pisces]. ... This is the reason for each of the pains in each of the signs'. This corresponds to *Ṭ*(II), §4.10:1–7, pp. 214–15.

[43] *Mishpeṭei ha-Mazzalot,* MS Paris, BNF héb. 1058, fols 17a–17b: 'The Ancients mentioned the pains of each planet in each sign. ... I offer you a comprehensive method to understand them. ... I have now disclosed to you a secret; the Ancients concealed it and did not reveal it in their books'.

Astrological Digressions

As already mentioned, in both versions of *Ṭeʿamim* Ibn Ezra applies the same interpretive methodology as that employed in his biblical commentaries: brief notes that comment on quotes from an underlying text, interspersed with long digressions or asides. For modern historians of astrology, these long digressions are the most interesting part of the two versions of the *Book of Reasons*. The underlying idea is that astrology cannot possibly be elucidated by astrology itself but must be explained on the basis of other branches of the sciences, notably astronomy and mathematics.

An outstanding case is the explanation in *Ṭeʿamim* I of the bright and dark degrees. These are two categories of degrees in each of the zodiacal signs endowed with astrological influence, which are mentioned in the introductions to astrology composed by Abū Maʿshar, al-Bīrūnī, and al-Qabīṣī, as well as in Ibn Ezra's own *Reshit Ḥokhmah*; in all these sources these degrees are simply listed separately in the sections on each of the twelve zodiacal signs.[44] Now, to Ibn Ezra's mind, the 'reasons' behind the bright and dark degrees have to do less with their astrological properties, to which he pays little attention, than with the eminently astronomical problem of locating them in the zodiac. Since the position of the bright and dark degrees is given with respect to the images of the zodiacal constellations, an adjustment is necessary when an astrologer wants to locate them in the zodiac using astronomical tables that take account of the motion of the fixed stars (and the zodiacal constellations) with respect to the equinoxes. Hence, Ibn Ezra embarks on a long excursus that discusses the following topics: first, the start and length of the solar year, where Ibn Ezra offers the opinions of Hipparchus, Ptolemy, the Arab scientists, and the Indian scientists;[45] second, the controversy about the motion or stasis of the fixed stars,

---

44 See Abū Maʿshar, *Kitāb al-Madkhal*, V:20, v, p. 207; al-Bīrūnī, *The Book of Instruction in the Elements of the Art of Astrology*, ed. and trans. R. Ramsay Wright (London: Luzac & Co., 1934), §458, p. 270; al-Qabīṣī, *The Introduction to Astrology*, I:50, p. 43; Abū Maʿshar, *The Abbreviation of the Introduction to Astrology*, pp. 139–41; Levy and Cantera, *The Beginning of Wisdom*, chapter II (Hebrew part), p. xi, lines 5–10 et passim.

45 *Ṭ*(I), §2.12:4–6, pp. 50–51: 'Hipparchus said that the solar year is 365¼ days, but he said that the quarter is deficient, although he did not know by how much. Ptolemy said that the deficit is the 300th part of a day; the Arab scientists investigated closely and found that the deficit is 110th of a day; and someone said that it is 106th of a day. But the truth is that the deficit is 131st of a day. The Indian scientists pay no attention to the intersection of the two circles, for their year runs from the moment the Sun enters into conjunction with an

where Ibn Ezra presents the theory of trepidation,[46] the Indian theory that the zodiacal signs do not move,[47] as well as the Ptolemaic theory of the precession of the equinoxes, which Ibn Ezra endorses;[48] third, the controversy about how to divide the zodiac;[49] and finally, instructions on the use of astronomical tables to locate the bright and dark degrees.[50]

Other notable digressions focus on the following topics: the number and order of the orbs and the motion, number, and names of stars and constellations, where Ibn Ezra presents a comprehensive, concise, and remarkable demonstration (or deduction) of a nine-orb universe;[51] the names and sizes of the signs, where the Ptolemaic theory of the precession of the equinoxes is invoked;[52] the nature of the zodiacal signs, where Ibn Ezra ostensibly subscribes to the Aristotelian view of the physical composition of the bodies of the supra- and the sublunary domains but subsequently deviates from it by giving heat

---

upper star until it [i.e., the Sun] returns once more to conjunction with it [i.e., with the same upper star]'.

46 *Ṭ*(I), §2.12:7, pp. 50–51: 'There is another disagreement among the Ancients, for some say that the poles of the orb of the zodiacal signs ascend and descend eight degrees, and others say that there are two circles at the head of Aries and Libra'.

47 *Ṭ*(I), §2.12:7, pp. 50–51: 'The Indian scientists drew the right conclusions from <the principles of> their art, for they say that the stars of the orb of the zodiacal signs do not move'.

48 *Ṭ*(I), §2.12:9–10, pp. 50–51: 'The Ancients said, and Ptolemy <agreed> with them, that they move one degree in 100 years; those who investigated closely after them found that their motion is one degree in 66 years. The correct <value> is that the motion is <one degree in> 70 years'. The latter is the rate proposed by al-Ṣūfi for the motion of the eighth orb'.

49 *Ṭ*(I), §2.12:13, pp. 52–53: 'In fact, the Indian scientists divided the signs into equal parts relying on observation alone, meaning the shapes <of the constellations>, but Ptolemy and his colleagues <divided the signs> according to what is appropriate by the method of <giving> proofs'.

50 *Ṭ*(I), §2.12:14, pp. 52–53: 'So the expert in the zodiacal signs can find out the degree of the ascendant and the positions of the planets according to the reckoning of the tables of the scholars who rely on experience. But if he wants to pass <astrological> judgment by the method of the shapes [i.e., the zodiacal constellations], the bright and dark degrees, and the pits (so-called because they are very dark stars, as if a man had fallen into a pit), this year, which is the year <5>908, he should subtract eight whole degrees'. This corresponds to *Ṭ*(II), §8.7:2–4, pp. 254–55.

51 *Ṭ*(II), §1.2:1–7, pp. 182–85; this corresponds to *Ṭ*(I), §1.3:1–12, pp. 30–33.

52 *Ṭ*(I), §1.2:1–6, pp. 28–31.

primacy over cold;[53] the nature of the planets, where he criticizes Ptolemy's opinion;[54] the rationale behind the planetary houses, where Ibn Ezra reviews a variety of theories and discusses the relative locations of Mercury and Venus with respect to the Sun.[55] Finally, in an excursus on the astrological aspects, he offers first a geometrical justification and then an arithmetical explanation, for which he takes explicit credit, and which exploits features of the integers: pairs of integers separated by the constant 4 (1 and 5, 2 and 6, etc.) are harmonious; pairs separated by the constant 2 (1 and 3, 2 and 4, etc.) are also harmonious but to a lesser degree; and pairs separated by the constant 3 (1 and 4, 2 and 5, etc.) are disharmonious.[56]

Harmonizing Astrology with Medieval Science

To Ibn Ezra's mind, however, not only should astrology be explained by science, it must also be in harmony with science. Therefore, one burning issue that provokes Ibn Ezra's active intervention has to do with astrological doctrines that he believes contradict major aspects of his scientific world view. Most conspicuous is his concern that the standard astrological view of the physical natures of the planets (i.e., the Sun is hot and the Moon is cold), and the standard astrological understanding of the physical natures of the zodiacal signs (i.e., that the signs of the fiery triplicity are hot) may not be compatible with the rigid Aristotelian separation between the super- and sublunary domains, which he accepts without reservation. Ibn Ezra appears to be haunted by this quandary in both versions of *Ṭeʿamim*;[57] he also seems to be obsessed by this topic in his

53 *Ṭ*(II), §2.1:1–13, pp. 184–87; this corresponds to *Ṭ*(I), §1.4:1–7, pp. 30–33.

54 *Ṭ*(I), §1.5:1–17, pp. 32–37.

55 *Ṭ*(I), §2.4:1–12, pp. 42–45; §2.5:1–12, pp. 44–47; this corresponds to *Ṭ*(II), §2.5:1–10, pp. 194–97; §2.6:1–7, pp. 196–97.

56 *Ṭ*(I), §3.1:1–6, pp. 58–61; §3.2:1–12, pp. 60–63; this corresponds to *Ṭ*(II), §4.6:1–6, pp. 210–13; §4.7:1–8, pp. 212–13; §4.8:1–3, pp. 212–13.

57 *Ṭ*(I), §1.5:6–7, pp. 34–35: 'Others said that they knew these natures <of the planets> by experience. But the truth is that there is neither a planet nor an upper star that is either cold or hot, because they are made of a fifth element, as Aristotle explained with incontrovertible proofs'. *Ṭ*(I), §2.7:3, pp. 46–47: 'They assigned Saturn as <their> partner because it is cold, and inasmuch as the sign is hot its nature is tempered. Know that when I said cold and hot I referred only to what they generate and put it this way to make it easier for students': see also *Ṭ*(II), §2.1:1, pp. 184–85; *Ṭ*(II), §8.7:8, pp. 254–55.

non-scientific work, notably the biblical commentaries.[58] In addition to endorsing the Aristotelian fifth element he also espouses the theory that all the planets emit heat by virtue of their motion and are neither hot nor cold in themselves. Similarly the Moon, which is taken to be cold, emits heat but to a lesser extent, because cold is not the opposite of heat but only a lesser degree of heat (he offers the flesh of the ox as an example of this).[59]

Ibn Ezra also finds fault with a number of astrological doctrines of Indian origin that depend on the theory that the fixed stars are motionless. This applies to the Indian version of the exaltations, which are localized in specific degrees in the signs and not in entire signs,[60] and to the doctrines of the bright and dark degrees and of the pits, which assign astrological properties to degrees with respect to the images of the zodiacal signs and not with respect to the equinoxes (see above, p. 467 and 468, n. 50). Ibn Ezra endorses the Greco-Arabic tradition that the fixed stars move very slowly with respect to the equinoxes (a theory that had been advanced in many different versions); hence, he believes, these

---

58 See long commentary on Exod. 33:21; first commentary on Gen. 1:1; second commentary on Gen. 1:1; commentary on Eccles. 1:4.

59 *Ṭ*(I), §1.5:11–12, pp. 34–24: 'The general rule is that neither the planets nor the luminaries generate cold, <but> only heat, on account of their motion and the nature of the light emitted by them. <Consequently,> they concluded that the Moon is cold only because it does not generate sufficient heat as compared to the complexion of human beings, just as the physicians concluded that the flesh of the ox is cold, although it is known that all flesh is hot but it is <considered> cold as compared to the complexion of human beings, and harms them'. This corresponds to *Ṭ*(II), §2.1:2–3, pp. 184–85. The elements of this passage may be found in a passage of Ibn Ezra's *Liber de rationibus tabularum* that comments on Ptolemy's opinion about the nature of the Moon: see José M. Millás Vallicrosa, ed., *El Libro de los Fundamentos de las Tablas Astronómicas de R. Abraham Ibn Ezra* (Madrid and Barcelona: CSIC, 1947), p. 97: 'Bene autem cognovimus omnes stellas in se neque calidas neque frigidas esse. Motu tamen et lumine effectivas esse caloris. Sed quia corpus lune parvum est nec equiparatur soli in effectu caloris nec reddit calorem sufficientem complexioni humane, ideo in comparatione dicta est frigida et humida. Qua ratione magistri philosophice carnem bovinam frigidam dicunt, cum tamen omnis caro calida et humida sit'.

60 *Ṭ*(I), §2.6:1–2, pp. 46–47: 'This sign [i.e., Aries] is the house of exaltation of the Sun because that is where it begins to incline towards the ecumene and its [the Sun's] power becomes perceptible in the world. The Indian scientists said that the degree of its exaltation is 19° from <the beginning of> this sign, because in this place there is a star with the complexion of Jupiter and Venus; but if this was correct the degree has changed, as I shall explain when I discuss the bright and dark degrees'.

degrees should be regarded as constantly changing their location, by virtue of the motion of the fixed stars of the eighth orb.

We should highlight that even though Ibn Ezra criticizes some astrological tenets and censures the 'science of the images'—that is, the making of idols or talismans, as 'forbidden by the law of God, because it resembles idolatry'[61]—the two versions of the *Book of Reasons* do not include any defence of or attack on astrology. For Ibn Ezra, evidently, just as the biblical text cannot be explained by the biblical text alone, so too astrology cannot be explained by astrology alone. Astrology is only one branch of the sciences of his age; as such it should be explained in their light but must also be in agreement with them.

61 *Ṭ*(II), §8.3:2, pp. 250–51.

DR REASON AND DR EXPERIENCE: CULPEPER'S ASSIGNATION OF PLANETARY RULERS IN THE ENGLISH PHYSITIAN

Graeme Tobyn

The English Physitian (1652), commonly known as Culpeper's Herbal, is the most famous work of the leading translator of medical texts into English in the seventeenth century, Nicholas Culpeper (1616–1654).[1] The herbal sold without illustrations for three pence, found its way into the homes of a large section of the English reading public and, it has been claimed, had more influence over the practice of medicine in England for the hundred years following his death than the writings of the famous William Harvey, demonstrator of the circulation of the blood, or of Thomas Sydenham, the 'English Hippocrates'.[2]

Culpeper's Herbal is distinctive not only for making easily available in the vernacular sound knowledge on the uses of native plant medicines, but also in its consistent correlation of these plants with the seven planets of pre-modern astrology. In *The English Physitian Enlarged* (1653)—an augmented version released within a year of the first edition to distinguish the work from the numerous pirated editions which were printed, and the template for most later editions down to the present day—there are 328 separate entries of plant descriptions, all but six of which are apportioned a planetary ruler.[3] Thirty-eight plants are correlated with both a planet and a zodiac sign. Some of the plant entries have a dominant astrological theme woven into the description of the

---

[1] Nicholas Culpeper, *The English Physitian: Or, an Astrologo-Physical Discourse of the Vulgar Herbs of This Nation: Being a Compleat Method of Physick* (London: Peter Cole, 1652). Reference will be made to the expanded edition *The English Physitian Enlarged* (London: Peter Cole, 1656) in my possession, a reissue of the first 1653 edition. Quotations taken from the preface of this version match those of *The English Physitian* (1652). For Culpeper generally, see Benjamin Woolley, *The Herbalist: Nicholas Culpeper and the Fight for Medical Freedom* (London: HarperCollins , 2004); Graeme Tobyn, *Culpeper's Medicine: A practice of Western Holistic Medicine* (London: Singing Dragon, 2013).

[2] F.N.L. Poynter, 'Nicholas Culpeper and his Books', *Journal of the History of Medicine* 17 (1962): pp. 152–67.

[3] The six herbs without a planetary ruler are: nailwort (Whitlow grass) p. 170, oats p. 284 [i.e., p. 184 but misprinted], parsley piert [p. 288], meadow rue p. 324, rye p. 327 and blackthorn p. 357.

herbs' medicinal actions, and these are proportionately more frequent among the new entries which augmented the original text. Therefore, references here will be made to this enlarged edition.

This study will explore the basis on which the assignations of a particular planet to each native herb were made. Why was Culpeper so assiduous and thorough in this matter? How was the knowledge of the correspondences to be employed? What sources did he draw on for his assignations and do their correspondences of herbs and planets match his own? How does Culpeper himself explain the attributions? In histories of herbals, Culpeper's 'astrological botany' has been derided or condemned as 'a travesty rather than a reflection of the ancient astrological lore' but with little actual analysis applied to the detail of the astrological content.[4] This is what will be undertaken now.

Why did Culpeper assiduously categorise the herbs according to the planets?

The English Physitian and its enlarged version of the following year were the culmination of original output and among the final writings undertaken by Culpeper, who died within six months of publication of the latter.[5] He had commenced his writing career with the controversial release of his translation from Latin of the pharmacopoeia of the College of Physicians, *A Physical Directory* (1649).[6] His main astrological work appeared two years later: *Semeiotica Uranica; Or, An Astrological Judgment of Diseases from the Decumbiture of the Sick* (1651).[7] In the same way that Culpeper produced a new work in the vernacular by translating the physicians' *Pharmacopoeia* and appending his own commentary, so the *Semeiotica Uranica* was based on astrological works by the twelfth-century biblical scholar and philosopher Abraham Ibn Ezra (1089/92–1164/67) and the more recent but obscure Noel (Natalis) Durret, recorded as having been a 'professor of sciences and mathematics' and a protégé of Cardinal

---

[4] Agnes Arber, *Herbals, Their Origin and Evolution: A Chapter in the History of Botany, 1470–1670,* 3rd ed. (Cambridge: Cambridge University Press, 1986), ch. VIII; Eleanour Sinclair Rohde, *The Old English Herbals* (New York: Dover Publications, 1971 [1922]), pp. 163–67.

[5] Mary Rhinelander McCarl 'Publishing the Works of Nicholas Culpeper, Astrological Herbalist and Translator of Latin Medical Works in Seventeenth-Century London', *Canadian Bulletin of Medical History* Vol.13 (1996): pp. 225–76.

[6] Nicholas Culpeper, *A Physical Directory* (London: Peter Cole, 1649).

[7] Nicholas Culpeper, *Semeiotica Uranica; Or, An Astrological Judgment of Diseases from the Decumbiture of the Sick* (London: Nathaniell Brookes, 1651).

the Duke of Richelieu.[8]

Culpeper draws on Ibn Ezra's medical-astrological *Sefer Ha-Me'orot* (The Book of Lights), which he would have known by its sixteenth-century Latin title *De luminaribus seu de diebus creticis*, for the introductory section on the critical days of a disease and its astrological interpretation,[9] and Durret's *De crisium mysterio tractatus* from his *Novae motuum celestium ephemerides Richelianae* (1641).[10] The focus of Culpeper's work is medical prognosis using astrology to provide an answer to the sick person's inquiry 'What is wrong with me and what will happen?'[11] Since the *Pharmacopoeia* described the Galenic simples and compound prescriptions of seventeenth-century England, and taking note of the positions of the stars was one of the observations that a physician in Tudor and Stuart England could make in relation to the patient consulting him,[12] the subject matter of these works of Culpeper's was hardly different from orthodox medical theory and practice at that time. While Galen himself had the considerable technical ability to calculate the positions of the heavenly bodies, he did not consider them responsible for the commencement and course of diseases, but rather the climatic conditions which derived from their positions in the heavens.[13] Seemingly, among those medical sects into which Galen had divided ancient medicine, there was little concern with astrology.[14]

---

8 Avner Ben-Zaken, 'The Heavens of the Sky and the Heavens of the Heart: the Ottoman Cultural Context for the Introduction of Post-Copernican Astronomy', *British Journal for the History of Science*, 37 (2004): pp. 6–7. Culpeper, *Semeiotica Uranica*, pp. 1, 15. Culpeper described 'Avenezra' as a physician and astrologer.

9 Shlomo Sela, ed. and trans., *Abraham Ibn Ezra on Elections, Interrogations and Medical Astrology* (Leiden: Brill, 2011): pp. 451–83.

10 Ben-Zaken, 'The Heavens of the Sky', pp. 2, 7; Chanita Goodblatt, 'The Presence of Abraham Ibn Ezra in Seventeenth-Century England', *ANQ*, 22, no.2 (2009): pp. 18–19; Renate Smithuis, 'Abraham Ibn Ezra's Astrological Works in Hebrew and Latin: New discoveries and exhaustive listing', *Aleph* 6 (2006): pp. 239–338; *Novae motuum celestium ephemerides Richelianae…Authore N.Durret Montebrisono* (Paris: sumptibus authoris, 1641).

11 Jim Tester, *A History of Western Astrology* (Woodbridge: Boydell & Brewer, 1987), pp. 222–24.

12 Lauren Kassell, *Medicine and Magic in Elizabethan London* (Oxford: Oxford University Press, 2005), p. 7.

13 Vivian Nutton, 'Greek Medical Astrology and the Boundaries of Medicine', in *Astro-Medicine: Astrology and Medicine, East and West*, eds. Anna Akasoy, Charles Burnett and Ronit Yoeli-Tlalim, Micologus' Library 25 (Florence: SISMEL, 2008), p. 21.

14 Nutton, 'Greek Medical Astrology', pp. 18–19. According to Nutton, the Empiricists were not concerned with the causes of disease but with which medicines were effective once and may work again in a similar case, while the Methodists grouped all disease

Evidence from later Arabic medicine also featured the application of astrology to medical diagnosis and prognosis. In a book on astrological medicine by Yūḥannā ibn al-Ṣalt, there is consideration of the lunar and astral influences on generation and corruption, the correlation of signs and planets with humours and diseases, the apportioning of significations of the angles of a decumbiture to a patient, disease and therapeutic mode in the style of Dorotheus of Sidon, the election of an appropriate day for treatment and the observation of constellations forbidding the prescribing of medicines.[15] However, two of the most famous Arabic physicians, Avicenna and Averroes, refuted astrology altogether, while al-Rāzī included only a short section on the influence of the stars on the crises of illness.[16]

It is clear, then, that in the Greco-Arabic tradition the alliance of astrology with medicine was not fully accepted and, where it was employed, it did not normally extend to the identification of specific remedies for a given case. Instead, the medical art of prescribing was left open to allow the physician-astrologer to take into account all the relevant signs, physical and celestial, before determining the treatment.[17] Indeed, the only mention of medicinal agents in the *Semeiotica Uranica,* based as it was on the work of Ibn Ezra and Durret, occurs in the one example of the diagnostic and prognostic method from Culpeper's own practice, where he counters a French physician's mis-prescribing of the exotic purgative scammony (*Convolvulus scammonia*) with a standard clyster or enema whose ingredients go unmentioned.[18] The other example cases in the book, translated from Durret's medical horoscopes attributed to the famous Italian physician Girolamo Cardano (1501–76), the Spanish Jesuit philosopher Benedictus Pererius (1535–1610), Thomas Bodier, physician and author of *De ratione et usu dierum criticorum* (1555), Giovanni Magini (1555–1617), the Italian astronomer and mathematician who wrote *De astrologica ratione ac usu dierum criticorum seu decretiorum* (1607), and that of a

---

presentations into three categories of manifestations and the course of the stars synchronous with any one presentation were so distant as to be irrelevant.

15 Felix Klein-Franke, *Iatromathematics in Islam: a Study on Yuhanna ibn al-Salt's book on Astrological Medicine* (Hildesheim: G. Olms, 1984).

16 Manfred Ullmann, *Islamic Medicine* (Edinburgh: Edinburgh University Press, 1997), p. 112; Erwin H. Ackerknecht, *Therapeutics from the Primitives to the 20th Century* (New York: Hafner Press, 1973), p. 48.

17 Note for example the absence of discussion concerning actual remedies to be used in the chapters on Western astrological medicine from Galen to Pico della Mirandola in *Astro-Medicine*, eds. Akasoy, Burnett and Yoeli-Tlalim, pp. 17–142.

18 Culpeper, *Semeiotica Uranica*, pp. 58–69.

certain John Baptista Triandula, also contain no specific indications for particular herbs or medicaments.[19]

Culpeper's assiduous linking of herb to ruling planet in *The English Physitian* suggests a different orientation, outside that of the mainstream of Greco-Arabic medicine. Clues exist in some of his other works. Since his working life as a writer only lasted seven years at most, Culpeper's output was prolific; he must have worked on several texts at once and he had cause to engage an amanuensis in the last few years before his death.[20] One of the texts he worked on in 1651–2 was a translation of the new dispensatory of the College of Physicians, which had been published in 1650.[21] In Culpeper's English edition—which was issued in 1653, most likely between the dates of publication of *The English Physitian* and its enlarged version—he inserted some new material into the catalogue of simples to help the reader apply his understanding of Culpeper's *Key to Galen and Hippocrates, their method of Physick* to the medicinal herbs listed.[22] Thus the physicians' materia medica was analysed in terms of their manifest qualities (whether heating or cooling, drying or moistening and to what degree), their therapeutic properties such as an astringent or analgesic action and, significantly, the part of the body to which each was assigned.[23]

In introducing the section on assignements of herbs to parts of the body Culpeper referred to the different opinions of ancient physicians. Some rejected, he wrote, 'any specifical vertues at all in medicines, or any congruity to certain parts of the body'—if a herb strengthened or harmed the brain it must do the same to all parts of the body—but they were 'ignorant of the influence of the heavens'; others recognized that certain herbs possessed 'distinct operations upon distinct parts of the body' and this 'by an hidden quality' but lacked a knowledge of astrology to explain this quality; and a third group steered a

19 These horoscopes are only mentioned in *Semeiotica Uranica* (p.143) and not translated and reproduced until the second edition, i.e., *An Astrological Judgment of Diseases* (1655) because, Culpeper wrote, he lacked in 1650-51 the relevant ephemerides to generate accurate horoscopes.

20 Tobyn, *Culpeper's Medicine*, pp. 14, 63. I have reckoned on a writing period between 1647–54; Ibid., p. 23.

21 McCarl, 'Publishing the Works of Culpeper', *Canadian Bulletin of Medical History*, 13 (1996): pp. 225–76. See the chronology of publication of Culpeper's works on pp. 263–76.

22 Nicholas Culpeper, *Pharmacopoeia Londinensis: or, The London Dispensatory* (London: Peter Cole, 1653), pp. 187–325 [incorrect pagination]. Culpeper's *Key to Galen and Hippocrates, their method of Physick* had first been appended to the third edition of his translation of the old *Pharmacopoeia* (1650) and was now transferred into the new one.

23 Culpeper, *Pharmacopoeia Londinensis*, pp. 35–54.

middle course by agreeing that the effect of a herb was on the whole body but could strengthen a particular part 'because the substance of the medicine agrees with the substance of that part which it strengthens...and the substance of all parts of the body are not alike'.[24] Culpeper judged that this last argument had some weight to it but fell short of recognizing 'a certain truth, the sympathy and antipathy in the creation is the cause both of all diseases and also of the operations of all medicines'.[25]

Complementing this material, Culpeper placed a new two-page introduction in the 1653 *Pharmacopoeia Londinensis*, a 'Premonitory Epistle To The Reader'.[26] Here Culpeper linked the universe created by God as one united body to the body of Man as macrocosm-microcosm; he deduced that the three realms of the physical elements, the stars and God (the elementary, celestial and intellectual worlds within this universe) must have their counterparts in the human body and asserted that, since disease was understood to be natural, the stars should have some influence on the body. In this respect he could write of a celestial Moon and its corresponding microcosmic Moon regulating certain aspects of the human body. The theme of three was reiterated by the argument that 'if there be a trinity in the deity (which is denied by none but Ranters), then must there be a trinity also in all his works, and a dependency between them' namely 'that every inferior world is governed by its superior'. Culpeper proved these points by citing scripture on the rulership of the day by the Sun and of the night by the Moon, and by reasoned argument where he contended that elementary bodies are subject to constant change and must therefore be in nature passive; whereas the stars are unchanging and so in nature active, effecting alterations over time in the elementary worlds by their celestial motions and configurations. He concluded that 'he and he only is a physician who knows which of these qualities [in the world of elements] offends, by which of the celestial bodies it is caused, and how safely and speedily to remedy it. All the rest that practise physick are but mountebanks'. Development in the intellectual world, through fearing God, proclaiming his glory and studying his great books, 'the book of the scripture' and 'the book of the creatures' would in its turn bring wisdom that would free the human soul from the necessity of celestial causation.[27]

Culpeper had already shown which organs and functions in the body were associated with each planet in his *Astrologo-Physical Discourse of the Human*

---

24 Ibid., p. 305.
25 Ibid.
26 Ibid., C1r-v.
27 Ibid., C1v.

Vertues in the Body of Man that first appeared in print in his *Ephemeris for 1651*.[28] Now, in *The English Physitian* Culpeper provided the correspondences between planets and medicinal herbs. Citing in the preface from Romans 1.20 'the invisible things of Him from the creatures of the world are clearly seen, being understood by the things that are made, even His eternal power and Godhead, so that they are without excuse' and a poet's couplet 'because out of thy thoughts God should not pass, his image stamped is on every grass', Culpeper suggested that in the Book of the Creatures, i.e., the study of nature, signs of the planetary correspondences of herbs are readily apparent. He had made such a study, though with no help from the authors he had read on the subject, and his herbal contained the fruits of his discoveries:

> I knew well enough the whole world and everything in it was formed of a composition of contrary elements, and in such a harmony as must needs show the wisdom and power of a great God. I knew as well, this creation, though thus composed of contraries, was one united body, and man an epitome of it. I knew those various afflictions in Man in respect of sickness and health were caused naturally by the various operations of the microcosm; and I could not be ignorant, that as the cause is, so must the cure be; and therefore he that would know the reason of the operations of herbs must look up as high as the stars. I always found the disease vary according to the various motions of the stars; and this is enough one would think to teach a man by the effect where the cause lay. Then to find out the reason of the operation of herbs, plants etc. by the stars went I, and herein I could find but few authors, but those as full of nonsense and contradiction as an egg is full of meat; this being little pleasing and less profitable to me, I consulted with my two brothers, Dr. Reason and Dr. Experience and took a voyage to visit my mother Nature, by whose advice, together with the help of Dr. Diligence, I at last obtained my desires, and being warned by Mr. Honesty a stranger in our daies to publish it to the world, I have done it.[29]

Although Culpeper's explanation for the 'reason of the operation of herbs' is couched mainly in religious allusions, the macrocosm-microcosm link and the three worlds indicate the influence of Neoplatonic ideas that were part of the cosmology of Paracelsian medicine. That Culpeper was interested in the

---

28 Culpeper's publisher Peter Cole inserted this *Discourse* into subsequent posthumous editions of the *Pharmacopoeia Londinensis*: Culpeper, *Pharmacopoeia Londinensis* (London, 1654), A1r–B1v. Possible reasons for the *Discourse* not appearing in the 1653 *Pharmacopoeia* include technicalities of printing—this edition is in small quarto format while the 1654 one is in quarto—may be Culpeper's illness, which had worsened at this time, and the publisher's rationalisation of his Culpeper material only after the author's death.

29 Culpeper, *The English Physitian Enlarged*, C1r-v.

harmonisation of Galenic medicine and its materia medica of herbal simples and Paracelsian medicine which emphasised God-given healing powers and the use of pharmaceutical forms in which the stronger herbal remedies could be prepared for safe use by his reading public is affirmed by another translation he was preparing, *A New Method of Physick, or A short View of Paracelsus and Galen's Practice* (1654).[30] The author was an obscure German Physician from Spitzburg, Simeon Partliz, who attempted to reconcile Galenic and Paracelsian medicine 'ex doctissimorum medicorum, tum dogmaticorum, tum Hermeticorum scriptis', according to the title-page of the original 1625 Latin text.[31] The translation had apparently been ready for the press as early as 1651, when Culpeper must have started work on *The English Physitian*.[32] Additionally, Culpeper lists among his sources for the herbal 'a manuscript', which he credits in his comments on Aqua mellis, the quintessence of honey of Paracelsus, in the *Pharmacopoeia Londinensis* to a certain Mr. Charles Butler of Hampshire.[33]

In England in the 1650s there was a renewed interest in Paracelsian medicine stirred by the arrival and subsequent translation of the works of the Flemish chemical physician Jan Baptist van Helmont (1580–1644), which encouraged translations of more works by Paracelsus.[34] The former 'Elizabethan compromise' in which English practitioners studied the new chemical remedies as additions to the pharmacopoeia but rejected the mystical, Hermetic aspects of Paracelsian philosophy was now overturned in a more violent conflict with the cruel practices and crude compounds of Galenic medicine.[35] Culpeper had written as early as 1649 that 'your best way to learn to still chymicial oyls is to learn of an alchymist'.[36] Yet he himself was 'more attracted to the transcendental than to the practical side of Paracelsian doctrine, for it accorded well with his devoutly religious outlook'.[37] W.R., the anonymous author of the biographical sketch of Culpeper's life, wrote that he had 'bent his inclinations from the time that he was but ten years of age to…studies of astrology and occult philosophy'

---

[30] F.N.L. Poynter, 'Nicholas Culpeper and the Paracelsians' in *Science, Medicine and Society in the Renaissance: Essays to Honor Walter Pagel*, ed. Allen G. Debus (London: Science History Publications, 1972), pp. 201–20. Walter Pagel, *Paracelsus: An Introduction to Philosophical Medicine in the Era of the Renaissance*, 2nd Edition. (Basel: Karger, 1982), p. 333.
[31] Simeon Partliz, *Medici Systematis Harmonici…*(Frankfurt: Aubrius, 1625).
[32] Tobyn, *Culpeper's Medicine*, pp. 64–65.
[33] Culpeper, *Pharmacopoeia Londinensis* (1653), p. 184.
[34] Allen G. Debus, *The English Paracelsians* (New York: Oldbourne, 1965), p. 181.
[35] Ibid.
[36] Culpeper, *A Physical Directory*, p. 317.
[37] Poynter, *Nicholas Culpeper and the Paracelsians*, p. 219.

and asserted that he occupied a position where 'he was not only for Galen and Hippocrates, but he knew how to correct and moderate the tyrannies of Paracelsus'.[38] Culpeper's Herbal is evidence of his interest in both these competing medical philosophies.

How was the knowledge of the correspondences to be employed?

The planetary assignations in *The English Physitian* were to be used to help his readers identify which herbs were required in the treatment of any condition, by recourse to Galenic principles of treatment by opposites with respect to the herbs' medical indications and to astrological significations derived from a decumbiture or horoscope cast for the moment the sick person fell ill or consulted the astrologer. In order to facilitate the latter judgment, Culpeper included an example horoscope in the final chapter of his herbal, 'The Way of Mixing Medicines according to the Cause of the Disease and the part of the Body afflicted', which he deemed the key to the whole work.[39]

Of the five herbs Culpeper selected from indications in this horoscope as necessary to treat the condition of the sick person, two were to be used for their sympathetic virtues, healing like with like, and three by antipathy to the disease. Moreover, the herbal assigned to three of the stated herbs both a planet and a zodiac sign. These double symbols allowed the selection of what should be a precisely attuned remedy for the organ affected in the given case or else a sharing of both sympathetic and antipathetic effect. As an example here, the 'tough phlegm and melancholy' diagnosed in the lungs through the symbol in the horoscope of Saturn in Cancer (a pernicious placing), could be removed by the use of sundew (*Drosera rotundifolia*): this 'herb of the Sun and under the celestial crab may do very well'; because it was a sympathetic remedy for the lungs as indicated by the zodiac sign Cancer, it was antipathetical to the cold of Saturn through its solar nature and, as a herb hot and dry in the extreme, could cut and help expectorate the phlegm by the treatment of contraries.[40]

Since only thirty-eight of the 328 plants in the herbal were given a

---

38 W.R. 'The Life of the Admired Physician and Astrologer of our Times, Mr. Nicholas Culpeper' in *Culpeper's School of Physick* (London: Peter Cole, 1659), Cc2v and C4v. A posthumous publication under Culpeper's name further connected him with Paracelsian medicine: *Mr. Culpepper's Treatise of Aurum Potabile* (London, 1656), but the true author of the treatise remains in doubt; see Tobyn, *Culpeper's Medicine*, pp. 33–36, Woolley, *The Herbalist*, p. 326; McCarl, 'Publishing the works of Nicholas Culpeper', p. 260, n. 56.

39 Culpeper, *The English Physitian Enlarged*, pp. 394–98.

40 Ibid, pp. 398, 319.

corresponding zodiac sign as well as a planetary ruler, such close working of the symbolism appears to have had a limited applicability. The assignations of zodiac signs as well as planets may have been a work in progress for Culpeper, a job that was never completed. These double correspondences, however, were not needed for the second aspect of Culpeper's application of astrology to medicine: the potentising of remedies to resolve the astrological cause of the disease by gathering or preparing each plant medicine under the right celestial conditions. As well as the practical concerns to select a herb in good condition and at the appropriate phase of growth according to the part required, it should be picked 'in what place they most delight to grow in' and at a time when its ruling planet is strongly activated in the zodiac, in harmonious alignment with the moon and in the hour of the planet which rules it.[41] Since the need of the remedy may have been pressing, Culpeper gave alternative instructions to avoid delay yet 'observe the like in gathering the herbs of other plan[e]ts and you may happen to do wonders'. Marsilio Ficino himself had emphasised the value of such preparations: 'at least do not neglect medicines which have been strengthened by some sort of heavenly aid, unless perhaps you would neglect life itself. For I have found by long and repeated experience that medicines of this kind are as different from other medicines made without astrological election, as wine is from water'.[42]

What sources did Culpeper draw on for his attributions?

How did Culpeper arrive at his assignations of planets to herbs? Was it a result of his study of the book of nature or did he follow the work of another author? There is a list among the prefatory material in *The English Physitian* of 'authors made use of in this treatise', a simple list of many of the greatest names in the history of the transmission of knowledge of herbs in Greco-Arabic medicine, together with Culpeper's own close 'colleagues', Dr. Reason and Dr. Experience.[43] I have suggested elsewhere that these authors' names have been

---

41 Ibid, p. 381; Tobyn, *Culpeper's Medicine*, pp. 198–200 where the exact astrological instructions and examples for the herbal are cited.

42 Marsilio Ficino, *Three Books on Life*, trans. Carol V. Kaske and John R. Clark (Binghampton, NY: Center for Medieval and Early Renaissance Studies, 1989), pp. 239–41.

43 *The English Physitian Enlarged*, C2v. More obscure names in Culpeper's list of authors are 'Pona', presumably Giovanni Pona who wrote a study of herbal simples growing in the region around Verona, entitled *Plantae, seu Simplicia, ut vocant, quae in Baldo monte, et in via ab Verona ad Baldum reperiuntur* (Basel: Zetzner, 1608), 'Pena', i.e., Pierre Pena who

elided and gathered by Culpeper as he abbreviated chapters on English herbs from his central source for the herbal, the apothecary John Parkinson's *Theatrum Botanicum* (1640).[44] Neither Parkinson, nor any of the other authors of herbals, which make up the majority of the names listed, included astrological correspondences for the herbs they described. Culpeper was critical of this written tradition, anyway, complaining in his preface that:

> ...all the authors that have written of the nature of herbs gave not a bit of a reason why such an herb was appropriated to such a part of the body, nor why it cured such a disease... neither Gerard nor Parkinson nor any that ever wrote in the like nature ever gave one wise reason for what they wrote and so did nothing else but train up young novices in physick in the School of Tradition and teach them just as a parrot is taught to speak: an author saith so, therefore 'tis true. And if all that authors say be true, why do they contradict one another?[45]

But among the authors are two notable astrologers, namely 'Avenaris' or Abraham Ibn Ezra (already discussed here), and the French physician and astrologer Antoine Mizauld (1510–1578), professor of medicine in Paris, doctor and astrologer to Marguerite de Valois, and author of numerous tracts on medical astrology and sympathy and antipathy in nature. That Mizauld was one of the authors with whose contradictory views Culpeper found fault is evident from the latter's discussion of the rulership of henbane (*Hyoscyamus niger*):

> I wonder in my heart how astrologers could take on them to make this an herb of Jupiter, and yet Mizaldus, a man of a penetrating brain, was also of that opinion as well as the rest. The herb is indeed under the dominion of Saturn, and I prove it by this argument: all the herbs which delight to grow in saturnine places are

co-wrote with Matthias de L'Obel, *Stirpium adversaria nova* (London: Thomas Purfoot, 1570–71) and 'Bellus', presumably Onorio Belli (d. 1604), a Venetian doctor known for his correspondence with the Flemish botanist Charles de L'Escluse, *Ad Carolum Clusium aliquot epistolae de rarioribus quibusdam plantis agentes*, which was appended to L'Escluse's *Rariorum Plantarum Historia* (Antwerp: ex Officina Plantiniana apud Ioannem Moretum 1601).

44 Graeme Tobyn, 'An anatomy of *The English Physitian*', in *Critical Approaches to the History of Western Herbal Medicine*, eds. Susan Francia and Anne Stobart (London: Bloomsbury Academic Publishing, 2014), pp. 87–103.

45 *The English Physitian Enlarged* C1r-v. The original passage in the 1652 edition (A4v) is softer: 'In this art the worthies of our own nation Gerard, Johnson and Parkinson are not to be forgotten, who did much good in the study of this art, yet they and all others that wrought of the nature of herbs gave not a bit of reason why...'

> saturnine herbs…and whole cartloads of [henbane] may be found near the places where they empty the common jakes, and scarce a stinking ditch to be found without it growing by it. Ergo tis an herb of Saturn.[46]

However, there is no extensive list in Mizauld's works that I have consulted showing the correspondences between herbs and planets. His astrological works include lists of those diseases that planets might signify or of the organs of the body which they rule but not of the herbs to which they correspond. [47] The works on sympathy and antipathy source Pliny, Galen, Fracastoro, Cardan and other writers ancient and contemporary on observations of attractions and repulsions between animals, birds, fish, stones and plants or between these and the Sun and Moon as the physical determinants of day and night, light and darkness.[48] In his *Secrets de la lune* (1571), Mizauld reveals, for instance, that cucumbers visibly increase in size at full moon and that herbs gathered when the moon increases in light are of much greater efficacy and virtue than during her decrease in light or the dark of the Moon; and he repeats the traditional association between the twelve signs and the body from head to feet and the warning from the ancients not to perform surgery on a part of the body when the Moon occupies its associated zodiac sign.[49]

Thus Dr Reason had consulted with Dr Experience to determine a more

---

[46] Ibid, pp. 124–25.

[47] *Antonii Mizaldi Monslucianі planetologia, rebus astronomicis, medicis, et philosophicis erudite referta* (Lyon: apud Mathiam Bonhomme, 1551) and *Aesculapii et Uraniae medicum simul et astronomicum ex colloquio conjugium, harmoniam microcosmi, cum macrocosmo, sive humani corporis cum caelo, paucis figurans, & perspicue demonstrans* (Lyon: apud J. Tornaesium, 1550). Other astrological works by Mizauld that I have consulted are: *Zodiacus, sive duodecim signorum coeli hortulus; Asterismi, sive Stellatarum octavi coeli imaginum Officina;* and *Planetae, sive planetarum collegium* printed in one volume (Paris: C. Cuillard, 1553).

[48] *Memorabilium aliquot naturae arcanorum sylvula, rerum variarum sympathias & antipathias…libellis duobus complectens. Autore Antonio Mizaldo Monsluciano* (Paris: apud Jacobum Kerver, 1554) and the excerpted *Catalogi septem sympathiae et antipathiae…rerum aliquot memorabilium* (Paris: apud Jacobum Kerver, 1554). In the former, *Memorabilium aliquot*, p.60, Mizauld mentions henbane ('hyoscyamus'), writing: pigs which have eaten 'hyoscyamus' are torn by impending danger unless they immediately rinse themselves inside and out with copious amounts of water, as Aelian attests [sues sumpta herba hyoscyamo praesenti periculo convelluntur: nisi copiosa aqua statim se foris et intus proluerunt ut Aelianus attestatur].

[49] Antoine Mizauld, *Secrets de la Lune* (Paris: Frederic Morel, 1571), ch. IIII, pp. 12–13, ch. VIII pp. 20–21.

accurate correlation of henbane with Saturn than Mizauld proposed, a correlation strengthened by the fact that henbane has narcotic and poisonous properties. Culpeper had already stated in the preface to his herbal that he knew by sight most of the plants he discussed, a practical knowledge and experience that had started in his childhood in the Sussex countryside. He challenged Mizauld a second time in the herbal, together with 'almost al astrologo-physitians' who held that plantain (*Plantago spp.*) was a herb of Mars:

> They give a very simile of a truth for it too, viz. because it cures diseases of the head and privities which are under the houses of Mars, Aries and Scorpio. All diseases of the head coming of heat are caused by Mars, for Venus is made of no such hot mettle, or at least deals in inferior parts. The truth is it is under the command of Venus and cures the head by antipathy to Mars, and the privities by sympathy to Venus.[50]

In the herbal Mizauld is mentioned a third and final time, reporting that houseleek preserves from fire and lightning whatever structure they grow upon. The statement is coupled in one sentence with Culpeper's determination of the plant as a herb of Jupiter, seemingly as an explanation or qualification of the assignation. It is probable that whatever influence Mizauld's writings had on Culpeper's planetary assignations, it amounted to no more than a noted sympathy or antipathy in nature that Culpeper sometimes worked into his formal assignation of the symbolically appropriate planet (for houseleek, Jupiter as protector 'father Zeus' who carries a thunderbolt) to the herb in question. But since it appears—from the fact that out of three citations of Mizauld's correlations between macrocosm and microcosm in the herbal Culpeper did not accept two of them—that Mizauld may be one of the authors 'full of nonsense and contradiction', then we need to look closely not at Culpeper's list of authors but at his own qualifications of his planetary assignations. As he wrote in 1651: 'let every one that desires to be called by the name of artist have his wits in his head (for that's the place ordained for them) and not in his books'.[51]

Culpeper's own explanations and qualifications

I have analysed each entry in *The English Physitian Enlarged* for indications of Culpeper's reasoning concerning the herbs' astrological signatures. Nearly every

---

50 Culpeper, *The English Physitian Enlarged*, p. 300.

51 Culpeper, *Semeiotica Uranica*, p. 102.

attribution is found at the beginning of the section on medicinal virtues in each herb entry. An effect of the editing of Parkinson's lists of therapeutic actions and indications to compose the substance of the majority of Culpeper's descriptions of medicinal virtues is that an entry can appear to be a disjointed amalgam of Parkinson's list prefaced by Culpeper's assignation of a ruling planet. Often, however, the assignation is immediately qualified by comments which I have taken as evidence of Culpeper's reasoning for the assignation. A small number of entries, indeed, are thoroughly astrological in theme and have not been sourced from Parkinson's herbal.[52]

I have thus found that Culpeper's reasoning for the assignations falls into one of four groupings. In the first two groupings there is explicit indication of a central 'sympathetic' use of the herb either by way of a hidden power to strengthen the organs or faculties ruled by the planet assigned to it or, more obviously to the eye, by a doctrine of signatures that links the appearance of a herb—its colour, shape or key feature such as thorns—or where it grows to one of the planets. Examples are the sea-holly (*Eryngium maritimum*): 'the plant is venusian and breedeth seed exceedingly, and strengthens the spirit procreative' for sympathetic effect on the reproductive organs under Venus; and docks (*Rumex spp.*) for the doctrine of signatures: 'al docks are under Jupiter; of which the red dock which is commonly called bloodwort cleanseth the blood, and strengthens the liver; but the yellow dock root is best to be taken when either the blood or liver is afflicted by choler'.[53]

In the second two groupings, an impression of antipathetic use is created. Either the reasoning includes the description and explicit linking of the planetary ruler with the herb's manifest qualities—which are not routinely listed in the herbal but which are a necessary part of the standard Galenic theory of cure by contraries—or there is an absence of any reasoning to connect the planetary ruler with the list of indications drawn from the Galenic tradition. Examples of these two groups include blue-bottle (*Centaurea cyanus*): 'as they are naturally cold, dry and binding, so they are under the dominion of Saturn' who shares these qualities; and the scarlet pimpernel (*Anagallis arvensis*): 'it is a gallant solar herb. This is of a cleansing and attractive quality, whereby it draweth forth thorns and splinters...'[54]

Culpeper promised in his preface that 'if you view it with the eye of reason, you shall see a reason for every thing that is written, whereby you may find the

[52] Tobyn, 'An anatomy of *The English Physitian*', pp. 98–99.
[53] Culpeper, *The English Physitian Enlarged*, pp. 87, 95.
[54] Ibid, pp. 40, 298.

very ground and foundation of physick'.[55] However, the majority of entries according to my analysis are of this last type, seemingly devoid of an explanation that connects a ruling planet to the medicinal indications of the herb. A breakdown of the 322 herb entries which are assigned a planetary ruler yields the following totals:[56]

Explanations of connection between herb and its planetary ruler				
	Sympathetic use		Antipathetic use	
	Strengthening related organs	By doctrine of signatures	According to manifest qualities	Seemingly without explanation
from total of 322 herb entries	83	18	50	171

Table 1: Explanation of the planetary assignations given to herbs listed in The English Physitian Enlarged.

Taking the numbers in each grouping as percentages of the total, it is also possible to analyse the groupings related to each planetary ruler. In such a breakdown, it appears that Culpeper was much more likely than average to attribute a saturnine or martial rulership to a herb's cold and binding or hot and biting qualities respectively. A strengthening effect through sympathy of plant, planet and organ was relatively more often attributed to solar remedies for the heart and Venusian herbs for gynaecological use. Herbs under Mercury were significantly more frequently described as treating diseases of the lungs by antipathy to Jupiter, ruler of that organ, than by strengthening the brain by the power of sympathy. Indeed, there are no herbs of Mercury in Culpeper's text which are explained by either their manifest qualities or by the doctrine of signatures.

By way of examples, Culpeper writes of agrimony (*Agrimonia eupatoria*): 'It is a herb under Jupiter and the sign Cancer; and strengthens those parts under that planet and sign, and removes diseases in them by sympathy, and those under Saturn, Mars and Mercury by antipathy, if they happen in any part of the body governed by Jupiter, or under the signs Cancer, Sagittary or Pisces, and therefore must needs be good for the gout'. Comfrey's (*Symphytum officinale*)

---

55 Ibid, C1v.

56 Ibid, (p.1) and n.3.

manifest qualities stand out: 'this is also an herb of Saturn, and I suppose under the sign Capricorn, cold, dry and earthy in quality'. The prickly bramble bush (*Rubus fructicosus*) has a suitable signature for a sharp and wounding plant with sweet fruit, 'It is a plant of Venus in Aries...If any ask the reason why Venus is so prickly? Tell them, 'tis because she is in the house of Mars'. Figwort or throatwort (*Scrophularia nodosa*), hot and dry in the second degree, has its main therapeutic use represented even in its later Linnaean binomial: 'some Latin authors call it Cervicria because 'tis appropriated to the neck; and we throatwort... Venus owns the herb and the celestial bull will not deny it, therefore a better remedy cannot be for the king's evil, because the Moon that rules the disease is exalted there, nor for any disease in the neck'. With lovage (*Levisticum officinale*) Culpeper shows us how this herb may become the specific treatment for a disease with a particular celestial cause: 'it is an herb of the Sun under the sign Taurus. If Saturn offend the throat, (as he always does, if he be occasioner of the malady, and in Taurus is the genesis), this is your cure'. Motherwort (*Leonurus cardiaca*) predominantly demonstrates treatment by sympathy: 'Venus owns the herb and it is under Leo. There is no better herb to drive melancholy vapours from the heart, to strengthen it, and make a merry, cheerful, blithe soul than this herb'.[57]

Generally, the notion of sympathy and antipathy viewed through the traditional teachings on the natures of the planets and their friendships and enmities—where, for instance, Mercury is an enemy to Jupiter and Venus to Mars (because each rules the zodiac signs opposite to those under the command of the other) and Saturn is an enemy to both the moon and Venus (signs opposing or at right angles together with contrary qualities)—frequently supplies on close reading of the herb entries the explanations which Culpeper has not spelled out. Thus, many herbs under Venus treat inflammations, burns and wounds by antipathy and are gentle, or sweet to taste and restore beauty or stir up lust. A number of purges and vomits are under violent Mars. Some Jupiter herbs are wholesome and healthy. Lunar herbs counter inflammation and Saturn herbs are 'anti-venereal'.

This astrological reasoning appears to be more prevalent in Culpeper's herbal than the appeal to a doctrine of signatures which requires first-hand knowledge of the plants. Yet the two are not mutually exclusive; rather they compound the picture of the herb's true essence. Living close to nature and having familiarity with the herbs Culpeper discussed would have allowed his readers easily to connect thorny bushes and thistles with Mars and the knowledge of their

[57] Ibid, pp. 6, 73, 37, 101, 147, 164.

medicinal virtues which the herbal taught would confirm it. Equally familiar to readers must have been the fact that the flowers of the scarlet pimpernel, designated above as a solar herb 'without explanation' with respect to its medicinal indications, open only when the sun is shining and close in wet or humid weather, earning the plant the common names of 'poor man's weather-glass' and 'shepherd's sundial'.[58] Its assignation to the sun was so obvious Culpeper felt no need to allude to it by quoting such common names nor make a formal link to its medicinal actions. The names of some herbs which designate their main therapeutic indications, such as goutwort (*Aegopodium podagraria*) and dropwort (*Filipendula vulgaris*, for urinary problems) also attracted the relevant planetary ruler (Saturn and Venus respectively).

Local names, familiarity in nature and the 'eye of reason' were combined with the medicinal knowledge supplied in Culpeper's Herbal of native plants to provide explanations for his planetary assignations, which had little or no need of supplementation by a foreign text full of classical Southern European observations of the kind that Antoine Mizauld wrote.

Conclusion

In conclusion, I have shown that Culpeper's application of astrological medicine partook of both Galenic and Paracelsian teachings. He remained steadfast in his use of native herbal simples that all his readers could hope to access cheaply or for free. But the philosophical and transcendental aspects of the Paracelsianism that was in vogue during the 1650s chimed with his devout puritan outlook and his faith in reading signs in the heavens, while its rejection of authorities in favour of new approaches to knowledge, of the sort promoted by Dr. Reason and Dr. Experience, must have carried political and intellectual appeal. Thus he sought to teach his fellow countrymen not only about the healing benefits of the herbs around them, but how to use them most efficiently through heavenly aid. The assignations of planets to herbs facilitated their therapeutic application and the understanding of the method was available to any who could use the 'eye of reason'.

The macrocosm-microcosm concept and the associated notions of sympathy and antipathy between the celestial and physical worlds were not part of a new doctrine but had ancient roots. Regarding the astrological lore concerning plants in antiquity, however, Ducourthial has argued that the instructions of astrologers of that period were in no way comparable to occasional comments concerning celestial signs in, say, Pliny or Dioscorides. These latter made

---

58 Geoffrey Grigson, *The Englishman's Flora* (London: Phoenix House, 1960), pp. 268–69.

reference to the stars for determining the most favourable moments for achieving different agricultural tasks, which may have included the gathering of certain non-cultivated plants, although in Hesiod's *Works and Days* there is no consecration of the most favourable moments for the harvest of non-cultivated plants. But the majority of observations by those involved in the transmission and teaching of knowledge of medicinal plants are drawn from nature itself. Astrologers seem scarcely to have thought of integrating these into their system, which tended to remain at the level of theory regarding elemental composition.[59] Such correspondences between the elemental and celestial worlds had concerned the human mind since the time of the Pre-Socratic philosophers and of Plato, but it was Paracelsus who first undertook the systematic application of such speculation to a study of Nature.[60] Culpeper was directly inspired by the revival in mid-seventeenth century England of this approach to promote his own synthesis of astrological medicine.

---

[59] Guy Ducourthial, *Flore Magique et Astrologique de L'Antiquite* (Paris: Belin, 2003), p. 274.
[60] Pagel, *Paracelsus*, p. 50.

SELF-GOVERNANCE AND THE BODY POLITIC IN RENAISSANCE ANNUAL PROGNOSTICATIONS

Steven Vanden Broecke

Introduction

Extant texts which we might identify as annual prognostications appear to be no older than the middle of the fourteenth century.[1] However, there is ample evidence that the genre fits into a much older tradition of 'mundane astrology' (also known as 'general' astrology) which was already well-represented in Book II of Claudius Ptolemy's *Tetrabiblos*. From at least the thirteenth century onwards, medieval textbooks on mundane astrology contain extensive discussions of forms of astrological prediction which are strongly reminiscent of the preserved annual prognostications.[2] Moreover, there is some evidence of proto-prognostications for the late twelfth century.[3]

Lodovica Braïda has pointed out how, as early as the eighteenth century, European elites began to adopt a strangely bifurcated interpretation of the astrological almanacs and prognostications which annually came off the European presses.[4] On the one hand, these productions were interpreted as reflections of a popular culture and folk psychology possessed by superstition and fear. On the other hand, they were approached as utilitarian instruments distributing useful knowledge amongst the masses. Any choice between these

---

[1] Cf. Lynn Thorndike, 'Extracts from Augustine of Trent on the Year 1340: Latin Text', in *A History of Magic and Experimental Science*, 8 vols. (New York: Columbia U.P., 1923–58), III: pp. 699–707.

[2] Notable early examples include (ps.-?)Albertus Magnus, *Speculum astronomiae* (c. 1260); Guido Bonatti, *Liber astronomiae* (c. 1277); John of Eschenden, *Summa iudicialis de accidentibus mundi* (1347–48).

[3] For instance, the so-called Toledo letter of 1179. On this document and its impact, see now Gerd Mentgen, *Astrologie und Öffentlichkeit im Mittelalter* (Stuttgart: Anton Hiersemann, 2005), pp. 17–134.

[4] Lodovica Braïda, 'Les almanachs italiens du XVIIIe siècle: véhicules de "faux préjugés" ou "puissants moyens d'éducation"?' in *Les lectures du peuple en Europe et dans les Amériques du XVIIe au XXe siècle*, ed. Hans-Jürgen Lüsenbrink (Editions Complexe, 2003), pp. 259–70.

competing interpretations is intimately entwined with the interpreter's decisions about which features of these texts will count as typical or fundamental, as well as about the social origins and legitimacy of these features. The very presence of astrology in these texts, for instance, could be classified on the side of the superstitious or the legitimate.

Interestingly, the interpretive tension between the prognostication as site of information or representation of anxiety has been carried over into the historiography of astrology. Anthony Grafton's *Cardano's Cosmos*, for instance, approached the Renaissance prognostication as a tool which served the utilitarian interests of the prognosticator and his audience. The prognosticator, Grafton asserted, 'probably hoped to' gain credibility for his medical services by recruiting the astrological beliefs of his audience, while the audience gained 'practical advice for farmers, doctors, and others concerned with short-term futures and theoretical advice for the rulers of church and state'.[5] It comes as no surprise, then, that the Renaissance prognostication was presented as the early modern analogue of the contemporary weather prediction or economic forecast.[6] At the same time, Grafton found himself confronted with frequent instances where the early modern prognostication offers 'sweeping generalizations, sonorous, deliberately frightening language, and banal details about rain and snow' or 'the gravest and most pompous prose to predict the obvious'. Switching over to a portrait of the prognostication as arising from a 'sharply competitive prophetic ecology', this genre now represented the objective political and religious turmoil of the early modern world.[7]

The basic nature of the Renaissance prognostication thus oscillates between its being a symptom of anxiety and a tool of instrumental reason, while the Renaissance prognosticator is cast in the alternative roles of shouting prophet and sedate knowledge-maker.[8] In this paper, I would like to question both interpretations by portraying the early Renaissance prognostication as an instrument of self-governance. Renaissance self-governance, I would like to

---

[5] Anthony Grafton, *Cardano's Cosmos: The Worlds and Works of a Renaissance Astrologer* (Cambridge MA: Harvard U.P., 1999), pp. 42, 48.

[6] Anthony Grafton, 'Starry Messengers. Recent work in the History of Western Astrology', *Perspectives on Science* 8 (2000): pp. 70–83.

[7] Grafton, *Cardano's Cosmos*, pp. 44, 48–50.

[8] A hysteria supposedly stimulated by popular belief in prophecy and divine punishment.

suggest, differs from more modern models of self-conduct in two important ways. On the one hand, it primarily addresses a situation of being governed by an Other with superior force. In the case of astrology, this Other is the visible heavens, and its government manifests itself in the form of fortunate or unfortunate gifts being added to the self's life story. This is the anthropological background against which Renaissance prognostications annually unveiled what one must reasonably hope and fear. To interpret the latter revelations as symptoms of an underlying pessimism or anxiety overlooks both the prognosticator's revelations of good fortune and his profound concern with the stability of the body politic.

On the other hand, Renaissance self-governance did not seek to extract or protect the self from its lifelong relation to the stars; instead, it sought to inject some measure of resistance and agency *inside* this reality, thus turning the self into something which was not *only* governed by the stars, but also by God, the intellect and the will. Accordingly, it may be anachronistic to interpret Renaissance astrology as a modern project of technical rationality which approaches the heavens as an external realm threatening the self's proper domain of possessions and acquisitive acts.

Preaching God's Book in the Heavens

Giuseppe Bezza has already pointed out how fifteenth-century astrological discourse spoke of the heavens as a legible book, sometimes—erroneously—attributing this to the authority of Abū Ma'shar.[9] Such claims were certainly prevalent in early Renaissance prognostications, where they were often cast in the language of divine providence and care for humankind. In his prognostication for 1486, Martin Pollich of Mellerstadt thus presented the visible heavens as a legible surface

> . . . in which [God] has written all things. He has fashioned a book in which we may read and acknowledge what is to happen to us, warning us for the evil future sooner than she arrives.[10]

---

[9] Giuseppe Bezza, 'Liber scriptus et liber vivus. Antecedenti astrologici alla metafora galileiana del Libro dell'universo', accessed 24 July 2012, http://www.cieloeterra.it/articoli.liber/liber.html.

[10] Martin Pollich of Mellerstadt, *Practica Lipcensis* (Nürnberg, 1485), fol. [A1r]: 'Der Erwirdige got (. . .) haut auss gestrecket das fel der hymel sam ein permet in welches er

The very availability of this book, Pollich continued, was a sign of unspeakable divine mercy (*unausssprechliche barmhertzicheit*). It was a gift which allowed humans to negotiate their helplessness in the face of corporeal corruption (*verderben*) by offering them a content of 'coming histories' (*zukunftigen geschichten*). Johann Virdung's *Judicium Lipczense* for 1492 emphasized that it was God's will for there to be a relation of subjection between man and the stars, because it is 'they from whom cognition of many future events can be obtained'. Moreover, Virdung continued:

> In *Timaeus,* Plato testified that 'those things which God wanted us to know he wrote down in the heavens as if in a book'. Albumasar alludes to this when he says 'God made the heavens like a parchment on which the species of all inferior things are written down'.[11]

A clear echo of the readable-book approach to the heavens can be overheard in the preface to Gaspar Laet's prognostication for 1524:

> And the natural force of the position of the stars is not at all the primary cause of inferiors, but the instrument of the divine mind and a secondary cause: an instrument by which God gives us an understanding of the conceptions in His mind, just as the voice by which a man imparts the conceptions of his heart.[12]

On the one hand, such interpretations of the visible heavens easily closed the gap between the astrologer and the prophet. This had already been prepared in

---

alle ding geschriben hat. Und hot gemacht ein buch darynne wir mügen lesen und erkennen was uns schedlich sey, Warnende uns vor böser czukunft ee danne sy kummet'. Hain *13313

[11] Johannes Virdung of Hassfurt, *Iudicium Lipczense (. . .) 1493 (. . .)* (Leipzig, 1493), fol. [A1r]: 'Ipsa namque sunt ex quibus futurorum plurima haberi potest cognitio (. . .). Testante Platone in thimeo inquientis: ea quae a nobis deus scieri voluit scripsit in celo quasi in libro. Cui alludit et albumasar cum dicit: fecit deus celum ut pellem in quo omnium inferiorum rerum species sunt descripte'. Hain *8372.

[12] Gaspar Laet, *Pronosticum (. . .) pro anno domini millesimo quingentesimo vigesimo quarto* (Antwerp: Michael Hillenius, 1524), fol. [A1r]: 'Et vim positionis siderum naturalem causam inferiorum non omnino primariam esse, sed instrumentum divinae mentis et secundariam causam, mediante quo instrumento deus dat nobis inteligere mentis conceptum, sicut homo conceptus cordis per voces'.

the early fifteenth century by Pierre d'Ailly, who approached the heavens as a legible book in which God announced the same basic events which Scripture codified into a closed narrative.[13] D'Ailly put this presupposition to use by correlating Apocalyptic 'end of the visible world' prophecies with specific astrological phenomena and situating the latter in a given chronological framework. In doing so, D'Ailly re-used the regularity of celestial motion so as to offer a more secure and credible revelation of which events one should expect inside the spiritual relation to God.

On the other hand, these interpretations also turned the prognostication into a starting-point for negotiating God's supernatural mercy and assistance. At the end of an extensive doxography of the ancient defense of a 'fatal disposition' in the cosmos, the preface to Paul of Middelburg's prognostication for 1482 emphasized two reasons for accepting the existence of fate while rejecting its 'necessity in compelling'. On the one hand, Paul invoked the fact that 'the influxes of the stars can be stopped by a nudge of the omnipotent God'; on the other hand, there was the certainty that 'the actions of the stars are not received except in suitably disposed matter'.[14]

Acknowledgment of this first possibility was not unexceptional among the prognosticators. Consider the following passage, which appears in the preface to Johannes Laet's prognostication for 1479:

> With the highest God as my witness, the present [prognostication] was only written so that the hearts of men would convert to the good, and would wholly guard themselves from coming threatening evils. Whenever the stars threaten us with approaching terrestrial evils, we, forewarned, could implore God with devote minds for Him to convert to good those evil starry influences which we fear, and this out of His infinite goodness. For the divine will and human prudence both change and lift the starry influences on earth.[15]

---

[13] Cf. Laura Ackerman Smoller, *History, Prophecy, and the Stars: The Christian Astrology of Pierre d'Ailly, 1350–1420* (Princeton NJ: Princeton U.P., 1994), p. 98, on pagans knowing of Christ's birth on the basis of a Saturn–Jupiter conjunction.

[14] Paul of Middelburg, *Iudicium pronosticum (. . .) anni 1482*, fols. [A2r/v]: Hain 11144. For more on Paul of Middelburg's prognostications, see the contribution of Stephan Heilen in this volume.

[15] Johannes Laet, *Prenosticata (. . .) 1479* (Cologne: Johannes Guldenschaff, 1479), fol. [A1r]: 'Cum teste altissimo presentia scripta ad alium finem scripta non sunt quam ut hominum corda ad bonum convertat et de futuris malis comminatis possetenus precaveant. Ut cum

Likewise, the section on war and peace in a *Practica* for 1488 by Martin Pollich of Mellerstadt was concluded with 'But here I end, imploring the aid of the omnipotent God to assist the just and mercifully safeguard his people'.[16] In his *Practica* for 1493, Marcus Schinnagel explained that the astrologer publicly foretells evils to come because 'the evils being foreknown, we should immediately and without delay implore the omnipotent God with a devote mind and supplication, with fasting and weeping, so that he would deign to avert evils known beforehand from us, wretches'.[17] Pietro Bono Avogadro's prognostication for 1495 advised the people of Bologna to 'plead with God for the divine fabricator to safeguard this most renowned city'.[18] And in the section on war and peace of Gaspar Laet's prognostication for 1525, we hear:

> (. . .) if strife would not be suspended before the summer, [I have] little hope for the rest of the year—unless God, omnipotent founder of the stars, from whom the stars have a force and power of influencing these inferior things, averts or suspends their laws, or disposes the minds of men in such a way that they do not welcome the malign influences of the stars.[19]

Likewise, the difference between divine *potentia absoluta* and *potentia ordinata* was often couched in the theological language of 'grace'. Laet concluded his

---

stelle nobis de futuris malis comminentur super terram ut tunc avisati devotis mentibus deum deprecemur ut ipse sua bonitate infinita malas stellarum influentias quas formidamus velit in bonum commutare. Quoniam voluntate dei et prudencia hominum stellarum influentie super terram alterantur atque tolluntur (. . .)'. Sole known copy: British Library IB4240.

[16] Martin Pollich, *Practica Lipcensis* (Leipzig, 1487), fol. [A7v]: 'Sed hec et quamplura missa facio, dei omnipotentis auxilium implorans ut sit adiutor iustorum et suos misericorditer tueatur'.

[17] Marcus Schinnagel, *Pregnosticum (. . .) 1492*, fol. A2v: '(. . .) illa non est mea nec alicuius astrologi intentio, sed ut statim et illico malis precognitis omnipotentem deum devota mente et oratione ieiunio et fletu implorare debeamus ut mala prius cognita a nobis miseris avertere dignetur'. Hain *14539.

[18] Pietro Bono Avogadro, *Prognostico dell'anno 1495* (Venezia: Cristoforo de' Pensi(?), 1494), fol. A4v: 'Bononienses deum deprecent ut divinus fabricator hanc celeberrimam custodiat civitatem'. GW 245 (cf. http://www.gesamtkatalogderwiegendrucke.de).

[19] Gaspar Laet, *Pronosticum* (Antwerp: Michiel Hillen van Hoochstraten, [1523]), fol. [A2v]. Wouter Nijhoff and M.E. Kronenberg, *Nederlandsche bibliografie van 1500–1540* ([Nijhoff]'s-Gravenhage, 1923–71), 8 vols., n° 3338.

prognostication for 1478, for instance, by expressing his hope that:

> (. . .) the most glorious God would deign, out of his most benign grace, to convert and change all evil future things to good, and liberate us from unforeseen death and enemies. Amen.[20]

The prognosticator's art of embodiment

Despite the frequency of the prognosticator's emphasis on divine mercy it was the second possibility, mentioned by Paul of Middelburg in 1482, that would be the default option in carving out corporeal non-helplessness. The basic contours of this second option were set down in a highly influential commentary on Alcabitius's *Libellus isagogicus* by John of Saxony (fl. 1327–1355), who put the point rather clearly:

> One is to heed the way in which a wise man can impede or help the operations of the stars. It is certain that we cannot simply block off the celestial influence, just as we cannot [stop] the general fact that fire combusts. But we can dispose the passive so as to receive the celestial influence in such or such a way. For we see that the very same solar heat dissolves ice, while hardening mud.[21]

Notice John of Saxony's emphasis on the fact that there is nothing to be done about the *fact* of one's body being affected by the cosmic play of influence. Instead, our commentator's hopes were strictly limited to an endless refashioning of the 'passive' recipient of this play. The same set of expectations was voiced in the extremely influential *Introductorium maius* (in the standard

20 Johannes Laet, *Pronosticatio anno presentis lxxvii (. . .)* (Paris: Richard Blandin and Guillaume Février, 1478), fol. B8r: '(. . .) deus gloriosus sua benignissima gratia dignetur omnia futura mala in bonum convertere et immutare et nos ad [sic] morte improvisa et inimicis liberare amen'. Hain 9827.

21 Al-Qabisi, *Alkabitius Astronomie iudiciarie principia tractatus cum Joannis saxonij commentario* (Paris, 1521), fol. a2v: 'Sed advertendum est de modo per quem sapiens potest impedire vel adiuvare opus stellarum. Certum est quod nos non possumus simpliciter impedire influentiam celestem: sicut nec combustione ignis. Sed possumus disponere passum ad recipiendum alio vel alio modo influentiam celestem. Videmus enim quod idem calor solis glacies dissolvit et constringit lutum'. On John of Saxony's astrological work, see Lynn Thorndike, *A History of Magic and Experimental Science*, 8 vols. (New York: Columbia U.P., 1923–58), III: pp. 253–67.

Latinized version of Hermann of Carinthia) of Abū Ma'shar (Albumasar). In his attack on the supposed uselessness of astrology (chapter I.5), the Latin Albumasar conceded that the coming of (good or bad) things cannot be hastened nor changed, but asserted that a warning does allow one to impede or at least lighten the 'force of the thing', and this either by fashioning a more robust body for oneself, or fleeing.[22] The third tract of Leopold of Austria's *Compilatio* likewise stated that the utility of astrology was to 'evade a foreknown danger, if this is possible, or to provide for its coming if this is impossible'.[23]

Such assumptions appear to have been widely shared among early prognosticators. Johannes Laet's printed prognostication for 1476 found that

> (. . .) the death of some great prelates is discerned for this year: bishops and abbots of great renown, who are under the direct will and command of great princes (. . .). And this mortal accident will come out from acute fevers, or from the burning of the blood which generates such fevers. Hence, if any prelate, bishop, or abbot would meet such an accident, he is advised to take recourse to venesection, and a purging of the body by drugs.[24]

In this passage, it was not so much the 'accident' as such, but rather its effects in the recipient which were to be turned around by a work on the body. In a similar vein, Johann Virdung of Hasfurt's *Practica* for 1495 claimed that

> (. . .) foreseen blows hurt less. Thus, if we were to know that a great cold will come, we would furnish our house so that our bodies would not be bound in cold.[25]

---

22 Abū Ma'shar, *Introductorium in astronomiam Albumasaris abalachi* (Augsburg: Erhard Ratdolt, 1489), fol. b2v.

23 [Leopold of Austria], *Compilatio Leupoldi ducatus Austrie filij de astrorum scientia* (Venice: Erhard Ratdolt, 1489), fols. C1v–C3r.

24 Johannes Laet, *Pronosticationes (. . .) eventuum futurorum (. . .) 1476* (Louvain: Johannes de Westfalia, 1475/6), fols. A2r/v: '(. . .) quod hoc an[n]o percipietur mors aliqorum magnorum prelatorum, episcoporum scilicet et abbatum magni nominis qui subsunt voluntati seu ditioni magnorum principum (. . .). Et illud accidens mortis eveniet ex febribus acutis, seu ex adusto sanguine qui generabit tales febres. Quapropter si alicui prelato episcopo vel abbati tale accidens evenerit: consulendum est sibi quod statim faciat sibi fieri minutionem sanguinis, et corpus purgari per medicinam'. Sole known copy Oxford, Bodleian Library, MS. Arch.Seld. B 25 (fols. 253–262).

25 Johann Virdung of Hassfurt, *Practica Cracoviensis super anno M.cccc.cxv (. . .)* , fol. [A1r]:

The preface to Domenico Maria de Novara's Italian prognostication for 1497, meanwhile, asserted that 'the operation of the stars in this world is similar to the force of the magnet which attracts the iron unless it is impeded by the vapor of garlic or the virtue of a diamond'.[26] It is precisely this focus on sublunary passion and the mode of expression—rather than the fact—of celestial influence which also underlay Novara's emphasis, in the preface to his prognostication for 1492, on the need for astrologers to 'adapt the passive virtues of subject parts to the agents [of the virtues of celestial bodies]'.[27] The same attitude probably underlay the claim of John of Glogau (c. 1445–1507) that

> (. . .) The best astronomer can prohibit much evil which is to come from the stars, if only he would know *the nature of these [stars]* [my italics].[28]

John of Glogau's assertions were repeated almost verbatim in a prognostication for 1495 by his Ferrarese colleague Pietro Bono Avogadro, who duly identified this as stemming from the pseudo-Ptolemaic *Centiloquium*.[29]

Hope, fear, and governance of the self

Contrary to what many historians have claimed about the Renaissance prognosticator, this art of embodiment was not specifically, and certainly not exclusively, obsessed with misfortune and calamity. Consider the opening section of book IV of Guido Bonatti's *Liber astronomiae* (c. 1277), one of the

---

'Nam iacula previsa minus ledent: sicuti si cognoverimus frigus grande eventurum, domum lignis exornemus ne nostra frigoribus constrigantur corpora'. Hain *8373.

[26] Domenico Maria de Novara, *I pronostici di Domenico Maria de Novara*, eds. Fabrizio Bònoli, Giuseppe Bezza, Salvo de Meis and Cinzia Colavita (Firenze: Leo S. Olschki, 2012), p. 209: '(. . .) la operatione de le stelle in questo mondo è simile a la virtù de la calamita che tira a sé el ferro, se non è impedita dal vapore de l'aglio, overo dalla virtù del diamante'.

[27] Novara, *Pronostici*, p. 182: 'Mondanorum effectuum naturam prescire desiderans non solum vires celestium corporum contemplatur verum subiectarum partium debet virtutes passivas agentibus adaptare'.

[28] Malgorzata H. Malewicz, 'Johannis de Glogovia "Persuasio brevis quomodo astrologiae studium religioni christianiae non est adversum"', *Studia Mediewistyczne* 22 (1985), pp. 153–75.

[29] Pietro Bono Avogadro, *Prognostico dell'anno 1495* (Venezia: Cristoforo de' Pensi(?), 1494), fol. A1r.

standard authorities of the prognosticators, where Bonatti discusses the usefulness of mundane astrology through 'revolutions of the years of the world':

> By the revolutions of the years of the world, it is known what good or bad is to be in that year; whether the year will be tranquil or importune; whether there will be wars in the revolved year or not, and likewise for peace; what is the future state of kings or princes, of rich men or magnates, of the populace and the mean religious; also, the well-being of anyone whatsoever, as well as of any sort whatsoever, and this universally according to the customs of men. Likewise, it is known what is to be concerning crops, whether abundance or penury is expected, and what is to come forth from them: a mean or mediocre price, as is said in the section on lots.[30]

Part VI of *Liber astronomiae*, which dealt with weather prediction, spoke of the cognition of 'fortunate' and 'infortunate' things (in the plural), but not in the sense of effects of a given relation to something called 'fortune'.[31] Likewise, Johannes Laet's dedication of his prognostication for 1477–8 to prince-bishop Louis de Bourbon of Liège approached the visible heavens as the source of fortune and infortune, and this with the accord of God.[32] In his dedication of a Latin edition of Ptolemaic and Arabic astrological works (1493) to Domenico Maria de Novara, Girolamo Salio of Faventino not only approached the phenomenon of celestial motion as the ultimate source of the sublunary phenomena of generation and corruption, but also as the source of differentiation in the ultimate fortunes of humans. The importance which Salio attached to this is underlined by the fact that he identified such differentiation,

---

[30] Guido Bonatti, *De astronomia tractatus X* (Basel: Nicolaus Pruckнerus, 1550), col. 489. I will be referencing this edition throughout this paper. The literature on Bonatti is undeservedly small, but includes: Bernardo Boncompagni, *Della vita e delle opere di Guido Bonatti astrologo ed astronomo del secolo decimoterzo* (Roma: Tipografia delle Belle Arti, 1851); Mario Tabanelli, *Un Astrologo Forlivese dal 1200: Guido Bonatti* (Brescia: Magalini Editrice, 1978); Cesare Vasoli, 'L'Astrologo Forlivese Guido Bonatti', *Atti del Convegno Internazionale di studi Danteschi (. . .) (Ravenna, 10–12 Settembre 1971)* (Ravenna: Longo, 1979), pp. 239–60.

[31] Bonatti, *De astronomia*, col. 830.

[32] Johannes Laet, *Pronosticatio anno presentis lxxvii (. . .)* (Paris: Richard Blandin and Guillaume Février, 1478), fol. A1r: '(. . .) et fortuna vel impedimentum operatio seu destructio fit ex motibus planetarum ex operibus eorum et hec nutu dei est totumque opus planetarum eorumque fortuna et infortunium'. Hain 9827.

when correlated with differences in human birth charts, as the basis for astrology's primeval experiential tradition.[33]

Such passages suggest that pessimism was not as 'typical' of the prognosticators as is often suggested. Even if it is true that astrological productions of this period assign a privileged position to the possibility of foretelling misfortune, this does not necessarily imply a 'pessimistic' outlook. At the beginning of *Liber astronomiae*, Bonatti thus explained that astrology responds to a desire to know

> (. . .) what must happen to someone concerning a specific thing. Through this, an evil thing which threatens someone *can* be avoided by that person, while a profitable thing that is promised, *can actually* be apprehended [my italics].[34]

This passage anticipated a claim with which Domenico Maria de Novara introduced his prognostication for 1484:

> For only the art of coming things of the stars gives us foresight and similitude to the immortal God; for knowing the end of things through her, we may embrace things which are coming, or flee coming danger and damnation.[35]

Likewise, the prognosticator John of Glogau identified astrology as that art which opens up the possibility for men to

> (. . .) declare the passion of future events to mortals from the site and motion of the stars; that is, what good is to be hoped for from the stars, and what evil is to be abhorred.[36]

It is interesting to read such statements with an actual Renaissance prognostication in hand. Doing so enables one to understand how Johannes

---

33 Claudius Ptolemaeus, *Liber quadripartiti Ptholemei (. . .)* (Venice: Bonetus Locatellus, 1493), dedicatory letter, col. 1. Hain *13544.

34 Bonatti, *De astronomia*, col. 12: 'quid debeat ei evenire de re illa. Unde si minetur ei damnum, poterit illud evitare; et si promittat ei lucrum, poterit illud apprehendere'.

35 Novara, *Pronostici*, p. 133: 'Sola namque astrorum peritia nos futurorum praescios immortali deo similimos reddit per hanc enim cognito rerum fine poterimus quae praefutura sunt complecti, periculum vero aut dannum allatura subterfugere'.

36 Malewicz, 'Johannis de Glogovia', p. 167.

Canter's promise of a planet Saturn which, beginning in September 1489, would 'administer better fates to his kin' might not have been read as the announcement of a future fact, but rather as a warning of a future *possibility*, whose materialisation would depend on the willingness of Canter's Saturnine readers to seek out such good fortune, as well as on their capability of doing so by knowing that it would be a reasonable expectation in the first place.[37]

Glogau's statement not only qualifies historians' claims about the endemic pessimism of Renaissance prognostications; it also calls for carefulness in reading these texts as informative predictions of future trends and events, wielded so as to minimise the possibility of loss. Glogau's liberal use of the language of passions, hopes and fears suggests a far less detached outlook on celestial influence, which we must now try to unpack.

Ladislaus of Cracow, an *émigré* prognosticator working in Rome, opened his prognostication for 1494 with the claim that both philosophers and theologians defended the opinion that '*this inferior world* is governed by celestial causes [my italics]', and that this was adopted as a working assumption in 'all judgments of the stars'. Worries about a distancing of God were handled by Ladislaus by asserting that the celestial influences were contained by His absolute rule, which 'added or diminished' these influences at will.[38]

While this last statement echoes the aforementioned emphasis on divine mercy and supernatural intervention, the rest of Ladislaus's text highlights the extent to which prognosticators approached the visible heavens as intermediaries ('secondary causes') in a single web of the divine governance of creation. The prognosticators specialised in the intimate relations of rule obtaining between the visible heavens and the four sublunary elements. In the preface to his prognostication for 1477–8, Johannes Laet thus spoke for many of his colleagues when he wrote that

> [God] instituted the earth immobile and neither declined to the right nor to the left. He also made the four elements changeable, and led them—and each creature along with them—to be changed by the motion of the seven planets. Thus,

[37] Johannes Canter, *Prognosticatio anno 1489* (Rome: Stephan Planck, 1489), fol. [A3v]. Hain *4353.

[38] Ladislaus de Cracovia, *Iudicium anno 1494* (Rome: Andreas Freitag de Argentina, 1494), fol. A1v. Hain *5800.

everything which happens in this world, is effected by the motion of the planets.[39]

In the preface to his vernacular *Practica Lipcensis* for 1486, Martin Pollich of Mellerstadt began by pointing out that 'the honorable God of the heavens, who governs and universally rules over this entire world by His will and power', created the heavens and the stars, endowing them with light, motion, and influence. This God, Pollich continued, 'moves the heavens around the terrestrial realm', situating and fixing the latter in the middle 'so that through these, the lower world would be ordered and ruled'. It is not surprising, then, to find that the prognostications of the Bolognese prognosticator Domenico Maria de Novara habitually described man's relation to the stars in terms of 'being ruled' or 'being governed' (*regi, gubernari*) and 'governing oneself' (*se gubernare*).[40] Similar statements were made in Gaspar Laet's Dutch prognostication for 1503.[41] In this way, Renaissance prognostication culture comes forth as a primary instance of what Michel Foucault referred to as the Renaissance culture of governmentality: one organised around the practice of turning to the visible heavens, *rather than something else,* in order to organise the self's relation to fortune and change.[42]

Such statements confirm how the Renaissance prognostication annually renewed man's insight into the inevitable and constant changes which followed from the embeddedness of sublunary bodies in a relation of governance by the stars. As we have seen, prognosticators did not consider this relation to be something which one could oppose, let alone extract the self from. Instead, the

---

[39] Johannes Laet, *Pronosticatio anno presentis lxxvii (. . .)* (Paris: Richard Blandin and Guillaume Février, 1478), fol. A1r: '[Deus] posuit terram immobilem in circuitu eius et non declinate ad dexteram neque ad sinistram et posuit quattuor elementa mobilia et movere fecit ea per motum septem planetarum ita omnis creatura et universa que fiunt in hoc mundo efficiuntur a motu planetarum (. . .)'. Hain 9827.

[40] See e.g., Novara, *Pronostici*, pp. 139, 170, 178, 187.

[41] Gaspar Laet, *Pronosticacie (. . .) MCCCCCiij* (Antwerpen: Adriaen van Berghen, 1503), fol. a1v: 'Ghesien dat de werelt geregeert wort bijden lope des hemels ende dat die dingen opter aerden hen veranderen ende muteren naden loop des hemels als philosophus seit Methaurorum primo. Ende dat wi vinden in vele ende menige vande dingen (. . .)'. Wouter Nijhoff and M.E. Kronenberg, *Nederlandsche bibliografie van 1500–1540* (Gravenhage, 1923–71), 8 vols., n° 3344.

[42] Michel Foucault, *Sécurité, territoire, population. Cours au Collège de France (1977–78)* (Paris: Gallimard/Seuil, 2004).

rationality of their productions hinged on their enabling a work of preparing the body to receive or alter celestial gifts. A good example of this occurs in the *Iudicium* for 1505 by Georg Tannstetter, which emphasized that God endowed man with reason and art, by which he could '(. . .) easily choose to flee sicknesses, wars, hunger, and many more of this kind, and to embrace health and a temperate air'.[43] This is also why prognosticatory predictions were typically voiced as revelations of what one could hope and fear for the coming year. Domenico Maria de Novara's prognostications were often styled as sources of advice on what one should reasonably fear (*timere*) in one's relation to fortune. More often than not, this was not a matter of anxiety or pessimism but of the organisation of self-governance. It is in this way that one should read the typical prediction for the city of Mechlin in Johannes Laet's prognostication for 1479:

> To those of Mechlin, I declare that nothing special is to come out, different from how the years usually pass by; nevertheless, drowning of some people is to be feared, as are fire and messengers arriving at unusual times (. . .).[44]

Conversely, one should also be careful in associating the Renaissance prognostication with utilitarian and informative discourses about the future, designed to minimise the danger of loss in human actions. Such a picture does not allow us to sufficiently appreciate the prognosticator's emphasis on a given governance of the embodied self inside a hierarchically structured creation; his understanding of the prognostication as an annual revelation of new episodes in the story of such governance; his uptake of human agency as a means of altering these celestial passions (rather than of modifying one's own projects in light of information about the future).

---

[43] Georg Tanstetter Collimitius, *Iudicium Viennense (. . .) super anno M.ccccc.v (. . .)*, fol. [A1r]: 'Altissimus ille deus (. . .) humanum genus arte rationeque dotavit, qua aegritudines, bella, famem, et id genus plura fugere, pacem vero sanitatem et temperamentum aeris eligere facile queat'.

[44] Johannes Laet, *Prenosticata (. . .) 1479* (Cologne: Johannes Guldenschaff, 1479), fol. A5v: 'Mechlinensibus non assigno aliquam rem specialem eventuram aliter quam anni communiter solent pertransire. Sed est timendum de submersione aliquarum personarum et igne et nuncijs advenientibus ex temporis alienis et est particulare'.

Celestial Passions, the Lower Soul, and the Social Body

An emphasis on divine governance of corporeal creation through the secondary causes of the stars was hardly exclusive to the prognosticators. In *Summa theologica* Ia.q115.a4, which detailed the participation of celestial bodies in the divine government of the world, Aquinas even invoked the successes of mundane astrology as evidence for the reality of such governance. Considering that 'astrologers often foretell the truth concerning the coming of wars, and other human actions, of which the intellect and will are principles', Aquinas explained

> The majority of men follow their passions, which are movements of the sensitive appetite, in which movements heavenly bodies can co-operate; but few are wise enough to resist these passions. Consequently astrologers are able to foretell the truth in the majority of cases, especially in a general way. But not in particular cases, for nothing prevents man resisting his passions by his free-will. And so the astrologers themselves say that the wise man is stronger than the stars, in so far as, that is, he conquers his passions' (ST.Ia.q115.a4.ad 3).[45]

Likewise, his letter *De iudiciis astrorum* made it amply clear that there was an entire realm of what Aquinas called 'corporeal effects': that is, of 'things which depend on natural and corporeal causes'. His examples of these clearly evoked the realm of mundane astrology: 'storminess and serenity of the air, health or infirmity of the body, or abundance and sterility of crops'.[46] Aquinas also asserted that 'all men use some observation of the celestial bodies regarding effects of this kind', providing a list of examples that would inform the pastoral-theological category of 'natural astrology' for many centuries to come:

---

[45] 'Ad tertium dicendum quod plures hominum sequuntur passiones, quae sunt motus sensitivi appetitus, ad quas cooperari possunt corpora caelestia, pauci autem sunt sapientes, qui huiusmodi passionibus resistant. Et ideo astrologi ut in pluribus vera possunt praedicere, et maxime in communi. Non autem in speciali, quia nihil prohibet aliquem hominem per liberum arbitrium passionibus resistere. Unde et ipsi astrologi dicunt quod sapiens homo dominatur astris, inquantum scilicet dominatur suis passionibus'. Acc. 24 July 2012, http://www.corpusthomisticum.org/sth1103.html#33271.

[46] '(. . .) prenoscendum corporales effectus, puta tempestatem et serenitatem aeris, sanitatem uel infirmitatem corporis, uel ubertatem et sterilitatem fructuum'. Accessed 24 July 2012, http://www.corpusthomisticum.org/ote.html.

> (. . .) farmers sow and reap at a specific time, which is observed through the motion of the sun; sailors abstain from sailings at full or new moon; physicians observe the critical days in the case of diseases, determined in accordance with the course of sun and moon.[47]

Like the prognosticators, Aquinas assumed that the lower faculties of the human soul, animals, plants, and the elements were all equally governed by the stars. However, the evidence collected in the preceding sections also allows us to understand that, unlike Aquinas, the prognosticators did not approach such celestial passions as a natural fact which required no more than a privileging of the intellect and the will. The key difference lay in the prognosticator's focus on the realities of fortune and historical vicissitude. This focus invited them to re-use the Thomistic model of celestial passions as the natural-philosophical basis for a work of constructing prognostications and distributing these, so as to enable a relation of self-governance in relation to fortune.

There is good evidence that such self-governance was not modeled on the ideal of the modern, individual, rational actor seeking to protect or maximise his own domain of possessions. Consider the structure and content of early Renaissance prognostications. Although there is considerable geographical variation in order and completeness (especially in the fifteenth century), it is fair to say that the archetypical Renaissance prognostications treated the following five topics:

(1) accidents relative to other bodies: weather, the well-being of crops and livestock;

(2) accidents relative to the health of human individual or social bodies: health and disease, peace and war;

(3) accidents of specific kinds of members of the social body, relative to a distribution of these kinds over different planetary rulerships: men of arms and military leaders are under the rule of Mars, women are under

[47] '(. . .) sicut agricole seminant et metunt certo tempore quod obseruatur secundum motum solis; naute nauigationes uitant in plenilunio, uel in lune defectu; medici circa egritudines creticos dies obseruant, qui determinantur secundum cursum solis et lune'. Accessed 24 July 2012, http://www.corpusthomisticum.org/ote.html.

Venus, lawyers, philosophers, and artists are under Mercury, worldly princes under the Sun, etc.;

(4) accidents of individual prelates or princes, relative to their natal horoscope;

(5) accidents of individual cities or provinces, relative to their foundation horoscope and/or planetary rulership.

In the case of the first sections, the prognostication narrated the state, in any given year, of beings which, as Domenico Maria de Novara put it in 1497, 'are agitated by a certain fatal connexion of causes'. Like other prognosticators, however, Novara also emphasized that the human will was capable of resisting such causes, even if this was difficult. Accordingly, it did not belong to the prognosticator 'to announce the effects, but the influxes and celestial impressions'.[48] Seen from this perspective, the second section stands out by introducing the presence of celestial passions in the social body and 'body politic'. Typical of this was the following passage from Marcus Schinnagel's prognostication for 1493:

> Mars coursing through the tenth house, signifies discord, betrayal, and enmity between powerful men and magistrates. It is to be feared that many men will perish this year from war. It is also to be feared that soldiers will die a sorry death (. . .). Noblemen, kings, and potentates will be inclined to war.[49]

As for the third section of the early Renaissance prognostication, consider the following passage from Johannes Canter's prognostication for 1489:

> Those governed by the most dire ray of Saturn, such as Jews, farmers, old men, those pursuing vile professions – as well as, according to Guido [Bonatti], monks, especially those in black garments. These persons will be well in the beginning of

---

[48] Novara, *Pronostici*, p. 209.

[49] Marcus Schinnagel, *Prognosticon anno 1493* (s.l., [1493]), fol. [A2r]: 'Mars in decima decurrens discordias simulatas et inimicicias multas inter homines potentes et magistratus esse significat. Et timendum est multos homines hoc anno bello perire. Timendumque milites mala morte extingui. (. . .) Nobiles, reges, potentes, ad bellum excitabuntur'. Hain *14539.

> the year, and will flourish for the most part, since their significator will find itself well-disposed in its own house. However, its retrogradation, from 19 April until 2 September, will rightly lead them to consider themselves unlucky, being vexed by diverse furies and infirmities. When Saturn escapes from its great misfortune, in the beginning of September, he will administer better fates to his kin.[50]

Although Canter adresses the reader directly, it is significant that he does so as the bearer of a specific societal (and planetary) name. Distribution of planetary rulership over various parts of human society was hardly typical of the textual tradition of mundane astrology before the thirteenth century; it is not to be found in *Tetrabiblos* nor in the major Arabic authorities with which the prognosticators were familiar.[51] Clearly, early Renaissance prognostications manifested a stronger tendency to approach the social body as an association and incorporation of different classes or—more accurately—'social regions'. Even in this case, the prognosticator set out to offer an annually renewed revelation of the celestial life of the social body. Consider the following passage, taken from Martin Pollich of Mellerstadt's preface to his prognostication for 1488:

> There are various estates of men and their artifices which the heavens do not influence [lit. 'flow directly into'], just as they do not for the rational part of man as a whole, nor for that which falls under this part – the individual intellectual habits, justice, and whatever is part of that, such as exchanges and distributions of things, all of which are willful due to the freedom of the rational appetite. Nevertheless, the heavens can act indirectly in this part, and this through most strong inclinations of the entire sensual faculty and inferior appetite. Because of the latter's linkage to the body, it is agitated so much and with such a great stimulus

---

[50] Johannes Canter, *Prognosticatio anno 1489* (Roma: Stephan Planck, 1489), fol. [A3v:]: 'Saturni durissimi radio gubernati: quales sunt hebrei rustici agricole senesque homines et vilia exercicia sectantes, Monachi item teste Guidone maxime nigris indumentis induti. In principio anni bene se habebunt, plurimumque fortunabuntut, quum eorum significator in domo propria gaudioque erit. Verum propter eius retrogradationem quam faciet a xix aprilis usque ad ij septembris, diversis furijs vexari infirmitatibusque infelices etiam se reputantes non errabunt. Post tamen principium septembris evasus ex infortunio maximo saturnus, fata meliora suis etiam parabit'. Hain *4353.

[51] A brief survey suggests that planetary rulership over different parts of society appears neither in Albumasar's *Flores*, nor in Messahallah's *De revolutionibus annorum mundi*, nor in Haly Abenragel's *De iudiciis astrorum*.

> and sweet caress – so to speak – from the celestial bodies, that it would be hard to kick back this fatal stimulus and difficult to resist such a strong inclination, just as it is most arduous to navigate against the stream. This is particularly the case for men who guide their lives according to the sensual faculty. But the heavens can do much less in those who live by reason. The present prognostication is instituted for the benefit of that inclination in diverse men.[52]

The similarities with Aquinas's language are clear; but these metaphors and concepts are here deployed to address the challenges of a social body, rather than of embodied individuals. For both the social body as a whole and its specific social 'estates', the prognosticator set himself the task of predicting their 'state' (*status*) or well-being in the coming year. Accordingly, the ideal reader was expected to identify with this social body and with one of these categories, and to take the content of the prognostication as a guide to organising his celestial life.

The crucial importance of reader identifications with a limited set of social categories and 'roles' casts an interesting light on the intended use and meaningfulness of the prognostication. More specifically, it suggests that the aforementioned five-fold structure was carefully constructed as a mirror of the various identities and predicates which a prognostication reader was expected to adopt. If this hypothesis is correct, then the typical structure yields an ideal reader who defined himself as situated in the cosmos through relations of dependency on other, non-human beings (section 1), as a member of a social body (section 2), and as a specific kind of member of a social body (section 3).

---

52 Martin Pollich of Mellerstadt, *Practica Lipsiensis* (Leipzig, 1487), fols. [A7v–A8r]: 'Sicut sunt diversi hominum status et varia ipsorum artificia quibus celum non per se influit, quemadmodum nec toti parti rationali. Neque his que huic parti insunt quales sunt singuli intellectuales habitus cum iusticia et que illi insunt ut commutationes et rerum distributiones que omnia arbitraria sunt propter libertatem rationalis appetitus. Sed nihilominus celum in hanc partem agere poterit indirecte et secundum quondam fortissimam inclinationem totius sensualitatis et inferioris appetitus qui propter colligationem sui ad corpus tanto stimulo et dulci palpamine (ut ita loquar) a corporibus celestibus adeo agitatur ut durum sit recalcitrare fatali stimulo et difficile resistere tam forti inclinatione quemadmodum gravissimum est contra torrentem navigare: presertim hominibus qui secundum sensualitatem vitam ducunt. Qui enim ratione vivunt in hos celum minus potest. Ad illam ergo inclinationem diversorum hominum presens prognosticum est institutum'. Hain *11055.

If this reading has some virtue to it, then the ideal reader of the Renaissance prognostication may very well have been expected to take responsibility for the presence of good fortune in each of these regions of existence, gradually working his way towards his identity as a city-dweller. This would also mean that the first sections of the Renaissance prognostication in fact targeted members of a kind of undefined, universal social body situated in the natural world. Contrary, then, to what often obtained in older mundane astrology, prognosticatory discourse was no longer *primarily* aimed at kings and princes. The art of negotiating celestial passions was no longer just the responsability of Big Men. If the prefaces of early Renaissance prognostications still primarily targeted kings and princes, then it was mainly by virtue of expecting them to support and protect the legitimacy of the prognostication as such. Instead, the early Renaissance prognostication counted on its being received and wielded by individual 'everymen'.

However, all of this still leaves open the last two sections on political 'particulars': specific rulers, kingdoms, counties, cities. These sections were often based on annual revolutions of particular horoscopes, rather than the chart of the vernal ingress on which the first three sections were based. At the very least, then, these sections appear to involve more than a simple differentiation of the non-particularised social body of the first three sections towards nameable realities. These sections may not have been primarily targeted at 'ordinary' subjects of particular rulers (section 4) or members of particular social bodies (section 5). Indeed, a cursory inspection (although this would repay further study) of a random selection of early Renaissance prognostications suggests that these last two sections were, quite simply, directed at specific detainers of rule: kings, counts, dukes, and city magistrates.

Conclusion

This paper has tried to show that early Renaissance prognosticators are best interpreted as creative adopters of widespread analyses of divine governance through the secondary causes of the stars. Adopting these theological and natural-philosophical anthropologies as a key to the secrets and vicissitudes of human fortune, their productions offered an annually renewed insight in the celestial life of embodiment and the lower soul, so as to allow self-governance amongst the members of the Christian body politic and render the latter less passionate in its relation to fortune.

This result strongly qualifies two dominant interpretations of the early modern prognostication. On the one hand, historians have suggested that these texts are best interpreted as printed commodities in an early modern information economy, providing individuals with a tool for fine-tuning the rationality of their acquisitive actions by taking in credible knowledge of the future. On the other hand, historians have also portrayed the early Renaissance prognostication as a site where 'popular' fears and anxieties, stimulated by the objective uncertainty and disorder of an entire age, manifested themselves in the form of 'pessimistic' predictions which could easily cross over into the language and imagery of apocalyptic prophecy.

As we have seen, there is good evidence that early prognostication culture is best interpreted as part of a late medieval culture of political governance which had begun to carve itself out within the older theological discourse of divine care and guidance of his people. The early prognostication was deeply conversant with this older discourse in its emphasis on the heavens as a divinely given book which demonstrated His mercy; in its easy adoption of the language of grace and divine supplication as a source of assistance for natural man; in its manifold borrowings from scholastic analyses of divine governance of creation through the secondary causes of the stars; in its deep concern with the reality of celestially induced passions of the lower soul. Contrary to what is often suggested, prognosticators did not seek to protect individual readers from celestially induced misfortune. Instead, they tried to inject a measure of stability and rationality inside the constant play of celestially induced passions and effects. As far as the individual self was concerned, the early Renaissance prognosticators were much more akin to Joan Quigley, the infamous astrological consultant to the Reagans, who claimed of astrology that 'it is like being in the ocean: you should go with the waves, not against them'.[53]

At the same time, early prognostication culture also testifies to a novel interest in the body politic, rather than the more homogeneous and universal social body of Christ, as the ultimate focus of its attention. The ideal reader of the prognostication was expected to identify himself as a member of the natural realm of elements, plants and animals, of the social body of Christendom, and of a body politic consisting of different social estates under the guidance of specific

53 TIME Magazine, 16 May 1988, accessed 25 July 2012: http://www.time.com/time/magazine/article/0,9171,967410-1,00.html.

secular rulers. Without entirely disavowing the importance of individualised consumption through booksellers and peddlers, it should be noted that some of the most solid evidence we have about 16th-century consumption and distribution of prognostications, points in the direction of city councils buying large parts of a print run and distributing these as new year's gifts.[54] Although this will require much additional research, the self-image of the prognosticator as offering guidance to the body politic, which Patrick Curry so meticulously unearthed for 17th-century England, may have been much older and widespread than we suspect.

---

[54] This situation was convincingly demonstrated in Jeroen Salman's study of Dutch prognostication culture. See Jeroen Salman, 'Populair drukwerk in de Gouden Eeuw. De almanak als handelswaar en lectuur' (PhD dissertation, Leiden University, 1997), pp. 56–67, 102–19, 155–59, 177–85, 207–13.

Contributors

†Giuseppe Bezza was an historian of astronomical and astrological culture and the author of the recently published *Commento al Centiloquio tolemaico* (2013), as well as *Arcana Mundi: Antologia del pensiera astrologico antico* (1995), *Commento al primo libro della Tetrabiblo di Tolomeo* (1991) and many other publications in the history and practice of astrology.

Jean-Patrice Boudet is professor of Medieval History at the University of Orléans. His major publications include *Lire dans le ciel. La bibliothèque de Simon de Phares, astrologue du XVe siècle* (Brussels, 1994), *Le 'Recueil des plus celebres astrologues' de Simon de Phares* (2 vols, Paris, 1997-1999), and *Entre science et* nigromance. *Astrologie, divination et magie dans l'Occident médiéval (XIIe-XVe siècle)* (Paris, 2006). He is currently preparing a critical edition of the 12th century Latin translations of Pseudo-Ptolemy's *Centiloquium*.

Bernadette Brady has a PhD in Anthropology (2012) and MA in Cultural Astronomy and Astrology (2005). She is currently a tutor in the Sophia Centre for the Study of Cosmology in Culture at the University of Wales Trinity Saint David, UK. Her research interests are in the cultural significance of astrology both historically as well as in contemporary life. Her publications in this area include previous work on Galileo's astrology, 'Four Galilean Horoscopes: An Analysis of Galileo's Astrological Techniques' in *Galileo's Astrology* (*Culture and Cosmos* 7.1, 2003); and her recent book, *Cosmos, Chaosmos and Astrology: Rethinking the Nature of Astrology*. (London: Sophia Centre Press, 2014). She currently lives in Bristol, UK.

Charles Burnett holds an MA and PhD from the University of Cambridge, and is Professor of the History of Islamic Influences in Europe at the Warburg Institute, University of London (since 1999). He has written extensively on the translations of Arabic texts into Latin in the Middle Ages and their impact on European culture. He has edited major works of the astrologer Abū Maʻshar (with Keiji Yamamoto) and texts on arithmetic, geometry, music, philosophy and alchemy, as well as documenting the process of transmission of learning in the Mediterranean basin.

Geoffrey Cornelius is a practising astrologer. He holds a PhD in Theology and Religious Studies from the University of Kent, and is currently teaching at Canterbury Christchurch University on its MA in Myth, Cosmology and the Sacred. His research focus is in the hermeneutics of divination.

Meira B. Epstein has been researching Abraham Ibn Ezra's astrological texts since the late 1980s. Her published translations are *The Beginning of Wisdom* (1998), *The Book of Reasons* (1991) and *The Book of Nativities and revolutions* (2008). In preparation are *The Book of Elections* and *The Book of Interrogations.* She is a certified professional astrological consultant and a principal teacher for the NCGR education and certification program, focusing on science, astronomy and history. Meira lectures and teaches internationally on all aspects of astrology. A college degree and a career in teaching ESL (English as a Second Language) in Israel was followed by a full-cycle career in computer programming on Wall Street. Her website is www.bear-star.com.

Miquel Forcada is Titular Professor of Arabic and Islamic Studies in The Department of Semitic Philology of the University of Barcelona and main researcher of the Grup Millàs Vallicrosa of History of Arabic Science of the same university. He has published extensively on several topics about the History and Philosophy of Science in al-Andalus (Muslim Iberian Peninsula). His current research is focused on the scientific doctrines of the physician philosophers of 12th century al-Andalus and the debates among Aristotelism, Galenism and Ptolemaism.

Dorian Gieseler Greenbaum (PhD 2009, the Warburg Institute, London) is a tutor at the University of Wales Trinity St David. She has recently published 'Astronomy, Astrology and Medicine', in Springer's *Handbook of Archaeoastronomy and Ethnoastronomy* (2014); with Franziska Naether, 'Astrological Implications in the "Lot Oracle" *PGM* 50', *MHNH* 11 (2011): pp. 484-505; and, with Micah Ross, 'The Role of Egypt in the Development of the Horoscope' in *Egypt in Transition: Social and Religious Development of Egypt in the First Millennium BCE* (2010). Her book, *The Daimon in Hellenistic Astrology: Origins and Influence,* will appear in Brill's Magic and Divination Series in 2015.

ROBERT HAND is an astrologer and historian. He received his PhD in History from The Catholic University of America. His doctoral fields of concentration were late medieval and early modern religious life and science. Hand is currently Chairman of the Board of Kepler College, a former Chairman of the National Council for Geocosmic Research, and holds memberships in other organizations including the History of Science Society and the American Historical Association; he is a patron of the Faculty of Astrological Studies. In 1997 he co-founded Arhat Media. Its purpose is to procure, protect and publish historical astrological texts. He also translates medieval Latin works into English from early modern printed editions and manuscripts.

STEPHAN HEILEN is Professor of Classics at the University of Osnabrück, Germany. His main fields of research are the history of astrology in antiquity and in the Renaissance, Neo-Latin poetry, and the history of classical scholarship. His German doctoral thesis was the first critical edition of Lorenzo Bonincontri's Neo-Latin poem *De rebus naturalibus et divinis,* an imitation of Lucretius and Manilius in six books (Teubner 1999). His German *Habilitationsschrift,* an edition with commentary of the astrological fragments of Antigonus of Nicaea (2nd c. A.D.), will be published by De Gruyter in 2015. For more information, see his homepage at the University of Osnabrück.

JAN P. HOGENDIJK is Professor of History of Mathematics at the University of Utrecht, Netherlands. He teaches undergraduate mathematics courses and his research interests are history of the mathematical sciences in medieval Islamic civilization, as well as the history of mathematics in the Netherlands until 1850. In addition, he has had administrative positions such as Director of Teaching of the bachelor program in mathematics at the University of Utrecht (2009–2012 and 2015–). He often travels to the Middle East. Before coming to Utrecht, he was a member of the History of Mathematics Department in Brown University, RI, USA, and the History of Science Department of the J.W. Goethe University in Frankfurt am Main (Germany). For more information see his website www.jphogendijk.nl.

PIERGABRIELE MANCUSO received his doctoral degree in Jewish

Studies from University College London, 2009. He studied in Oxford and has been a fellow of the Warburg Institute, London. He taught at Boston University Abroad Programs, Ca' Foscari University (Venice) and the University of Kentucky (Lexington). He is the director of the Eugene Program in Jewish Studies at the Medici Archive Project, Florence and the Venetian Centre for International Jewish Studies. He is the author of several studies and monographs on medieval Italian Jewry and Jewish music.

Dr **JOSEFINA RODRÍGUEZ-ARRIBAS** (PhD 2004) is a researcher at the Friedrich-Alexander Universität, Erlangen-Nürnberg and has substantial research experience in the history of medieval science, medieval Hebrew, and Jewish divination. Since 2009 her research has focused on the relationships between the textual and the material scientific cultures of Jews, notably, the cultural role of astrolabes among Jews between the 12th and 17th centuries. She has given over 40 lectures at international congresses in Europe, USA, Japan, and Israel on topics related to her expertise, and has published a book (*El cielo de Sefarad: los judíos y los astros*, 2011) and several chapters and articles on medieval astronomy, astrology, and astrolabes. She also contributed several entries to the *Encyclopaedia of Jews in the Islamic World* (2010).

H. DARREL RUTKIN is Associate lecturer in the History of Science in the Unit for History and Philosophy of Science at the University of Sydney. He is a Historian of Science specializing in the history of medieval, Renaissance and early modern astrology with a PhD from Indiana University (2002). He is the recipient of pre- and post-doctoral fellowships—including a Rome Prize from the American Academy in Rome, Villa I Tatti, Harvard University's Center for Italian Renaissance Studies in Florence, the Dibner Institute for the History of Science and Technology at M.I.T. and in its current incarnation at the Huntington Library, and most recently at the Friedrich-Alexander Universität, Erlangen-Nürnberg. Among other articles, he has also contributed to the *Cambridge History of Science* and the *Harvard Companion to the Classical Tradition.*

JULIO SAMSÓ is Emeritus Professor of Arabic and Islamic Studies of the University of Barcelona. He obtained his MA and PhD degrees at the same university and also studied at Muhammad V's

University (Rabat, Morocco) and the University of Alexandria (Egypt). He has also been professor at the University of La Laguna and the Universidad Autónoma de Barcelona. He is a specialist in the history of Medieval science, and particularly the history of astronomy in al-Andalus and the Maghrib. He has published fourteen books and about 200 articles. Among his most relevant publications are the following: *Las Ciencias de los Antiguos en al-Andalus* (2nd ed. Almería: Fundación Ibn Tufayl de Estudios Árabes, 2011), *Islamic Astronomy and Medieval Spain* (Aldershot: Ashgate Variorum, 1994), *Astronomy and Astrology in al-Andalus and the Maghrib* (Aldershot: Ashgate Variorum, 2007) and *Astrometeorología y astrología medievales* (Barcelona: Publications i Edicions de la Universitat de Barcelona, 2008).

PETRA G. SCHMIDL works as a postdoctoral research assistant at the Exzellenzcluster "Normative Orders" at the Goethe University in Frankfurt. Her research interests lie in the field of pre-modern astronomy and astrology in Islamicate societies, and astronomical instruments, mainly the astrolabe, in both the orient and the occident. She mainly concentrates on folk astronomical traditions and descriptive astrological methods and is interested in the interdependencies between astronomy and astrology, and religion and power.

SHLOMO SELA teaches in Bar Ilan University's Department of Jewish Thought. His research focuses on Jewish attitudes towards the sciences, with special interest in the history of astrology in the Middle Ages. He has recently published *Abraham Ibn Ezra on Nativities and Continuous Horoscopy,* A Parallel Hebrew-English Critical Edition of the Book of Nativities and the Book of Revolution, Edited, Translated and Annotated by Shlomo Sela (Leiden and Boston: Brill, 2013). This volume continues his edition of Ibn Ezra's complete works on astrology. Email: shelomo.sela@gmail.com

GRAEME TOBYN is a medical herbalist with 25 years in practice, a senior lecturer in the School of Health at the University of Central Lancashire where he leads an MSc Herbal Medicine programme and a member of the Company of Astrologers, London. He is the author of *Culpeper's Medicine* (1997/2013) and co-author of *The*

Western Herbal Tradition (2011) and contributor of a chapter 'An Anatomy of The English Physitian' to Francia and Stobart's *Critical Approaches to the History of Western Herbal Medicine* (2014). He is currently completing a PhD at Lancaster University on the promotion of native herbal medicines in the early modern period and is the Visiting Botanical Medicine Scholar at Bastyr University, Seattle, WA, for 2015.

STEVEN VANDEN BROECKE (PhD in History, K.U. Leuven, 2000) teaches in the History department of Ghent University (Belgium). He has authored papers and books on the history of early modern humanist mathematics, cosmography, astronomy, and astrology. He is currently preparing a second monograph on early modern astrological culture, which turns to the history of astrology as a privileged means of detecting long-term shifts in the way that hermeneutics and governance of self and others have been problematized. He is also interested in comparative approaches to the broader phenomenon of early modern 'discourses of possession' (e.g., divine grace, witchcraft, demonology, celestial influence, powers of the imagination, sympathy).

INDEX

Index of names of persons, names of books (where authors are anonymous or debated), and some peoples, places and institutions. In the alphabetical order the Arabic definite article ('al') and the letter '`ayn' (`) are ignored, as is the prefix 'pseudo-'. An 'n' after the number indicates that the reference occurs in one of the notes on that page.

THE SOPHIA CENTRE

The Sophia Centre was set up with funding from the Sophia Trust and is located within the University of Wales, Trinity St. David's School of Archaeology, History and Anthropology. It has a wide-ranging remit to investigate the role of cosmological, astrological and astronomical beliefs, models and ideas in human culture, including the theory and practice of myth, magic, divination, religion, spirituality, politics and the arts. The Centre teaches the MA in Cultural Astronomy and Astrology via distance learning online, and also supervises MPhil and PhD research. There is no need to live in the UK to study at the Sophia Centre.

Much of the Centre's work is historical, but it is equally concerned with contemporary culture and lived experience. If you are interested in the way the sky is used to create meaning and significance, then the Sophia Centre may be the best place for you to study. By joining the Sophia Centre, you enter a community of like-minded scholars whose aim is to explore humanity's relationship with the cosmos.

For further information about the Sophia Centre see the website at www.tsd.ac.uk/en/sophia or contact Nick Campion, the Course Director, at the details below.

The Sophia Centre
Department of Archaeology and Anthropology
University of Wales, Trinity Saint David
Ceredigion
Wales SA48 7ED
United Kingdom
Email: n.campion@tsd.ac.uk

CPSIA information can be obtained
at www.ICGtesting.com
Printed in the USA
BVOW03s2039081217
501839BV00006B/183/P

9 781907 767